Ching Lai

5/15/92

DESIGN AND VALIDATION

OF COMPUTER PROTOCOLS

Gerard J. Holzmann

AT&T Bell Laboratories
Murray Hill, New Jersey 07974

PRENTICE HALL
Englewood Cliffs, New Jersey 07632

Library of Congress Cataloging-in-Publication Data

Holzmann, Gerard J.
    Design and validation of computer protocols / Gerard J. Holzmann.
        p.   cm. -- (Prentice Hall software series)
    Includes bibliographical references and indexes.
    ISBN 0-13-539925-4
    1. Computer network protocols--Design.   I. Title. II. Series.
    TK5105.5.H645 1991
    004.6'2--dc20   90-40822
                                                              CIP

Prentice Hall Software Series
Brian W. Kernighan, Advisor

The publisher offers discounts on this book when ordered in large quantities. For more information, write:

> Special Sales/College Marketing
> Prentice-Hall, Inc.
> College Technical and Reference Division
> Englewood Cliffs, NJ 07632

This book is typeset in Times Roman by the author, using a 200P Linotronic phototypesetter and a DEC VAX 8550 running the 10th Edition of the UNIX® operating system.

DEC and VAX are trademarks of Digital Equipment Corporation. UNIX is a registered trademark of AT&T.

Printed in the United States of America

10 9 8 7 6 5 4 3 2 1

ISBN 0-13-539925-4

Prentice-Hall International (UK) Limited, *London*
Prentice-Hall of Australia Pty. Limited, *Sydney*
Prentice-Hall Canada Inc., *Toronto*
Prentice-Hall Hispanoamericana, S.A., *Mexico*
Prentice-Hall of India Private Limited, *New Delhi*
Prentice-Hall of Japan, Inc., *Tokyo*
Simon & Schuster Asia Pte. Ltd., *Singapore*
Editora Prentice-Hall do Brasil, Ltda., *Rio de Janeiro*

CONTENTS

FOREWORD

It is now over 15 years since the first, tentative efforts were made to assemble theories and tools that could help with the development of communications protocols — the rules and procedures that control and manage the flow of information within computer networks.

During the intervening years, a significant body of knowledge has been accumulated that can be successfully applied to the various phases of protocol development. There are now international standards for languages designed for the formal specification of the protocols upon which we will build our future computer networks. We have learned that even the most carefully developed protocol specifications contain subtle errors unless they are subjected to a thorough error analysis. Much progress has been made in the development of automated tools to support this. There have also been significant advances in testing techniques that make it possible to build reliable heterogeneous networks using hardware and software from a wide spectrum of manufacturers and development organizations.

We are fortunate that Gerard Holzmann has made the effort to write this book that summarizes much of what we know about designing protocols and documents his own considerable experience in the field. His book has four major sections. The first gives an introduction to the problems that are encountered during the development of protocols and discusses the principles of protocol design. The historical examples used to introduce the subject are a delight. The second section discusses ways in which a protocol can be modeled and specified. The third explains how protocol models can be analyzed to determine their properties and evaluate their correctness. The final section presents protocol design tools which complement the material in the earlier sections of the book. This is an important section. Protocols have proved to be extremely difficult to understand without automated analysis tools. The serious student of the field will learn a great deal by using the tools presented here to build and analyze his own protocols.

Colin H. West

x

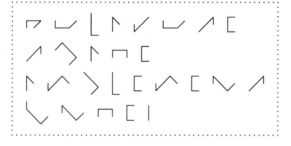

PREFACE

Protocols are sets of rules that govern the interaction of concurrent processes in distributed systems. Protocol design is therefore closely related to a number of established fields, such as operating systems, computer networks, data transmission, and data communications. It is rarely singled out and studied as a discipline in its own right. Designing a logically consistent protocol that can be proven correct, however, is a challenging and often frustrating task. It can already be hard to convince ourselves of the validity of a sequentially executed program. In distributed systems we must reason about concurrently executed, interacting programs.

Books about distributed systems, computer networks, or data communications often do no better than describe a set of standard solutions that have been accepted as correct by, for instance, large international organizations. They do not tell us why the solutions work, what problems they solve, or what pitfalls they avoid.

This text is intended as a guide to protocol design and analysis, rather than as a guide to standards and formats. It discusses design issues instead of applications. Two issues, therefore, are beyond the scope of this text: network control (including routing, addressing, and congestion control) and implementation. There is, however, no shortage of texts on both topics. The design problem is addressed here as a fundamental and challenging issue, rather than as an irritating practicle obstacle to the development of reliable communication systems. The aim of the book is to make you familiar with all the issues of protocol validation and protocol design.

The first part of the book covers the basics. Chapter 1 gives a flavor of the types of problems that are discussed. Chapter 2 deals with protocol structure and general design issues. Chapters 3 and 4 discuss the basics of error control and flow control.

The next four chapters cover formal protocol modeling and specification techniques, beginning in Chapters 5 and 6 with the introduction of the concept of a protocol validation model, that serves as an abstraction of a design and a prototype of its implementation. In Chapter 5 a terse new language called PROMELA is introduced for the description of protocol validation models, and in Chapter 6 it is extended for the specification of protocol correctness requirements. In Chapter 7 we use

PROMELA to discuss a number of standard design problems in the development of a sample file transfer protocol. Part II closes with a discussion, in Chapter 8, of the extended finite state machine, a basic notion in many formal modeling techniques.

The third part of the book focuses on protocol synthesis, testing, and validation techniques that can be used to battle a protocol's complexity. Both the capabilities and the limitations of the formal design techniques are covered.

The fourth and last part of the book gives a detailed description of the design of two protocol design tools based on PROMELA: an interpreter and an automated validator. Based on these tools, an implementation generator is simple to add. Source code for the tools is provided in Appendices D and E. The source is also available in electronic form. Ordering information can be found in Appendix E.

LECTURE PLAN

The core of this book is contained in Chapters 2, 5, 6, 7, and 11. These chapters explore a design discipline that is supported by the tools discussed in Chapters 12 to 14. The remaining text is meant to make the book relatively self-contained. Chapter 3 on error control, Chapter 4 on flow control, and Chapter 8 on finite state machines give background information that should be part of the working knowledge of every protocol designer. Chapters 9 and 10 bring the reader up-to-date with the latest techniques in closely related fields of protocol engineering.

For a one-semester course in protocol design the following sequence of chapters and appendices is suggested: 1, 2, A, 3, B, 4, 5 & C, 6-14. A shorter course, for instance embedded in full semester course on operating systems or data networks, would consist of Chapters 1, 2, 5, 6, 7-11, 14. The software discussed in the book can be used for class projects in the design and validation of sample protocols. Suggestions for exercises are included throughout the text.

ACKNOWLEDGMENTS

Many people have helped in the preparation of this book. Friendly readers who worked their way through earlier drafts include Jon Bentley, Geoffrey Brown, Tom Cargill, John Chaves, Mohamed Gouda, Paul Haahr, Brian Kernighan, David Lee, Doug McIlroy, Sally McKee, Norman Ramsey, Howard Trickey, and Colin West.

The validation software was developed over many years. Crucial help in the derivation of the basic algorithm of supertrace was given by Doug McIlroy, Rob Pike, Jim Reeds, and Ken Thompson. Costas Courcoubetis and Mihalis Yannakakis extended the software with algorithms for analyzing liveness properties.

I am also grateful to Greg Chesson, Tony Dabhura, Sandy Fraser, Joop Goudsblom, Andrew Hume, Mike Lesk, Don Mitchell, Beate Oestreicher, John Peterson, Björn Pehrson, Dave Presotto, S. Purushothaman, Krishan Sabnani, Ravi Sethi, and M. Sullivan for references and valuable suggestions.

Gerard J. Holzmann

INTRODUCTION **1**

1.1 EARLY BEGINNINGS

The problem of designing efficient and unambiguous communication protocols existed long before the first computers were built. There is a long history of attempts to construct systems for transferring information quickly over long distances. From a protocol designer's point of view, the mishaps that were caused by misinterpreted communications are fascinating. Of course, the problems of the early systems were not always documented as diligently as the features.

BEACONS AND ALARUMS

Anything that is detectable over a large distance is a potential means of communication. In the play *Agamemnon* from 458 B.C., for instance, Aeschylus describes in detail how fire signals were used, supposedly, to communicate the fall of Troy to Athens over a distance of more than 300 miles. But the number of different messages that can be transferred by a single big fire is limited. A detailed account of that problem was given by the Greek historian Polybius in the 2nd century B.C.[1] It is probably one of the first explicit descriptions of data transmission methods. Polybius starts by explaining why a signaling method is useful in the first place.

> *"It is evident to all that in every matter, and especially in warfare, the power of acting at the right time contributes very much to the success of enterprises, and fire signals are the most efficient of all the devices which aid us to do this. For they show what has recently occurred and what is still in the course of being done, and by means of them anyone who cares to do so even if he is at a distance of three, four or even more days' journey can be informed. So that it is always surprising how help can be brought by means of fire messages when the situation requires it."*

---

1. *The Histories*, Book X, Chapter 43. The translation is by W.R. Patton and was published by Harvard University Press in 1925.

1

The use of fire signals must have been commonplace in Polybius' days. But, there were a few problems to solve.

> *"Now in former times, as fire signals were simple beacons, they were for the most part of little use to those who used them. For the service should have been performed by signals previously determined upon, and as facts are indefinite, most of them defied communication by fire signals. To take the case I just mentioned, it was possible for those who had agreed on this to convey information that a fleet had arrived at Oreus, Peparethus, or Chalcis, but when it came to some of the citizens having changed sides or having been guilty of treachery or a massacre having taken place in the town, or anything of the kind, things that often happen, but cannot all be foreseen — **and it is chiefly unexpected occurrences which require instant consideration and help** — all such matters defied communication by fire signal. For it was quite impossible to have a preconcerted code for things which there was no means of foretelling."*

The crucial observation is the part in bold. Throughout this book we will see that it is still a problem. It is the unexpected sequences of events that lead to protocol failures, and the hardest problem in protocol design is precisely that we must try to expect the unexpected.

Polybius continues his account with a description of a new signaling method that he believed solved the communication problem. It is remarkably sophisticated, though it only partly solves the problem. The new system used two sets of five torches. By lighting between one and five torches in each set, a total of 5^2 characters could be encoded, sufficient to transmit arbitrary messages as a sequence of encoded letters.

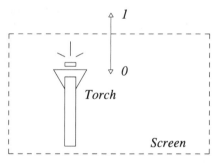

Figure 1.1 — Torch Telegraph

As shown in Figure 1.1, the torches could be used to send a binary torch code. A torch could be made visible to the remote receiver by raising it above a screen, and it could be hidden by lowering it. Polybius describes the torch code as follows.

> *"We take the alphabet and divide it into five parts, each consisting of five letters. There is one letter fewer in the last division, but it makes no practical difference. Each of the two parties who are about to signal to each other must now get ready*

five tablets and write one division of the alphabet on each tablet, and then come to an agreement that the man who is going to signal is in the first place to raise two torches and wait until the other replies by doing the same. This is for the purpose of conveying to each other that they are both at attention. These torches having been lowered, the dispatcher of the message will now raise the first set of torches on the left side indicating which tablet is to be consulted, i.e., one torch if it is the first, two if it is the second, and so on. Next he will raise the second set on the right on the same principle to indicate what letter of the tablet the receiver should write down."

No real improvements over Polybius' telegraph were made for almost twenty centuries, though there was no lack of inferior alternatives. In 1684, the English scientist Robert Hooke described a rather clumsy optical system that worked with large wooden characters. The characters could be displayed at a signaling station and observed from a distance with a telescope.[2] As far as we know, it was never put into practice.

In 1796, the German G. Huth invented an equally unsuccessful system that he named "telephone." The idea was to place men with "speaking tubes" on roof tops and have them shout messages to each other. In fact, Huth's idea had been tried before. Alexander the Great (356-323 B.C.) is said to have used a twelve foot megaphone to shout commands to his armies from nearby hills. Not surprisingly, Polybius did not spend much time discussing this system.

Another remarkable device was used during the American Revolutionary War (1775-1783). It consisted of a pole from which any combination of three different objects could be displayed. With a barrel, a flag, and a basket, $2^3 - 1$ different messages could be transmitted, though obviously not in very rapid succession.

OPTICAL SYSTEMS

The first successful pre-electric telegraph system was developed by the French engineer Claude Chappe in 1793. His system consisted of large wooden constructions built on hill tops or church towers and was operated by civil servants equipped with telescopes. The semaphore had three movable parts, *regulator* and two *indicators*, as illustrated in Figure 1.2. The regulator was roughly 15 ft long, the indicators measured approximately 7 by 1 ft each.

It is not clear from the reports what the precise signaling "alphabet" was or how it was encoded in the positions of regulator and indicators. The semaphore arms could be moved only in 45° increments. Theoretically, with three movable parts, each semaphore could be set in 256 (8×8×4) different positions. Particularly confusing combinations were not used, for instance positions where the indicators duplicate the angle of the regulator. Reportedly, about half of the valid semaphore

---

2. The telescope was also a recent invention at the time. It was described by Galileo in *Siderius Nuncius* (The Starry Messenger) in 1610.

positions were used to encode digits, punctuation marks, upper- and lower-case letters, and the other half were used for special control codes. The civil servants were hired to read the semaphore position from the neighboring stations and to copy it onto their own semaphore to relay messages.

At the peak of its success, shortly before electric telegraphs took over, Chappe's system had grown into a complete network of no less than 556 semaphore stations covering more than 3000 miles and reaching nearly every part of France. Little is known about the specific operating procedures employed or the coordination problems that must have plagued the semaphore operators. What, for instance, was a semaphore operator supposed to do when two messages came in simultaneously from opposite directions?

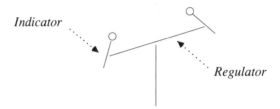

Figure 1.2 — Chappe's Semaphore

Almost every country had one or more variations of Chappe's optical telegraph in this period. The British admiralty, for instance, used a six-shutter semaphore designed by a Lord George Murray. Each shutter could be either opened or closed to transmit a message: a 6-bit binary code. The use of control messages is also documented for this system. All six shutters closed was used to signal *not ready*, all six shutters open meant *ready to send*.

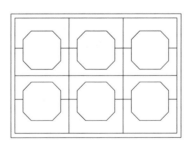

Figure 1.3 — George Murray's Six-Shutter Telegraph

A similar system, using ten shutters, was developed in Sweden. The Swedish system is documented in detail in a publication of its inventor, the Swedish Chancery Secretary A.N. Edelcrantz, called *Avhandling om Telegrapher* published in 1796.

A coding table, based on a simple system for assigning numbers to shutter positions, was included.

> *"All telegraphic correspondence is started with a signal indicating that you want to speak, or a speak sign, which is left up until the receiver has given the corresponding alert sign. (...) When this is done, the speak sign is taken down and the first signal in the message is given. The receiver then takes down the alert sign and repeats the signal from the sender to show that it has read it correctly. The same procedure is repeated for all signals in the message.*

In 1796 this telegraph connected Stockholm and Åland. One shutter telegraph station, built in Furusund in 1836, has survived and can still be visited today (see also Bibliographic Notes). The signaling codes used on the Swedish system include codes for session control (start, stop), error control, flow control (repeat), rate control (slower, faster), and even a negative acknowledgment, which was named appropriately "cannot see."

The transmission speed of the optical telegraphs varied. On Chappe's telegraph the semaphore position was changed once every 15-20 seconds. With a subset of 128 possible symbols (or 7 bits of information) this gave a transmission speed of roughly 0.5 bits/sec. The 10-bit code of the Swedish shutter telegraph was changed every 8-10 seconds, and the 6-bit code of the British system every 5 seconds, both giving a signaling speed of approximately 1 bit/sec.

The visibility of the semaphores must have been another concern of the operators. On an average of twenty days per year, for example, weather conditions prevented the usage of a shutter semaphore that connected five cities in The Netherlands between 1831 and 1839.

After 1840, the electric telegraph finally proved to be faster, more reliable, and less conspicuous than optical telegraphs.

ELECTROMAGNETISM

The principle of an electric telegraph was described as early as 1753 by a mysterious "C.M." in a letter to the *Scots' Magazine*.[3] The identity of the author has never been fully established. Some sources say that the initials are those of a Charles Marshall from Renfrew (the letter was mailed from Renfrew). Others claim that the author was someone called Charles Morrison of Greenock. The letter describes an electric telegraph with a number of parallel wires: one for each different code, or character, to be transmitted. Small pithballs were placed at the receiver near the terminals of each wire. The sender could place a static electric charge on one of the wires (by discharging a Leyden jar) and cause the corresponding pithball at the receiver to move.

---

3. The *Scots' Magazine*, February 17, 1753, Vol. XV, p. 73. The letter was titled *An expeditious method for conveying intelligence.*

Shortly after 1830 a new insight into electromagnetic induction was obtained through the work of Michael Faraday in England and Joseph Henry in the United States. In England, the principle was used in 1837 by William Cooke in the construction of the first electric telegraph. Cooke used an electric charge to deflect a compass needle in a small magnetic field at the receiving instrument. The idea for such a ''needle telegraph'' was perfected by Cooke in cooperation with Sir Charles Wheatstone. It was patented in 1837 as a *Method of Giving Signals and Sounding Alarums at Distant Places by Means of Electric Currents Transmitted through Metallic Circuits*. In the United States similar work was done by Samuel Morse and Theodore Vail.

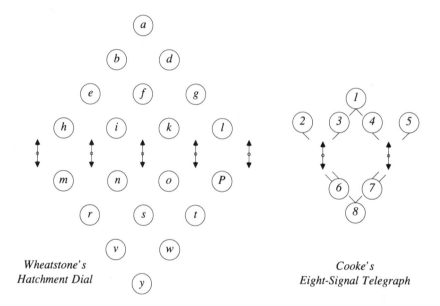

Wheatstone's Hatchment Dial   *Cooke's Eight-Signal Telegraph*

Figure 1.4 — The First Multiple-Needle Telegraphs

The first patent, dated 12 June 1837, was for a telegraph system with five magnetic needles. Any combination of two out of the five needles could be deflected either left or right, enough to signal twenty different letters. In Figure 1.4 a five-needle and a two-needle telegraph are shown. On both instruments only two needles would be deflected at a time. Together the two needles would point at the character or the code being transmitted. A little later, Cooke and Wheatstone also developed transmission codes for single-needle telegraphs that included a small number of control codes, such as *repeat* and *wait*. The *repeat* code, for instance, was sent on a single-needle telegraph as a sequence of ten clicks of the needle to the right.

William Cooke made great efforts to sell his system to the railway companies in England as a method for traffic control. In 1842, Cooke published an amusing booklet with a long title,[4] which documents his lobbying. He was perhaps a little too optimistic about the potential benefits:

> *"... trains might proceed fearlessly, whether in time or out of time, whether on the right or on the wrong line, as their speed could always be slackened soon enough to avoid a collision."*

The system was readily adopted and used on several lines of the Great Western Railways in England. The first experiments showed that the operating expenses were only one-tenth of those for optical telegraphs, and the transmission speeds were much higher.

Unfortunately, one of the first applications of the electric telegraph was to protect notoriously dangerous stretches of railroad, such as single-track lines and tunnels. Many railway accidents from this period were caused by subtle misunderstandings between the signalmen using the new equipment.

TRAIN CRASHES

The cause of a railway accident is usually investigated and documented in minute detail, so there is no shortage of material on the early protocol design problems. A single example may suffice to illustrate how major accidents could result merely from an unexpected combination of events. To be sure, the accident to be described could have been prevented if an adequate protocol had been used for the communication between the signalmen.

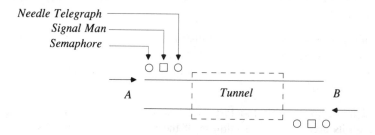

Figure 1.5 — Clayton Tunnel

The accident occurred in the Clayton tunnel, which must have been one of the best protected railway sections in England. On each end of the 1.5 mile long tunnel, 24 hours per day, signalmen were on duty. Furthermore, in 1841, the tunnel was equipped with a new space-interval block-signaling system. There were semaphore

---

4. *Telegraphic Railways or the single way recommended by safety, economy, and efficiency, under the safeguard and control of the electric telegraph — with particular reference to railway communication with Scotland, and to Irish Railways.* (Cooke [1842]).

signals on each end of the tunnel, and the block-interval system guaranteed that any train passing a green signal automatically set that signal to red. It was up to the signalmen to reset the signals to green, but before doing so they were required to make certain that trains that had entered the tunnel on one side had indeed emerged again at the other end.

There were two tracks through the tunnel: one for each direction. At all times, only one train was allowed per track in the tunnel. As a further safety measure the tunnel had been equipped with a single-needle telegraph. This system was set up for the exchange of a small number of predefined messages between the signalmen on both ends of the tunnel.

Typically, after allowing a train to enter one side of the tunnel, the signalman at that side transmitted the code *train in tunnel* to his colleague. When (and if) the train emerged from the tunnel at the other end, his colleague responded with the code *tunnel is free*. Upon the receipt of that message, the first signalman could reset the entrance signal to allow the next train to enter.

To make the system foolproof, yet a third message code had been added with which a signalman could ask his colleague: *has the train left the tunnel?* The presence of the two signalmen guaranteed that the tunnel could be used safely even if, for any reason, the semaphore signal on either side of the tunnel malfunctioned. If a semaphore failed to show red after a train had passed, the signalman was warned by a bell. He could then use red and white flags to signal trains and keep the traffic going.

Still, the protocol turned out to be incompletely specified. Here is what happened in August 1861.

□ A first train passes semaphore A and fails to set the signal to red. As expected, the bell warns the signalman at A (call him signalman A). He dutifully first transmits the code *train in tunnel* to his colleague, and then fetches the red flag to warn the next train.

□ A second train, however, is too fast, and has already passed the green signal. Fortunately, its driver catches a glimpse of the red flag just in time as he enters the tunnel. A third train is warned in time and comes to a full stop before the tunnel entrance.

□ Signalman A returns to his box and again signals *train in tunnel* to indicate that there are now two trains in the tunnel. The protocol did not account for this event so the meaning of two subsequent *train in tunnel* messages had not been specified. However, since it was unlikely that the second train could overtake the first one, no real problem existed. The only problem for signalman A was to find out from his colleague when both trains had left the tunnel, so that the third one could enter.

☐ To alert his colleague to the problem, signalman A transmits the only other appropriate message he has: *has the train left the tunnel?* At this point there is no hope of recovery. Even if the signalman at B could understand precisely what the problem was, he had no way of communicating this. After seeing the first train emerge from the tunnel he responds, in full agreement with his instructions, *tunnel is clear.*

☐ Signalman A cannot know if he should wait for two subsequent *tunnel is clear* messages or whether the message can be taken literally. He decides that both trains must have left the tunnel and allows the third train to enter by waving a white flag. The driver of the second train, though, had seen the red flag while entering the tunnel and has come to a full stop in the middle of the tunnel. After some deliberation the driver decides to play it safe and back out of the tunnel.

☐ In the collision that followed 21 people died and 176 were injured.

It is hard to assess who would be to blame for this accident. Once, by a freak combination of events, it had become possible for the second train to enter the tunnel before the first one had left it, there was no way to recover. The common sense of both the signalmen and the driver of the second train could not prevent the accident. The set of instructions given to the signalmen was incomplete. At the time, though, some were more eager to blame the relatively new block signaling method or the telegraph instruments than the men who had drafted the operating procedures for the signalmen's interactions.

In the early days of the railways, many accidents and near accidents were the result of an outright lack of means for communication. Later, when the right tools were available, it was discovered how surprisingly difficult it can be to establish unambiguous rules for communication. A historian of railway disasters (Nock [1967]) described the problem as follows, much in line with Polybius' earlier observations:

> *"One can almost hear the same comment being made time after time. 'I could not imagine that could ever happen.' Yet bitter experience showed that it could, and gradually the regulations and railway engineering practice were elaborated."*

The problem was to design a practical, common sense set of rules that was efficient to use under normal circumstances and that allowed for a safe recovery from unexpected events.

1.2 THE FIRST NETWORKS

Though originally the electric telegraph was mostly used for railway signaling, it did not take long before it became more generally available. In 1851 the stock exchanges in London and Paris had been connected by telegraph, and the first public telegraph companies were founded. By 1875 almost 200,000 miles of telegraph line were in operation. At first, the telegraphs were operated with either needle instruments or Morse signaling keys. The most frequently used signaling code was a modified Morse code. The original Morse code used three signaling elements of varying duration: dots, dashes, and long dashes. The modern version was introduced in 1851, using a variable length binary code of the two familiar signaling elements: dots and dashes.

A first improvement made to this still manually operated system was the paper tape punch reader. In 1858 Wheatstone built the *Wheatstone Automatic*, with which transmission speeds of 300 words per minute could be achieved (about 30 bits/sec). It was used until very recently. After 1920 special "tele-typewriter" keyboards and printers were connected directly to the telegraph wires. The 5-bit code that was used on these machines was developed by the Frenchman Emil Baudot in 1874. By 1925 complete "telex" (telegraph-exchange) networks were in operation.

In the same period, between 1850 and 1950, two other now familiar methods of communication were developed: telephone and radio. Elisha Gray and Alexander Graham Bell, for instance, filed their applications for a patent on the invention of the telephone[5] in 1876, and in 1897 Guiglielmo Marconi built and used the first radio telegraph.

MASTER-SLAVE PROTOCOLS

The demands for the thoroughness of new communication protocols increased dramatically after 1950, when protocol execution was first automated on large mainframe computers.

One of the earliest programmable computers, the ENIAC, was built at the University of Pennsylvania in 1946. It weighed in at 30 tons. As we know, after the invention of the transistor in 1947 by J. Bardeen, W.H. Brattain, and W. Shockley of AT&T Bell Laboratories, subsequent systems quickly became both smaller and faster. Though size is not really an issue in protocol design, speed is. Even today, it continues to change the nature of the protocol design problem.

The first computers had to be connected to peripheral devices, such as paper tape readers and teletype keyboards. Since computers were initially large, expensive, and scarce, one single "intelligent" mainframe was often connected to large arrays of "dumb" peripherals.

At first, the peripherals were at fairly close range, say within the same room as the mainframe computer, connected by multidrop lines. If there were no data to transfer to the peripherals, the mainframe would "poll" the peripherals to see if any of them had data to return or a status report to file.

Already in 1956 the first experiments took place with long-distance data transmission from computer to computer across telephone wires, causing fundamentally dif-

---

5. Bell's patent, in fact, did not mention the word "telephone" at all; it was titled *Improvements in Telegraphy*.

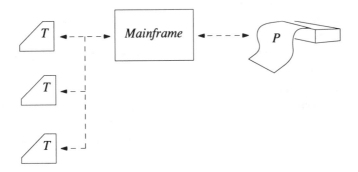

Figure 1.6 — Master-Slave Protocols

ferent types of control problems. Six years later the first data transmission via a satellite (Telstar) took place.

The first data communications protocols run on computers were rather simple encodings of the heuristics of manual operations. The procedures were used to solve a traditional master-slave coordination problem. At all times one of the two parties involved in the communication was in control and responsible for all data transfer, recovery, synchronization, and connection management tasks. Many of the older protocols were designed with this concept in mind. IBM's *Bisync* protocol, for example, dates from this period. In the 1960s, with direct connections of mainframe computers via data networks, the protocol design problem became more important. The data speeds were higher, the traffic load larger, and much of the convenience of master-slave relations was lost. Mainframes were now talking directly to each other, connected in networks of peers.

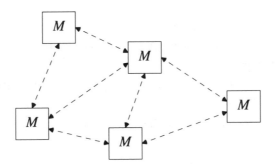

Figure 1.7 — Network of Peers

PEER PROTOCOLS

The first large-scale computer networks were the airline reservation systems from the early 1960s. The SABRE system from American Airlines, for instance, was built in 1961. In 1969 a large general-purpose packet-switching network was developed, sponsored by the U.S. Department of Defense. This ARPA (Advanced Research Projects Agency) network connected almost 1200 nodes by 1985. The Internet, a successor to the ARPA network, grew from about 25,000 nodes in 1987 to an estimated 250,000 nodes towards the end of 1989.

The number of private and public data networks is expected to continue to grow rapidly. The technology available for the construction of these systems is often sophisticated, at least as far as the hardware and the basic operating procedures are concerned. Yet, though the systems may now operate with optical fibers and satellite links, the problems that have to be solved to utilize a communication system effectively are essentially the same as in the days of Polybius.

The protocol design problem is to establish agreement about the usage of shared resources in a network of peers. It is not immediately clear which process is responsible for which task; those responsibilities may have to be negotiated. If more than one process erroneously assumes responsibility for a task, havoc can result. The network designers of the 1960s learned the hard way that very unlikely sequences of events really do happen and can ruin the best design.

Entire networks can be paralyzed by faulty or incomplete protocols. Although a collision of two data streams on a satellite channel seems harmless compared to a head-on collision of two trains, in both cases the damage can be substantial.

1.3 PROTOCOLS AS LANGUAGES

The term *protocol* for a data communications procedure was first used by R.A. Scantlebury and K.A. Bartlett at the National Physical Laboratory in England, in a memorandum that was written in April 1967. The memorandum was titled *A protocol for use in the NPL data communications network*.

We already know that a protocol is a kind of agreement about the exchange of information in a distributed system. A full protocol definition, in fact, looks much like a language definition.

□ It defines a precise *format* for valid messages, such as the dots and dashes that make up the Morse code (a syntax).

□ It defines the *procedure rules* for the data exchange (a grammar).

□ And it defines a *vocabulary* of valid messages that can be exchanged, with their meaning (semantics).

We will come up with a slightly extended definition of a protocol in the next chapter. But note that the grammar of the protocol must be logically consistent and complete: under all possible circumstances the rules should prescribe in unambiguous terms what is allowed and what is forbidden. In practice, this is a difficult requirement to meet.

Although protocols, in one form or another, have been used on long-distance communication systems throughout history, until recently there was always a human
operator who could be relied upon to make common sense decisions to resolve
unexpected problems. In the 5-bit telex-code there are even two special symbols to
invoke human action: the code `10010` means *who is there?*, and the code `11010`
rings a bell.

In using machines rather than human operators, we have the same communication
and coordination problems, but this time the errors can happen faster, and we can
no longer rely on human intervention to recover from the unexpected cases.

One important hidden requirement of protocol design is now obvious: not only
should there be rules for the exchange of information, there should also be an
agreement between the sender and the receiver about those rules. IBM's *Bisync*
protocol, for instance, had been implemented on many different systems, and on
each new system it was embellished with the inevitable common sense of the
implementer for shortcuts and improvements. These slightly differing interpretations of the rules of the *Bisync* protocol ruled out any hope that two arbitrarily
chosen implementations of the same protocol could really communicate. Instead of
leading to stricter guidelines for the design, specification, and implementation of
protocols, this led to the institution of international standardization bodies.

1.4 PROTOCOL STANDARDIZATION

Many standardization bodies are active in the area of data communications. Exam-
ples are the National Institute of Science and Technology (NIST, formerly the
National Bureau of Standards or NBS), the Federal Telecommunications Standards
Committee (FTSC), and the Institute of Electrical and Electronics Engineers
(IEEE). The two most important standardization bodies in this area, however, are
the ISO and the CCITT.

☐   The International Standards Organization (ISO) includes many national stan-
    dards bodies, such as the American National Standards Institute (ANSI). ANSI
    is responsible for important standards such as the ASCII character code and the
    RS232 interface definition. The ISO is organized in technical committees (TC),
    each organized in subcommittees (SC), and working groups (WG). TC97, for
    instance, is concerned with standards for computers, TC97/SC6 deals with
    telecommunications, and TC97/SC6/WG1 works on standards for data link pro-
    tocols. The ASCII code is formally known as ISO standard 646. Unlike the
    CCITT, the ISO is not a treaty organization and membership is voluntary.

☐   The Comité Consultatif International Télégraphique et Téléphonique (CCITT) is
    part of the International Telecommunications Union (ITU). The CCITT is a
    U.N. treaty organization that was formed in 1956 by the union of two separate
    entities: the CCIT (telegraph systems) and the CCIF (telephone systems).
    Today it includes many of the public telephone companies, such as the Euro-

pean PTTs and America's AT&T. The U.S. Department of State is also an official member of the organization. The CCITT is organized in study groups (SG) and working parties (WP). SGVII, for instance, is concerned with data communication networks, and SGVII/WP2 works on network interfaces. The 5-bit telex code is officially known as CCITT-Alphabet No. 2. The best known protocol recommendations published by the CCITT are X.21 and X.25 (see also Chapter 2). X.21 has the dubious honor (see Bibliographic Notes to Chapter 11) of being the first reference protocol to be validated by exhaustive reachability analysis.

Another organization that does important work in this area, though it is not directly involved with protocol standardization, is the International Federation for Information Processing (IFIP). One of IFIP's aims is to serve as a bridge organization that connects the work performed in bodies such as the CCITT and the ISO. Like the ISO the IFIP is organized in Technical Committees (TC), where each Technical Comittee is further subdivided into Working Groups (WG). TC6, for instance, is devoted to data communications, and WG 6.1 studies *Architecture and Protocols for Computer Networks*. IFIP was established in 1960.

Of course, protocol standardization still does not solve the protocol design problem itself. After all, what good is an international standard that is incomplete or even faulty? The standardization bodies face the same problem as all other protocol designers, and one can well say that "design by committee" does not always guarantee the best results.

Before this problem can be solved, we will need convincing methods to *design* and *describe* protocols, and effective methods to *check* that any protocol submitted to a standardization body is correct. Clearly, to design and describe a protocol we need to be able to express its design criteria, and to verify a protocol effectively we need to be able to check that its design criteria are met.

The problem to define a common format for the specification protocols in standardization documents has been studied for many years. Three protocol specification languages have now been developed: SDL, Lotos, and Estelle. They are commonly referred to as the three FDTs, or Formal Description Techniques.

☐   The Specification and Description Language (SDL) was developed by study groups SGXI and SGX of the CCITT. It is meant specifically for the specification and design of telecommunications systems, such as telephone switches. The study was started in 1968. A first version became CCITT Recommendation Z101-Z104 in 1976, and revised versions were published in 1982 and in 1985. A final, stable version was approved in 1987. There are two, largely equivalent, variants of SDL in use: a graphical form and a program form. The flow charting language used in the first part of this book is loosely based on the graphical form (see Appendix B).

☐ The Language of Temporal Ordering Specifications (Lotos) is being developed within the ISO, TC97/SC21/WG1. Lotos is also called a ''process algebra.'' It is based on the Calculus of Communicating Systems (CCS) developed by Robin Milner at the University of Edinburgh. The main goal of the process algebras is the formal specification of process behaviors on a high level of abstraction. The algebras define a rigorous set of transformation rules and equivalence relations that can allow a designer to reason formally about behaviors. Lotos was issued as ISO international standard IS8807 in February 1989.

☐ Estelle is a second formal description technique being developed within another subgroup of ISO TC97/SC21/WG1. A total of three subgroups of WG1 studying formal description techniques have been active since 1981. (The third subgroup studies architectural methods.) The language Estelle is based on an extended finite state machine concept (see Chapter 8). It was issued as ISO international standard IS9074 in July 1989.

Lotos is the only FDT from this range that specifically also addresses the design problem. We can learn quite a lot from the experience gained here. None of the FDTs, however, have addressed also the problem that complete designs must be verifiable at the protocol specification level. We must be able to check, preferably with automated tools, that a design meets its requirements. As it stands, verifiability cannot be guaranteed for any of the FDTs. Both Lotos and SDL specifications, for instance, can specify infinite systems, which renders many verification problems formally undecidable. There is an active area of research to develop tools for subsets of the languages, but also here the problems to be solved are formidable.

1.5 SUMMARY

Protocol design is not a new problem. It is as old as communication itself. Only when the interpretation of the protocol rules had to be automated on high-speed machines, was it discovered that protocol design in itself can be a challenging problem. The protocols being developed today are larger and more sophisticated than ever before. They try to offer more functionality and reliability, but as a result they have increased in size and in complexity. The problem that a designer now faces is fundamental: how to design large sets of rules for information exchange that are minimal, logically consistent, complete, and efficiently implemented. The problem can be approached from two sides.

☐ Given a problem, how can a designer solve it systematically so that design requirements are realized?

☐ Given a protocol, how can an analyzer demonstrate convincingly that it conforms to the correctness requirements?

In this book we study the fundamental problem of designing and analyzing protocols that formalize interactions in distributed systems. Typically, these will be interactions of computers, but they apply equally well to the interaction of people with torch telegraphs. The problem in all such systems is to come up with an unambiguous set of rules that allows one to initiate, maintain, and complete information exchanges reliably.

DESIGN DISCIPLINE

First we need to understand what the basic problems are, and we spend the first few chapters studying that. Next, we need to establish a design discipline, a set of self-imposed constraints that can help us avoid trouble. But that is not all. All freshly designed protocols, no matter how disciplined their designers have been, must be treated with suspicion.

> *Every protocol should be considered to be incorrect until the opposite is proven.*

We will argue that to prove the correctness or incorrectness of protocols, a good set of efficient and automated design tools is indispensable.

DESIGN TOOLS

Not even the best set of rules can prevent all errors. That is a simple fact of life. We must require, however, that protocol rules always provide for a graceful recovery from the errors that do occur. It is not good enough if the protocol rules *allow* for an interpretation that prevents disaster in unexpected circumstances. We must require that the rules *preclude* interpretations that may lead to disaster.

The design methods we develop in this book are based on the concept of a *validation model*. A validation model expresses the essential characteristics of the protocol, without going into the details of its implementation. Automated tools can interpret these validation models and find the flaws in the design with relentless precision.

In the next chapters we begin exploring the general structure of communication protocols and some of the basic issues involved in protocol design.

EXERCISES

1-1 The transmission code developed by Polybius for his torch telegraph divided the 24-letter Greek alphabet into five groups. The first four groups had five letters each, and the fifth group had the remaining four.
    The telegraph worked with two groups of torches: one was used to encode the group number, the other to transmit the character number within that group. Transmission took place character by character, by raising and lowering torches in the two groups. There were no codes for spaces to separate words, nor for any kind of punctuation. (Punctuation was not used yet in written Greek either.) There was, however, one additional control message to signal the start of a message: two torches raised simultaneously (see the quotation from Polybius on page 3).
    What are the possible synchronization problems, in the absence of a proper agreement on the order in which the torches in the two groups are to be lowered and raised?

1-2 Estimate the transmission speed of the torch telegraph and compare it with Chappe's system. How long does it take to transmit the message "protocol failure?"

1-3 Polybius recommended the compaction of messages to reduce transmission time and thus the number of errors. Comment on this discipline. Hint: consider the opposite technique of increasing redundancy to protect against transmission and interpretation errors.

1-4 If the signalmen at the Clayton tunnel had had the complete character set on their needle telegraphs, consider how they could have used it to resolve the problem. The length of the tunnel is 1.5 miles, the speed of the trains was approximately 45 miles per hour, and the transmission speed of a needle telegraph is about 25 symbols per minute.
The problem for the signalmen was to establish the whereabouts of the second train. At the crucial moment the second train was backing out of the tunnel to where the third train was waiting. The signalman at A assumed that the second train had already left the tunnel; the signalman at B did not know that a second train was involved.

1-5 Try to revise the protocol for the Clayton Tunnel to avoid completely the possibility of the accident. Do not assume that the number of trains in the tunnel is always either zero or one, and do not assume that trains always travel in one direction.

1-6 The complete code for the needle telegraph had a *repeat* message that could be used to request the retransmission of the last message sent by the other station. Consider what would happen if this discipline was strictly enforced and the *repeat* message itself was the last transmitted message of both stations.

1-7 (Jon Bentley) If a telephone call is unexpectedly terminated, there is an informal "telephone protocol" which says that the caller should redial the call. If the called party is unaware of this protocol a curious problem results. A "Lover's Paradox" prevents contact from being made when both parties try to establish it simultaneously. What is the protocol flaw? Assume the callers are machines, how could the machines be programmed to prevent the problem from repeating itself ad infinitem? What happens to this protocol if both parties have a "call interrupt" feature (the ability to take an extra call when already offhook)?

BIBLIOGRAPHIC NOTES

The French engineer Claude Chappe was born in Brûlon, France, in 1763. He originally joined a religious order as a monk, but in 1791 was forced to leave the order. Together with his brother Ignace he set up a shop to work on the telegraph. His only publication was a short note on the optical telegraph from 1798 (Chappe [1798]). His life is described in a book by his brother, published in 1824 (Chappe [1824]). Claude Chappe committed suicide in 1805, supposedly when others claimed credit for his inventions.

The shutter telegraph used in England was designed by Lord George Murray in 1794. It is described in Reid [1886] and Michaelis [1965]. The system was in operation until 1816. The Edelcrantz system, and its signaling code, is described in Edelcrantz [1796]. Malmgren [1964] and Herbarth [1978] write that the optical system coexisted with the first electric telegraphs for a period of about five years.

Herbarth [1978] includes a detailed history of the optical telegraph networks that were built in France, Sweden, England, and Germany. A photo of the telegraph station in Furusund provided the logo for the 11th conference on Protocol Specification, Testing and Verification, held in Stockholm in 1991.

The needle telegraphs of Cooke and Wheatstone were used for signaling on British railways until well into the twentieth century. A description of the early telegraphs, such as the one installed in the Clayton tunnel, can be found in Hubbard [1965], Marland [1964], Michaelis [1965], Prescott [1877], and Bennet and Davey [1965]. Only two of the five-needle telegraph instruments shown in Figure 1.4 were ever built. One of these is now in the London Science Museum; the other is in the Berlin Postal Museum.

It is still not uncommon, though less frequent, that railway signaling procedures are revised after a major accident has demonstrated that unlikely events do occur in practice. The cause of even minor railway accidents is usually studied in great detail and well documented; see for instance Nock [1967], Rolt [1976], Schneider and Mase [1968], and Shaw [1978].

Much is also known about the sometimes elaborate drum signaling methods used by African and Australian tribes and the smoke and fire signals of the American Indians. Descriptions can be found in Mallery [1881] and Hodge [1910]. Hooke's optical telegraph and the American "basket telegraph" are described in Still [1946].

The first use of the term "protocol" for data communications systems was attributed to Scantlebury and Bartlett in Campbell-Kelly [1988]. He writes:

"Bartlett's recollection is that the term 'procedure' had been used up to that point but was now objected to on the grounds that it had acquired a special meaning in the ALGOL report."

The term became a permanent part of computer jargon when it was adopted in the early 1970s by the developers of the ARPA network (Pouzin and Zimmerman [1978]).

The specification language SDL is documented in CCITT [1988]; see also Saracco, Smith, and Reed [1989], Rockstrom and Saracco [1982], and Saracco and Tilanus [1987]. The construction of an automated validator for a subset of SDL is discussed in Holzmann and Patti [1989]. Excellent introductions to Lotos can be found in Brinksma [1987, 1988], Bolognesi and Brinksma [1987], and Eijk, Vissers, and Diaz [1989]. An overview of the calculus for communication systems CCS can be found in Milner [1980].

For a different perspective of protocol standardization work and the development of the three FDTs see also Bochmann [1986] and Vissers [1990]. Estelle is described in Budkowski and Dembinski [1987].

PROTOCOL STRUCTURE **2**

2.1 INTRODUCTION

In the first chapter we have seen some general examples of the protocol design problem. Having chosen a transmission medium, be it a torch telegraph or an optical fiber, we have to write down a set of rules for its proper use, defining how messages are encoded, how a transmission is initiated and terminated, and so on. Two types of errors are hard to avoid: designing an incomplete set of rules, or designing rules that are contradictory.

In this chapter we look at ways to make sure that the set of rules is both complete and consistent. It requires us to be very precise in specifying *all* the relevant pieces of a protocol. It also requires some discipline in separating orthogonal issues, using modularity and structure.

Let us first look at the general types of services that a computer communications protocol must be able to provide. Assume we have two computers, *A* and *B*. *A* is connected to a file store device *d*, and *B* connects to a printer *p*. We want to send a text file from the file store at *A* to the printer at *B*.

Figure 2.1 — File Server and Print Server

Obviously, to be able to communicate at all, the two machines must use the same physical wires, use compatible character encodings, and transmit and scan the signals on the wires at roughly the same speed. But, assuming that those issues have been resolved, there is still more to the problem than sending signals down a wire.

A must be able to check whether or not the printer is available. It must be able to adapt the rate at which it is sending the characters to the rate at which the printer can handle them. Specifically, the machine must be able to suspend sending when the printer runs out of paper or is switched off line.

It is important to note that, even though the actual data flow in only one direction, from *A* to *B*, we need a *two-way* channel to exchange control information. The two machines must have reached prior agreement on the meaning of control information and on the procedures used to start, suspend, resume, and conclude transmissions. In addition, if transmission errors are possible, control information must be exchanged to guard the transfer of the data. Typical control messages, for instance, are positive and negative acknowledgments that can be used by the receiver to let the sender know whether or not the data were received intact.

All rules, formats, and procedures that have been agreed upon between *A* and *B* are collectively called a *protocol*. In a way, the protocol formalizes the interaction by standardizing the use of a communication channel. The protocol, then, can contain agreements on the methods used for:

○ Initiation and termination of data exchanges
○ Synchronization of senders and receivers
○ Detection and correction of transmission errors
○ Formatting and encoding of data

Most of these issues can be defined on more than one level of abstraction (Figure 2.2). At a low level of abstraction, for instance, any synchronization concerns apply to the synchronization of the sender's and receiver's clock that is used to drive or to scan the physical transmission line. At a higher level of abstraction, it is concerned with the synchronization of message transfers (for example, in flow control and rate control methods), and at a still higher level it deals with the synchronization and coordination of the main protocol phases.

At the lowest level a format definition can consist of a method for encoding bits with analog electrical signals. One level up, it may consist of methods for encoding the individual characters of a transmission alphabet into bit patterns. Next, character codes can be grouped into message fields, and message fields into frames or packets, each with a specific meaning and structure.

The error control methods required in a protocol depend on the specific properties of the transmission medium used. This medium may insert, delete, distort, or even duplicate and reorder messages. Depending on the specific behavior, the protocol designer can devise an error control strategy.

The protocol descriptions we have discussed so far have been fairly informal and fragmented. Unfortunately, this is not unusual. It is all too tempting to rely on the

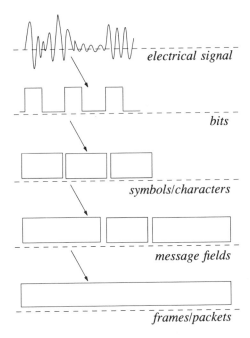

Figure 2.2 — Sample Levels of Abstraction: Formatting

goodwill and common sense of the reader (or implementer) to fill in the details that have been omitted, to understand the hidden assumptions, and to disambiguate the language. A first step towards more reliable protocol design is to formalize and to structure the descriptions, to make explicit all assumptions.

In the next section we begin this process by considering what the essential elements in a protocol definition are.

2.2 THE FIVE ELEMENTS OF A PROTOCOL

A protocol specification consists of five distinct parts. To be complete, each specification should include explicitly:

1. The *service* to be provided by the protocol
2. The *assumptions* about the environment in which the protocol is executed
3. The *vocabulary* of messages used to implement the protocol
4. The *encoding* (format) of each message in the vocabulary
5. The *procedure rules* guarding the consistency of message exchanges

The fifth element of a protocol specification is the most difficult to design and also the hardest to verify. The larger part of this book is therefore devoted to precisely that topic: the design and validation of unambiguous sets of procedure rules.

Each part of the protocol specification can define a hierarchy of elements. The protocol vocabulary, for example, can consist of a hierarchy of message classes. Similarly, the format definition can specify how higher-level messages are constructed from lower-level message elements, and so on.

As noted in Chapter 1, a protocol definition can be compared to a language definition: it contains a *vocabulary* and a *syntax* definition (i.e., the protocol format); the procedure rules collectively define a *grammar*; and the service specification defines the *semantics* of the language.

There are some special requirements we have to impose on this language. Like any computer language the protocol language must be *unambiguous*. Unlike most programming languages, however, the protocol language specifies the behavior of concurrently executing processes. This concurrency creates a new class of subtle problems. We have to deal with, for example, *timing*, *race conditions*, and possible *deadlocks*. Since the precise sequence of events cannot always be predicted, the number of possible orderings of events can be so overwhelming that it defeats any attempt to analyze the protocol by simple manual case analysis.

The next section gives an informal example of the definition of the five protocol elements, and the types of errors that can linger in a design. Following that, we consider each of the five main protocol elements in more detail. The chapter is concluded with a discussion of protocol design techniques that can help to structure a design, so that it ultimately can be implemented efficiently and proven correct with automated tools.

2.3 AN EXAMPLE

The following protocol was described by W.C. Lynch [1968] as

> *"... a reasonable looking but inadequate scheme published by one of the major computer manufacturers in a system information manual."*

We discuss this protocol here to see how we can identify the basic building blocks in a specification discussed above. Let us first consider the service specification.

SERVICE SPECIFICATION

The purpose of the protocol is to transfer text files as sequences of characters across a telephone line while protecting against transmission errors, assuming that all transmission errors can in fact be detected. The protocol is defined for full-duplex file transfer, that is, it should allow for transfers in two directions simultaneously (see also Appendix A). Positive and negative acknowledgments for traffic from A to B are sent on the channel from B to A, and vice versa. Every message contains two parts: a message part, and a control part that applies to traffic on the reverse channel.

ASSUMPTIONS ABOUT THE ENVIRONMENT

The "environment" in which the protocol is to be executed consists minimally of two users of the file transfer service and a transmission channel. The users can be assumed to simply submit a request for file transfer and await its completion. The transmission channel is assumed to cause arbitrary message distortions, but not to lose, duplicate, insert, or reorder messages. We will assume here that a lower-level module (see Chapter 3) is used to catch all distortions and change them into undistorted messages of type *err*.

PROTOCOL VOCABULARY

The protocol vocabulary defines three distinct types of messages: *ack* for a message combined with a positive acknowledgment, *nak* for a message combined with a negative acknowledgment, and *err* for a message with a transmission error. The vocabulary can be succinctly expressed as a set:

$$V = \{ \ ack, err, nak \ \}.$$

Each message type can further be refined into a class of lower-level messages, consisting for instance of one sub-type for each character code to be transmitted.

MESSAGE FORMAT

Each message consists of a control field identifying the message type and a data field with the character code. For the example we assume that the data and control fields are of a fixed size.

The general form of each message can now be represented symbolically as a simple structure of two fields:

{ *control tag, data* }

which in a C-like specification may be specified in more detail as follows:

```
enum control { ack, nak, err };

struct message {
        enum control    tag;
        unsigned char   data;
};
```

The line starting with the keyword enum declares an enumeration type named control with three possible values: one for each message type used. The message structure itself contains two fields: a tag of type control, and a data field declared as an unsigned character (one byte).

PROCEDURE RULES

The procedure rules for the protocol were informally described as follows:

"1. If the previous reception was error-free, the next message on the reverse channel will carry a positive acknowledgment; if the reception was in error it will carry

a negative acknowledgment.''

''2. If the previous reception carried a negative acknowledgment, or the previous reception was in error, retransmit the old message; otherwise fetch a new message for transmission.''

To formalize these rules, we can use state transition diagrams, flow charts, algebraic expressions, or program-form descriptions. In Chapters 5 and 6 we develop a new language to describe procedure rules like these in protocol validation models. For the time being, though, we can use simple flow charts, such as the one shown in Figure 2.3. An overview of the flow chart language is given in Appendix B.

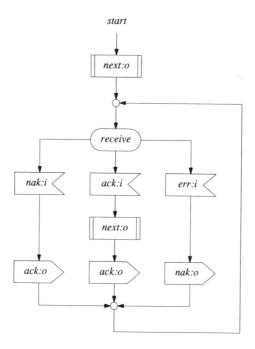

Figure 2.3 — Lynch's Protocol

The box labeled *receive* symbolizes a state in which the reception of a new message from the channel is awaited. Depending on the type of message received, one of three execution paths is then chosen. The dented box represents the recognition of a message of the type that matches its label. The pointed box indicates the transmission of a message with the corresponding type.

The box labeled *next:o* indicates an internal action to obtain the next data item (character) to be transferred. The data item is stored in variable *o*, which is used in the output operations. For instance, *ack:o* sends data item *o* with a positive acknowledgment of the last received message. Incoming data is stored in variable *i*.

As we might expect, there are some p⋯⋯eed to be considered.

DESIGN FLAWS

First we have the problem that data⋯⋯continue if data transfer in the other direction al⋯⋯ercome this problem by having the processes us⋯⋯data are to be transferred.

Another problem that has to be solv⋯⋯is to decide how a data transmission is to be in⋯⋯cedure rules specify normal data transfer, but not⋯⋯res.

We can try to initiate the data tran⋯⋯cesses send a fake error message. Note that if b⋯⋯e protocol in this way, it is hard to bring the tw⋯⋯te the transfer when the processes have ended u⋯⋯ever, requires extra control messages.

A more important deficiency of th⋯⋯ration has been omitted from the specification. ⋯⋯ide whether or not a data item that was received⋯⋯in variable i, is to be accepted (and, for instance,⋯⋯ed duplicates of previously received messages sh⋯⋯ain. This problem seems to have no solution i⋯⋯dure rules listed above.

Consider what can happen if ev⋯⋯accepted, that is, data appended to *ack* and *nak* ⋯⋯nded to *err* messages is not. The extension ⋯⋯tunately does not solve the problem. The follov⋯⋯ance, leads to the acceptance of a duplicate messz⋯⋯ransfer by sending a deliberate error message to B⋯⋯smit the characters a to z, and that B responds by⋯⋯reverse order, from z to a. Consider then the seq⋯⋯e sequence diagram of Figure 2.4. The two solid⋯⋯cutions of the two processes. The dotted lines s⋯⋯. The dashed lines show message transfers that ⋯⋯o messages are distorted in this manner: a posit⋯⋯and a negative acknowledgment from B to A.

At the end of the sequence, ⋯⋯from B, it cannot tell whether the message is new⋯⋯essage that contained this information was corrup⋯⋯erroneously accepts the message.

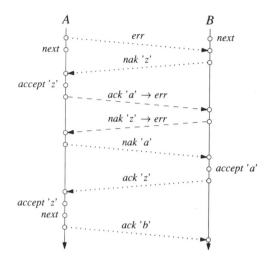

Figure 2.4 — Time Sequence Diagram

It must be noted that, even though the protocol is simple, it is disproportionately hard to discover the error. To assume that the error, if overlooked in the design phase, will sooner or later reveal itself in practice would be naive. The error only occurs in the rare event that two transmission errors occur in sequence. As Lynch observed:

> "Such errors, while rare, do occur, and their rareness will make it extremely difficult to catch the flaw in the system. This inadequate scheme will work 'almost' all of the time."

The example protocol is simple. The informal description is convincing, and based on that description alone few would doubt the protocol's correctness. Yet the specification is incomplete, and any straightforward implementation allows subtle errors during the exchange of the data. If anything, this example should convince us that, even for the simplest of protocols, a good design discipline and effective analytical tools are indispensable.

In the next sections we return to the five elements of a protocol specification defined in Section 2.2, and consider the corresponding structuring methods and design criteria that we could use. First, in Section 2.4, we consider the structuring of service specifications and the explicit assumptions that must be made about a protocol's environment. In Section 2.5, we look at the protocol vocabulary and data format, and in Section 2.6 we talk in more detail about the issues involved in the design of protocol procedure rules.

2.4 SERVICE AND ENVIRONMENT

To accomplish a higher-level task like file transfer, a protocol must perform a range of lower-level functions such as synchronization and error recovery. The specific realization of a service depends on the assumptions that are made about the environment in which the protocol is to be executed. Error recovery, for instance, should correct for the assumed behavior of the transmission medium. Particulars on the types of assumptions one can make about transmission channels are given in Appendix A and in Chapter 3. Here we concentrate on the structure of service specifications proper.

Common sense tells us that if a problem is too large to solve we must partition it into subproblems that are either easier to solve or that have been solved before. Software, and in particular protocol software, is then most conveniently structured in *layers*. More abstract functions are defined and implemented in terms of lower-level constructs, where each layer hides certain undesirable properties of the communication channel and transforms it into a more idealized medium.

As an example, assume we want to implement a data transmission protocol that provides for the encoding of characters into tuples of 7 bits each, and for some rudimentary error detection scheme to protect the bytes against transmission errors, for instance by the addition of one parity bit to each 7-bit byte. This protocol then provides two *services*: encoding and error detection. We can separate these two services into two functional submodules, an encoder and a parity module, and invoke them sequentially. At the other end of the line, there will be a decoder and a parity checker. For full-duplex transmission, we can conveniently combine the function of the encoder and decoder into one module, say P_2, and similarly we can combine the parity adder and checker into a single module P_1.

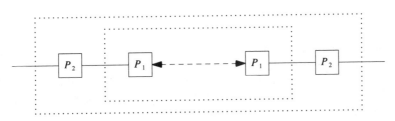

Figure 2.5 — Building a Virtual Channel

Figure 2.5 illustrates the principle. The channel (the dashed line) is wrapped in two layers. In effect, each layer provides a different service and implements a separate protocol. The first layer implements the P_1 protocol; the second layer implements the P_2 protocol. The data format of the P_2 protocol is a 7-bit byte. The data format of the P_1 protocol is an 8-bit byte.

The P_2 protocol does not see and does not know about the eighth bit that is added to its bytes. The only thing it cares about is that the channel its 7-bit bytes travel on is more reliable than the raw channel at the lower level. The P_1 protocol provides a virtual channel for the P_2 protocol, but is transparent to the P_2 protocol. The two keywords are *transparent* and *virtual*. "Transparent" is something that exists but seems not to. "Virtual" is something that seems to exist but does not.

To the P_1 protocol, any data format that is enforced by the P_2 protocol is invisible (transparent). As far as P_1 is concerned, it is an uninterpreted sequence of data, of which only the length is known. Similarly, neither the P_2 nor the P_1 protocol layer knows anything about the format imposed by possible higher layers in the hierarchy (e.g., a P_0 layer), or lower layers (e.g., P_3).

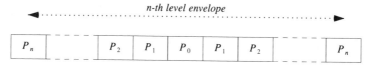

Figure 2.6 — Data Envelopes

As shown in Figure 2.6, each layer can enclose the data to be transmitted in a new data *envelope*, consisting of a header and/or trailer, before passing it to the next layer. The original data format from the upper layers need not even be preserved by the lower layers. The data may well be divided up differently, in larger or in smaller portions, as long as the original format can be restored by the receiving protocol module.

The principle of hierarchical design is well-known in sequential programming, but is relatively new for distributed systems. The advantages are clear:

☐ A layered design helps to indicate the logical structure of the protocol by separating higher-level tasks from lower-level details.

☐ When the protocol must be extended or changed, it is easier to replace a module than it is to rewrite the whole protocol.

In 1980 the International Standards Organization (ISO) recognized the advantages of standardizing a hierarchy of protocol services as a reference model for protocol designers. The ISO recommendation defines seven layers, as illustrated in Figure 2.7. The layers are listed below with a short descriptive phrase explaining their place in the hierarchy.

   1. *Physical* layer: transmission of bits over a physical circuit
   2. *Data link* layer: error detection and recovery
   3. *Network* layer: transparent data transfer and routing
   4. *Transport* layer: user to user higher-level data transfer
   5. *Session* layer: coordination of interactions in user sessions
   6. *Presentation* layer: interpretation of user-level syntax
       for instance for encryption or compression of data
   7. *Application* layer: entry point for application processes
       such as electronic mail or file transfer demons

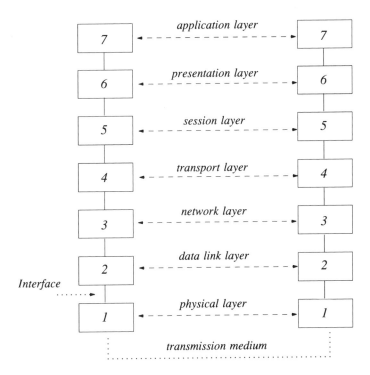

Figure 2.7 — ISO Reference Model for Open Systems Interconnection

The first layer contains all protocol functions that apply to the actual transmission of bits over a physical connection. It specifies, for instance, whether a connection is a copper wire, a coaxial cable, a radio channel, or an optical fiber. The physical medium could be a *point-to-point* channel, dedicated to communication between two specific machines, or it could be a shared *broadcast* channel, such as the University of Hawaii's *Aloha* network, or an Ethernet link. All relevant properties of raw data channels and of the modems that are used to drive them (see Appendix A) are defined here. The first layer also defines the encoding of bits in, for instance, electrical, optical, or radio signals. It also defines and standardizes the mechanical requirements of cables, switches, and connectors, including pin assignments and the like. The physical layer protocols hide all these details from the subsequent layers and transform the physical line into a rudimentary data link.

The next three layers are the most important ones. Their relative function is illustrated in Figure 2.8. The boxes represent network nodes or hosts, the circles represent user-level processes executing at these hosts, and the lines represent the logical connections viewed at three different levels of abstraction.

The data link layer uses the service provided by the physical layer and transforms a raw data link into a reliable one by adding error handling. It connects two hosts, possibly but not necessarily hosts that function as nodes in a network (see Figure 2.8). It transmits the data in blocks (frames) and can provide for the multiplexing of independent data streams over a single data link. It may provide a flow control service to guarantee that frames can only be received from the link in the precise order in which they were sent, despite channel errors. Protocols that operate on the data link level are known as *link-level protocols*.

The network layer takes care of typical network functions, such as the addressing and routing of messages. It can try to avoid bottlenecks in the network by using adaptive routing schemes, or it can try to reduce congestion in the network with rate control methods. The network layer provides the means to set up and release network connections, potentially spanning multiple data links, or hops, through the network, e.g., from node A to node B in Figure 2.8.

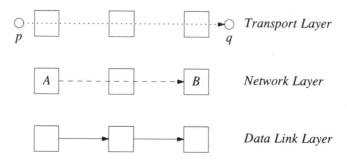

Figure 2.8 — Relative Function of Three Layers

The transport layer connects user-level processes, such as p and q in Figure 2.8, transparently through a network. Network and transport layer protocols are sometimes called *end-to-end protocols*, and data link protocols are called *hop-by-hop*. Either the network or the transport layer may provide a flow control service, which is now called end-to-end, instead of the hop-by-hop flow control that can be implemented at the data link layer. It can, in fact, make quite a difference which of these two types of flow control is used (see Chapter 4, Rate Control).

Each layer in the hierarchy defines a distinct service and implements a different protocol. The format used by any specific layer is largely independent of the formats used by the other layers. The network layer, for instance, sends data *packets*, the data link layer casts them into *frames*, and the physical layer translates them into *byte* or *bit* streams. The receiver decodes the raw data on layer 1, interprets and deletes the frame structure on layer 2, so that layer 3 can again recognize the packet structure. The format enforced by the lower layers is transparent to the higher layers.

Officially the model sketched above is called the ISO *Reference Model of Open Systems Interconnection.* It has, however, quickly become known as ISO's OSI model.

The first layers of the OSI model are the most frequently used. A layer 1 protocol was standardized by the CCITT[1] as Recommendation X.21. The recommendation for the second layer is largely based on the HDLC protocol we mentioned earlier (see Section 2.5, Bit Stuffing). The first three OSI layers together are defined in CCITT Recommendation X.25. The X.25 protocol defines the interaction of a computer, or DTE for *data terminal equipment* in CCITT terminology, and a network link, or DCE for *data circuit terminating equipment.* Computer-to-computer interaction is not defined until the fourth layer in the OSI reference model: the transport layer. A well-known transport layer protocol is the Transmission Control Protocol (TCP) that was standardized by the U.S. Department of Defense. The corresponding network layer protocol is called the Internet Protocol (IP).

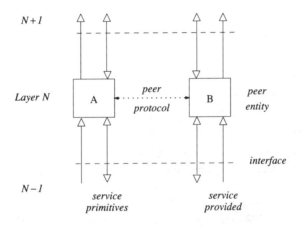

Figure 2.9 — Protocol Layering

The precise functions performed on each layer of the OSI model and the definition of the X.25 protocol are of little interest to us here (see Bibliographic Notes). More important is the structuring method itself. Software layering is a design principle that can be powerful when used properly, but it defeats its purpose when carried to extremes.

□ A layer defines a level of abstraction in the protocol, grouping closely related functions and separating them from orthogonal ones. By decoupling layers, future changes made in one layer need not affect the design of the other layers. The correct choice of the required levels of abstraction necessarily depend on the specific protocol being designed.

---

1. Comité Consultatif International Télégraphique et Téléphonique.

□ An interface separates distinct levels of abstraction. A correctly placed interface is small and well-defined. A badly placed interface causes unnecessary complexity, it causes code duplication, and it may degrade performance.

Figure 2.9 illustrates the main concepts of a layering technique. The protocol functions on the N-th layer form a logical entity. In the model they are referred to as *peer entities*. By convention the vertical boundary between two adjacent layers is called an *interface*, and the horizontal boundary between two entities in different systems is called a *peer protocol*. Since the local implementation details of the layer interfaces can easily be hidden from the environment, only the peer protocols must be standardized among systems.

The interface between two adjacent layers is defined as a collection of *service access points* implemented by the lower layer and available to the higher layer. The information to be exchanged is formatted incrementally by the various layers in *data units* or *data envelopes*. In sequence, the information is passed from the sender down from the highest layer used, to the physical layer, transmitted via the actual physical circuit from system to system, and interpreted step by step while being passed up the protocol hierarchy again to the highest layer used by the receiver.

In this framework, we can recognize the first two elements of the five-part protocol specification discussed in this section

○ the *service* to be provided by the protocol, and
○ the *assumptions* made about its environment

as formal specifications of the upper and lower interface of a given protocol layer. The service is provided to the upper layer protocols, or to the user at the top layer. The assumptions made are assumptions about the services provided by the lower layer protocols. At the lowest protocol layer these assumptions concern the bare service provided by the physical transmission medium, i.e., an optical fiber, a copper wire, or a torch telegraph.

The protocol hierarchy is an excellent example of the application of design discipline. Design issues are separated from one another and solved independently. The problems of error control, error recovery, addressing and routing, flow control, data encryption etc., can be solved step by step in a disciplined manner. From a designer's point of view, though, it is not predetermined that every design problem is always best subdivided as suggested in Figure 2.7. The specifics of the protocol system and the environment in which it is executed determine how a design problem can best be decomposed into smaller problems.

2.5 VOCABULARY AND FORMAT

We first look, on a fairly low level of abstraction, at some protocol formatting methods. These formats must underly all higher-level structures, for example, the structures that are used to encode the protocol message vocabulary. The three main formatting methods are:

- ○ Bit oriented
- ○ Character oriented
- ○ Byte-count oriented

BIT ORIENTED

A bit-oriented protocol transmits data as a stream of bits. To allow a receiver to recognize where a message (a frame) starts and ends in the bit stream, a small set of unique bit patterns, or *flags*, is used. Of course, these bit patterns can be part of the user data too, so something has to be done to ensure that they are always interpreted properly. If a framing flag, for instance, is defined as a series of six one bits enclosed in zeros, `01111110`, series of six adjacent ones in the user data must be intercepted. This can be done by inserting an extra zero after every series of five ones in the user data.

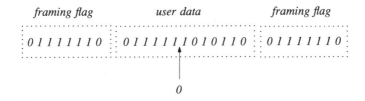

Figure 2.10 — Bit Stuffing

The receiver can now correctly detect the structure enforced by the flags in the bit stream by inspecting the first bit after every series of five ones: if it is a zero it must be deleted, else the pattern being scanned must be part of a true frame delimiter. This *bit stuffing* technique is used in ISO's layer 2 protocol (see Section 2.6) for *High Level Data Link Control*, HDLC, which is in turn based on IBM's *Synchronous Data Link Control* protocol, SDLC. Once the basic low-level flag structure is in place, it can be used to support higher-level structures.

CHARACTER ORIENTED

In a character-oriented protocol some minimal structure is enforced on the bit stream. If the number of bits per character is fixed to *n* bits (typically 7 or 8), all communication takes place in multiples of *n* bits. These data units are then used to encode both user data and control codes. Examples of control codes are the ASCII[2] start of text *STX* and end of text *ETX* messages that can serve as delimiters and can be used to enclose the user data.

---

2. American Standard Code for Information Interchange.

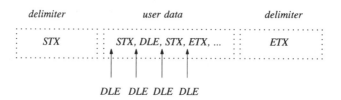

Figure 2.11 — Character Stuffing

Again, if raw data are transmitted (for example, binary object code), care must be taken that the delimiters do not accidentally occur in the user data. In IBM's *Bisync* protocol, for instance, every control character, such as *STX* and *ETX*, is preceded by an extra code, the data link escape character *DLE*. If any control message, such as *STX*, *ETX*, or even *DLE* itself, happens to occur literally in the user data, it is preceded by an extra *DLE* character. The *DLE* code is interpreted by the receiver as a control code that turns off any special meaning of the first character that follows it. The receiver deletes the first *DLE* code that it sees in the character stream, and passes on the following character uninterpreted. Only if the special meaning of an *STX* or *ETX* code is not suppressed by a preceding *DLE* character is it interpreted as a delimiter. The technique is called *character stuffing*.

Figure 2.11 shows where the *DLE* codes would be inserted in a stream that consists of four subsequent control characters in the user data.

BYTE-COUNT ORIENTED

The flags of a bit-oriented protocol and the control characters of a character-oriented protocol are used to structure a raw data stream into larger fragments. One reason for such structuring is to indicate to a receiver where a data stream begins and ends. In byte-count oriented protocols a slightly different method is chosen. In a known place after the *STX* control message, the sender includes the precise number of bytes (characters) that the message contains. An *ETX* message is now superfluous, and techniques such as bit stuffing or character stuffing are no longer needed. Most protocols in use today are of this type. A specific example is DEC's *Digital Data Communication Message Protocol*, DDCMP.

HEADERS AND TRAILERS

With the basic structuring methods we have discussed above, more systematic higher-level data formatting methods can be built. So far we have silently assumed the absence of transmission errors. If a byte-count field is distorted, or a *DLE* character is lost, these techniques fail. In the absence of an error detection and error recovery strategy, therefore, the techniques are of little use.

As we will see in more detail in Chapter 3, error detection schemes require transmission of redundant information, typically in the form of a *checksum*. If flow control techniques are added, for instance to detect loss or reordering of text frames, a *sequence number* field is appended. If more than one type of message is used we further have to include an indication of the type of message being transferred. And then, if we are transmitting redundant information anyway we might as well add other potentially useful data such as the name of the sender or the priority of the message.

All this overhead is most conveniently grouped into separate structures that encapsulate the user data: a mere *STX* control message thus expands into a *header* structure, and similarly the simple *ETX* grows into a composite message *trailer*.

For obvious reasons, byte counts are typically placed in message headers and checksums are placed in the trailer. The message format may then be defined as an ordered set of three elements:

format = { *header, data, trailer* }.

The header and trailer again define ordered subsets of control fields, which may be defined as follows:

header = { *type, destination, sequence number, count* },
trailer   = { *checksum, return address* }.

The length of the data field is defined by the last field in the header. The destination and the return address can again be defined by substructures.

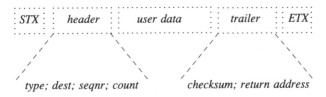

Figure 2.12 — Message Format

The *type* field can be used to identify the messages that make up the protocol vocabulary. Depending on the particular structure of the protocol vocabulary, this field can be refined still further.

2.6 PROCEDURE RULES

Up to this point, we have stressed the similarity of the protocol design task and normal software development. It is time to look at one of the differences. An important aspect of the protocol design problem is that the procedure rules are interpreted concurrently by a number of interacting processes. The effect of each new rule we add to the set is often much larger than can be foreseen. Many different interleavings in time of the interpretation of these rules by the various processes will be possible. Precisely because of this concurrency a protocol behavior is not always reproducible. To convince ourselves of the correctness of a design we need something better than informal reasoning. The most popular tool for reasoning about protocols, unfortunately, is the time sequence diagram, like the one used in Figure 2.4. To be sure, the time sequence diagram is convenient for reporting a single known error. But it is woefully inadequate for reasoning about the working of a protocol in general. To allow this we must, at least, be able to express behavior unambiguously in a convenient formal notation. Transition tables, or formal finite state machines (see Chapter 8), for instance, can be used for this purpose. In addition, we must be able to express arbitrary correctness requirements on the behaviors that we specify (see Chapters 5 and 6).

There is no general methodology that can guarantee *a priori* the design of an unambiguous set of procedure rules (we discuss this in more detail in Chapter 10). There are, however, tools with which we can, even automatically, verify the logical consistency of the rules (see Chapter 11) and the observance of the correctness requirements. And, of course, there is common sense and plain good engineering practice that can help us to keep the protocol rules manageable. We look at some of those issues in the next section.

2.7 STRUCTURED PROTOCOL DESIGN

Protocol design touches on a broad range of issues. Some of these issues are well understood; others we are only beginning to understand. Protocol design is partly an engineering problem that can be addressed by the application of well-known techniques. At the physical layer of the ISO hierarchy, for instance, we know precisely what the characteristic behaviors of different types of information carriers are, how fast we can transmit data on them and what the resulting average bit error rate will be.

There are various techniques for encoding binary data into the analog signals that can be carried by the various media, and there are well-known techniques for synchronizing transmitters and receivers at this level. We do not have to reinvent and revalidate those techniques for each new protocol, and indeed they can be considered so standard that we need not discuss them in this book. For the interested reader, the details are included in Appendix A.

Much higher up in the protocol hierarchy, we face problems of network design: routing data through networks, the precise dimensioning of network structures, the interconnection of multiple networks with gateways, and the development of higher-level disciplines for congestion control and congestion avoidance. In between this high level *network view* and the low level view of transmission codes and data carriers there is a large unknown territory, where there are few techniques that can help us through the design process. There is still a range of well-known error control and flow control techniques that can be used to build reliable data links, but this is only where real protocol design problem begins: the actual problem of devising unambiguous and complete sets of rules for the exchange of information in a distributed system.

Before this ''gray area'' of protocol design can become a true engineering discipline, it has to be established what the principal design tools are, what rules are to be followed, and what mistakes are to be avoided.

The development of a new engineering discipline often happens in two phases. In the first phase, the new technology is explored, and the designers seek tools that restrict them as little as possible in their exploration of its possibilities. If difficulties are encountered the capability of the tools is *expanded* to allow the user to cope with the growing set of problems. The trend in this first phase, then, is to remove constraints rather than to impose them.

In the second phase, after a better understanding of the nature of the problems develops, a new set of tools appears. These tools deliberately impose a carefully selected set of *constraints* upon the user. These constraints are meant to enforce a design discipline that is based upon the history of mistakes, collectively called ''experience,'' from the first development phase. In protocol design we are still waiting to make the transition to the second phase of development. Below we discuss some central concepts in the new design discipline for protocols that is emerging.

A designer will adhere to the discipline only if in return, provably and reproducibly, a more reliable product can be obtained. Below we give an overview of what is likely to become part of a general set of principles of sound design, which will allow us to enter the second phase of development in the field of protocol engineering. It is important to recognize that all these notes are variations on two common themes: simplicity and modularity.

SIMPLICITY — THE CASE FOR LIGHT-WEIGHT PROTOCOLS

A well-structured protocol can be built from a small number of well-designed and well-understood pieces. Each piece performs one function and performs it well. To understand the working of the protocol it should suffice to understand the working of the pieces from which it is constructed and the way in which they interact. Protocols that are designed in this way are easier to understand and easier to implement efficiently, and they are more likely to be verifiable and maintainable. A light-weight protocol is simple, robust, and efficient. The case for light-weight protocols directly supports the argument that efficiency and verifiability are not orthogonal, but complementary concerns.

MODULARITY — A HIERARCHY OF FUNCTIONS

A protocol that performs a complex function can be built from smaller pieces that interact in a well-defined and simple way. Each smaller piece is a light-weight protocol that can be separately developed, verified, implemented, and maintained. Orthogonal functions are not mixed; they are designed as independent entities. The individual modules make no assumptions about each other's working, or even presence. Error control and flow control, for instance, are orthogonal functions. They are best solved by separate light-weight modules that are completely unaware of each other's existence. They make no assumptions about the data stream other than what is strictly necessary to perform their function. An error-correction scheme should make no assumptions about the operating system, physical addresses, data encoding methods, line speeds, or time of day. Those concerns, should they exist, are placed in other modules, specifically optimized for that purpose. The resulting protocol structure is open, extendible, and rearrangeable without affecting the proper working of the individual components.

WELL-FORMED PROTOCOLS

A *well-formed* protocol is not *over-specified*, that is, it does not contain any unreachable or unexecutable code. A well-formed protocol is also not *under-specified* or incomplete. An incompletely specified protocol, for instance, may cause *unspecified receptions* during its execution. An unspecified reception occurs if a message arrives when the receiver does not expect it or cannot respond to it.

A well-formed protocol is *bounded*: it cannot overflow known system limits, such as the limited capacity of message queues.

A well-formed protocol is *self-stabilizing*. If a transient error arbitrarily changes the protocol state, a self-stabilizing protocol always returns to a desirable state within a finite number of transitions, and resumes normal operation. Similarly, if such a protocol is started in an arbitrary system state, it always reaches one of the intended states within finite time.

A well-formed protocol, finally, is *self-adapting*. It can adapt, for instance, the rate at which data are sent to the rate at which the data links can transfer them, and to the rate at which the receiver can consume them. A *rate control* method, for instance, can be used to change either the speed of a data transmission or its volume.

ROBUSTNESS

As Polybius (Chapter 1) noted,

> *"it is chiefly unexpected occurrences which require instant consideration and help."*

It is not difficult to design protocols that work under normal circumstances. It is the unexpected that challenges them. It means that the protocol must be prepared to deal appropriately with every feasible action and with every possible sequence of actions under all possible conditions. The protocol should make only minimal assumptions about its environment to avoid dependencies on particular features that could change. Many link-level protocols that were designed in the 1970s, for instance, no longer work properly if they are used on very high speed data lines (in the Gigabits/sec range). A robust design automatically scales up with new technology, without requiring fundamental changes. The best form of robustness, then, is not *over-design* by adding functionality for anticipated new conditions, but *minimal* design by removing non-essential assumptions that could prevent adaption to unanticipated conditions.

CONSISTENCY

There are some standard and dreaded ways in which protocols can fail. We list three of the more important ones.

☐ *Deadlocks* — states in which no further protocol execution is possible, for instance because all protocol processes are waiting for conditions that can never be fulfilled.

☐ *Livelocks* — execution sequences that can be repeated indefinitely often without ever making effective progress.

☐ *Improper terminations* — the completion of a protocol execution without satisfying the proper termination conditions.

In general, the observance of these criteria cannot be verified by a manual inspection of the protocol specification. More powerful tools are needed to prevent or detect them. Such tools are discussed in Part III.

2.8 TEN RULES OF DESIGN

The principles discussed above lead to ten basic rules of protocol design.

1. Make sure that the problem is well-defined. All design criteria, requirements and constraints, should be enumerated before a design is started.

2. Define the service to be performed at every level of abstraction before deciding which structures should be used to realize these services (*what* comes before *how*).

3. Design *external* functionality before *internal* functionality. First consider the solution as a black-box and decide how it should interact with its environment. Then decide how the black-box can internally be organized. Likely it consists of smaller black-boxes that can be refined in a similar fashion.

4. Keep it simple. Fancy protocols are buggier than simple ones; they are harder to implement, harder to verify, and often less efficient. There are few truly complex problems in protocol design. Problems that appear complex are often just simple problems huddled together. Our job as designers is to identify the simpler problems, separate them, and then solve them individually.

5. Do not connect what is independent. Separate orthogonal concerns.

6. Do not introduce what is immaterial. Do not restrict what is irrelevant. A good design is "open-ended," i.e., easily extendible. A good design solves a class of problems rather than a single instance.

7. Before implementing a design, build a high-level prototype (Chapters 5 and 6) and verify that the design criteria are met (Chapters 11 to 14).

8. Implement the design, measure its performance, and if necessary, optimize it.

9. Check that the final optimized implementation is equivalent to the high-level design that was verified (Chapter 9).

10. Don't skip Rules 1 to 7.

The most frequently violated rule, clearly, is Rule 10.

2.9 SUMMARY

A protocol includes more than an agreement on the meaning of signals for data. Minimally, the protocol must include agreements on the use of control information, which is needed to standardize the use of the channel itself.

To be complete, the definition of a protocol should include the five main elements listed in Section 2.2. Protocol failures are often caused by hidden assumptions about events or about the possible sequences of events. It is the responsibility of the protocol designer to make these assumptions explicit. Again: it is not sufficient if a correct interpretation of the specification is merely possible. It is required that no incorrect interpretation is possible.

The main protocol structuring techniques are the layering of control software and the structuring of data. The OSI model is given as an example of this approach. Beware, it is not a recipe. Similarly, the ten rules of design are guidelines, not commandments. A structured and sound approach to the design of consistent procedure rules must always be a self-imposed discipline.

In the next two chapters we first cover the basics of protocol design, the known techniques for building reliable channels out of unreliable ones. The remainder of the book is devoted to the study of the protocol design problem itself. It does not discuss network design issues, nor the specific encoding or usage of the protocol standards that are in use today. Instead, our goal is to discuss how protocols can be designed using a simple discipline based on the rules given above.

EXERCISES

2-1 Identify the five protocol elements from Section 2.2 for the torch telegraph of Polybius, discussed in Chapter 1. List at least three cases of incompleteness in the protocol.

2-2 Give an informal description of the procedure rules of a protocol that manages the data transfer from a file server to a printer (Section 2.1). Make sure that the protocol can recover when the printer runs out of paper or is switched off line.

2-3 Explain what the equivalents of control and data messages are in a telephone call. Write down a complete (Section 2.2) protocol specification for a phone call, taking into account all possible signals and exception conditions. Consider the case where two people try to call each other simultaneously and consider the best procedure rules for redialing after a busy signal.

2-4 Extend Lynch's protocol to avoid the duplication error, and show with a rigorous argument that the revised version works.

2-5 Explain why a byte count is most conveniently placed in a message header (Section 2.5).

2-6 Explain the difference between bit stuffing and character stuffing.

2-7 Calculate the optimal length for a framing flag in a bit oriented protocol. Note that a longer series of ones in the framing flag reduces the probability of its occurrence in the user data and thus the overhead in the number of stuffed bits, at the expense of a higher overhead in the framing flag itself. Assume random user data. (See Bertsekas and Gallager [1987, p. 78-79]).

2-8 In your favorite programming language, write a function that performs *STX — ETX* framing and character stuffing on an arbitrary byte stream. Provide the matching receive function and test it.

BIBLIOGRAPHIC NOTES

That control messages are vital to a reliable operation of communication lines was already known in the days of the pre-electric telegraphs. Even the torch telegraph had a *start of text* message, and most later systems had at least special control codes for *repeat* and *wait*. The same control signals are defined on nearly every data link in use today. Hubbard [1965], reports yet another type of control message, devised by ''an anonymous French inventor'' for an early electro-static telegraph system. He suggested using the static charge of the telegraph line to ignite a small amount of gunpowder in the receiving station to *wake* a sleeping attendant.

The system described by Marland [1964] wins the prize for the best control messages ever devised. It noted a telegraphic system that was described in the *Mechanics' Magazine* of June 11, 1825 (Vol. IV, p.148). In this system the electro-static shocks are administered directly to the operator. And, if that is not enough, it suggests a most original solution to the problem of a drowsy telegraph operator:

> *''Let the first shock pass through his elbows, then he will be quite awake to attend the second.''*

Excellent introductions to the problems of protocol design can be found in Pouzin and Zimmerman [1978] and in Merlin [1979]. The formalism for describing protocols as an abstract language, with vocabulary, formal grammar, and syntax was introduced in Puzman and Porizek [1980].

Perhaps the greatest importance of the paper by Lynch [1968] is that it sparked a famous paper by Bartlett, Scantlebury, and Wilkinson from the National Physical Laboratory in England, defining one of the simplest and best known protocols in use today: *the alternating bit protocol*. We discuss it in Chapter 4.

The symbols used in the flow chart in Figure 2.3 are from the CCITT specification language SDL. The language is quickly gaining popularity as a specification method for communication protocols. For an overview see, for instance, Rockstrom and Saracco [1982] and SDL [1987]. The official SDL language definition is in CCITT [1988]. The flow charting ''language'' used here is more fully described in Appendix B. The best reference to the C language, referred to briefly in Section 2.3, is Kernighan and Ritchie [1978, 1988].

The principal ideas of structured programming and software layering stem from E.W. Dijkstra [1968a, 1968b, 1969a, 1969b, 1972, 1976] and N. Wirth [1971, 1974]. They are closely related to the technique of design by stepwise refinement Wirth [1971], see also Gouda [1983]. That the principle of stepwise refinement was known long before program design became an issue is illustrated by the following quote from E.F. Moore.

> *''One way of describing what engineers do in designing actual machines is to say that they start with an overall description of a machine and break it down successively into smaller and smaller machines, until the individual relays or vacuum tubes are ultimately reached.''* (Moore [1956])

The ideas on protocol design expressed here are also inspired by discussions with many others, most notably Jon Bentley, John Chaves, Peter van Eijk, Rob Pike, and Chris Vissers. The importance of the service concept in protocol design is eloquently explained in Vissers and Logrippo [1985].

The term *self-stabilization* was also coined by Dijkstra, see for example, [1974, 1986], see also Kruijer [1979]. Lamport discussed self-stabilization in several papers, Lamport [1984, 1986]. Multari wrote his thesis on self-stabilizing protocols, Multari [1989]. Other pioneering work in this area is done at the University of Texas at Austin by M.G. Gouda [1987] and at Cornell University by G.M. Brown [1989].

The study of light-weight protocols was pioneered in the 1970s by a research group at the Computer Laboratory of the University of Cambridge, involved with the design of the Cambridge Ring Network, e.g., Needham and Herbert [1982], and a little later by a group at AT&T Bell Labs, including Sandy Fraser, Greg Chesson, and Bill Marshall, involved with the design of the hardware and software for the Datakit® switch.

The term *light-weight* protocol was coined by the Cambridge group, who also developed the first serious contender in this class: the *byte stream protocol* that is used on the Cambridge Ring. The work at Bell Labs led ultimately to the design of the standard Universal Receiver Protocol (URP), Fraser and Marshall [1989], and its successors the PSP and MSP packet switch protocols.

A complete description of the OSI model can be found in ISO [1979]. The X.25 protocol, finally, is documented in CCITT [1977] and explained in, for instance, Lindgren [1987], and Stallings et al. [1988]. More about data networking problems can be found in Tanenbaum [1981, 1988] or in Stallings [1985].

ERROR CONTROL 3

3.1 INTRODUCTION

The number of errors caused by data transmission is typically orders of magnitude larger than the number of errors caused by hardware failures within a computer system. The bit error probability for internal circuits is usually below 10^{-15}. On an optical fiber link the average probability of errors is approximately 10^{-9}. That is, on the average, one in every 10^9 bits transmitted (or processed) is distorted, six orders of magnitude more than for hardware circuits. Similarly, on a coaxial cable the probability of bit errors is approximately 10^{-6}. For a switched telephone line, the numbers are even higher, between 10^{-4} and 10^{-5}.

The difference in magnitude between an error probability of 10^{-15} and one of 10^{-4} should not be underestimated. A bit error rate of 10^{-15} on a transmission line would be immeasurably small at today's transmission rates. At a rate of 9600 bits per second, it would cause one single bit error every 3303 years of continuous operation. At the same data rate, a bit error rate of 10^{-4} causes a bit error, on average, once a second.

Depending on line and network characteristics, transmitted data may be reordered, distorted, or deleted, and occasionally noisy lines may even insert new data into transmissions. The errors introduced in data transmissions are, of course, not entirely unpredictable or inexplicable. The errors have two main causes, discussed in more detail in Appendix A:

○ Linear distortion of the original data, for instance, as caused by bandwidth limitations of the raw data channel

    ○ Non-linear distortion that is caused by echoes, cross-talk, white noise, and impulse noise

The effect of these distortions can be remedied, to a certain extent, with cable insulation and hardware compensation filters. The errors that remain must be caught in software by the communications protocol.

There are several ways in which the error characteristics of a data line can be expressed. The first, and most important, is the long-term average bit error rate. But, since this is only an average, there are two other factors in use:

    ○ The percentage of time that the average bit error rate does not exceed a given threshold value

    ○ The percentage of error-free seconds

The last two measures give an indication of the overall quality of a line or a network. For the design of an error control method one commonly uses only the average bit error rate, as an indication of the expected performance.

No error control method can be expected to catch all errors that can possibly occur. We can, however, require that an error control scheme increase the reliability of the transmissions, preferably to the level of reliability of the stand-alone operation of a computer.

An often overlooked issue is that an effective error control scheme should match the error characteristics of the channels to be used. If a channel only produces *insertion* errors, it would be unwise to design a protocol that protects against *deletions*. Similarly, if a channel produces independent, single-bit errors with a relatively low probability, even the simplest parity scheme (Section 3.6) can easily outperform the most sophisticated error control methods. And, finally, if the error rate of the channel is already lower than that of peripheral equipment, the inclusion of *any* error control scheme needlessly degrades performance and may even turn out to decrease rather than increase the protocol's reliability.

3.2 ERROR MODEL

For a channel with a long-term average bit error rate of p, it is theoretically most convenient if we assume a random distribution of the errors over the sequence of bits transmitted. The probability of n subsequent bit errors in a message is then simply p^n, and the probability of one or more bit errors in a message of n bits is $1 - (1 - p)^n$. Though this ignores the effect of impulse noise, it gives us a good starting point for the study of error control disciplines. The formal model for a channel of this type is the *discrete memoryless channel* shown in Figure 3.1.

The channel is called discrete because it recognizes only a finite number of distinct signal levels. It is called memoryless because the probability of an error is assumed to be independent of all occurrences of previous errors. Since we have

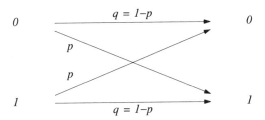

Figure 3.1 — Discrete Memoryless Channel

assumed that the probability of a bit error is the same for both signal elements, the channel in Figure 3.1 is also called a *symmetric channel*.

Many different variations to this basic model are possible, accompanied by increasingly complex calculations to predict the effect of error control methods. In an asymmetric channel, for instance, the probability of an error may depend on the signal value being transmitted. The distribution of error probabilities can also be defined as a process with memory: if the last n bits transmitted were in error it is very probable that the next few will be wrong too. It is difficult to capture this behavior in a predictive model. The error model provided by the binary symmetric channel predicts that the probability of a series of at least n contiguous error-free bit transmissions, called an "error-free interval" (EFI), is equal to

$$Pr(EFI \geq n) \quad = \quad (1-b)^{n}, \quad n \geq 0 \tag{3.1}$$

where b is the long-term average bit error rate.

The probability decreases linearly with the length of the interval. Similarly, the probability that the duration of a burst exceeds n bits decreases linearly with n. To express that the probability of an error-free interval decreases exponentially with its duration, we can replace formula (3.1) with a Poisson distribution:

$$Pr(EFI \geq n) \quad = \quad e^{-b(n-1)}, \quad n \geq 1 \tag{3.2}$$

The best way to verify the accuracy of this prediction is, of course, to compare it against empirical data. Such studies indicate indeed that formula (3.2) predicts error free intervals better than (3.1). A still better match can be found if a correction factor is added to (3.2). We thus obtain the following approximation, which is due to Benoit Mandelbrot (see Bibliographic Notes):

$$Pr(EFI \geq n) \quad = \quad \left[n^{(1-a)} - (n-1)^{(1-a)} \right] e^{-b(n-1)}, \quad 0 \leq a < 1, \quad n \geq 1 \tag{3.3}$$

The parameter a determines how serious the clustering effect is predicted to be. When a is zero, formula (3.3) reduces to the Poisson distribution in (3.2). For non-zero a, the probability of longer error-free intervals decreases more than the probability of shorter intervals. With growing a this effect becomes more pronounced. Of course, if the error characteristics are independent of the bit rate they can be expressed in seconds.

With different parameter values a and b, functions of type (3.2) and (3.3) can be used to predict both the duration of error-free intervals and the duration of bursts independently. We will use this method in Chapter 7. For the remainder of this chapter, however, we will restrict ourselves to the model of a binary symmetric channel.

3.3 TYPES OF TRANSMISSION ERRORS

Many different types of errors can occur on data lines. The most important transmission errors show up as data

- ○ Insertion
- ○ Deletion
- ○ Duplication
- ○ Distortion
- ○ Reordering

Inserted and deleted data may be caused by the temporary loss of synchronization between sender and receiver. Deletion errors may also be caused artificially by inadequate flow control disciplines. A receiver, for instance, may run out of buffers to hold incoming messages and lose messages that it cannot store. Data duplication may even be performed intentionally, for instance by a sender that implements a retransmission protocol. If data are routed through networks, potentially via many different routes, also data reordering may occur.

Data sequencing problems, such as deletion, duplication, and reordering, are solved with proper flow control schemes (Chapter 4). But, in all cases where data distortion or insertion can occur, no matter what the cause is, we need methods to verify the consistency of the data. We discuss such methods below.

3.4 REDUNDANCY

An error detection method can only work by increasing the redundancy of messages in some well-defined way. By checking the consistency of a message the receiver can then assess the reliability of the information it contains. Apart from detecting transmission errors, though, the receiver must also be able to correct the errors. There are two ways in which this can be done:

- ○ Forward error control
- ○ Feedback error control

If the redundancy is made large enough the receiver may be able to reconstruct a message from the distorted signal. This method is called *forward* error control. The corresponding transmission codes are named *error-correcting codes*.

The alternative is to use an *error-detecting code* and arrange for the retransmission of corrupted messages. This is called *feedback* error control. A retransmission request can be an explicit negative acknowledgment sent from receiver to sender or, when the probability of error is sufficiently low, it can be implicit in the absence of a positive acknowledgment for correctly received data. In that case the receiver simply ignores any corrupted data and waits for the sender to time out waiting for the acknowledgment and retransmit the message.

The purpose of error control is to bring the channel error rate down. Not all errors can be detected, so there is always a *residual error rate*. Assume that the probability of a transmission error in a message is p and that the error control method catches a fraction f of all errors. For a given f and p, we can then calculate the residual error rate $p \cdot (1 - f)$ and convince ourselves that it is, for instance, in the order of 10^{-9} or less.

If probability p is very close to zero, an error-correcting code is generally ill-advised: it merely slows down the data transfer. If, on the other hand, p approaches one, a retransmission scheme would be a bad choice: almost every message, including the retransmitted ones, would be hit. Of course there are exceptions to these rules. If p is small, and the cost of retransmission high, a forward error control scheme may still be profitable. In other cases still, a combination of forward and feedback error control may be a good compromise: the receiver corrects frequently occurring errors and asks the sender for the retransmission of messages that contain less frequent errors.

In the next section we first look at the main types of error-correcting and error-detecting codes that have been developed.

3.5 TYPES OF CODES

The two basic types of codes are

- ○ Block codes
- ○ Convolution codes

In a *block code* all code words have the same length, and the encoding for each possible data message can be statically defined. In a *convolution code* the code word produced depends on both the data message itself and a given number of previously encoded messages: the encoder changes its state with every message processed. The length of the code words is usually constant. We can further distinguish between

- ○ Linear codes
- ○ Cyclic codes
- ○ Systematic codes

Linear and cyclic block codes are the most commonly used codes in data communication protocols. In a linear code every linear combination of valid code words (such as a modulo-2 sum) produces another valid code word. A cyclic code is a code in which every cyclic shift of a valid code word also produces a valid code word. A *systematic* code, finally, is a code in which each code word includes the data bits from the original message unaltered, either followed or preceded by a separate group of check bits.

In all cases the code words are longer than the data words on which they are based. If the number of original bits is d and the number of additional bits is e, the ratio $d/(d+e)$ is called the *code rate*. Improving the quality of a code often means increasing its redundancy and thus lowering the code rate. To reduce the channel error rate by a factor of $5 \cdot 10^2$ by forward error control, for instance, may require a code with a code rate of 0.5 or less.

The remainder of this chapter is organized as follows. Section 3.6, gives a general introduction to parity check codes. In Section 3.7, we extend the code into a forward error control method. Section 3.8 discusses a simple linear block code, due to R. Hamming, that offers protection against independent single bit errors. Section 3.9 focuses on cyclic block codes, using the popular cyclic redundancy check as an example. Section 3.10 discusses a simple alternative to a cyclic redundancy check: the arithmetic checksum method.

3.6 PARITY CHECK

If the probability of multiple bit errors per message is sufficiently low, all the error control needed on a binary symmetric channel is a parity check code. To every message we add a single bit that makes the modulo-2 sum of the bits in that message equal to one. The overhead is merely one bit per message. If any single bit, including the check bit, is distorted by the channel the parity at the receiver comes out wrong and the transmission error can be detected.

If we set $q = 1 - p$, the probability of an error-free transmission of n message bits plus one parity bit is $q^{(n+1)}$, and the probability of a single bit error in $n+1$ bits transmitted is the binomial probability $(n+1) \cdot p \cdot q^n$. Under these assumptions (i.e., a memoryless channel) the residual error rate of a one-bit parity check is

$$1 - q^{(n+1)} - (n+1) \cdot p \cdot q^n$$

For $n = 15$ and $p = 10^{-4}$ this leaves a residual error rate on the order of 10^{-6} per message, or about 10^{-7} per bit.

The solid line in Figure 3.2a shows how the residual error rate per code *word* increases as a function of the *bit* error rate p. The dotted line shows what the error rate per code word would be without the parity check bit: $1 - q^n$. When p is sufficiently small, therefore, the parity check code can indeed bring the error rate of the channel down. The curve in Figure 3.2b shows the difference between the error rate of the uncorrected and the corrected code. It reaches a maximum for $p \simeq 0.06$.

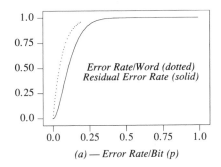
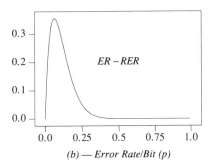

Figure 3.2 — Residual Error Rate of a 1-bit Parity Check, n=15

3.7 ERROR CORRECTION

A forward error control scheme uses only a small subset of the available bit combinations to encode messages. The codes are chosen such that it takes a relatively large number of bit errors to convert one valid message into another. By mapping an erroneous message onto the "closest" valid message in the coding scheme, a receiver can try to correct for occasional transmission errors. The closest valid message in this case is the message that differs from the code word received in the fewest number of bits.

The code rate of an error-correcting code is in general lower than that of a mere error-detecting code. In principle, therefore, forward error correction is only considered to be useful when the communication of control messages from a receiver back to a sender is difficult. The difficulty may be

- ○ A very long transmission delay
- ○ The absence of a return channel
- ○ A high bit-error rate

A good example of the first problem is the communication between a space probe and its remote control center on earth. A control signal, for instance to release a camera shutter or to make a course adjustment, may take several minutes to reach the distant probe. There may not be enough time to repeat a signal in case of a transmission error. The signal either gets through or is lost forever.

The second problem can exist in radio broadcast transmission systems with one sender and multiple receivers. A more perverse, but very real, example is when transmission sequences are stored on a backup-device and played back later. At the time of transmission the original data may no longer be available for retransmission.

The third problem, a high bit error rate, may mean that even the probability that a request for *re*transmission can be received correctly is unacceptably low. In all three cases, adding redundancy to a message may be the only way to avoid the irrevocable loss of some of the messages transmitted.

Even a single parity check per code word can be extended easily from a single-error detecting code into a single-error correcting code. Every sequence of seven bits is first extended with a single parity bit that makes the number of one bits in each sequence even. The parity bit is called a *longitudinal* redundancy check, or LRC bit. By adding an extra sequence of eight bits to every series of n codes, we can include a *vertical* redundancy check, or VRC bit, for the set of bits that occupy the same bit position in each sequence. For instance, with ASCII coding, for $n = 4$:

$$
\begin{array}{llll}
         &   &   & LRC \\
D & = & 1000100 & 0 \\
A & = & 1000001 & 0 \\
T & = & 1010100 & 1 \\
A & = & 1000001 & 0 \\
\hline
  &   & 0010000 & 1 \quad VRC
\end{array}
$$

A faulty VRC bit encodes the column number and a faulty LRC bit the corresponding row number for an error bit so that any single bit error per series of 40 transmitted bits can indeed be corrected. We have used 12 check bits to protect a sequence of 28 data bits, which corresponds to a code *rate* of $28/(12+28) = 0.7$.

Now, let us forget about parity checks and develop an error-correcting code from scratch. The following example is based on J.H. van Lint [1971].

EXAMPLE

Suppose we would like to standardize the generation of random numbers. The method we choose is to appoint an impartial person to be our standard random number generator. He performs this task by flipping a standard coin A times per second. The results are transmitted to all four corners of the earth via a standard binary symmetric channel that operates at a maximum speed of $2A$ bps (bits per second), with a bit error rate of $2 \cdot 10^{-2}$.

Clearly, the result of each flip of the standard coin can be encoded in one bit of information. Transmitting the raw bits can be done at a rate of A bps, but causes the receivers to get an average 2% of the numbers deviating from the "random standard."

The first thing we may come up with to solve this problem could be to transmit each result not once but twice, that is we encode each result in two bits instead of one. The receivers are now able to detect most transmission errors, but clearly there is no time left to correct them. An error-correcting code is in order. We can now try to encode two flips of the coin, as a pair, into four bits of data, using Table 3.1.

Table 3.1 — Coding

Result	Code
hh	0000
th	1001
ht	0111
tt	1110

The receivers use a different table, shown as Table 3.2, that allow them to decode any code word received as one of the four possible messages.

Table 3.2 — Decoding

Valid Codes				Result
0000	1000	0100	0010	hh
1001	0001	1101	1011	th
0111	1111	0011	0101	ht
1110	0110	1010	1100	tt

The code is resistant to single bit errors in the first three bits of each code word sent. The first column in Table 3.2 contains the original code word sent, and the next three columns contain the codes that result after an error in the first, second, or third bit, respectively. Multiple bit errors, or a single error in the fourth bit, still lead to the reception of a non-standard random number. What are the odds that this happens? A code is received correctly if, with probability q^4, it has no errors or, with probability $3p \cdot q^3$, it has exactly one error among the first three bits.

$$q^4 + 3p \cdot q^3 = 0.9788$$

We started out with an error rate of 2% per single bit, that is a 4% chance of at least one error in a series of two bits. The error rate is reduced to $1 - 0.9788 = 0.0212$ or 2.12% for two subsequent bits. We used four bits to encode two flips, giving a code rate of 0.5. We wasted twelve out of sixteen possible code words to accomplish this reduction in the error rate, but we are still transmitting the codes as fast as the results are produced by our standard random number generator.

Without changing the effective signaling speed, or the code rate, we could boost the amount of waste still further by using eight bits to encode series of four data bits. To select the 2^4 valid code words needed from the range of 2^8 available we can again attempt to reduce the possibility that one valid word is transformed into another by transmission errors.

HAMMING DISTANCE

The *difference* between two code words can be defined as the number of bits in which they differ. The minimum difference between two words in a code is called its *Hamming distance*. If we succeed in finding a code with a Hamming distance of n, any combination of up to $n - 1$ bit errors can be detected. Better still, any combination of up to $(n-1)/2$ errors per code word can be corrected if we tell the receiver to interpret every nonvalid code word as the closest valid code word. The receiver will guess wrong for higher numbers of bit errors, but if the probability of these is sufficiently low the overall error rate of the channel may still be reduced.

Formally, this method is called *maximum likelihood decoding*, or also *nearest neighbor decoding*. By increasing the Hamming distance, choosing longer and longer code words, we should then be able to increase the reliability of a code as much as we want.

The following question now comes up: is this true for any transmission rate and for any channel? The answer can be found in a paper published by Claude Shannon in 1948, *A Mathematical Theory of Communication*. Assuming a bandwidth limited channel with white noise, Shannon proved that only for transmission rates up to a certain limit can the error rate of the channel be made arbitrarily small (Appendix A). The limit is called the *channel capacity*.

Shannon's argument is based on the observation that the amount of information transferred by a channel can never exceed the entropy of the information source nor the entropy of the channel itself caused by noise. Below that limit it is theoretically always possible to derive reliable information from the channel. Informally, Shannon found that when the signal-to-noise ratio gets smaller, each signal must last longer to make it stand out from the noise, which in turn reduces the maximum signaling speed that can be obtained.

The effort required in coding the data, however, normally prohibits the operation of a channel near the theoretical limit. For a telephone line, for instance, with a bandwidth of 3.1 kHz and a signal-to-noise ratio of 30 dB (that is, 8:1), the Shannon limit is roughly 30 Kbit/sec, which is much more than the maximum rate used in practice.

3.8 A LINEAR BLOCK CODE

We saw in the last section that the redundancy of a code determines its power to detect and correct transmission errors. The redundancy can be defined as the number of bits used over the minimum required to encode a message unambiguously. To encode one of n equally likely messages, for instance, requires $\log_2 n$ bits, rounded up to the nearest integer value. We call this quantity m.

$$m = \lceil \log_2 n \rceil$$

Table 3.3 — Parity Protection

c	m	m/(m+c)
1	0	0.00
2	1	0.50
3	4	0.57
4	11	0.73
5	26	0.84
6	57	0.90
7	120	0.94
8	247	0.97

We can protect these m bits by adding c check bits and choosing the n codes used from the $2^{(m+c)}$ codes now available in such a way that each combination of two valid codes differs in as many bits as possible.

To be able to correct all single bit errors, we know that we need a Hamming distance of at least three between code words, but how many check bits will this minimally cost? For every code word of $m+c$ bits, there are precisely $m+c$ codes that can result from single bit errors. For every word from the range of 2^m possible data codes, therefore, we need $m+c+1$ words to protect it against single bit errors. The total number of words in the code then is $(m+c+1) \cdot 2^m$, which should be equal to the $2^{(m+c)}$ words with which we started.

Setting

$$(m+c+1) \cdot 2^m = 2^{(m+c)}$$

gives

$$m+c+1 = 2^c$$

allowing us to calculate the minimal number of check bits c for any given number of data bits m. For $m=8$, we find a minimum of $c=3.66$ or 4 check bits per message, giving a code *rate* of $8/(8+4) = 0.66$.

Alternatively, we can find the maximum number of data bits m for a given number of check bits c. The first eight numbers are listed in Table 3.3, with the corresponding maximum code rates. The same effect is illustrated for up to 16 checkbits in Figure 3.3.

With good approximation, the number of data bits that can be protected goes up exponentially with the number of check bits that are available.

HAMMING CODE

An example of a code that realizes this protection is a code developed by R. Hamming. In Hamming's code, included as an example of a perfect single-error correcting code in Shannon's 1948 paper, the bits in a code word are numbered

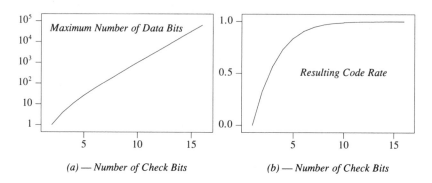

(a) — Number of Check Bits   *(b) — Number of Check Bits*

Figure 3.3 — Parity Protection

from 1 to $m+c$. The i-th check bit is placed at the bit position 2^i for $1 \leq i \leq \log_2(m+c)$.

The check bits have been placed in the code word in such a way that the sum of the bit positions they occupy points at the erroneous bit for any single bit error. To catch a single bit error the check bits are used as parity bits.

When a bit position is written as a sum of powers of two, for example, $(1+2+4)$, it also points at the check bits that cover it. Data bit $7 = (1+2+4)$, for instance, is counted in the three check bits at positions 1, 2, and 4. A single bit error that changes the seventh data bit changes the parity of precisely these three checks. The receiver can therefore indeed determine which bit is in error by summing the bit positions of all check bits that flagged a parity error. An error that changes, for instance, the second bit only affects that single bit and can also be corrected.

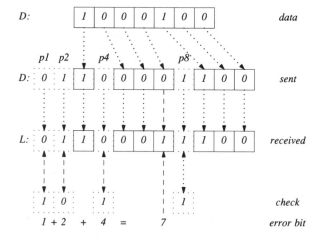

Figure 3.4 — Correction of a Transmission Error

As an example, the ASCII character code for the letter D is `1000100`. Figure 3.4 shows how the data and parity bits are placed in a Hamming code. If a transmission error changes bit position 7 from a 0 into a 1 the code arrives as the ASCII code for an L `1001100`. But, the first three parity bits transmitted now differ from the values the receiver can calculate and reveal the faulty seventh bit.

It is of course not really relevant to the code as such in what order the code bits are placed in a code word. By rearranging the bits, for instance, every binary Hamming code can be changed into a systematic code or into a cyclic code.

MATRIX REPRESENTATION

There is a convenient method to define the linear block parity check codes in matrix form. As an example, consider a code with three data bits, named `D1`, `D2`, and `D3`, and three check bits, `C4`, `C5`, and `C6`. We can define the three check bits as the modulo-2 sum of the data bits, for instance as follows:

$$
\begin{aligned}
C4 &= D1 + D2 \\
C5 &= D1 \qquad\;\; + D3 \\
C6 &= \qquad\;\; D2 + D3
\end{aligned}
$$

These three functions can be defined in matrix form as follows:

$$
\begin{bmatrix} C4 \\ C5 \\ C6 \end{bmatrix} = \begin{bmatrix} 1 & 1 & 0 \\ 1 & 0 & 1 \\ 0 & 1 & 1 \end{bmatrix} \begin{bmatrix} D1 \\ D2 \\ D3 \end{bmatrix}
$$

Taking this one step further, we can also express the three defining functions as follows:

$$
\begin{aligned}
D1 + D2 + \qquad + C4 \qquad\qquad\quad &= 0 \\
D1 + \qquad + D3 \qquad + C5 \qquad\quad &= 0 \\
D2 + D3 \qquad\qquad + C6 &= 0
\end{aligned}
$$

which leads to the following matrix representation.

$$
\begin{bmatrix} 1 & 1 & 0 & 1 & 0 & 0 \\ 1 & 0 & 1 & 0 & 1 & 0 \\ 0 & 1 & 1 & 0 & 0 & 1 \end{bmatrix} \cdot C^t = \begin{bmatrix} 0 \\ 0 \\ 0 \end{bmatrix}
$$

In this formula, C^t is the transpose of the data word, written as a vector of bits. According to the definition, the matrix multiplication must produce a zero vector. Note that the right side of the matrix is a unit submatrix, with ones only on the diagonal. The matrix can always be written in this form by grouping all the check bits on the right side of the defining formulas.

$$
H \cdot C^t = \mathbf{0}
$$

H is called a *parity check matrix*. Transmission errors can be formalized as an error vector **E** that is added to the code word. When the receiver performs the check now, it may find a non-zero result **s**.

$$H \cdot (C^t + \mathbf{E}) = \mathbf{s}$$

The vector $\mathbf{s}$ is called a *syndrome*. In this code every modulo-2 sum of valid code words produces another valid code word. Therefore, if the error vector $\mathbf{E}$ happens to match any valid code word, the syndrome is zero and the error goes undetected.

BURSTS

Until now we have focused mainly on the detection and correction of single bit transmission errors, assuming that errors would be mutually independent. In practice, we know that transmission errors are not mutually independent: they tend to come in *bursts*.

Noise spikes, echoes, and cross-talk all affect series of subsequent bits whenever they occur. For a switched telephone line the average probability of a bit error may be 10^{-5}. But, if one bit in an arbitrary message has been distorted the probability that the next bit is also wrong can be as high as 0.5. The result is that relatively few messages are distorted overall, but the ones that are distorted are more seriously hurt. Clearly, it is rather pointless to develop an error control scheme that can flawlessly detect and correct a rare single bit error if the burst errors are more common.

Though the definition of the Hamming code is relatively simple, it is surprisingly hard to extend it into a code that can correct multiple bit errors per word. To guarantee the detection of even numbers of bit errors per code word the Hamming code can be extended with a single longitudinal parity check. A more general solution, however, is more difficult.

CODE INTERLEAVING

A general method to counter burst errors is code *interleaving*, One interleaving method is to change the order in which bits are transmitted across the channel.

Assume we have messages of n bits each, protected against single bit errors. Assuming further that traffic is non-interactive, we can intercept burst errors up to a length of k bits by buffering each block of k subsequent messages, placing them in a matrix of $k \times n$ bits and transmitting the bits in this matrix column by column instead of row by row. At the receiver end the original matrix is restored column by column and read row by row. A burst error of length k or less then only causes a single bit error per row and can be corrected properly.

True double-error correcting codes, not based on interleaving schemes, were first published by Hocquenghem [1959], and Bose and Ray-Chaudhuri [1960]. These codes, collectively known as BCH codes, require substantially more theoretical justification than can be given here. A further generalization of the BCH codes is known as the Reed-Solomon code. It has found application, for instance, in the digital encoding of sound on compact disks.

In a study performed at IBM in 1964, it was found that in almost all cases feedback error control can be superior to forward error control in both throughput and in residual error rates. We therefore continue with a discussion of a cyclic block code that is used for *feedback* error control.

3.9 CYCLIC REDUNDANCY CHECKS

The cyclic redundancy check, or CRC, method is also based on the addition of series of check bits to code words. In this case the added bits guarantee that, in the absence of transmission errors, the code word plus check bits is divisible by a given factor. The specific division method and the factor used determine the range of transmission errors that can be detected. To simplify the algebraic manipulation of code words we can define a mapping of codes onto polynomials. A sequence of N bits can then be interpreted as a polynomial of maximum degree $N-1$:

$$\sum_{i=0}^{N-1} b_i \cdot x^i$$

where each b_i takes the value of the bit in position i in the sequence, with bits numbered right to left. The code word 10011, for instance, defines polynomial

$$x^4 + x + 1$$

We are working in a binary system so all operations, including division and multiplication, are defined modulo-2. Modulo-2 addition is defined as follows:

$$0 + 0 = 0 - 0 = 0$$
$$0 + 1 = 0 - 1 = 1$$
$$1 + 0 = 1 - 0 = 1$$
$$1 + 1 = 1 - 1 = 0$$

In longer additions there is no carry, and in subtractions there is no borrow. In polynomial form, therefore, for any i we have $x^i + x^i = 0$, since both $1+1=0$ and $0+0=0$. To multiply two code words, we can multiply the corresponding polynomials.

Table 3.4 — A Cyclic Code

Data Word	Polynomial	Multiplied By	Produces	Code Word
0 0 0	0	$x+1$	0	0 0 0 0
0 0 1	1	$x+1$	$x+1$	0 0 1 1
0 1 0	x	$x+1$	x^2+x	0 1 1 0
0 1 1	$x+1$	$x+1$	x^2+1	0 1 0 1
1 0 0	x^2	$x+1$	x^3+x^2	1 1 0 0
1 0 1	x^2+1	$x+1$	x^3+x^2+x+1	1 1 1 1
1 1 0	x^2+x	$x+1$	x^3+x	1 0 1 0
1 1 1	x^2+x+1	$x+1$	x^3+1	1 0 0 1

For example,

$$(x^4+x+1) \times (x^3+x^2) = x^7+x^6+x^4+x^2$$

We can use this mechanism easily to define a code. Consider, for instance, a code with three data bits. We encode the data in four bits by multiplying every data word with the polynomial $x+1$, as shown in Table 3.4. The resulting code is a parity check code with a code rate of 3/4. It is also a cyclic code, but not a systematic one.

If we can add, subtract and multiply polynomials, we can of course also divide them. Let us try dividing the polynomial $x^7+x^6+x^3+x^4+x^2$ by a factor x^5+x^2+1.

$$
\begin{array}{l}
x^5+x^2+1 \quad / \quad x^7+x^6+x^4+x^3+x^2 \quad \backslash \quad x^2+x \\
\qquad \underline{x^7+0\ +x^4+0\ +x^2} \\
\qquad \quad x^6+0\ +x^3 \\
\qquad \quad \underline{x^6+0\ +x^3+x} \\
\qquad \qquad \qquad x
\end{array}
$$

To make the original polynomial divisible by factor x^5+x^2+1, we could simply subtract the residual x from it. But, although the receiver would then be able to detect transmission errors, it would not be able to recover the original message from the code word. Better is to append the residual as a checksum. The factor used to generate a checksum is called the *generator polynomial* of the code.

We now first multiply the message polynomial by a factor equal to the highest degree of the generator polynomial, in this case x^5, to make room for the checksum. It simply means shifting the bits in the code word five places to the left. Then we divide the message polynomial by the generator polynomial and subtract the residual.

Since the CRC is a linear code, every error pattern E must be equal to some valid code word T. For a known code this property can be used to calculate the residual error rate. If P is the message polynomial and G a generator polynomial of degree r, the residual R has degree $r-1$ and is defined to be the remainder of

$$\frac{P \cdot x^r}{G}$$

The code word T to be transmitted is

$$T = P \cdot x^r - R$$

A transmission error in effect adds an error polynomial E to the transmitted code. When the receiver divides the code by the generator polynomial it finds the error term

$$\frac{T+E}{G} = \frac{T}{G} + \frac{E}{G} = \frac{E}{G}$$

A transmission error is only undetected if the remainder of the division of the error pattern E by the generator polynomial G is zero. If E is nonzero and of a lower degree than G, the division always leaves a remainder. This means that all burst errors of length r and less are detected perfectly. Note carefully that this is independent of the position of the burst within the code word T. The error pattern E cannot turn into a multiple of G simply by multiplication with a factor x^i (assuming, of course, that G is not equal to x^i).

Longer burst errors only go undetected if the error pattern E is an integer factor times the generator polynomial. If we assume random error patterns, the probability of this can easily be calculated. With $n+r$ code bits transmitted, there are a total of 2^{n+r} possible error patterns. The number of integer multiples of a generator polynomial of degree r in a code word of length $n+r$ is equal to 2^n. Each multiple can be considered as a finite sum of n factors, where each factor is obtained by a left shift of the generator polynomial into the data word. The generator can be shifted left by n bit positions. Each of these n factors is either present or absent in the final multiple, giving 2^n possible multiples. This means that a fraction

$$\frac{2^n}{2^{n+r}} = \frac{1}{2^r}$$

of all random errors are missed. For $r=16$, this corresponds to 10^{-5} of all error patterns.

STANDARDIZED GENERATOR POLYNOMIALS

The problem of designing a cyclic redundancy check code is clearly to find generator polynomials that trap the largest class of transmission errors. One such polynomial is known as CRC-12:

$$x^{12} + x^{11} + x^3 + x^2 + 1$$

It generates a 12-bit checksum.

The CCITT has recommended the following generator polynomial for 16-bit checksums, usually referred to as CRC-CCITT:

$$x^{16} + x^{12} + x^5 + 1$$

The highest degree of the polynomial is sixteen so this code detects all burst errors up to 16 bits in length. In modulo-2 arithmetic, this polynomial can also be written as follows:

$$(x+1) \times (x^{15} + x^{14} + x^{13} + x^{12} + x^4 + x^3 + x^2 + x + 1)$$

Now, it is easy to see that any polynomial multiplied by the factor $x+1$ must have an even number of terms (that is, non-zero bits). This means that any E with an odd number of terms, produced by any odd number of single bit transmission errors, is not divisible by $x + 1$, and can be detected. For this reason most standard generator polynomials have at least a factor $x + 1$. The CCITT polynomial can also be shown to trap all double bit errors, 99.997% of burst errors of 17 bits, and 99.998% of all burst errors longer than 17 bits.

Another frequently used generator polynomial is the one used in IBM's *Bisync* protocol, known as CRC-16 (which also has the factor $x + 1$):

$$x^{16} + x^{15} + x^2 + 1$$

There is also a 32-bit checksum polynomial, CRC-32, defined by an IEEE standards committee (IEEE-802):

$$x^{32} + x^{26} + x^{23} + x^{22} + x^{16} + x^{12} + x^{11} + x^{10} + x^8 + x^7 + x^5 + x^4 + x^2 + x + 1$$

THE ANSI FDDI STANDARD

The 32-bit checksum CRC-32 is also the polynomial used in the Fiber Distributed Data Interface (FDDI) standard, defined by ANSI in 1986. In the FDDI standard, though, the calculation of the checksum is somewhat different from the standard method explained above. The calculation is as follows. Let p be the degree of the message polynomial P, and let L be a polynomial representing a sequence of 32 bits, all with value one. The checksum is calculated as the *complement* of the remainder of

$$\frac{(L \cdot x^p + P) \cdot x^{32}}{G}$$

First the pattern L is prepended to the code word. The resulting word is shifted left by 32 bits to make room for the checksum. The checksum is then calculated as before and complemented before transmission. The complement can be obtained in modulo-2 arithmetic by adding the pattern L to the remainder. Since the resulting checksum is obviously different from the earlier

$$\frac{P \cdot x^{32}}{G}$$

a division of the transmitted code word T by the generator polynomial G no longer yields zero in the absence of errors. To perform the check, the FDDI receiver does a different calculation. Let M be the code word as it is received, that is,

$$M = T + E$$

The receiver now checks that the remainder of the division

$$\frac{(L \cdot x^p + M) \cdot x^{32}}{G}$$

equals

$$\frac{L \cdot x^{32}}{G}$$

that is, it must equal the pattern L that was added to the checksum at the FDDI sender to invert it before the transmission. The addition of the pattern L and the inversion of the checksum guarantee, among other things, that a transmitted code word never consists of only zero bits.

EFFICIENCY

The encoding and decoding of CRC checksums can be a time consuming task that may degrade the performance of a protocol. The implementation is therefore typically done either in hardware with shift registers or in software with lookup tables storing precomputed values for parts of the CRC sum.

The following C program, by Don Mitchell of AT&T Bell Laboratories, generates a lookup table for an arbitrary checksum polynomial. Input for the routine is an octal number, specified as an argument, that encodes the generator polynomial. Bits are numbered left to right from zero to $r - 1$, where r is the degree of the generator polynomial. The r-th bit itself is omitted from the code word (it is implicit in the length).

Using Mitchell's program takes two separate steps. First, the program is compiled and run to generate the lookup tables. Then the checksum generation routine can be compiled, with the precalculated lookup tables in place. If, on a UNIX® system, Mitchell's program is compiled as

```
$ cc -o crc_init crc_init.c
```

lookup tables for the three most popular CRC-polynomials can be generated as follows:

```
$ crc_init 05401   > crc_12.h
$ crc_init 0120001 > crc_16.h
$ crc_init 0102010 > crc_ccitt.h
```

This is the text of `crc_init.c`:

```
main(argc, argv)
        int argc; char *argv[];
{
        unsigned long crc, poly;
        int n, i;
        sscanf(argv[1], "%lo", &poly);
        if (poly & 0xffff0000)
        {       fprintf(stderr, "polynomial is too large\n");
                exit(1);
        }
        printf("/*\n *  CRC 0%o\n */\n", poly);
        printf("static unsigned short crc_table[256] = {\n");
```

```
      for (n = 0; n < 256; n++)
      {       crc = n;
              if (n % 8 == 0)
                      printf("     ");
              for (i = 0; i < 8; i++)
              {       if (crc & 1)
                      {       crc >>= 1;
                              crc ^= poly;
                      } else
                              crc >>= 1;
              }
              printf("0x%x, ", crc);
              if (n % 8 == 7)
                      printf("\n");
      }
      printf("};\n\n");
      exit(0);
}
```

The table can now be used to generate checksums:

```
unsigned short
cksum(s, n)
      register unsigned char *s;
      register int n;
{
      register unsigned int crc;

      for (crc = 0; n > 0; n--)
         crc = crc_table[(crc ^ *s++) & 0xff] ^ (crc>>8);

      return crc;
}
```

The CRC checksum, using a lookup table with the algorithm shown above, is computed in approximately 1.1 msec of CPU time (for a 512-bit message, when running on a DEC/VAX-750). For comparison, the following is the checksum routine from the UNIX system uucp code.

```
cksum(s,n)
      register char *s;
      register n;
{
      register short sum;
      register unsigned short t;
      register short x;
      sum = -1;
      x = 0;
      do {
              if (sum<0) {
                      sum <<= 1;
                      sum++;
              } else
                      sum <<= 1;
```

```
                    t = sum;
                    sum += (unsigned)*s++ & 0377;
                    x += sum^n;
                    if ((unsigned short)sum <= t) {
                            sum ^= x;
                    }
            } while (--n > 0);

            return(sum);
    }
```

The method is a simple and somewhat ad hoc hashing scheme. It takes slightly more CPU time for a checksum computation (1.8 msec per call), yet the protection it provides against transmission errors is smaller than that of the cyclic redundancy check.

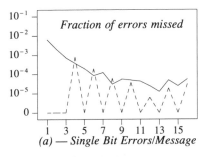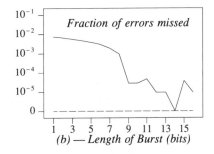

(a) — Single Bit Errors/Message   (b) — Length of Burst (bits)

Figure 3.5 — Comparison of Checksumming Methods
Uucp Checksum, solid; CRC-16 Checksum, dashed

The data for Figure 3.5 were obtained by randomly distorting 164,864 messages of 512 bits each. In a first test (shown in Figure 3.5a) independent single bit errors were introduced. In a second test (Figure 3.5b) burst errors were simulated. Checksums were calculated for both the distorted and the undistorted messages. A distorted message was accepted only if its checksum was the same as for the undistorted message.

The CRC-16 catches all odd numbers of bit errors and properly rejects all burst errors up to 16 bits. The two methods have a comparable performance only for even numbers of single bit errors and for burst errors longer than 16 bits long (not shown). In all other cases the CRC-16 method is superior.

3.10 ARITHMETIC CHECKSUM

Each checksumming method has an overhead in bits that is expressed as its code rate. It also has a hidden overhead in the CPU-time that is required to calculate the checksum bits, which erodes the maximum transmission rate. The time requirements can be reduced by using lookup tables, as shown above, or by developing special purpose hardware for the checksum calculation. In applications where the

requirements for the residual error rate do not justify a CRC implementation, it can
be attractive to find a simple alternative that can still provide serious error protection.

A very interesting method of this type was published by John Fletcher in 1982.
The checksum in Fletcher's algorithm requires only addition and modulo operations
and is trivially simple. Here is the code of a version that has been adopted for the
ISO Class 4 transport protocol standard (TP4).

```
unsigned short
cksum(s, n)
        register unsigned char *s;
        register int n;
{
        register int c0=0, c1=0;
        do {
                c0 = (c0 + *s++)%255;
                c1 = (c0 + c1)%255;
        } while (--n > 0);
        return (unsigned short) (c1<<8+c0);
}
```

It is remarkably simple, yet it turns out to have a respectable error detection capability. Figure 3.6 compares the performance of Fletcher's algorithm with that of
the uucp checksum.

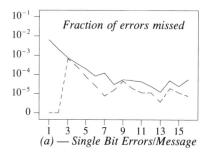
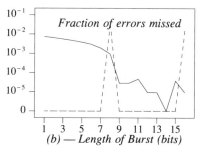

(a) — Single Bit Errors/Message   *(b) — Length of Burst (bits)*

Figure 3.6 — Comparison of Checksumming Methods
Uucp Checksum, solid; Arithmetic Checksum, dashed

Given the simplicity of the algorithm, the return in error detection capability is certainly worthwhile.

3.11 SUMMARY

One functional module in the protocol hierarchy is error control. The inclusion of
an error control scheme can and should be transparent to the rest of the protocol.
Its function is to transform a channel with error rate p into one with a lower (residual) error rate $p \cdot (1-f)$, where f is the fraction of the errors that is intercepted by
the error code.

An error control scheme requires overhead that is measured by the number of redundant bits that are added to each code word. Redundancy is rarely equal to protection (see Exercise 3-1), but a small amount of redundancy is a prerequisite to any error control scheme.

With proper encoding and at the price of lower transfer rates, the receiver can use an error-correcting code to recover from the characteristic errors introduced by the channel. With lower overhead an acceptable performance can be achieved with error-detecting codes that rely on flow control schemes for the retransmission of distorted data. Flow control schemes are studied in Chapter 4.

The adequacy of an error control scheme, however, can only be assessed properly when the error characteristics of the transmission channel, the required transfer rate (i.e., code rate), and the required level for the residual error rate are known.

EXERCISES

3-1 A phone company recently considered running new 56 Kbit/sec data lines at an end-to-end data rate of 9600 bits/sec, using the extra bandwidth to enhance reliability. The method chosen was to transmit each single byte five times in succession. By a majority vote, comparing the five successive bytes and choosing the most frequent one from each set, the receiver would then decide which byte had been transmitted. Comment on the code rate and the protection against burst errors.

3-2 A simple error control scheme has the receiver retransmit all the messages it receives back to the sender. Each message then has to survive two successive transmissions to be accepted. Try to build a protocol that works this way.

3-3 The protocol of Exercise 3-2 is modified to have the receiver merely return a CRC checksum field to the sender by way of acknowledgment. The checksum is returned for every message received, distorted or not, and is used by the sender to decide upon retransmission. Comment upon this improvement.

3-4 (Jon Bentley) The two sentences ''the dog runs'' and ''the dogs run'' are both valid in English. The sentences ''the dogs runs'' and ''the dog run'' are both invalid. Would this classify English grammar as a feedback or as a forward error control method?

3-5 The message 101011000110 is protected by a CRC checksum that was generated with the polynomial $x^6 + x^4 + x + 1$. The checksum is in the tail (the right side) of the message. (a) How many bits is the checksum? (b) If no transmission errors occurred, what would the original data be? (c) Were there any transmission errors?

3-6 List the circumstances under which an error-correcting code with a code rate of 0.1 can be more attractive than an error-detecting code with feedback error control? Consider error rates and roundtrip message propagation delays.

3-7 Another method to adapt a single error-correcting code for protection against burst errors is to use n error codes for a sequence of n messages, where the i-th code word covers only the i-th bit from each message. To protect against burst errors of up to k bits this method attempts to separate the bits that make up one new ''code word,'' spanning n messages, by more than k bit positions. Work out the details of this method and apply it to a sample message.

3-8 CRC checksum polynomials that contain the factor $x + 1$ catch all odd numbers of bit errors. Think of a method to catch all even numbers of bit errors as well, for instance, by deliberately introducing a bit error in a second transmission, and comment upon this scheme. Consider the code rate as well.

3-9 How would you classify Fletcher's algorithm? (See Section 3.4)

BIBLIOGRAPHIC NOTES

More information on the various types of transmission errors and their causes can be found in, for instance, Tanenbaum [1981], Fleming and Hutchinson [1971], and Bennet and Davey [1965]. An application oriented treatment of data transmission techniques can be found in Tugal and Tugal [1982].

The Hamming code was first described by Claude Shannon [1948] as an example of a perfect code. Hamming's paper on error-correcting codes followed a few years later, Hamming [1950]. Slepian [1973] gives an overview of the theory inspired by Shannon's work. An excellent introduction to coding theory can be found in J.H. van Lint's lecture notes, Lint [1971].

Other good reference works on the theory of error-correcting and error-detecting codes, including discussions of BCH and Reed-Solomon codes, are Berlekamp [1968], Kuo [1981], Peterson and Weldon [1972], and MacWilliams and Sloane [1977]. The results of the IBM study of error-correcting and error-detecting codes, mentioned at the conclusion of Section 3.7, were presented in IBM [1964]. A simple method to generate a CRC lookup table was described in Perez [1983]. Alternative methods to generate CRC-16 and CRC-32 checksums using look-ahead tables can be found in Griffiths and Stones [1987]. Methods to generate CRC checksums with shift registers are given in e.g., MacWilliams and Sloane [1977], Adi [1984], and Stallings [1985].

The results of a survey held in 1969-1970 to measure the error characteristics of switched lines was reported in Fleming and Hutchinson [1971] and Balkovic et al. [1971]. An overview of the results of measurements on T1 lines, performed by AT&T in 1973 and 1974, is given in Brilliant [1978]. More general discussions or various ways for interpreting and analyzing the measurement data can be found in, for instance, Decina and Julio [1982] or in Ritchie and Scheffler [1982].

Fletcher's arithmetic checksumming method was first described in Fletcher [1982], and is discussed in Nakassis [1988]. The ISO transport protocol series was standardized in ISO [1983]. The predictive model for error clustering, discussed in Section 3.2 is described in Bond [1987] and is due to Benoit Mandelbrot [1965] (the inventor of fractals).

FLOW CONTROL 4

4.1 INTRODUCTION

The simplest form of a flow control scheme merely adjusts the rate at which a sender produces data to the rate at which the receiver can absorb it.[1] More elaborate schemes can protect against the deletion, insertion, duplication, and reordering of data as well. But let us first look at the simpler version of the problem. It is used

○ To make sure that data are not sent faster than they can be processed.
○ To optimize channel utilization.
○ To avoid data clogging transmission links.

The second and the third goals are complementary: sending the data too slowly is wasteful, but sending data too fast can cause congestion. The data path between sender and receiver may contain transfer points with a limited capacity for storing messages shared between several sender-receiver pairs. A prudent flow control scheme prevents one such pair from hogging all the available storage space.

In this chapter we build up a full flow control discipline in a sequence of modifications of a simple, basic model. The procedure rules of these protocols are specified with the flow charting language introduced in Chapter 2 and summarized in Appendix B. The notation *mesg:o* in an input or output statement, for instance, indicates that a message of type *mesg* with data field *o* is received or sent, respectively. The statement *next:o* indicates the internal retrieval of data item *o* to be transmitted in the next output message. Similarly, *accept:i* indicates the acceptance (storage) of *i* as correctly received data.

---

1. At the lowest level such synchronization must already take place to drive a physical line. See *Synchronous and Asynchronous Transmission* in Appendix A.

Figure 4.1 illustrates a protocol without any form of flow control. Note that it is a *simplex* protocol: it can be used for transfer of data in only one direction (see Figure 2.1 and Appendix A).

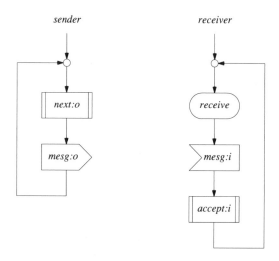

Figure 4.1 — No Flow Control

The protocol in Figure 4.1 only works reliably if the receiver process is guaranteed to be faster than the sender. If this assumption is false, the sender can overflow the input queue of the receiver. The protocol violates a basic law of program design for concurrent systems:

Never make assumptions about the relative speeds of concurrent processes.

The relative speed of concurrent processes depends on too many factors to base any design decisions on it. Apart from that, the assumption about the relative speed of sender and receiver is often not just dangerous but also invalid. Receiving data is generally a more time-consuming process than sending data. The receiver must interpret the data, decide what to do with it, allocate memory for it, and perhaps forward it to the appropriate recipient. The sender need not find a provider for the data it is transmitting: it does not run unless there are data to transfer. And, instead of allocating memory, the sender may have to free memory after the data are transmitted, usually a less time-consuming task. Therefore, the bottleneck in the protocol is likely to be the receiver process. It is bad planning to assume that it can always keep up with the sender.

The oldest and least reliable flow control technique that can be used to address this synchronization problem requires no prior negotiation between sender and receiver about the pace at which messages can be transmitted. The method uses two control messages: one to *suspend* and one to *resume* traffic. The messages are sometimes

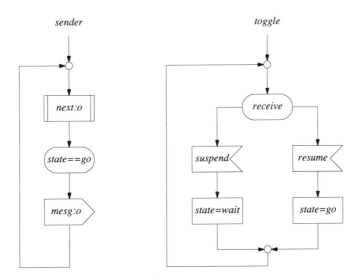

Figure 4.2 — X-on/X-off Protocol: Sender Processes

called *x-off* and *x-on*.[2] Assume, then, that we have an error-free channel and a protocol vocabulary of the following three message types:

$V = \{ \textit{ mesg, suspend, resume } \}$

where the control messages *suspend* and *resume* are used to implement the flow control discipline. The procedure rules of the protocol can now be added. We implement them here with two additional processes, one in the sender and one in the receiver, as shown in Figure 4.2.

After receiving a *suspend* message, the *toggle* process in the sender sets the value of a variable *state* to *wait*. It resets the variable to its initial value *go* after the arrival of a *resume* message. The sender process simply waits (at the oval box) until *state* has the proper value before transmitting the next message.[3]

The receiver is also split into two parts. After the arrival of a data message a counter process increments a variable *n*, and upon the acceptance of the message, an acceptor process decrements it. The data messages are passed from the counter process to the acceptor process via an internal queue. The count remembers the number of messages that have been received from the sender and the number that are waiting to be accepted by the receiver. If its value increases beyond some predefined limit, a *suspend* message is sent to the sender. If it drops below a lower bound, the *resume* message is sent, as shown in Figure 4.3. To split the receiver

---

2. The *control-s* and *control-q* codes on many data terminals provide the same two functions.

3. Recall that the oval box indicates a potential delay. The process waits for a message to arrive when the box is labeled *receive*, or else it waits until the condition specified becomes true. Cf. Figure 2.1.

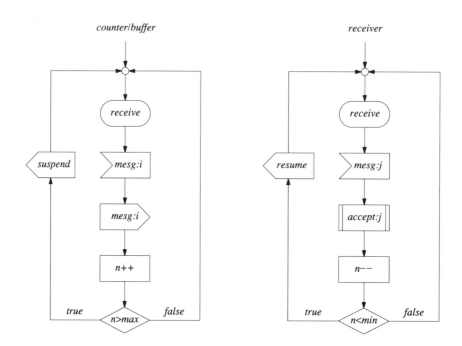

Figure 4.3 — X-on/X-off Protocol: Receiver Processes

into two processes, of course, only makes sense if *accept* is a relatively time-consuming operation.

There are some problems to be resolved. The correct working of the protocol depends on the properties of the transmission channel. If a *suspend* message is lost or even delayed, the overflow problem recurs. The working of a protocol should not depend on the time it takes a control message to reach the receiver. Worse still, if a *resume* message is lost, the four-process system comes to a complete halt.

We have these two problems to solve:

○ Protect against overrun errors in a more reliable way.
○ Protect against message loss.

A standard method of solving the first problem is to let the sender explicitly wait for the acknowledgment of transferred messages. An example is the *Ping-Pong* protocol of Figure 4.4. This method is often called a *stop and wait* protocol. The overflow problem has disappeared, but the system still deadlocks if either a control or a data message is lost. The sender and receiver are too tightly coupled. Let t be the message propagation time on the channel, a the time it takes the receiver to process and accept an incoming message, and p the time it takes the sender to prepare a message for transmission. With the above scheme the sender incurs a delay of $2t + a - p$ units of time for every message transmitted.

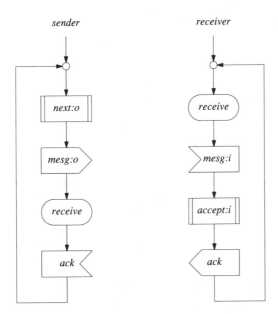

Figure 4.4 — Ping-Pong Protocol

Typically $p < a$ and, obviously, t increases at least linearly with the distance between sender and receiver. Note, however, that the acknowledgment message does not just signify the arrival of the last message, it is also used as a *credit* that the receiver extends to the sender to transmit the next message. This idea directly leads to a solution that can alleviate the delay problem: the window protocol.

4.2 WINDOW PROTOCOLS

In a call-setup phase, the receiver can tell the sender exactly how much buffer space it is prepared to reserve for incoming messages. The sender is then given *credit* for a fixed number of outstanding messages. The credit can be updated dynamically when the amount of available buffer space changes.

Let us not worry about message loss just yet and first look at the basic working of a window protocol. Each message received is acknowledged with a single *ack* control message on a return channel. All we have to do is to keep count of the number of messages in transit.

The initial credit can either be negotiated, or it can be set to a fixed number of messages W. For each message sent the sender decrements its credit, and for each message received the receiver extends a new credit to the sender via the return channel. The example protocol shown in Figure 4.5 illustrates this. The quantity $W - n$ gives the number of unused credits.

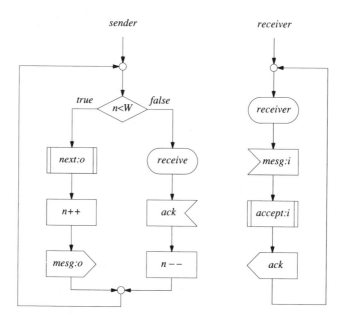

Figure 4.5 — Window Protocol for an Ideal Channel

Let $a(t)$ be the number of credit messages received by the sender at time t after initialization, let $m(t)$ be the number of messages sent to the receiver, and let $n(t)$ be the value of n at time t. The maximum number of messages that the sender can have outstanding, waiting acknowledgment, is

$$W - n(t) + m(t) - a(t)$$

where $W - n(t)$ is the number of unused credits and $m(t) - a(t)$ the number of used credits. We would like to convince ourselves that

$$W - n(t) + m(t) - a(t) \leq W$$

or

$$m(t) - a(t) \leq n(t)$$

Initially all variables in this inequality are zero and the condition is trivially true. Every send action in the sender increments both sides of the inequality, right side first, and preserves its validity. Similarly, with every receive action the receiver process decrements both sides by one, the left side first, again preserving the correctness.

MESSAGE LOSS

The maximum credit W is called the *window size* of the protocol. During a transfer, the current credit varies between zero and W, depending on the relative speeds of sender and receiver. The sender is only delayed when the credit is reduced to zero. This flow control discipline can optimize communication on channels with long transit delays by enabling the sender to transmit new messages while waiting for the acknowledgment of old ones.

The problems of lost, inserted, duplicated, or reordered messages do, of course, still exist. If, for instance, a set of acknowledgment messages is lost, both parties may hang: the sender waiting for the acknowledgments that were lost, the receiver waiting for the messages it credited.

TIMEOUTS

To protect against the loss of essential messages the sender has to keep track of elapsed time. In the Ping-Pong protocol of Figure 4.4, for instance, the sender can try to predict the worst turn-around time for each acknowledgment. If the response has not arrived within that period, the sender can *time out* and assume that it was lost.

In practice, the "worst" turn-around time is often calculated with a heuristic:

$$T_{worst} = \overline{T} + N \cdot \sqrt{var(T)}$$

where T is the round-trip delay N is usually one, and rarely larger than two. The round-trip delay is simply the time it takes a message to go from sender to receiver plus the time it takes a response to return to the sender (see Exercise 4-12). $\overline{T}$ and $var(T)$ are, respectively, the *average* and the *variance* of T. The factor N is thus a multiplication factor for standard deviation of the turn-around time (the square root of the variance).

In many cases, the behavior of the receiver process at the far end of a transmission channel can be modeled by an M/M/1 queueing system.[4] We then assume that, from the receiver's point of view, the distribution function of the interarrival times of messages is a Poisson process and the distribution time for the processing of these messages is a simple exponential function. For an M/M/1 queueing system, it can be shown that the variance of the time spent in the system is the square of the mean. This means that for our transmission channel the variance of both the one-way and the round-trip delay is also the square of the mean, $var(T) = \overline{T}^2$. This leads to the simple rule of thumb that an approximation for the retransmission time can be obtained by doubling the average round-trip delay T (assuming a factor $N = 1$ in the above estimate:

$$T_{worst} \approx 2 \cdot \overline{T}$$

A timeout after a deletion error certainly looks straightforward. A common mistake, however, is to let both the sender *and* the receiver use timeouts. Consider the extension of the Ping-Pong protocol shown in Figure 4.6.

---

4. The notation is due to D.G. Kendall [1951].

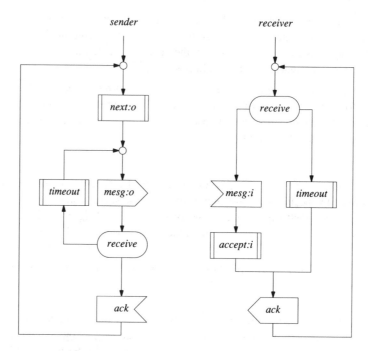

Figure 4.6 — Ping-Pong Protocol with Timeouts

Figure 4.7 shows what can happen with this protocol if a deletion error occurs. Both sender and receiver decide to retransmit the last sent message when a deletion error is assumed. When the first *ack* message reaches the sender, it cannot possibly tell whether it acknowledges the lost or the retransmitted message. The sender ends up matching the wrong *ack* and *mesg* messages indefinitely.

One lesson to be learned from this is that sender and receiver should not both be able to initiate retransmissions. It is sufficient to place this responsibility with one

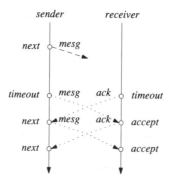

Figure 4.7 — Time Sequence Diagram of An Error

of the two processes. Traditionally, this is the sender process, since only the sender can know for certain when new data has been sent. Another lesson is that we must be able to tell from an acknowledgment exactly which message is being acknowledged, even if we only intend to send one message at a time, as in the Ping-Pong protocol. We can do this by adding *sequence numbers* to each data and control message. By doing so, we also obtain a mechanism for solving other classes of transmission problems in a fairly straightforward way: duplication errors and out-of-sequence messages.

Since sequence numbers necessarily have a restricted range,[5] we must have a way to verify that recycled numbers cannot disturb the correct working of the protocol. We will see below that if sequence numbers are used in combination with a window protocol this requirement can be fulfilled relatively easily. Before we make that combination, the *sliding* window protocol, let us take a closer look at the use of timeouts and sequence numbers.

4.3 SEQUENCE NUMBERS

As an example of a better use of a timeout, and a one-bit sequence number, we can consider an extended version of the alternating bit protocol (a famous protocol, see the Bibliographic Notes). The protocol continues to surface in so many different disguises in the protocol literature that it is worthwhile to first look at the original specification from Bartlett, Scantlebury and Wilkinson [1969]. In their paper, the protocol is defined with two finite state machines of six states each, as shown in Figure 4.8. The original protocol, therefore, can be in no more than 36 different states, substantially fewer than all other variations that have been studied.

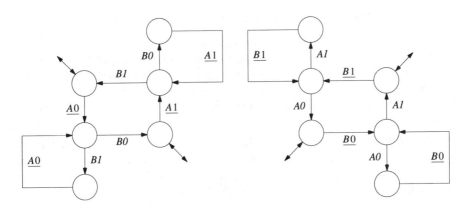

Figure 4.8 — Original Alternating Bit Protocol

---

5. There is only a finite number of bits to store them in the message headers.

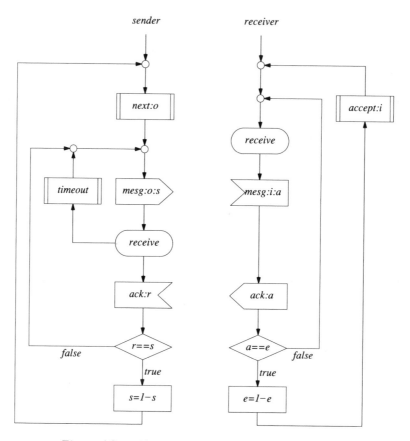

Figure 4.9 — Alternating Bit Protocol with Timeouts

Figure 4.8 specifies the behavior of two processes, *A* and *B*. The notation is from Bartlett, Scantlebury and Wilkinson [1969]. The edge labels specify the message exchanges. Each label consists of two characters. The first specifies the origin of the message being received or transmitted, and the second specifies the sequence number, called the *alternation bit* in the original paper. Send actions are underlined.

The double headed arrows indicate states where input is to be accepted in the receiver or where a new message is fetched for output in the sender. Erroneous inputs, i.e., messages that carry the wrong sequence number, prompt a retransmission of the last message sent. It is relatively easy to extend the protocol with timeouts to allow for recovery from message loss. A flow chart version of this extension is shown in Figure 4.9.

We have used two types of messages, *mesg* and *ack*, with, for instance, the format

   { *mesg, data, sequence number* }

and

  { *ack, sequence number* }

respectively. In the flow chart, *mesg:o:s* indicates a message *mesg* with data field *o* and sequence number field *s*.

We have also used four single-bit variables: *a*, *e*, *r*, and *s*. Variable *s* is used by the sender to store the last sequence number sent, and *r* holds the last sequence number received. The receiver uses *e* to hold the next number expected to arrive and variable *a* to store the last actual sequence number received. All variables have an initial value zero.

Figure 4.10 illustrates what happens if the deletion error from Figure 4.7 occurs in the alternating bit protocol. The protocol recovers from the error when the sender process times out and retransmits the lost message.

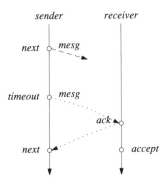

Figure 4.10 — Time Sequence Diagram of Error

Consider also what happens if an acknowledgment is delayed long enough for the sender to time out and retransmit the last message (see Exercise 4-6).

MESSAGE REORDERING

Now let us consider the duplication and reordering of messages, as may happen in, for instance, datagram networks where messages can travel along different routes to their destination. The obvious solution is to encode the original order of the messages in a larger sequence number that is attached to each message. With a 16-bit field for the sequence numbers we can number 65,536 subsequent messages. Assuming a message length of 128 bits and an effective line speed of 9600 bps (bits per second), we could run out of numbers within 15 minutes. Fortunately, this range problem readily disappears if we limit the maximum number of messages that can be in transit at any one time: the sender's credit. Clearly, the range of the sequence numbers has to be larger than the maximum credit used so that a receiver can always distinguish duplicate messages from originals.

Assume a range M of available sequence numbers and an initial credit of W messages. We assume for the time being that M is sufficiently larger than W to avoid confusion of recycled sequence numbers. The sender must do some bookkeeping for every outstanding message within the current window. We use two arrays for this purpose. Boolean array element *busy[s]* is set to *true* if a message with sequence number s was sent and has not yet been acknowledged. The second array *store[s]* remembers the last message with sequence number s that was transmitted. Initially, all elements of array *busy* are set to *true*.

There are many problems to solve to get this version of the window protocol to work. The task can be split into three subtasks: transmitting messages, processing acknowledgments, and retransmitting messages that remain unacknowledged for too long. In addition to the constants W and M, the following four variables are used, all with an initial value of zero:

- ○ s, the sequence number of the next message to send
- ○ *window*, the number of outstanding unacknowledged messages
- ○ n, the sequence number of the oldest unacknowledged message
- ○ m, the sequence number of the last acknowledged message

First consider the transmission process in Figure 4.11. As long as all credits have not been used up, messages can be transmitted. Each message transmitted increments the number of outstanding messages, and by doing so, it implicitly decrements the credit for the transmission of new messages. A sequence number s is assigned, the message contents are stored in *store[s]* for possible retransmission later, the flag is set in *busy[s]*, and s is incremented modulo the range of the sequence numbers M (using the '%' operator).

The acknowledgment process is even simpler. It receives the incoming acknowledgments and sets the *busy[m]* flag to *false*. The order in which these acknowledgments are received is irrelevant.

The retransmission process waits until there are messages in transit by checking that *window* is non-zero. Each message that is sent must ultimately be acknowledged and have its *busy[n]* flag reset to *false*. The retransmission process waits for this to happen at the second wait clause. If it does, the window size is decremented, and n is incremented to point to the next oldest unacknowledged message. If the *busy* flag is not reset to *false* within a finite amount of time, the retransmission process times out and retransmits the message. The oval box delays the process until the condition specified becomes *true* or, as in the current case, until a timeout occurs (cf. Appendix B). The way we have specified it here, the retransmission timer repeats just one message, the oldest unacknowledged message.

The receiver for the sliding window protocol is given in Figure 4.12. It is split into two processes. One process receives and stores the incoming messages in whatever order they may happen to arrive. A second process accepts and acknowledges the messages, using the sequence numbers to restore their proper order. Messages can-

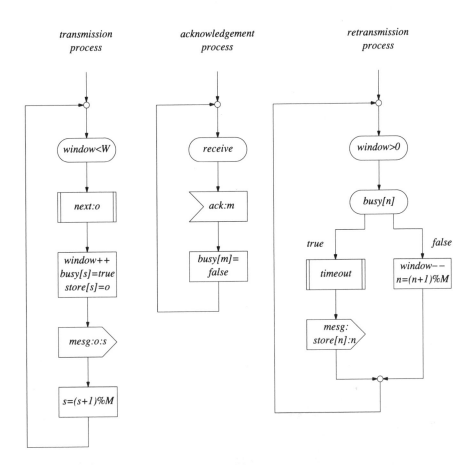

Figure 4.11 — Sender Processes, Sliding Window Protocol

not be acknowledged until they are accepted, to avoid the risk of running out of buffers to store messages if the accepting process turns out to be slower than the sender. We use a boolean array *recvd[M]* to remember the sequence numbers of messages that have been received, but not yet accepted, and an array *buffer[M]* to remember the contents of those messages. There is one extra variable to keep track of the protocol's progress: *p*, the sequence number of the next message to be accepted. It has an initial value of zero.

The accept process is straightforward. It waits for the *received* flag of the next message to be accepted to become *true*, accepts and acknowledges the message, and increments *p*. The receiver checks whether a newly arrived message is an original or a duplicate. For a new message, the *received* flags are set, and the message is stored in array *buffer*. Two flags must be updated, one for the message that

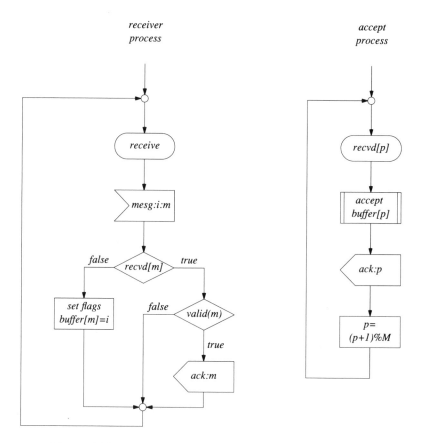

Figure 4.12 — Receiver Processes, Sliding Window Protocol

was just received and one for a message that we now know can no longer be received because it is outside the current window (see Exercise 4-14.)

$$recvd[m] \; = \; true$$

and

$$recvd[(m-W+M)\%M] \; = \; false$$

or equivalently

$$recvd[(m-W)\%M] \; = \; false$$

A duplicate message is recognized by the fact that the *received* flag was set to *true* before. There are two possible reasons for the arrival of a duplicate message:

○   The message was received, but not yet acknowledged.

○ The message was received and acknowledged, but the acknowledgment somehow did not reach the sender.

Only in the second case should the acknowledgment be repeated. The current value of variable p should be sufficient to figure out which of the two cases applies. If the sequence number count was not modulo M, the test would simply be:

$$valid(m) \ = \ m < p$$

since only values smaller than p were acknowledged before. Taking the modulo M effect into account, this becomes:

$$valid(m) \ = \ (0 < p - m \leq W) \ \| \ (0 < p - M - m \leq W)$$

The window protocol guarantees that a retransmitted message cannot have a sequence number that is more than W smaller than the last message that was acknowledged. The only case, then, where we can have $m > p$ or $p - m > W$ is when p has wrapped around the maximum M, and m has not.

MAXIMUM WINDOW SIZE

If M is the range of the sequence numbers, what is the maximum number of outstanding messages W that we can use and still guarantee that the window protocol works properly? If all messages that arrive out of order were simply rejected by the receiver, the answer would be $M - 1$. As long as a sequence number is not recycled before the last message using it is acknowledged, all is well. This means that if messages may be received out of order, as in Figure 4.12, the window size cannot exceed $M/2$ (cf. Exercise 4-9).

As an example, consider the following case. Let H be the highest sequence number (modulo M) that the receiver has read and acknowledged. It signifies to the receiver that the sender has at least processed an acknowledgment for the W-th message preceding the one numbered H (observation 1). The receiver also knows that at best the sender has processed all acknowledgments up to and including the one for the message numbered H (observation 2).

□ Observation 1 means that the sender may decide to retransmit any one of the $W - 1$ messages preceding H, and H itself. The oldest message that could be retransmitted would carry sequence number $(H - W + 1) \% M$.

□ Observation 2 means that the sender may also transmit up to W of the messages that succeed the message numbered H. The first $W - 1$ of these messages may even be lost on the transmission channel so that the message with number $(H + W) \% M$ is the first new message to arrive.

The highest-numbered message that may succeed H must be distinguishable from the lowest-numbered message that may be retransmitted preceding sequence number H. This means $M > 2W - 1$, or a maximum window size of $W = M/2$.

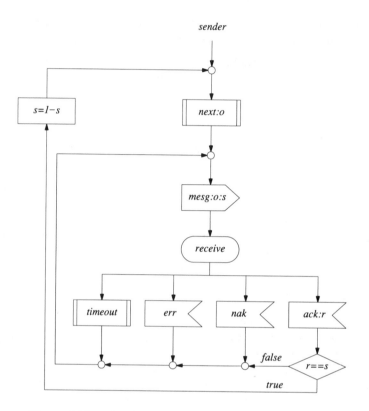

Figure 4.13 — Sender, Extended Alternating Bit Protocol

4.4 NEGATIVE ACKNOWLEDGMENTS

So far, we have used acknowledgments as a method of flow control, not of error control. If a message is lost or damaged beyond recognition, the absence of a positive acknowledgment would cause the sender eventually to time out and retransmit the message. If the probability of error is high enough, this can degrade the efficiency of the protocol, forcing the sender to be idle until it can be certain that an acknowledgment is not merely delayed, but is positively lost. The problem can be alleviated, though not avoided completely, with the introduction of *negative* acknowledgments.

The negative acknowledgment is used by the receiver whenever it receives a message that is damaged on the transmission channel. How the receiver may be able to establish that is discussed in Chapter 3. When the sender receives a negative acknowledgment, it knows immediately that it must retransmit the corresponding message, without having to wait for a timeout. The timeout itself is still needed, of course, to allow for a recovery from messages that disappear on the channel.

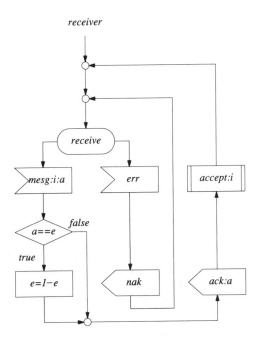

Figure 4.14 — Receiver, Extended Alternating Bit Protocol

Figures 4.13 and 4.14 show an extension of the alternating bit protocol from Figure 4.9 with negative acknowledgments. In this simple case, the *nak* needs no sequence number. (See also Exercise 4-3.)

TERMINOLOGY

The method of using acknowledgments to control the retransmission of messages is usually referred to as an *ARQ* method, where ARQ stands for Automatic Repeat Request. There are three main variants:

- ○ Stop-and-wait ARQ
- ○ Selective repeat ARQ
- ○ Go-back-N continuous ARQ

The Ping-Pong protocol of Figure 4.4, possibly extended with negative acknowledgments, classifies as a *stop-and-wait ARQ*. After each message is sent, the sender must wait for a positive or a negative acknowledgment, or perhaps a timeout.

The use of acknowledgments in the sliding window protocol of Figures 4.11 and 4.12 is a *selective repeat ARQ* method. In Figure 4.11 implemented a "one-at-a-time" selective repeat method where only the oldest unacknowledged message is retransmitted. In general, however, any message that triggers either a negative acknowledgment or a timeout may be retransmitted, independently of any other out-standing message. The generalized method is called "continuous" selective repeat.

The last strategy, *go-back-N continuous ARQ*, could be implemented in the above protocol by having the sender retransmit the corrupted message and all subse-quently sent messages. In that case the design of the receiver can be simplified. The accept processor from Figure 4.12, for instance, can now be deleted and the buffer becomes superfluous. In a go-back-N discipline the receiver refuses to accept all messages that arrive out of order, and waits for them to arrive in the proper sequence. It will not acknowledge any out-of-order messages. An ack-nowledgment with sequence number s can now be understood to acknowledge all messages *up to* and including s. Such an acknowledgment is therefore sometimes called a *cumulative acknowledgment*.

BLOCK ACKNOWLEDGMENT

A variation that can be used with the selective repeat and the go-back-N strategy to reduce the number of individual acknowledgment messages that must be sent from receiver to sender is known as *block acknowledgment*. In this case each positive acknowledgment can specify a range of sequence numbers of messages that have been received correctly. The block acknowledgment can be sent periodically or at the sender's request. Block acknowledgment can be seen as an extended form of cumulative acknowledgment.

4.5 CONGESTION AVOIDANCE

At the start of this chapter we gave two main reasons for the inclusion of flow con-trol schemes in protocols: synchronization and congestion avoidance.

Up to this point we have mostly ignored congestion avoidance and focused on end-to-end synchronization. One important issue in particular has not been dis-cussed yet: For a given data link, how is the actual window size and the corresponding range of sequence numbers chosen? It is relatively easy to set an upper limit on the window size: at some point increasing it can no longer improve the throughput if the channel is already fully saturated.

Assume it takes 0.5 seconds for a message to travel from sender to receiver, and another 0.5 seconds for the acknowledgment to come back to the sender. The sender can then fully saturate the channel if it can keep sending data for 1 second. If the data rate of the channel is S bps the sender should be able to transmit S bits before it needs to check for acknowledgments. If there are M bits in each message that is transmitted, the best window size is trivially S/M. And, of course, we had better make certain that $M<S$. A larger window size than S/M is wasteful: by the time the last message in the current window is transmitted, the acknowledgment for the oldest outstanding message should have arrived, and if it has not, it may be time to start considering the retransmission of that message.

There is a danger in the type of calculation we have performed here. It reduces the flow control problem to a link-level issue, while ignoring the network that contains the data link. Consider, for example, the two-hop data link shown in Figure 4.15.

Figure 4.15 — Two-Hop Link

There are two ways of defining a flow control protocol for transfers from the sender to the receiver in this two-link network:

○   Hop-by-hop (also called node-to-node)

○   End-to-end

In a hop-by-hop protocol, the window size is calculated separately for each link to try to saturate each one. The first link is 100 times faster than the second. But if we succeed in saturating both channels we have only succeeded in creating a bigger problem. Data arrive at the transfer point about 100 times faster than they can be passed on to the receiver. No matter how much buffer space the transfer point initially has, it eventually runs out of space, and unless it can throttle down the sender, it will start losing messages.

The only way the transfer point can control the sender is to refuse to acknowledge messages. The sender, however, tries to saturate the channel and will do so, either with retransmissions or with new data. If the number of acknowledgments drops, the sender will continue to saturate the channel by retransmitting data.

A flow control scheme, then, must be designed to optimize the utilization of two separate resources:

○ The buffer space in the network nodes
○ The bandwidth of the links connecting the nodes

The simple scheme above fails on both counts: it wastes buffer space in the transfer point, thereby potentially blocking other traffic that may be routed through that node, and it wastes bandwidth by triggering a deluge of retransmissions on the link from the sender to the transfer point. Optimal use of the two-link data path can only be achieved if the sender offers data at the data rate of the slowest link in the path: just 1% of the saturation point of the first link, which implies some type of feedback scheme from the second link back to the first.

In an end-to-end protocol this problem does not exist. The end-to-end capacity of the network path equals the capacity of the slowest link, and the window size can be set accordingly. The problem is that in a complicated network there is no hope that a sender can easily predict where the slowest link in its path to the receiver will be. The safest thing to do would be to derive a maximum window size for the whole network that is based on its slowest link. But that is hardly an inspiring solution, not to mention a wasteful one. Furthermore, in a larger network the capacity of a data link depends not just on the hardware but also on the number of competing users. If ten users start transferring large files over the fastest link in the network, that link can suddenly become the slowest one for all other users.

Going back to the original problem, even though we have pretended otherwise up to this point, flow control is not a static problem, but a dynamic one. In a static flow control protocol a sender always assumes that a message was either lost or distorted if its acknowledgment does not arrive with the round-trip message delay time. The appropriate response of the sender, in that case, is to retransmit the message. It can, however, also mean that the network is overloaded. The appropriate response of the sender is then to *reduce* the amount of traffic it offers to the network. The simplest method the sender has for doing this is to decrease its window size.

DYNAMIC FLOW CONTROL

A *dynamic window flow control* method makes the protocol self-adapting, one of the principles of sound design we listed in Chapter 2. A simple and commonly used method is to force a sender to decrease its window size whenever a retransmission timeout occurs. Once the timeouts disappear, the sender can be allowed to gradually increase the window size back to its maximum value. There are different philosophies about the precise parameters to be used in such a technique. Three popular variations are listed below.

☐ Decrease the window by *one* for every timeout that occurs, and increase it by one for *every* positive acknowledgment.

☐ Decrease the window to *half* its current size upon every timeout, and increase it by one message for every N positive acknowledgments received.

☐ Decrease to its *minimum* value of one, immediately when a timeout occurs, and increase the window by one for every N positive acknowledgments received.

All methods assume a minimum window size of one. The maximum size can be calculated as before, or it can be set to a heuristic value, such as the number of hops on the link through the network between sender and receiver. The heuristic guarantees that in normal operation every intermediate node stores just one message per connection.

With all three techniques it is assumed that the protocol by default uses its precalculated maximum window size. The *slow start* protocol developed by Van Jacobson also removes that assumption: the protocol starts with the minimum window size of one, and only starts increasing the effective window size once the first acknowledgment has been received. In the slow start protocol the round-trip delay is continuously measured, and it, rather than the retransmission timeout, is used as a measure for increasing or decreasing the window size.

RATE CONTROL

With the dynamic window flow control schemes above, we have touched upon more specific network design issues, which are outside the range of this book. From a network operator's point of view, the best congestion avoidance technique is to control the amount of traffic that *enters* the network under overload conditions, rather than attempting to minimize the damage for the traffic that has already been accepted, for instance, with timeouts and retransmissions. These methods are collectively called *rate control methods*. Figure 4.16 shows a well-known throughput versus traffic load chart that illustrates the need for rate control.

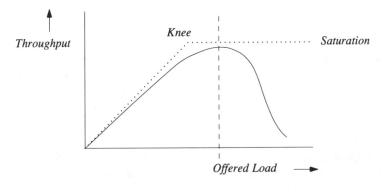

Figure 4.16 — Network Congestion

Ideally, the throughput of the network increases linearly with the offered load until it is fully saturated. In practice, network control algorithms eat away a little from the network capacity and a somewhat lower throughput is realized. Close to the saturation point, a growing offered load leads to an increasing degradation of service caused by the network congestion. The effect is comparable to a busy highway where traffic slowly comes to a complete standstill under peak loads. Congestion, then, is usually defined as a condition in the network where an increase in traffic load causes a decrease in throughput. The best point at which to operate the network is to the left of the dashed line in Figure 4.16, by controlling the offered load directly with, for instance, a rate control method. In some studies it was found that the optimal point is at the *knee* of the curve in Figure 4.16: the saturation point of the network under ideal conditions. Optimization is then interpreted as the maximization of throughput divided by measured round-trip message delay.

Rate control and flow control can be applied independently of one another. A standard rate control method is to give the sender a *permit* to offer data to the network at a specific average number of bytes per second. It can specify two parameters:

○ The average data rate R in bytes per second
○ The averaging interval that is used to calculate R

In the XTP protocol (see the Bibliographic Notes to Chapter 2) a third parameter is used:

○   The maximum data burst rate

Rate control is important as an efficiency and network control issue. It cannot, however, affect the logical consistency of a protocol definition, which is the primary focus of this book.

4.6 SUMMARY

Problems such as the ones we have discussed in this chapter have been discovered in many real-life protocols, and protocol designers will continue to be confronted with them over and over again. We have presented them here in their most basic form, to identify where the potential design flaws are.

Flow control and error control are often hard to distinguish. A flow control scheme can be used to coordinate the rate of transmission of messages between the processes in a distributed system. It can be used to avoid bottlenecks, and to recover from transmission errors. The strategies we have explored include the use of timeouts, the extension of messages with sequence numbers, and the use of positive and negative acknowledgments. A logical extension of static window flow control mechanism is dynamic window flow control. It allows protocols to become self-adapting, a principle of sound design. Flow control methods can be used to solve a variety of problems. They can be used in an end-to-end protocol to synchronize a sender and a receiver. They can be used in link level protocols to optimize buffer management and bandwidth utilization. Finally, they can be used as specific congestion avoidance techniques to match the capacity of a sender to the capacity of the network that carries the traffic.

Throughout this chapter we have assumed that a receiver process can establish whether incoming messages should be acknowledged and accepted, or should be rejected due to transmission errors. Refer to Chapter 3 to see how this can be accomplished.

EXERCISES

4-1 Describe in detail the conditions under which an *X-on/X-off* protocol and a *Ping-Pong* (stop-and-wait) protocol can fail.

4-2 Consider the adequacy of the alternating bit protocol under message loss, duplication, and reordering.

4-3 Change the extended alternating bit protocol from Figures 4.13 and 4.14 by also sending a negative acknowledgment when a message is received with the wrong sequence number. Show precisely what can go wrong.

4-4 Extend the X-on/X-off protocol for full-duplex transmissions. Consider the extra problems that the loss of control messages can now cause.

4-5 Show what happens if the timeout period in the alternating bit protocol is not chosen correctly.

4-6 If the acknowledgment message in the alternating bit protocol is delayed long enough to trigger the sender's timeout, a duplicate *mesg* from the sender is created, which in turn triggers a duplicate *ack* message, and so on. How would you change the protocol to solve this problem?

4-7 Describe your favorite traffic control problem (for example, grid lock, right of way problems, traffic circles) as a protocol problem.

4-8 Two divisions of an army are encamped to the south and to the north of a guerrilla force that is slightly stronger than either of the two divisions separately. Together, however, the two divisions can launch a surprise attack and defeat their adversaries. The problem for them is to coordinate their plans such that neither will mistakenly attack alone. It is decided beforehand that division *A* will notify division *B* of the plan for attack by sending a messenger. The messenger, though, must pass guerrilla-held territory to reach his goal. This "communication channel" between *A* and *B* is expected to have a substantial loss rate, and at least a potential for message distortion and insertion. Assume that message distortion can be dealt with by using proper encoding techniques. There is a flow control problem caused by the disappearance and reappearance of detained messengers. It is decided that to confirm the safe arrival of a messenger from *A* to *B* a second messenger will be sent from *B* to *A* with an acknowledgment. But, when can division *B* be sure that its acknowledgment arrived? The acknowledgment has to survive the same channel behavior as the original message. Therefore, the acknowledgment must itself be acknowledged. But in that case, the acknowledgment of acknowledgments would have to continue *ad infinitum*. What is the flaw in this reasoning? (This is a "folk" problem in protocol theory; for instance, see Bertsekas and Gallager [1987, pp. 28-29.]).

4-9 In a sliding window protocol where messages are not accepted out of order, show what can happen when the window size *W* equals to the range of the sequence numbers *M* (see Figure 4.11).

4-10 Show how you can reduce the dimensions of all four arrays in the protocol of Figure 4.11 to the maximum window size.

4-11 Consider the following problem on a channel that can reorder messages. A message with sequence number *N* is sent and acknowledged by the receiver, but the acknowledgment suffers a very long delay in the channel. A timeout occurs, and the message numbered *N* is retransmitted. The new acknowledgment overtakes the old one. The window of the sliding window protocol advances, and after it has advanced one full cycle, a new message with sequence number *N* is transmitted. By this time, the old acknowledgment finally makes it back to the sender and is confused for a new acknowledgment for the last message sent. Can you devise a solution to this problem?

4-12 An alternative method for the calculation of a retransmission timeout, used in the TCP protocol, is based on the following formula Stallings [1985, p. 508], Zhang [1986],

Karn and Partridge [1987]: $\beta \cdot (\alpha \cdot \overline{T} + (1 - \alpha) \cdot T_{last})$, where T_{last} is the last observed round-trip delay. Compare this method with the one given in this chapter. Explain the effect of parameters α and β.

4-13 The original alternating bit protocol, shown in Figure 4.8, is only partially specified. Provide the missing pieces.

4-14 Consider in detail what might happen if, in Figure 4.12, *recvd[p]* would be reset to *false* in the accept process immediately after an acknowledgment is sent.

BIBLIOGRAPHIC NOTES

The "alternating bit protocol," introduced in this chapter, is one of the simplest, best documented, and most thoroughly verified protocol designs. It was first described in a paper by three people from the National Physical Laboratory in England, Bartlett, Scantlebury and Wilkinson [1969], in response to an article by W.C. Lynch [1968]. Variations of the NPL protocol are still popular as a litmus test for new protocol validation and specification methods. Cerf and Kahn [1974] first extended the alternating bit protocol into a go-back-N sliding window protocol. The selective repeat strategy is due to Stenning [1976]. The block acknowledgment strategy was first described in Brown, Gouda, and Miller [1989].

A general introduction to flow control techniques can be found in, for instance, Pouzin [1976], Tanenbaum [1981, 1988], or Stallings [1985]. An excellent survey and comparison of flow control techniques was published in Gerla and Kleinrock [1980]. An early attempt at rate control is described in Beeforth et al. [1972]. It distinguishes between two types of acknowledgment: one acknowledges to the sender that a message was correctly received and need not be retransmitted, and another signals to the sender that the buffer space occupied by that message was released (e.g., because the packet was forwarded), and that the window of sequence numbers can advance a notch.

Various versions of Figure 4.16 have been published over the years. It is discussed in detail in, for instance, Gerla and Kleinrock [1980] and Jain [1986].

The XTP, or Express Transfer Protocol is described in Chesson [1987]. The protocol was designed to survive applications in high speed data networks. It is promoted by the company "Protocol Engines," founded by Greg Chesson. Other important work on protocols for high-speed data networks is reported in Clark [1985], and Clark, Lambert and Zhang [1988]. Dynamic window flow control methods are described in, for instance, Gerla and Kleinrock [1980], Jain [1986]. Jacobson's slow start protocol is described in Jacobson [1988].

More on the choice of timeout intervals for network protocols can be found in Zhang [1986] and Karn and Partridge [1987]. For an introduction to general network control issues refer to McQuillan and Walden [1977], Tanenbaum [1981, 1988], Cole [1987], or Stallings [1985, 1988].

VALIDATION MODELS   **5**

5.1   INTRODUCTION

In Chapter 2 we discussed the five main elements of a protocol definition: a service specification, explicit assumptions about the environment, the protocol vocabulary, format definitions, and procedure rules. Most of these elements can be structured in a hierarchical manner. The service specification, for instance, can be divided into layers, each new layer building upon the ones below it and providing a higher-level service to the user. To realize the service at a given layer, a consistent set of procedure rules must be derived and described in some formal language. The design of a complete and consistent set of procedure rules, however, is one of the hardest problems in protocol design.

A PROTOCOL VALIDATION LANGUAGE

In this chapter we introduce a notation for the specification and verification of procedure rules. Since the focus is on the procedure rules, these specifications provide only a partial description of a protocol. We call such a partial description a protocol *validation model*. The language we use to describe validation models is called PROMELA.

Our aim is to model protocols as succinctly as possible in order to be able to study their structure and to verify their completeness and logical consistency. Doing so, we deliberately abstract from other issues of protocol design, such as message format. A validation model defines the interactions of processes in a distributed system. It does not resolve implementation details. It does not say how a message is to be transmitted, encoded, or stored. By simplifying the problem in this way we can isolate and concentrate on the hardest part: the design of a complete and consistent set of rules to govern the interactions in a distributed system.

This chapter gives an introduction to the use of PROMELA for specifying system behavior in formal validation models. The next chapter discusses specific methods for defining the precise correctness criteria that can be applied to the validation of these models. A brief reference manual to PROMELA can be found in Appendix C. Chapter 7 gives an example of a serious application of PROMELA in the design of a file transfer protocol. Chapter 12 discusses the design of an interpreter/simulator for the language, and Chapter 13 discusses how this software can be extended with an automated analyzer for PROMELA models.

5.2 PROCESSES, CHANNELS, VARIABLES

We describe procedure rules as formal programs for an abstract model of a distributed system. Of course, we want this model to be as simple as possible, yet sufficiently powerful to represent all types of coordination problems that can occur in distributed systems. As far as descriptive power is concerned, it would suffice to define just one type of object: the finite state machine. The state machine can model all other objects that we may be interested in, including finite variables and message channels (bounded FIFO queues). Though such a model may be sufficient, it is not very convenient to work with. We therefore define validation models directly in terms of three specific types of objects:

- *processes*
- message *channels*
- state *variables*

For the purpose of analysis, each of these objects may be translated into a finite state machine by a simple translation process that is considered in Chapter 8. For now, however, we can pretend to have the luxury of working directly with these higher-level objects. All processes are by definition global objects. Variables and channels represent data that can be either global or local to a process.

5.3 EXECUTABILITY OF STATEMENTS

In PROMELA there is no difference between conditions and statements. Even isolated boolean conditions can be used as statements. The execution of a statement is conditional on its *executability*. All PROMELA statements are either executable or blocked, depending on the current values of variables or the contents of message channels. Executability is the basic means of synchronization. A process can wait for an event to happen by waiting for a statement to become executable. For instance, instead of writing a busy wait loop:

```
while (a != b) skip     /* wait for a == b */
```

we can achieve the same effect in PROMELA with the statement

```
(a == b)
```

The condition can only be executed (passed) if it holds. If the condition does not hold, execution blocks until it does. Arithmetic and boolean operators in conditions such as these are the same as in C. As we will see below, assignments to variables are always executable.

5.4 VARIABLES AND DATA TYPES

Variables in PROMELA are used to store either global information about the system as a whole or information that is local to one specific process, depending on where the declaration for the variable is placed. A variable can be one of the following six predefined data types:

```
bit, bool, byte, short, int, chan.
```

The first five types in this list are called the basic data types. They are used to specify objects that can hold a single value at a time. The sixth type specifies message channels. A message channel is an object that can store a number of values, grouped in user-defined structures. We discuss the basic data types first. Message channels are discussed separately in Section 5.6.

The declarations

```
bool    flag;
int     state;
byte    msg;
```

define variables that can store integer values in three different ranges. The scope of the variable is global if it is declared outside all process declarations, and local if it is declared within a process declaration. Table 5.1 summarizes the basic data types, sizes, and the corresponding value ranges on DEC/VAX computers.

Table 5.1 — Basic Data Types

Name	Size (bits)	Usage	Range
bit	1	unsigned	0..1
bool	1	unsigned	0..1
byte	8	unsigned	0..255
short	16	signed	$-2^{15}..2^{15}-1$
int	32	signed	$-2^{31}..2^{31}-1$

The names bit and bool are synonyms for a single bit of information. A byte is an unsigned quantity that can store a value between 0 and 255. shorts and ints are signed quantities that differ only in the range of values they can hold.

ARRAYS

Variables can be declared as arrays. For instance,

```
byte state[N]
```

declares an array of N bytes that can be accessed in statements such as

```
state[0] = state[3] + 5 * state[3*2/n]
```

where n is a constant or a variable declared elsewhere. The index to an array can be any expression that determines a unique integer value. The valid range of indexes is 0 .. N-1. The effect of the use of an index value outside that range is undefined; most likely it will cause a runtime error.

So far we have seen examples of a variable declaration and of two basic types of statements: boolean conditions and assignments. Declarations and assignments are always *executable*.

5.5 PROCESS TYPES

To execute a process we have to be able to name it, define its type, and instantiate it. Let us first look at the definition and naming of processes. All types of processes that can be instantiated are defined in proctype declarations. The following, for instance, declares a process with one local variable named state.

```
proctype A() { byte state; state = 3 }
```

The process type is named A. The body of the declaration, enclosed in parentheses, consists of local variable or channel declarations and statements. The declaration above contains one local variable declaration and a single statement: an assignment of the value 3 to variable state.

The semicolon is a statement *separator* (not a statement terminator, hence there is no semicolon after the last statement). PROMELA defines two different statement separators: an arrow, ->, and a semicolon, ;. The two separators are equivalent. The arrow is sometimes used as an informal way to indicate a causal relation between two statements. Consider the following example.

```
byte state = 2;
proctype A() { (state == 1) -> state = 3 }
proctype B() { state = state - 1 }
```

In this example we declared two process types, A and B. Variable state is now a global, initialized to the value 2. Process type A contains two statements, separated by an arrow. Process type declaration B contains a single statement that decrements the value of the state variable by 1. Since the assignment is always executable, processes of type B can always terminate without delay. Processes of type A, however, are delayed until the variable state contains the proper value.

THE INITIAL PROCESS

A `proctype` definition only declares process behavior, it does not execute it. Initially, just one process is executed: a process of type `init` which must be declared explicitly in every PROMELA specification. The `init` process is comparable to the function `main()` of a standard C program. The smallest possible PROMELA specification is

```
init { skip }
```

where `skip` is a null statement. Only slightly more complicated is the PROMELA equivalent of the famous ''hello world'' program from C:

```
init { printf("hello world\n") }
```

More interestingly, however, the initial process can initialize global variables, create message channels, and instantiate processes. An `init` declaration for the two-process system in Section 5.5, for instance, might look as follows.

```
init { run A(); run B() }
```

This `init` process starts two processes, which will run concurrently with the `init` process from then on. In the above case, the `init` process terminates after starting the second process, but it need not do so. Run is a unary operator that instantiates a copy of a given process type (for example, A). It does not wait for the process to terminate. The `run` statement is executable and returns a positive result only if the process can effectively be instantiated. It is unexecutable and returns zero if this cannot be done, for instance if too many processes are already running. Since PROMELA models finite state systems, the number of processes and message channels is always bounded. The precise value of the bound is hardware-dependent and therefore undefined in PROMELA. The value returned by `run` is a run-time process number, or `pid`. Because `run` is defined as an operator, `run A()` is an expression that can be embedded in other expressions. It would therefore be valid, though perhaps not too useful, to use it in a composite expression such as

```
i = run A() && (run B() || run C())
```

Since communication between processes is defined on named channels, the process numbers (`pids`) are usually irrelevant. There is one important exception that we discuss in Chapter 6, Section 6.7.

The `run` operator can pass parameter values to the new process, for instance as follows:

```
proctype A(byte state; short set)
{       (state == 1) -> state = set
}
init { run A(1, 3) }
```

Only message channels, discussed later, and instances of the five basic data types can be passed as parameters. Arrays and process types cannot be passed.

Run can be used in any process to spawn new processes, not just in the initial process. An executing process disappears when it terminates (i.e., reaches the end of the body of its process type declaration), but not before all the processes that it has instantiated (its "children") have terminated first.

Going back to the earlier example, note that using run we can create any number of copies of the process types A and B. If, however, more than one concurrent process is allowed both to read and write the value of a global variable a well-known set of problems can result (see Bibliographic Notes). Consider, for instance, the following system of two processes, sharing access to the global variable state.

```
byte state = 1;
proctype A() { (state == 1) -> state = state + 1 }
proctype B() { (state == 1) -> state = state - 1 }
init { run A(); run B() }
```

If one of the two processes terminates before its competitor has started, the other process will block forever on the initial condition. If both pass the condition simultaneously, both can terminate, but the resulting value of state is unpredictable. It can be 0, 1, or 2.

Many solutions to this problem have been considered, ranging from the abolition of global variables to the provision of special machine instructions that can guarantee an indivisible test-and-set sequence on a shared variable. The example below was one of the first solutions published. It is due to the Dutch mathematician T. Dekker. It grants two processes mutually exclusive access to an arbitrary *critical section* in their code by manipulating three global state variables. The first four lines in the PROMELA specification below are C-style macro definitions. The first two macros define true to be a constant value equal to 1 and false to be a constant 0. Similarly, Aturn and Bturn are defined as boolean constants.

```
 1 #define true      1
 2 #define false     0
 3 #define Aturn     1
 4 #define Bturn     0
 5
 6 bool x, y, t;
 7
 8 proctype A()
 9 {    x = true;
10      t = Bturn;
11      (y == false || t == Aturn);
12      /* critical section */
13      x = false
14 }
15 proctype B()
16 {    y = true;
17      t = Aturn;
18      (x == false || t == Bturn);
```

```
19      /* critical section */
20      y = false
21 }
22 init { run A(); run B() }
```

The conditions on lines 11 and 18 are used to synchronize the processes. They can only be executed if they hold. The algorithm can be executed repeatedly and is independent of the relative speeds of the two processes.

ATOMIC SEQUENCES

In PROMELA there is another way to avoid the *test-and-set* problem: atomic sequences. A sequence of statements enclosed in parentheses prefixed with the keyword atomic indicates that the sequence is to be executed as one indivisible unit, non-interleaved with any other processes. It is an error if any statement, other than the first one, can block in an atomic sequence. The executing process will abort in that case. Here is the earlier example, rewritten with two atomic sequences.

```
byte state = 1;
proctype A() { atomic { (state == 1) -> state = state + 1 } }
proctype B() { atomic { (state == 1) -> state = state - 1 } }
init { run A(); run B() }
```

In this case the final value of state is either 0 or 2, depending on which process executes. The other process will be blocked forever.

Atomic sequences can be an important tool in reducing the complexity of a validation model. An atomic sequence restricts the amount of interleaving that is allowed which can effectively render complex validation models tractable, without loss of generality. The example below illustrates this.

```
proctype nr(short pid, a, b)
{       int res;

atomic  {       res = (a*a+b)/2*a;
                printf("result %d: %d\n", pid, res)
        }
}
init { run nr(1,1,1); run nr(1,2,2); run nr(1,3,2) }
```

The init process starts up three copies of the process type nr. Each process computes some number and prints it. The manipulations of the variables within these processes are all local and cannot affect the behavior of the other processes. Defining the body of the process as an atomic sequence dramatically reduces the number of cases that would need to be considered in a validation (Chapter 11), without changing the possible behaviors of the processes in any way. It is usually trivial to identify statement sequences that can be rewritten with atomic sequences.

5.6 MESSAGE CHANNELS

Message channels are used to model the transfer of data from one process to another. They are declared either locally or globally, just like variables of the basic data types, using the keyword `chan`. For instance,

```
chan a, b; chan c[3]
```

declares the names a, b, and c as channel identifiers, the last one as an array. A channel declaration can have an initializer field as well:

```
chan a = [16] of { short }
```

initializes channel a. The initializer says that the channel can store up to 16 messages of type `short`. Similarly,

```
chan c[3] = [4] of { byte }
```

initializes an array of 3 channels, each with a capacity of 4 message slots, each slot consisting of one message field of type `byte`.

If the messages to be passed by the channel have more than one field, the declaration looks as follows:

```
chan qname = [16] of { byte, int, chan, byte }
```

This time, we have defined a single channel that can store up to 16 messages, each consisting of 4 fields: an 8-bit value, a 32-bit value, a channel name, and another 8-bit value.

The statement

```
qname!expr
```

sends the value of expression `expr` to the channel we just created, that is, it appends the value to the tail of the channel.

```
qname?msg
```

retrieves a message from the head of the channel, and stores it in the variable `msg`. Channels pass messages in first-in first-out order. In the above cases, only a single value is passed through the channel. If multiple values are transferred per message, they are specified in a comma-separated list

```
qname!expr1,expr2,expr3
qname?var1,var2,var3
```

If more parameters are sent per message than the message channel can store, the redundant parameters are lost. If fewer parameters are sent then the message channel can store, the value of the remaining parameters is undefined. Similarly, if the receive operation tries to retrieve more parameters than are available, the value of the extra parameters is undefined; if it receives fewer than the number of parameters that was sent, the extra information is lost.

By convention, the first message field is often used to specify the message type (a constant). An alternative and equivalent notation for the send and receive operations is therefore to specify the message type, followed by a list of message fields enclosed in parentheses. In general:

```
qname!expr1(expr2,expr3)
qname?var1(var2,var3)
```

The send operation is executable only when the channel addressed is not full. The receive operation, similarly, is only executable when the channel is non-empty.

Optionally, some of the arguments in the receive operation can be constants:

```
qname?cons1,var2,cons2
```

In this case, a further condition on the executability of the receive operation is that the value of all message fields that are specified as constants match the value of the corresponding fields in the message that is at the head of the channel.

Here is an example that uses some of the mechanisms introduced so far.

```
proctype A(chan q1)
{        chan q2;
         q1?q2;
         q2!123
}
proctype B(chan qforb)
{        int x;
         qforb?x;
         printf("x = %d\n", x)
}
init
{        chan qname[2] = [1] of { chan };
         chan qforb = [1] of { int };
         run A(qname[0]);
         run B(qforb);
         qname!qforb
}
```

Note that channel qforb is not declared as an array and therefore the send operation and the end of the initial process does not need an index. The value printed by the process of type B will be 123.

A predefined unary operator len(qname) takes the name of a channel qname as an operand and returns the number of messages that it currently holds. Note that if len is used as a condition, rather than on the right side of an assignment, it is unexecutable if the channel is empty: it returns a zero result, which by definition means that the statement is temporarily unexecutable.

Send and receive operations cannot be evaluated without potential side-effects. Composite conditions such as

```
(qname?var == 0)
```

or

```
(a > b && qname!123)
```

are therefore invalid in PROMELA. For the receive operation, however, there is an alternative notation, using square brackets around the clause behind the question mark. For instance,

```
qname?[ack,var]
```

is evaluated as a condition and can be combined with other boolean expressions. It returns a positive result (1) if the corresponding receive statement

```
qname?ack,var
```

would be executable, i.e., if there is indeed a message `ack` at the head of the channel. It returns zero otherwise. It has no side-effect; specifically, it does not remove the message from the channel.

Note carefully that in non-atomic sequences of two statements such as

```
(len(qname) > 0) -> qname?msgtype
```

or

```
qname?[msgtype] -> qname?msgtype
```

the second statement is not necessarily executable after the first one has been executed. There may be race conditions if access to the channels is shared between several processes. In both cases, a second process can steal the message just after the current one determined its presence. PROMELA does not, and indeed cannot, prevent the user from writing these specifications. On the contrary, these are precisely the types of problems we want to model in our validation language.

RENDEZVOUS COMMUNICATION

So far we have talked about asynchronous communication between processes via message channels created in statements such as

```
chan qname = [N] of { byte }
```

where N is a positive constant that defines the buffer size. Using a channel size of zero, as in

```
chan port = [0] of { byte }
```

defines a rendezvous port that can only pass, and not store, single-byte messages. Message interactions via such rendezvous ports are synchronous, by definition. Consider the following example:

```
#define msgtype 33

chan name = [0] of { byte, byte };

byte name;
```

```
proctype A()
{        name!msgtype(124);
         name!msgtype(121)
}
proctype B()
{        byte state;
         name?msgtype(state)
}
init
{        atomic { run A(); run B() }
}
```

The two run statements are placed in an atomic sequence to enforce that the two processes start simultaneously. Of course, they need not terminate simultaneously, and they need not have run to completion before the atomic sequence terminates. Channel name is a global rendezvous port. The two processes synchronously execute their first statement: a handshake on message msgtype and a transfer of the value 124 to local variable state. The second statement in process A is unexecutable, because there is no matching receive operation in process B.

If the channel name is defined with a non-zero buffer capacity, the behavior is different. If the buffer size is at least two, the process of type A can complete its execution before its peer even starts. If the buffer size is one, the sequence of events is as follows. The process of type A can complete its first send action, but it blocks on the second, because the channel is now filled to capacity. The process of type B can then retrieve the first message and terminate. At this point, A becomes executable again and terminates, leaving its last message as a residual in the channel.

Synchronous ports can be declared as arrays, just like asynchronous channels. Rendezvous communication is binary: only two processes, a sender and a receiver, can be synchronized in this way. We will see an example of a way to exploit this to build a semaphore below. But first, let us introduce a few more control flow structures.

5.7 CONTROL FLOW

Between the lines, we have already introduced three ways of defining control flow: concatenation of statements within a process, parallel execution of processes, and atomic sequences. There are three other control flow constructs in PROMELA to be discussed:

○ Case selection
○ Repetition
○ Unconditional jumps

CASE SELECTION

The simplest construct is the selection structure. Using the relative values of two variables a and b to choose between two options, for instance, we can write

```
if
:: (a != b) -> option1
:: (a == b) -> option2
fi
```

The selection structure contains two execution sequences, each preceded by a double colon. Only one sequence from the list is executed. A sequence can be selected only if its first statement is executable. The first statement is therefore called a *guard*.

In the example above the guards are mutually exclusive, but they need not be. If more than one guard is executable, one of the corresponding sequences is selected at random. If all guards are unexecutable, the process blocks until at least one of them can be selected. There is no restriction on the type of statement that can be used as a guard. The following example uses input statements:

```
#define a 1
#define b 2

chan ch = [1] of { byte };

proctype A() { ch!a }
proctype B() { ch!b }
proctype C()
{       if
        :: ch?a
        :: ch?b
        fi
}
init { atomic { run A(); run B(); run C() } }
```

This example defines three processes and one channel. The first option in the selection structure of the process of type C is executable if the channel contains a message a, where a is a constant with value 1, as defined in a macro definition at the start of the program. The second option is executable if it contains a message b, where b is a constant. Which message will be available depends on the relative speeds of the processes.

A process of the following type either increments or decrements the value of variable count once.

```
byte count;

proctype counter()
{       if
        :: count = count + 1
        :: count = count - 1
        fi
}
```

REPETITION

A logical extension of the selection structure is the repetition structure. We can modify the above program to obtain a cyclic program that randomly increments or decrements the variable.

```
byte count;

proctype counter()
{       do
        :: count = count + 1
        :: count = count - 1
        :: (count == 0) -> break
        od
}
```

Only one option can be selected for execution at a time. After the option completes, the execution of the structure is repeated. The normal way to terminate the repetition structure is with a break statement. In the example, the loop can be broken when the count reaches zero. It need not terminate since the other two options remain executable. To force termination, we could modify the program as follows:

```
proctype counter()
{       do
        :: (count != 0) ->
                if
                :: count = count + 1
                :: count = count - 1
                fi
        :: (count == 0) -> break
        od
}
```

JUMPS

Another way to break the loop is with an unconditional jump: the infamous goto statement. This is illustrated in the following implementation of Euclid's algorithm for finding the greatest common divisor of two positive numbers:

```
proctype Euclid(int x, y)
{       do
        :: (x >  y) -> x = x - y
        :: (x <  y) -> y = y - x
        :: (x == y) -> goto done
        od;
done:
        skip
}
```

The goto in this example jumps to a label named done. A label can only appear before a statement. Above, we want to jump to the end of the program. In this

case a dummy statement skip is useful: it is a place holder that is always executable and has no effect. The goto statement itself is always executable.

5.8 EXAMPLES

The following example specifies a filter that receives messages from a channel in
and divides them over two channels large and small depending on the values
attached. The constant N is defined to be 128, and size is defined to be 16 in two
macro definitions.

```
#define N     128
#define size  16

chan in    = [size] of { short };
chan large = [size] of { short };
chan small = [size] of { short };

proctype split()
{       short cargo;

        do
        :: in?cargo ->
                if
                :: (cargo >= N) -> large!cargo
                :: (cargo <  N) -> small!cargo
                fi
        od
}
init {  run split() }
```

A process type that merges the two streams back into one, most likely in a different
order, and writes it back to the channel in could be specified as

```
proctype merge()
{       short cargo;

        do
        ::      if
                :: large?cargo
                :: small?cargo
                fi;
                in!cargo
        od
}
```

With the following modification to the init process, the split and merge processes
can busily perform their duties forever.

```
init
{       in!345; in!12; in!6777; in!32; in!0;
        run split(); run merge()
}
```

As a final example, consider the following implementation of a Dijkstra semaphore, using binary rendezvous communication.

```
#define p       0
#define v       1

chan sema = [0] of { bit };
proctype dijkstra()
{       do
        :: sema!p -> sema?v
        od
}
proctype user()
{       sema?p;
        /* critical section */
        sema!v
        /* non-critical section */
}
init
{       atomic {
                run dijkstra();
                run user(); run user(); run user()
        }
}
```

The semaphore guarantees that only one user process can enter its critical section at a time. In the example, each user process accesses its critical section only once. If repeated access could be requested, the semaphore would not necessarily prevent one process from monopolizing access to the critical section.

5.9 MODELING PROCEDURES AND RECURSION

Procedures, even recursive ones, can be modeled as processes. The return value can be passed back to the calling process via a global variable or via a message. The following program illustrates this.

```
proctype fact(int n; chan p)
{       int result;

        if
        :: (n <= 1) -> p!1
        :: (n >= 2) ->
                chan child = [1] of { int };
                run fact(n-1, child);
                child?result;
                p!n*result
        fi
}
```

```
init
{        int result;
         chan child = [1] of { int };

         run fact(7, child);
         child?result;
         printf("result: %d\n", result)
}
```

The process `fact(n, p)` recursively calculates the factorial of n, communicating the result to its parent process via channel p.

5.10 MESSAGE-TYPE DEFINITIONS

We have seen how constants can be defined using C-style macros. As a mild form of syntactic sugar, PROMELA allows for message type definitions of the form

```
mtype = { ack, nak, err, next, accept }
```

The definition is equivalent to the following sequence of macro definitions.

```
#define ack      1
#define nak      2
#define err      3
#define next     4
#define accept   5
```

A formal message-type definition is the preferred way of specifying the message types since it defers any decision on the specific values to be used. At the same time, it makes the names of the constants, rather than the values, available to an implementation, which can improve error reporting. There can be only one message-type definition per specification.

5.11 MODELING TIMEOUTS

We have already discussed two types of statements with a predefined meaning in PROMELA: `skip` and `break`. Another predefined statement is `timeout`. The `timeout` statement allows a process to abort the waiting for a condition that can no longer become true, for example, an input from an empty channel. The timeout provides an escape from a hang state. It can be considered an artificial, predefined condition that becomes true only when no other statements in the distributed system are executable. Note that it carries no value: it does not specify a timeout interval, but a timeout possibility. We deliberately abstract from absolute timing considerations, which is crucial in validation work, and we do not specify how the timeout should be implemented. A simple example is the following process that sends a reset message to a channel named `guard` whenever the system comes to a standstill.

```
proctype watchdog()
{       do
        :: timeout -> guard!reset
        od
}
```

The timeout, as defined here, does not model errors caused by premature timeouts in a real system. If this is required, it can be achieved by redefining the keyword in a macro, for instance as follows.

```
#define timeout 1        /* always enabled, arbitrary delay */
```

More examples are given in Chapter 7.

STATEMENT TYPES

With the exception of `assert` statements and temporal claim primitives (see Chapter 6) we have now discussed all basic types of statements defined in PROMELA:

- ○ Assignments and conditions
- ○ Selections and repetitions
- ○ Send and receive
- ○ `Goto` and `break` statements
- ○ `Timeout`

Note that `run` and `len` are not statements but unary operators that can be used in assignments and conditions.

The `skip` statement was introduced as a filler to satisfy syntax requirements. It is not formally part of the language but a *pseudo-statement*, a synonym for another statement with the same effect. Trivially, `skip` is equivalent to the condition (1); it is always executable and has no effect.

5.12 LYNCH´s PROTOCOL REVISITED

Now that we have a language, let us try to describe the example protocol from Chapter 2. The version below is based on Figures 2.1 and 2.3, with the trial extension for accepting messages and for initializing the data transfer discussed in Section 2.4.

```
mtype = { ack, nak, err, next, accept }
proctype transfer(chan in, out, chin, chout)
{       byte o, i;

        in?next(o);
        do
        :: chin?nak(i) -> out!accept(i); chout!ack(o)
        :: chin?ack(i) -> out!accept(i); in?next(o); chout!ack(o)
        :: chin?err(i) -> chout!nak(o)
        od
}
```

```
init
{       chan AtoB = [1] of { byte, byte };
        chan BtoA = [1] of { byte, byte };
        chan Ain  = [2] of { byte };
        chan Bin  = [2] of { byte };
        chan Aout = [2] of { byte };
        chan Bout = [2] of { byte };

        atomic {
                run transfer(Ain, Aout, AtoB, BtoA);
                run transfer(Bin, Bout, BtoA, AtoB)
        };
        AtoB!err(0)
}
```

The channels `Ain` and `Bin` are to be filled with token messages of type `next` and arbitrary values (e.g., ASCII character values) by unspecified background processes: the users of the transfer service. Similarly, these user processes can read received data from the channels `Aout` and `Bout`. The processes are initialized in an atomic statement and started with the dummy `err` message.

As a last example, below is a listing in PROMELA of a viciously complex procedure to calculate Ackermann's function, which is defined recursively as

```
ack(0,b) = b+1
ack(a,0) = ack(a-1, 1)
ack(a,b) = ack(a-1, ack(a,b-1))
```

The PROMELA version is as follows.

```
/***** Ackermann's function *****/

proctype ack(short a, b; chan ch1)
{       chan ch2 = [1] of { short };
        short ans;
        if
        :: (a == 0) ->
                ans = b+1
        :: (a != 0) ->
                if
                :: (b == 0) ->
                        run ack(a-1, 1, ch2)
                :: (b != 0) ->
                        run ack(a, b-1, ch2);
                        ch2?ans;
                        run ack(a-1, ans, ch2)
                fi;
                ch2?ans
        fi;
        ch1!ans
}
```

```
init
{       chan ch = [1] of { short };
        short ans;

        run ack(3, 3, ch);
        ch?ans;
        printf("ack(3,3) = %d\n", ans);
        assert(0)        /* a forced stop, (Chapter 6) */
}
```

Seems simple enough? It takes 2433 process instantiations to produce the answer. The answer, by the way, is 61.

5.13 SUMMARY

We have introduced a notation for describing protocol procedure rules in a specification and modeling language named PROMELA. In this chapter we have discussed PROMELA features for describing system behavior only. In the next chapter we discuss the remaining language features that are specifically related to the specification of correctness criteria.

The validation modeling language has several unusual features that make it suited for modeling distributed systems. All communication between processes takes place via either messages or shared variables. Synchronous and asynchronous communication are modeled as special cases of a general message-passing mechanism.

Every statement in PROMELA can potentially model delay: it is either executable or not, in most cases depending on the state of the environment of the running process. Process interaction and process coordination are thus at the very basis of the language. The semantics of the language make a mapping from the flow chart language used in the first part of the book to PROMELA programs straightforward. It is probably good to keep in mind that PROMELA is a modeling language, not a programming language. There are no abstract data types, and only a few basic types of variables. A validation model is an abstraction of a protocol implementation. The abstraction maintains the essentials of the process interaction so that it can be studied in isolation. It suppresses implementation and programming detail. An overview of the language can be found in Appendix C.

In the next chapters we find good use for the language. In Chapter 7 it is used in the design of a file transfer protocol. In Part IV we show how to develop the software for analyzing protocol models written in PROMELA.

EXERCISES

5-1 Assume the statement run A() is unexecutable, for instance because there were too many processes running. Can you say if b = run A() is executable?

5-2 If the statement (qname?var == 0) were allowed in PROMELA, what would its effect be? Hint: consider the side-effects of the receive operation.

5-3 Revise the two programs from Section 5.6 to incorporate the use of messages of type eot to signify the end of an input stream.

5-4 Rewrite the declaration for process types fact() and ack() to use a global variable instead of messages to communicate the result of the calculation from a child process to its parent.

5-5 Rewrite the fact() program to return the n-th Fibonacci number, f(n) = f(n-1) + f(n-2), instead of a factorial. By definition, f(0) = 0 and f(1) = 1.

5-6 Rewrite your program for generating Fibonacci numbers to reduce the number of processes that is required. (Hint: make the program singly recursive; every process creates no more than one child.)

5-7 Extend the model of Lynch's protocol with two user processes that use the transfer service.

5-8 Extend the same program with a process type modeling a faulty transmission channel between the two users.

5-9 Write a PROMELA program that performs a *bubble* sort on the elements of a channel that is initialized with messages of type int, each carrying a value. A bubble sort is done by scanning through a list of numbers repeatedly, swapping any pair of adjacent numbers that are out of order.

5-10 Write a PROMELA program that sorts integers by building a binary tree of processes. Each process holds one integer in the sequence. It has one parent process and up to two children processes, left and right. The integers enter the sorter via the process at the root of the tree. All processes follow the same discipline. If the next integer received is larger than the one held by the receiver, it is routed to the left. If it is smaller, it is routed to the right. Children processes are created only when necessary. When the last integer has been processed, the values stored in the tree must be retrieved in the right order and printed.

5-11 With distributed processes, it is relatively easy to design resource managers that can, for instance, provide user programs mutually exclusive access to devices or services. Write a sample printer server that "owns" a display channel and allows processes to submit a sequence of messages to it (e.g., anything up to an eot) in fragments, without the possibility of interruption by other processes.

5-12 Rewrite the example using the Dijkstra semaphore with rendezvous communication into a solution using asynchronous communication between the monitor process and the user processes.

5-13 Consider in detail why the C data types real or double are not defined in PROMELA.

5-14 (Paul Haahr) Many processors use "interrupt priority levels" to ensure that some devices get handled before others (e.g., disks are usually treated as more urgent that keyboards). The current priority level is stored in a special CPU register, usually a 3-bit or 4-bit integer. During normal operation, the priority level is zero. Each hardware device that can interrupt the CPU is assigned a priority level. When a hardware interrupt occurs, if the processor is currently running at a level less than that of the device, the processor starts running the appropriate interrupt handler; if not, the device waits until the priority drops and then interrupts. When the interrupt handler starts, the priority level is set to the device's priority. It is reset to the previous level when the handler terminates.

The processor can also set the priority level independently of the interrupt handlers, e.g., with an instruction spl(x). This can be used to prevent an interrupt handler from being interrupted in the middle—when its data structures are not necessarily in a proper state—by another interrupt that will use the same structures. It is also used by operating systems to assure mutual exclusion. For example, if a device (say a disk) interrupts at level six, the device driver that runs the disk has to set the priority level temporarily to six before using data structures that may be altered by a disk interrupt.

Model the interrupt priority scheme in PROMELA for three processes, modeling the behavior of a CPU, a disk process and a terminal process. (Hint: use an array to model the stack of priority levels.)

5-15 Modify the validation model for Lynch's protocol to model the possibility of transmission errors.

BIBLIOGRAPHIC NOTES

PROMELA is an extension of a smaller language named Argos that was developed in 1983 for protocol validation, e.g., Holzmann [1985]. The syntax of PROMELA expressions, declarations, and assignments is loosely based on the language C, Kernighan and Ritchie [1978]. The language was influenced significantly by the ''guarded command languages'' of E.W. Dijkstra [1975] and C.A.R. Hoare [1978]. There are, however, important differences. Dijkstra's language had no primitives for process interaction. Hoare's language was based exclusively on synchronous communication. Also in Hoare's language, the type of statements that could appear in the guards of an option was restricted. The semantics of the selection and cycling statements in PROMELA is also rather different from other guarded command languages: the statements are not aborted when all guards are false but they block, thus providing the required synchronization.

The mutual exclusion (or ''critical section'') problem, referred to briefly in this chapter, has been studied for many years. The following intriguing series of articles documents some of the improvements that have been made: Dijkstra [1965], Knuth [1966], deBruyn [1967], Dijkstra [1968], Eisenberg and McGuire [1972], Lamport [1974, 1976, 1986]. More elaborate discussions can also be found in Bredt [1970] or Holzmann [1979].

CORRECTNESS REQUIREMENTS 6

6.1 INTRODUCTION

In Chapter 5 we developed a language for modeling behavior in distributed systems. The language is deliberately defined at a high level of abstraction to allow us to focus on design rather than on implementation issues. The programs that can be written in this language are therefore called *validation models*. The details required to convert a validation model into an implementation could presumably be filled in with relatively little effort, perhaps even mechanically. But the primary purpose of PROMELA is validation, not implementation.

To validate a design, we need to be able to specify precisely what it means for a design to be correct. A design can be proven correct only with respect to specific correctness criteria. Three fairly standard criteria were listed in Chapter 2: the absence of deadlocks, livelocks, and improper terminations. It is, for instance, never enough to just ''know'' that a design is free of deadlocks.

  *A good design is **provably** free of deadlocks.*

There are many protocol properties that one might be interested in proving for any given design. But the problems we are dealing with are complex. It is not too hard to show that the problem of verifying even the simplest protocol properties, such as absence of deadlock, is PSPACE hard (see Bibliographic Notes), even for a finite state model. In attempting to prove the correctness of a protocol, we have to be aware of these complexity bounds. Since it is our goal to develop a validation methodology that can be applied to protocols of arbitrary size, we need to develop methods for battling the complexity from two different sides:

☐ We need a formalism for specifying correctness requirements that is not so inherently complex that effective analysis for larger models becomes impossible.

☐ We need a method for reducing the complexity of models that are beyond the range of our validation methods.

The second point, reduction, is discussed in Chapters 8 and 11 (see Section 8.9, Generalization of Machines, and Section 11.7, Complexity Management). The first point will be addressed here. It says that the more expressive we make our notation for specifying correctness requirements, the less useful it will be in practice. The set of correctness criteria that can be expressed in PROMELA is therefore chosen carefully. This set is deliberately not restricted to a single all-powerful mechanism. Several independent levels of complexity are supported. The simplest, most frequently used requirements, such as absence of deadlock, are expressed straightforwardly and checked independently of other properties. They can be analyzed mechanically with fast and frugal algorithms even for very large systems. Slightly more complicated types of requirements, such as absence of livelocks, are expressed independently, and carry an independent price-tag in computational expense when validated mechanically. The most sophisticated requirements are inevitably also the most expensive to check. In Chapter 11 we discuss the best known algorithms for the automated validation of each type of correctness requirement and quantify the size of systems that they can validate.

In the next section we give an overview of the types of correctness criteria that can be expressed for PROMELA models. Each of the sections that follow it elaborates one of these properties in detail. It shows the PROMELA language structures that are needed to express each property and gives some examples of its use.

6.2 REASONING ABOUT BEHAVIOR

We formalize correctness criteria as claims about the behavior of a PROMELA validation model. Two general types of claims are then that a given behavior is either

○ Inevitable or
○ Impossible

Since the number of possible behaviors of any given PROMELA model is finite, however, a claim of either type implicitly defines a complementary and equivalent claim of the other type. It therefore suffices to support just one.

> *All correctness criteria that can be expressed in PROMELA define behaviors that are claimed to be **impossible**.*

To state that a given behavior is inevitable, for instance, we can state that all deviant behaviors are impossible. Similarly, if a correctness assertion states that a condition is invariantly true, the correctness claim states that it is impossible for the assertion to be violated, independent of the system behavior.

Before we can continue, however, we will have to be more precise about the terms we are using. What, for instance, is a behavior, and how can we make claims about it?

The *behavior* of a validation model is defined completely by the set of all the execution sequences it can perform, where an *execution sequence* is simply a finite, ordered set of states. A *state*, in turn, is completely defined by the specification of all values for local and global variables, all control flow points of running processes, and the contents of all message channels. We say that a validation model can *reach* a given state by the execution of PROMELA statements, using the earlier defined semantics of executability. A validation model can also *be placed* in a given state by an assignment of the appropriate values to variables, control flow points and channels.

Of course, not just any arbitrary collection of states is also a valid execution sequence. A finite, ordered set of states is said to be *valid* for a given PROMELA model M if it satisfies the following two criteria:

☐ The first state of the sequence, i.e., the state with ordinal number 1, is the initial system state of M, with all variables initialized to zero, all message channels empty, with only the init process active, and set in its initial state.

☐ If M is placed in the state with ordinal number i, there is at least one executable statement that can bring it to the state with ordinal number $i+1$.

We will consider two special types of sequences, called terminating and cyclic sequences.

☐ An execution sequence is said to be *terminating* if no state occurs more than once in the sequence, and the model M contains no executable statements when placed in the last state of the sequence.

☐ An execution sequence is said to be *cyclic* if all states except the last one are distinct, and the last state of the sequence is equal to one of the earlier states.

Cyclic sequences define potentially infinite executions. All terminating and cyclic execution sequences that can be generated by executing a PROMELA model, together define the *system behavior* of that model. The union of all states included in the system behavior is called *the set of reachable states* of the model.

PROPERTIES OF STATES

Correctness claims for PROMELA models can be built up from simple propositions, where a proposition is a boolean condition on the state of the system. The propositions can refer to all the elements of a system state: local and global variables, control-flow points of arbitrary executing processes, and the contents of message channels. Some of the notation for this was discussed in Chapter 5; the remaining features will be introduced shortly.

The propositions implicitly define a labeling of states. In any given state a proposition is either true or false. Correctness criteria then can be expressed in terms of states, e.g., by defining explicitly in which states a given proposition is required to hold. Some of these requirements can be specified in PROMELA with, for instance, *assertion* statements that are embedded in the model. This mechanism by itself, however, is not sufficient. If more than one proposition is used, we may want to express a correctness requirement as a temporal ordering of propositions, i.e., by specifying the order in which propositions are required to hold, irrespective of the state the system is in. Alternatively, the temporal ordering can define the order in which propositions should never hold. As indicated above, these two alternatives for defining temporal orderings are complementary. Only the second alternative is supported in PROMELA. The formalism to support this is a new language feature called a *temporal claim*.

TEMPORAL CLAIMS

In the formalization of temporal claims we specify an ordering of propositions. It is important to note that the semantics of these *proposition* orderings is different from the semantics of *statement* orderings elsewhere in a PROMELA model. Within proctype definitions, a sequential ordering of two statements implies that the second statement is to be executed after the first one terminates. Since we are not allowed to make any assumptions about the relative speeds of concurrently executing processes, the only valid interpretation of the word *after* in the above sentence is *eventually after*. Correctness claims, however, may have to be more specific. In a temporal claim a sequential ordering of two propositions defines an *immediate* consequence. We will show later how other types of temporal relations can also be specified with this mechanism.

The types of correctness requirements we make can be different for terminating and cyclic sequences, as are the algorithms we will ultimately need to check these claims. An important requirement that applies to terminating sequences is, for instance, absence of deadlock. Not all terminating sequences, however, correspond to deadlocks. We will have to be able to express which properties the final state in a sequence must have to make that sequence acceptable as a non-deadlocking terminating sequence. For cyclic sequences, finally, we should be able to express general conditions such as the absence of livelock.

OVERVIEW

The remainder of this chapter is devoted to a more detailed discussion of the formalization of correctness criteria in PROMELA. It will introduce the last few language constructs that specifically deal with validation:

○ The assert() statement, which can be used to express both local assertions and global system invariants

○ Three types of labels that can be used to define a small class of frequently used correctness claims for terminating and cyclic sequences

○ The formalization of general temporal claims

○ The notation that can be used in assertions and in temporal claims to refer to the control-flow states and the local variables of arbitrary running processes

We begin by taking a closer look at the specification of the correctness properties of states.

6.3 ASSERTIONS

Correctness criteria can often be expressed as boolean conditions that must be satisfied whenever a process reaches a given state. The PROMELA statement

```
assert(condition)
```

is always executable and can be placed anywhere in a PROMELA model. The condition can be an arbitrary boolean expression. If the condition is true, the statement has no effect. The validity of the statement is violated, however, if there is at least one execution sequence in which the condition is false when the `assert` statement becomes executable.

Consider the following example from Chapter 5.

```
byte state = 1;
proctype A() { (state == 1) -> state = state + 1 }
proctype B() { (state == 1) -> state = state - 1 }
init { run A(); run B() }
```

We could try to claim that when a process of type `A()` completes the value of variable `state` must be 2, and when a process of type `B()` completes it must be 0. This could be expressed as follows.

```
byte state = 1;

proctype A()
{       (state == 1) -> state = state + 1;
        assert(state == 2)
}
proctype B()
{       (state == 1) -> state = state - 1;
        assert(state == 0)
}
init { run A(); run B()  }
```

The claims are, of course, false, and an automated validator would demonstrate that quickly.

6.4 SYSTEM INVARIANTS

A more general application of the `assert` statement is to formalize system invariants, i.e., boolean conditions that, if true in the initial system state, remain true in *all* reachable system states, independently of the execution sequence that leads to each specific state. To express this in PROMELA, it suffices to place the system invariant by itself in a separate, monitor process.

```
proctype monitor() { assert(invariant) }
```

Once an instance of the process type `monitor` has been started (the name is immaterial), with a regular `run` statement, it executes independently of the rest of the system. It can decide to evaluate the assertion at any time; its `assert` statement is executable precisely once for every state of the system.

For a simple application of this type of correctness claim, consider the `dijkstra` semaphore validation model, introduced in Chapter 5.

```
#define p       0
#define v       1

chan sema[0] of { bit };
proctype dijkstra()
{       do
        :: sema!p -> sema?v
        od
}
proctype user()
{       sema?p;
        /* critical section */
        sema!v
        /* non-critical section */
}
init
{       atomic {
                run dijkstra();
                run user(); run user(); run user()
        }
}
```

The semaphore guarantees mutually exclusive access of user processes to their critical sections. We can modify the user processes as follows, to count the number of processes in the critical section in a global variable `count`.

```
byte count;
proctype user()
{       sema?p;
        count = count+1;
        skip;   /* critical section */
        count = count-1;
        sema!v
        skip;   /* non-critical section */
}
```

The following system invariant can now be used to verify the correct operation of the semaphore:

```
proctype monitor() { assert(count == 0 || count == 1) }
```

An instantiation of the monitor must be included in the initial process, to allow it to perform the correctness check.

```
init
{        atomic {
                  run dijkstra(); run monitor();
                  run user(); run user(); run user()
         }
}
```

6.5 DEADLOCKS

In a finite state system, all execution sequences either terminate after a finite number of state transitions, or they cycle back to a previously visited state. Not all terminating sequences, however, are necessarily deadlocks. In order to define what a deadlock in a PROMELA model is, we must be able to distinguish the expected, or *proper*, end-states from the unexpected ones. The unexpected end-states will include not just deadlock states, but also many error states that are the result of a logical incompleteness of the protocol specification. The classic example of the latter is the *unspecified reception*.

The final state in a terminating execution sequence must minimally satisfy the following two criteria to be considered a proper end-state:

○ Every process that was instantiated has terminated
○ All message channels are empty

But not all processes necessarily terminate. It can be perfectly valid, for instance, for server processes to stay alive after user processes terminate. We must be able, therefore, to identify individual process states in `proctype` definitions as proper end-states. In PROMELA this can be done with *end-state* labels. In the semaphore example from Chapter 5, for instance, we can write

```
proctype dijkstra()
{
end:     do
         :: sema!p -> sema?v
         od
}
```

to define that any process of type `dijkstra` is considered to be in a proper end-state when it is in the state labeled `end`.

If there is more than one proper end-state within a single `proctype` definition, all label-names must still be unique. An end-state label is defined to be any label-name that has a three-character prefix `end`. So it is valid to use variations such as `enddne`, `end0`, `end_war`. We can now revise the first criterion from the definition of a proper end-state:

○ Every process that was instantiated has either terminated or has reached a state marked as a proper end-state

Any final state in a terminating execution sequence that does not satisfy the two criteria for proper end-states is automatically classified as an improper end-state.

An implicit correctness claim that is made about all validation models will be that the behaviors they define do not include any improper end-states.

Refer to Chapter 14 and Appendix F for some examples of the use of end-state labels in a real validation.

6.6 BAD CYCLES

Two properties of cyclic sequences can be expressed in PROMELA, corresponding to two standard types of correctness requirements. Both properties are based on the explicit marking of states in a validation model. The first property specifies that

  ○ There are no infinite behaviors of only unmarked states

that is, the system cannot infinitely cycle through unmarked states. The marked states are called *progress-states*, and the execution sequences that violate the above correctness claim are called *non-progress cycles*. The second property is the opposite of the first. It is used to specify that

  ○ There are no infinite behaviors that include marked states

Execution sequences that violate this claim are called *livelocks*. We discuss each type of correctness claim in more detail below.

NON-PROGRESS CYCLES

To claim the absence of non-progress cycles, we must be able to define the system states within the PROMELA model that denote progress. These progress states are defined much like end-state labels.

A progress-state label marks a state that *must* be executed for the protocol to make progress. An example can be the incrementing of a sequence number, or the delivery of data to a receiver. In the semaphore example we can label the successful passing of a semaphore test as "progress." Simply by marking it as a progress state we can express the correctness criterion that the passing of the semaphore guard cannot be postponed infinitely long, e.g., by an infinite execution cycle that does not pass the progress state.

```
proctype dijkstra()
{
end:      do
          :: sema!p ->
progress:          sema?v
          od
}
```

An automated validator can readily confirm that indeed this claim cannot be violated. If more than one state carries a progress-state label, variations with a common prefix are again valid: progress0, progressisslow, and so on.

LIVELOCKS

Suppose we wanted to express the opposite of a progress condition, e.g., we want to formalize that something cannot happen infinitely often. We can express properties like this with the third, and last, class of special PROMELA labels. In addition to the end-state, and progress-state labels introduced earlier, we now define acceptance-state labels. An *acceptance-state label* is any label starting with the character sequence "accept." It marks a state that *may not* be part of a sequence of states that can be repeated infinitely often.

For example, if we replace the progress-state label in `proctype dijkstra()` with an acceptance-state label

```
proctype dijkstra()
{
end:     do
         :: sema!p ->
accept:           sema?v
         od
}
```

we claim that it is impossible to cycle through a series of p and v operations. We know, of course, that this claim is false. We can either prove that it is false manually, or we can use an automated validator to provide a counter-example.

Again, all variations, such as `acceptor`, `acceptable`, and `accept_yo`, are allowed. In principle, we could make the best use of an acceptance state if we could use it to express complete behaviors that are required to be impossible, rather than only the absence of a designated state in all cycles. We will do precisely that by using the labels to define the acceptance states of special claim automata that model error behaviors. (This also explains the choice of the term "accept.") These automata express general temporal claims.

6.7 TEMPORAL CLAIMS

Up to this point we have talked about the specification of correctness criteria with assertions and with three special types of labels that can be used to mark end states, progress states, and acceptance states. Powerful types of correctness criteria can already be expressed with these tools, yet so far our only option is to add them to `proctype` definitions. Suppose that, within this framework, we want to express the temporal claim "every state in which property P is true is followed by a state in which property Q is true." We noted before that two different interpretations of the term "followed by" are possible, depending on whether the two states must *immediately* or *eventually* follow each other. It is basic to the semantics of PROMELA that no assumptions whatsoever can be made about the relative timing of process executions. This means that, so far, the only legitimate interpretation of the above term is that two steps "eventually" follow each other (including "immediately'' as a special case). That, however, leaves us with the problem to express the other types of properties. For this we need a different type of validation primitive.

Temporal claims define temporal orderings of *properties* of states. To express the requirement that ''every state in which property *P* is true is followed by a state in which property *Q* is true,'' we could write

```
P -> Q
```

But, it's not quite that simple. There are two snags.

☐ Since all our correctness criteria are based on properties that are claimed to be *impossible*, the temporal claims we use must also express *orderings* of properties that are impossible.

☐ The temporal claims are defined on complete execution sequences. Even if a prefix of the sequence is irrelevant, it must still be represented as a trivially-true sequence of propositions.

With that in mind we can now express the requirement above properly as

```
never { do :: skip od -> P -> !Q }
```

that is, independent of the initial sequence of events, it is impossible for a state in which property *P* is true to be followed by a state in which property *Q* is false..

The PROMELA notation for a temporal claim is

```
never  { ... }
```

where the dots contain the details of the claim.

Temporal claims can be primed with assertions, progress-state labels, or acceptance-state labels to catch more types of errors that just a complete match of the behavior expressed. The never claims can be expressed, for instance, as special finite state machines that cycle through an acceptance state if the undesirable behavior is recognized.

Suppose we wanted to express the temporal property that condition1 can never remain true infinitely long. To catch violations of this property, we must find a representation in a temporal claim of all behaviors where condition1 may be false initially, becomes true eventually, and remains true. It is expressed as follows

```
    never {
            do
            :: skip
            :: condition1 -> break
            od;
    accept: do
            :: condition1
            od
    }
```

The tricky part is to remember the inclusion of the `skip` (a condition that is always true) in the first loop. Note that sequences where the truth value of `condition1` first changes from true to false a few times are permitted by the claim.

The claim itself is simply a finite state machine, with a proposition defined in every state. For every state transition elsewhere in the validation model, i.e., by the execution of a PROMELA statement, the claim machine must change its state and move from one proposition to the next. To match a temporal claim, at every state in a sequence of states the proposition at corresponding state in the claim machine must be true.

For instance, if we write erroneously

```
never {
        do
        :: skip
        :: condition1 -> break
        od;
accept:
        condition1
}
```

the claim contains just one more state transition after `condition1` becomes true. The claim is then completely matched if there is at least one execution sequence in which `condition1` holds in two subsequent states.

The finite state machines specified in the claims above contain three states each: the initial state, the state labeled `accept` and the normal end state. The first, correct, version of the claim specifies that it would be an error (a livelock) if the machine can stay in the second state infinitely long. The second version specified that it would be an error if the third state is reachable.

`Never` claims, used in combination with acceptance-state labels, can express also the absence of non-progress cycles. The claims are therefore more general than progress-state labels. The expense (complexity) of finding non-progress cycles directly with progress-state labels, however, is smaller than the expense of the validation of a claim that specifies the same property.

To get the full benefit of temporal claims, we must be able to refer to the control-flow states and the variable values of running processes. As an example, consider the following version of the alternating bit protocol.

```
1 #define MAX 3
2
3 mtype = { msg0, msg1, ack0, ack1 };
4
5 chan        sender  =[1] of { byte };
6 chan        receiver=[1] of { byte };
7
```

```
 8 proctype Sender()
 9 {   byte any;
10 again:
11     do
12     :: receiver!msg1;
13             if
14             :: sender?ack1 -> break
15             :: sender?any /* lost */
16             :: timeout    /* retransmit */
17             fi
18     od;
19     do
20     :: receiver!msg0;
21             if
22             :: sender?ack0 -> break
23             :: sender?any /* lost */
24             :: timeout    /* retransmit */
25             fi
26     od;
27     goto again
28 }
29
30 proctype Receiver()
31 {   byte any;
32 again:
33     do
34     :: receiver?msg1 -> sender!ack1; break
35     :: receiver?msg0 -> sender!ack0
36     :: receiver?any /* lost */
37     od;
38 P0:
39     do
40     :: receiver?msg0 -> sender!ack0; break
41     :: receiver?msg1 -> sender!ack1
42     :: receiver?any /* lost */
43     od;
44 P1:
45     goto again
46 }
47
48 init { atomic { run Sender(); run Receiver() } }
```

Processes Receiver and Sender communicate here via the message channels receiver and sender. Each channel can hold one message at a time of type byte.

Message loss is modeled explicitly in the sender and the receiver processes with a clause that can steal an incoming message before it is processed (lines 15, 23, 36, and 42). We may want to express the claim ''it is always true that when the sender transmits a message, the receiver will eventually accept it.'' Our first job is again to find the corresponding undesirable property that can be expressed in a temporal claim. To be able to specify this, however, we need to be able to refer to

states inside the sender and receiver processes. The required notation is used in the
following formalization of the claim.

```
never {
        do
        :: len(receiver) == 0
        :: receiver?[msg0] -> goto accept0
        :: receiver?[msg1] -> goto accept1
        od;
accept0:
        do
        :: !Receiver[2]:P0
        od;
accept1:
        do
        :: !Receiver[2]:P1
        od
}
```

The claim above is a four-state machine: the inital state, the two states that were
labeled, and the normal end state. At least one of three conditions must be true in
the initial system state. The claim remains in this state as long as channel
receiver is empty. If it contains a message[1] msg0 or msg1 it will change state to
either accept0 or accept1, depending on the message that was matched. Once
the transition to, for instance, state accept0 has been made, the claim can only
remain in that state if the receiver process will never accept a message with the
same sequence number, i.e., if the receiver process never passes the state labeled
P0.

There can be many instantiations of the process type Receiver so we need some
way of specifying exactly which particular instantiation we mean when we refer to
the state of a process. This is the only time that we need to be able to refer to the
instantiation number or the pid of a process. The pid of a process is the number
that is returned by the run operator, when a process is instantiated. The pids are
assigned in the order in which processes are started, but they may be recycled when
processes die. The initial process always has pid zero, and its number is never
recycled. A pid can usually easily be inferred from the program text. Since the
receiver process is the second process that is instantiated in this system, its pid is
two. We can refer to the receiver process unambiguously as Receiver[2]. The
condition that the receiver is currently in the state labeled P0 is expressed as
Receiver[2]:P0. The condition is false whenever the second process that was
instantiated is in any state other than at label P0 of process type Receiver.

The notation Receiver[2]:P0 is a special case of a more general construct which
allows temporal claims to refer to internal conditions of the asynchronous processes
defined within a PROMELA model. A reference to the current value of local variable

---

1. The notation for a side-effect free inspection of the contents of a message channel was introduced in
Chapter 5 on page 100.

any in the receiver process, for instance, is written `Receiver[2].any`. It can be used in arbitrary expressions, such as

```
assert(Receiver[2].any < 0)
```

In process references, a colon is used to refer to labels (i.e., control flow states) and a period is used to refer to local variables. In the first case, the value returned is a boolean. In the second case it is the integer value of the variable specified.

The example claim can be proven for the alternating bit protocol as specified, using the default semantics of `timeout`. This means that the claim is matched provided that the retransmission timers behave as intended: there will be no retransmission unless a message was lost. To check also the rather perverse case where timeouts can fire at any time, independently of message loss, we could add the macro definition

```
#define timeout skip
```

Now the temporal claim can be violated. Counter-examples are easily produced with an automated validator, such as the one discussed in Chapters 11-14.

6.8 SUMMARY

In this chapter we have introduced all the remaining language features of the validation modeling language PROMELA. All are directly related to the specification of the correctness requirements of a model. They are

○ Assertion statements

○ End-state, progress-state, and acceptance-state labels

○ The temporal claim `never`

○ The notation for referring to the control-flow states and local variable values of running processes within assertions and temporal claims

The order in which we have introduced the tools for expressing correctness properties corresponds roughly to an increasing level of sophistication in performing validations.

In the initial stages of a design, a user is unlikely to use more than assertions and perhaps end-state labels. In the final stages of a design, when all initial flaws have been corrected and a more precise qualitative assessment of the design can be made, validations with explicit temporal claims may be developed. In many cases this level of sophistication in a validation is never required and all the necessary properties can be established without it.

It is almost impossible to manually verify correctness requirements such as the ones we have discussed. The behavior of even very simple protocol systems is of a staggering complexity that no designer can be expected to assess accurately. Tools are needed not only to express the correctness requirements of a protocol design, but also to verify them reliably. In the next chapters we show how we can work with a language such as PROMELA in the design of protocols and how automated systems can be developed to support an efficient validation of all correctness claims.

In the literature, correctness criteria are often classified as *safety* and *liveness* properties. Informally, a safety property is something bad that should never happen (i.e., is ''impossible,'' cf. page 113). Deadlocks, unspecified receptions, and assertion violations would all be classified as violations of safety properties. A liveness property, on the other hand, expresses something desirable that should eventually happen (i.e., is ''inevitable,'' cf page 113). A standard example of a liveness property is the performance of a service, such as the transfer of data in a flow control protocol. The ''something desirable'' that should eventually happen, however, is typically not restricted to a single event. It is, for instance, not enough to show that a service can be performed once, e.g., that the first message sent via the flow control protocol is always transferred correctly. The service must be performed consistently, which means that we are really checking for a series of related events. Fortunately, in finite state systems, desirable and undesirable behavior are complementary; in a formal validation language it suffices to support one basic concept only. In PROMELA we have chosen to support safety claims. More significant than the distinction between safety and liveness is the difference in expressive power between properties of states and properties of sequences of states, or temporal claims. We have used this distinction to classify the validation features that are defined in PROMELA.

EXERCISES

6-1 The assertion used to verify mutual exclusion in the semaphore example was formalized as a global system invariant. Find another place for the assertion to perform the same check without an extra monitor process.

6-2 Find the temporal claim `never` that expresses the same correctness requirement as the ''ordinary'' `proctype` definition
```
proctype monitor() { (invariant) -> assert(invariant) }
```
Explain the difference in semantics of the semicolon (or arrow).

6-3 Consider Dekker's algorithm from Chapter 5. Make a new PROMELA model, where the processes repeatedly access their critical sections. Express the correctness requirement that no two processes can be in their critical sections simultaneously, with
   o An assertion
   o A system invariant
   o End-state labels
   o A temporal claim `never` (combined with acceptance-state labels)
End-state labels can be used in this problem, for instance, by forcing the system into an improper end-state when the exclusion is violated. You are allowed to introduce extra global ''state'' variables, e.g., to count the number of processes inside the critical section.

6-4 Repeat Exercise 6-3, but this time do not use any global variables in the assertions or in the temporal claim. Define extra ''ordinary'' labels to define control flow points in the program bodies that can be monitored in assertions and claims.

6-5 For the model from Exercise 6-4, express the correctness requirement that no single process can monopolize access to the critical section. Express the claim that within finite time after access is attempted, access is granted. Use

    ○ Progress-state labels

    ○ Acceptance-state labels

    ○ A temporal claim `never` combined with acceptance-state labels

(Three different solutions.) Add variables and labels as needed.

6-6 All ''linear-time propositional temporal logic formulas'' (see Bibliographic Notes) can be expressed in PROMELA with acceptance-state labels and temporal claims. To illustrate this, find PROMELA representations of the following requirements

    ○ Eventually, proposition p always remains true

    ○ p is always true until q becomes true

    ○ Eventually, p is always true until q becomes true

Can you discover a pattern in the modeling of these formulas into PROMELA temporal claims? Could it be automated?

6-7 Find a way translate arbitrary temporal claims back into temporal logic formulas.

6-8 In temporal claims, consider if the construction

```
accept:    do :: skip od
```

is equivalent to assert(0).

BIBLIOGRAPHIC NOTES

The definition of terminating and cyclic execution sequences to reason about the behavior of a distributed system is described in Owicki and Lamport [1982], Manna and Wolper [1984], and Snepscheut [1985]. The formalization of correctness requirements in a notation that is based on temporal logic formulas was first explored in Pnueli [1977]. It was soon also applied to the study of concurrent systems. Early applications are the French validation system Cesar, Queille [1982], and Clarke's model checking system, Clarke [1982], Browne, Clarke, Dill, and Mishra [1986].

Formally, the temporal claims defined in this chapter describe nondeterministic Büchi automata, a special class of the ∀-automata described in Manna and Pnueli [1987]. In Wolper [1981] it was shown that Büchi automata have the expressive power of an extended type of temporal logic formulas.

PSPACE hardness is a measure for the complexity of algorithms. Informally, a problem that is PSPACE hard is known to have no efficient solution. For a detailed discussion see Garey and Johnson [1979].

The terms safety and liveness were first defined in Lamport [1977].

PROTOCOL DESIGN 7

7.1 INTRODUCTION

So far, our discussion of protocol design has covered specification and structuring methods, design principles, and solutions to a set of standard protocol problems. It is time to see how we can apply all this to a real design problem. As an example, in this chapter we undertake the design of a protocol for the transfer of files between two asynchronous machines.

Our purpose in this chapter is to use a disciplined method to specify the five essential elements of the protocol (Chapter 2, Section 2.2). For the protocol procedure rules our aim is to construct a high level prototype with explicit correctness criteria. Later, we will then be able to show convincingly that the design criteria are either satisfied or violated, using automated tools.

We will try to do this by applying the rules of design that are listed in Chapter 2, Section 2.8. Most important among those for validation purposes is Rule 7:

Before implementing a design, build a high level prototype and verify that the design criteria are met.

Our prototype is a validation model, as defined in Chapters 5 and 6. A verification that the design criteria are met is done in Chapter 14, with the tools that are developed in Chapters 11 to 13.

We make two crucial assumptions about the design process.

☐ Protocol design is an iterative process. The design is not likely to be correct the first time it is written down, and very likely it will not be quite correct the second or third time around either.

☐ Worse, each time a design phase is completed, we, the designers, will be convinced that it is error-free. A manual walk-through of the code can reveal the biggest blunders, but cannot be expected also to reveal the subtle ones. Almost by definition, we will overlook the unexpected cases that can cause errors.

The construction of a formal validation model (a prototype) and a fast and unbiased automated correctness checker is therefore indispensable for all but the simplest designs. Chapters 11 and 13 discuss how a correctness checker for PROMELA models can be constructed. In Chapter 14 the validation tool is applied to the design of this chapter, either to verify that it meets the specifications or to reveal where it is flawed. Our concern in this chapter is design and correctness. In the discussion that follows it is important to keep in mind that we are building a validation model, not an implementation. The model is an abstraction, and as such it is a design tool in itself.

A full listing of the protocol developed here can be found in Appendix F. The validation of the design with a tool called SPIN is discussed in Chapter 14.

A FILE TRANSFER PROTOCOL

The file transfer protocol we develop can be classified in a number of different ways. It is a *point-to-point* protocol, that is, it has one sender and one receiver. Protocols with more than one receiver are sometimes called *multi-point* or broadcast protocols. The file transfer protocol provides an *end-to-end* service between two users on two different machines, possibly communicating through many intermediate machines.[1]

The procedure rules for the protocol are developed as a sequence of validation models that can be checked on their correctness properties either individually or in combination. The assumption throughout this part of the design is that adequate tools are available for verifying the consistency of the intermediate validation models, and that they can be refined and adjusted with the help of those tools.

First we will make sure that the problem is completely defined. We explicitly specify the other four elements of the protocol: the service specification, the assumptions about the environment (the transmission channel), the protocol vocabulary, and the message format.

7.2 SERVICE SPECIFICATION

The protocol must implement a reliable end-to-end file transfer service. This service includes connection establishment and termination, recovery from transmission errors, and a flow control strategy to prevent the sender from overflowing the receiver. The protocol must be able to transfer ASCII text files, one at a time, with the probability of an undetected bit error being less than a modest 1 in 10^8 bits transmitted. We require that the user be able to abort a file transfer in progress, and that the protocol be able to recover from message loss.

---

1. Cf. the OSI hierarchy in Chapter 2, Section 2.6. Only layers 4 to 7 provide end-to-end service.

7.3 ASSUMPTIONS ABOUT THE CHANNEL

The protocol is to be designed for full-duplex transfer of messages over voice-grade, switched telephone lines. Having a dedicated line, rather than a network connection, we can safely ignore specific networking issues such as routing, congestion control, queueing delays, etc., and focus on concurrency control. To make it interesting, we assume that the transfers take place between New York and Los Angeles, a distance of approximately 4500 km. Given that the propagation time of an electrical signal in a cable is about 30,000 km/sec (Appendix A), the minimal time for a message to travel from sender to receiver is then approximately 0.15 seconds.

The bandwidth and average signal-to-noise ratio of a voice-grade telephone line allow us to transmit comfortably at a signaling speed of 1200 bps, using a standard modem (cf. Chapter 3 and Appendix A). We assume that transmission is character-oriented, using ASCII character encoding (Chapter 2, Section 2.5).

Most errors on telephone lines are caused by noise spikes, echoes and cross-talk. The resulting bit errors are not uniformly distributed: they come in bursts. Therefore, to describe the error characteristics, we must know some error distribution functions. In Chapter 3 (page 46) we gave several methods for predicting the probability of error-free intervals and burst durations. For the error-free intervals we are mostly interested in the average duration, not in the precise error distributions, so we will assume a simple Poisson distribution

$$Pr(EFI = n) = f \cdot e^{-f \cdot n}, \quad n \geq 0$$

where $1/f$ gives us the average duration of the error-free interval. We will use $f = 8 \cdot 10^{-6}$, which corresponds to an average error-free interval of 125,000 bit transmissions (or about 100 seconds).

For the error bursts we are interested in a more accurate prediction of the probability that a given burst lasts at least n bit transmissions. We use Mandelbrot's function:

$$Pr(Burst \geq n) = \left[n^{(1-a)} - (n-1)^{(1-a)} \right] e^{-g(n-1)}, \quad 0 \leq a < 1, \quad n \geq 1$$

where a and g are parameters. The parameter values that we choose here will determine the type of error control method that will be needed. The precise values should be derived from measurements on the telephone channels used. They are, however, largely irrelevant to the discussion that follows. We will assume $a = 0.9$ and $g = 0.009$, a choice that matches our intuition about the behavior of burst errors. The average duration of a burst error that can be calculated for these parameter values is roughly 12 bit transmission times (10 msec). Figure 7.1 shows how the probability of a burst depends on its length, using the above prediction. The y-axis is logarithmic.

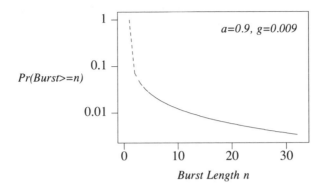

Figure 7.1 — Probability of Burst Errors

If we succeed in reducing the residual error rate to no more than 1 in 10^8 transmitted bits, at 1200 bps this gives and expectation of no more than one undetected error for every 23 hours of continuous operation.

7.4 PROTOCOL VOCABULARY

Consider the protocol as a black box. To perform its function, the protocol has to communicate with its environment. It exchanges messages with the remote system via a data link, and with the local user and a local file server via internal message channels.

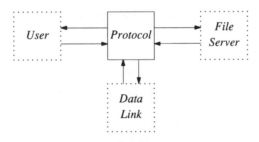

Figure 7.2 — Protocol Environment

Without going into the details of the protocol itself just yet, let us see what types of messages are needed to build it.

The black box accepts two types of messages from the local user. The first message type is used to initiate a file transfer. It can have a single parameter:

```
transfer(file_descriptor)
```

The second message type can be used by the user to interrupt a transfer in progress.

```
abort
```

The `transfer` message must trigger a message to the local file server to verify that the file to be transferred really exists, and if so, what the size of the file is. We call that message

    open(file_descriptor)

If the file can be opened, its size is determined, and a connection is made with the remote system. To communicate the connection request from the local to the remote system we use the message

    connect(size)

At the remote side, an incoming `connect` request again triggers a message to the file server, this time to verify that a new file of the given size can be stored. The message for that can be

    create(size)

We need at least two more messages from the file server to indicate whether an `open` or a `create` request can be accepted or must be rejected:

    accept(size)

and

    reject(status)

In response to an `open` request, the `accept` message returns the file size to the calling process. If the request is rejected, an integer parameter can be used to carry information about the reason. The message types `accept` and `reject` can also be used to inform the local user about the success or failure of an outgoing file transfer. And similarly, they can be used by the local system to inform a remote system whether an incoming file transfer is accepted.

To transfer a file, four things have to happen in a specific order:

○ Establishment of a connection with the local file server
○ Establishment of a connection with the remote system
○ Transfer of data
○ Orderly termination of the connection

Each protocol phase has its own vocabulary of messages and its own rules for interpreting them. Each phase may again have to be sub-divided into still smaller steps. The second phase, for instance, will consist of two steps: (1) an initialization of the flow control protocol, and (2) a handshake with the remote system using the `connect` and `accept` or `reject` message. The synchronization of the local and the remote flow control layer protocols is necessary to guarantee that they agree on the initial sequence numbers to be used. We can use the message

    sync

and its acknowledgment

    sync_ack

for this purpose.

In the third protocol phase we need messages for retrieving the data from the file server and transmitting them to the remote system. For example, we can use a message

```
data(cnt, ptr)
```

to transfer `cnt` bytes of information, available in a data buffer that is identified by the second parameter. This, of course, is not necessarily the way in which interactions with the file server have to be implemented in a final design. For now, however, it suffices that it accurately models the essentials of these interactions.

Another message,

```
eof
```

can be used by the file server to signify the end of a file. The correct completion of a file transfer, with the `eof` message, can be confirmed by the remote system with a single message

```
close
```

So far, the only assumption we have made about the file server is that it recognizes six messages: `open`, `create`, `accept`, `reject`, `data`, and `eof`. To avoid synchronization problems between the local system and the local file server, we assume that the above six messages are exchanged by rendezvous communication (i.e., they are equivalent to local procedure calls). This guarantees that, for instance, unused `data` messages from or to the file server do not accumulate. After the successful completion of both a local `open` and a remote `create` request, the `data` messages are used to transfer data from local file server to the remote file server, using the protocol to be developed.

We need one extra message to implement a simple flow control discipline that acknowledges correctly received data:

```
ack
```

The complete protocol vocabulary then consists of thirteen distinct message types. Nine of these messages can be exchanged by the two remote machines: `accept`, `ack`, `close`, `connect`, `data`, `eof`, `reject`, `sync_ack`, and `sync`. The other four, `abort`, `create`, `open`, and `transfer`, are internal messages only.

7.5 MESSAGE FORMAT

It should now be decided what the right format for the above messages is. The messages minimally require a type field and an optional data field. To implement a flow control discipline, the messages sent to the remote system must also carry sequence numbers, and to implement error control they must carry a checksum field. Since the transmission channel is byte oriented, we can format each message as a sequence of bytes. Clearly, we would like these sequences to be as short as

possible. Let us see how we can calculate the minimal size required, knowing only
what we know so far about the protocol and the transmission channel to be used.

At the highest level, a message can be encoded into a series of bytes, indicating its
type and the value of its parameters. Before the message is sent, the flow control
appends a sequence number, and the error control appends a checksum field. At
the lowest level, just before the message is placed onto the transmission line, a line
driver appends the message delimiters, to enable the remote system to recognize
where a message starts and stops. The ASCII 8-bit patterns STX (start of text) and
ETX (end of text) can be used for this purpose. With byte stuffing (Chapter 2),
misinterpretation message delimiters that are part of the data itself can be avoided.

The remote receiver strips the STX and ETX characters and removes the stuffed
characters. The remote error control strips and interprets the checksum, and the
remote flow control strips and interprets the sequence number. If all is well, the
message finally arrives at its peer as the original series of bytes again.

The best position of the various message fields in the byte sequence depends to
some extent on the encoding of the protocol routines at the lowest level (the physical layer) in the hierarchy. Placing the checksum field at the end of a message has
the advantage that the sender can compute it on the fly while transmitting the body
of the message. There can also be a small difference in performance depending on
where the message-type field is placed. It can either be placed at the front of the
message, in a fixed place behind the STX symbol, or at the end, in a fixed place
before the ETX symbol. Since we have variable length messages, the position of
the ETX symbol is less predictable than that of the STX symbol. Placing the type
field at the start of the message can therefore make it easier to parse an incoming
message.

We thus arrive at the message format shown in Figure 7.3, where the *Data* field is
absent in control messages.

Figure 7.3 — Message Format

In Figure 7.3, a symbol representing the length of each field in bits is indicated in
the lower-righ corner. D bytes of information in the data field corresponds to a
field width of 8D bits. How are the numbers h1, h2, D, and t1 determined?

THE MESSAGE TYPE FIELD

This is the easiest of the four numbers to calculate. We have 13 different types of
message. Since $2^3 < 13 \leq 2^4$, 4 bits for the type field suffice.

$$h_1 = 4$$

THE SEQUENCE NUMBER FIELD

Now, let us derive an appropriate width for the sequence number field h_2. The message propagation time is 0.15 seconds, long enough to transmit 180 bits. If a message would be bounced back by the receiver without processing delays, the sender could transmit 360 bits before receiving the return message. We would like to design the protocol in such a way that the sender can completely saturate the channel whenever the receiver consumes the data as fast as the sender produces data. We must therefore make certain that the sender will not have to wait idly for acknowledgments when it could be sending messages. This means that the sender should be able to be at least 360 bits ahead of the receiver under normal circumstances. The number of messages that this corresponds to depends on the number of bytes in the data field and in the header and trailer.

If we use a selective repeat continuous ARQ method (Chapter 4), the most flexible flow control method we have discussed, the maximum number of outstanding messages with a sequence number field of h_2 bits is 2^{h_2-1}. With a one-bit sequence number only one message can be outstanding at a time, forcing the sender to remain idle for at least 0.3 seconds, waiting for the acknowledgment on that message (twice the message propagation time). With a two-bit sequence number, two messages may be outstanding, meaning that the sender can transmit one message while awaiting the acknowledgment for another. If that message is at least 360 bits long, no time is lost. Below we will see that it is indeed advantageous to use a data field longer than 360 bits. So, we have

$$h_2 \geq 2$$

Assuming again that the receiver is at least as fast as the sender, we could organize the flow control as follows. All messages within the current window are sent before the acknowledgment for the oldest outstanding message is checked. If no acknowledgment is received by that time, the oldest message is retransmitted. If an acknowledgment is received, the window slides up one notch and a new message can be transmitted. The sender is never idle, and the channel is saturated.

Note carefully that if the receiver is slower than the sender it is prudent not to try to saturate the channel: the receiver needs time to catch up with the sender. For this case we can include a timer. If no acknowledgment for the oldest outstanding frame is received by the time the sender checks for one, the sender now waits at least an additional timeout period for the acknowledgment to arrive. The appropriate value for the timeout count can be estimated, or it can be adjusted dynamically with a *rate control* method. We shall restrict ourselves to the optimal case, with a fully saturated channel.

THE DATA FIELD

The length of the data field is expressed in the byte count D and is variable per data message. It is not to our advantage to make a message too long, since the expectation that a message contains bit errors trivially increases with its length. On the other hand, if we make the messages too small, the overhead[2] of the header and trailer becomes too large. The average duration of an error-free interval was estimated at approximately 125,000 bit transmissions, so we certainly should not make a message longer than that. Somewhere between these 125 Kbits and the 360 bits we derived earlier there must be an optimal length for the data field. We can approximate this optimum as follows.

OPTIMAL DATA SIZE

Let t be the length of the data message overhead in bits (header plus trailer) and d the length of the data field, also in bits: $d=8D$. Further, let a be the length of an ack control message, p_d the probability of a data message being distorted or lost, and p_a the probability of the same error for an acknowledgment.

Let us first consider the case where $p_d=p_a=0$. The transmission of one message requires one data message and one acknowledgment message, a total of $d+t+a$ bits. The overhead is $t+a$, and the protocol efficiency is

$$E \;=\; \frac{d}{d+t+a}$$

So in the absence of errors, it is best to chose d as large as possible.

Now consider the case where p_d and p_a are non-zero. The probability that neither the data message nor its acknowledgment is hit by a transmission error is $(1-p_d)(1-p_a)$. Therefore, the probability that the message must be retransmitted is

$$p_r \;=\; 1-(1-p_d)(1-p_a)$$

The probability that it takes i subsequent transmissions to get the data message across, $i-1$ retransmissions and one successful transmission, is

$$p_i \;=\; (1-p_r)\,p_r^{i-1}$$

The expected number of transmissions per message R is then given by

$$R \;=\; \sum_{i=1}^{\infty} i p_i$$

$$\;=\; \sum_{i=1}^{\infty} i(1-p_r)p_r^{i-1}$$

2. See also "code rates" defined in Chapter 3, Section 3.5.

$$= (1-p_r) \sum_{i=1}^{\infty} i p_r^{i-1}$$

$$= (1-p_r) \sum_{j=0}^{\infty} \sum_{i=j}^{\infty} p_r^i$$

$$= (1-p_r) \sum_{j=0}^{\infty} \frac{p_r^j}{1-p_r}$$

$$= \frac{1}{1-p_r}$$

The relative efficiency E, in the presence of errors, is then

$$E = \frac{d}{R(d+t+a)}$$

The optimal value for d can be found by setting the derivative of E with respect to d to zero: $\delta E / \delta d = 0$. Alternatively, we can simply fill in the known or approximate values for R, t, and a, and plot E as a function of d.

With the values we derived earlier, and counting 8 bits each for the STX and ETX message delimiter, we have

$$a = h_1 + h_2 + t_1 + 16$$

$$= 4 + 2 + 16 + 16 = 38$$

and trivially

$$t = a = 38$$

We earlier assumed that an error-free interval would last an average of 125 Kbits. This corresponds to $(125 \cdot 10^3)/(d+t)$ messages or $(125 \cdot 10^3)/a$ acknowledgments. A first-order approximation can then be obtained by taking

$$p_d = (d+38)/(125 \cdot 10^3)$$

and

$$p_a = 38/(125 \cdot 10^3) = 3.04 \ 10^{-4}$$

We now have

$$R = \frac{1}{1-p_r}$$

$$= \frac{1}{(1-p_d)(1-p_a)}$$

Substituting in the last expression for E gives:

$$E = \frac{d \cdot (1 - p_d)(1 - p_a)}{d + t + a}$$

$$= \frac{d \cdot (1 - (d + 38)/(125 \cdot 10^3))(1 - 38/(125 \cdot 10^3))}{d + 76}$$

In Figure 7.4 the protocol efficiency E is plotted as a function of the length of the message data field d.

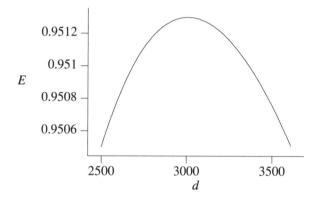

Figure 7.4 — Protocol Efficiency versus Data Size in Bits

There is clearly an optimum value for d. The maximum efficiency of 95.13% is achieved for a data size of 3004 bits, or 376 bytes. So we have now derived the third value D for Figure 7.3.

In reality, of course, the probability of lost and distorted data should be derived from the error distribution functions. We should have solved the more difficult equations

$$p_d = \sum_{i=0}^{d+38} Pr(EFI = i) \quad p_a = \sum_{i=0}^{38} Pr(EFI = i)$$

To see how large the mistake is we made, we set $d = 3004$ and calculate

$$p_d = \sum_{i=0}^{3004+38} Pr(EFI = i) = 240.42 \ 10^{-4}$$

and

$$p_a = \sum_{i=0}^{38} Pr(EFI = i) = 3.039 \ 10^{-4}$$

The earlier approximations give for the same value of d

$$p_d = (3004 + 38)/(125 \cdot 10^{3)} = 243.36 \ 10^{-4}$$

and

$$p_a = 38/(125 \cdot 10^{3)} = 3.04 \ 10^{-4}$$

Our first estimate is within 1.2 percent of the recalculated values. Since we have no reason to trust the predictive value of the error distribution function with that degree of accuracy, we settle for the first estimate.

THE CHECKSUM FIELD

All that remains is to derive the value for t_1, the width of the checksum field. The channel has deletion and distortion errors, but is not expected to produce insertions or message reorderings. The error rate is low enough that we do not need an error correcting code. For a reasonable message length, well below 125 Kbits, most messages get through without transmission errors. We must, however, be able to correct for the characteristic errors of the channel: burst errors. This makes a cyclic redundancy check a good choice. The average duration of a burst error was assumed to be 10 msec, affecting a sequence of 12 bits. The degree of the generator polynomial therefore at least has to be larger than 12 to catch these errors.

The target residual bit error rate is 10^{-8}. To be able to check if we can comply with this requirement by choosing the 16-bit CRC-CCITT checksum polynomial, we have to look at the distribution of burst-error durations. We know that the CRC-CCITT checksum catches all single and double bit errors, all odd numbers of bit errors, all burst errors up to 16 bits long, 99.997% of burst errors of 17 bits, and 99.998% of all burst errors longer than 17 bits.

We assumed that burst errors occur on the average once every 100 seconds. A burst of roughly 12 bits long then corresponds to a long-term average bit error rate of 10^{-4}. Of the bursts longer than 16 bits, two or three out of every 10^5 bursts will go undetected. If *every* burst was longer than 16 bits, this would mean that two or three burst errors per 100×10^5 seconds would get through, corresponding to a long-term average bit error rate of roughly 10^{-6} (there are more than ten bits in every burst). We can therefore only realize a target residual bit-error rate of 10^{-8} if burst errors longer than 16 bits occur less than once out of every 10^2 bursts, or fewer than once every 10,000 seconds. Using the probability distribution function, we find (cf. Figure 7.1):

$$Pr(Burst \geq 17) = 0.08.e^{-0.08 \cdot 17} = 0.007$$

The result is within range of the target. We can choose the 16-bit checksum, and have our last value:

$$t_1 = 16$$

For the control messages it seems like overkill to include even a 16-bit checksum for a message that carries only two small numbers. Note, however, that a burst error can wipe out the complete message, so with the same redundancy an error correcting code could not perform better.

As an aside, the message format, with all the field widths we have now derived, can be defined in C as follows.

```
struct {
        unsigned type  : 4;
        unsigned seqno : 2;
        unsigned char data[376];
        unsigned char checksum[2];
} message;
```

We used bit-fields for the fields in the message header and unsigned characters (8 bits wide) for the data field and the checksum. The message delimiters STX and ETX were omitted. This is, however, not necessarily the way in which a C compiler would arrange for the bits to be stored in memory. Some padding may occur to align bit-fields with word or byte boundaries.

EFFECTS OF ROUNDING

In Figure 7.4 we see that the protocol efficiency is not very sensitive to variations in the data size near the optimum. We are also stuck with the peculiar values for h_1 and h_2 that we calculated earlier. Multiples of 8 bits would be more convenient for the receiver to process. Let us see how badly the efficiency would be affected if we used the nearest multiple of 8 for all field widths, as shown in Table 7.1.

Table 7.1 — Rounding

Symbol	Old	New
h_1	4	8
h_2	2	8
t_1	16	16

The recalculated values for E as a function of d for these new values are indicated by the lower curve in Figure 7.5. The effect of adding 10 bits of overhead is a reduction of E by less than one percent, which should be considered insignificant compared to the errors introduced by earlier approximations. The new optimum is reached for a data length of 3370 bits, or about 422 bytes (46 bytes more than before).

After rounding, the message format can be written without bit-fields

```
struct {
        unsigned char type;
        unsigned char seqno;
        unsigned char data[422];
        unsigned char checksum[2];
} message;
```

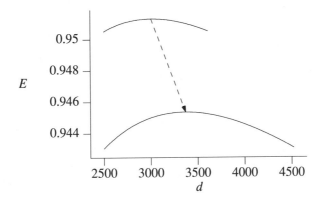

Figure 7.5 — Degradation of Protocol Efficiency by Rounding

7.6 PROCEDURE RULES

We are now ready to start with the description of the procedure rules. In this part of the design, few things can be calculated or measured. Yet the rules have to be complete and consistent. Before committing ourselves directly to an implementation, we would like to be able to design and debug the rules in an intermediate form, for instance as a validation model. PROMELA was designed for precisely this purpose. We first look at some of the abstractions we have to make in the modeling of the messages. Then we look at the layering of the protocol and derive a rough global structure. Finally, from the highest layer down to the lowest we refine each layer and combine them into the final design. The correctness requirements for each layer are formalized using the notation developed in Chapter 6.

ABSTRACTION

The precise encoding for the messages, derived in the previous sections, contains too much information for the problem we are now facing. Manipulating messages at this level of detail would needlessly complicate the design, description, and validation of the procedure rules. To derive the procedure rules we build a model of the communication system in which we consider only the semantics of the protocol, not its precise syntax. To the model, for instance, the contents of transferred files are irrelevant. The variable length `Data` field from Figure 7.3, therefore, need not be represented, nor (as we will argue below) the checksum field. We use a message template of just two fields in the validation model.

```
fld1, fld2
```

The first field represents the generic message type, e.g., `data`, and the second field carries a parameter, such as a sequence number. Both fields can be of PROMELA type `byte`.

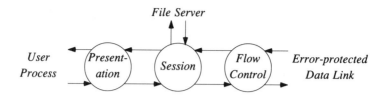

Figure 7.6 — Protocol Hierarchy

What we are designing from this point on is a validation model, not an implementation. If we do our job right though, it should be simple to remove the abstractions from the model, refine it where necessary, and derive an implementation.

LAYERS

To structure the design, we divide it into several layers. The user interacts with a presentation layer protocol. Below that we place a session control layer, and below that a data link layer that enforces a general flow control discipline. The data link is the physical data line, equipped with modems, for encoding binary data into analog signals, and providing error detection on every message transmitted using CRC-CCITT checksumming. The data link we work with from this point on, therefore, can lose but not distort messages.

Each layer in this hierarchy is managed by one or more PROMELA processes, as indicated with the protocol ''pipeline'' in Figure 7.6.

PROTOCOL ENVIRONMENT

Our first job in building a validation model is to make explicit all relevant assumptions about the behavior of the environment, as illustrated in Figures 7.2 and 7.6. The environment consists of three entities:

- ○ User process
- ○ File server
- ○ Data link

The minimal assumptions we must make about the behavior of each of these three is formalized in PROMELA code.

First consider the user level protocol. There can be two user processes: one on each end of the data link. The users can submit a transfer request at any time by passing a file descriptor to the presentation layer of the protocol. At any time after the transfer request, the originating user may also decide to abort a transfer. We assume that the user then waits for a response from the lower protocol layers, signaling either the successful or unsuccessful completion of the transfer. We can model these assumptions with the following PROMELA process.

```
proctype userprc(bit n)
{       use_to_pres[n]!transfer;
        if
        :: pres_to_use[n]?accept -> goto Done
        :: pres_to_use[n]?reject -> goto Done
        :: use_to_pres[n]!abort  -> goto Aborted
        fi;
Aborted:
        if
        :: pres_to_use[n]?accept -> goto Done
        :: pres_to_use[n]?reject -> goto Done
        fi;
Done:
        skip
}
```

The binary argument n identifies the user and the channels that it accesses. The message transfer would ordinarily carry a parameter that points to the file to be transferred (e.g., a file-descriptor). To a validation, however, the value of that parameter is irrelevant, and it is therefore not present in the model. Clearly, the correctness of the file transfer protocol should not depend on the particular file-descriptors used.

The message channels we use in the model can be defined globally. Every arrow in Figure 7.6 corresponds to two such channels, one for each side of the protocol. Using a simple naming scheme to indicate which layers each channel connects, we can define the following types of channels. There are two users, and QSZ is a queue size of at least one (cf. Figure 7.6).

```
chan use_to_pres[2] = [QSZ] of { byte };
chan pres_to_use[2] = [QSZ] of { byte };
chan pres_to_ses[2] = [QSZ] of { byte };
chan ses_to_pres[2] = [QSZ] of { byte, byte };
chan ses_to_flow[2] = [QSZ] of { byte, byte };
chan flow_to_ses[2] = [QSZ] of { byte, byte };
chan dll_to_flow[2] = [QSZ] of { byte, byte };
chan flow_to_dll[2] = [QSZ] of { byte, byte };
```

The channels for the synchronous communication between the session layer protocol and the file server are defined with zero buffer capacity, as follows:

```
chan ses_to_fsrv[2] = [0] of { byte };
chan fsrv_to_ses[2] = [0] of { byte };
```

This brings the total to ten different types of message channels, with one copy being instantiated for each side of the connection. The channels used for the higher protocol layers can be defined with a simpler message format than the lower layers. The sequence number field, for instance, is used only by the flow control layer.

Next we must formalize our assumptions about the behavior of the file server. Again, no design decisions are made yet. The aim is merely to make explicit what must minimally be assumed about the external behavior of the file server process.

An incoming file transfer begins with a `create` message. The file server responds
with either a `reject` or an `accept` message. As far as the validation model is
concerned, either choice is equally likely, so it can be modeled as a nondeterministic one. If the request is accepted, zero or more `data` messages follow, and the file
server falls back into its initial state upon the reception of the final `eof` or, in case
of an abort, the `close` message. In first approximation, disregarding what we said
earlier about abstraction, we may try to describe this behavior in a PROMELA validation model as follows.

```
proctype fserver(bit n)
{       int fd, size, ptr, cnt;
        do
        :: ses_to_fsrv[n]?create(size) ->         /* incoming */
                if       /* nondeterministic choice */
                :: fsrv_to_ses[n]!reject
                :: fsrv_to_ses[n]!accept ->
                        do
                        :: ses_to_fsrv[n]?data(cnt,ptr)
                        :: ses_to_fsrv[n]?eof -> break
        /* abort */     :: ses_to_fsrv[n]?close -> break
                        od
                fi
        :: ses_to_fsrv[n]?open(fd) ->    /* outgoing */
                ...
        od
}
```

But we are on the wrong track with this model. Notice that local variables and
message parameters `fd`, `size`, `cnt`, and `ptr` really provide unwanted detail in the
model. We are designing the procedure rules for the interaction of the file server
with the session layer protocol. We want to specify how these two modules
interact, i.e., the types of messages that they will exchange and the inherent expec-
tations about the order in which the different types of messages will arrive and will
be sent. Important to specify at this level of abstraction is *when* data can be
passed, not *which* data will be passed. The size and contents of data transferred are
therefore still irrelevant at this level of modeling (cf. Chapter 14 about the formal
generalization of models).

A better way to model the relevant behavior of the file server for incoming data is

```
proctype fserver(bit n)
{       do
        :: ses_to_fsrv[n]?create ->       /* incoming */
                if
                :: fsrv_to_ses[n]!reject
                :: fsrv_to_ses[n]!accept ->
                        do
                        :: ses_to_fsrv[n]?data
                        :: ses_to_fsrv[n]?eof -> break
                        :: ses_to_fsrv[n]?close -> break
                        od
```

```
                      fi
         :: ses_to_fsrv[n]?open ->          /* outgoing */
                        ...
         od
    }
```

The model for outgoing data is similar. After the server receives an open message, it may respond with either an accept or a reject message. If the request is accepted, a series of data messages is transferred, followed by a single eof message. The file transfer can be aborted again by a close message from the session layer to the file server.

```
    :: ses_to_fsrv[n]?open ->                      /* outgoing */
            if
            :: fsrv_to_ses[n]!reject
            :: fsrv_to_ses[n]!accept ->
                    do
                    :: fsrv_to_ses[n]!data
                    :: fsrv_to_ses[n]!eof -> break
                    :: ses_to_fsrv[n]?close -> break
                    od
            fi
```

The last piece of the environment is the data link. Again, we must make explicit all our assumptions about its behavior, in so far as it relates to the protocol we are designing.

The data link is assumed to be protected with an error detection protocol. The details of the checksum calculation can be found in Chapter 3, Section 3.7, but for this part of the design problem these details are irrelevant. The checksum calculation is a computation, and not an interaction pattern. It would be folly to try to model it in detail in PROMELA as if it were a procedure rule.

All we are interested in here is the external behavior of the data link. The data link, then, can arbitrarily omit messages from the sequences that it passes, using some hidden oracle to decide the fate of each message. The choice can be modeled as a nondeterministic one.

```
proctype data_link()
{   byte type, seq;
    do
    :: flow_to_dll[0]?type,seq ->
        if
        :: dll_to_flow[1]!type,seq
        :: skip /* lose */
        fi
    :: flow_to_dll[1]?type,seq ->
        if
        :: dll_to_flow[0]!type,seq
        :: skip /* lose */
        fi
    od
```

}

We have now completed the formalization of all assumptions about the environment in which the protocol must be used. We are now ready to design the three core protocol layers: the presentation, the session layer, and the flow control layer.

7.6.1 PRESENTATION LAYER

The presentation layer provides the interface to the user. Its job is to take care of the details of the file transfer, providing, for instance, for the resubmission of the request for file transfer when a non-fatal error occurs. We can anticipate five different reasons for an outgoing file transfer request to fail.

1. The local system is busy serving an incoming file transfer.
2. The local file server rejects the request, for instance because the file to be transferred does not exist.
3. The remote file server rejects the request, for instance because it cannot allocate sufficient space.
4. There is a collision between an incoming and an outgoing file transfer request.
5. The file transfer was aborted by the user.

Two of these five possible causes of a failure are transient (1 and 4) and may disappear if the transfer request is repeated. The presentation layer can further try to protect itself against repeated abort requests from the user processes by filtering out any duplicates.

To get started on a design for the presentation layer we can draw a tentative state diagram. The presentation layer, then, can be given two main states: an IDLE state and a busy, or TRANSFER state. The process moves from IDLE to TRANSFER upon the reception of the user's transfer request. It returns to the IDLE state upon the successful completion of the transfer or the detection of a fatal error. This initial outline is shown in Figure 7.7.

Figure 7.7 — Partial State Transition Diagram: Presentation Layer

Using Figure 7.7 as a guideline we can fill in the relevant details in a validation model as follows.

```
#define FATAL          1       /* failure types */
#define NON_FATAL      2       /* repeatable    */
#define COMPLETE       3       /* success       */
```

```
proctype present(bit n)
{       byte status, uabort;

IDLE:
        do
        :: use_to_pres[n]?transfer ->
                uabort = 0;
                goto TRANSFER
        :: use_to_pres[n]?abort ->
                skip    /* ignore */
        od;
TRANSFER:
        pres_to_ses[n]!transfer;
        do
        :: use_to_pres[n]?abort ->
                if
                :: (!uabort) ->
                        uabort = 1;
                        pres_to_ses[n]!abort
                :: (uabort) ->
                        skip
                fi
        :: ses_to_pres[n]?accept ->
                goto DONE;
        :: ses_to_pres[n]?reject(status) ->
                if
                :: (status == FATAL || uabort) ->
                        goto FAIL
                :: (status == NON_FATAL && !uabort) ->
                        goto TRANSFER
                fi
        od;
DONE:
        pres_to_use[n]!accept;
        goto IDLE;
FAIL:
        pres_to_use[n]!reject;
        goto IDLE
}
```

The file transfer request is repeated until it succeeds or until it triggers a fatal error. The main assumption that the presentation layer makes about the session layer protocol is that it will eventually respond to a transfer request with either an accept or a reject message. It also assumes that the session layer can accept an abort message at any time.

Correctness Requirements: As a correctness requirement for the presentation layer we will identify its valid end-states. There is one valid end-state only, the IDLE state. By adding the prefix "end," i.e. replacing the name IDLE with endIDLE, we can specify the requirement that the presentation layer must be in the given state when a protocol transfer terminates. Provided that our assumptions about the session layer and the user layer are true, it is not too hard to show that

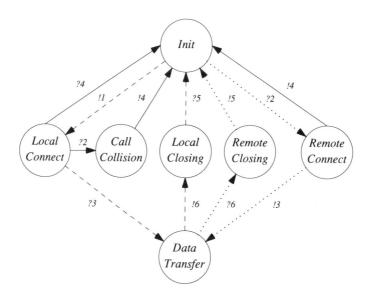

Figure 7.8 — Partial State Transition Diagram: Session Layer
1: transfer, 2: connect, 3: accept, 4: reject, 5: closed, 6: eof

this requirement is satisfied. The presentation layer can be blocked only in a small number of unexecutable statements. The assumptions about the user and session layers guarantee that none of those statements can remain unexecutable forever. But an informal argument, such as the one above, is not a proof. In Chapter 14 we use an automated prover to show that the assumptions we have made and the conclusions we have drawn from them are not just convincing but also correct.

7.6.2 SESSION LAYER

Earlier we decided that the protocol would have four phases:

- ○ Initialization of the file server
- ○ Connection establishment
- ○ Data transfer
- ○ Call completion

The messages in the protocol vocabulary that we looked at earlier are, of course, not unrelated; they imply a certain ordering. A transfer request should precede a connection confirmation, just as connection establishment should precede data transfer. We can make some of these implied relations explicit with the outline shown in Figure 7.8.

The transitions are labeled with numbers that refer to some, though not all, of the messages that are exchanged. Incoming messages are prefixed with a question mark, outgoing messages with an exclamation point. The dashed arrows indicate the expected sequence of events for a successful outgoing file transfer; the dotted lines indicate a normal incoming file transfer. Writing down the state transition diagram has forced us to make some further design choices. In the call establishment phase, for instance, a connection request may come from the remote system directly after the processing of a local connection request has started. In Figure 7.8 we have chosen to reject both requests when such a call collision occurs. The call completion phase is entered when a file has been successfully transferred, and the `eof` message has been sent. Alternatively, the transfer can be interrupted when the user sends the `abort` message. In the following paragraphs we consider each protocol phase separately and fill in the details.

CALL ESTABLISHMENT PHASE

The session layer sits between the presentation and the flow control layer. After the local `transfer` message from the presentation layer arrives, the session layer must perform a number of crucial tasks. It must try to open the file for reading on the local system, it must create a file for writing on the remote system, and in between it must establish a connection with the remote system. Any of these three tasks may fail. The local file server takes care of all file access.

This leads to the following descriptions for the call establishment phase. First, there are only two messages that can trigger a file transfer: the local `transfer` message and the remote `connect` message. Everything else should be ignored by the session protocol. Instead of explicitly specifying all non-valid messages, we can make the session layer receive a message of arbitrary type and check only for a match with the expected message, which in state `IDLE` is either a `transfer` message coming from the upper protocol layer or a `connect` message from the lower layer.

```
proctype session(bit n)
{       bit     toggle;
        byte    type, status;

IDLE:
        do
        :: pres_to_ses[n]?type ->
                if
                :: (type == transfer) ->
                        goto DATA_OUT
                :: (type != transfer)
                        /* ignore */
                fi
        :: flow_to_ses[n]?type ->
                if
                :: (type == connect) ->
                        goto DATA_IN
                :: (type != connect)
                        /* ignore */
                fi
```

```
            od;
DATA_OUT:
            ...
DATA_IN:
            ...
    }
```

It seems best to separate the data transfer phases for incoming and outgoing files. The easier case is the preparation for an incoming file. There is only one interaction with the local file server.

```
DATA_IN:                    /* prepare local file server */
        ses_to_fsrv[n]!create;
        do
        :: fsrv_to_ses[n]?reject ->
                ses_to_flow[n]!reject;
                goto IDLE
        :: fsrv_to_ses[n]?accept ->
                ses_to_flow[n]!accept;
                break
        od;
        ... incoming data transfer ...
        ... close connection etc.  ...
```

An outgoing transfer is done in three steps, each of which can fail:

○ Handshake on a local open request with the file server
○ Initialization of the flow control layer
○ Handshake with the remote system on a connect request

The first step can be specified as follows.

```
DATA_OUT:                   /* 1. prepare local file */
        ses_to_fsrv[n]!open;
        if
        :: fsrv_to_ses[n]?reject ->
                ses_to_pres[n]!reject(FATAL);
                goto IDLE
        :: fsrv_to_ses[n]?accept ->
                skip    /* proceed */
        fi;
```

The second step is harder. We must make sure that we cannot accidentally accept an old sync_ack message from a previous initialization attempt. We use a one-bit sequence number to solve that problem (see Exercise 7-12.)

```
                        /* 2. initialize flow control */
        ses_to_flow[n]!sync,toggle;
        do
        :: flow_to_ses[n]?sync_ack,type ->
                if
                :: (type != toggle) /* ignore */
                :: (type == toggle) -> break
                fi
```

```
:: timeout ->   /* failed */
        ses_to_fsrv[n]!close;
        ses_to_pres[n]!reject(FATAL);
        goto IDLE
od;
toggle = 1 - toggle;
```

In the third and last step, we must consider the possibility of a call collision.

```
                    /* 3. prepare remote file */
ses_to_flow[n]!connect;
if
:: flow_to_ses[n]?accept ->
        skip     /* success */
:: flow_to_ses[n]?reject ->
        ses_to_fsrv[n]!close;
        ses_to_pres[n]!reject(FATAL);
        goto IDLE
:: flow_to_ses[n]?connect ->
        ses_to_fsrv[n]!close;
        ses_to_pres[n]!reject(NON_FATAL);
        goto IDLE
:: timeout ->   /* got disconnected? */
        ses_to_fsrv[n]!close;
        ses_to_pres[n]!reject(FATAL);
        goto IDLE
fi;
... outgoing data transfer...
... close connection etc. ...
```

When a call collision is detected both parties close their files and return to the initial state, leaving it up to the presentation layers to make another attempt to transfer
their files. Prudence dictates that we include a timeout clause in every state
where we wait for events that can only be supplied by the remote system. In case
all communication is lost, e.g., on carrier loss, it gives us a way back to the initial
state.

DATA TRANSFER PHASES

The design of the data transfer phases is relatively straightforward. For outgoing
transfers we obtain data from the file server and transfer them to the flow control
layer. The only things that can complicate the design are the messages that can
interrupt the transfer: a timeout or an abort message from the user.

```
do                          /* outgoing data */
:: fsrv_to_ses[n]?data ->
        ses_to_flow[n]!data
:: fsrv_to_ses[n]?eof ->
        ses_to_flow[n]!eof;
        status = COMPLETE;
        break   /* goto call termination */
```

```
    :: pres_to_ses[n]?abort ->          /* user aborts */
            ses_to_fsrv[n]!close;
            ses_to_flow[n]!close;
            status = FATAL;
            break    /* goto call termination */
    od;
```

For incoming file transfers, we obtain data messages from the flow control layer
and transfer them to the file server. Only the remote user can abort an incoming
transfer. When the remote user aborts, the local system receives a `close` message
from the remote system (see above). This leads to the following PROMELA model.

```
    do                          /* incoming data */
    :: flow_to_ses[n]?data ->
            ses_to_fsrv[n]!data
    :: flow_to_ses[n]?eof ->
            ses_to_fsrv[n]!eof;
            break
    :: pres_to_ses[n]?transfer -> /* sorry, busy */
            ses_to_pres[n]!reject(NON_FATAL)
    :: flow_to_ses[n]?close ->       /* remote user aborts */
            ses_to_fsrv[n]!close;
            break
    :: timeout ->   /* got disconnected? */
            ses_to_fsrv[n]!close;
            goto IDLE
    od;
```

All the necessary character stuffing and byte encoding operations (Chapter 2, Section 2.5) are again irrelevant to the validation model. We can safely assume that
they happen elsewhere, e.g., in the modem that connects us to the physical line.

CALL TERMINATION PHASE

We complete the high-level design of the data transfer phase by adding the processing of call termination messages. The call termination phase can only be entered
from the data transfer phase, as shown above. First let us consider the normal termination of an outgoing file transfer session.

```
    /* close connection, outgoing transfer */
    do
    :: pres_to_ses[n]?abort /* too late, ignored */
    :: flow_to_ses[n]?close ->
            if
            :: (status == COMPLETE) ->
                    ses_to_pres[n]!accept
            :: (status != COMPLETE) ->
                    ses_to_pres[n]!reject(status)
            fi;
            break
```

```
    :: timeout ->    /* disconnected? */
            ses_to_pres[n]!reject(FATAL);
            break
    od;
    goto IDLE
```

The code for responding to the termination of an incoming file transfer is simpler:

```
    /* close connection, incoming transfer */
    ses_to_flow[n]!close;    /* confirm it */
    goto IDLE
```

Correctness Requirements: The main correctness requirement for the session control layer protocol is that it satisfies the assumptions made by the presentation layer protocol: it always responds to a transfer message, within a finite amount of time, with either an accept or a reject message. Similarly, a remote connect message should be followed by an accept or a reject message to the remote presentation layer, within a finite amount of time. We can formalize both these requirements in a temporal claim by defining behavior that is required to be absent. A first attempt is shown below.

```
    never {
            do
            :: !pres_to_ses[n]?[transfer]
            && !flow_to_ses[n]?[connect]
            :: pres_to_ses[n]?[transfer] ->
                    goto accept0
            :: flow_to_ses[n]?[connect] ->
                    goto accept1
            od;
    accept0:
            do
            :: !ses_to_pres[n]?[accept]
            && !ses_to_pres[n]?[reject]
            od;
    accept1:
            do
            :: !ses_to_pres[1-n]?[accept]
            && !ses_to_pres[1-n]?[reject]
            od
    }
```

where n is either zero or one. An automated validation of the session layer protocol based on this claim is discussed in Chapter 14. We can also identify the IDLE state in the session layer as a valid end-state, again by simply replacing the name with endIDLE.

To complete the design, we now provide the data link layer, which comes in two parts: one layer implementing a flow control discipline and one providing error control.

7.6.3 FLOW CONTROL LAYER

We can model a full sliding window protocol, as discussed in Chapter 4, by
directly encoding Figures 4.11 and 4.12. To make things interesting, we will restrict ourselves to an encoding with a single process instead of five. In this case we
cannot get away with an abstraction for parameters such as the window size and the
range of sequence numbers used, without losing essential information about the
operation of this protocol layer. All data in PROMELA is initialized to zero by
default. We discuss the model step by step.

```
#define true    1           /* for convenience */
#define false   0
#define M        4           /* range sequence numbers  */
#define W        2           /* window size: M/2         */
```

As we saw in Chapter 4, and will prove in Chapter 11, the maximum number of
outstanding messages in a protocol of this type is equal to half the range of the
sequence numbers.

```
proctype fc(bit n)
{       bool    busy[M];       /* outstanding messages    */
        byte    q;             /* seq# oldest unacked msg */
        byte    m;             /* seq# last msg received  */
        byte    s;             /* seq# next msg to send   */
        byte    window;        /* nr of outstanding msgs  */
        byte    type;          /* msg type                */
        bit     received[M];   /* receiver housekeeping   */
        bit     x;             /* scratch variable        */
        byte    p;             /* seq# of last msg acked  */
        byte    I_buf[M], O_buf[M];    /* message buffers */
```

The `fc` model contains code for independent sender and receiver actions in full-
duplex communications. Some of the housekeeping, then, has to do with keeping
track of outgoing messages and some with incoming messages on the return channel.

Outgoing messages are stored in a message buffer `O_buf`, indexed by their
sequence number. Buffering the outgoing messages allows the protocol to
retransmit old messages when they are not acknowledged. A boolean array `busy` is
used to remember which slots in the array of outgoing data are free and which are
taken.

The main body of the flow control layer is a single `do` loop that checks for outgoing messages from the session layer, adds sequence numbers, forwards the messages to the error control layer, and keeps track of their acknowledgment. In
separate clauses it checks for incoming messages from the error control layer, strips
sequence numbers, and forwards the remainders to the session layer. Sending of
messages can be modeled as follows. A message is only sent if it is available, i.e.,
if the message channel `ses_to_flow` is non-empty, and if the lower protocol layer
is free to accept it, i.e., if the message channel `flow_to_dll` is non-full.

```
do
:: (window < W   && len(ses_to_flow[n]) >  0
                  && len(flow_to_dll[n]) < QSZ) ->
        ses_to_flow[n]?type;
        window = window+1;
        busy[s] = true;
        O_buf[s] = type;
        flow_to_dll[n]!type,s;
```

There is a little extra dance to be done if the message sent is a message of type
sync, which is used by the session layer to reset the flow control layer protocol.
In that case, all busy flags are cleared, and the sequence number returns to zero.

```
if
:: (type != sync) ->
        s = (s+1)%M
:: (type == sync) ->
        window = 0;
        s = M;
        do
        :: (s > 0) ->
                s = s-1;
                busy[s] = false
        :: (s == 0) ->
                break
        od
fi
```

When an ack message arrives, its sequence number m points to the message that is
being acknowledged. The status of that message, kept in array busy[m], is reset to
zero, meaning that the slot has become free. In the receiver code discussed below
this is included as follows:

```
:: dll_to_flow[n]?type,m ->
        if
        :: (type == ack) ->
                busy[m] = false
        ...
```

If the message that was acknowledged is the oldest outstanding message, the window can slide up one or more notches and make room for more messages to be
transmitted. This is modeled with two independent conditional clauses in the outer
execution loop. The advancement of the window is guarded with a timeout clause
to protect against lost messages.

```
:: (window > 0 && busy[q] == false) ->
        window = window - 1;
        q = (q+1)%M
:: (timeout && window > 0 && busy[q] == true) ->
        flow_to_dll[n]!O_buf[q],q
```

All that remains is the modeling of the clauses for the receiver part of the flow control layer. The messages are received in a generic clause

```
:: dll_to_flow[n]?type,m ->
```

followed by a switch on the message type. Incoming data are buffered to protect against messages that are received out of order, e.g., as a result of message loss and retransmission, and to allow the flow control layer to forward these messages to the session layer in the right order. The boolean array `received` is used to keep track of which messages have arrived and which are pending.

Let us first look at the processing of `sync` and `sync_ack` messages.

```
if
...
:: (type == sync) ->
        m = 0;
        do
        :: (m < M) ->
                received[m] = 0;
                m = m+1
        :: (m == M) ->
                break
        od;
        flow_to_dll[n]!sync_ack,0
:: (type == sync_ack) ->
        flow_to_ses[n]!sync_ack,0
```

The `sync` message is meant to initialize the flow control layer. In this case, the message comes from the remote peer and should be acknowledged with an `sync_ack` when the re-initialization is completed. If an `sync_ack` message arrives from the remote peer, it is passed on to the session layer protocol. To avoid circularity, the synchronization messages do not carry sequence numbers.

All other messages are considered to be data messages:

```
:: (type != ack && type != sync && type != sync_ack)->
    if
    :: (received[m] == true) ->
            x = ((0<p-m   && p-m<=W)
            ||   (0<p-m-M && p-m-M<=W));
            if       /* ack was lost? */
            :: (x) -> flow_to_dll[n]!ack,m
            :: (!x) /* else skip */
            fi
    :: (received[m] == false) ->
            I_buf[m] = type;
            received[m] = true;
            received[(m-W+M)%M] = false
    fi
```

When a data message arrives, we must first check whether or not it was received before. If it was received before, we have `received[m]==true`, and we must check to see if it has been acknowledged yet. Messages are only acknowledged after they have been passed on to the session layer and have freed up the buffer space that they held. A message that has not been received before is stored, and the appropriate flag is set in array `received`.

The same clause is used to reset the received flag to false for the message that is one full window size away from the last received message: only at this point in the protocol can we be certain that this message cannot be transmitted again. The acknowledgment for that message must have been received or we could not have received the current message.

If the current message was received before, a check on the sequence number tells us if it was previously acknowledged or not. If it was, the fact that it was retransmitted indicates that the acknowledgment was lost, and needs to be repeated. One more clause remains: the one that encodes the accept process from Figure 4.12.

```
    :: (received[p] == true && len(flow_to_ses[n])<QSZ
                            && len(flow_to_dll[n])<QSZ) ->
            flow_to_ses[n]!I_buf[p];
            flow_to_dll[n]!ack,p;
            p = (p+1)%M
    od
}
```

The flow control layer is now complete. It takes some time to convince ourselves that it really works. Though the protocol is only about a hundred lines of code, the behavior it specifies can be complex, especially in the presence of transmission errors.

Correctness Requirements: The main correctness requirement for this protocol layer is that it transfers messages without deletions and reorderings, despite the behavior of the underlying transmission channel. To express, or check, this requirement we could label each message transferred by the sender, and check at the receiver that no labels are lost and that the relative ordering of the labels is undisturbed. In a way, such a label acts like just another sequence number.

Given a flow control protocol with a window size W and a range of sequence numbers M, how many distinct labels would minimally be needed to check the correctness requirement? The answer, due to Pierre Wolper (see Bibliographic Notes), is surprising. The number is independent of W and M: three different labels suffice for any protocol. Consider the following checking experiment. We transmit sequences of messages through the flow control layer, carrying just the label, and no other data. The three different types of labels are arbitrarily called red, white, and blue. For convenience we call the corresponding messages red, white, and blue messages as well. To construct a range of test sequences, one red and one blue message are placed randomly in an infinite sequence of white messages. If the flow control protocol can ever lose a message, it will be able to lose the red or the blue message in at least one of the test sequences. Similarly, if the protocol can ever reorder two messages, it will be able to change the order of the red and the `blue` message in at least one sequence. The test sequences can be generated by a fake session layer protocol module.

```
proctype test_sender(bit n)
{       do
        :: ses_to_flow[n]!white
        :: ses_to_flow[n]!red -> break
        od;
        do
        :: ses_to_flow[n]!white
        :: ses_to_flow[n]!blue -> break
        od;
        do
        :: ses_to_flow[n]!white
        :: break
        od
}
```

The matching test model, which receives the test messages at the remote end of the protocol, can be defined as follows.

```
proctype test_receiver(bit n)
{       do
        :: flow_to_ses[n]?white
        :: flow_to_ses[n]?red -> break
        od;
        do
        :: flow_to_ses[n]?white
        :: flow_to_ses[n]?blue -> break
        od;
        do
        :: flow_to_ses[n]?white
        od
}
```

The correctness requirement can now be formalized with a temporal claim or even more simply by adding some assertions to the receiver process.

```
proctype test_receiver(bit n)
{       do
        :: flow_to_ses[n]?white
        :: flow_to_ses[n]?red -> break
        :: flow_to_ses[n]?blue -> assert(0)     /* error */
        od;
        do
        :: flow_to_ses[n]?white
        :: flow_to_ses[n]?red -> assert(0)       /* error */
        :: flow_to_ses[n]?blue -> break
        od;
        do
        :: flow_to_ses[n]?white
        :: flow_to_ses[n]?red -> assert(0)       /* error */
```

```
                :: flow_to_ses[n]?blue -> assert(0)      /* error */
                od
      }
```

This completes the design of the three main protocol layers. We have designed a protocol model that has sufficient detail to allow us to express and verify a set of formal correctness requirements about the protocol. It is not an implementation. The issue, however, need not come up until after the design itself has been validated (Chapter 14). Only then, the task of deriving an efficient implementation from the design will become relevant. We only take a quick peek at some of the issues here.

AN ASIDE ON IMPLEMENTATION

It is not relevant to the design of the validation model, but just out of curiosity we can look at how we could implement the parsing of messages at the lowest level in the protocol, just below the error control layer, or perhaps even combined with it. In C, for instance, the bytes obtained from the line can be stored, without processing, in a buffer raw that is large enough to hold one complete data message. We assume that the line drivers take care of character stuffing and de-stuffing, so we have a pure message delimited by STX and ETX control bytes.

If we use the protocol with the fields in the message header rounded to the nearest multiple of eight (Table 7.1), the maximum buffer size required is 428 bytes (422 data bytes plus 6 bytes overhead). The bytes are read into the buffer in a tight loop that can be coded as follows. We use a union of a raw buffer, a data message, and a non-data message. The code below assumes that the low-order byte of a 16-bit number, such as the checksum, is sent before the high-order byte.

```
typedef struct DATA_MSG {
        unsigned char type;
        unsigned char seqno;
        unsigned char tail[424];           /* includes checksum */
} DATA_MSG;

typedef struct NON_DATA_MSG {
        unsigned char type;
        unsigned char seqno;
        unsigned char checksum[2];
} NON_DATA_MSG;

union {
        unsigned char    raw[426];         /* data+header+trailer */
        DATA_MSG         data;
        NON_DATA_MSG     non_data;
} in;
```

Assuming that protection against the accidental occurrence of the STX and ETX message delimiters is provided by the sender by inserting (stuffing) a DLE (data link escape) character before all data that matches one of the three special characters

STX, ETX, or DLE, we can write the byte scanning and de-stuffing routine as follows.

```
recv()
{       unsigned char c;
        unsigned char *start = in.raw;
        unsigned char *stop = start+428;
        unsigned char *ptr  = start;
scan:
        for (;;)                                        /* forever    */
        {       if ((c = line_in()) == STX)             /* next byte */
                        ptr = start;                    /* reset ptr */
                else if (c == ETX)
                        goto check;                     /* have msg  */
                else if (ptr < stop)
                {       if (c == DLE)                   /* escape     */
                                *ptr++ = line_in();
                        else
                                *ptr++ = c;     /* store     */
                }
        }
check:
        ...
}
```

When the ETX marker has been seen we must check for a valid message by calculating the checksum, for instance by calling the CRC routine discussed in Chapter 3. If indeed the low-order byte of the checksum is sent first, a recalculation of the checksum of all the raw data as received, *including* the checksum field, should come out zero in the absence of transmission errors:

```
check:
        if (cksum(in.raw, ptr-start) == 0)
                /* good message, accept */
        else
                /* distorted message, ignore */
        goto scan;      /* resume scanning for messages */
```

When the checksum is nonzero, the buffer contents must be discarded; otherwise it can be copied to a safe place and passed to the upper protocol layer.

7.7 SUMMARY

In this chapter we have discussed a protocol design, leading up to a hierarchy of validation models written in PROMELA. The function of each layer in this hierarchy is largely independent of the functions performed by the other layers. Each layer adds some functionality, and helps to transform the underlying physical channel into a virtual one with a progressively more idealized behavior.

With the derivation of the validation models the design process is not complete. The behavior of the model will have to be formally validated, perhaps revised, and finally implemented. Finding unspecified receptions, unexecutable code segments, or deadlocks is almost impossible to do by inspection alone. The normal, expected sequences of events can be checked easily. The errors, however, usually hide in the unexpected combinations of events: execution sequences that have a low probability of occurring. In Chapter 14, we consider the validation of the models we have derived.

If the implementation is not derived automatically from the validated model, we must add another validation step to guarantee that the implementation and the model are equivalent: conformance testing (see Chapter 8, Section 8.6, and Chapter 9).

EXERCISES

7-1 Compare the protocol hierarchy derived in this chapter to the OSI reference model discussed in Chapter 2, Section 2.6. Which layers are missing?

7-2 Describe precisely in which order framing (using STX and ETX symbols), byte stuffing, and checksum calculations must be performed at the receiver and at the sender.

7-3 Which layer would have to be modified to include a rate control method in this protocol? Which layer would have to be modified to include a dynamic flow control method? Describe a simple version of each method.

7-4 Consider the possibility of recalculating the optimal data size D at run time and using the information gained to make the protocol adapt to dynamically changing channel characteristics.

7-5 Complete the state transition diagram from Figure 7.8, adding transitions and states for all messages in the protocol vocabulary.

7-6 Redesign the protocol for a transmission rate of 2400 bps.

7-7 Redesign the protocol for a channel with zero error rate and zero signal propagation delay.

7-8 (Doug McIlroy) Extend the protocol to allow for the file transfer to resume where it left off after carrier loss. Consider the option to use a status parameter in the accept and reject messages sent by the presentation layer to indicate how much of the file was successfully transferred. Hint: there can be no acknowledgment for the last data received and stored at the remote system at the moment of carrier loss.

7-9 Is there a possibility that the two parties in the file transfer protocol can be caught in an execution cycle, or *livelock*, where both continue to send messages, but neither party succeeds in reaching the data transfer phase? If true, suggest a way to amend the protocol to avoid this problem.

7-10 Redesign the file server process to allow for asynchronous communication with the session layer.

7-11 Try to merge the two data link layers into one layer, performing both flow control and error control.

7-12 Show that the one-bit toggle session number protects against the misinterpretation of sync_ack messages. Hint: compare with the alternating bit protocol.

7-13 Suppose that the channel assumptions are changed to include the possibility of data reordering on the transmission channel. Does the one-bit connection set up method from Exercise 7-12 still work? Hint: a standard solution to this generalized version of the problem is known as the *three-way handshake*, see for instance, Stallings [1985, p. 490].

7-14 Consider what would need to be changed in the implementation (see "An Aside on Implementation") for transmissions in which the high-order byte of a 16-bit quantity is sent before the low-order byte.

7-15 Express the correctness requirement for the flow control layer in a temporal claim. Hint: first express a requirement on the correct behavior; then reverse it to specify all invalid behaviors. Use a do-loop labeled with an acceptance-state label as the specification of the error state that is reached (and never exited) whenever the correct behavior is violated.

7-16 Check the ten design rules from Chapter 2 and verify how they were applied to this design. Criticize the design where the rules were violated.

BIBLIOGRAPHIC NOTES

Software layering is a concept that is primarily due to E.W. Dijkstra (see Bibliographic Notes, Chapter 2). More on the derivation of protocol parameters, such as the optimal data length, can be found in Field [1976], Tanenbaum [1981], or Arthurs, Chesson and Stuck [1983].

In spirit at least, the design borrows many ideas from the world of light-weight protocols (see Chapter 2). The importance of a judicious placement of control information in either the header or the trailer of a protocol, was first emphasized by Greg Chesson, one of the initiators of light-weight protocol design.

In many standards all control information is by default placed in one single control block that is placed at the header of each message. The term "trailer protocol" was coined by Chesson in an effort to show that the opposite discipline, of placing all control information in the trailer and none, except perhaps a routing address, in the header, could lead to more efficient encodings of both sender and receiver. For instance, both the byte count and the checksum of a message can then be computed on the fly by the sender. The receiver can similarly compute checksums on the fly (starting at an STX control flag), and after spotting the matching ETX flag the receiver can find the byte count close by. The checksum can be verified immediately.

The correctness criterion that we specified for the flow control layer was first discussed in Wolper [1986]. It is also discussed in Aggarwal, Courcoubetis, and Wolper [1990].

FINITE STATE MACHINES **8**

8.1 INTRODUCTION

At a low level of abstraction, a protocol is often most easily understood as a state machine. Design criteria can also easily be expressed in terms of desirable or undesirable protocol states and state transitions. In a way, the protocol state symbolizes the assumptions that each process in the system makes about the others. It defines what actions a process is allowed to take, which events it expects to happen, and how it will respond to those events.

The formal model of a communicating finite state machine plays an important role in three different areas of protocol design: formal validation, protocol synthesis, and conformance testing. This chapter introduces the main concepts. First the basic finite state machine model is discussed. There are several, equally valid, ways of extending this basic model into a model for communicating finite state machines. We select one of those models and formalize it in a definition of a generalized communicating finite state machine. The model can readily be applied to represent PROMELA specifications and to build an automated validator.

There exist many variations of the basic finite state machine model. Rather than list them all, we conclude this chapter with a discussion of two of the more interesting examples: the Petri Net and the FIFO Net.

8.2 INFORMAL DESCRIPTION

A finite state machine is usually specified in the form of a transition table, much like the one shown in Table 8.1 below.

Table 8.1 — Mealy[1]

Condition		Effect	
Current State	In	Out	Next State
q0	–	1	q2
q1	–	0	q0
q2	0	0	q3
q2	1	0	q1
q3	0	0	q0
q3	1	0	q1

For each control state of the machine the table specifies a set of transition rules. There is one rule per row in the table, and usually more than one rule per state. The example table contains transition rules for control states named q0, q1, q2, and q3. Each transition rule has four parts, each part corresponding to one of the four columns in the table. The first two are conditions that must be satisfied for the transition rule to be executable. They specify

○ The control state in which the machine must be

○ A condition on the "environment" of the machine, such as the value of an input signal

The last two columns of the table define the effect of the application of a transition rule. They specify

○ How the "environment" of the machine is changed, e.g., how the value of an output signal changes

○ The new state that the machine reaches if the transition rule is applied

In the traditional finite state machine model, the environment of the machine consists of two finite and disjoint sets of signals: input signals and output signals. Each signal has an arbitrary, but finite, range of possible values. The condition that must be satisfied for the transition rule to be executable is then phrased as a condition on the value of each input signal, and the effect of the transition can be a change of the values of the output signals. The machine in Table 8.1 illustrates that model. It has one input signal, named In, and one output signal, named Out.

A dash in one of the first two columns is used as a shorthand to indicate a "don't care" condition (that always evaluates to the boolean value *true*). A transition rule, then, with a dash in the first column applies to all states of the machine, and a transition rule with a dash in the second column applies to all possible values of the input signal. Dashes in the last two columns can be used to indicate that the exe-

---

1. This example first appeared in two seminal papers on finite state machines, published by George H. Mealy [1955] and Edward F. Moore [1956].

cution of a transition rule does not change the environment. A dash in the third column means that the output signal does not change, and similarly, a dash in the fourth column means that the control state remains unaffected.

In each particular state of the machine there can be zero or more transition rules that are executable. If no transition rule is executable, the machine is said to be in an *end-state*. If precisely one transition rule is executable, the machine makes a deterministic move to a new control state. If more than one transition rule is executable a nondeterministic choice is made to select a transition rule. A *nondeterministic* choice in this context means that the selection criterion is undefined. Without further information either option is to be considered equally likely. From here on, we will call machines that can make such choices *nondeterministic machines*.[2] Table 8.2 illustrates the concept. Two transition rules are defined for control state q1. If the input signal is one, only the first rule is executable. If the input signal is zero, however, both rules will be executable and the machine will move either to state q0 or to state q3.

Table 8.2 — Non-Determinism

Current State	In	Out	Next State
q1	–	0	q0
q1	0	0	q3

The behavior of the machine in Table 8.1 is more easily understood when represented graphically in the form of a state transition diagram, as shown in Figure 8.1.

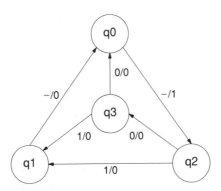

Figure 8.1 — State Transition Diagram

---

2. The nondeterministic formal automata (NFA) from automata theory are often defined differently. (See for instance, Aho, Sethi and Ullman [1986, p. 114].) Unlike our nondeterministic machines, an NFA can be in more than one state at the same time.

The control states are represented by circles, and the transition rules are specified as directed edges. The edge labels are of the type *c/e*, where *c* specifies the transition condition (e.g., the required set of input values) and *e* the corresponding effect (e.g., a new assignment to the set of output values).

TURING MACHINES

The above definition of a finite state machine is intuitively the simplest. There are many variants of this basic model that differ in the way that the environment of the machines is defined and thus in the definition of the conditions and the effects of the transition rules. For truly finite state systems, of course, the environment must be finite state as well (e.g., it could be defined as another finite state machine). If this requirement is dropped, we obtain the well-known *Turing Machine* model. It is used extensively in theoretical computer science as the model of choice in, for instance, the study of computational complexity. The Turing machine can be seen as a generalization of the finite state machine model, although Turing's work predates that of Mealy and Moore by almost two decades.

The "environment" in the Turing machine model is a tape of infinite length. The tape consists of a sequence of squares, where each square can store one of a finite set of tape symbols. All tape squares are initially blank. The machine can read or write one tape square at a time, and it can move the tape left or right, also by one square at a time. Initially the tape is empty and the machine points to an arbitrary square. The condition of a transition rule now consists of the control state of the finite state machine and the tape symbol that can be read from the square that the machine currently points to. The effect of a transition rule is the potential output of a new tape symbol onto the current square, a possible left or right move, and a jump to a new control state.

The tape is general enough to model a random access memory, be it an inefficient one. Table 8.3 illustrates this type of finite state machine.

Table 8.3 — Busy Beaver[3]

Condition		Effect	
Current State	In	Out/Move	Next State
q0	0	1/L	q1
q0	1	1/R	q2
q1	0	1/R	q0
q1	1	1/L	–
q2	0	1/R	q1
q2	1	1/L	q3
q3	–	–	–

This machine has two output signals: one is used to overwrite the current square on the tape with a new symbol, and one is used to move the tape left or right one square. State q3 is an *end* state.

It is fairly hard to define an extension of this variant of the model with a practical method for modeling the controlled interaction of multiple finite state machines. The obvious choice would be to let one machine read a tape that is written by another, but this is not very realistic. Furthermore, the infinite number of potential states for the environment means that many problems become computationally intractable. For the study of protocol design problems, therefore, we must explore other variants of the finite state machine.

COMMUNICATING FINITE STATE MACHINES

Consider what happens if we allow overlap of the sets of input and output signals of a finite state machine of the type shown in Table 8.1. In all fairness, we cannot say what will happen without first considering in more detail what a "signal" is.

We assume that signals have a finite range of possible values and can change value only at precisely defined moments. The machine executes a two-step algorithm. In the first step, the input signal values are inspected and an arbitrary executable transition rule is selected. In the second step, the machine changes its control state in accordance with that rule and updates its output signals. These two steps are repeated forever. If no transition rule is executable, the machine will continue cycling through its two-step algorithm without changing state, until a change in the input signal values, effected by another finite state machine, makes a transition possible. A signal, then, has a state, much like a finite state machine. It can be interpreted as a variable that can only be evaluated or assigned to at precisely defined moments.

The behavior of the machine from Table 8.1 is now fully defined, even if we assume a feedback from the output to the input signal. In this case the machine will loop through the following sequence of three states forever: q0, q2, q1. At each step, the machine inspects the output value that was set in the previous transition. The behavior of the machine is independent of the initial value of the input signal.

We can build elaborate systems of interacting machines in this way, connecting the output signals of one machine to the input signals of another. The machines must share a common "clock" for their two-step algorithm, but they are not otherwise synchronized. If further synchronization is required, it must be realized with a subtle system of handshaking on the signals connecting the machines. This problem,

---

3. This table is Tibor Rado's classic entry into the busy beaver game. The object of the game is to create an N-state (here $N = 3$) finite state machine that, when started on an empty tape (i.e., with all squares zero) reaches a known end state in a finite number of steps, leaving the longest possible sequence of ones on the tape.

as we saw in Chapter 5, has three noticeable features: it is a hard problem, it has been solved, and, from the protocol designer's point of view, it is irrelevant. Most systems provide a designer with higher-level synchronization primitives to build a protocol. An example of such synchronization primitives are the send and receive operations defined in PROMELA.

ASYNCHRONOUS COUPLING

In protocol design, finite state machines are most useful if they can directly model the phenomena in a distributed computer system. There are two different and equally valid ways of doing this, based on an asynchronous or a synchronous communication model. With the asynchronous model, the machines are coupled via bounded FIFO (first-in first-out) message queues. The signals of a machine are now abstract objects called messages. The input signals are retrieved from input queues, and the output signals are appended to output queues. All queues, and the sets of signals, are still finite, so we have not given up the finiteness of our model.

Synchronization is achieved by defining both input and output signals to be conditional on the state of the message queues. If an input queue is empty, no input signal is available from that queue, and the transition rules that require one are unexecutable. If an output queue is full, no output signal can be generated for that queue, and the transition rules that produce one are similarly unexecutable.

From this point on we restrict the models we are considering to those with no more than one synchronizing event per transition rule; that is, a single rule can specify an input or an output, but not both. The reason for this restriction is twofold. First, it simplifies the model. We do not have to consider the semantics of complicated composites of synchronizing events that may be inconsistent (e.g., two outputs to the same output queue that can accommodate only one of the two). Second, it models the real behavior of a process in a distributed system more closely. Note that the execution of a transition rule is an atomic event of the system. In most distributed systems a single send or receive operation is guaranteed to be an atomic event. It is therefore appropriate not to assume yet another level of interlocking in our basic system model.

Table 8.4 — Sender

State	In	Out	Next State
q0	–	mesg0	q1
q1	ack1	–	q0
q1	ack0	–	q2
q2	–	mesg1	q3
q3	ack0	–	q2
q3	ack1	–	q0

As an example of asynchronous coupling of finite state machines, Tables 8.4 and 8.5 give transition table models for a simple version of the alternating bit protocol (see also Chapter 4, Figure 4.8). The possibility of a retransmission after a timeout is not modeled in Table 8.4. We could do so with spontaneous transitions, by adding two rules:

State	In	Out	Next State
q1	–	mesg0	–
q3	–	mesg1	–

The table can model the *possibility* of retransmissions in this way, though not their *probability*. Fortunately, this is exactly the modeling power we need in a system that must analyze protocols independently of any assumptions on the timing or speed of individual processes (see also Chapter 11).

Table 8.5 — Receiver

State	In	Out	Next State
q0	mesg1	–	q1
q0	mesg0	–	q2
q1	–	ack1	q3
q2	–	ack0	q0
q3	mesg0	–	q4
q3	mesg1	–	q5
q4	–	ack0	q0
q5	–	ack1	q3

The last received message can be accepted as correct in states q1 and q4. A state transition diagram for Tables 8.4 and 8.5 is given in Figure 8.2. The timeout option in the sender would produce and extra self-loop on states q1 and q3.

We do not have parameter values in messages just yet. In the above model the value of the alternating bit is therefore tagged onto the name of each message.

SYNCHRONOUS COUPLING

The second method for coupling machines is based on a synchronous model of communication, like the one discussed briefly in Chapter 5. The transition conditions are now the "selections" that the machine can make for communication. Again we allow only one synchronizing event per transition rule. The machine can select either an input or an output signal for which a transition rule is specified. To make a move, a signal has to be selected by precisely two machines simultaneously, in one machine as an output and in the other as an input. If such a match on a signal occurs, both machines make the corresponding transition simultaneously and change their selections in accordance with the new states they reach.

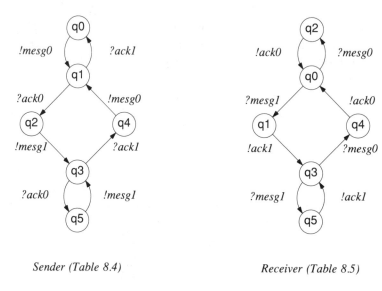

Sender (Table 8.4)   Receiver (Table 8.5)

Figure 8.2 — State Transition Diagrams, Tables 8.4 and 8.5

Tables 8.6 and 8.7 give an example of synchronously coupled finite state machines. The machine in Table 8.6 can make just one input selection P in state q0 and one output selection V in state q1.

Table 8.6 — User

State	In	Out	Next State
q0	P	–	q1
q1	–	V	q0

The second machine is almost the same as the first, but has the inputs and outputs swapped (Table 8.7).

Table 8.7 — Server

State	In	Out	Next State
q0	–	P	q1
q1	V	–	q0

If we create two machines of type 8.6 and combine them with one machine of type 8.7, we can be certain that for all possible executions the first two machines cannot both be in state q1 at the same time. Note that synchronous communication was defined to be binary: exactly two machines must participate, one with a given input selection and the other with the matching output selection. Typically, a parameter value will be passed from sender to receiver in the synchronous handshake. The value transfer, however, is not in the model just yet.

We can again consider the synchronous communication as a special case of asynchronous communication with a queue capacity of zero slots (see also Chapters 5 and 11). In the remainder of this chapter we therefore focus on the more general case of a fully asynchronous coupling of finite state machines.

8.3 FORMAL DESCRIPTION

Let us now see if we can tidy up the informal definitions discussed so far. A communicating finite state machine can be defined as an abstract demon that accepts input symbols, generates output symbols, and changes its inner state in accordance with some predefined plan. For now, these symbols or "messages" are defined as abstract objects without contents. We will consider the extensions required to include value transfer in Section 8.8. The finite state machine demons communicate via bounded FIFO queues that map the output of one machine upon the input of another. Let us first formally define the concept of a queue.

A *message queue* is a triple (S, N, C), where:

S is a finite set called the queue vocabulary,
N is an integer that defines the number of slots in the queue, and
C is the queue contents, an ordered set of elements from S.

The elements of S and C are called messages. They are uniquely named, but otherwise undefined abstract objects. If more than one queue is defined we require that the queue vocabularies be disjoint. Let M be the set of all messages queues, a superscript $1 \leq m \leq |M|$ is used to identify a single queue, and an index $1 \leq n \leq N$ is used to identify a slot within the queue. C_n^m, then, is the n-th message in the m-th queue. A system vocabulary V can be defined as the conjunction of all queue vocabularies, plus a null element that we indicate with the symbol ε. Given the set of queues M, numbered from 1 to $|M|$, the system vocabulary V is defined as

$$V = \bigcup_{m=1}^{|M|} S^m \cup \varepsilon$$

Now, let us define a communicating finite state machine.

A *communicating finite state machine* is a tuple (Q, q_0, M, T), where

Q is a finite, non-empty set of states,
q_0 is an element of Q, the *initial state*,
M is a set of message queues, as defined above, and
T is a state transition relation.

Relation T takes two arguments, $T(q,a)$, where q is the current state and a is an action. So far, we allow just three types of actions: inputs, outputs, and a null action ε. The executability of the first two types of actions is conditional on the state of the message queues. If executed, they both change the state of precisely one message queue. Beyond this, it is immaterial, at least for our current purposes, what the precise definition of an input or an output action is.

The transition relation T defines a set of zero or more possible successor states in set Q for current state q. This set will contain precisely one state, unless nondeterminism is modeled, as in Table 8.2. When $T(q,a)$ is not explicitly defined, we assume $T(q,a) = \varnothing$.

$T(q,\varepsilon)$ specifies spontaneous transitions. A sufficient condition for these transitions to be executable is that the machine be in state q.

8.4 EXECUTION OF MACHINES

Consider a system of P finite state machines, with overlapping sets of message queues. The union of the sets of all message queues is again called M. This system of communicating finite state machines is executed by applying the following rules, assuming asynchronous coupling only. The elements of finite state machine i are referred to with a superscript i.

ALGORITHM 8.1 — FSM EXECUTION

1. Set all machines in their initial state, and initialize all message queues to empty:

$$\forall(i), 1 \leq i \leq P \quad \rightarrow \quad q^i = q_0^i$$

$$\forall(i), 1 \leq i \leq |M| \quad \rightarrow \quad C^i = \varnothing$$

2. Select an arbitrary machine i and an arbitrary transition rule T^i with

$$T^i(q,^i a) \neq \varnothing \quad \text{and} \quad a \text{ is executable}$$

and execute it.

3. If no executable transition rules remain, the algorithm terminates.

Action a can be an input, an output, or it can be the null action ε. Let $1 \leq d(a) \leq |M|$ be destination queue of an action a, and let $m(a)$ be the message that is sent or received, $m(a) \in S^{d(a)}$. Further, let N^i represent the number of slots in message queue i. In an asynchronous system, for instance, the following three rules can be used to determine if a is executable.

$$a = \varepsilon \tag{1}$$

or

$$a \text{ is an input and } m(a) = C_1^{d(a)} \tag{2}$$

or

$$a \text{ is an output and } |C^{d(a)}| < N^{d(a)} \tag{3}$$

Algorithm 8.1 does not necessarily terminate.

Table 8.8 — Receiver-II

Condition		Effect	
Current State	In	Out	Next State
q0	mesg1	–	q1
q0	mesg0	–	q2
q1	–	ack1	q0
q2	–	ack0	q0

8.5 MINIMIZATION OF MACHINES

Consider the finite state machine shown in Table 8.8, with the corresponding state transition diagram in Figure 8.3. Though this machine has three states fewer than the machine from Table 8.5, it certainly looks like it behaves no differently. Two machines are said to be *equivalent* if they can generate the same sequence of output symbols when offered the same sequence of input symbols. The keyword here is *can*. The machines we study can make nondeterministic choices between transition rules if more than one is executable at the same time. This nondeterminism means that even two equal machines *can* behave differently when offered the same input symbols. The rule for equivalence is that the machines must have equivalent choices to be in equivalent states.

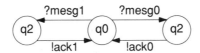

Figure 8.3 — State Transition Diagram for Table 8.8

States within a single machine are said to be equivalent if the machine can be started in any one of these states and generate the same set of possible sequences of outputs when offered any given test sequence of inputs. The definition of an appropriate equivalence relation for states, however, has to be chosen with some care. Consider the following PROMELA process.

```
proctype A()
{       if
        :: q?a -> q?b
        :: q?a -> q?c
        fi
}
```

Under the standard notion of language equivalence that is often defined for deterministic finite state machines, this would be equivalent to

```
proctype B()
{       q?a;
        if
        :: q?b
        :: q?c
        fi
}
```

since the set of all input sequences (the language) accepted by both machines is the same. It contains two sequences, of two messages each:

```
{ q?a;q?b , q?a;q?c }
```

The behavior of the two processes, however, is very different. The input sequence q?a;q?b, for instance, is always accepted by process B but may lead to an unspecified reception in process A. For nondeterministic communicating finite state machines, therefore processes A and B are not equivalent. The definitions given below will support that notion.

In the following discussion of equivalence, state minimization, and machine composition, we will focus exclusively on the set of control states Q and the set of transitions T of the finite state machines. Specifically, the internal "state" of the message queues in set M is considered to be part of the environment of a machine and not contributing to the state of the machine itself. That this is a safe assumption needs some motivation. Consider, as an extreme case, a communicating finite state machine that accesses a private message queue to store internal state information. It can do so by appending messages with state information in the queue and by retrieving that information later. The message queue is internal and artificially increases the number of states of the machine.

When we consider the message queue to be part of the environment of a machine in the definitions that follow, we ignore the fact that the information that is retrieved from such a private queue is always fixed (i.e., it can only have been placed in the queue by the same machine in a previous state). If we say that two states of this machine are equivalent if they respond to the same input messages in the same way, we do in fact place a *stronger* requirement on the states than strictly necessary. We require, for instance, that the two states would respond similarly to messages that could never be in a private queue for the given state. To suppress state information that could be implicit in the messages queue contents therefore does not relax the equivalence requirements. As we will see, it does lead to simpler algorithms.

Using this approach, the set of control states of a communicating finite state machine can be minimized, without changing the external behavior of the machine, by replacing every set of equivalent states with a single state. More formally, we can say that this equivalence relation defines a partitioning of the states into a finite set of disjoint equivalence classes. The smallest machine equivalent to the given one will have as many states as the original machine has equivalence classes.

We can now define a procedure for the minimization of an arbitrary finite state machine with $|Q|$ states.

ALGORITHM 8.2 — FSM MINIMIZATION

1. Define an array E of $|Q| \times |Q|$ boolean values. Initially, every element $E[i,j]$ of the array is set to the truth value of the following condition, for all actions a:

$$T(i,a) \neq \varnothing \quad \Leftrightarrow \quad T(j,a) \neq \varnothing$$

Two states are not equivalent unless the corresponding state transition relations are defined for the same actions.

2. If the machine considered contains only deterministic choices, T defines a unique successor state for all *true* entries of array E. Change the value of all those entries $E[i,j]$ to the value of

$$\forall(a), \quad E[T(i,a),T(j,a)]$$

It means that states are not equivalent unless their successors are also equivalent. When $T(i,a)$ and $T(j,a)$ can have more than one element, the relation is more complicated. The value of $E[i,j]$ is now set to *false* if either of the following two conditions is *false* for any action a.

$$\forall(p), \ p \in T(i,a) \quad \rightarrow \quad \exists(q), q \in T(j,a) \text{ and } E[p,q]$$

$$\forall(q), \ q \in T(j,a) \quad \rightarrow \quad \exists(p), p \in T(i,a) \text{ and } E[q,p]$$

This means that states i and j are not equivalent unless for every possible successor state p of state i there is at least one equivalent successor state q of state j, and vice versa.

3. Repeat step 2 until the number of *false* entries in array E can no longer be increased.

The procedure always terminates since the number of entries of the array is finite and each entry can only be changed once, from *true* to *false*, in step 2. When the procedure terminates, the entries of the array define a partitioning of the $|Q|$ states into equivalence classes. State i, $1 \leq i \leq |Q|$, is equivalent with all states j, $1 \leq j \leq |Q|$, with $E[i,j] = true$.

Table 8.9 — Equivalence

	q0	q1	q2	q3	q4	q5
q0	1	0	0	1	0	0
q1	0	1	0	0	0	1
q2	0	0	1	0	1	0
q3	1	0	0	1	0	0
q4	0	0	1	0	1	0
q5	0	1	0	0	0	1

If we apply this procedure to the finite state machine in Table 8.5, we obtain the stable array of values for E shown in Table 8.9 after a single application of the first two steps. A one in the table represents the boolean value *true*. From the table we see that state pairs (q0, q3), (q1, q5), and (q2, q4) are equivalent. We can therefore reduce Table 8.5 to the three-state finite state machine that was shown in Table 8.8. It is necessarily the smallest machine that can realize the behavior of Table 8.5.

The procedure above can be optimized by noting, for instance, that array E is symmetric: for all values of i and j we must have $E(i,j)=E(j,i)$. Trivially, every state is equivalent with itself.

8.6 THE CONFORMANCE TESTING PROBLEM

The procedure for testing equivalence of states can also be applied to determine the equivalence of two machines. The problem is then to determine that every state in one machine has an equivalent in the other machine, and vice versa. Of course, the machines need not be equal to be equivalent.

A variant of this problem is of great practical importance. Suppose we have a formal protocol specification, in finite state machine form, and an implementation of that specification. The two machines must be equivalent, that is the implementation, seen as a black box, should respond to input signals exactly as the reference machine would. We cannot, however, know anything with certainty about the implementation's true internal structure. We can try to establish equivalence by systematically probing the implementation with trial input sequences and by comparing the responses with those of the reference machine. The problem is now to find just the right set of test sequences to establish the equivalence or non-equivalence of the two machines. This problem is known in finite state machine theory as the *fault detection* or conformance testing problem. Chapter 10 reviews the methods that have been developed for solving this problem.

Carrying this one step further, we may also want to determine the internal structure of an unknown finite state machine, just by probing it with a known set of input signals and by observing its responses. This problem is known as the *state verification* problem. Without any further knowledge about the machine, that problem is alas unsolvable. Note, for instance, that in Figure 8.1 state q3 cannot be distinguished from state q2 by any test sequence that starts with an input symbol one. Similarly, state q1 cannot be distinguished from state q3 by any sequence starting with a zero. Since every test sequence has to start with either a one or a zero there can be no single test sequence that can tell us reliably in which state this machine is.

8.7 COMBINING MACHINES

By collapsing two separate finite state machines into a single machine the complexity of formal validations based on finite state machine models may be reduced.

The algorithm below is referred to in Chapter 11 in the discussion of an incremental protocol validation method, and in Chapter 14 in the discussion of methods for stepwise abstraction.

The problem is to find a tuple (Q, q_0, M, T) for the combined machine, given two machines (Q^1, q_0^1, M^1, T^1) and (Q^2, q_0^2, M^2, T^2).

ALGORITHM 8.3 — FSM COMPOSITION

1. Define the product set of the two sets of states of the two state machines. If the first machine has $|Q^1|$ states and the second machine has $|Q^2|$ states the product set contains $|Q^1| \times |Q^2|$ states. We initially name the states of the new machine by concatenating the state names of the original machines in a fixed order. This defines set Q of the combined machine. The initial state q_0 of the new machine is the combination $q_0^1 q_0^2$ of the initial states of the two original machines.

2. The set of message queues M of the combined machine is the union of the sets of queues of the separate machines, $M^1 \cup M^2$. The two original sets need not be disjoint. The vocabulary V of the new machine is the combined vocabulary of M^1 and M^2, and the set of actions a is the union of all actions that the individual machines can perform.

3. For each state $q^1 q^2$ in Q, define transition relation T for each action a as the non-deterministic choice of the corresponding relations of M^1 and M^2 separately, when placed in the individual states q^1 and q^2. This can be written:

$$\forall(q^1 q^2)\,\forall(a), \quad \rightarrow \quad T(q^1 q^2, a) = T^1(q^1, a) \cup T^2(q^2, a)$$

The combined machine can now be minimized using Algorithm 8.2. Algorithm 8.3 can be readily adapted to combine more than two machines.

The greatest value of the composition technique from the last section is that it allows us to simplify complex behaviors. In protocol validations, for instance, we could certainly take advantage of a method that allows us to collapse two machines into one. One method would be to compose two machines using Algorithm 8.3, remove all their internal interactions, i.e., the original interface between the two machines, and minimize the resulting machine.

There are two pieces missing from our finite state machine framework to allow us to apply compositions and reductions in this way. First, the finite state machine model we have developed so far cannot easily represent PROMELA models. In the next section we show how the basic finite state machine model can be extended sufficiently to model PROMELA models elegantly. The second piece that is missing from our framework is a method for removing internal actions from a machine without disturbing its external behavior. We discuss such methods in Section 8.9.

8.8 EXTENDED FINITE STATE MACHINES

The finite state machine models we have considered so far still fall short in two important aspects: the ability to model the manipulation of variables conveniently

Table 8.10 — Finite State Variable

Current State	In	Out	Next State
q0	s0	–	–
q0	s1	–	q1
q0	s2	–	q2
q0	rv	–	r0
r0	–	0	q0
q1	s0	–	q0
q1	s1	–	–
q1	s2	–	q2
q1	rv	–	r1
r1	–	1	q1
q2	s0	–	q0
q2	s1	–	q1
q2	s2	–	–
q2	rv	–	r2
r2	–	2	q2

and the ability to model the transfer of arbitrary values. These machines where defined to work with abstract objects that can be appended to and retrieved from queues and they are only synchronized on the access to these queues.

We make three changes to this basic finite state machine model. First, we introduce an extra primitive that is defined much like a queue: the variable. Variables have symbolic names and they hold abstract objects. The abstract objects, in this case, are integer values. The main difference from a real queue is that a variable can hold only one value at a time, selected from a finite range of possible values. Any number of values can be appended to a variable, but only the last value that was appended can be retrieved.

The second change is that we will now use the queues specifically to transfer integer values, rather than undefined abstract objects. Third, and last, we introduce a range of arithmetic and logical operators to manipulate the contents of variables.

The extension with variables, provided that they have a finite range of possible values, does not increase the computational power of finite state machines with bounded FIFO queues. A variable with a finite range can be simulated trivially by a finite state machine. Consider the six-state machine shown in Table 8.10, that models a variable with the range of values from zero to two. The machine accepts four different input messages. Three are used to set the pseudo variable to one of its three possible values. The fourth message, rv, is used to test the current value of the pseudo variable. The machine will respond to the message rv by returning one of the three possible values as an output message.

Thus, at the expense of a large number of states, we can model any finite variable without extending the basic model, as a special purpose finite state machine. The extension with explicit variables, therefore, is no more than a modeling convenience.

Recall that the transition rules of a finite state machine have two parts: a condition and an effect. The conditions of the transition rules are now generalized to include boolean expressions on the value of variables, and the effects (i.e. the actions) are generalized to include assignment to variables.

An *extended finite state machine* can now be defined as a tuple (Q, q_0, M, A, T), where A is the set of variable names. Q, q_0, and M are as defined before. The state transition relation T is unchanged. We have simply defined two extra types of actions: boolean conditions on and assignments to elements of set A. A single assignment can change the value of only one variable. Expressions are built from variables and constant values, with the usual arithmetic and relational operators.

In the spirit of the validation language PROMELA, we can define a condition to be executable only if it evaluates to *true*, and let an assignment always be executable. Note carefully that the extended model of communicating finite state machines is a *finite* state model, and almost all results that apply to finite state machines also apply to this model.

EXTENDED I/O

Input and output actions can now be generalized as well. We will define I/O actions as finite, ordered sets of values. The values can be expressions on variables from A, or simply constants. By definition the first value from such an ordered set defines the destination queue for the I/O, within the range $1..|M|$. The remaining values define a data structure that is appended to, or retrieved from, the queue when the I/O action is performed. The semantics of executability can again be defined as in PROMELA.

EXAMPLE

Consider the following PROMELA fragment, based on an example from Chapter 5.

```
proctype Euclid
{       pvar x, y;

        In?x,y;
        do
        :: (x >  y)  -> x = x - y
        :: (x <  y)  -> y = y - x
        :: (x == y)  -> break
        od;
        Out!x
}
```

The process begins by receiving two values into variables x and y, and it completes by returning the greatest common divisor of these two values to its output queue. The matching extended finite state machine is shown in Table 8.11, where we combine all conditions, assignments and I/O operations in a single column.

Table 8.11 — Extended Finite State Machine

Current State	Action	Next State
q0	In?x,y	q1
q1	x>y	q2
q1	x<y	q3
q1	x=y	q4
q2	x=x-y	q1
q3	y=y-x	q1
q4	Out!x	q5
q5	–	–

Set A has two elements, x and y.

We now have a simple mapping from PROMELA models to extended finite state machines. Algorithm 8.3, for instance, can now be used to express the combined behavior of two PROMELA processes by a single process. We noted before that this technique could be especially useful in combination with a *hiding* method that removes internal actions from a machine without disturbing its external behavior. We take a closer look at such methods in the next section.

8.9 GENERALIZATION OF MACHINES

Consider the following PROMELA model.

```
1 proctype generalize_me(chan ans; byte p)
2 {   chan internal[1] of { byte };
3     int r, q;
4
5     internal!cookie;
6     r = p/2;
7     do
8     :: (r <= 0) -> break
9     :: (r > 0) ->
10             q = (r*r + p)/(2*r);
11             if
12             :: (q != r) -> skip
13             :: (q == r) -> break
14             fi;
15             r = q
16     od;
```

```
17     internal?cookie;
18     if
19     :: (q <  p/3) -> ans!small
20     :: (q >= p/3) -> ans!great
21     fi
22 }
```

A process of this type will start by sending a message `cookie` to a local message channel. It will then perform some horrible computation, using only local variables, read back the message from the channel `internal`, and send one of two possible messages over an external message channel `ans`.

Now, for starters, nothing detectable will change in the external behavior of this process if we remove lines 2, 5 and 17. The message channel is strictly local, and there is no possible behavior for which any of the actions performed on the channel can be unexecutable. Lines 5 and 17 are therefore equivalent to `skip` operations and can be deleted from the model. Reductions, or *prunings*, of this type produce machines that have a equivalent external behavior to the non-reduced machines. This is not true for the next type of reduction we discuss: generalization.

The horrible computation performed by the process, between lines 6 and 16, does not involve any global variables or message interactions. Once the initial value of variable `p` is chosen, the resulting message sent to channel `ans` is fixed. If we are interested in just the external behavior of processes of type `generalize_me`, independently of the precise value of `p`, the model could be rewritten as

```
proctype generalized(chan ans; byte p)
{
        if
        :: ans!small
        :: ans!great
        fi
}
```

This specification merely says that within a finite time after a process of this type is instantiated, it sends either a message of type `small` or a message of type `great` and terminates. To justify the reduction we must of course show that the loop in the original specification will always terminate. If this is not the case, or cannot be proven, the correct reduction would be

```
proctype generalized(chan ans; byte p)
{
        if
        :: (0)
        :: ans!small
        :: ans!great
        fi
}
```

where the possibility of blocking is preserved explicitly.

We call a reduction of this type, where uninteresting but strictly local, behavior is removed, a *generalization*. A process of type `generalized` can do everything that a process of type `generalize_me` can do, but it can do more. The generalized process can, for instance, for any given parameter p, return either of the two messages, while the non-generalized processes will pick only one. The generalized processes is *only* more general in the way it can produce output, not in the way it can accept input, or in general in the way other processes can constrain its behavior via global objects.

The usefulness of generalizations in protocol validation can be explained as follows. Consider two protocol modules A and B whose combined behavior is too complex to be analyzed directly. We want to validate a correctness requirement for the processes in module A. We can do this by simplifying the behavior in module B, for instance by combining, pruning, generalizing, and minimizing machines. If the behavior in module B is generalized as discussed above, the new module B will still be capable of behaving precisely like the unmodified module B, but it can do more. If we can prove the observance of a correctness requirement for module A in the presence of the generalized module B, which may be easier, the result will necessarily also hold for the original, more complex, module B, because the original behavior is a subset of the new behavior.

Two things should be noted. First, if we are interested in proving a property of module A we simplify its environment, which in this case is module B. We do not change module A itself. Second, it is important that the modified behavior of module B does not, by virtue of the modifications, allow module A to pass its test. This is guaranteed by the fact that the generalized module B continues to adhere to all constraints that can be imposed by A, via global objects, such as message channels and variables. The validation, then, gives us the best of both worlds. It performs a stronger test, since it validates properties for more general conditions than defined in the original protocol, yet it is easier to perform, since a generalized process can be smaller than its original.

A general method for the reduction of an arbitrary PROMELA `proctype` definition can be described as follows.

☐ Identify selection and repetition structures in which all the guards are conditions on local variables only, and in which the union of all guards is `true`.

☐ Replace each of the guards identified in the first step with the PROMELA statement `skip`.

☐ Replace all assignments to local variables that are no longer part of any condition, with `skip`.

☐ Remove all redundant declarations and minimize or simplify the new `proctype` body, for instance, by combining equal clauses in selection and repetition structures, and by removing redundant `skip` statements.

If we apply this method to the process type `generalize_me`, after pruning away the interactions on channel `internal`, we can reduce it to

```
proctype generalized_2(chan ans; byte p)
{
        do
        :: break
        :: skip
        od;
        if
        :: ans!small
        :: ans!great
        fi
}
```

which is similar to and has the same external behavior as the (second) version we derived earlier with a little more handwaving. Note that the loop in the above version does not necessarily terminate.

A more substantial application of this generalization technique and the resulting reduction in complexity is discussed in Chapter 14.

8.10 RESTRICTED MODELS

To conclude this chapter, we look at two other interesting variants of the basic finite state machine model that have been applied to the study of protocol problems. Many variations of the basic finite state machine model have been used for the analysis of protocol systems, both restrictions and extensions. The restricted versions have the advantage, at least in principle, of a gain in analytical power. The extended versions have the advantage of a gain in modeling power. The most popular variants of the finite state machine are formalized token nets, often derived from the Petri Net model. Below we briefly review the Petri Net model and discuss one of the variations, the FIFO Net.

PETRI NETS

A Petri Net is a collection of *places*, *transitions*, and directed *edges*. Every edge connects a place to a transition or vice versa. Places are graphically represented by circles, transitions by bars, and edges by directed arcs. Informally, a place corresponds to a condition and a transition corresponds to an event. The *input places* of transition T are the places that are directly connected to T by one or more edges. The input places correspond to conditions that must be fulfilled before the event corresponding to T can occur. The output places of a transition similarly correspond to the effect of the event on the conditions represented by the places.

Each place that corresponds to a fulfilled condition is marked with one or more *tokens* (sometimes called a *stone*). The occurrence of an event is represented in the Petri Net as the *firing* of a transition. A transition is enabled if there is at least one token in each of its input places. The effect of a firing is that one token is added to the markings of all output places of the firing transition, and one token is removed from the markings of all its input places.

Two transitions are said to *conflict* if they share at least one input place. If the shared place contains precisely one token, both transitions may be enabled to fire, but the firing of one transition disables the other. By definition the firing of any combination of two transitions is always mutually exclusive: only one transition can fire at a time.

By assigning zero or more tokens to each place in the net we obtain an initial marking. Each firing creates a new marking. A series of firings is called an *execution sequence*. If for a given initial marking all possible execution sequences can be made infinitely long, the initial marking, and trivially all subsequent markings, are said to be *live*. If in a certain marking no transition is enabled to fire, the net is said to *hang*. An initial making is said to be *safe* if no subsequent execution sequence can produce a marking where any place has more than one token.

A number of properties has been proven about Petri Nets, but mostly about still further simplified versions. Two examples of such variants are:

☐ Petri Nets in which precisely one edge is directed to and from each place. Such nets are called *marked graphs*. In a marked graph there can be no conflicting transitions.

☐ Petri Nets in which all transitions have at most one input place and one output place. These nets are called *transition diagrams*.

Figure 8.4 gives an example of a Petri Net modeling a deadlock problem. Initially, the two top transitions *t1* and *t2* are enabled. After *t1* fires, transition *t3* becomes enabled. If it fires, all is well. If in this marking, however, transition *t2* fires, the net will *hang*.

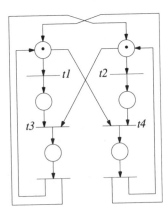

Figure 8.4 — Petri Net with hang state

A token in a Petri Net symbolizes more than the fulfillment of a *condition*, as described above. It also symbolizes a *control flow point* in the program, and it symbolizes a *privilege* to proceed beyond a certain point. A token models a shared resource that can be claimed by more than one transition. All these abstractions symbolize the enforcement of partial orderings on the set of possible execution sequences in the system modeled. Especially relevant to the protocol modeling problem is that mixing these abstractions can make it more difficult than necessary to distinguish computation from communication in a Petri Net model.

The complexity of a Petri Net representation rises rapidly with the size of the problem being modeled. It is virtually impossible to draw a clear net for protocol systems that include more than two or three processes. This makes the Petri Net models relatively weak in modeling power compared to communicating finite state machines, without offering an increase in analytical power. There are, for instance, no standard procedures, other than reachability analysis, to analyze a Petri Net for the presence of hang states. Neither are there standard procedures for simplifying a large Petri Net into one or more smaller, equivalent ones.

One final note on the modeling power of basic Petri Nets. We observed above that the places in a Petri Net can be used to model conditions. It is fairly easy to model logical *and* and *or* tests on places using multiple edges, but there is no general way to model a logical *not*-operation (negation). With a logical *not*-operation it would be possible to define that a transition can fire if a place holds no tokens.

Of course, there are many good applications of Petri Net theory. They have been applied successfully to the study of a range of theoretical problems in parallel computation. For the above pragmatic reasons, however, we conclude that Petri Nets do not give us an advantage in the study of protocol design and validation problems.

FIFO NETS

FIFO Nets are an interesting generalization of Petri Nets and a relatively recent addition to the range of tools proposed for studying distributed systems (see Bibliographic Notes).

A FIFO Net, like a Petri Net, has places, edges, and transitions, but the places contain symbols rather than tokens. The symbols are appended to and reclaimed from the places by transition firings. They are stored by the places in FIFO queues. Both incoming and outgoing edges of transitions are labeled with symbol names. A transition can only fire if the queue of each of its input places can deliver the symbol that corresponds to the edge connecting the transition to that place. Upon firing the labels on the outgoing edges specify which symbols are to be appended to the queues of the corresponding output places.

The generalization of FIFO Nets is strong enough to make them equivalent in computational power to the finite state machines that we defined earlier. Alas, there are no better procedures to analyze FIFO Nets for interesting protocol errors, such as deadlock. In some cases, procedures do exist for restricted versions of FIFO Nets, but again the restrictions generally reduce the modeling power too severely to make them of interest as a general tool for designing or analyzing protocol systems.

8.11 SUMMARY

The formal model of a finite state machine was developed in the early 1950s for the study of problems in computational complexity and, independently, for the study of problems in the design of combinatorial and sequential circuits. There are almost as many variants of the basic model of a finite state machine as there are applications. For the study of protocol design problems we need a formalism in which we can model the primitives of process interactions as succinctly as possible. With this in mind we developed an extended finite state machine model that can directly model message passing and the manipulation of variables. Its semantics are closely linked to the semantics of PROMELA.

There are three main criteria for evaluating the adequacy of formal modeling tools:

○ Modeling power
○ Analytical power
○ Descriptive clarity

The main purpose of the modeling is to obtain a gain in analytical power. It should be easier to analyze the model than it is to analyze the original system being modeled. We have chosen the finite state machine as our basic model. There is a small set of useful properties that can easily be established with a static analysis of finite state machine models. More importantly, however, the manipulation of finite state machines can be automated, and more sophisticated dynamic analysis tools can be developed. We study such tools in Part IV of this book. The descriptive clarity of the finite state machines is debatable. It can well be argued that they trade descriptive clarity for analytical power. By using PROMELA as an intermediate form of an extended finite state machine, however, we can circumvent this problem.

The Turing machine model falls short on all three criteria listed above when applied to the study of protocol problems. In particular, the definition of the ''environment'' is hard to exploit in the modeling of communications. Perhaps even more importantly, many problems of interest, such as absence of deadlock, are intractable for Turing machine models. The model is too powerful for our purpose.

Petri Nets have been used for the study of distributed systems since their inception in the early 1960s. The Petri Net and the FIFO Net have an appealing conceptual simplicity that is mostly based on the graphical representation of the mechanism of process interaction. This advantage in descriptive clarity, however, is lost when the size of the problem exceeds a modest limit. Beyond roughly fifty states per process, the nets become inscrutable. Another, more subtle problem is to distinguish synchronization aspects from the control flow aspects in a Petri Net model. Both are modeled with the same tool: the token. It can be argued that descriptive clarity is traded here for conceptual simplicity. For the modeling of protocol systems this turns out to be an unfortunate trade-off. Protocols of a realistic size typically have many times the numbers of states beyond which a Petri Net becomes unusable. The restrictions of the model imply a loss of modeling power that is not offset by a comparable gain in analytical power.

EXERCISES

8-1 Explain the difference between the dash introduced as a notational convenience in Section 8.2 and the ε introduced in Section 8.3.

8-2 Apply Algorithm 8.1 to Table 8.1.

8-3 Define the rules for the executability of a in Algorithm 8.1, assuming a synchronous instead of asynchronous coupling of machines.

8-4 Change Algorithm 8.3 to combine any number of machines.

8-5 Implement Algorithms 8.1 to 8.3 in your favorite programming language. Invent a syntax for specifying a system of finite state machines. Specify Tables 8.4 and 8.5 in this formalism and use your programs to minimize the corresponding machines, to combine them into one single machine, and to simulate the execution of the resulting description.

8-6 Model the behavior of Tables 8.6 and 8.7 in PROMELA.

8-7 Do the *run* and *chan* operators in PROMELA make the systems modeled unbounded?

8-8 Find an algorithm that detects which message queues from the definition of a communicating finite state machine are only used internally, to store state information, and that removes them from the specification by increasing the number of states.

8-9 (S. Purushothaman) Are two machine states equivalent if one of the two states contains an unexecutable transition that the other state lacks (cf. a receive from an always-empty message queue) ?

8-10 Derive a formal finite state machine description for the example processes A and B on page 173 and show that they are not equivalent.

BIBLIOGRAPHIC NOTES

The theory of finite state machines has a long history and at least parts of it can be found in many computer science text books, e.g., Aho, Hopcroft and Ullman [1974], Aho, Sethi and Ullman [1986]. The original idea of the finite state machine is attributed to McCulloch and Pitts [1943]. Most tightly connected to the theory that was subsequently developed are the names of D.A. Huffman, G.H. Mealy, E.F. Moore and A.M. Turing. The original paper on Turing machines is Turing [1936]. For a more recent discussion see, for instance, Kain [1972]. Huffman's early work on the concept of finite state machines and state equivalence was published in Huffman [1954] and reprinted in Moore [1964]. Edward Moore's first paper on finite state machines is Moore [1956]. In Moore's model the output of a finite state machine depends only on its current state, not on the transition that produced it.

The early papers by Moore are collected in Moore [1964]. George Mealy's original paper, on the finite state machine model can be found in Mealy [1955]. Mealy's model is slightly more general than Moore's. In his model the output of a finite state machine depends on the last transition that was executed, not necessarily on the current state.

For a more general introduction to the basic theory and its application to circuit design, refer to, for instance, Harrison [1965, Hartmanis and Stearns [1966], Kain [1972], Shannon and McCarthy [1956]. The "busy beaver problem" was introduced in Rado [1962] and further studied in Lin and Rado [1965].

The formal model of a finite state machine has been applied to the study of communication protocols since the very first publications, e.g., Bartlett, Scantlebury and Wilkinson [1969]. It has long been the method of choice in almost all formal modeling and validation techniques, cf. Bochmann and Sunshine [1980]. The model was first applied to a protocol validation problem in Zafiropulo [1978]. A very readable introduction the theory of communicating finite state machines can be found in Brand and Zafiropulo [1983].

An excellent overview of various methods for deriving equivalence relations for concurrent processes, and the complexity of the corresponding algorithms, can be found in Kanellakis and Smolka [1990]. The generalization of machines is closely related to the concept of a "protocol projection" that was introduced in Lam and Shankar [1984].

Petri's model was first described in Petri [1962]. See also Agerwala [1975] for a discussion of the Petri Net's modeling power and for some extensions. A discussion of FIFO Nets can be found in Finkel and Rosier [1987]. There are, of course, many other interesting analytical models for concurrent systems. An overview and assessment can be found in, e.g., Holzmann [1979].

CONFORMANCE TESTING 9

9.1 INTRODUCTION

The goals of protocol conformance testing and of protocol validation are easily confused.

☐ A *conformance test* is used to check that the external behavior of a given implementation of a protocol is equivalent to its formal specification.

☐ A *validation* is used to check that the formal specification itself is logically consistent.

If a formal specification has a design error, a faithful implementation of that specification should *pass* a conformance test if and only if it contains the same error. A conformance test should fail only if implementation and specification differ. A consistency validation of the protocol, however, must always reveal the design error. In this chapter we study conformance testing methods. Chapters 11 and 13 are devoted to consistency validation.

Figure 9.1 — Conformance Testing

We are given a known reference specification, for instance in finite state machine format, and an unknown implementation. For all practical purposes, the implementation is a black box with a finite set of inputs and outputs. The only type of experiment we can do with the black box is to provide it with sequences of input signals (messages) and observe the resulting output signals. The implementation under test, commonly referred to as the *IUT*, passes the test only if all observed outputs match those prescribed by the formal specification. A series of input sequences that is used to exercise the protocol implementation in this way is called a *conformance test suite*. The test is derived from the reference specification, ideally by a mechanical procedure (Figure 9.1).

There are two main problems to be solved.

☐ Finding a generally applicable, efficient procedure for generating a conformance test suite for a given protocol implementation.

☐ Finding a method for applying the test suite to a running implementation.

The second problem looks simpler than it is. The IUT may be a single layer in a hierarchy of protocol functions with two interfaces to surrounding layers, as illustrated in Figure 2.12 on page 31. To test this layer we may need both an upper and a lower tester, and some systematic method for coordinating the sequences they generate. Another complicating factor exists when the IUT and the tester are physically separated from each other, as illustrated in Figure 9.2.

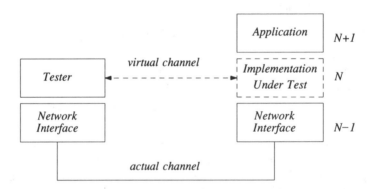

Figure 9.2 — The General Conformance Testing Problem

The tester may only be able to access the IUT via a remote network connection, and may not be able to supply inputs and retrieve outputs from the IUT in a completely reliable manner. In this chapter we discuss only the first problem: the problem of deriving high-quality conformance test sequences.

9.2 FUNCTIONAL TESTING

Protocol conformance testing became an issue when the administrators of the first public data networks had to determine the adequacy of commercial equipment that was to be used on their networks. The problem was to verify the conformance of the equipment to the network standard without having access to the, often proprietary, internal details of the equipment. In the early 1980s, the first attempts to build effective protocol test suites, therefore, had two main goals.

☐ To establish that a given implementation realizes all functions of the original specification, over the full range of parameter values.

☐ To establish that a given implementation can properly reject erroneous inputs in a way that is consistent with the original specification.

An example of a functional test of the first type could be a basic *interconnection test*, meant to establish that the IUT is minimally able to set up and to tear down a standard connection. An example of a test of the second type could be a *format test*, used to verify that the IUT properly rejects violations of the required packet format and violations of the consistency of the packet content (e.g., checksum or byte-count errors).

The problem encountered in these tests is a conflict between complexity and standardization. It is virtually impossible to exhaustively test all possible behaviors of an unknown implementation by simply probing it and observing its responses. There is always a possibility that some untried sequence of probes would reveal a new behavior that is unacceptable. The specific test suite selected for a conformance test of this type, therefore, is always a small selection of the infinite set of all possible test suites. To prevent a manufacturer from rigging a device to pass a given conformance test rather than making it equivalent to the specification proper, the test suites for functional conformance testing cannot be standardized or published.

There is, however, a basic unfairness in requiring a manufacturer to pass a test without making public what the test is, or without standardizing the test in such a way that all competing manufacturers have to submit their equipment to the same test. Ultimately, the complexity of conducting the tests, the difficulty of standardizing them, and the uncertainty of their value has led to a new approach to conformance testing. This new approach has the following purpose.

☐ To establish that the control *structure* of the implementation conforms to the structure of the specification. Implementation and specification have the same structure if they model equivalent sets of states and allow for the same state transitions.

Though a test suite of this type can easily be standardized, there are no methods available yet that will work for protocols of arbitrary complexity, taking into account, for instance, internal variables, message parameter values, and timer settings. Good methods are known only for a restricted class of protocols that can be specified by non-extended finite state machines. The remainder of this chapter is devoted to a discussion of those methods.

9.3 STRUCTURAL TESTING

No data or parameter values are considered in this type of test. Instead, the emphasis is on the control structure of the protocol. Again, probing an unknown device to compare its internal structure with that of a reference specification is generally impossible. We have to make some simplifying assumptions.

1. The IUT models a deterministic finite state machine with a known maximum number of states and with a known input and output vocabulary.

2. The IUT produces a response to an input signal within a known, finite amount of time.

3. The states and the transitions of the IUT form a strongly connected graph: every state in the graph is reachable from every other state in the machine via one or more state transitions.

A *state* of the IUT, for the purposes of this discussion, is defined as a stable condition in which the IUT is waiting for a new input signal. A *transition* is defined as the consumption of an input signal, the possible generation of an output signal, and the possible move to a new state. For a reproducible test result the move must be a deterministic one, which means that the model of a finite state machine that we can use is a subset of the model discussed in Chapter 8. However, since we are discussing concrete implementations rather than abstract designs, the determinism is not likely to be a restriction.

The three properties listed above are requirements. Without them a conformance test of the type to be discussed is not possible. In the remainder we also assume that the IUT corresponds to a completely specified finite state machine.

4. In each state the IUT can accept and respond to all input symbols from the complete system vocabulary. A null response, i.e., a transition back to the same state, is a valid response.

This *completeness assumption* allows us to generalize the algorithms below by removing a special case, but it is not a requirement. In many cases, a conformance test can even be shortened if not all possible input combinations need to be tested.

The IUT can also have properties that can simplify the task of conformance testing itself. Unlike the first three requirements, the following three properties are convenient but not essential.

5. *Status property.* When a "status" message is received, the IUT responds with an output message that uniquely identifies its current state. The IUT does not change state.

6. *Reset property.* When a "reset" message is received, the IUT responds by making a transition to a known initial state, independent of its current state. The IUT need not produce an output.

7. *Set property.* When a "set" message is received in the initial system state, the IUT responds by making a transition to the state that is specified in a parameter of that message. The IUT need not produce an output.

Given a machine with all seven properties listed above, a conformance test can be performed as follows.

ALGORITHM 9.1 — CONFORMANCE TESTING

1. For all possible combinations of a state i and an input signal j, perform the following three steps.

2. Use the *reset* message to bring the IUT to the initial state, and then use the *set* message to transfer the IUT to state i.

3. Apply input signal j. Verify that any output received, including the null output, matches the output required by the specification.

4. Use the *status* message to interrogate the IUT about its final state. Verify that this final state matches the one required by the specification.

The test verifies that the IUT is capable of correctly performing all state transitions in the formal specification. The set of input signals tested should, of course, include the *set*, *reset*, and *status* messages. If the IUT passes these tests, it is *capable* of reproducing the behavior of the formal specification, but it remains unknown if the IUT is capable of any other behavior. Specifically, if the IUT is faulty, it may violate the first requirement for conformance testing that we listed above. The acceptance of an input signal that is outside the official input vocabulary may then cause a transition of the faulty IUT into a set of states that produces erroneous behavior.

Within these constraints, the result of Algorithm 9.1 is the best we can hope to achieve with a conformance test. But is it also the best possible algorithm? The cost of the test can be expressed as the length of the test suite, that is as the total number of messages that is sent to the IUT. Assume that the formal specification contains $S = |Q|$ states and has an input vocabulary of V distinct messages, which includes the set, reset, and status messages. The length of the test suite for Algorithm 9.1 then is

$$4SV$$

After every test the IUT is forced back into the initial state. We can avoid that if we can find a sequence of state transitions that passes through every state and every transition at least once. Such a sequence of transitions is called a *transition tour*. At best such a transition tour starts with a single reset message and exercises every transition exactly once, each time followed by a status message to verify the destination state. A set message is no longer required. The length of the test suite is now minimally

$$1 + 2SV$$

The problem is now to find the minimal transition tour or one that is as close as possible to it. It is a standard problem from graph theory. An *Euler tour* in a directed graph is a sequence of transitions that starts and ends at the same state and contains every transition exactly once. A sufficient condition for the existence of an Euler tour is that the graph (the finite state machine) be both strongly connected and *symmetric*, that is, every vertex (state) must be the destination and the origin of the same number of edges (transitions).

Given a symmetric and strongly connected graph, an Euler tour can be found with a standard procedure that is summarized in Algorithm 9.2. In the first step, the algorithm derives a simple spanning tree of the graph. A spanning tree of a graph contains all its vertices, but only a subset of the edges. In the spanning tree that is constructed in Algorithm 9.2 any vertex can have multiple incoming edges, but is restricted to only one outgoing edge, as illustrated in Figure 9.3. In graph theory, a spanning tree with this property is called a *spanning arborescence*.

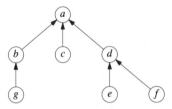

Figure 9.3 — A Spanning Arborescence

Every directed edge represented in the spanning arborescence must be present in the original graph. In Figure 9.3, for instance, there must exist edges in the original graph from vertex b to a, from g to b, and so on. In the second step of Algorithm 9.2, the tree is used to decide in which order edges should be added to the transition tour. Edges in the spanning arborescence are added last.

An edge i in the graph that starts at vertex s is written (s,i). Its destination is written $dest(s,i)$. The set of vertices that are represented in the spanning arborescence is called T. After the first step of Algorithm 9.2 is completed T should equal the set of vertices (states) in the original graph Q.

ALGORITHM 9.2 — DERIVING A TRANSITION TOUR

1. Spanning Arborescence — Choose an arbitrary vertex of the original graph and add it to set T. This vertex will become the root of the spanning arborescence. Next, select an edge (s,i) with $s \notin T$ and $dest(s,i) \in T$ add vertex s and edge (s,i) to the spanning arborescence. Vertex s is added to T. Continue to grow the tree until no more vertices can be added.

2. Transition Tour — Beginning at the vertex that was chosen as the root node of the spanning arborescence, select an outgoing edge and move to the corresponding destination vertex. The lowest priority in the selection of outgoing edges is given to the edges that are part of the spanning arborescence. The other edges can be chosen in arbitrary order. Continue to grow the transition tour until no more edges can be added.

As an example, consider the symmetric graph in Figure 9.4. To identify the edges, we have labeled them with letters. Multiple labels represent multiple edges. There are, for instance, three directed edges from q0 to q2, named *d*, *e*, and *f*.

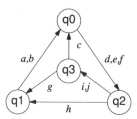

Figure 9.4 — A Symmetric Graph

A spanning arborescence with root q3 could contain, for instance, edges *i*, *d*, and *b*. Using Algorithm 9.2, two different transition tours based on this spanning arborescence are then *c*, *e*, *j*, *g*, *a*, *f*, *h*, *b*, *d*, *i* and *g*, *a*, *f*, *j*, *c*, *e*, *h*, *b*, *d*, *i*.

If the graph we are considering is not symmetric, we must first transform it into a symmetric graph by duplicating edges. Every edge that is duplicated then corresponds to a transition that will be executed more than once in the final transition tour. In graph theory, the duplication is called an *augmentation* of the original graph. Algorithm 9.3 is a simple way to derive such an augmentation (cf. Exercise 9-12).

ALGORITHM 9.3 — GRAPH AUGMENTATION

1. Label every vertex in the graph with an integer that represents the difference between the number of outgoing and incoming edges for that vertex. This number can be positive, zero, or negative. Since, by definition, every edge has both an origin and a destination, the sum of all label values must be zero.

2. Select a vertex *A* with a negative label and a vertex *B* with a positive label. Find the shortest path from *A* to *B* by traversing the fewest number of edges in the *original* graph. Duplicate the edges along this path. Update the labels of *A* and *B*. The labels on the intermediate vertices do not change.

3. If the augmented graph is symmetric the algorithm terminates. The cost of the augmentation is the total number of edges that have been duplicated. If the graph is not symmetric, return to step 2.

Verify, for instance, that the graph in Figure 9.4 is a symmetric augmentation of the state transition diagram in Figure 8.1 (cf. Exercise 9-4).

Step 2 of the algorithm calls for the calculation of the shortest distance between two vertices. A range of algorithms has been studied to solve this problem efficiently. Refer to the Bibliographic Notes at the end of this chapter for an overview. The ultimate cost of the augmentation depends in a subtle way on the choice of vertices that is made in step 2 of Algorithm 9.3. Fortunately, there is only a finite number of ways in which these choices can be made each time step 2 is executed. Therefore, we could try to find the minimum-cost augmentation by exhaustive search. There are, however, better methods. One method is to study graph augmentation as a network flow problem. The problem can then be represented as a *minimum-cost flow* problem, which can be solved in polynomial time (see Bibliographic Notes).

After a symmetric augmentation Algorithm 9.2 can be used to derive a transition tour. For a minimum-cost augmentation, the transition tour produced by Algorithm 9.2 will also be the shortest, and therefore the lowest cost test suite for the IUT. The problem of finding a transition tour in a non-symmetric graph, where every transition is exercised at least once, and possible more than once, is known as the *Chinese Postman Problem*. As indicated above, the problem can be solved in polynomial time.

To derive the test sequence with Algorithms 9.1 we assumed that the IUT has three properties: a reset message, a set message, and a status message. The set message is an oddity that is not likely to be present in many IUTs, but fortunately, in the construction of test sequences based on a transition tour with Algorithm 9.2, we did not need it anymore.

The absence of the *reset* and the *status* messages are more problematic. The reset message can be replaced by a sequence of transitions, called a *homing sequence*, that is known to bring the system back to the initial state, whatever its current state may be. In general, a homing sequence is defined as an adaptive procedure, where the responses generated by the machine can be used to determine what the next input message should be. It can be shown that every strongly connected finite state machine must have such an adaptive homing sequence. Better still, the homing sequence can be derived algorithmically. It can be shown that it need never take more than $S(S-1)/2$ transitions before the machine reaches a known state (see Bibliographic Notes). To reach the initial system state after that point is reached requires between zero and $S-1$ extra transitions. Consider, for example, the machine in Table 9.1.

The machine has two states, so $S=2$ and $S(S-1)/2 = 1$. A sequence of length one can tell us in which state the machine is. It never takes more than $(S-1) + S(S-1)/2 = 2$ inputs to reset the machine to state q0 with certainty.

Table 9.1 − Example

Current State		In	
q0	0	0	q1
q0	1	0	q1
q1	0	1	q0
q1	1	1	q0

A more significant challenge is posed by the omission of the *status* message. The status property is also not likely to be present in an IUT, if it is not needed for the normal operation of the protocol. To replace the status message, we can use a sequence of transitions called a *state signature* or *Unique Input/Output* (UIO) sequence. A UIO sequence can determine whether the IUT is in a given state when the UIO begins. A UIO sequence then has the opposite goal of a homing sequence: it identifies the first instead of the last state in the sequence. To be able to verify every state in the IUT, we must be able to derive a UIO sequence for every state separately.

Not all UIO sequences are necessarily different. In fact, it may be possible to derive a single UIO sequence that can be used to identify any state in a finite state machine. Such a sequence is called a *distinguishing sequence*. The finite state machine that was discussed in Chapter 8 (cf. Figure 8.1) illustrates, however, that not all finite state machines have such a distinguishing sequence. It can also be shown, in much the same way, that not all states have a UIO sequence. In the next two sections we first assume that a UIO sequence can be derived for all states in the specification. We show how these UIO sequences can be used to replace the status messages in a transition tour.

The method discussed below is popular, but it must be remembered that, with the replacement of the status message by a UIO sequence, the fault-detecting power of the transition tour is reduced. The UIO sequences, after all, assume a correct implementation. A faulty machine could in principle fool an observer into believing that a given state has been reached by accidentally generating just the right responses to a precomputed UIO sequence. An alternative method that is not based on UIO sequences is discussed in Section 9.6.

9.4 DERIVING UIO SEQUENCES

In this section we first show how UIO sequences can be derived, assuming that they exist. In the next section we show how the transition tour can be modified to counter the side-effect of the application of UIO sequences.

So far, the best known method to find UIO sequences is to enumerate all possible I/O sequences and to check them for the UIO property. Algorithm 9.4 accomplishes that by building an exponentially expanding tree of I/O sequences. The nodes in the tree at distance N from the root correspond to the I/O sequences of length N. Each node has associated with it two sets of states. The first set, P, contains a partitioning of the set of S states into classes, where S, by definition, is equal to $|Q|$. Two states are in the same class of the partitioning P if and only if they cannot be distinguished from one another by the application of the I/O sequence represented by the node: the specification produces the same outputs under this sequence, no matter which of these states is chosen as an initial state. The members of the second (ordered) set T define for each state in S what the final state will be if the I/O sequence represented by the node were applied with that state as an initial state.

Let $dest(i,j)$ again be the state that the IUT should reach if input j is received while in state i, and let $output(i,j)$ define the output signal that is generated during the transition, if any. Further, let $T[i]$ define the i-th element of set T for the current node, and $T_j[i]$ the i-th element of set T for its j-th successor node.

ALGORITHM 9.4 — UIO DERIVATION

1. Initially, partitioning P consists of a single set that includes all S states of the specification. Set T has S members. The initial value for the i-th member in T, with $1 \leq i \leq S$, is i. The tree of I/O sequences is initialized to a single node, called the root node, which corresponds to the null sequence. Initially, the root node is the only leaf node in the tree. (A leaf node is a node without successors.)

2. Sort the leaf nodes of the tree in a list and delete duplicates. To every leaf node now assign V successor nodes in the tree, one for every possible input signal. Set $T_j[i] = dest(T[i],j)$.

3. The partitioning P_j for the j-th successor node is derived from the current partitioning P as follows. Let set O define the output signals associated with each of the S states for the last transition. Consider each class in P separately. Make a list of all distinct output signals that are generated by the states that are included in the class considered. This class in P is now split into sub-classes in such a way that all states that generated the same output signal are assigned to the same sub-class. If all states within the class considered generated the same output signal for the last input symbol applied, they all remain in the same class of the partitioning.

4. If there is a class in the partitioning of P at this point that contains just one state, the node that holds this partitioning will define a UIO sequence for that state.

5. Steps 2 to 4 are repeated until UIO sequences for all states have been found (or until available memory is exhausted).

This algorithm searches UIO sequences for all states in the specification at the same time. Because it exhaustively checks all possible input sequences, with the shortest sequences being inspected first, it finds the shortest UIO sequences first. The algorithm requires a rapidly growing amount of space to pursue the search for sequences beyond the first few levels. In the worst case the number of nodes in the tree for sequences of length n is

$$\sum_{i=0}^{n} V^i$$

This means that for an input alphabet of ten messages or more it becomes impractical to search for sequences that are longer than five or six steps. The problem of determining if a state has a UIO sequence was proven to be PSPACE hard, and similarly the problem of determining the shortest possible UIO sequence, given that at least one such sequence exists (see Bibliographic Notes). In practice, however, UIO sequences can often be found within the limits of the algorithm.

9.5 MODIFIED TRANSITION TOURS

Next it must be shown how the UIO sequences can be incorporated into a transition tour to construct a conformance test. A problem is that a UIO sequence will in general leave the IUT in a state different from the one that is being verified and thus interferes with the transition tour.

Call the UIO sequence that identifies state i UIO_i, and call its final state $dest(UIO_i)$. For every state i we now augment the graph of the original specification with a "pseudo-transition" for each input symbol j in state i:

$$(i, dest(UIO_{dest(i,j)}))$$

This pseudo-transition consists of the edge traversed for the test of input signal j followed by the verification of the target state, using the UIO sequence for that state. With S states and V input symbols, there are trivially SV pseudo-transitions. The problem of modifying an existing transition tour for the inclusion of UIO sequences, then, is really the problem of finding a new transition tour through the pseudo-transitions only. Call the graph containing only pseudo-transitions the pseudo-graph.

We make a symmetric augmentation of the pseudo-graph and then compute an Euler tour with Algorithm 9.2. For the augmentation we can use Algorithm 9.3, but with one important exception: the calculation of the shortest distance in step 2 is based on the original graph without the pseudo-transitions.

This problem of finding a transition tour through a subset of the edges of a graph (i.e., the pseudo-edges) is known as the *Rural Chinese Postman Problem*.

9.6 AN ALTERNATIVE METHOD

The method based on UIO sequences can be used to produce conformance tests of good quality, but it has some drawbacks. First, not all states in a finite state machine necessarily have a UIO sequence, and even if they do, the UIO sequence may be too long to be derived algorithmically. The problem of deriving UIO sequences is PSPACE-complete, which means that only very short UIO sequences can be found in practice. Second, the UIO sequences can only reliably identify states in a correct IUT. It is unknown, and unknowable, what their behavior is for faulty IUTs. In particular, they cannot guarantee that any type of fault in an IUT remains detectable with the modified transition tours.

If further assumptions can be made about the types of faults in the IUT, the construction of a reliable test is possible, and can be done with a polynomial time algorithm. The main assumption is that no fault can increase the number of reachable states or the number of input signals of the IUT. The method we discuss below is based on the use of *characterizing sequences*.

CHARACTERIZING SEQUENCES

Assume that the original protocol specification corresponds to a minimized finite state machine. For every two states from this machine there exists a finite sequence of inputs that triggers a different sequence of outputs. Such a sequence is called a *characterizing sequence*. It can be shown that every characterizing sequence has a length smaller than S steps, the number of states in the machine. Though there are $S(S-1)/2$ distinct pairs of states in a machine, it is easy to see that no more than $(S-1)$ different characterizing sequences are needed to separate any combination of two states. The $S-1$ characterizing sequences can be selected from the maximal set of $S(S-1)/2$ sequences as follows.

ALGORITHM 9.5 — SELECTING CHARACTERIZING SEQUENCES

1. Select two arbitrary states from the machine and find a sequence that separates them. The different output sequences in response to this sequence can be used to partition the S states into at least two different sets. The sets are blocks in a partitioning of states.

2. Select one of these blocks containing more than one state. Select two states from that block and find a sequence from the original collection that can separate them.

3. The number of state sets (blocks in a partitioning of the states) is increased by at least one extra set for each new characterizing sequence that we find. The procedure, therefore, can be repeated at most $S-1$ times.

At this time each block in the partitioning contains just a single state. For any two states in two different blocks we have now selected a sequence that can separate them. The set of $S-1$ characterizing sequences selected from the original collection can be used to distinguish between any pair of states in the machine.

Let $CS(i,j)$ be the characterizing sequence that distinguishes state i from state j. Let $P(i)$ be a sequence of inputs that leads the machine from the initial state to state i in the reference specification, and let R be the reset message that returns the machine to the initial state. The conformance test can now be performed as follows. The algorithm starts by numbering the states of the finite state machine in breadth-first search order. The numbers are later used to make sure that states that can be reached in the fewest number of transitions from the initial state are tested first.

ALGORITHM 9.6 — CONFORMANCE TESTING

1. Number the states of the machine in breadth-first order. This can be done by constructing a spanning tree of the states. The initial state of the machine becomes the root node of the tree. Initially it is the only leaf in the tree (a node without successors) and it gets the lowest number in the breadth-first search order.

2. To every leaf of the tree we connect all states that can be reached by a single transition in the finite state machine. No state, however, can be added to the tree more than once. The new leafs are numbered consecutively, in arbitrary order. Step 2 is repeated until all states from the machine are represented.

3. The k-th state in breadth-first search order, $1 \leq k \leq S$, is tested with the input sequence.

$$\forall (i), i < k \quad \rightarrow \quad R \ P(i) \ CS(i,k) \ R \ P(k) \ CS(i,k)$$

The test sequence checks that the k-th state can be distinguished from all states with a lower breadth-first search number, i.e., from all states that were checked before. Passing the k-th test in this series shows that the IUT has at least k distinct states and that transitions along the edges of the tree, from the initial state to each one of these states, are correctly implemented.

4. Next, all remaining transitions of the machine must be verified. In general, for every state i and transition j, we must perform the following test

$$R \ P(i) \ j$$

We can skip testing transitions that correspond to edges in the breadth-first search tree; they were already tested in step 3. After the output in response to input j has been verified, the new state that has been reached must again be checked, using the method from step 3, by comparing it systematically against all other states in the specification.

The breadth-first search order guarantees that the paths $P(i)$ are verified one transition at a time. If state i can only be reached from the initial state after passing through some other state j, the search order guarantees that state j is verified first.

The total cost of identifying the S states is $O(S^3)$. The cost of verifying a single transition is $O(S^2)$, and since there are VS transitions the total cost is $O(VS^3)$. The cost, finally, of deriving the characteristic sequences (another standard graph theory problem) is $O(VS^2)$.

This cost of the conformance test, therefore, is still polynomial in S and V, and, unlike the UIO based method, the cost of its construction is also polynomial in S and V. Also, unlike the UIO based method, a conformance test such as this can always be constructed and is guaranteed to detect any fault in the IUT other than those that increase the number of states or input signals. Algorithm 9.6 assumes the existence of a reliable reset message. Yannakakis and Lee have shown that for a machine without a reset message there still exists a polynomial length conformance test with the same fault coverage as Algorithm 9.6 (see Bibliographic Notes). No polynomial time algorithm is known, however, to derive such a test sequence for a reset-less machine.

9.7 SUMMARY

A conformance test is designed to verify whether an unknown implementation of a protocol can be considered to be equivalent to a known specification. The test can never produce an answer that is completely reliable. Only the presence of desirable behavior can be tested for, not the absence of undesirable behavior. It is therefore always possible that an implementation is capable of responses that are not part of the specification.

In principle, there are two approaches to the conformance testing problem. One is a rather *ad hoc* approach where, by trial and error, the correct provision of the main protocol functions is verified for as broad a range of parameter values as possible. For example, if the purpose of the protocol is connection management, we can test randomly chosen sequences for connection setup and tear-down. A second method is to systematically probe the implementation with test sequences to establish whether its internal structure, seen as a finite state machine, conforms to the structure of the specification. Parameter and data values are not considered in this type of test. Instead the focus is on the control structure of the protocol proper. Most of the progress in the development of protocol conformance testing tools has been made with the second type of testing.

Not surprisingly, an effective conformance test can be greatly facilitated if specification and implementation were developed with the feasibility of a test in mind. A systematic conformance test is only possible if the IUT has at least the three properties listed in Section 9.3. A particularly simple algorithm (Algorithm 9.1) can be applied if, in addition, the IUT has a reset, status, and set transition on every state. The hard work in conformance testing comes when one or more of the desirable properties are missing.

Without the set property, the best method is to find a transition tour of all states using Algorithms 9.2 and 9.3, testing the response of the IUT to all possible input signals. A status message can be replaced by a test sequence, called a UIO sequence, that can similarly reveal the state of the machine. Algorithm 9.4 can be used to derive these UIO sequences. The main problem to be solved here is that the UIO sequences disturb the state of the IUT when they are applied. Section 9.5 shows how a transition tour can be constructed that avoids this problem.

An alternative method, that also avoids the use of status and set messages is discussed in Section 9.6. All methods discussed can fail when an implementation error in the IUT increases the number of reachable states or the number of input signals. In the absence of such errors, the conformance testing sequence produced by Algorithm 9.6 can guarantee the detection of all faults. The length of the test sequence, however, can be considerably larger than the one based on UIO sequences.

EXERCISES

9-1 Explain in detail why it is essential that each of the first three requirements on the structure of an IUT be fulfilled for a conformance test to be feasible.

9-2 Is it necessary that the finite state machine modeled by the IUT has been minimized?

9-3 How will the algorithms in this chapter have to be changed for incompletely specified finite state machines?

9-4 Is the symmetric augmentation of Figure 8.1 shown in Figure 9.4 unique. If not, is it an augmentation with the lowest cost?

9-5 Can a conformance test detect whether the IUT has more states than the formal specification? Fewer states?

9-6 Can the fault coverage of a conformance test ever reach 100%?

9-7 Explain the difference between a distinguishing sequence, a homing sequence, a characterizing sequence, and a UIO sequence.

9-8 How would the fault coverage of a conformance test be affected if the application of a status message, or its equivalent, were deleted from a transition tour?

9-9 Write an algorithm for finding homing sequences.

9-10 Write an algorithm for finding characterizing sequences.

9-11 How does the cost of the above two algorithms (the number of operations to be performed in the worst case) depend on the number of edges and vertices in the graph? Can you derive upper bounds?

BIBLIOGRAPHIC NOTES

Conformance testing methods are of interest to all protocol users who want to assess the quality of protocol implementations. They are also of interest to international standardization bodies, who aim to provide a neutral third party certification of protocols and protocol implementation. Organizations such as the ISO and the CCITT are in the process of developing standards and guidelines for the certification of protocols meant to comply with, for instance, the reference model for Open Systems Interconnection discussed in Chapter 2, Rayner [1987].

The general conformance testing problem, i.e., the problem of testing implementations of arbitrary extended finite state machines, using remote testers across a data network, is an active research area. Progress is reported in the yearly IFIP Working Group 6.1 Symposia on Protocol Specification, Testing and Verification, IFIP [1982-present]. An excellent overview of the general problem can be found in Rayner [1987]. Work is also underway to standardize a notation for conformance test suites, named the *Tree and Tabular Combined Notation* or TTCN, see ISO [1987].

One of the first efforts to develop an independent center for the assessment and certification of protocol implementations was begun by the National Physical Laboratory (NPL) in England, in the early 1980s, Rayner [1982, 1987]. In the U.S.A., this work was undertaken by the National Institute of Science and Technology (NIST, formerly the National Bureau of Standards or NBS), Nightingale [1982]. An overview of other test and certification centers is given in Wang and Hutchinson [1987].

Two issues complicate the work of the certification centers. First, the certification centers should be able to perform remote testing of implementations, across a trusted data network. Second, the certification tests sometimes have to be applied to a single protocol layer in a hierarchy of otherwise trusted layers.

The certification centers have concentrated mainly on service, or functional, conformance testing. Structural testing, as described here, is a more recent development. The conformance testing work we have described is based on both finite state machine theory and on graph theory. The concept of a test sequence was studied as early as 1956 by E.F. Moore in one of his first papers on finite state machines, Moore [1956]. Moore was also the first to define homing sequences and distinguishing sequences. The concept of a distinguishing sequence was further developed in Gill [1962] and in Hennie [1964]. Huffman independently studied problems similar to those in Moore [1956]. His results can be found in Huffman [1964]. A complete discussion of homing sequences and characterizing sequences can be found in Kohavi [1978].

Naito [1981] and Sarikaya [1984] were among the first to study systematic protocol test generation techniques using transition tours. The concept of a UIO sequence, was introduced in Hsieh [1971], and was discussed in Friedman and Menon [1971]. Independently it was also discovered by Gobershtein [1974]. K.K. Sabnani and A.T. Dahbura [1985, 1988] rediscovered the principle and applied it to the conformance testing problem. The term UIO sequence was coined by them. Hsieh used the term *simple I/O* sequence; Gobershtein used *check word*. Yannakakis and Lee [1990] introduced the term *state signature*.

A method to reduce the length of a conformance test sequence by computing multiple UIO sequences per state is described in Shen and Lombardi [1989].

COMPLEXITY

The problem of finding the minimum length transition tour of a finite state machine, described for instance in Klee [1980], can be solved in polynomial time. Algorithm 9.2 comes from Edmonds and Johnson [1973] and was applied to the conformance testing problem in Uyar and Dahbura [1986]. A symmetric augmentation of a graph can also be found in polynomial time with network flow algorithms. An Euler tour can be found in a time that is linear in the number of transitions in the symmetric graph. The corresponding algorithm can be found in Edmonds and Johnson [1973].

The problem of finding a transition tour through a subset of the transitions in a graph, for instance the pseudo-transitions corresponding to UIO sequences in a modified transition tour, can be shown to be NP-complete. If, however, the graph consisting of pseudo-transitions is weakly connected, the problem reduces to one that can be solved in polynomial time, as shown in Aho, Dahbura, Lee and Uyar [1988]. Efficient algorithms for the derivation of transition tours for restricted classes of finite state machines are studied in Edmonds and Johnson [1973]. The algorithms were first applied to protocol conformance testing in Uyar and Dahbura

[1986] and extended in Aho, Dahbura, Lee and Uyar [1988]. The Chinese Postman Problem was first described by the Chinese mathematician M-K. Kuan [1962].

In general, the cost of traversing a transition in the finite state machine machine can be given by a real number. A well-known algorithm for finding the shortest distance (i.e., lowest cost path) between two vertices in a graph, given those constraints, is Dijkstra's shortest path algorithm, e.g., Dijkstra [1959], Aho [1974], Price [1971]. There are, however, also faster methods, see for instance Tarjan [1983]. In conformance testing it is often possible to associate simply a unit cost with the traversal of all transitions. In this case, the best algorithm for finding shortest paths is breadth-first search.

Efficient solutions to minimum-cost — maximum-flow problems are also discussed in detail in Tarjan [1983] and Gibbons [1985]. An overview can be found in Aho, Dahbura, Lee and Uyar [1988].

Algorithm 9.6, and the analysis of its complexity, was described in Yannakakis and Lee [1990]. It is similar to the W-method from Chow [1978]. A proof of the PSPACE hardness of the UIO derivation problem can also be found in Yannakakis and Lee [1990].

An issue not discussed here is the problem of estimating the quality or fault coverage of a conformance test. Note that, despite the first three requirements from Section 9.3, a faulty IUT may well have more states or more inputs than our reference specification. In Vasilevskii [1973] it was shown that a checking sequence becomes inherently exponential if faults increase the number of states. The machine may also have nondeterministic responses, or it may not be strongly connected, as required. There is always an infinite number of such implementations that can pass a given conformance test without being equivalent to the reference specification. In theory, therefore, the fault coverage of every conformance test of the type we have described must approach zero. Yet, the relative fault coverage of individual conformance test methods may well differ. Empirical methods to measure such differences are illustrated in Dahbura and Sabnani [1988] and Sidhu and Leung [1989]. By randomly modifying transitions in a finite state machine description of the IUT it can be measured what percentage of this restricted class of errors is caught by a conformance testing method. As yet, however, such tests have only been used successfully to confirm results that can also be proven theoretically.

Not discussed in this chapter are two alternative methods for conformance testing that have been explored. The W-method was introduced in Vasilevskii [1973] and elaborated in Chow [1978]. The method is also explained in Shih and Sidhu [1986]. The second method is based on the use of grammars to generate test sequences and was explored in Linn and McCoy [1983], and Probert and Ural [1983]. A general overview of test methods is given in Sidhu [1990]. An interesting formal study of the conformance testing problem is described in Brinksma et al. [1989].

PROTOCOL SYNTHESIS   **10**

10.1 INTRODUCTION

One of the toughest open problems in protocol design is finding a discipline of programming that can guarantee *a priori* the derivation of a functionally correct protocol that is free of dynamic errors such as deadlock. A proper design discipline will lead to a smaller and more effective product that is easier to maintain and modify. As yet, little progress has been made in this area. This chapter is therefore necessarily tentative.

We briefly discuss three methods for interactively building correct protocol specifications. The first two of these methods focus on the functionality of a protocol design; the third emphasizes structure.

Bear in mind that a protocol synthesis method cannot synthesize service specifications. No automated tool can determine the purpose of a new protocol. The design problem is to find a protocol that (1) realizes a *given* service, and (2) does so in an error-free manner. All three methods discussed below assume that a service specification exists, either in a formalized form or informally in the mind of the user of the synthesis tool.

In the next section we illustrate a protocol derivation method that allows us to synthesize the protocol components from a formal specification. We do this by formalizing the service specification in such a way that a skeleton structure for the protocol procedure rules of each communicating process can be extracted from it. The synthesized processes can then be fine-tuned manually.

10.2 PROTOCOL DERIVATION

In protocol validation we may want verify assertions that the user makes about the structure of possible dialogues between processes. A dialogue is a sequence of message exchanges that can be observed at a given interface, e.g., a set of channels.

Consider the problem of designing a connection management protocol.

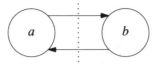

Figure 10.1 — Interface

There are two processes, *a* and *b*, that share access to a full-duplex data link, indicated with two arrows in Figure 10.1. Processes *a* and *b* have to coordinate the beginning and the ending of data transfers across the link.

Typically, the designer is asked to supply two process specifications, one for each side of the connection, in an attempt to constrain the possible dialogues to a well-defined set. An assertion about these constraints can be formalized and verified by an automated protocol validator. In protocol synthesis we can try to turn this problem around by beginning with a specification of the set of allowable dialogues and deriving the processes from them so that, by construction, these processes will be unable to exhibit any other than the stated behavior.

We provide a specification for two processes. Either side can initiate a connection; if both processes try to do so at the same time the attempt fails. The behavior can be specified as a six-state machine, as follows, in an informal notation resembling PROMELA. The notation a->b informally encodes the direction in which a message flows.

```
spec manager
{
idle:
        if
        :: b->a!connect -> goto b_opens
        :: a->b!connect -> goto a_opens
        fi;
a_opens:
        if
        :: b->a!accept -> goto connected
        :: b->a!connect -> goto idle    /* conflict */
        fi;
b_opens:
        if
        :: a->b!accept -> goto connected
        :: a->b!connect -> goto idle    /* conflict */
        fi;
connected:
        if
        :: b->a!disconnect -> goto b_closes
        :: a->b!disconnect -> goto a_closes
        fi;
```

```
a_closes:
        b->a!disconnect -> goto idle;
b_closes:
        a->b!disconnect -> goto idle
}
```

This specification describes the message exchanges that are visible at the interface between *a* and *b*, i.e., at the dotted line in Figure 10.1. There may be other messages that are handled by *a* or *b*, and there may be many other tests and data manipulations to be performed. The above specification is therefore partial.

Some of the messages are to be sent by process *a* and some are to be received by *a*. We can derive a skeleton process description from the specification that describes precisely the constraints for process *a*. Mechanically, we can then derive the following state machine for process *a*. We can say it is the derivative of specification *manager* with respect to *a*.

```
proctype D_manager_D_a()
{
R0:     if
        :: b!connect -> goto R1
        :: a?connect -> goto R2
        fi;
R1:     if
        :: a?connect -> goto R0
        :: a?accept -> goto R3
        fi;
R2:     if
        :: b!connect -> goto R0
        :: b!accept -> goto R3
        fi;
R3:     if
        :: b!disconnect -> goto R4
        :: a?disconnect -> goto R5
        fi;
R4:     a?disconnect -> goto R0;
R5:     b!disconnect -> goto R0
}
```

The state machine for process *b* is similar, since the protocol specification is symmetric. The derivation is trivial in this case and can easily done by hand. In general, though, the derivation is more subtle.

Consider the following example that describes the behavior of a simple alternating bit protocol. The interface is the same as shown in Figure 10.1. The specification for the messages that cross the interface at the dotted line, however, is now formalized as follows.

```
spec abp
{       do
        :: a->b!msg0;
```

```
            do
            :: b->a!ack0; break
            :: b->a!ack1; a->b!msg0
            od;
        a->b!msg1;
            do
            :: b->a!ack0; a->b!msg1
            :: b->a!ack1; break
            od
    od
}
```

This single specification completely describes the behavior of two protocol machines, the sender *a* and the receiver *b*. The two derivations produce the following results.

```
proctype D_abp_D_a()
{
R0:     b!msg0 -> goto R1;
R1:     if
        :: a?ack0 -> goto R2
        :: a?ack1 -> goto R0
        fi;
R2:
        b!msg1 -> goto R1
}
proctype D_abp_D_b()
{
R0:     b?msg0 -> goto R1;
R1:     if
        :: a!ack0 -> goto R2
        :: a!ack1 -> goto R0
        fi;
R2:     b?msg1 -> goto R1
}
```

According to this specification the wrong acknowledgment may be repeated by the receiver and will be ignored by the sender. As a result, the skeleton state machine for *b* includes behavior that is permissible, but not desirable. To avoid this, we must rewrite the derived process, manually, as follows, splitting state R1 into two halves:

```
proctype D_abp_D_b()
{
R0:     b?msg0 -> goto R11;
R11:    if
        :: a!ack0 -> goto R2
        fi;
R12:    if
        :: a!ack1 -> goto R0
        fi;
R2:     b?msg1 -> goto R12
}
```

which can be simplified via

```
proctype D_abp_D_b()
{
R0:      b?msg0 -> goto R11;
R11:     a!ack0 -> goto R2;
R12:     a!ack1 -> goto R0;
R2:      b?msg1 -> goto R12
}
```

to its final form:

```
proctype D_abp_D_b()
{
R0:      b?msg0 -> a!ack0;
         b?msg1 -> a!ack1;
         goto R0
}
```

Now let us see how the derivation is affected if we expand the specification with a message to a third process *c* that logs all correctly transmitted and acknowledged messages with sequence number zero.

```
spec abp2
{
        do
        :: a->b!msg0;
                do
                :: b->a!ack0; a->c!log; break
                :: b->a!ack1; a->b!msg0
                od;
                a->b!msg1;
                do
                :: b->a!ack0; a->b!msg1
                :: b->a!ack1; break
                od
        od
}
```

The derivative of the specification for *c* is simply

```
proctype D_abp2_D_c()
{
R0:      c?log -> goto R0
}
```

The derivative for *b* remains unchanged, but the derivative for *a* becomes

```
proctype D_abp2_D_a()
{
R0:      b!msg0 -> goto R1;
R1:      if
         :: a?ack0 -> goto R2
         :: a?ack1 -> goto R0
         fi;
```

```
    R2:        c!log -> goto R3;
    R3:        b!msg1 -> goto R4;
    R4:        if
               :: a?ack0 -> goto R3
               :: a?ack1 -> goto R0
               fi

    }
```

10.3 DERIVATION ALGORITHM

The skeleton machine can be derived from a specification in two steps. First, if we derive a machine for process p, all messages in the specification that are not either sent or received by p are replaced by skip. Next, all specifications of the type

```
        q->p!message
```

are translated into

```
        p?message
```

and, similarly, all specifications

```
        p->q!message
```

become

```
        q!message
```

The last step is to handle cases such as these

```
    R0:        if
               :: p?message0 -> goto R1
               :: skip -> goto R2
               fi
```

where the skip was inserted in the first step. In this case, an event outside the derived process can make the system change state, presumably changing the future behavior of the environment of the derived process. The derived process does not, and cannot, know when or if this invisible transition takes place. It must, however, be capable of accepting any incoming messages that may arrive after the invisible transition takes place. Therefore, for the above example, state R0 of the derived process *inherits* all receive operations from state R2, together with the corresponding transitions.

If state R2 is specified

```
    R2:        p?message1 -> goto R3
```

the new state R0 becomes

```
    R0:        if
               :: p?message0 -> goto R1
               :: p?message1 -> goto R3
               fi
```

If state R2 offers a choice

```
R2:     if
        :: p?message1 -> goto R3
        :: q!message2 -> goto R0
        :: p?message3 -> goto R0
        fi
```

we inherit only the receive operations and write

```
R0:     if
        :: p?message0 -> goto R1
        :: p?message1 -> goto R3
        :: p?message3 -> goto R0
        fi
```

The only remaining possibility is if state R2 specifies only a send operation:

```
R2:     q!message2 -> goto R0
```

In this case the `skip` transition is omitted, and we write

```
R0:     if
        :: p?message0 -> goto R1
        fi
```

which simplifies to

```
R0:     p?message0 -> goto R1
```

This last case may be flagged as a potential inconsistency in the specification. The specification in this case requires a process to wait for an event that it cannot observe.

The last derivation step above is repeated until all the "hidden" transitions have been removed. Note that if the target state R2 has its own `skip` transitions the last derivation step may require the inspection of still more states.

```
R2:     if
        :: p?message1 -> goto R3
        :: skip -> goto R0
        :: skip -> goto R4
        fi
```

The derivation algorithm can produce skeleton state machines for the target processes that adhere to the constraints of the specification. It illustrates one of the purposes of a protocol synthesis procedure: offering automated assistance to a protocol designer. The designer can concentrate on defining just one central item: the protocol specification itself.

Unfortunately, this design procedure gives no guarantee that the interaction of the derived processes will not lead to dynamic errors, such as deadlocks. Concentrating on that aspect of the design problem leads to a different type of design procedure, which we discuss next.

10.4 INCREMENTAL DESIGN

The following design method, originally published in 1980, is often used as a guideline for attempts to build protocol synthesis procedures. The procedure is interactive, and assumes the existence of an independent service specification that the designer will follow while developing the protocol processes.

The user specifies only message transmissions. The system deduces where in the protocol the corresponding receive actions are required. Initially, all processes, i.e., the "skeleton state machines" from the first method, are assigned a dummy initial state. The designer can now select one of the states in the system and extend it with a message transmission. The designer must specify the name of the message, its parameters, and its destination. For the process that is to transmit the message, the designer must also specify a successor state for the send action: either an existing or a newly created process state.

For each transmission edge added to one of the processes in this way, the synthesis software traces all possible states of the destination process in which the message can be received, and updates the state machine for that process automatically. The user has to name the successor states for all message receptions events that are added.

After each update, the incremental design procedure can warn the designer which *stable state tuples* have been created. A stable state tuple is defined as a composite system state in which no messages are in transit or stored in buffers. If such a composite system state is reachable, the state must persist until one of the processes sends a message. If none of the processes can transmit a message, the reachable stable state tuple corresponds to a deadlock.

The designer in this method can only specify send actions. The place where the corresponding receive actions are required is deduced by the synthesis software. This avoids unspecified receptions and certain types of deadlock, but it cannot guarantee the *functional* correctness of the protocol. That is, the synthesis method cannot guarantee that a protocol synthesized in this way will realize a given service.

10.5 PLACE SYNCHRONIZATION

The third approach can be considered a compromise between the first two methods discussed above. This method starts with a service specification written as a regular expression of synchronization requirements. The symbols in the service expression are the names of service primitives. The operators of the expression determine how the execution of these primitives is to be synchronized. In the expression

$$a^1 ; (b^2 \| c^3) \tag{1}$$

the superscripts denote service access points, the physical places where the service primitives are executed. The semicolon is used to indicate a sequential execution:

the execution of service primitive a, at the place represented by 1, must have been completed before the primitives b or c can be executed at places 2 or 3, respectively. The parallel bars are used to indicate that the two subexpressions can be executed simultaneously. Parentheses are used for grouping. A single bar between two subexpressions implies alternation, either one of the two subexpressions can be executed, but not both.

To enforce the synchronization requirements formalized in the service expression, the synthesis algorithm can derive a protocol that controls the execution of the service primitives. The sequential execution in expression (1), for instance, can be enforced by having the first primitive a^1 complete by transmitting a unique message from place 1 to places 2 and 3, and by delaying the execution of primitives b^2 and c^3 until that message has arrived.

The synthesis method is appealing, but it also has drawbacks. The method can derive protocols for only a limited class of global synchronization requirements. Not all protocol specifications can easily be expressed in those terms. Consider a reader/writer protocol for a data base shared between multiple processes. One method to secure the integrity of the data is to allow multiple readers to be active, but to allow access to at most one writer process at a time, and then only when no reader processes are active.

If a reader process i, requiring access to item n, is represented by the symbol r^{n_i}, and the corresponding writer process is represented by w^{n_i}, the design problem is now to write a regular expression on these symbols, using the operators ;, ||, and |. To properly describe the solution, we must count the number of active processes of each type and express the synchronization requirement as conditions on those counts. But the regular expression does not allow us to do that. If a synchronizing expression can be found, it may not be easier to find it than to invent the final protocol directly.

10.6 SUMMARY

An ideal method for protocol design would be to build a model from scratch that can be proven correct by construction. No such method exists, although many interesting attempts have been made. In this chapter we have given an overview of three such attempts. The first method allows one to extract skeleton state machines from a single, formalized statement of a correctness requirement. The method has drawbacks, the most important of which are:

☐ The method does not provide any help in the correct formalization of the protocol specification itself.

☐ The derived processes must, in some cases, be tuned to remove permissible but undesirable behavior. The method offers no help here, nor can it help us to verify that the alterations preserve the correctness of the derivations.

The second method interactively guides the protocol designer to a complete design and issues warnings on potential deadlocks. The most important drawbacks of this approach are:

☐ The method does not guarantee that the protocol constructed realizes a given service.

☐ The method does not guarantee absence of dynamic errors such as deadlocks. It can only warn for the possibility of a deadlock. When the number of possible deadlock states rises, as it does in a design of a realistic size, it quickly becomes impossible for a human designer to verify manually that all potential deadlock states are effectively unreachable.

The third method derives protocols from concise expressions of global synchronization requirements. Its main drawback is:

☐ Only a restricted class of protocol design problems can be expressed in the regular expression language on which the method is based.

All three methods share one other drawback that is perhaps of even greater importance: they do not really seem to facilitate the design process.

EXERCISES

10-1 Try to derive Lynch's protocol (Chapter 2) and parts of the file server protocol (Chapter 7) with a protocol synthesis method.

10-2 Some protocol synthesis methods that have been described in the literature guarantee "correctness by construction" with the help of an exhaustive reachability analysis algorithm that is run over partial specifications during the design. Consider the possible drawbacks of this method.

10-3 Compare the place synchronization method with the protocol derivation method. Both start out with an abstract "service specification" from which a protocol is derived. How do the two types of service specifications differ? Do they have the same expressive power?

10-4 Develop a workable protocol synthesis method and mail the solution to the author for the next edition of this book.

BIBLIOGRAPHIC NOTES

This chapter has given only a brief overview of synthesis methodologies since, alas, none exist that can adequately solve the protocol design problem.

The best known method for protocol synthesis is the incremental method from Section 10.4. It was first described in Brand and Zafiropulo [1980]. The method has many variations and has even been applied in protocol validation algorithms. The place synchronization method from Section 10.5 is a formal method to derive parts of a lower-level protocol from a higher-level service specification. The method is fully developed in Gotzheim and Bochmann [1986]. A variant can also be found in Chu and Liu [1988].

The derivation method from Section 10.2 can be seen as an extension of earlier work on methods to derive the description of a protocol entity from a specification of its communication partner, see Zafiropulo et al. [1980], Gouda [1983], Merlin and Bochmann [1983].

Not studied here is a potentially interesting, recent application of control theory to the protocol synthesis problem that was reported in Rudie and Wonham [1990]. In this approach, the original protocol system is first described as an uncontrolled process in which all feasible actions, such as message transfers, happen chaotically. A high-level service specification details the constraints for the system. Assuming that the process contains a sufficient number of control points, a protocol can then be derived as a minimal restriction of the chaotic process behavior that satisfies the system constraints.

Several methods have also been studied for partitioning a sequential program into a distributed program, preserving functionality and correctness, e.g., Moitra [1985, Prinoth [1982]. These algorithms require an initial solution to the problem, through the derivation of a sequential program, before the synthesis method itself can be applied.

A general overview of protocol synthesis methods can be found in Chu [1989].

PROTOCOL VALIDATION 11

11.1 INTRODUCTION

In Chapter 9 we studied the problem of checking that the implementation of a protocol conforms to a formal specification. We now discuss the problem of verifying the logical consistency of the formal specification itself, independent of an implementation. For consistency we assume that the specification is formalized as a validation model in PROMELA, although this is not essential to many of the algorithms we discuss. We first describe a manual proof method based on the notion of state invariants only. We then show how the same principle can be used to build an automated validation system. Finally, we extend the algorithms to support also the verification of the other correctness requirements that can be expressed in PROMELA (see Chapter 6).

Most automated validation systems are based on exhaustive reachability analysis. To establish the observance of state invariants, then, it suffices to verify their correctness with a simple boolean test for each state that is reachable from a given initial system state. The main problem that must be addressed in the design of such a system is the "state space explosion problem." For protocols of a realistic size, the number of reachable system states is usually too large for purely exhaustive analyses. We discuss the nature of this problem and some of the counter-strategies that have been developed.

11.2 A MANUAL PROOF METHOD

Consider a simple transmission system with a sender S and a receiver R. Process S sends messages to process R over an unreliable transmission medium that can lose but not insert, reorder, or distort messages. Every message transmitted carries a sequence number. Initially, this number is zero, and it is incremented by one for every new message transmitted. It can grow arbitrarily large. The receiver acknowledges the receipt of messages by echoing the sequence numbers over a similarly unreliable return channel. The receiver stores the largest sequence number it has received in a local variable B. The sender tries to keep track of that number by maintaining a count in a local variable A. The value of A is equal to the largest sequence number that the sender can be certain R has received. Initially, we have

$$A = B = 0$$

In the following we assume that sender and receiver simply exchange sequence numbers and no other data. The protocol is then defined by four atomic operations, two in each process. They can be formalized in PROMELA as follows, where for the time being we will pretend that data of the type int have unbounded range. W is an arbitrary positive constant.

```
mtype = { mesg, ack }
proctype S()
{       int A;
        do
        :: R!mesg(A + rand()%W)          /* S1 */
        :: S?ack(A)                      /* S2 */
        od
}
proctype R()
{       int B, b;
        do
        :: S!ack(B)                      /* R1 */
        :: atomic {                      /* R2 */
                R?mesg(b);
                B = fct(b,B);
           }
        od
}
```

Transition R2 consists of two statements that are, at least conceptually, executed in one indivisible step. In the first step a new message is received. In the second step a new value for B is obtained via a function fct(). The function records the reception of a message numbered b and returns a value $X \geq B$ for which it can guarantee that all messages with numbers smaller than X were recorded by fct() before. It could accomplish this, for instance, by setting

```
if
:: (b == B+1) -> B = b
:: (b != B+1) -> skip
fi
```

forcing messages to be received in sequence, but it could also be more liberal (see Chapter 4).

Assuming that there are r messages in queue R and s acknowledgments in S, with

$$r \geq 0 \quad \text{and} \quad s \geq 0$$

the following condition holds invariantly for the acknowledgments that are buffered in S:

$$A \leq S[1] \leq S[2] \leq \cdots \leq S[s] \leq B \tag{1}$$

The correctness of this system invariant is proven by induction. First notice that in the initial state the channels are empty and the invariant reduces to $A \leq B$, which holds trivially since $A = B = 0$. Next observe that if the invariant holds in an arbitrary system state it must hold in all its successor states, since it cannot be invalidated by the four atomic operations:

☐ S1 does not change any of the variables in (1).
☐ S2 transforms (1) into

$$A = S[1] \leq S[2] \leq \cdots \leq S[s] \leq B$$

which must hold if (1) holds.

☐ R1, assuming that the acknowledgment is not lost, transforms (1) into

$$A \leq S[1] \leq S[2] \leq \cdots \leq S[s] \leq S[s+1] = B$$

which also must hold if (1) held before R1 was executed.

☐ R2 can increase, but never decrease, the value of B, and thus cannot invalidate the invariant either.

Together, this proves the validity of invariant (1). The next invariant applies to the r messages waiting in queue R:

$$R[i] < R[j] + W, \quad \text{for} \quad 0 \leq i \leq r \text{ and } i < j \leq r+1 \tag{2}$$

where, for convenience, we define

$$R[0] = B \quad \text{and} \quad R[r+1] = A$$

In the initial state, with $r = 0$, the queue is empty, and the invariant becomes $B < A + W$ which trivially holds for all $W > 0$, since $A = B = 0$. We must check again that the correctness of the invariant is unaffected by the four atomic operations.

☐ S1 can add an element $r+1$ to queue R (if the message is not lost):

$$A \leq R[r+1] < A + W \tag{2a}$$

and then increment r. There are only two cases to consider where the invariant could now be violated: $i = r$ and $j = r$. For $i = r$, invariant (2) states

$$R[r] < R[r+1] + W$$

By definition, this means

$$R[r] \ < \ A + W$$

which (2a) clearly cannot violate. For $j = r$, invariant (2) states

$$R[i] \ < \ R[r] + W, \quad \text{for} \quad 0 \leq i < r$$

Since (2a) guarantees that $R[r] \geq A$, after S1 completes, this reduces to

$$R[i] \ < \ A + W, \quad \text{for} \quad 0 \leq i < r$$

which must hold if it held before S1 was executed.

☐ S2 can only increase the value of A, as a direct result of (1).

☐ R1 does not change any of the variables in (2).

☐ R2 deletes a message from the queue, thus removing one of the conditions from the invariant. Either it has no effect or it sets $R[0] = R[1]$, which also cannot disturb the correctness of (2).

This completes the proof of invariant (2).

THE WINDOW PROTOCOL INVARIANT

Invariants (1) and (2) can be used to prove a more general property of the window protocol.

$$B - W \ \leq \ R[i] < B + W \quad \text{for} \quad 1 \leq i \leq r \tag{3}$$

☐ To prove this, first note that by invariant (2) we have

$$R[i] \ < \ A + W \quad \text{for} \quad 1 \leq i \leq r$$

Since by invariant (1) we also have $A \leq B$ the right side of (3) is easily proven.

☐ Second, by invariant (2) we have

$$B \ < \ A + W \quad \text{or} \quad B - W \ < \ A$$

Since by invariant (1) we also have $A \ \leq \ R[i]$ the left side of (3) is also proven.

Invariant (3) implies that the receiver can deduce the true value of a message (i.e., its sequence number) even if only part of the value is transmitted, for instance the value modulo $2W$. It is an elegant demonstration that the selective repeat ARQ protocol, discussed in Chapter 4, needs a range of sequence numbers that is twice the window size W.

DISCUSSION OF MANUAL PROOFS

The proof technique we have discussed was first described by Stein Krogdahl and later refined by Donald Knuth. It is based on the notion of state invariants. Unlike the methods used in most automated validation systems, this method is not based on the inspection of reachable system states, but on the inspection of state transitions. There are usually far fewer state transitions than reachable system states. The example system illustrates this nicely: since the sequence numbers are unbounded, the number of reachable system states is infinite, but the number of state transitions is restricted to four. The effort required to verify that a transition cannot invalidate an arbitrary system invariant, however, can be substantial.

In independent work, Mohamed Gouda (see Bibliographic Notes) has argued that all manual proofs can be build on just two basic notions:

- ○ System invariants, and
- ○ Well-founded formulas

A well-founded formula can be used, for instance, to prove termination or to build induction proofs. To construct such a proof we must find a quantity that is inevitably decreased during the lifetime of the program and that forces a desirable outcome of the program when it reaches a minimum. To find the right invariants and well-founded formulas can be hard. In general, the manual proofs must be structured carefully, requiring the user to find and to prove a series of intermediate invariants before the correctness of a more general property can be demonstrated. The advantage of this approach is that it forces the user to thoroughly understand both the design problem and the suggested solution.

This advantage, however, can turn into a disadvantage when the method is applied to larger problems. The manual proofs can be tedious, and they are inevitably susceptible to human error, much like the protocol design that is the subject of the proof. For each invariant that is to be proven the method may require a manual inspection of all atomic state transitions within the system. The manual techniques break down in cases where validation is needed most, i.e., for larger protocols. We accept here, therefore, that there is a need for automatic tools to help us either in constructing proofs, or in finding counter-examples to correctness claims (a euphemism for ''debugging''). After all, even a proof is not a proof unless its validity can be checked. To quote Lamport [1977]:

> ''A formal proof is one which is sufficiently detailed, and carried out in a sufficiently
> precise formal system, so that it can be checked by a computer.''

Although there is no simple algorithm that could automate the manual proof methods we have discussed, there is, at least for finite state systems, an alternative. The alternative becomes possible if we base our proof method directly on reachable system states, rather than indirectly on the transitions that connect them. Methods of this type can be used to validate both properties of states and properties of sequences of states, as discussed in Chapter 6. The remainder of this chapter is devoted to a discussion of these methods.

11.3 AUTOMATED VALIDATION METHODS

Let us look at the general structure of automated validation systems based on reachability analysis. Initially, we will consider only the validation of state properties, such as assertion violations and improper terminations. We discuss in some detail the limitations of the reachability analysis methods and the strategies that have been developed to exploit them. In later sections we show how the method can be extended to validate properties of sequences of states, such as non-progress conditions and temporal claims, as discussed in Chapter 6.

REACHABILITY ANALYSIS ALGORITHMS

A reachability analysis algorithm tries to generate and inspect all the states of a distributed system that are reachable from a given initial state. Implicitly, it will construct all possible execution sequences, although, depending on the type of algorithm used, not all information about state sequences is necessarily available for analysis. There are three main types of reachability analysis algorithms. In the order in which they are listed here, they can be applied to systems of increasing complexity:

○ Full search (systems up to 10^5 states)
○ Controlled partial search (systems up to 10^8 states)
○ Random simulation (larger systems)

The full search is the simplest algorithm. It performs the most thorough analysis of the three types of algorithm, but it can only analyze the smallest class of protocols. We quantify the limitations later in this chapter. If the full search method exceeds its limits, it effectively reduces to an uncontrolled partial search method, and the quality of the analysis deteriorates quickly.

The controlled partial search tries to optimize the quality of the reachability analysis specifically for those cases where a full search is infeasible. It attempts this by selecting an optimal fraction of the full state space that can be searched within given constraints of memory and time.

Random simulation techniques are specifically meant for the validation of systems of a complexity that defeats even the controlled partial search. The system state space for these systems can be estimated to be so large that no partial search technique can make a sensible selection. The best possible search in these cases is a random, or biased random, walk of the state space.

There are two different measures for expressing the capabilities of a reachability analysis tool: *coverage* and *quality*. The search coverage is easily quantified as the number of system states tested divided by the number of states in the full state space. A perhaps more appropriate, but less easily quantified measure, is the search's ability to find errors: the number of distinct errors found divided by the total number of errors present. In the comparison of the three basic search methods below we use both measures. In Chapter 13 we develop an automated protocol validation system for PROMELA models that can perform reachability analysis in all three basic modes: random simulations and either fully exhaustive or partial state space searches.

11.3.1 FULL STATE SPACE SEARCH

The standard full, or exhaustive, search algorithm explores all reachable composite system states of a set of interacting finite state machines. How precisely the interaction among the machines is defined is largely irrelevant to the design of the search algorithm. The basic state machine model can be extended with finite message queues, or local and global variables. As discussed in Chapter 8, these additions do not extend the power of the finite state machine model, provided that they are defined over a finite domain.

A state machine, in this model, is defined by a finite number of states and state transitions. Each state transition has two parts: a pre-condition and an effect. The pre-condition is typically a boolean condition on the state of the machine, the queues, and the variables. The transition is enabled, and can be executed, only if the pre-condition holds. The effect of an execution can change the state of the system, for instance the states of the local machine, the queues, and the variables, and perhaps even the state of other machines (e.g., in a multi-party rendezvous system).

The system as a whole is defined by the composite of all individual machine, variable, and queue states, and the combination of all simultaneously enabled local state transitions. From here on, the term *state* is used as a short-hand for *composite system state*. Where this can cause confusion we use the terms *machine state* or *system state*. Given an initial state for each machine in the system, the sets of machine states and system states can each be divided into two disjoint classes: reachable states and unreachable states. Normally it is required that the system not contain any unreachable *machine* states: they would correspond to unexecutable code in an implementation. Normally, also, the set of unreachable *system* states is several orders of magnitude larger than the set of reachable system states. The set of unreachable system states should include all error states.

An exhaustive reachability analysis tries to determine which states are reachable and which are not. Every reachable state and every sequence of reachable states can be checked for a given set of correctness criteria. These criteria can be general safety conditions that must hold for any protocol, such as the absence of deadlocks or buffer overruns, or they can be protocol-specific requirements such as a temporal claim about the proper working of a message retransmission discipline. In many cases protocol-specific requirements can be formalized as state invariants, the correctness of which can be verified with a simple boolean test in every reachable system state.

In the algorithm below, the reachability analysis starts with a small routine named start() that initializes two sets: a working set of system states to be analyzed, called W, and a set of states that have been analyzed, called A.

```
start()
{       W = { initial_state };  /* work set:   to be analyzed */
        A = { };                /* previously analyzed states */
        analyze();
}
```

Set `A` is also referred to as the *system state space*. When the algorithm terminates, it should include all the reachable system states The basic structure of the reachability analysis algorithm is as follows.

```
analyze()        /* exhaustive or full search */
{       if (W is empty) return;
        q = element from W;
        add q to A;
        if (q == error_state)
                report_error();
        else
        {       for each successor state s of q
                        if (s is not in A or W)
                        {       add s to W;
                                analyze();
                        }
        }
        delete q from W;
}
```

The order in which states are retrieved from working set `W` seems irrelevant at first, but it turns out to be an important control point. If states are stored in set `W` in *first-in first-out* order, the algorithm performs a breadth-first search of the state space tree. If states are stored in *first-in last-out* (i.e., stack) order, this changes into a depth-first search. A breadth-first search has the advantage that it finds the shortest error sequences first. A depth-first search, however, has the advantage that it requires a smaller work set `W`. An intuitive explanation for this is that the size of `W` in a depth-first search is a function of the depth of the search tree, but a function of its width in a breadth-first search. The depth of the search tree depends on the maximum length of a unique execution sequence. The width of the tree, however, is determined by the maximum number of distinct execution sequences, which is usually a much larger number.

As an example, consider a protocol where every state has two successors. The state space is then equivalent to a binary expanding tree. After n transitions, the breadth of the search tree is 2^n states. The depth of the tree, however, is only n states.

There is one other important advantage to the depth-first search discipline. When an error is discovered we would like the algorithm to be able to produce an execution sequence that leads to the error via a valid sequence of state transitions, starting from the initial system state. With a breadth-first search method, the path from the initial system state must be reconstructed from information stored in the state space set A. With a depth-first search, however, such a path need not be reconstructed: a sequence is implicitly defined by the stack order of set W.

DISCUSSION OF THE FULL SEARCH METHOD

The main problem with the full search strategy is its restricted applicability. It is important to note that the coverage of the full state space search technique is not necessarily 100%: it depends on the size of the state space and the amount of memory that is available for the search. If the size of the state space is R and the maximum number of states that can be stored in memory during the search is A both the coverage and the search quality can only reach 100% when $R \leq A$. When $R > A$ the coverage reduces to A/R, but the search *quality* is likely to be worse.

For large protocols the exhaustive search algorithm deteriorates into a low-quality partial search.

Consider a protocol for two processes, each having 100 states, one message queue, and each accessing five local variables. The two message queues are restricted to five slots each, and the effective range of the local variables is assumed to be limited to ten values. The number of distinct messages exchanged is ten. In this relatively small example system, there are $10^{5 \cdot 2}$ possible states of the protocol variables. Each process can be in one of 10^2 different states, so two processes can maximally be in 10^4 different composite system states. Finally, each queue can hold between zero and five messages, where each message can be one out of ten possible messages. The total number of system states in the worst case then is

$$10^{10} \cdot 10^4 \cdot \left[\sum_{i=0}^{5} 10^i \right]^2$$

or in the order of 10^{24} different states. If we assume, quite unrealistically, that each state can be encoded in 1 byte of memory and can be analyzed in 10^{-6} sec of CPU time, we would still need a machine with at least 10^{15} times as much memory as currently available, and would need roughly 10^{11} *years* of CPU time to perform an exhaustive analysis.

Fortunately, the number of effectively reachable states is usually much smaller than the total number of system states calculated above. After all, it is the purpose of a protocol to restrict the the behavior of the protocol processes, and thus the number of effectively reachable states, in order to realize the desired functionality. Still, even relatively small protocol systems can easily generate anywhere from 10^5 to 10^9 reachable system states. The number of states grows dramatically if, for instance, the size of a message queue is increased, or if the assumptions about the behavior of the "environment" in which the protocol is executed (e.g., the channel characteristics) are relaxed.

The exhaustive search method unavoidably breaks down when the state space grows beyond approximately 10^5 states. A quick "back of the envelope" calculation can illustrate this.

> If one system state can be stored in S bytes of memory, and we have a machine with M bytes available, we can generate and analyze no more than M/S states. M is a machine-dependent constant that is typically in the range from 10^6 to 10^7. Values for S are typically in the range 10 to 10^2 bytes, with larger values corresponding to the larger numbers of reachable states. This leads to an estimate for the maximum state space size of about 10^5 states. This value can also be found experimentally by running the full search algorithm until it has exhausted available memory.

This means that in many cases the full search method is feasible only if we can reduce the complexity of our validation models to the maximum that a given machine can analyze. The complexity of protocol models can be reduced substantially by structuring and layering techniques, but in some cases, even after such reductions, the problems to be analyzed remain inherently complex and cannot be further reduced without losing essential features.

As one example, consider the window protocol described in Chapter 7. It is a simple protocol, with no obvious further simplification. In its basic form this protocol is well within the range of the full search method. As illustrated in Chapter 14, however, the complexity of the search goes up dramatically if the assumptions about channel behavior are relaxed and can make a full search impossible.

11.3.2 CONTROLLED PARTIAL SEARCH

If the state space is larger than the available memory can accommodate, the exhaustive search strategy discussed above effectively reduces to a partial search, without guaranteeing that the most important parts of the protocol are inspected. This observation has led to the development of a new class of algorithms that specifically try to exploit the benefits of a partial search. They are based on the premise that in most cases of practical interest the maximum number of states that can be analyzed, A, is only a fraction of the total number of reachable states R. A controlled partial search, then, has the following objectives:

○ To analyze precisely A states, with $A = M/S$

○ To select these A states from the complete set of reachable states R in such a way that all major protocol functions are tested

○ To select the A states in such a way that the search *quality*, i.e., the probability of finding any given error, is better than the *coverage* A/R

An algorithm for the partial search looks exactly like the earlier algorithm for an exhaustive search, with only one difference: not all successor states are analyzed.

```
analyze()       /* partial search */
{       if (W is empty) return;
```

```
            q = element from W;
            add q to A;
            if (q == error_state)
                    report_error();
            else
            {       for some successor state s of q
                            if (s is not in A or W)
                            {       add s to W;
                                    analyze();      /* recursive */
                            }
            }
            delete q from W;
    }
```

It is interesting to note that even a random selection of successor states is superior to an uncontrolled partial search, since it guarantees that the complete state space is sampled, rather than the unknown fragment that happens to be generated first in a full search. The selection can also be based on a heuristic that favors executions that are likely to reveal design errors fast. Many different ways of organizing a controlled partial search have been studied. They include methods based on:

○ Depth-bounds
○ Scatter searches
○ Guided searches
○ Probabilistic searches
○ Partial orders
○ Random selections

We discuss the first five methods briefly below. The last method, based on random selections, is developed in the remainder of this chapter. References to more detailed descriptions of all techniques are included in the Bibliographic Notes.

DEPTH-BOUNDS

A fairly standard and simple partial search technique is the placement of a bound on the length of the execution sequences that are analyzed. It limits the search to a useful subset of behaviors, ruling out, for instance, degenerate cases of multiple overlapping executions. In the full search algorithm, for instance, it allows us to restrict the maximum size of working set W.

SCATTER SEARCH

In a scatter search, executions are selected that lead closer to potential deadlock states. One of the requisites of a deadlock state, for instance, is that there are no messages pending (all channels are empty). The algorithm therefore favors receive operations over send operations. The goal of the method is to increase the probability of finding errors fast.

GUIDED SEARCH

In a guided search, the state selection criterion is a cost function that is dynamically evaluated for each successor state. The cost function can be fixed, as in a scatter search, or it can be changed dynamically during the search. Not much is known about the types of cost functions, or "guiding expressions," that could prove to be useful.

PROBABILISTIC SEARCH

In a probabilistic search, successor states are explored in decreasing order of their probability of occurrence. All transitions in the system are labeled, minimally with a tag that gives them a "high" or a "low" probability of occurrence, and these tags are used as the selection criteria.

PARTIAL ORDERS

The main factor that is responsible for the state space explosion problem is the large number of possible interleavings of concurrent events. As shown in Chapter 5 (page 97), not all interleavings are necessarily relevant in the search for error states.

There are several ways of exploiting partial orders. A first method is based on the definition of a heuristic for either

  ○ *Fair progress* state exploration or
  ○ *Maximum progress* state exploration

Both heuristics work by assigning a search priority to the protocol processes. The number of transitions that are inspected during the search is limited, with preference given to the transitions that belong to high-priority processes. Transitions in lower-priority processes are only considered if all higher-priority processes are blocked. In a *fair* progress exploration technique, the relative priority of a process is *decreased* when one of its transitions is executed during the search; in the *maximum* progress exploration technique the relative priority is *increased*.

A second, more recent, method to exploit partial orders is based on formal definitions of equivalence relations on system behavior. The goal is then to prune away that part of a search that can be *proven* to be irrelevant. (References to these and the other techniques are collected in the Bibliographic Notes.)

RANDOM SELECTIONS

In a controlled partial search based on random selections of successor states, no effort is made to predict where likely errors in the state space are to be found. We will argue below that this is not only the simplest technique to implement, but is also likely to produce the highest quality search. It is the only technique that can satisfy all three requirements for a controlled partial search that were listed at the start of this section.

DISCUSSION OF CONTROLLED PARTIAL SEARCH METHODS

The first four techniques for controlling the partial search that we discussed above have one main problem in common. All four methods try to predict where the errors in a protocol can be found. This is an inherently risky approach. As a corollary of Murphy's law, the errors are likely to hide where a designer or a validator has decided *not* to look. Next to the random selection of successor states, the techniques based on partial orders can, in principle, avoid that problem. The dependencies between processes, however, can be subtle. Consider, for instance, a system of three processes A, B, and C, where A and B interact with C, but not with each other. It would be tempting to conclude that since A and B are disjoint, all possible interleavings of their behaviors are necessarily equivalent. But, alas, this assumption is invalid. Note that the behavior of process A can depend on B's behavior indirectly through their mutual interaction with C. Every distinct interleaving of the actions of A and B can be significant in determining the outcome.

To determine mechanically, therefore, which particular interleavings can safely be ignored in state space searches can be non-trivial. An accurate assessment may well be more expensive that a full blast exhaustive search, and thus be self-defeating as an optimization technique.

A final problem with the first five methods is that, although they can reduce the size of the state space, none of these methods provides a tool for matching the size of the state space to the size of available memory. For all these methods the size of the fraction of the state space that is effectively searched can only be determined experimentally, and is protocol dependent. This means that we may have to perform many validations, with different selection criteria, before we can find the optimal one that analyzes precisely M/S states. In Section 11.4 we will develop the idea of the random selection of successor states and show that it can be used to effectively solve also this problem.

Before doing so, we discuss a final state space exploration method, also based on the random selection of successor states, but this time without any attempt to build a state space

11.3.3 RANDOM SIMULATION

The controlled partial search methods have wide applicability. There are applications, however, where also a controlled partial search becomes infeasible. One can attempt, for instance, to apply a protocol validation algorithm directly to highly-detailed, compiled code that runs in a machine. In those cases, the parameter S, measuring the size of a single composite system state in bytes, can range anywhere from 10^3 to 10^5 bytes of memory.

Even on a larger machine, the largest number of states that can be maintained by a partial search then drops to a few hundred system states at best, in a state space that is many orders of magnitude larger. In cases like these, the only sensible approach is to discard sets A and W from the search algorithm and to explore the state space with a random simulation or 'random walk.' The algorithm is as follows.

```
analyze()          /* random simulation */
{       q = initial state;
        while (1)          /* forever */
        {       if (q is error_state)
                {       report_error();
                        q = initial state;
                } else
                        q = a successor state of q;
        }
}
```

This technique works largely independent of the size and complexity of the system being modeled; even "infinite size" systems can be explored in this manner. The coverage of the method, of course, cannot be measured, though in principle an exhaustive coverage of finite state spaces is guaranteed, given a sufficient amount of time. In practice this is not a very useful guideline, since a "sufficient" amount of time can easily mean a century of computation time or worse. In experiments, however, Colin West was able to show that even for an immeasurably small search *coverage* the *quality*, or error-finding capability, of the search can be adequate.

The remainder of this chapter is devoted to the development and motivation of a controlled partial search technique that was named *supertrace*. An implementation in C of an exhaustive search algorithm for PROMELA, with a supertrace option for large problems, is discussed in Chapters 12 to 13.

11.4 THE SUPERTRACE ALGORITHM

Given M bytes of memory, how can we organize a state space search to use precisely M bytes, no more and no less, and perform the largest search possible within that arena? To answer that question we look in a little more detail at the memory storage methods that are traditionally used. The standard way to maintain the state space set A in either a full or a partial search algorithm is to use a storage technique called *hashing*. Hashing allows us to determine quickly whether or not a new state s is already a member of set A and can be discarded or is not yet in A and needs to be inserted. The method is to use the contents of s to calculate a hash value $h(s)$, which is used as an index into a lookup table of states. The table is organized as shown in Figure 11.1.

Assume that we have H slots in the hash table. Hash function $h(s)$ is defined such that it returns an arbitrary value in the range $0..(H-1)$. For the same state $s \in A$, $h(s)$ always returns the same value. But there is also a possibility that two different states produce the same hash value. In the case we are studying, the hash table will have to accommodate a large number of states, which means $A > H$. The hash function will then produce the same hash value for an average of A/H dif-

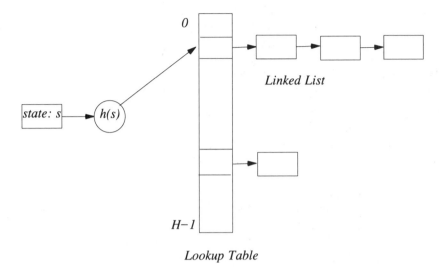

Figure 11.1 — Hash Table Lookup

ferent states. All states that hash to the same value are stored in a linked list that is accessible via the lookup table under the calculated index (the hash value). On the average then, when the table is full, each new state must be compared to A/H other states before it is either inserted into the linked list, or discarded as redundant. When A grows beyond the first H states, the number of comparisons required grows steadily, and the search efficiency degrades: there is a time penalty for analyzing systems of more than H states.

A typical value for H is 10^4 slots. The table itself takes up $H{\times}B$ bytes of memory, plus B bytes for each state that is inserted, where B is the size of an address pointer. On most machines $B=4$, which means that a table with say 256,000 slots requires more than 1 Mbyte of overhead that can no longer be used to store states. To accommodate the largest possible state space, therefore, a small value for H is required. As shown above, however, a small value for H means a low search efficiency.

If we could somehow manage to use a very large value for H, the number of hash conflicts could be minimized and thus the speed of the search algorithm could be optimized. Let us assume we can use the full search algorithm with a value for H in the order of 10^8 slots. In a state space of up to 10^5 states we can expect to have fewer than $10^5/10^8$ hash conflicts, or less than one conflict in a thousand states. This means that there will rarely be more than a single state in the linked list that is connected to each slot in the hash table. But this means that we do not have to store complete state descriptions in the hash table: in all but a few cases the hash table index (the hash value) uniquely identifies a state. The only bookkeeping required is to remember if a slot in the hash table is filled or not. A single bit of storage per state will suffice. If we have M bytes of memory available, we have $8M$ bits for the state space (assuming 8 bits per byte). A 10 Mbyte machine can thus give us a state space large enough to hold 80 million states. The hash function $h(s)$ is used to calculate the position of a bit in the available memory arena M. A bit value of 1 will now indicate that the state corresponding to this hash value has been previously analyzed. The state itself is not stored.

Since no states are stored, there are no states to compare a new state against: the bit position uniquely identifies the state. The method can be expected to work well if the state space is sparse and indeed H is very large. A large value of H makes hash conflicts rare for all cases where $A < H$. Most importantly, however, when $A > H$ the hashing automatically defines a randomized partial search method that matches the coverage of the search to the available memory. The method therefore approximates an exhaustive search for smaller protocols and slowly changes into a controlled partial search method for larger protocols. For smaller protocols, however, we do not need a partial search method: we can use a traditional exhaustive search technique.

> *Supertrace is a controlled partial-search technique that is **only** meant for the validation of protocol systems that cannot be analyzed exhaustively.*

As an exhaustive search technique the supertrace algorithm would compare unfavorably with almost any other standard depth-first search method, simply because it cannot guarantee 100% coverage due to the possibility of unresolved hash conflicts (cf. Tables 13.1 and 13.2 in Chapter 13). We will show, however, that as a partial search technique, the new algorithm is superior to other methods.

HASH CONFLICTS

The overhead of the lookup table with a supertrace algorithm reduces from

$$HB + (S + B)A$$

bytes to

$$H/8$$

bytes. However, since the states are no longer stored we can no longer compensate for hash conflicts. Remarkably, this defect has a positive effect on the overload behavior of the algorithm during partial searches. Here is how it works.

If a new state s is generated and it is found that the flag is set at index $h(s)$, we must conclude that state s was analyzed before and should be ignored. When a hash conflict occurs, the above conclusion is wrong, and the search will ignore a state that should have been analyzed: the search is truncated. As $A/H \rightarrow 0$, the number of hash conflicts that will be encountered approaches zero, and the method approaches (but can never guarantee to be) a fully exhaustive search. Indeed, therefore, it is best to choose H as large as possible.

The maximum value for H that we can choose for given memory size M is $H = 8M$. Let us see how this algorithm compares to a traditional partial search.

The memory requirements are the same. The limit to the coverage of the traditional search, however, is $A = M/S$. Storing the same M/S states in the hash table of the modified algorithm, with $H = 8M$, gives a ratio

$$A/H = M/(8MS) = 1/(8S)$$

For a typical value of $S \approx 100$, the probability of a hash conflict then approaches 10^{-3}. But the new algorithm is not restricted to a maximum of M/S states. It can analyze a maximum of H distinct states. The hash conflicts, which increases as the state space fills up, now work to scatter the states that are selected for analysis across the set of reachable states in an approximately random manner.

There are two cases to consider. For $R < M/S$, the coverage of the traditional algorithm will be the same as or slightly better than the new algorithm, since it avoids the effect of the hash conflicts. However, when $R < M/S$ we do not need a partial search algorithm at all since we can still perform an exhaustive (traditional) search in memory. The supertrace algorithm should not be used in these cases.

For problems with $R > M/S$, the coverage of the new algorithm, i.e., the total number of effectively analyzed states compared to the total number of reachable states, is substantially higher than the coverage of the traditional algorithm. For $R \gg M$ it approaches $8M/R$, compared to $M/(S\,R)$ for the traditional algorithm (see also Figure 11.2).

If state description S becomes larger the traditional algorithm can analyze fewer and fewer states, but the performance of the new algorithm stays the same. If, for M fixed at 10^7 bytes of memory, S grows from 100 to 1000 bytes per state, the coverage of a traditional partial search algorithm *drops* from 10^5 to 10^4 analyzable states. The coverage of the new algorithm, however, remains constant at a maximum of $H = 8 \cdot 10^7$ analyzable states.

The effect is illustrated, for a fixed size S, in Figure 11.2. Increasing S is equivalent to moving the dotted and the dashed line to the left: the behavior of the traditional algorithm changes, but the behavior of the supertrace algorithm remains constant.

For state spaces that are larger than an exhaustive search algorithm can accommodate, the traditional method breaks down very rapidly, its coverage dropping by a factor of ten for every tenfold increase in the number of reachable states. The coverage of the new algorithm is substantially better.

When $A \to R$, A is the same order of magnitude as H, which means that a large fraction of the state space can still be analyzed, the hash conflicts acting as a random pruning that scatters the search over the oversized state space. For still larger protocols with $A > H$ the coverage of the search approaches H/A, or $8M/R$.

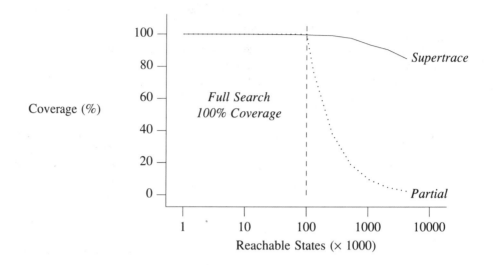

Figure 11.2 — Comparison of Two Algorithms

MULTIPLE HASHINGS

The hash functions helps us to make a fast random selection of states from a large state space, and thus implements an efficient controlled partial search. Assume a hypothetical 10 Mbytes of memory available for the search and a state space of 800 million states of 100 bytes each. The coverage of all traditional search methods, except supertrace and random simulation, is limited to the analysis of $10^7/100$ in $8 \cdot 10^8$ states or 0.0125 %. A single run of supertrace would give a maximum coverage of $8 \cdot 10^7/8 \cdot 10^8$ or 10%. The question is: Can we ever achieve a still better coverage with the same system constraints? Surprisingly, the answer for the supertrace algorithm is: Yes.

The hash function can be used as a parameter in repeated searches. Suppose the first search with hash function $H1$ selected 80 million states are random from the 800 million reachable states. A second search with a different hash function $H2$ will also select 80 million states, but it will make a different selection. We may expect that there will be a 10% overlap between the two state sets, but the combined coverage of the two searches has now gone up to $80+72$ million states out of the 800 million candidates, or 19%. Continuing this process, we can in theory get arbitrarily close to a coverage of 100% of the state space, provided that a sufficient number of independent hash functions can be found.

The validator developed in Chapter 13 uses this principle to increase the coverage of searches. It uses two hash functions in each single run.

11.5 DETECTING NON-PROGRESS CYCLES

So far, we have only discussed the validation of state properties, using a straight-forward reachability analysis algorithm. The complexity of the algorithm, even for this simple case, is in PSPACE. We have therefore made a deliberate effort to find the fastest, most frugal implementation so that the range of problems we can apply it to is as large as possible. But we are not done. There are other properties that we may be interested in proving, specifically for PROMELA validation models. If, as we have argued above, the efficiency of a straight reachability analysis is a concern, the efficiency of the more subtle types of validation is crucial.

A straightforward check for non-progress conditions could be based on the construction and inspection of all strongly connected components in the reachability graph that is implicitly defined by the state space of the system being analyzed. This approach, though commonly used, fails when the state space is too large to be stored completely. Here we explore a different option that has a modest expense and, most importantly, that can be used in combination with a supertrace algorithm to do partial validations of very large systems.

Our first problem is to detect cycles in the reachability graph that do not pass through any states marked as progress-states. The algorithm we develop is only for identifying non-progress cycles. We will not try to combine it with a simultaneous search for assertion violations and improper terminations. A first attempt to find the non-progress cycles is to perform a standard depth-first reachability analysis where all sequences are truncated when a progress-state is reached. That is, progress-states are treated as if they have no successors. All cycles that can be constructed in a search of this type, must be non-progress cycles. The size of the state space that is created in this search is at most equal to the size of a straight depth-first search. It is likely to be smaller due to the truncations at progress states.

> To see how this may be implemented, refer to the algorithm for the full state space search given in Section 11.3.1. A cycle is detected if the depth-first search reaches a state that is already in work-set W, assuming that states are extracted from set W in last-in first-out order.

The flaw of this method is that it does not allow us to detect cycles that do not pass through the initial system state. There may well be a cyclic execution sequence (as defined in Chapter 6) that first passes through a finite number of states, some of which may be marked as progress states, before entering a cycle of strictly non-progress states. This observation, however, immediately leads to a new algorithm that does work.

A non-progress cycle might start in any reachable system state. So we must inspect two distinct state spaces: one created by the original depth-first search, and one that is created when transitions from progress states are disabled. The task of our search algorithm is to inspect every possible prefix of a cyclic sequence in the original state space and see if it can be continued into a cycle in the second state space. The implementation is simple. We can add a two-state demon to our validation model that defines in which mode the search will operate, as follows

```
proctype demon() { bit magic = 0; magic = 1 }
```

The initial state of demon process is just before the assignment, with variable magic equal to zero. The second, and final, state of the demon is immediately after the assignment, with magic equal to one. The demon process can switch from the initial state to the final state nondeterministically, and once it has switched it cannot go back. The value of variable magic defines in which mode the search is performed. When magic is zero, a normal depth-first search is performed, without any error checking. When magic is one, all transitions that originate in progress states are disabled. All subsequent execution sequences should be terminating. If there is any cycle of states that are reachable while magic is one, it must be a non-progress cycle.

> The value of magic can only change once in any given execution sequence, and it can only change from zero to one. Let us assume that, after magic has changed value, a cycle of states is detected that is not a non-progress cycle. By definition that cycle contains at least one transition originating at a progress state. This transition can only occur when magic is equal to zero. This means that the value of variable magic changes from zero to one and back at least once each time through the cycle. This contradicts the earlier observation that magic only changes value once.

The algorithm we have constructed further has the property that if any non-progress cycle exists, at least one will be detected. To prove that, let us assume that there exists a reachable strongly connected component that contains only non-progress states. (A strongly connected component is any set of states in which every member can reach every other member of the set via one or more transitions.)

> The algorithm generates two copies of every reachable state; there is one copy in which magic is equal to zero, and one copy with magic equal to one. There is a transition from the first copy to the second that corresponds to the one transition that the demon process can make. Consider the case where no state from the strongly connected component has been generated with magic equal to one. Consider the first such state that is generated. Since the strongly connected component is assumed to be reachable, and the transition of the demon process is always executable, this must happen at some point in the search. Call this state the *seed* state.

> The depth-first search tree that is rooted at the seed has all states from the strongly connected component as successors, including itself (by the definition of a strongly connected component). Since the seed state is also reachable from itself (by the same definition) via non-progress states only (by our original assumption), it must be revisited. The moment the seed is revisited, a cycle is detected. By our earlier proof, that cycle must be a non-progress cycle.

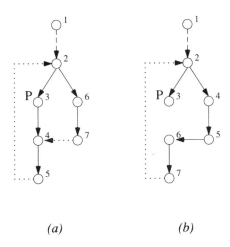

(a)   *(b)*

Figure 11.3 — Detection of a Non-Progress Cycle

There can, of course, be many different paths through a strongly connected component, each one of which may represent a different type of non-progress cycle. The algorithm above does not guarantee that all variants are detectable in a single execution of the search. It does guarantee that at least one variant is detected. If no non-progress cycles are detected, therefore, we can be certain that none exist.

Figure 11.3 illustrates how a difficult case of a non-progress cycle is detected. The circles represent system states and the arrows represent transitions. The states are numbered in the order in which they are visited during a search. The state marked P is a progress-state. State 1 is the initial system state. The dashed line from state 1 to state 2 is an arbitrary execution sequence. The dotted lines indicate state matches. Remember that after the creation of every state our depth-first search algorithm checks to see if the state was created before. If a match is found the search is truncated. If the match occurs in work set w, i.e., on the stack, a cycle is detected.

In Figure 11.3a a fragment of the state space is shown as it would be created in a normal depth-first search. In Figure 11.3b the same states are shown after the transition of the demon process to the state in which transitions starting at progress states are disabled. The numbers indicate the order in which states are visited.

Before the transition of the demon process, in Figure 11.3a, just one cycle is detected by the normal depth-first search method. It is detected when the fifth state visited is found to match the second state, which is on the stack. The loop is benign, since it contains the progress-state. The search continues, after removing states 4, 3, and 2 from the stack, with the new state 6. The seventh state visited matches the fourth one, and the search is completed. The last match does not produce a cycle, because state 4 is no longer on the stack.

The non-progress loop through the states marked 2, 6, 7, 4, and 5 therefore remains undetected in the standard depth-first search. After the transition of the demon process, all transitions from the state marked P are disabled. This means that the states are now visited in the order indicated in Figure 11.3b. The first, harmless, cycle can now no longer be constructed, but the second cycle can, and is correctly detected.

With the addition of a simple two-state demon process, the algorithm is trivial to implement. An implementation in C is given in Appendix E. Its expense is a doubling of the time and space requirements. Perhaps the most important advantage of the algorithm, however, is that it can be used in combination with any controlled partial search method. Specifically it can be used with a bit state space technique, as used in the supertrace algorithm.

11.6 DETECTING ACCEPTANCE CYCLES

The detection of acceptance cycles (see Chapter 6, page 120) is substantially harder than the detection of non-progress cycles, discussed in the last section. This time, all execution cycles that pass through at least one acceptance state must be detected. We are interested in finding an algorithm that continues to work with supertrace, so that its application to very large problems is not excluded.

The following algorithm is due to Mihalis Yannakakis (see the Bibliographic Notes). The expense of the algorithm is at worst a doubling of the time and space requirements of the basic search. We conduct a depth-first search with two state spaces instead of one (i.e., two copies of set A). Call the second state space set C. When no acceptance state is encountered, set C remains unused, and the search is precisely the same as before. For every acceptance state that is removed from work set W and added to set A (i.e., after all its successor states have been visited) the algorithm switches sets A and C and begins a new search. Call the acceptance state the *seed* of that search. If at any time during this search the seed state can be revisited, an acceptance cycle is found, and an error can be declared (i.e., the temporal claim is satisfied, which means that an undesirable behavior is possible). When no such error is found, the second search terminates when all successors of the seed have been added to set C. At this point, sets A and C are swapped again, and the depth-first search continues as before.

No state will be visited more than twice in this search, once in set A and once in set C. It is not hard to convince ourselves that any cycle found by this algorithm is necessarily an acceptance cycle. It is harder to show, however, that in the absence of hash collisions any acceptance cycle that exists is also found.

Assume that there are acceptance states that belong to one or more strongly connected components in the reachability graph. If all states in the reachability graph are numbered in the order in which they are added to set A, consider the acceptance state with the lowest number. Call that state the *seed*. Because the seed belongs to a strongly connected component it is reachable from itself. The acceptance cycle is detected if and only if none of the intermediate states along that path have been added to set C before the seed. If there is any such state, however, it necessarily has a lower search number than the seed.

All states along the path we are interested in belong, by definition, to the same strongly connected component as the seed. If any one of those states has a lower search number, and was added to set C before, its complete set of successors must have been analyzed as well, *before* we reach the seed. This means that all these successor states have a lower search number than the seed. The set of successors, however, includes the seed, because they all belong the same strongly connected component. This means that this is not the first visit to the seed, which contradicts our assumption.

11.7 CHECKING TEMPORAL CLAIMS

To check temporal claims, as they were defined in Chapter 6, every state transition in the reachability graph for the original system, without the temporal claim, must be matched with a state transition in the finite state machine that represents the temporal claim.

Fortunately, this requirement is relatively easy to meet, and compatible with supertrace. After the generation of a successor state during the standard search we include one extra test, a forced transition of the temporal claim process to a new state. If such a transition cannot be made, the search can be truncated as if a state match was found. It means that the undesirable behavior that is expressed in the claim cannot be realized after the last transition in the system is made. The details of an implementation in C are given in Appendix E. In the best possible case, if no transition from the initial system state can be matched by a transition in the claim, the time and space requirements of the new algorithm reduce to almost zero. In the worst possible case, however, the size of the state space is multiplied by the number of reachable states of the claim.

The worst-case expense of the validation of temporal claims increases linearly with the size of the claim, measured as the number of states of the extended finite state machine that defines the claim. With the discussion of the last two sections, we can compare the complexity of the validation of different types of PROMELA correctness requirements. The minimum expense is incurred for the validation of properties of states, such as assertions and improper terminations. It can be twice as hard to check for non-progress properties, and $2N$ times as hard to check a temporal claim of N states.

If we turn this argument around, we can say that, with the same search quality, for the validation of state properties the system can be $2N$ times larger than for the validation of temporal claims. It is therefore important that a validation system, such as PROMELA, allows us to validate each type of property separately,[1] so that the simpler requirements do not incur the expense of the more complicated ones. The system size determines in all cases precisely which types of validation of a given quality can be performed. If the best search quality that can be realized for a given system is insufficient, we can do two things:

○ Express the correctness requirement differently so that it can be checked more efficiently

○ Express the system behavior differently in an effort to reduce its final size

We discuss the second method in more detail below.

11.8 COMPLEXITY MANAGEMENT

The validation of protocol systems that generate up to a few hundred thousand states is well within reach of of the automated validation systems we have described. The validation of larger systems, however, can be a substantial challenge in the management of complexity. It could well be claimed that complexity management itself is the most important issue in the design of a validation strategy. In this section we review some of the main issues.

The discussion of partial search techniques (page 228) was the primary motivation for the complexity management technique that we have chosen as the basis of the supertrace algorithm. Two other important issues remain to be discussed:

○ Reduction methods

○ Incremental composition

Both methods are applied before a state space search is started, instead of taking effect during a search as in the partial searches. They therefore apply to all search methods, from fully exhaustive searches to random walks. We discuss them in more detail below.

REDUCTION METHODS

The design of a validation model trivially determines the complexity of the validation that is to be performed. If protocol layering and structuring techniques are applied, it is often possible to separate, without loss of generality, the validation of multiple orthogonal protocol functions. An example of that is given in Chapter 14, where the validation of the flow control protocol from Chapter 7 is separated from the validation of the session control protocol.

In Chapter 8, Section 8.9, we discussed a technique to further reduce the complexity of a validation model by systematic generalizations that do not affect the scope

---

1. Temporal claims could be used to express state properties, and even non-progress conditions, and could therefore be used as a single default mechanism for specifying correctness requirements.

of a validation. Similar ideas have been based on the notion of "protocol projections," as first described by Lam and Shankar.

In some cases, however, it may still be hard or impossible to find the ideal behavior preserving reduction. In those cases we have one more complexity management option. There are many modeling parameters that control the range of possible behaviors defined by a model. The determining factors for the complexity of PROMELA models, for instance, are the number of processes, message queues, and variables, and the size of the message queues. Decreasing the number of slots in message queues can reduce the maximum amount of asynchrony in a concurrent system and dramatically decrease the number of reachable composite system states, without necessarily decreasing its scope. A validation model often can be analyzed exhaustively by restricting some of these parameters. The model, of course, becomes a partial one when the parameter settings are decreased. This means that we often have a choice between performing an exhaustive search for a partial model, or a partial search for a full model. Which approach is the most appropriate naturally depends on the problem being studied.

INCREMENTAL COMPOSITION

In the reachability analysis algorithms we have discussed up to this point, we have assumed that all asynchronous processes that contribute to the global behavior of the protocol are combined in a single step in the generation of the global system state space. In some cases, an *incremental composition* method can be used to reduce the size of the state space that is being constructed. (See Algorithm 8.3, and see also Chapter 8, Section 8.7.) With this method we first generate the set of all reachable composite system states of two or more of the protocol processes. This partial state space is then reduced by standard state machine minimization and then composed with the remaining processes, again in an incremental fashion.

In a typical application of this method, at each step two separate state machines are replaced by one state machine, which is reduced in size before it is combined with the other machines. To work, this method obviously requires that the validation model consist of *more* than two state machines (asynchronous processes). It further relies crucially on the user's ability to find precisely those combinations of state machines that can produce the greatest reductions. The reduction is meant to remove behavior that is internal to the machines that are combined. It reduces the combined machine to the *external* behavior of the machines that were collapsed.

This means that the method works best if it is applied to machines that are tightly coupled (that is, they exchange a lot of messages) and that are relatively independent of the rest of the system. If the user, by mistake, combines two machines that are disjoint, the state space explosion problem is worsened: effectively the two machines would be replaced by an irreducible composite state machine that defines the complete Cartesian product of all states in the two individual state machines. A

Several researchers have implemented the incremental composition method and applied it to validation models that only use *rendezvous* communications. The advantage here is that the rendezvous points can disappear in the reduction steps. It is not clear if the method can still be effective when it is applied to systems such as PROMELA that allow asynchronous, buffered message exchanges. In these cases the internal buffers may complicate the minimization process.

11.9 BOUNDEDNESS OF PROMELA MODELS

It is not immediately obvious that any given PROMELA model can be reduced to a finite state system and validated with the algorithms we have discussed in this chapter. A PROMELA validation model allows an arbitrary number of process instantiations and an arbitrary number of message queues to be created. The following program, for instance, is valid in PROMELA.

```
proctype A()
{       chan Ain = [1024] of { int, int };

        do
        :: run A()
        od
}
init { run A() }
```

To simulate the execution of this model would require an infinite amount of memory and an infinite length of time. Any real execution of the model, however, can only take place on a finite machine. Most models are therefore finite by design, and it can even be argued that the possibility of infinite growth is a design error.

PROMELA restricts the maximum number of processes and message queues that can be created. The precise limit is not defined. At some point during the execution of the example program above the run statement will become unexecutable and block the last process that was created. Every PROMELA model is therefore by definition a finite state system and can be analyzed with a standard reachability analysis algorithm. Each process has a fixed number of states, each message queue has a fixed number of slots, and the range of all variables used in the system is fixed. When the model is executed, it can only reach a finite number of possible states. At some point in the execution of process A() above, for instance, the run statement becomes unexecutable and prohibits further growth.

In Chapters 12 and 13 we discuss the implementation of a program that converts PROMELA specifications into the required finite state models. The program implements all three basic search modes we have discussed: random simulation, bit state space search, and the full state space search.

ments all three basic search modes we have discussed: random simulation, bit state space search, and the full state space search.

11.10 SUMMARY

Given a new, carefully designed protocol, how can we gain confidence that it will not fail in some unexpected way? For instance, we may want to prove that the protocol is robust under adverse channel behavior, or we may want to show that certain undesirable events, such as system deadlocks, cannot occur. The methods we have described in this chapter are based on the verification of correctness requirements that can be expressed as system invariants: properties that remain invariantly true for all possible executions of the system.

The manual proof method we gave is based on an exhaustive inspection of state transitions, and the automated variant is based on an exhaustive inspection of system states. The manual validation procedure can be expected to work for systems of up to ten or twenty state transitions, but is largely independent of the number of reachable states. The credibility of these manual proofs, however, is at best inversely proportional to their length.

The automated procedure does not have this drawback, but its applicability depends crucially on the number of reachable system states. For relatively small systems, up to approximately 10^5 reachable system states, we can apply a fully exhaustive state space search. The purpose of the exhaustive search is to show the *absence* of errors. If it can be completed without reporting any errors, it is certain that the protocol cannot violate any of the correctness criteria.

For larger systems, up to approximately 10^8 reachable system states, the best validation that can be performed is a controlled, partial search. The purpose of a partial search is to show the *presence* of errors, not the absence. The partial search is designed in such a way that if it is applied to a protocol that contains an error, it optimizes our chances of exposing it within the constraints of the machine on which the validation algorithm is run. We have discussed three different ways of achieving this objective:

☐ Using search heuristics to restrict the partial search to system states that are likely to contain the errors.

☐ Using a hashing technique that dramatically increases the number of system states that can be manipulated.

☐ Using reduction methods to simplify validation models before they are subjected to a search.

The first method has the disadvantage that it tries to predict where the errors are likely to be, an inherently dangerous strategy. The second strategy does not have this problem, and turns out to be the only one that allows us to match the scope of the analysis to the constraints of the system on which the validation algorithm is executed, whatever they may be. The application to PROMELA is elaborated in the next two chapters.

For exceptionally large validation problems, finally, the only workable validation method is a random simulation that tries to explore as many system states as possible, trying to home in on those states that can violate the system invariants.

EXERCISES

11-1 Use the manual proof technique to show that the alternating bit protocol preserves the correctness of the window protocol invariant for a window size of one.

11-2 Modify the partial search algorithm to include a maximum or fair state space exploration heuristic.

11-3 The following solution to Dijkstra's mutual exclusion problem (see Chapter 2, and Dijkstra [1965]) appeared in the *Communications of the ACM*, Hyman [1966]. It is reproduced here as it was published (in pseudo Algol).

```
 1  Boolean array b(0;1) integer k, i, j,
 2  comment process i, with i either 0 or 1;
 3  C0:   b(i) := false;
 4  C1:   if k != i then begin
 5  C2:   if not (b(j) then go to C2;
 6        else k := i; go to C1 end;
 7        else critical section;
 8        b(i) := true;
 9        remainder of program;
10        go to C0;
11        end
```

Show that the solution is incorrect by modeling the solution in PROMELA, and performing an automated validation with one of the reachability analysis algorithms discussed in this chapter.

11-4 The reachability analysis algorithms we have considered verify the observance of system *state* invariants. Consider possible extensions to the basic full-search algorithm to check for properties of system state *sequences*: paths through the global state space. What extensions are necessary, for instance, to be able to prove or disprove for the alternating bit protocol that there is no infinite sequence of transitions in which the 1-bit sequence number remains unchanged?

11-5 There are algorithms that can find all strongly connected components in a directed cyclic graph, e.g., Aho, Hopcroft & Ullman [1974, p. 192]. Consider how such an algorithm could be used to extend the capabilities of the reachability analyzers, what the cost in added time and space complexity would be, and how these extensions would be affected by partial searching.

BIBLIOGRAPHIC NOTES

The manual proof technique based on system invariants is due to Krogdahl [1978] and Knuth [1981]. The proof of the window invariant discussed here was also first given in Knuth [1981]. The method was also used more recently in Brown, Gouda, and Miller [1989]. Gouda's manual validation method based on state invariants and well-founded formulas is inspired by Floyd's seminal paper Floyd [1967].

Several other attempts have been made to develop automated protocol validation tools that are not based on reachability analysis. Early experience with some automated versions of these tools was reported in Schwabe [1981] and Sunshine and Smallberg [1982]. A promising new manual proof theory is based on the Oxford specification language z. See for instance Duke, Hayes, King and Rose [1988], Duke, Hayes and Rose [1988], and Hayes, Mowbray and Rose [1989].

Work on automated protocol validation methods was pioneered by Brand and Joyner [1978], Hajek [1978], West and Zafiropulo [1978], West [1978], Zafiropulo [1978], and Razouk and Estrin [1980]. The work of Colin West and Pitro Zafiropulo West and Zafiropulo [1978] provided a first demonstration that with automated tools even protocols that have withstood the scrutiny of years of development in an international standardization organization can, within a few seconds of computer time, be shown to be flawed. In this case, the protocol was the CCITT Recommendation X.21, and the validation tool was a straightforward implementation of the validation theory developed in Zafiropulo [1978]. Important subsequent work was reported in Zafiropulo et al. [1980], Rubin and West [1982]. Excellent surveys of the work on protocol validation can be found in IFIP conference proceedings such as IFIP [1983], or the April 1980 special issue on "Computer Network Architectures and Protocols" of the *IEEE Transactions on Communications*, which contains the standard reference Bochmann and Sunshine [1980].

There are many results on the computational complexity of the validation task of a communicating finite state machine model, see for instance Cunha and Maibaum [1981], Brand and Zafiropulo [1983], Apt and Kozen [1986], Reif and Smolka [1988]. In general, the problem of finding deadlocks in a system of communicating finite state machines is PSPACE complete at best, and becomes formally undecidable when the message channels are unbounded.

This result, of course, does not mean that any further analysis of finite state machine models is pointless. It does mean that the complexity of a protocol validation algorithm is a main concern. These algorithms can carry no more overhead than strictly necessary to solve the problem. Though it can be tempting to extend a search algorithm to capture more subtle features, it is generally ill-advised to do so if the method is to survive application to problems of a realistic size.

The necessity of partial search techniques was first described in West [1986b] and in Holzmann [1985, 1987a]. An overview of a range of search heuristics that have since been invented for partial searches can be found in Lin, Chu and Liu [1987]. The random state space exploration method as first studied by Colin West [1986b, 1989]. Probabilistic partial search techniques were described by Maxemchuck and Sabnani [1987]. A scatter search technique with guiding expressions was introduced in Pageot and Jard [1988]. A heuristic for partial orders was first suggested in Holzmann [1985]. Several more formal approaches have been investigated in the last few years, e.g., Probst [1990], Valmari [1990] and Godefroid [1990]. The fair progress state exploration heuristic was first suggested in Rubin and West [1982], and further explored in Gouda and Han [1985]. Maximum progress state exploration was described in Gouda and Yu [1984]. The concept of "protocol projections" was introduced in Lam and Shankar [1984].

The bit state space technique was first described in Holzmann [1987b] and elaborated in Holzmann [1988]. The hashing technique is based on a much older technique called "scatter storage," described in Morris [1968], and applied earlier in McIlroy [1982]. The bit state space search technique can easily be applied to all FSM based models, e.g., Rafiq and Ansart [1983], Estelle, e.g., Richier et al. [1987], the S/R model, Aggarwal, Kurshan and Sharma [1983], and Petri Net models, e.g., Bourguet [1986], to name just a few.

The extension of the exhaustive search algorithm with assertion proving capabilities was described in Holzmann [1987a]. An comparison of search algorithms based on reachability analysis appeared in Holzmann [1990].

The algorithm for the detection of non-progress cycles has not been published before. The algorithm for the detection of acceptance cycles, for instance in the context of a temporal claim, is due to Mihalis Yannakakis of AT&T Bell Laboratories. It was first described in Courcoubetis, Vardi, Wolper, and Yannakakis [1990]. A standard algorithm for detecting strongly connected components in a graph can be found in Aho, Hopcroft and Ullman [1974, p. 192].

The application of pure finite state models to the protocol validation problem can be found in, for instance, Brand and Zafiropulo [1983], Bochmann [1983], or Knudsen [1983].

Many interesting approaches to the protocol validation problem could not be discussed here. In particular this goes for the work on the S/R model and omega regular languages, Aggarwal, Kurshan and Sharma [1983], Har'El and Kurshan [1990], and model checking systems for circuit verification, e.g., Clarke [1982], Browne, Clarke, Dill, and Mishra [1986].

A PROTOCOL SIMULATOR 12

12.1 INTRODUCTION

Without the proper tools it may be possible to design a correct protocol, but in most cases it will be impossible to formally establish its correctness with any measure of reliability. So far, we have occupied ourselves mainly with the development of a design discipline based on the usage of formal validation models. In this chapter we extend this discipline with a software tool for simulating the behavior of validation models written in PROMELA. The tool is called SPIN, which is short for: simple PROMELA interpreter[1]. SPIN can simulate the execution of a validation model by interpreting PROMELA statements on the fly. It can be used on either partial or complete protocol designs, at any level of abstraction. It can quickly tell us whether or not we are on the right track with a design and as such it can be a valuable design tool.

The program that we develop in this chapter will not try to validate correctness requirements. That is a task for a validator (Chapter 13). A small exception to that rule is made for PROMELA `assert` statements, since the corresponding requirements are validated as a mere side-effect of their execution. The validation of non-progress cycles, invalid end-states, and temporal claims, however, is outside the scope of a simulator. The complete program for the simulator contains about 2000 lines of text. It includes a lexical analyzer, a parser, and a process scheduler. It does require a fair amount of explanation and some familiarity with C and UNIX to get through this chapter. But, rest assured, it is not necessary to understand the details of the implementation to be able to use the simulator. Below we first dis-

---

1. The terms *simulator*, *interpreter*, and *evaluator* are used as synonyms in this chapter.

cuss the general structure and the type of output the simulator can generate. Then we discuss a small version of the program, only for evaluating PROMELA expressions, and show how it works. Finally, we extend this program into a complete interpreter, by adding the missing pieces one by one. In the next chapter SPIN is extended with an option for performing fast automated protocol validations. A source listing for the final version of SPIN can be found in Appendices D and E.

12.2 SPIN – OVERVIEW

To build the interpreter we rely on the UNIX programming tools *yacc*, *lex*, and *make*. A casual familiarity with these tools is therefore assumed. We concentrate here on what the tools can do for us, rather than explain how they work inside. In case of emergency consult a UNIX manual or refer to the Bibliographic Notes at the end of this chapter for pointers to other literature that may be helpful.

A SAMPLE SIMULATION RUN

Consider the example program from Chapter 5 for calculating the factorial of a positive integer number.

```
proctype fact(int n; chan p)
{       int result;

        if
        :: (n <= 1) -> p!1
        :: (n >= 2) ->
                chan child = [1] of { int };
                run fact(n-1, child);
                child?result;
                p!n*result
        fi
}
init
{       int result;
        chan child = [1] of { int };

        run fact(12, child);
        child?result;
        printf("result: %d\n", result)
}
```

Running the analyzer on this program produces the following output:

```
$ spin factorial
result: 479001600
13 processes created
```

where $ is a UNIX system prompt. And fortunately,

```
12*11*10*9*8*7*6*5*4*3*2*1 = 479001600
```

Running the simulator in verbose mode gives us a little more information about the run, for instance by printing all message transmissions, with the number of the pro-

cess performing them, the contents of the message being sent, and the name of the
destination channel.

```
$ spin -s factorial
proc 12 (fact)   line    5, Send 1          -> queue 12 (p)
proc 11 (fact)   line   10, Send 2          -> queue 11 (p)
proc 10 (fact)   line   10, Send 6          -> queue 10 (p)
proc  9 (fact)   line   10, Send 24         -> queue 9 (p)
proc  8 (fact)   line   10, Send 120        -> queue 8 (p)
proc  7 (fact)   line   10, Send 720        -> queue 7 (p)
proc  6 (fact)   line   10, Send 5040       -> queue 6 (p)
proc  5 (fact)   line   10, Send 40320      -> queue 5 (p)
proc  4 (fact)   line   10, Send 362880     -> queue 4 (p)
proc  3 (fact)   line   10, Send 3628800    -> queue 3 (p)
proc  2 (fact)   line   10, Send 39916800 -> queue 2 (p)
proc  1 (fact)   line   10, Send 479001600 -> queue 1 (p)
result: 479001600
13 processes created
```

The column with the message value now implicitly gives us a running count of the
factorial being computed. If still more information is needed, we can also run the
simulator with additional flags to print, for instance, message receptions or the
values of variables. But the above example suffices for now.

12.3 EXPRESSIONS

One specific function that the simulator must perform is the evaluation of expressions. In a statement such as

```
crunch!data(3*12+4/2)
```

the simulator must evaluate three expressions:

○ The value of the destination `crunch`
○ The value of the message type `data` and
○ The value of the argument `3*12+4/2`

The evaluation of expressions may seem insignificant at first, but since PROMELA is
founded on the concept of executability, the evaluation of statements in general is
really at the core of the simulator. To keep things simple, let us therefore begin
with a small program that can do no more than evaluate PROMELA expressions.

We have to tell our program what valid expressions look like and how they should
be evaluated. The first issue calls for a grammar specification. If we ignore variable names for a while, the simplest form of expression is a number, say an integer
constant. We write a constant as a series of one or more digits, where a digit is
any symbol in the range '0' to '9'. If we formalize this we can write

```
digit    :       '0' | '1' | '2' | '3' | '4'
         |       '5' | '6' | '7' | '8' | '9'
```

The term we are defining is on the left side of the colon, and the defining symbols are on the right side where the vertical bar ' | ' is used to separate alternatives. Recursively then, we can define a constant as a series of one or more digits, as follows:

```
const    :       digit
         |       digit const
```

And, similarly, we can specify that a simple expression is just a number by writing

```
expr     :       const
```

It is now easy to tag on more interesting types of expressions. From any two valid expressions we can make another valid one by adding, subtracting, multiplying, or dividing them. Recursively again, we define

```
expr     :       const
         |       expr '+' expr
         |       expr '-' expr
         |       expr '*' expr
         |       expr '/' expr
         |       '(' expr ')'
```

The last line is for good form: if 2+5 is a valid expression, then so is (2+5). It also allows us to force the order of evaluation of subexpressions, but more about that later.

Formally, what we have defined here are three *production rules*. On the left side of the rule (before the colon) we write the phrase we want to define. On the right side we write a number of alternative ways in which the phrase can be constructed, separated by vertical bars. Quoted characters are called *literals*. Names written in capitals are called *terminals* or *tokens*. Everything else is called a *non-terminal* and must be defined, that is, it must occur somewhere on the left side of a production rule. A lexical analyzer is used to recognize the terminals and literals and pass them on to a parser. The parser can then restrict itself to checking the grammar, and building a "parse tree." This general structure is illustrated in Figure 12.1.

Figure 12.1 — General Structure of the Simulator

The scheduler evaluates the program by walking down the parse tree, evaluating its nodes in accordance with the semantics of the language. So it is important that the parser delivers a tree structure to the scheduler that is connected in such a way that it can be evaluated on the fly. But, more about the parser and the scheduler later; let us first look at the lexical analyzer.

A first specification of the lexical analyzer is fairly straightforward to define with the UNIX tool *lex*. In fact, with *lex*, it is easy to consider numbers a special class of token named CONST (uppercase, because it is now a terminal), with their numeric value attached as an attribute. In this way the grammar specification can assume the existence of the number tokens, rather than having to parse and check them for syntax. This is what the specification of the lexical analyzer looks like. We call this first version of the program spine (SPIN expression evaluator). As always, the line numbers are not part of the program text.

```
 1 /***** spine: lex.l *****/
 2
 3 %{
 4 #include "spin.h"
 5 #include "y.tab.h"
 6
 7 int lineno = 1;
 8 %}
 9
10 %%
11 [ \t]          { /* ignore white space */ }
12 [0-9]+         { yylval.val = atoi(yytext); return CONST; }
13 \n             { lineno++; }
14 .              { return yytext[0]; }
```

The program skips over white space (line 11), counts newlines (line 13), calculates the value of sequences of digits (line 12) and returns it as part of a token of type CONST. Everything else is passed on as a literal (line 14), i.e., as a single character. We rely on *yacc* to produce the definition of the name CONST. It is contained in the header file y.tab.h that is included on line 5. But before we discuss the input for *yacc*, we have to go back briefly to the grammar definition.

We still have to define what an expression such as 2+5*3 means. As far as our program is concerned, it could equally well mean either (2+5)*3 or 2+(5*3). The convention is that multiplication and division have a higher precedence than addition and subtraction, which means that the second interpretation is the correct one. We will see below how these precedence rules can be stated formally in a grammar specification.

All rules and definitions given so far can be expressed with the UNIX parser generator *yacc*. A complete *yacc* specification for the grammar defined so far looks as follows:

```
 1 /***** spine: spin.y *****/
 2
 3 %{
 4 #include "spin.h"           /* defines what Nodes are etc */
 5 %}
 6
```

```
 7 %union{                        /* defines the data type of   */
 8     int val;                   /* the internal parse stack   */
 9     Node *node;
10 }
11
12 %token     <val>    CONST      /* token CONST has a value    */
13 %type      <node>   expr       /* expressions produce nodes  */
14
15 %left      '+' '-'             /* left associative operators */
16 %left      '*' '/'             /* idem, highest precedence   */
17 %%
18
19 /** Grammar Rules **/
20
21 program : expr                 { printf("= %d\n", eval($1)); }
22            ;
23 expr    : '(' expr ')'         { $$ = $2; }
24         | expr '+' expr        { $$ = nn( 0, '+', $1, $3); }
25         | expr '-' expr        { $$ = nn( 0, '-', $1, $3); }
26         | expr '*' expr        { $$ = nn( 0, '*', $1, $3); }
27         | expr '/' expr        { $$ = nn( 0, '/', $1, $3); }
28         | CONST                { $$ = nn($1, CONST, 0, 0); }
29            ;
30 %%
```

Parts of this specification will look familiar. Lines 23 to 29 define the structure of expressions, and lines 15 and 16 define the precedence rules. Line 12 defines CONST to be a token with an attribute of type val. Line 21 defines that, in this version, we expect a PROMELA program to consist of a single expression.

There are also some new phrases. Line 13, for instance, contains the definition for the internal representation of an expression: a data structure named node. We use *yacc* to build a parse tree of a PROMELA program, or in this case a parse tree of an expression. For example, parsing the expression 2+5*3 produces the tree shown in Figure 12.2.

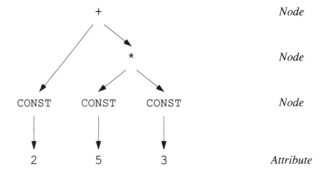

Figure 12.2 — Parse Tree for 2+5*3

The parse tree defines the structure of the program and will help us later to determine how it is to be interpreted.

The *yacc* file is used to generate what is called an *LALR(1)* parser that can build the tree in Figure 12.2. The parser scans its input in one pass from *left*-to-right. It builds a *rightmost derivation in reverse*, using at most *one look-a*head token. Each node in the parse tree is represented by a data structure that is defined in the include file spin.h, on lines 3 to 7. The structure is referred to in spin.y on lines 9 and 13.

```
 1 /***** spine: spin.h *****/
 2
 3 typedef struct Node {
 4     int     nval;           /* value attribute      */
 5     short   ntyp;           /* node type            */
 6     struct Node *lft, *rgt; /* children parse tree */
 7 } Node;
 8
 9 extern Node *nn();          /* allocates nodes      */
10 extern char *emalloc();     /* allocates memory     */
11 extern void exit();
```

We have used only binary arithmetic operators so each node in the tree needs to point to at most two descendants. In spin.h these are called lft and rgt, two pointers to structures of type Node. The definition of a Node also contains a field for storing the node type, which can be an operator such as '+', and '*', or it can be a terminal node of type CONST. Terminal nodes, of course, have no descendants (cf. Figure 12.2), but they do have an attribute of type nval which is used to store the numerical value of the constant calculated by the lexical analyzer and passed on to the parser in the yylval.val field of the token (line 12 of lex.1).

Now, back to the parser. Whenever a subexpression is recognized it is remembered in a structure of type Node. In our example we use the function nn() to prepare such a structure. Its type is declared in spin.h on line 9. The definition of the procedure itself looks as follows:

```
Node *
nn(v, t, l, r)
        Node *l, *r;
{
        Node *n = (Node *) emalloc(sizeof(Node));
        n->nval = v;
        n->ntyp = t;
        n->lft  = l;
        n->rgt  = r;
        return n;
}
```

The routine allocates memory for a new node in the parse tree, relying on emalloc() to check for error conditions and it returns a pointer to the initialized structure. For instance, when expression 5*3 is parsed, line 28 in spin.y is invoked twice, once for 5, once for 3. Each call produces a sub-expression of type CONST that is passed to line 26. The nodes of type CONST have no descendants, but the attribute fields are set to the value of the constant. The value produced by lex.1 is available in a predefined parameter named $1, where the 1 refers to the first field in the production rule on line 28. In this case there is only one field on the right side of that rule, so $1 is also the only valid parameter. The type of the field is an integer in this case, as defined on lines 8 and 12.

On line 26 a new node is constructed of type ′*′ with the two sub-expressions of type CONST as descendants. Arithmetical operators, such as ′*′, are passed as literals from the lexical analyzer to the parser. The data structures representing the two sub-expressions for the multiplication are again passed by *yacc* in two parameters, named $1 and $3. They point at the first and the third field of the production rule.

When the complete parse tree has been built it is passed to the production rule on line 21 and it can be interpreted. Here is the code for the interpreter.

```
eval(now)
        Node *now;
{
        if (now != (Node *) 0)
        switch (now->ntyp) {
        case CONST: return now->nval;
        case    '/': return (eval(now->lft) / eval(now->rgt));
        case    '*': return (eval(now->lft) * eval(now->rgt));
        case    '-': return (eval(now->lft) - eval(now->rgt));
        case    '+': return (eval(now->lft) + eval(now->rgt));
        default   : printf("spin: bad node type %d\n", now->ntyp);
                    exit(1);
        }
        return 0;
}
```

The default clause defends against unknown node types. The known types of nodes are evaluated recursively until the final answer is produced.

If we put all these pieces together we get the PROMELA expression evaluator. Here is a complete listing, together with the remaining routines that escaped mention above.

```
 1 /***** spine: spin.h *****/
 2
 3 typedef struct Node {
 4      int    nval;              /* value attribute    */
 5      short  ntyp;              /* node type          */
 6      struct Node *lft, *rgt; /* children parse tree */
 7 } Node;
 8
 9 extern Node *nn();            /* allocates nodes    */
10 extern char *emalloc();       /* allocates memory   */
11 extern void exit();
```

```
12
13 /***** spine: lex.l *****/
14
15 %{
16 #include "spin.h"
17 #include "y.tab.h"
18
19 int lineno = 1;
20 %}
21
22 %%
23 [ \t]          { /* ignore white space */ }
24 [0-9]+         { yylval.val = atoi(yytext); return CONST; }
25 \n             { lineno++; }
26 .              { return yytext[0]; }
27
28 /***** spine: spin.y *****/
29
30 %{
31 #include "spin.h"           /* defines what Nodes are etc */
32 %}
33
34 %union{                     /* defines the data type of    */
35     int val;                /* the internal parse stack    */
36     Node *node;
37 }
38
39 %token      <val>   CONST   /* token CONST has a value     */
40 %type       <node>  expr    /* expressions produce nodes   */
41
42 %left       '+' '-'         /* left associative operators  */
43 %left       '*' '/'         /* idem, highest precedence    */
44 %%
45
46 /** Grammar Rules **/
47
48 program : expr              { printf("= %d\n", eval($1)); }
49         ;
50 expr    : '(' expr ')'      { $$ = $2; }
51         | expr '+' expr     { $$ = nn( 0, '+', $1, $3); }
52         | expr '-' expr     { $$ = nn( 0, '-', $1, $3); }
53         | expr '*' expr     { $$ = nn( 0, '*', $1, $3); }
54         | expr '/' expr     { $$ = nn( 0, '/', $1, $3); }
55        | CONST             { $$ = nn($1, CONST, 0, 0); }
56        ;
57 %%
58
59 /***** spine: run.c *****/
60
61 #include "spin.h"
62 #include "y.tab.h"
63
64 eval(now)
65     Node *now;
```

```
66 {
67      if (now != (Node *) 0)
68      switch (now->ntyp) {
69      case CONST: return now->nval;
70      case  '/': return (eval(now->lft) / eval(now->rgt));
71      case  '*': return (eval(now->lft) * eval(now->rgt));
72      case  '-': return (eval(now->lft) - eval(now->rgt));
73      case  '+': return (eval(now->lft) + eval(now->rgt));
74      default   : printf("spin: bad node type %d\n", now->ntyp);
75                  exit(1);
76      }
77      return 0;
78 }
79
80 /***** spine: main.c *****/
81
82 #include "spin.h"
83 #include "y.tab.h"
84
85 main()
86 {
87      yyparse();
88      exit(0);
89 }
90
91 yywrap()     /* a dummy routine */
92 {
93      return 1;
94 }
95
96 yyerror(s1, s2)      /* called by yacc on syntax errors */
97      char *s1, *s2;
98 {
99      extern int lineno;
100     char buf[128];
101     sprintf(buf, s1, s2);
102     printf("spine: line %d: %s\n", lineno, buf);
103 }
104
105 char *
106 emalloc(n)
107 {   extern char *malloc();   /* library functions */
108     extern char *memset();
109
110     char *tmp = malloc(n);
111     if (!tmp)
112     {       printf("spine: not enough memory\n");
113             exit(1);
114     }
115     memset(tmp,0,n);          /* clear memory */
116     return tmp;
117 }
118
119 Node *
```

```
120 nn(v, t, l, r)
121     Node *l, *r;
122 {
123     Node *n = (Node *) emalloc(sizeof(Node));
124     n->nval = v;
125     n->ntyp = t;
126     n->lft  = l;
127     n->rgt  = r;
128     return n;
129 }
```

To compile this set of programs, the following *makefile* can be used.

```
# ***** spine: makefile *****
CC=cc             # ANSI C compiler
CFLAGS=           # no flags yet
YFLAGS=-v -d -D # verbose, debugging
OFILES= spin.o lex.o main.o run.o
spine:  $(OFILES)
        $(CC) $(CFLAGS) -o spine $(OFILES)
%.o:    %.c spin.h      # all files depend on spin.h
        $(CC) $(CFLAGS) -c $%.c
```

The *makefile* defines which flags must be passed to *yacc* and *cc* and it records the dependencies among the source files. It states, for instance, that when spin.h changes, all object files must be recreated. The *makefile* is read by another UNIX utility called *make* to produce the executable program spine. Here is the dialogue that is printed on my system if this program is compiled and invoked with a sample expression.

```
$ make
yacc -v -d -D spin.y
cc -c y.tab.c
rm y.tab.c
mv y.tab.o spin.o
lex  lex.l
cc -c lex.yy.c
rm lex.yy.c
mv lex.yy.o lex.o
cc -c main.c
cc -c run.c
cc -o spine spin.o lex.o main.o run.o
$ echo "2+5*3" | spine
= 17
$
```

The complete program must of course recognize quite a few other language features before it can simulate PROMELA programs. They can be grouped into five classes:

○ Variables
○ Statements
○ Control-flow constructs

○ Processes
○ Macro expansion

VARIABLES (Section 12.4, page 259)

We have to consider variable declarations, assignments to variables and references variables, generally in expressions built from the full range of arithmetic and logical operators, plus the special operators len and run. We consider variables of the five basic data types bit, bool, byte, short, and int, plus the declaration of channel type identifiers with the keyword chan.

STATEMENTS (Section 12.5, page 269)

There are two types of unconditional statements: assignments to variables and the print statement we added to the simulator. There are also five basic types of conditional statements: boolean conditions, timeouts, send and receive statements, and assert. The ''pseudo-statement'' skip can be implemented as the equivalent of the condition (1).

CONTROL FLOW (Section 12.6, page 277)

We have to consider the sequential control flow specifications: goto, break, selection, repetition, and atomic statements.

PROCESSES AND MESSAGE TYPES (Section 12.7, page 284)

Most importantly, we have to implement the code for parsing and interpreting global declarations for both process types and message types.

MACRO EXPANSION (Section 12.8, page 293)

One of the easier parts of the code. Macro expansion is achieved by routing the input to SPIN through the standard C preprocessor before parsing begins.

TO THE BRAVE

Each of the next four sections focuses on one of these four extensions of the little program spine, that was discussed above. This discussion ultimately leads us to the full simulator source of SPIN as it is listed in Appendix D. The discussion below is primarily meant for the benefit of those who would like to expand, or modify the code, or the language that it parses. Feel free to skip sections or to move directly to a safer part of the chapter, such as Section 12.9 explaining the general use of the program. The brave who delve into the code may occasionally want to refer back to this overview or to the previews at the beginning of each section. To see the code in context they may also want to refer to the appendix. Appendix D includes an index of all the code, together with references to the page numbers that explain it.

12.4 VARIABLES

Most of the code that is required for the manipulation of variables is contained in two files. The first file, sym.c, contains the definition of a general symbol table handler. The second file, vars.c, contains the code for storing and manipulating variables of the basic data types. We do not worry too much about variables of type chan just yet. The bulk of that will come in the next extension when message passing is implemented. For now, we will just parse the declarations. To fully implement the other types of variables, we need some new hooks in the lexical analyzer, the parser and in the expression evaluation routine. The next four subsections, then, focus on these extensions:

   ○ Extensions to the lexical analyzer (Section 12.4.1, page 259)
   ○ New symbol table routines (Section 12.4.2, page 261)
   ○ Extensions to the parser (Section 12.4.3, page 264)
   ○ New code for the evaluator (Section 12.4.4, page 267)

We begin by taking a look at the changes that have to be made in the lexical analyzer.

12.4.1 LEXICAL ANALYZER

There is a range of new tokens that must be added to recognize variable names and declarations in the input to the simulator. There are also several PROMELA operators that consist of more than one character and are best recognized in the lexical analyzer and converted into tokens. Let's first look at variable declarations. Recognizing the five basic data types and the keyword chan produces the following extra rules in lex.l.

```
"int"   { yylval.val =   INT; Token TYPE; }
"short" { yylval.val = SHORT; Token TYPE; }
"byte"  { yylval.val =  BYTE; Token TYPE; }
"bool"  { yylval.val =   BIT; Token TYPE; }
"bit"   { yylval.val =   BIT; Token TYPE; }
"chan"  { yylval.val =  CHAN; Token TYPE; }
```

Each declarator is passed as a token of type TYPE. The attribute is a constant, defined in spin.h, that specifies the width of each data type in bits (except for CHAN).

```
#define BIT     1        /* data types    */
#define BYTE    8        /* width in bits */
#define SHORT   16
#define INT     32
#define CHAN    64
```

The term Token is also defined in a macro

```
#define Token   if (!in_comment) return
```

which in combination with the following two lines

```
"/*"     { in_comment=1; }
"*/"     { in_comment=0; }
```

guarantees that no lexical tokens are passed to the parser within PROMELA comments.

The two-character operators are recognized by the following new *lex* rules.

```
"<<"    { Token LSHIFT; /* shift bits left  */ }
">>"    { Token RSHIFT; /* shift bits right */ }
"<="    { Token     LE; /* less than or equal to */ }
">="    { Token     GE; /* greater than or equal to */ }
"=="    { Token     EQ; /* equal to */ }
"!="    { Token     NE; /* not equal to */ }
"&&"    { Token    AND; /* logical and */ }
"||"    { Token     OR; /* logical or */ }
```

Most single character operators, such as '<' or '>' are still passed by the last line of the rules section:

```
{ Token yytext[0]; }
```

which was basically unmodified from the version used in spine. An exception is the assignment operator '=', which is converted into a real token, named ASGN. It is also given a value attribute that is set to the line number on which the assignment was found.

```
"="     { yylval.val = lineno; Token ASGN; }
```

To facilitate debugging, as many tokens as possible are tagged with a line number that refers back to the PROMELA source file. The above *lex* rule shows how that works for the assignment statement. The treatment of tokens for alphanumeric names is implemented slightly differently. To simplify the code that *lex* has to produce a little bit, we look up predefined alphanumeric names in a static table with procedure check_name(). The procedure is called from within the *lex* rule

```
[a-zA-Z_][a-zA-Z_0-9]* { Token check_name(yytext); }
```

An arbitrary name starts with an upper or lower case letter, and is followed by zero or more letters or digits. Underscores are allowed in names. To recognize the keywords len, run, and of (used in chan initializers), for instance, we can write:

```
static struct {
        char *s;        int tok;
} Names[] = {
        "len",          LEN,
        "run",          RUN,
        "of",           OF,
        0,              0,
};
```

```
check_name(s)
        char *s;
{
        register int i;
        for (i = 0; Names[i].s; i++)
                if (strcmp(s, Names[i].s) == 0)
                {       yylval.val = lineno;
                        return Names[i].tok;
                }
        yylval.sym = lookup(s); /* symbol table */
        return NAME;
}
```

Unrecognized names go through to the symbol table routines, all others come back immediately with a line number attached.

All new token names must be defined properly in the *yacc* grammar specification, but we will come to that later. Let us first look at the way in which names are stored in the symbol table. So far we have no separate processes, so all names are necessarily global. The routine lookup() is defined in a new file sym.c with a symbol table handler.

12.4.2 SYMBOL TABLE HANDLER

Each new name is stored in a data structure of type Symbol that is defined in the new version of spin.h.

```
typedef struct Symbol {
        char    *name;
        short   type;           /* variable or chan type   */
        int     nel;            /* 1 if scalar, >1 if array */
        int     *val;           /* runtime value(s), initl 0 */
        struct Node     *ini;   /* initial value, or chan-def */
        struct Symbol   *next;  /* linked list */
} Symbol;
```

The structure Symbol contains the full name of the symbol being stored as a pointer to a character string. It also holds its type and the number of elements that are accessible if the name is defined to be an array. The pointer ini points to a parse tree fragment that can be evaluated to initialize a new identifier: a channel initializer for message channels, or an integer expression for variables of the five basic data types. The integer pointer val points to a location where the runtime values of global variables are stored.

The last element of the structure, next, points to another symbol. In its simplest form then, the symbol table can be implemented as a single linked list pointed to by

```
Symbol *symtab.
```

Initially the list is empty:

```
symtab = (Symbol *) 0.
```

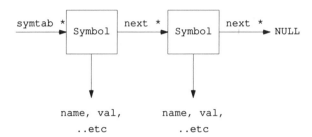

Figure 12.3 — Linked List for the Symbol Table

Inserting a new symbol `sp` at the front list takes just two assignments in C:

```
sp->next = symtab;
symtab = sp;
```

Linked lists will come back a few more times in the other extensions we make.
We use them, for instance, to implement message channels and for storing process
references in the scheduler. Figure 12.3 illustrates how the linked list is used for
the symbol table routines.

The complete lookup routine, using the linked list, can be written as follows:

```
Symbol *
lookup(s)
        char *s;
{
        Symbol *sp;
        /* check if symbol is already in the list */
        for (sp = symtab; sp; sp = sp->next)
                if (strcmp(sp->name, s) == 0)
                        return sp;       /* yes it is */
        /* if not, create a new symbol */
        sp = (Symbol *) emalloc(sizeof(Symbol));
        sp->name = (char *) emalloc(strlen(s) + 1);
        strcpy(sp->name, s);
        sp->nel = 1;                     /* scalar */
        /* insert it in the list */
        sp->next = symtab;
        symtab = sp;
        return sp;
}
```

The routine `emalloc()` allocates and clears memory for us, so by default the type
and the initial value of a new variable are both zero. The lookup routine is called
by the lexical analyzer that, as defined, has not enough context to determine the
type of a variable name or even if it is used as a scalar or as a vector. A separate
routine `settype()` is called by the parser to initialize the type field of variables
when that information has been collected. In the same check we can also make
sure that an array was not accidentally given a negative dimension. The first argu-

ment to settype() is a linked list of names, with a pointer into the symbol table
for each name.

```
settype(n, t)
        Node *n;
{
        while (n)
        {       if (n->nsym->type)
                    yyerror("redeclaration of `%s'", n->nsym->name);
                n->nsym->type = t;
                if (n->nsym->nel <= 0)
                    yyerror("bad array size for `%s'", n->nsym->name);
                n = n->rgt;
        }
}
```

The code maintains the same bookkeeping for all variables, scalars and arrays alike.
A scalar is simply an array of size one.

Using only a single linked list to store all names, however, makes the lexical
analyzer spend a disproportionate amount of time looking up variable names in the
initial for loop of routine lookup(). For each new name, the routine would be
forced to look at *all* previously entered names, before it can finally decide that a
new symbol must be created. The longer the list, the more severe the time penalty
becomes. A standard solution to this problem is to use a *hash-table* lookup
scheme. We use the name of the symbol to calculate a unique index into an array
of symbol tables (the hash-table), and store the symbol there. The average search
time goes down linearly with the size of the hash table. It leads to the following
version, with Nhash a constant defined in spin.h. The value of Nhash must be of
the type $2 \sup n - 1$, with arbitrary n.

```
Symbol  *symtab[Nhash+1];

hash(s)
        char *s;
{
        int h=0;
        while (*s)
        {       h += *s++;
                h <<= 1;
                if (h&(Nhash+1))
                        h |= 1;
        }
        return h&Nhash;
}

Symbol *
lookup(s)
        char *s;
{
        Symbol *sp;
        int h=hash(s);
```

```
              for (sp = symtab[h]; sp; sp = sp->next)
                            return sp;                      /* found */
              sp = (Symbol *) emalloc(sizeof(Symbol));      /* add */
              sp->name = (char *) emalloc(strlen(s) + 1);
              strcpy(sp->name, s);
              sp->nel = 1;
              sp->next = symtab[h];
              symtab[h] = sp;
              return sp;
      }
```

12.4.3 PARSER

Now let us look at the extensions that we must make in the parser to recognize variable names, declarations, and the new operators. First, recall that a token of type NAME has an attribute of type Symbol. We must therefore extend the definition of the parser's stack.

```
%union{
        int val;
        Node *node;
        Symbol *sym;
}
```

There are also some new token names and quite a few new precedence rules. Here is what we added.

```
%token   <val>    LEN OF
%token   <val>    CONST TYPE ASGN
%token   <sym>    NAME
%type    <sym>    var ivar
%type    <node>   expr var_list
%type    <node>   args arg typ_list
%right            ASGN
%left             OR
%left             AND
%left             '|'
%left             '&'
%left             EQ NE
%left             '>' '<' GE LE
%left             LSHIFT RSHIFT
%left             '+' '-'
%left             '*' '/' '%'
%left             '~' UMIN NEG
```

The assignment operator ASGN is right associative and gets the lowest precedence of all operators. The new token of type NAME has a symbol attribute pointing to a slot in the symbol table.

A sequence of zero or more variable declarations is parsed as follows:

```
any_decl: /* empty */              { $$ = (Node *) 0; }
        | one_decl ';' any_decl    { $$ = nn(0, 0, ',', $1, $3); }
        ;
one_decl: TYPE var_list            { settype($2, $1); $$ = $2; }
        ;
```

As soon as a complete variable declaration is recognized, in the last production above, the routine settype() is called to store the extra type information in the symbol table. Before we look at the definition of a var_list, note that a variable name can be followed by an array index. Variables are therefore defined in the grammar as a non-terminal var, of type sym.

```
var     : NAME                     { $1->nel =  1; $$ = $1; }
        | NAME '[' CONST ']'       { $1->nel = $3; $$ = $1; }
```

For the time being we just remember the array size specified, and check it for its validity later when a procedure settype() is called. A variable can also have an initialization field. An initialized variable can be defined as a non-terminal ivar, as follows:

```
ivar    : var                      { $$ = $1; }
        | var ASGN expr            { $1->ini = $3; $$ = $1; }
        | var ASGN ch_init         { $1->ini = $3; $$ = $1; }
        ;
ch_init : '[' CONST ']' OF '{' typ_list '}'
                                   { if ($2) u_async++; else u_sync++;
                                     cnt_mpars($6);
                                     $$ = nn(0, $2, CHAN, 0, $6);
                                   }
        ;
```

The initializer can be either an expression returning a value or a channel specification. The production rules above allow both. Some statistics are gathered about the number of message parameters used and the number of synchronous and asynchronous channels that are declared. The list of data types in a channel initializer is also quickly defined.

```
typ_list: TYPE                     { $$ = nn(0, 0, $1, 0,  0); }
        | TYPE ',' typ_list        { $$ = nn(0, 0, $1, 0, $3); }
        ;
```

The check that, for instance, a channel is not initialized with an expression can be placed in the code that performs the actual initializations. The set of production rules that deals with variable declarations can be completed by defining

```
var_list: ivar                     { $$ = nn($1, 0, TYPE, 0,  0); }
        | ivar ',' var_list        { $$ = nn($1, 0, TYPE, 0, $3); }
        ;
```

The node allocation routine nn() must now also handle the new symbol-table references. It is extended as follows:

```
Node *
nn(s, v, t, l, r)
        Symbol *s;
        Node *l, *r;
{
        Node *n = (Node *) emalloc(sizeof(Node));
        n->nval = v;
        n->ntyp = t;
        n->nsym = s;
        n->fname = Fname;
        n->lft  = l;
        n->rgt  = r;
        return n;
}
```

Next, we have to prepare to parse the new operators that we have added. Most of it is straightforward. The series of production rules for expressions merely grows a bit.

```
expr    : '(' expr ')'          { $$ = $2; }
        | expr '+' expr         { $$ = nn(0, 0,  '+', $1, $3); }
        | expr '-' expr         { $$ = nn(0, 0,  '-', $1, $3); }
        . . .
        | expr AND expr         { $$ = nn(0, 0,  AND, $1, $3); }
        | expr OR  expr         { $$ = nn(0, 0,   OR, $1, $3); }
        . . .
        | expr LSHIFT expr      { $$ = nn(0, 0,LSHIFT,$1, $3); }
        | expr RSHIFT expr      { $$ = nn(0, 0,RSHIFT,$1, $3); }
        | '~' expr              { $$ = nn(0, 0,  '~', $2,  0); }
        | '-' expr %prec UMIN   { $$ = nn(0, 0, UMIN, $2,  0); }
        | '!' expr %prec NEG    { $$ = nn(0, 0,  '!', $2,  0); }
        | LEN '(' varref ')'    { $$ = nn($3->nsym,$1,LEN,$3,0); }
        | varref                { $$ = $1; }
        | CONST                 { $$ = nn(0, $1, CONST, 0, 0); }
        ;
```

Perhaps the most interesting additions are the new types of expressions for the bit-wise, arithmetic and logical unary operations: bitwise complement ' ~ ', unary minus and boolean negation. Since the minus operator can also be used as a binary operator we have to set its precedence explicitly with the *yacc* keyword %prec. And, of course, the negation operator ' ! ' will double in one of the next extensions as a binary send operator, so its precedence in this grammar rule is also explicitly set. In the final version we replace the character token ' ! ' with a token SND, which is again labeled with a line number to improve error reporting.

The variable references, used in the last two production rules, are defined as follows:

```
varref  : NAME                  { $$ = nn($1, 0,  NAME,  0,  0); }
        | NAME '[' expr ']'     { $$ = nn($1, 0,  NAME, $3,  0); }
        ;
```

There are just two types of variable references, one for scalars and one for arrays.
They both return a node of type NAME with the first field referring to the symbol
that defines the variable name. The left pointer specifies the optional array index.
A null pointer in place of an index trivially evaluates to zero. It should produce an
error if we try to determine the "length" of anything other than a channel variable.
The parser, however, does not check this.

12.4.4 EVALUATOR

The last routine we must look at for the addition of variables is the evaluator code
in run.c Luckily, the extension is almost trivial. There are merely some new
cases in the switch. For instance:

```
switch (now->ntyp) {
...
case      NE: return (eval(now->lft) != eval(now->rgt));
case      EQ: return (eval(now->lft) == eval(now->rgt));
case      OR: return (eval(now->lft) || eval(now->rgt));
case     AND: return (eval(now->lft) && eval(now->rgt));
case LSHIFT: return (eval(now->lft) << eval(now->rgt));
case RSHIFT: return (eval(now->lft) >> eval(now->rgt));
...
case  ASGN: return setval(now->lft, eval(now->rgt));
case  NAME: return getval(now->nsym, eval(now->lft));
...
```

The only interesting new cases are the variable references on the last two lines
above. They are implemented with two procedure calls: getval() and setval().

To process an assignment, first the value to be assigned is determined by evaluating
the expression pointed to via now->rgt. Next, the target variable, and possibly its
index, must be found. All the information is available via the left pointer, which is
passed to setval(). A node of type NAME contains a pointer to the symbol table,
with the alpha-numeric variable name, and it contains an index for array references
or a null pointer for scalars. The routines getval() and setval() are defined in
vars.c. For global variables, the only type of variables we have so far, the routine
setval() hands the job to routine setglobal(), which checks the index and if
necessary allocates memory for the variables.

```
setglobal(v, m)
        Node *v;
{
        int n = eval(v->lft);
        if (checkvar(v->nsym, n))
                v->nsym->val[n] = m;
        return 1;
}
```

with checkvar() defined as follows:

```
checkvar(s, n)
        Symbol *s;
{
        int i;
        if (n >= s->nel || n < 0)
        {       yyerror("array indexing error, '%s'", s->name);
                return 0;
        }
        if (s->type == 0)
        {       yyerror("undecl var '%s' (assuming int)", s->name);
                s->type = INT;
        }
        if (s->val == (int *) 0)            /* uninitialized */
        {       s->val = (int *) emalloc(s->nel*sizeof(int));
                for (i = 0; i < s->nel; i++)
                {       if (s->type != CHAN)
                                s->val[i] = eval(s->ini);
                        else
                                s->val[i] = qmake(s);
        }       }
        return 1;
}
```

A plain variable is initialized by evaluating the expression in the initialization field
of the symbol. A null pointer in this field, again, trivially evaluates to the default
initial value zero. A channel variable is initialized by passing the initialization
pointer to a routine qmake() that is discussed in the next section. A type clash
between initializer and variable triggers an error in either the evaluator or in the
channel building routine.

The routine getval() hands off to getglobal().

```
getglobal(s, n)
        Symbol *s;
{
        if (checkvar(s, n))
                return cast_val(s->type, s->val[n]);
        return 0;
}
```

A zero result is returned if the checkvar routine fails, that is, if an indexing error
was detected. The routine cast_val() interprets the type of the variable and
masks or casts variable values accordingly.

```
cast_val(t, v)
{       int i=0; short s=0; unsigned char u=0;
        if (t == INT || t == CHAN) i = v;
        else if (t == SHORT) s = (short) v;
        else if (t == BYTE)  u = (unsigned char)v;
        else if (t == BIT)   u = (unsigned char)(v&1);
        if (v != i+s+u)
                yyerror("value %d truncated in assignment", v);
        return (int)(i+s+u);
}
```

It is considered an error if a value changes due to type casting. Variables are only cast to the right value when they are read. Internally, all values are stored in 32-bit integers.

12.5 STATEMENTS

Adding statements is relatively easy at this point. We discuss four sets of extensions:

- ○ Extensions to the lexical analyzer (Section 12.5.1, page 269)
- ○ Extensions to the parser (Section 12.5.2, page 270)
- ○ Extensions to the evaluation routines (Section 12.5.3, page 270)
- ○ The implementation of message passing (Section 12.5.4, page 272)

To implement message passing statements we add a new file `mesg.c`. We begin by adding five types of statements: boolean conditions, `timeouts`, assignments, `printf`, and `assert` statements, plus the pseudo-statement `skip`.

12.5.1 LEXICAL ANALYZER

Three of the statements, `assert`, `printf`, and `timeout`, produce new entries into the static lookup table of alphanumeric names in the lexical analyzer.

```
static struct {
        char *s;          int tok;
} Names[] = {
        "assert",         ASSERT,
        "printf",         PRINT,
        "timeout",        TIMEOUT,
        ...
};
```

The line number attached to the tokens by the routine `checkname()` allows us to produce the right feedback to a user when an `assert` statement fails during a simulation run.

The pseudo statement `skip` is translated into the equivalent constant with the *lex* rule

```
"skip"          { yylval.val = 1; return CONST; }
```

To implement the `printf` statement properly, we must define strings. The only place where string arguments are used is in `printf`'s, so we can treat it as a special token with a symbol attribute. The symbol pointer than holds the string, rather than the variable name. This produces one more *lex* rule.

```
\".*\"          { yylval.sym = lookup(yytext); return STRING; }
```

Finally, we add a rule for translating arrows into semicolons.

```
"->"                { return ';'; /* statement separator */ }
```

12.5.2 PARSER

To update the parser we must add some new production rules again for parsing statements. So far, a statement can be an assignment, a print statement, an assertion, a jump, or an expression (a condition). The `timeout` is implemented as a special predefined variable that can be part of a condition. It is added in the code for parsing expressions.

```
stmnt   : varref ASGN expr      { $$ = nn($1->nsym,$2, ASGN,$1,$3); }
        | PRINT '(' STRING prargs ')' { $$=nn($3, $1, PRINT,$4, 0); }
        | ASSERT expr           { $$ = nn(0, $1, ASSERT, $2, 0); }
        | GOTO NAME             { $$ = nn($2,$1,   GOTO,  0, 0); }
        | expr                  { $$ = nn(0,lineno, 'c', $1, 0); }
        ...
expr    : TIMEOUT               { $$ = nn(0, $1,TIMEOUT,  0, 0); }
        ...
```

We have made a separate production rule for parsing variable references, named `varref`. It can be used in a few more cases later.

A *sequence* of statements is defined as follows:

```
sequence: step                  { add_seq($1); }
        | sequence ';' step     { add_seq($3); }
        ;
step    : any_decl stmnt        { $$ = $2; }
        ;
```

There is no need to group declarations at the start of a program body in PROMELA, so in the rules above we have allowed each statement to be preceded by one or more declarations. The routine `add_seq()` is defined in `flow.c` to tag statements onto a linked list, but we look at that in more detail in Section 12.6. For now, a program body is just a sequence of statements, which is parsed as follows:

```
body    : '{'                   { open_seq(1); }
            sequence            { add_seq(Stop); }
        '}'                     { $$ = close_seq(); }
        ;
```

The first open brace starts a new linked list to store the statements via a call on routine `open_seq()`. When a complete sequence is recognized a special `Stop` node is tagged onto the end and the sequence is closed and passed up in the parse tree. We look at the routines for manipulating the sequences in `flow.c` in more detail later when we discuss compound statements. Let us first now consider the additions we have to make in the interpreter code to evaluate the statements added so far.

12.5.3 EVALUATOR

The additions are still modest. The interpreter only has to handle these new node types.

```
case TIMEOUT: return Tval;
case     'c': return eval(now->lft); /* condition */
case   PRINT: return interprint(now);
case  ASSERT: if (eval(now->lft)) return 1;
              yyerror("assertion violated", (char *)0);
              wrapup(); exit(1);
```

Timeouts are a modeling feature of PROMELA; they are implemented as a test on a predefined variable here. In the final simulator the scheduler can explicitly enable or disable timeout events to test if the protocol can recover from exception conditions. Conditions, identified by the internal node type 'c', are evaluated recursively and return a zero or non-zero status. The assert statement is interpreted directly and causes an error exit if it fails, printing the line number that was duly carried along as a token attribute. We have moved the grubby details of the implementation of the print statements into a separate procedure interprint(). It can be defined as follows:

```
interprint(n)
        Node *n;
{
        Node *tmp = n->lft;
        char c, *s = n->nsym->name;
        int i, j;
        for (i = 0; i < strlen(s); i++)
                switch (s[i]) {
                default:   putchar(s[i]); break;
                case '\"': break; /* ignore */
                case '\\':
                        switch(s[++i]) {
                        case 't': putchar('\t'); break;
                        case 'n': putchar('\n'); break;
                        default:  putchar(s[i]); break;
                        }
                        break;
                case '%':
                        if ((c = s[++i]) == '%')
                        {       putchar('%'); /* literal */
                                break;
                        }
                        if (!tmp)
                        {       yyerror("too few print args %s", s);
                                break;
                        }
                        j = eval(tmp->lft);
                        tmp = tmp->rgt;
                        switch(c) {
                        case 'd': printf("%d", j); break;
                        case 'o': printf("%o", j); break;
                        case 'u': printf("%u", j); break;
                        case 'x': printf("%x", j); break;
                        default:  break; /* ignore */
                        }
```

```
                          break;
                 }
         fflush(stdout);
         return 1;
     }
```

which recognizes a modest number of conversions of the UNIX library function
printf().

12.5.4 IMPLEMENTING MESSAGE PASSING

The synchronous and asynchronous message passing primitives are good for
another two to three hundred lines of source text. The easiest part is the extension
of the parser to pass the new statements on to the interpreter.

The sending and receiving get a relatively low evaluation priority, equivalent to
assignment. Three new types of statements are added.

```
    stmnt   : ...
            | varref RCV margs      { $$ = nn($1->nsym, $2, 'r',$1,$3); }
            | varref SND margs      { $$ = nn($1->nsym, $2, 's',$1,$3); }
```

with message arguments defined as follows:

```
    margs   : arg                   { $$ = $1; }
            | expr '(' arg ')'      { $$ = nn(0, 0, ',', $1, $3); }
            ;
    arg     : expr                  { $$ = nn(0, 0, ',', $1,   0); }
            | expr ',' arg          { $$ = nn(0, 0, ',', $1, $3); }
            ;
```

The arguments of a receive operation can only be constants or names, but it is
easier to verify that part of the syntax later. There is also one new type of expression

```
    expr    : ...
            | varref RCV '[' margs ']' { $$ = nn($1->nsym,$2, 'R', $1, $4); }
```

which corresponds to a side-effect free test of the executability of a receive statement (see Chapter 5).

The interpreter now has three extra clauses for the new internal node types 'r',
's', and 'R'. This corresponds to the following code in run.c.

```
         case LEN:       return qlen(now);
         case 's':       return qsend(now);
         case 'r':       return qrecv(now, 1); /* full-receive */
         case 'R':       return qrecv(now, 0); /* test only    */
```

The three procedures called here, together with the procedure for the initialization
of new channels qmake() mentioned in passing before, are expanded in the file
mesg.c. Let us first look at the implementation of qmake().

The descriptions of the message channels are stored in a linked list of structures of
type Queue, using the following definition from spin.h.

```
typedef struct Queue {
        short   qid;                /* runtime q index       */
        short   qlen;               /* nr messages stored    */
        short   nslots, nflds;      /* capacity, flds/slot   */
        short   *fld_width;         /* type of each field    */
        int     *contents;          /* the actual buffer     */
        struct Queue     *nxt;      /* linked list */
} Queue;
```

In mesg.c the head of the list is defined like this.

```
Queue *qtab = (Queue *) 0;         /* linked list */
int nqs = 0;                       /* number of queues      */
```

The rest is easy. We give zero length (rendezvous) channels one slot to temporarily hold a message as it is passed from a sender to a receiver.

```
qmake(s)
        Symbol *s;
{
        Node *m;
        Queue *q;
        int i; extern int analyze;
        if (!s->ini)
                return 0;
        if (s->ini->ntyp != CHAN)
                fatal("bad channel initializer for %s\n", s->name);
        if (nqs >= MAXQ)
                fatal("too many queues (%s)", s->name);
        q = (Queue *) emalloc(sizeof(Queue));
        q->qid = ++nqs;
        q->nslots = s->ini->nval;
        for (m = s->ini->rgt; m; m = m->rgt)
                q->nflds++;
        i = max(1, q->nslots);   /* 0-slot qs get 1 slot minimum */
        q->contents  = (int *) emalloc(q->nflds*i*sizeof(int));
        q->fld_width = (short *) emalloc(q->nflds*sizeof(short));
        for (m = s->ini->rgt, i = 0; m; m = m->rgt)
                q->fld_width[i++] = m->ntyp;
        q->nxt = qtab;
        qtab = q;
        ltab[q->qid-1] = q;
        return q->qid;
}
```

Of course, a channel can only be created if an initializer is provided. It is a fatal error if the initializer has the wrong type or if too many channels already exist. For efficiency only, an index to all active channels is also maintained in a linear list named ltab. Implementing qlen() is now straightforward.

```
qlen(n)
        Node *n;
{
        int whichq = eval(n->lft)-1;
```

```
        if (whichq < MAXQ && whichq >= 0 && ltab[whichq])
                return ltab[whichq]->qlen;
        return 0;
}
```

We check that the index calculated is within the correct range, that the corresponding queue exists, and return the length field from the corresponding data structure. The hard part remains: the implementation of synchronous and asynchronous versions of qsend() and qrecv(). We use a simple interface to decide which routine to use.

```
qsend(n)
        Node *n;
{
        int whichq = eval(n->lft)-1;
        if (whichq < MAXQ && whichq >= 0 && ltab[whichq])
        {       if (ltab[whichq]->nslots > 0)
                        return a_snd(ltab[whichq], n);
                else
                        return s_snd(ltab[whichq], n);
        }
        return 0;
}
qrecv(n, full)
        Node *n;
{
        int whichq = eval(n->lft)-1;
        if (whichq < MAXQ && whichq >= 0 && ltab[whichq])
                return a_rcv(ltab[whichq], n, full);
        return 0;
}
```

A rendezvous is triggered by the sender of a message. If, at that time, at least one process is blocked on the matching receive operation, a rendezvous can take place. The rendezvous receive operation, therefore, can be the same for both synchronous and asynchronous operations. First we consider the asynchronous case. Its basic form looks as follows (the version in Appendix D contains a few more features that are not relevant here):

```
a_snd(q, n)
        Queue *q;
        Node *n;
{
        Node *m;
        int i = q->qlen*q->nflds;       /* q offset */
        int j = 0;                      /* q field# */
        if (q->nslots > 0 && q->qlen >= q->nslots)
                return 0;       /* q is full */
        for (m = n->rgt; m && j < q->nflds; m = m->rgt, j++)
          q->contents[i+j] = cast_val(q->fld_width[j], eval(m->lft));
        q->qlen++;
        return 1;
}
```

If the channel is full, a zero status is returned, which means that the statement is currently unexecutable. If there is at least one free slot in the queue, the fields are copied and masked with the predefined field widths. The receive operation is a little more involved.

```
a_rcv(q, n, full)
        Queue *q;
        Node *n;
{
        Node *m;
        int j, k;
        if (q->qlen == 0) return 0;       /* q is empty */
        for (m = n->rgt, j=0; m && j<q->nflds; m = m->rgt, j++)
        {       if (m->lft->ntyp == CONST
                && q->contents[j] != m->lft->nval)
                        return 0;         /* no match */
        }
        for (m = n->rgt, j=0; j<q->nflds; m = (m)?m->rgt:m, j++)
        {       if (m && m->lft->ntyp == NAME)
                        setval(m->lft, q->contents[j]);
                for (k = 0; full && k < q->qlen-1; k++)
                        q->contents[k*q->nflds+j] =
                        q->contents[(k+1)*q->nflds+j];
        }
        if (full) q->qlen--;
        return 1;
}
```

The argument `full` is zero when the receive operation is used as a condition, as in qname?[ack], and non-zero otherwise. In the first case the procedure has no side-effects and merely returns the executability status of the receive. There are two `for` loops in the procedure. The first one checks that all message parameters that are declared as constants are properly matched and it checks that the other parameters are variable names. The second cycle copies the data from the queue into the variables specified and, as required, shifts message fields up one slot.

Only the synchronous version of the send operation remains to be expanded.

```
s_snd(q, n)
        Queue *q;
        Node *n;
{
        Node *m;
        int i, j = 0;   /* q field# */
        for (m = n->rgt; m && j < q->nflds; m = m->rgt, j++)
          q->contents[j] = cast_val(q->fld_width[j], eval(m->lft));
        q->qlen = 1;
        if (complete_rendez())
                        return 1;
        q->qlen = 0;
        return 0;
}
```

The sender first appends the message and then checks if there is a receiver that can execute the matching receive. There is no need to check the queue length here: when the send operation is executable, all rendezvous channels are guaranteed to be empty. If no matching receive is found, the send operation fails, cancels the message in the queue and returns a zero. If there is a matching receive operation, it will execute before the routine `complete_rendez()` returns, and both sender and receiver proceed to the next statement, again leaving the channel empty. The routine `complete_rendez()` is in fact a tiny portion of the scheduler and is listed in `sched.c`. It blocks all statements except a synchronous receive and the code that is required for evaluating expressions.

```
complete_rendez()
{       RunList *orun = X;
        Element *e;
        int res=0;
        Rvous = 1;
        for (X = run; X; X = X->nxt)
                if (X != orun && (e = eval_sub(X->pc)))
                {       X->pc = e;
                        res = 1;
                        break;
                }
        Rvous = 0;
        X = orun;
        return res;
}
```

The routine first sets a global flag `Rvous` to make sure that only receive operations are enabled. The variable `X` is then pointed to every runnable process to check if it can complete the rendezvous handshake. The evaluation routine that looks into every option of a compound for a possible match is called `eval_sub()`.

```
Element *
eval_sub(e)
        Element *e;
{
        Element *f, *g;
        SeqList *z;
        int i, j, k;
        ...
        if (e->sub)
        {       for (z = e->sub, j=0; z; z = z->nxt)
                        j++;
                k = rand()%j;   /* nondeterminism */
                for (i = 0, z = e->sub; i < j+k; i++)
                {       if (i >= k && f = eval_sub(z->this->frst))
                                return f;
                        z = (z->nxt)?z->nxt:e->sub;
                }
        } else
```

```
{               if (e->n->ntyp == ATOMIC)
                {       ...
                } else if (Rvous)
                {       if (eval_sync(e->n))
                                return e->nxt;
                } else
                        return (eval(e->n))?e->nxt:(Element *)0;
        }
        return (Element *)0;
}
```

The evaluation routine recursively searches through the options of compounds. If there is more than one option, the scheduler picks one at random, using the library routine rand(). When, at the lowest level in the recursion, it finds a statement instead of a compound to evaluate, it checks for the value of Rvous and calls this routine when it is set.

```
eval_sync(now)
        Node *now;
{       /* allow only synchronous receives
        /* and related node types      */
        if (now)
        switch (now->ntyp) {
        case TIMEOUT:   case PRINT:     case ASSERT:
        case RUN:       case LEN:       case 's':
        case 'c':       case ASGN:      case BREAK:
        case IF:        case DO:        case '.':
                return 0;
        case 'R':
        case 'r':
                if (!q_is_sync(now))
                        return 0;
        }
        return eval(now);
}
```

We will come back to the details later when we look more closely at the scheduler code itself.

12.6 CONTROL FLOW

Our next job is to bring some structure into the language by implementing the selection, repetition, break, goto and atomic statements. We have to build up a program as a coherent set of statements, with a control flow discipline that defines which statement from this set is to be evaluated by the scheduler at each execution step. All routines that deal explicitly with the control flow are placed in the file flow.c. This section discusses:

- Code for manipulating sequences (Section 12.6.1, page 278)
- Keeping track of labels (Section 12.6.2, page 280)
- Code for parsing compound statements (Section 12.6.3, page 282)

12.6.1 SEQUENCES

Recall the definition of the non-terminal `program` in `spin.y`, which we discussed before.

```
body:
           '{'                    { open_seq(1); }
              sequence            { add_seq(Stop); }
           '}'                    { $$ = close_seq(); }
sequence:
              step                { add_seq($1); }
           | sequence ';' step    { add_seq($3); }
```

A program body is a sequence of statements terminated by a special `Stop` node. But this time we have to carry around some extra information for compound statements. A compound statement is basically a fork in the execution sequence, where one sequence divides into a number of option sequences. We store each individual sequence in a structure of type `Sequence` defined in `spin.h`.

```
typedef struct Sequence {
        Element *frst;
        Element *last;
} Sequence;
```

A set of sequences is stored as a linked list, as follows:

```
typedef struct SeqList {
        Sequence        *this;   /* one sequence */
        struct SeqList  *nxt;    /* linked list  */
} SeqList;
```

And, of course the nodes of the parse tree will have to accommodate the new information, so the data structure for a `Node` is expanded somewhat more.

```
typedef struct Node {
        int     nval;           /* value attribute          */
        short   ntyp;           /* node type                */
        Symbol  *nsym;          /* new attribute            */
        Symbol  *fname;         /* filename of src          */
        struct SeqList  *seql;  /* list of sequences        */
        struct Node     *lft, *rgt; /* children in parse tree */
} Node;
```

Statements are added one by one to a sequence with `add_seq()`. The statements are most conveniently stored in structures of type `Element`. The definition in `spin.h` looks as follows:

```
typedef struct Element {
        Node    *n;                     /* defines the type & contents */
        int     seqno;                  /* uniquely identifies this el */
        unsigned char   status;  /* used by analyzer generator  */
        struct SeqList  *sub;    /* subsequences, for compounds */
        struct Element  *nxt;    /* linked list */
} Element;
```

Each element in a sequence is labeled with a unique sequence (or state) number, that will prove to be useful in building the validator in the next chapter. The numbers are handed out by routine new_el().

```
Element *
new_el(n)
        Node *n;
{
        Element *m;
        if (n && (n->ntyp == IF || n->ntyp == DO))
                return if_seq(n->seql, n->ntyp, n->nval);
        m = (Element *) emalloc(sizeof(Element));
        m->n = n;
        m->seqno = Elcnt++;
        return m;
}
```

The sub field of an element points to the options of a compound. It is set, only for those types of statements, in routine if_seq(), which is examined in detail in Section 12.6.3.

The sequence numbers are kept in a global counter Elcnt that is reset to one at the start of every new process. In the code below this happens when open_seq() is called with a non-zero argument.

The open brace of a body initializes a new sequence by a call on procedure open_seq(). The closing brace closes the sequence and passes it via close_seq(). Initializing a new sequence of elements or returning a completed one is fairly straightforward. In its simplest form it looks like this.

```
void
open_seq(top)
{       SeqList *t;
        Sequence *s = (Sequence *) emalloc(sizeof(Sequence));
        t = seqlist(s, cur_s);
        cur_s = t;
        if (top) Elcnt = 1;
}

Sequence *
close_seq()
{       Sequence *s = cur_s->this;

        cur_s = cur_s->nxt;
        return s;
}
```

The listing in Appendix D performs some extra checks that are relevant only to the validator.

The routine seqlist() attaches a new sequence to a linked list of sequences.

```
SeqList *
seqlist(s, r)
        Sequence *s;
        SeqList *r;
{
        SeqList *t = (SeqList *) emalloc(sizeof(SeqList));
        t->this = s;
        t->nxt = r;
        return t;
}
```

Adding an element to the current sequence happens as follows:

```
add_seq(n)
        Node *n;
{
        Element *e;
        if (!n) return;
        if (n->ntyp == ':')
        {       e = new_el(n->lft);
                set_lab(n->nsym, e);
                n = n->lft;
        } else
                e = new_el(n);
        if (n->ntyp != IF && n->ntyp != DO)
                add_el(e, cur_s->this);
}
```

The routine that allocates memory for a new element new_el() filters out the compound statements and does all the hard work for them, so that need not be repeated above. The routine add_el() which is used here is not too exciting.

```
add_el(e, s)
        Element *e;
        Sequence *s;
{
        if (!s->frst)
                s->frst = e;
        else
                s->last->nxt = e;
        s->last = e;
}
```

12.6.2 JUMPS AND LABELS

Routine add_seq() also catches labels, identified by a node type ':', and remembers them in another linked list.

```
typedef struct Label {
        Symbol  *s;
        Symbol  *c;
        Element *e;
        struct Label    *nxt;
} Label;
```

The code is again straightforward.

```
set_lab(s, e)
        Symbol *s;
        Element *e;
{
        Label *l; extern Symbol *context;
        if (!s) return;
        l = (Label *) emalloc(sizeof(Label));
        l->s = s;
        l->c = context;
        l->e = e;
        l->nxt = labtab;
        labtab = l;
}
```

When the scheduler has to determine the destination of a `goto` jump, it consults that list, and retrieves a pointer to the element that carried the label.

```
Element *
get_lab(s)
        Symbol *s;
{
        Label *l;
        for (l = labtab; l; l = l->nxt)
                if (s == l->s)
                        return (l->e);
        fatal("undefined label %s", s->name);
}
```

The routine is called at the top of every invocation of the generic evaluation routine `eval_sub()`, as follows:

```
        if (e->n->ntyp == GOTO)
                return get_lab(e->n->nsym);
```

Of course, to get the `goto` statements and labels at the right places into the parse tree, we must add a few more rules to the *lex* and *yacc* files. The lookup table in `lex.l` is expanded with

```
        "goto",         GOTO,
```

while adding a token `GOTO` to `spin.y`. The two production rules that recognize jumps and labels are:

```
        | GOTO NAME             { $$ = nn($2, $1, GOTO, 0, 0); }
        | NAME ':' stmnt        { $$ = nn($1, $3->nval, ':', $3, 0); }
```

The line number for a labeled statement is extracted from the node that is passed up through the third parameter `$3`. The `GOTO` token carries its own line number that is copied from `$1`.

12.6.3 COMPOUND STATEMENTS

The real challenge is to process the compound statements. There are a few new tokens to be handled, such as if, fi, do, od, ::, break, and atomic. The lexical analyzer is again extended with one line for each. Three new statement types and two new production rules are added to the production rules in spin.y.

```
stmnt    : ...
         | IF options FI { $$ = nn(0, $1, IF, 0, 0);
                             $$->seql = $2;
                         }
         | DO            { pushbreak(); }
           options OD    { $$ = nn(0, $1, DO, 0, 0);
                             $$->seql = $3;
                         }
         | BREAK         { $$ = nn(break_dest(),$1,GOTO,0,0); }
         | ATOMIC
           '{'           { open_seq(0); }
              sequence
           '}'           { $$ = nn(0,$1, ATOMIC, 0, 0);
                             $$->seql = seqlist(close_seq(), 0);
                             make_atomic($$->seql->this);
                         }
         ;
options  : option        { $$ = seqlist($1, 0); }
         | option options { $$ = seqlist($1, $2); }
         ;
option   : SEP           { open_seq(0); }
           sequence      { $$ = close_seq(); }
         ;
```

Every option in a compound statement can be a sequence of statements and is again captured in a data structure of type Sequence. Multiple options are again grouped into a linked list of sequences of the type SeqList that was defined before.

Repetition statements can be terminated with break statements. To keep track of the proper destinations we use pushbreak() to push an internal label onto a stack for every new repetition structure that is entered, and a routine breakdest() to retrieve the current destination of a break statement, much as with the labels and goto jumps we discussed earlier.

```
typedef struct Lbreak {
        Symbol  *l;
        struct Lbreak   *nxt;
} Lbreak;

pushbreak()
{       Lbreak *r = (Lbreak *) emalloc(sizeof(Lbreak));
        Symbol *l;
        char buf[32];
```

```
            sprintf(buf, ":b%d", break_id++);
            l = lookup(buf);
            r->l = l;
            r->nxt = breakstack;
            breakstack = r;
}

Symbol *
break_dest()
{        if (!breakstack)
                fatal("misplaced break statement", (char *)0);
         return breakstack->l;
}
```

A break statement, if it occurs, is translated with a call on break_dest() into a
jump to the last break statement that was pushed onto the stack.

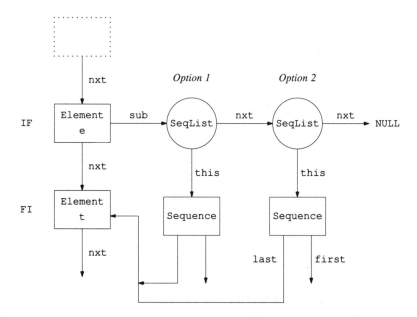

Figure 12.4 — Parse Tree for a Selection Structure

Now it is time to turn to one of the toughest procedures for parsing the compound
statements: if_seq(). A selection or repetition structure must push several elements into the statement sequence. Figure 12.4 illustrates the node structure that is
built by the procedure if_seq() to include selection statements into a sequence.
Only compound statements (selections and repetitions) attach any nodes to the sub
field of an Element. That field of sub-sequences starts a linked list (a SeqList) of
options, with one complete Sequence structure per option in the compound statement. Figure 12.4 shows a selection statement with two options.

The `last` pointer of the sub sequence that defines an option is connected to the element that immediately follows the one that contains the original `sub` field. In the figure this is the `Element` labeled t (for target). It formalizes that a selection sequence is terminated whenever an option terminates.

The structure build for a repetition statement is almost the same, with just one exception: the `last` field of each sub sequence is now pointed at an `Element` that is placed immediately preceding the compound, at the place of the dotted box in Figure 12.4. It formalizes that a repetition structure is repeated when an option terminates. The `break` statement in the repetition structure will still point to the target `Element` t. The code that makes all this happen looks as follows:

```
Element *
if_seq(s, tok, lnno)
        SeqList *s;
{
        Element *e = new_el((Node *) 0);
        Element *t = new_el(nn(0, lnno, '.', 0, 0)); /* target */
        SeqList *z;
        e->n = nn(0, lnno, tok, 0, 0);
        e->sub = s;
        for (z = s; z; z = z->nxt)
                add_el(t, z->this);
        if (tok == DO)
        {       add_el(t, cur_s->this);
                t = new_el(nn(0, lnno, BREAK, 0, 0));
                set_lab(break_dest(), t);
                breakstack = breakstack->nxt;    /* pop stack */
        }
        add_el(e, cur_s->this);
        add_el(t, cur_s->this);
        return e;          /* destination node for label */
}
```

12.7 PROCESSES AND MESSAGE TYPES

The main thing missing from our simulator at this point is the concept of a process. With that extension we can place some finishing touches on the software by also coding the scheduler, by adding the distinction between local and global variables. The code for the scheduler is confined to a file named `sched.c`. The extension of the lexical analyzer is minimal at this point: the mere addition of the keywords `proctype`, `init`, and `mtype`. The other extensions are more substantial:

12.7.1 PARSER

A complete PROMELA program is constructed from a series of program units defined as follows:

```
program : units                    { sched(); }
        ;
units   : unit | units unit
        ;
unit    : proc
        | init
        | claim
        | one_decl
        | mtype
        ;
proc    : PROCTYPE NAME             { context = $2; }
                  '(' decl ')'
          body                     { ready($2, $5, $7);
                                     context = (Symbol *) 0;
                                   }
        ;
mtype   : MTYPE ASGN '{' args '}' { setmtype($4); }
        | ';'    /* optional ; as separator of units */
        ;
        ...
decl    : /* empty */              { $$ = (Node *) 0; }
        | decl_lst                 { $$ = $1; }
        ;
decl_lst: one_decl                 { $$ = nn(0, 0, ',', $1,  0); }
        | one_decl ';' decl_lst { $$ = nn(0, 0, ',', $1, $3); }
        ;
```

A unit is either a process declaration, a list of message types, a temporal claim, or an init specification, each of which can be preceded by one or more global variable declarations. The init module and the temporal claims are defined as special type of processes:

```
init    : INIT                     { context = $1; }
          body                     { runnable($3, $1);
                                     context = (Symbol *) 0;
                                   }
        ;
claim   : CLAIM                    { context = $1;
                                     if (claimproc)
                                        yyerror("claim %s redefined",
                                                        claimproc);
                                     claimproc = $1->name;
                                   }
          body                     { ready($1, (Node *) 0, $3);
                                     context = (Symbol *) 0;
                                   }
        ;
```

There can be only one init and one temporal claim per specification. The first is required, the second optional. The presence of a claim is flagged in the global pointer claimproc.

Process declarations are placed in a ready queue of process bodies. To allow us to remember type declarations of formal parameters, declarations must now return a node containing the parameter list. Before the body of a process declaration is parsed, though, a context variable is set to identify any variable names and parameters to be recognized as local to the process declaration. Initially, only the init process is labeled runnable. Procedure setmtype() logically belongs in sym.c and can be implemented as follows:

```
Node *Mtype = (Node *) 0;
void
setmtype(m)
        Node *m;
{
        Node *n = m;
        if (Mtype)
                yyerror("mtype redeclared", (char *)0);
        Mtype = n;
        while (n)           /* syntax check */
        {       if (!n->lft || !n->lft->nsym
                || (n->lft->ntyp != NAME)
                ||  n->lft->lft)        /* indexed variable */
                        fatal("bad mtype definition", (char *)0);
                n = n->rgt;
        }
}
```

The procedure merely checks syntax and stores the arguments for later processing. The message-type definitions can be hidden completely from the rest of the program if we let the lexical analyzer check the list whenever it sees a NAME and map all message names found there onto constants. We can do that in procedure check_name().

```
check_name(s)
        char *s;
{
        register int i;
        for (i = 0; Names[i].s; i++)
                if (strcmp(s, Names[i].s) == 0)
                {       yylval.val = lineno;
                        return Names[i].tok;
                }
        if (yylval.val = ismtype(s))
                return CONST;
        yylval.sym = lookup(s); /* symbol table */
        return NAME;
}
```

The routine ismtype() looks up names in the list of message types.

```
ismtype(str)
        char *str;
{
        Node *n;
        int cnt = 1;
        for (n = Mtype; n; n = n->rgt)
        {       if (strcmp(str, n->lft->nsym->name) == 0)
                        return cnt;
                cnt++;
        }
        return 0;
}
```

12.7.2 SCHEDULER

The procedures `ready()` and `runnable()` require little imagination; they need merely store their arguments in linked lists where the scheduler can find them. The list of runnable processes is defined as follows:

```
typedef struct ProcList {
        Symbol  *n;             /* name       */
        Node    *p;             /* parameters */
        Sequence *s;            /* body       */
        struct ProcList *nxt;   /* linked list */
} ProcList;
```

And the routine that fills the list is

```
runnable(s, n)
        Sequence *s;    /* body */
        Symbol *n;      /* name */
{
        RunList *r = (RunList *) emalloc(sizeof(RunList));
        r->n = n;
        r->pid = nproc++;
        r->pc = s->frst;
        r->maxseq = s->last->seqno;
        r->nxt = run;
        run = r;
}
```

The actual runlist of executing processes has a program counter `pc` and a pointer to current values of local variables, which we call `symtab` again, since it is basically another symbol table list.

```
typedef struct RunList {
        Symbol  *n;             /* name                */
        int     pid;            /* process id          */
        int     maxseq;         /* used by analyzer generator */
        Element *pc;            /* current stmnt       */
        Symbol  *symtab;        /* local variables */
        struct RunList  *nxt;   /* linked list */
} RunList;
```

Inserting a process into the list is easy.

```
ready(n, p, s)
        Symbol *n;       /* process name */
        Node *p;         /* formal parameters */
        Sequence *s;     /* process body */
{
        ProcList *r = (ProcList *) emalloc(sizeof(ProcList));
        r->n = n;
        r->p = p;
        r->s = s;
        r->nxt = rdy;
        rdy = r;
}
```

Moving a process from the process list to the run list is a little more involved,
since also the parameter fields must be initialized.

```
enable(s, n)
        Symbol *s;       /* process name */
        Node *n;         /* actual parameters */
{
        ProcList *p;
        for (p = rdy; p; p = p->nxt)
                if (strcmp(s->name, p->n->name) == 0)
                {       runnable(p->s, p->n);
                        setparams(run, p, n);
                        return (nproc-nstop-1); /* pid */
                }
        return 0; /* process not found */
}
```

where

```
setparams(r, p, q)
        RunList *r;
        ProcList *p;
        Node *q;
{
        Node *f, *a;     /* formal and actual pars */
        Node *t;         /* list of pars of 1 type */
        for (f = p->p, a = q; f; f = f->rgt) /* one type at a time */
        for (t = f->lft; t; t = t->rgt, a = (a)?a->rgt:a)
        {       int k = eval(a->lft);        /* must be initialized*/
                if (typck(a, t->nsym->type, p->n->name))
                {       if (t->nsym->type == CHAN)
                                naddsymbol(r, t->nsym, k); /* copy */
                        else
                        {       t->nsym->ini = a->lft;
                                addsymbol(r, t->nsym);
                        }
                }
        }
}
```

with

```c
naddsymbol(r, s, k)
        RunList *r;
        Symbol  *s;
{
        Symbol *t = (Symbol *) emalloc(sizeof(Symbol));
        int i;
        t->name = s->name;
        t->type = s->type;
        t->nel  = s->nel;
        t->ini  = s->ini;
        t->val = (int *) emalloc(s->nel*sizeof(int));
        if (s->nel != 1)
        fatal("array in formal parameter list, %s", s->name);
        for (i = 0; i < s->nel; i++)
                t->val[i] = k;
        t->next = r->symtab;
        r->symtab = t;
}
```

and

```c
addsymbol(r, s)
        RunList *r;
        Symbol  *s;
{
        Symbol *t = (Symbol *) emalloc(sizeof(Symbol));
        int i;
        t->name = s->name;
        t->type = s->type;
        t->nel  = s->nel;
        t->ini  = s->ini;
        if (s->val)                  /* if initialized, copy it */
        {       t->val = (int *) emalloc(s->nel*sizeof(int));
                for (i = 0; i < s->nel; i++)
                        t->val[i] = s->val[i];
        } else
                checkvar(t, 0); /* initialize it */
        t->next = r->symtab;     /* add it */
        r->symtab = t;
}
```

To be able to create new process instantiations on the fly during a simulation, we expand the run statement in run.c as follows:

```c
        case   RUN: return enable(now->nsym, now->lft);
```

Processes can only be deleted from the run-list in reverse order of creation: a process can only disappear if all its children have disappeared first (Chapter 5). The pids can therefore be recycled in stack order. In the value returned by enable(), (nproc-nstop-1), the count nproc equals the total number of processes created, and nstop, the number of processes that deleted.

The most interesting routine left to discuss is the scheduling routine proper: sched(). Its relevant portion looks as follows:

```
sched()
{       Element *e, *eval_sub();
        RunList *Y;     /* previous process in run queue */
        int i=0;
        ...
        for (Tval = 0; Tval < 2; Tval++)
        {       while (i < nproc-nstop)
                for (X=run, Y=0, i=0; X; X = X->nxt)
                {       lineno = X->pc->n->nval;
                        Fname  = X->pc->n->fname;
                        if (e = eval_sub(X->pc))
                        {       X->pc = e; Tval=0;
                        } else  /* process terminated? */
                        {       if (X->pc->n->ntyp == '@'
                                && X->pid == (nproc-nstop-1))
                                {       if (Y)
                                                Y->nxt = X->nxt;
                                        else
                                                run = X->nxt;
                                        nstop++; Tval=0;
                                } else
                                        i++;
                        }
                        Y = X;
                }       }
        wrapup();
}
```

The scheduler executes one statement in each runnable process in round-robin fashion. It calls the routine eval_sub(), which we saw earlier, to recursively evaluate compound statements and atomic sequences. The evaluation of an atomic sequence only succeeds if the whole sequence can be completed. The code is part of eval_sub().

```
        if (e->n->ntyp == ATOMIC)
        {       f = e->n->seql->this->frst;
                g = e->n->seql->this->last;
                g->nxt = e->nxt;
                if (!(g = eval_sub(f)))
                        return (Element *)0;
                Rvous = 0;
                while (g && (g->status & (ATOM|L_ATOM))
                && !(f->status & L_ATOM))
                {       f = g;
                        g = eval_sub(f);
                }
                if (!g)
                {       wrapup();
                        lineno = f->n->nval;
                        fatal("atomic sequence blocks", (cha *)0);
                }
                return g;
```

```
    } else if (Rvous)
        ...
```

It is a fatal error if an atomic sequence blocks. If a process hits an unexecutable statement the scheduler checks to see if it is in a stop state. If so, the process is removed from the run queue and the count of terminated processes nstop is incremented. A global variable X points to the currently executing process. It is mainly used by the new routines for manipulating local variables, getlocal() and setlocal(), to determine in which process structure the variables are located. The scheduler also maintains a value Tval that is used by the interpreter in run.c to determine the executability of the timeout statement.

```
    case TIMEOUT: return Tval;
```

During normal execution, when the system is not blocked, Tval is zero and conditions that include a timeout are unexecutable. To recover from a potential deadlock, the scheduler can enable the timeout statements by incrementing Tval. If the system does not recover, the scheduler declares a true hang state and gives up.

12.7.3 LOCAL VARIABLES

Since local variables are created on the fly, upon the instantiation of new processes, the logical place for the code that manipulates them is in the scheduler. If a variable name is local, two special variants of getvar() and setvar() are used.

```
getlocal(s, n)
        Symbol *s;
{
        Symbol *r;
        r = findloc(s, n);
        if (r) return cast_val(r->type, r->val[n]);
        return 0;
}

setlocal(p, m)
        Node *p;
{
        int n = eval(p->lft);
        Symbol *r = findloc(p->nsym, n);
        if (r) r->val[n] = m;
        return 1;
}
```

The routine findloc() locates the name in the symbol table of the currently executing process, pointed to by X->symtab.

```
Symbol *
findloc(s, n)
        Symbol *s;
{
        Symbol *r;
```

```
        if (n >= s->nel || n < 0)
        {       yyerror("array indexing error %s", s->name);
                return (Symbol *) 0;
        }
        for (r = X->symtab; r; r = r->next)
                if (strcmp(r->name, s->name) == 0)
                        break;
        if (!r)
        {       addsymbol(X, s);
                r = X->symtab;
        }
        return r;
}
```

The local variables and the process states of any running process can be referred to
in assertions and temporal claims. The hooks in the parser that enable remote
referencing are simple. References to remote variables and process states require
the last two production rules:

```
        | NAME '[' expr ']' '.' varref  { $$ = rem_var($1, $3, $6); }
        | NAME '[' expr ']' ':' NAME    { $$ = rem_lab($1, $3, $6); }
```

with

```
    Node *
    rem_var(a, b, c)
            Symbol *a;
            Node *b, *c;
    {
            Node *tmp;
            tmp = nn(a, 0, '?', b, 0);
            return nn(c->nsym, 0, 'p', tmp, c->lft);
    }
```

and

```
    Node *
    rem_lab(a, b, c)
            Symbol *a, *c;
            Node *b;
    {
            return  nn(0, 0, EQ,
                    nn(lookup("_p"), 0, 'p', nn(a, 0, '?', b, 0), 0),
                    nn(c, 0, 'q', nn(a, 0, NAME, 0, 0), 0));
    }
```

The reference is implemented as a condition on the control flow state of a process,
represented by the internal variable _p, and the state value of a label name. The
value of the special variable _p is determined, just like the other remote variables,
using a node of type 'p'. The label name is determined with a new node of type
'q'. The node type '?' is only used as a temporary place holder.

In the evaluator two new node types trigger calls on these two routines:

```
case    'p': return remotevar(now);
case    'q': return remotelab(now);
```

The first routine, for referencing the current value of a local variable in a remote process, is implemented with a context switch in the scheduler, as follows:

```
remotevar(n)
        Node *n;
{
        int pno, i, j;
        RunList *Y, *oX = X;
        pno = eval(n->lft->lft);        /* pid */
        i = nproc - nstop;
        for (Y = run; Y; Y = Y->nxt)
        if (--i == pno)
        {       if (strcmp(Y->n->name, n->lft->nsym->name))
                        yyerror("wrong proctype %s", Y->n->name);
                X = Y; j = getval(n->nsym, eval(n->rgt)); X = oX;
                return j;
        }
        yyerror("remote ref: proc %s not found", n->nsym->name);
        return 0;
}
```

The second routine, for determining the control flow state in a remote process that corresponds to a given label name, is implemented with a search in the list of labels, as follows:

```
remotelab(n)
        Node *n;
{
        int i;
        if (n->nsym->type)
                fatal("not a labelname: '%s'", n->nsym->name);
        if ((i = find_lab(n->nsym, n->lft->nsym)) == 0)
                fatal("unknown labelname: %s", n->nsym->name);
        return i;
}
```

12.8 MACRO EXPANSION

The final version of SPIN in Appendix D has an expanded version of main() that properly interprets option flags, accepts a file argument and routes its input through the C preprocessor in /lib/cpp for macro expansion. The output of the preprocessor is dumped into a temporary file that is immediately unlinked to make sure that it disappears from the file system, even if the run of the simulator is interrupted. The parser, however, keeps a link to the file in the predefined file pointer yyin.

```
        if (argc > 1)
        {       char outfile[17], cmd[64];
                strcpy(filename, argv[1]);
                mktemp(strcpy(outfile, "/tmp/spin.XXXXXX"));
```

```
                    sprintf(cmd, "/lib/cpp %s > %s", argv[1], outfile);
                    if (system(cmd))
                    {        unlink(outfile);
                             exit(1);
                    } else if (!(yyin = fopen(outfile, "r")))
                    {        printf("cannot open %s\n", outfile);
                             exit(1);
                    }
                    unlink(outfile);
            } else
                    strcpy(filename, "<stdin>");
```

The preprocessor drops lines into the file that look like

```
    # 1 "spin.examples/lynch"
```

The lexical analyzer can pick them up and interpret them with an extra rule that is
defined as follows:

```
    \#\ [0-9]+\ \"[^\"]*\" {           /* preprocessor directive */
                    int i=1;
                    while (yytext[i] == ' ') i++;
                    lineno = atoi(&yytext[i])-1;
                    while (yytext[i] != ' ') i++;
                    Fname = lookup(&yytext[i+1]);
            }
```

The line number is remembered in variable lineno. The file name is stored in the
symbol table and a global pointer to it is kept in Fname. But most of these remaining features are cosmetic and can be either changed or ignored without undue risk.

12.9 SPIN — OPTIONS

The simulator recognizes eight command line options which can be used in any
combination. Two (flags *a* and *t*) are specific to the analysis code that we have yet
to develop in Chapter 13. The other six are discussed below.

spin −s

Prints a line on the display for every message that is sent. Example:

```
$ spin -s factorial
proc 12 (fact)  line   5, Send 1        -> queue 12 (p)
proc 11 (fact)  line  10, Send 2        -> queue 11 (p)
proc 10 (fact)  line  10, Send 6        -> queue 10 (p)
proc  9 (fact)  line  10, Send 24       -> queue 9 (p)
proc  8 (fact)  line  10, Send 120      -> queue 8 (p)
...
```

spin −r

Prints a line on the display for every message received. It prints the name and
pid of the running process, and a source line number for its current state.
Example:

```
$ spin  -s -r factorial
proc 12 (fact)  line   5, Send 1        -> queue 12 (p)
proc 11 (fact)  line   9, Recv 1        <- queue 12 (child)
proc 11 (fact)  line  10, Send 2        -> queue 11 (p)
proc 10 (fact)  line   9, Recv 2        <- queue 11 (child)
proc 10 (fact)  line  10, Send 6        -> queue 10 (p)
proc  9 (fact)  line   9, Recv 6        <- queue 10 (child)
....
```

spin −p

Prints a line on the display for every statement executed. Example:

```
$ spin -p factorial
proc  0 (_init) line 18 (state 2)
proc  1 (fact)  line 8 (state 4)
proc  1 (fact)  line 9 (state 5)
proc  2 (fact)  line 8 (state 4)
proc  2 (fact)  line 9 (state 5)
proc  3 (fact)  line 8 (state 4)
...
proc  3 (fact)  terminates
```

spin −l

Adds the value of all local variables to the output. This option, like the next
one, is most useful in combination with −p. Example:

```
$ spin -p -l factorial
...
proc 12 (fact)   line 12 (state 9)
                 queue 12 (p):
                 n = 1
proc 11 (fact)   line 4 (state 8)
                 result = 1
                 queue 12 (child):
                 queue 11 (p): [2]
                 n = 2
...
proc 12 (fact)   terminates
...
```

spin −g

Adds the current values of all global variables to the listings.

spin −t12345

Initializes the random number generator with the user specified seed 12345 to
secure a simulation run that can be reproduced exactly.

12.10 SUMMARY

The last version of SPIN contains about 2000 lines of source code, more than ten
times the size of the little expression evaluator that we started this chapter with.

To give an indication of the performance of SPIN we ran the following program to calculate Fibonacci numbers. It creates and runs a total of 1000 processes.

```
/***** Fibonacci Sequence *****/
proctype fib(short n)
{       short a = 0;
        short b = 1;
        short c;
        atomic
        {       do
                :: (b < n) ->
                        c = b;
                        b = a+b;
                        a = c
                :: (b >= n) ->
                        break
                od
        }
}
init
{       int i = 1;
        atomic
        {       do
                :: (i < 1000) -> i = i+1; run fib(1000)
                :: (i > 999) -> break
                od
        }
}
```

On a DEC-VAX/8550 computer, one simulation run takes about 7.6 second of user time. A program optimized for calculation can run a similar program two to ten times faster, but of course does not have the synchronization and multi-process features of PROMELA. The most expensive function calls of a simulation run can be found with the UNIX utility prof. For the Fibonacci test 80% of the runtime is spend in the following routines:

```
%     Time    #Calls      Name
23    2.633   433411      _eval
13    1.533   166433      _findloc
11    1.233   116950      _eval_sub
 9    1.050        0      _strcmp
 8    0.917        0      mcount
 6    0.717   117482      _getlocal
 5    0.617   117482      _cast_val
 5    0.617   117482      _getval
```

If at some point SPIN's efficiency must be improved, a good target for optimizations would be procedure eval(). (See also the Exercises.) For protocol simulations, however, the program is sufficiently fast.

In the next chapter we will see how we can extend SPIN's capabilities with a generator for exhaustive protocol validations. As discussed in Chapter 11, the potential performance bottlenecks in protocol validators do require careful attention if we are to produce a tool of practical value. We therefore shift most efficiency considerations to that part of the SPIN software.

EXERCISES

12-1 Change the semantics of the `timeout` statement by allowing a timeout count to be specified. Add a predefined variable `time` that is incremented once for each cycle through the list on running processes by the scheduler. Apply and test the new features with a sample protocol.

12-2 The simulator and the language PROMELA use a 32-bit signed quantity as the largest number. This puts restrictions on the use of SPIN as a calculator. What is the largest factorial that can be computed with the factorial program from Section 12.2?

12-3 Run the Fibonacci test on your system and measure the run-time. Make the atomic sequences non-atomic and repeat the test. Explain the result.

12-4 Model and simulate an arbitrary example PROMELA program from this book.

12-5 Add more features to PROMELA. For instance,
  ○ Allow inline C code fragments
  ○ Allow a keyword `else` in compound statements
  ○ Add C-like data structures
  ○ Add *device* channels
  A device channel is a prefined message queue that connects a PROMELA program to the outside world (for instance, add a terminal-screen and a keyboard channel).

12-6 Add a pre-simulation run optimizer that rewrites parts of the parse tree on the fly. Good candidates for optimization, for instance, are expressions involving only constant references, such as `(5*3+2)`.

12-7 Use the simulator to implement a random walk validation strategy. Consider the feasibility of validating each of the correctness criteria discussed in Chapter 6.

BIBLIOGRAPHIC NOTES

The best reference to the C programming language is still Kernighan and Ritchie [1978, 1988]. The second edition of this book, published in 1988, is an excellent reference to the new ANSI standard version of the C language. Another good discussion of the ANSI standard definition can be found in Harbison and Steele [1987].

Much more about the design of parsers and lexical analyzers can be found in the famous *dragon* books by Al Aho and others. See for instance Aho and Ullman [1977], and Aho, Sethi and Ullman [1986]. A very useful guide to the usage of the UNIX tools *yacc* and *lex* can also be found in Schreiner and Friedman [1985].

An outstanding tutorial on C program development can be found in Kernighan and Pike [1984]. Chapter 8 of that book is especially recommended.

A PROTOCOL VALIDATOR 13

13.1 INTRODUCTION

To extend the protocol simulator from Chapter 12 with an validator generator, all we have to do is to activate two command line options from the source listing in Appendix D:

-a, To generate a protocol specific SPIN analyzer
-t, To follow an error trail produced by that analyzer

To do this we have to replace the two dummy routines `gensrc()` and `match_trail()` in Appendix D with real code. To see how the analyzer is used refer to Section 13.8 or Chapter 14.

The analyzer described here is based on the discussion in Chapter 11. To keep the code reasonably simple, we will not discuss a complete implementation of the state vector model. Even without that, it takes a fair amount of code to produce a validator of good performance. But once the job is done right an efficient validator can be produced in a matter of seconds, and can be applied to problems of arbitrary complexity. The validators that are produced by SPIN in this way are among the fastest programs for exhaustive searching known to date. A full implementation of the state vector model can secure a still better performance, but that is well beyond the scope of this book.

The validators can be used in two different modes. For small to medium size models the validators can be used with an exhaustive state space. The result of all validations performed in this mode is equivalent to an exhaustive proof of correctness, for the correctness requirements that were specified (by default, absence of deadlock). For systems that are larger, the validators can also be used in *super-*

trace mode, with the bit state space technique as discussed in Chapter 11. In these cases the validations can be performed in much smaller amounts of memory, and still retain excellent coverage of the state space. The results of all validations performed in supertrace mode are superior to any other type of validation performed within the same physical constraints of the host machine (e.g., memory size and speed).

To produce an analyzer, the parse tree that is constructed by the SPIN simulator is translated into a C program, and extended with state space searching modules. The program that is generated is then compiled stand-alone. When it is executed it performs the required validation. If an error is discovered, the program writes a simulation trail into a file and stops. The simulation trail can be read by the original simulator, which can then reproduce the error sequence and allow the user to probe the cause of the error in detail.

Below we first discuss the general structure of the protocol analyzers that are generated. We then give an overview of the routines that extract the protocol specific information from the SPIN parse tree. Next we discuss the extensions of the simulator to provide for guided simulations. We conclude with some examples of the usage of the new tool.

13.2 STRUCTURE OF THE VALIDATOR

Figure 13.1 shows the main components of the analyzers that can be generated.

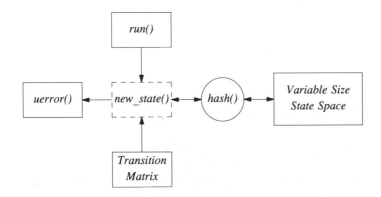

Figure 13.1 — Structure of SPIN Validators

A procedure called `run()` allocates memory and prepares all data structures that the validator will use during the search. It calls a single procedure `new_state()` to perform the actual search. The two main data structures used by this procedure `new_state()` are the state space and a large transition matrix that encodes the complete PROMELA validation model. Each statement in the model produces an entry in this matrix, defining precisely the executability predicate and the effect of the execution. Every `proctype` definition contributes entries to this matrix.

The current state of the system is maintained in a vector of values that can grow and shrink dynamically: a rubber state-vector. PROMELA `run` statements append new processes to the state-vector. The rubber state-vector, therefore, fulfills a role that is similar to that of the run queue in the simulator scheduler. Procedure `new_state()` performs a depth first search of all executable statements in the model. Instead of selecting just one executable statement from the list of runnable processes, as the simulator did, the validator's job is to test the effects of *all* executable statements, in all possible interleavings. Before starting the analysis for a new state `new_state()` consults the state space, via the `hash()` function and decides whether the current state was analyzed before and can be skipped.

If an error is found, procedure `uerror()` is called to produce an error trail for the simulator and, unless otherwise specified, analysis stops. An error can be any violation of the formal correctness requirements, for instance, a local assertion failure or a global system state in which all processes are permanently blocked.

Finding an inconsistency in the SPIN model and assisting the user in determining its causes, is done with two different tools: validator and simulator. The rationale behind this approach is the standard UNIX discipline: each tool we develop should do one thing, and do it well.

☐   The simulator is designed as an interactive tool. It has a short start-up time and can give a a detailed look at the working of the protocol.

☐   The validator is a non-interactive tool. It has a longer start-up time, since it requires the compilation of an intermediate program, but it is optimized for exhaustive searches.

13.3 THE VALIDATION KERNEL

Procedure `new_state()` is the core of the analyzer. It controls all executions, monitors progress, and performs the correctness checks. More than half of the run-time is spend in this routine, with the larger part of the remainder being used up in the calculation of hash values to access the state space.

The procedure is statically defined in a header file named `pangen1.h`. Different portions of the code are enabled or disabled depending on the presence or absence of rendezvous communications, temporal claims, acceptance states, or progress states, and depending on the type of state space storage that is selected. Ignoring, for the time being, all these options, the plain exhaustive state searching algorithm looks as follows:

```
 1 new_state()
 2 {    register Trans *t, *ta;
 3      char n, m, ot, lst;
 4      short II, tt;
 5      short From = now.nr_pr-1;
 6      short To = 0;
 7 Down:
 8      if (depth >= maxdepth)
 9      {        truncs++;
10               goto Up;
11      }
12      if (To == 0)
13      {        if (hstore((char *)&now, vsize))
14               {        truncs++;
15                        goto Up;
16               }
17               nstates++;
18      }
19      if (depth > mreached)
20               mreached = depth;
21      n = timeout = 0;
22
23 Again:
24      for (II = From; II >= To; II -= 1)
25      {        this = pptr(II);
26               tt = (short) ((P0 *)this)->_p;
27               ot = (unsigned char) ((P0 *)this)->_t;
28               for (t = trans[ot][tt]; t; t = t->nxt)
29               {
30 #include "pan.m"
31 P999:                   /* jumps here when move succeeds */
32                         if (m>n||(n>3&&m!=0)) n=m;
33                         depth++; trpt++;
34                         trpt->pr = II;
35                         trpt->st = tt;
36                         if (t->st)
37                         {        ((P0 *)this)->_p = t->st;
38                                  reached[ot][t->st] = 1;
39                         }
40                         trpt->o_t  =  t; trpt->o_n  = n;
41                         trpt->o_ot = ot; trpt->o_tt = tt;
42                         trpt->o_To = To;
43                         if (t->atom&2)
44                         {        From = To = II; nlinks++;
45                         } else
46                         {        From = now.nr_pr-1; To = 0;
47                         }
48                         goto Down;       /* pseudo-recursion */
49 Up:
50                         t = trpt->o_t; n = trpt->o_n;
51                         ot = trpt->o_ot; II = trpt->pr;
52                         tt = trpt->o_tt; this = pptr(II);
53                         To = trpt->o_To;
```

```
54 #include "pan.b"
55 R999:                       /* jumps here when done */
56                             depth--; trpt--;
57                             ((P0 *)this)->_p = tt;
58                 } /* all options */
59         } /* all processes */
60
61     if (n == 0)
62     {         if (!endstate() && now.nr_pr)
63             {         if (!timeout)
64                     {         timeout=1;
65                               goto Again;
66                     }
67                     uerror("deadlock");
68             }
69     }
70     if (depth > 0) goto Up;
71 }
```

The procedure is called once and does not return until either a complete search is performed or an error found. In this version, without all the trimmings of a full implementation, the only type of error checked for is an invalid end-state. The main work is done in two for loops. The first one, on line 24, loops over all currently executing processes. The second one, on line 28, exhaustively checks all executable statements in each process. The proctype of the current process is stored in a local variable ot, and the process state is kept in a local variable tt. These two variables together are used to index the *transition matrix*, trans[ot][tt], on line 28. A pointer T points to the definition of the transition itself: the condition, the effect and the next state. The execution of the transitions themselves are hidden in a file pan.m that is included on line 30. It is a simple case switch that records all transitions that are defined in the system. If a transition is executable, it leads to label P999. If it is unexecutable a continue is executed that brings us back into the inner loop on line 28.

A successful transition produces a new state that must be analyzed in precisely the same fashion as the current one. This is where normally a recursion step is executed. The time and space required for the recursive procedure calls, however, can easily be avoided if the recursion is replaced with iteration. Let us look at how this is implemented.

Lines 32 to 42 perform some housekeeping to prepare the validator for the analysis of a newly generated state. The depth count is increased, a pointer is incremented for the user level stack stptr, which maintains, among others, the execution trail. If the transition was labeled *atomic*, line 43 makes sure that the current process will continue executing in the next step, foregoing options for executions in the other processes. The default case is invoked on line 46, defining that all currently execution processes must be considered. The recursion step is replaced on line 48 with a jump to the label Down.

On the return from the pseudo recursion, with a jump to label Up on line 48, all relevant local variables are retrieved via the stack pointer stptr, which, if all is well, points at exactly the location where they were saved before the matching jump to Down. Then the state vector is restored to its original value by performing a reverse operation that undoes the effect of the last forward transition that was explored. The code that does this is hidden in a separate file pan.b that is included on line 48. This file also contains a case switch, that relies on the pointer to the transition matrix t to point the program to the right operation to execute.

The state itself, storing state information about all currently executing processes and all currently accessible queues and variables, is maintained in a global variable now, though that is not visible in the body of this procedure.

The label Again, on line 23, with the matching jump on line 65, is used to implement the timeout recovery mechanism. If the search gets stuck this is first noticed on line 61 by the zero value of variable n. A quick check is then performed to see if the deadlock is not in fact a valid endstate. If this test fails, the timeouts are enabled and second attempt is made to perform a transition with a return to label Again. If this also fails, the error routine uerror() is called, which can trigger the writing of an error trail and optionally abort the search.

The extensions that are needed to implement the full range of correctness checks discussed in Chapter 6 triple the size of the algorithm, though in a none too exciting way. To check temporal claims, for instance, the search alternately executes atomic statements in the model and in the claim. The toggle bit, which determines where to look for the next statement to execute, is piggybacked onto the variable tau. To implement rendezvous message passing, a global variable boq (short for "blocked on queue") is set after every rendezvous send operation. The variable blocks all operations other than a matching receive operation. Effectively, then, the send-receive handshake becomes one indivisible step, though the validator performs it as two distinct transitions. The other extensions similarly make the algorithm somewhat harder to read, but do not change it in a fundamental way. In the discussion we therefore restrict ourselves mainly to the basic version. A listing of the complete algorithm for exhaustive validation is given in Appendix E.

13.4 THE TRANSITION MATRIX

The transition matrix shown in Figure 13.1 performs a central role in the search. Some precautions are taken to make sure that it does not contain any spurious moves that could slow down the search. It is constructed from elements of the following type:

```
typedef struct Trans {
        short atom;     /* is this an atomic transition */
        int st;         /* the next state/statement     */
        int forw;       /* index for forward transition */
        int back;       /* index for return  transition */
```

```
        struct Trans *nxt;",
   } Trans;
```

Every proctype in the original SPIN specification defines a set of entries in the matrix: one for every control flow state. The following array is used to keep track of them.

```
   Trans *trans[NPROCS][NSTATES]
```

The transitions of a process of type 19 for control flow state 90 can be found through the pointer

```
   trans[19][90]
```

Figure 13.2 illustrates a typical use of the matrix elements.

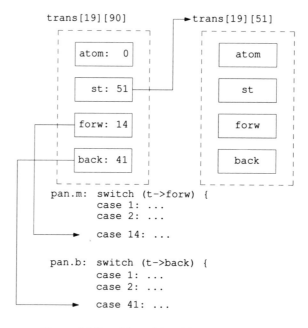

Figure 13.2 — Transition Matrix Elements

The first field of a Trans structure is used to label transitions that are atomic. A zero entry means that the transition is a normal, asynchronous one. Field st defines the successor state that is reached if a transition is successfully executed. The next field forw is an index that identifies the right operation to execute. It indexes a switch of transitions that is generated in the include file pan.m. Similarly, back is an index into the switch of pan.b that identifies the operation that can undo the effect of the forward transition and restore the state vector to its original state.

Whenever there is a nondeterministic choice of transitions to make, e.g., for SPIN selection and repetition structures, the options are placed in a linked list that is connected via the transition element's nxt pointer (not shown in Figure 13.2). To examine all executable options, the inner loop of new_state() simply walks down the linked list.

13.5 THE VALIDATOR-GENERATOR CODE

It would seem that all that is left to do to make the analyzer run is to generate the right transition matrix. Well, not quite. Since we are generating code anyway we can also generate protocol specific routines for manipulating the queues, instantiating process instances, and the like. It is a fairly substantial piece of code that generates all this information, but well worth it.

MESSAGE CHANNELS

Before discussing the code of the validator generator itself, let us look briefly at the code that it tries to produce. From the 25 relevant routines that are part of every analyzer generated, 7 deal with the message channels:

```
addqueue()
delq()
q_restor()
qsend()
qrecv()
unsend()
unrecv()
```

The first routine, for instance, implements the PROMELA chan statement, and the second routine removes a channel when it goes out of scope, that is, when the creating process has terminated. For every different type of message channel, a separate queue template is generated. For example,

```
typedef struct Q1 {
        unsigned char Qlen;        /* q_size */
        unsigned char _t;          /* q_type */
        struct {
                unsigned fld0 : 32;
        } contents[1];
} Q1;
```

defines a queue with one slot and one message field. Two queue fields are predefined: one specifies the type of the channel and the other the current number of messages that the corresponding queue stores. The routine q_restor() is used in backward moves to restore a deleted queue to its last known state, just before a deletion with qdel(). Messages are appended to a queue with the procedure qsend(into, fld0, ...). Parameter fld0 indicates the value of the first message parameter. Procedure qrecv(from, slot, fld, done) retrieves a single message field fld from slot slot in a queue from. The parameter done is set to one after all fields have been extracted and the message can be removed from the queue. Note that a single receive operation can have multiple side-effects by set-ting variables. The definition of a procedure that reads one message parameter at a time is a simple general solution to that problem.

Every action has an undo. The counterparts of send and receive are named unsend() and unrecv(), which, respectively, remove a complete message from the tail of a queue or put one back at its head.

PROCESSES

Three routines deal with processes.

```
addproc()
delproc()
p_restor()
```

Every type of process is again defined in a different template. For instance, for the factorial program we find

```
typedef struct P1 {       /* factorial */
        unsigned _t : 2;          /* proctype */
        unsigned _p : 4;          /* state    */
        int result;
        unsigned char child;
        int n;
        unsigned char p;
} P1;
```

The process type and the current process state are a standard part of the template. The required width of the bitfields is calculated by the generator. These first two fields are used to index the transition matrix. The remaining entries reserve slots for local variables. The procedure addproc() appends one of these templates to the state vector, and delproc() removes it. Procedure p_restor() is used in backward moves to restore a deleted process to its last known state.

STATE SPACE MAINTENANCE

The state space can be accessed in two different ways, selectable by a preprocessor directive named BITSTATE. Unless this name has been defined, a full state space is constructed with a traditional exhaustive search method. To access the state space the routine hstore() is used. Seen from procedure new_state() this looks as follows:

```
if (hstore((char *)&now, vsize))
{       truncs++;
        goto Up;
}
nstates++;
```

The variable vsize gives the current size of the state vector in bytes. The global now points to it. If hstore() returns the boolean value false, the state is new and must be analyzed. As a side effect of hstore(), the state is also stored in full in the state space. The next time that this same state is encountered the routine will return the boolean value `true`, which means that the state can be skipped. Internally `hstore()` uses a fast hash function called `s_hash()`.

If the name BITSTATE is explicitly defined during compilation, the more memory efficient supertrace, bit state space memory routines are used. The invoke a double value hashing function called `d_hash()`. The routine uses the state vector to calculate two different hash values (see Chapter 11, page 234). A check is then made on the two bit positions in the state space, and if a double match is found, the state is assumed to have been analyzed before. This is how it works:

```
d_hash((unsigned char *) &now, vsize);
j3 = (1<<(J1&7));  j1 = J1>>3;
j4 = (1<<(J2&7));  j2 = J2>>3;
if ((SS[j2]&j3) && (SS[j1]&j4))
{       truncs++;
        goto Up;
}
SS[j2] |= j3;  SS[j1] |= j4;     /* storage */
nstates++;
```

First `d_hash()` is called to produce two hash values for the first `vsize` bytes of the state vector, stored in `now`. The values are written into the integer global variables J1, and J2. The next few operations take the low order 3 bits from J1 and J2, using the bit mask 7, and assign them to j3 and j4. The remaining bits are shifted down by three bit positions and assigned to j1 and j2. The test

```
if ((SS[j2]&j3) && (SS[j1]&j4))
```

selects the calculated bit positions and only if both bits are on a match is assumed. The last line sets the two bits with a binary OR operation, to secure a future match on the same state. It is the only storage operation performed: a savings in memory of (8×`vsize`$-#2$) bits per state, assuming 8 bits per byte.

THE REMAINING ROUTINES

The remainder of the validation routines is fairly straightforward. There is a routine `endstate()` to determine if the current combination of process states is a valid end-state, by comparing them with the known stop states in each process. A routine `assert()` checks user defined assertions and produces an error trail if one is violated. There is a routine `r_ck()` for every process type in the system that performs the reachability check after the depth-first search by verifying that every relevant control flow state in the specification has indeed been reached by at least one of the executing processes. Two main routines deal with the transition matrix, `settable()` and `retrans()`. The first sets the table (matrix) to its default contents as produced by the generator, using the parse tree structure. The second quickly goes through the structure to optimize it a little for the validation task. Nested choices, for instance, are rewritten into single choices, without, of course, violating the semantics of PROMELA.

13.6 OVERVIEW OF THE CODE

The code for the generator is included in four C files. At the time of writing, a count of these routines produced:

```
$ wc pangen[1-4].c
    424    1341    8812 pangen1.c
    501    1784   13595 pangen2.c
    102     303    1659 pangen3.c
    170     583    4024 pangen4.c
```

Three header files contain fixed code that is included with every program generated:

```
$ wc pangen[1-2].h
    910    3363   22276 pangen1.h
    127     528    3389 pangen2.h
    108     348    2151 pangen3.h
```

And finally, one more file is used to implement the guided simulation option.

```
$ wc pangen5.c
    158     489    3292 pangen5.c
```

The complete code for the exhaustive validation option can be found in Appendix E. Here we highlight only the major parts.

The routine that is actually called by the simulator, if the command line option −a is given, is called gensrc(). It is included in pangen2.c. It starts by creating the five target files pan.[chtmb] and copying some code from pangen2.h into them. It then calls procedure putproc() once for every basic proctype that was parsed: once for the description of the init process, stored in the simulator's run queue, and once for every process in the ready queue. These calls generate all the code for the transition matrix and for the case switches with the transition statements. The remaining procedures to make the analyzer run are mostly included in the file pangen1.c and are invoked in calls at the close of gensrc().

The actual work of translating portions of the parse tree into C code happens in just two procedures: putstmnt() and undostmnt(). There is no magic here, just the generation of code, with some care taken to reduce the runtime requirements of validations. The state numbers are given by the seqno field in parse tree elements: every basic statement is assigned a unique sequence number by the parsing routines, as explained in Chapter 12. A set of transitions is assigned to every state to index the case switches. The transitions are numbered separately (note that there are likely to be more transitions than states if selection structures are used), and they are stored in the transition matrix.

Every sequence in a process body results in a call on procedure putseq(). The sequence is translated one statement at a time in a largely arbitrary order. Every element in the sequence that has been translated is labeled DONE in the status field. For the transitions the pointers between elements are followed, skipping as many intermediate steps as possible, using the routine huntini(). The actual code that

reproduces the effect of a forward transition is generated by putstmnt(), listed in
pangen2.c. The code that can undo the effect, when the depth first search
unwinds, is generated by undostmnt(), listed in pangen4.c. Rather then giving a
detailed expose of all the code being generated, let us consider the translation of
one specific type of statement: an assignment.

The routine putstmnt() contains code which, after macro substitutions, amounts
to the following:

```
case ASGN:          fprintf(fd, "(trpt+1)->oval = ");
                    putstmnt(fd, now->lft,m,pid);
                    fprintf(fd, ";\n\t\t");
                    putstmnt(fd,now->lft,m,pid);
                    fprintf(fd," = ");
                    putstmnt(fd,now->rgt,m,pid);
                    break;
```

Given the parse tree for the SPIN assignment

```
nips = 12+3*crunch;
```

this is translated into the sequence

```
case 34:            (trpt+1)->oval = now.nips;
                    now.nips = (12 + (3 * ((P1 *)this)->crunch));
                    m = 3; goto P333;
```

assuming that 34 is the number in the transition matrix assigned to the current
transition, nips is a global variable, a permanent part of the state vector now, and
crunch is a local variable that is accessible via the predefined pointer to the template of the current process in the state vector this. The first line is a backup of
the old value of global nips in a special field of the stack that is used to organize
the search in procedure new_state(). There is an offset of 1 to account for the
fact that officially we do not know yet if the transition is going to be executable or
not. Only if the execution is executable is the stack pointer increased, and the
backup value will be in the right place for the undo operation.

The code for the generation of the matching undo operation looks as follows:

```
case ASGN:          putstmnt(tb, now->lft, m, pid);
                    fprintf(tb, " = trpt->oval");
                    checkchan(now->rgt, m, pid);
                    break;
```

which for the same statement produces this code

```
case 28:            now.nips = trpt->oval;
                    goto R333;
```

assuming again that 28 is the index assigned to the current undo operation in the
transition matrix. The additional call on checkchan() in the undo code above is
to make sure that no channels were created as a side effect of the assignment. If
so, these channels are to be deleted again in the reverse transition.

13.7 GUIDED SIMULATION

The last extension to the simulator source code to be discussed is the implementation of procedure match_trail(). The code can be found in file pangen5.c. It looks for the simulation trail in file pan.trail, where the validator puts it. In its basic form, the trail has the following format:

```
0:0:1
1:0:2
2:0:3
3:0:4
4:0:5
5:0:6
6:0:8
7:3:15
```

Each line specifies a transition in three integer fields, separated by colons. The first field is a step number, counting up from zero to whatever the length of the error trail may be. The second field is the process number, with 0 for the init process, 1 for the first process that was started in a run statement, and so on. The last number on each line of the error trail identifies the state to which the process moves. The simulator's job is to follow the trail and touch upon all states listed. If, for now, we omit error recovery, temporal claim processes, and the treatment of stop states, the code looks as follows:

```
 1 match_trail()
 2 {    FILE *fd;
 3      int i, pno, nst;
 4
 5      if (!(fd = fopen("pan.trail", "r")))
 6      {       printf("spin -t: cannot find 'pan.trail'\n");
 7              exit(1);
 8      }
 9      Tval = 1; /* timeouts may be part of the trail */
10      while (fscanf(fd, "%d:%d:%d\n", &depth, &pno, &nst) == 3)
11      {       i = nproc - nstop;      /* number of running procs */
12              for (X = run; X; X = X->nxt)
13                      if (--i == pno) /* find process pno */
14                              break;
15              lineno = X->pc->n->nval;
16              do                              /* bring it to state nst */
17              {       X->pc = d_eval_sub(X->pc, pno, nst);
18              } while (X && X->pc && X->pc->seqno != nst);
19      }
20      printf("spin: trail ends after %d steps\n", depth);
21      wrapup();
22 }
```

After opening the trail file (lines 5-8), one directive at a time is read from the trail (lines 10). The right process is located (lines 12-14), and it is executed until the right state is reached (lines 16-18).

A stop state is identified by the new state 0, a non-existing state. It is executed as a removal of the process that was identified. The full code for `match_trail()` in Appendix E has extra checks to prepare it for cases where the validation model is unable to follow the trail, for instance if the model was changed since the trail was written. In these cases the simulator will report, for example,

```
step 23: lost trail (proc 4 state .13)
```

giving a rough indication where the simulation failed. In this case an inconsistency was discovered in step 23, just before process 4 reached state 13.

One case in which the simulator may lose track of the simulation trail, in a syntactically correct validation model, is illustrated by the following example.

```
do
:: (m >= N-1) -> break
:: (m <  N-1) -> m = m - 1
:: (m <  N-1) -> m = m - 1; n = n + 1
od
```

The two almost equal execution paths may, with the current implementation of the simulator, lead to an ambiguous trail. The problem can be avoided straightforwardly, by removing the ambiguity:

```
do
:: (m >= N-1) -> break
:: (m <  N-1) -> m = m - 1
        if
        :: skip
        :: n = n + 1
        fi
od
```

13.8 SOME APPLICATIONS

The analysis option is invoked from the original simulator with the flag -a, for instance, as follows:

```
$ spin -a factorial
```

At this point, typically within a second, we have generated a program that consists of five separate C files: a header file, the two case switches with forward and backward transitions, a main file with the main C routines, and a file with the transition matrix and some related routines.

```
$ wc pan.?
      55      197    1161 pan.b   # backward moves
     731     2159   14822 pan.c   # c routines
     108      409    2526 pan.h   # header
     120      482    2925 pan.m   # forward moves
     129      377    2580 pan.t   # transition matrix
    1143     3624   24014 total
```

The program can be compiled in two different ways. The default

```
$ cc -o pan pan.c
```

generates an analyzer that constructs a full state space, ruling out any chance of incompleteness. It provides 100% coverage, unless it runs out of memory. Optionally, a more frugal supertrace validator can be generated with the command

```
$ cc -DBITSTATE -o pan pan.c
```

In either case, the validation is started by typing

```
$ pan
pan: deadlock
pan: wrote pan.trail
...etc
```

If the validator finds an error it writes the simulation trail. The trail is used with the simulator in any of the modes discussed in Chapter 12, for instance with the -s option:

```
$ spin -t -s factorial
....etc.
```

where the new -t flag will tell the simulator to follow the trail in pan.trail rather than performing a random simulation.

Consider the following PROMELA version of Lynch's protocol, discussed in Chapters 2 and 5.

```
 1 #define MIN 9       /* first data message to send */
 2 #define MAX 12      /* last  data message to send */
 3 #define FILL        99      /* filler message */
 4
 5 mtype = { ack, nak, err }
 6
 7 proctype transfer(chan chin, chout)
 8 {    byte o, i, last_i=MIN;
 9
10      o = MIN+1;
11      do
12      :: chin?nak(i) ->
13              assert(i == last_i+1);
14              chout!ack(o)
15      :: chin?ack(i) ->
16              if
17              :: (o <  MAX) -> o = o+1       /* next */
18              :: (o >= MAX) -> o = FILL      /* done */
19              fi;
20              chout!ack(o)
21      :: chin?err(i) ->
22              chout!nak(o)
23      od
24 }
25
```

```
26 proctype channel(chan in, out)
27 {    byte md, mt;
28      do
29      :: in?mt,md ->
30              if
31              :: out!mt,md
32              :: out!err,0
33              fi
34      od
35 }
36
37 init
38 {    chan AtoB = [1] of { byte, byte };
39      chan BtoC = [1] of { byte, byte };
40      chan CtoA = [1] of { byte, byte };
41      atomic {
42              run transfer(AtoB, BtoC);
43              run channel(BtoC, CtoA);
44              run transfer(CtoA, AtoB)
45      };
46      AtoB!err,0      /* start */
47 }
```

A few integer data messages are inserted into the system to allow us to look at at least a few message exchanges. We have also added a process type to model the expected behavior of the communication channel: randomly distorting messages. We can simulate the behavior of the system with the old simulator code, for instance

```
$ spin -s lynch
proc  0 (_init)       line  46, Send err,0   -> queue 1 (AtoB)
proc  1 (transfer)    line  22, Send nak,10  -> queue 2 (chout)
proc  2 (channel)     line  31, Send nak,10  -> queue 3 (out)
proc  3 (transfer)    line  14, Send ack,10  -> queue 1 (chout)
...etc.
```

This may or may not hit the assertion violation, depending on how the nondeterminism is resolved at each step.

For a validation of the same specification, we generate and compile the validation program, let's assume in supertrace mode, as follows:

```
$ spin -a lynch
$ cc -o pan pan.c
```

We now have an executable program called pan. To see what options it accepts to perform the search, we can try

```
$ pan -?
unknown option
-cN stop at Nth error (default=1)
-l  find non-progress loops
-mN max depth N (default=10k)
-wN hash-table of 2^N entries (default=18)
```

We can, for instance, set the maximum search depth (the size of the backtrace stack) to another value than the default of 10,000 steps, or we can change the size of the hash table.

☐ With full state space storage, the size of the hash table should be chosen larger than or equal too the total number of reachable states that is expected, to avoid a serious time penalty for the resolution of the hash collisions (see Chapter 11).

☐ In supertrace mode the size of the hash-table is equal to the number of bits in the state space, so the -w flag really selects the actual size of the state space that is used for the search. By default this state space is set to $2^22 = 4,194,304$ bits = 524,288 bytes. The size of the state space determines the maximum number of states that can be analyzed. For the default case this is roughly 4,194,304/2 = 2,097,152 states, independent of the size of the state vector. (In this implementation two bits are used for every state stored.)

The coverage of the search will be smaller as we get closer to that limit. We discuss an indicator of that coverage, the hash factor, with a few other examples later. We first try the validator in exhaustive mode.

```
$ pan
assertion violated (i==(last_i+1))
pan: aborted (at depth 53)
pan: wrote pan.trail
full state space search for:
        assertion violations and invalid endstates
search was not completed
vector 56 byte, depth reached 53, errors: 1
        58 states, stored
        2 states, linked
        1 states, matched          total:        61
hash conflicts: 0 (resolved)
(size 2^18 states, stackframes: 0/16)
```

At the end of each run the validator prints the numbers of states stored, linked and matched. Stored states are states that have been added to the state space, either in full or in compressed form as two bits, depending on how the program was compiled. Linked states are states that were encountered within an atomic sequence, no state space checks are performed on them. Matched states are states that were analyzed and later revisited.

The validator found an error that is documented in the file pan.trail. We can now feed back this error trail to the simulator to look precisely at what goes on. For instance:

```
$ spin -t -s -r lynch
proc  0 (_init)        line  46, Send err,0    -> queue 1 (AtoB)
proc  1 (transfer)     line  21, Recv err,0    <- queue 1 (chin)
proc  1 (transfer)     line  22, Send nak,10   -> queue 2 (chout)
proc  2 (channel)      line  29, Recv nak,10   <- queue 2 (in)
proc  2 (channel)      line  32, Send err,0    -> queue 3 (out)
```

```
proc  3 (transfer)      line  21, Recv err,0    <- queue 3 (chin)
proc  3 (transfer)      line  22, Send nak,10   -> queue 1 (chout)
proc  1 (transfer)      line  12, Recv nak,10   <- queue 1 (chin)
proc  1 (transfer)      line  14, Send ack,10   -> queue 2 (chout)
....
proc  3 (transfer)      line  21, Recv err,0    <- queue 3 (chin)
proc  3 (transfer)      line  22, Send nak,99   -> queue 1 (chout)
proc  1 (transfer)      line  12, Recv nak,99   <- queue 1 (chin)
spin: "lynch" line 13: assertion violated
#processes: 4
                    _p = 3
proc  3 (transfer)      line 11 (state 15)
proc  2 (channel)       line 28 (state 6)
proc  1 (transfer)      line 13 (state 3)
proc  0 (_init) line 47 (state 6)
4 processes created
```

The simulator run can be repeated with different flags, e.g., printing variable values and process states, until the cause of the error is determined and can be repaired.

13.9 COVERAGE IN SUPERTRACE MODE

The coverage of the search in supertrace mode is determined by the number of hash collisions that occur. This number, of course, is usually unknown. It can be determined by comparing a run with full state storage to a run with a bit state space, but this is not always feasible. The number of hash collisions, however, depends critically on the ratio of the size of the hash-table, i.e., the number of bits in the state space, and the number of states that is stored. We call this factor the *hash factor*. It is calculated by the validator after each run as the size of the hash-table divided by the number of states stored. A high number (more than 100) correlates with good coverage. Low numbers (near 1) imply poor coverage.

Since we store two bits per state in supertrace mode, the hash factor can be anywhere from 2^N up to and including 0.5, where N can be set by the user to grab the maximum amount of memory that is available on the target machine. (For full state space storage the lower limit on the hash factor is zero.) By empirical testing with full and bit state space runs it can be confirmed that a hash-factor of 100 or more virtually guarantees a coverage of 99% to 100% of all reachable states. As an example, Table 13.1 gives the results of tests with a protocol model that has 334,151 reachable states.

The original run in this case was the full state space version, using 45.6 Mbyte of memory. It stored all states and resolved a total of 66,455 hash conflicts on the way. The run was repeated, first with a supertrace validation using the flag $-w25$, giving a hash factor of 100.9 and a coverage of 99.45%. By virtue of the double bit hash function, the number of hash conflicts is substantially lower than in the first run. The precise number can be found by subtracting the number of reached and stored states in the first run from the number of reached (but not stored) states in the second run. In each of the next three supertrace validations we halved the

Table 13.1 – Correlation between Hash Factor and Coverage

Search	Hash Factor	States Stored	Hash Collisions	Memory Used	Coverage
exhaustive	—	334,151	66,455	45.6 Mb	100%
supertrace	100.9	332,316	1,835	9.9 Mb	99.45%
supertrace	50.9	329,570	4,581	7.9 Mb	98.62%
supertrace	25.7	326,310	7,841	6.9 Mb	97.65%
supertrace	13.0	322,491	11,660	6.3 Mb	96.51%

hash factor by using the flags $-w24$, $-w23$, and $-w22$. The last run uses no more than 6.3 Mbyte of memory, of which 6 Mbyte, in both the full state space storage version and the supertrace version, is used for storing the backup trail which was 300,000 steps long for all runs of this test protocol. (This also explains why the amount of memory required does not precisely half each time the argument to the $-w$ flag is decremented.)

For comparison, a run of the full state space storage method that is restricted to 6.3 Mbyte of memory to store its state space, predictably, gets less coverage. The exhaustive search effectively degrades into an uncontrolled partial search, as illustrated in Table 13.2.

Table 13.2 – Coverage of Partial Searches

Search	Hash Factor	States Stored	Hash Collisions	Memory Used	Coverage
exhaustive	—	83,961	389,671	6.3 Mb	25.12%
supertrace	13.0	322,491	11,660	6.3 Mb	96.51%

The bit state space is clearly the method of choice here.

13.10 SUMMARY

Many automated validation tools require considerable effort from the user to translate a validation model into the low level code that is used to run the validator. The interpretation of error reports produced by those tools similarly can require considerable human ingenuity. With the simulator and validator generator SPIN, and the validation language PROMELA, we have tried to provide a high level design environment in which everything from simple protocols, up to complete designs for distributed message passing systems can be thoroughly tested and debugged before they are implemented. These tools can help us to deal effectively with the notoriously difficult problems of asynchrony and concurrency. The tools are portable, powerful, and efficient.

EXERCISES

13-1 Consider how the code must be changed to replace the depth-first search order with breadth-first. What are the memory requirements?

13-2 Modify the code to optimize the implementation of send and receive routines, and measure its effect.

13-3 Add an option to SPIN for restricting the validation runs to "fair" executions. This option is based on the assumption of a "fair process scheduler." This means that any process that can execute a statement is assumed to be enabled to do so within finite time. All infinite executions (cycles) that violate this fairness assumption can be ignored. All non-progress loops or acceptance cycles that violate this assumption should similarly be ignored. Hint: perform an extra check before reporting any error in cyclic sequences.

13-4 (E.A. Emerson - P. van Eijk) Implement a method that can give a better prediction of the coverage of partial supertrace validations. Do this by starting a supertrace validation by selecting 1000 states at random from the state space. (How?) Store those full states in a separate lookup table and check during the supertrace validation how many of those 1000 states are reached. The fraction of the states reached is an indication of the coverage. How reliable is the estimate? How expensive?

13-5 Modify the validator generator to allow for the automatic generation of protocol implementations from PROMELA code. Note that C code is already generated for all transitions and actions. Replace the search procedure `new_state()` with a scheduler, as used in the simulator code (Chapter 12), and allow for certain channels to be identified as special device channels (for example, files) that can be linked to C library routines that access the raw I/O channels. Your solution need not contain more than two pages of code.

BIBLIOGRAPHIC NOTES

The validator described has several predecessors of varying scope and performance. For those interested, the papers Holzmann [1984a, 1985, 1988] document the more significant changes. The last of these papers contains a detailed explanation of the state vector model and the bit state space method. The method described in Holzmann [1988] is the only version from this sequence that achieves a better performance, in terms of runtime and memory usage, than the method described here. It requires substantially more code to implement.

USING THE VALIDATOR 14

14.1 INTRODUCTION

It is time to put the tools we have developed in the last three chapters to use. First, to get our feet wet, let us look at two simple examples. The first is a reconstruction of a protocol used on the optical telegraphs in 1794 (see Chapter 1). The second is a small, but very important, example from Chapter 5: Dekker's algorithm for providing two competing processes. mutually exclusive access to a critical section in their code.

14.2 AN OPTICAL TELEGRAPH PROTOCOL

The details of the communications protocols used on the optical telegraphs built in the late 18th century are hard to find. The best source is a booklet published by the Swedish inventor of a shutter telegraph Edelcrantz [1796], which comes complete with coding tables and elaborate, informal descriptions of the required coding and signaling methods. All stations along a line, except the first and the last one, had to monitor two neighboring stations for incoming traffic. Two telegraph operators were therefore usually on duty. In the validation model we build for the optical telegraph we will therefore also use two asynchronous processes, one to model the actions of each operator.

To transfer a message, the sending operator had to set the telegraph on his station to a special start signal, which had to be confirmed with an attention signal from the receiving station. The start signal could then be removed, and the first message transfered. Each message had to be reproduced faithfully by the receiver before the sender could remove it from the telegraph. (Edelcrantz system also allowed for the use of a special error signal, but we will not model that here.) The end of a message was signaled with a special stop signal. After the stop signal was transfered, the telegraph was released for other traffic, for instance to traffic flowing in the opposite direction.

Clearly, an operator could not use the telegraph on his station for incoming or outgoing traffic if his colleague was already using it. We model the state of the telegraphs with a boolean array busy[N], where N is the number of telegraph stations. The validation model below puts three stations in a ring (it's unlikely that they were ever used that way), with two operators per station this gives a total of six processes.

```
 1 #define true        1
 2 #define false       0
 3
 4 bool busy[3];
 5
 6 chan   up[3] = [1] of { byte };
 7 chan down[3] = [1] of { byte };
 8
 9 mtype = { start, attention, data, stop }
10
11 proctype station(byte id; chan in, out)
12 {   do
13       :: in?start ->
14              atomic { !busy[id] -> busy[id] = true };
15              out!attention;
16              do
17              :: in?data -> out!data
18              :: in?stop -> break
19              od;
20              out!stop;
21              busy[id] = false
22       :: atomic { !busy[id] -> busy[id] = true };
23              out!start;
24              in?attention;
25              do
26              :: out!data -> in?data
27              :: out!stop -> break
28              od;
29              in?stop;
30              busy[id] = false
31       od
32 }
33
34 init {
35     atomic {
36             run station(0, up[2], down[2]);
37             run station(1, up[0], down[0]);
38             run station(2, up[1], down[1]);
39
40             run station(0, down[0], up[0]);
41             run station(1, down[1], up[1]);
42             run station(2, down[2], up[2])
43     }
```

```
44 }
```

If we run a random simulation on this protocol we quickly find a problem.

```
$ spin -r -s optical
proc  6 (station)      line  23, Send start    -> queue 3 (out)
proc  5 (station)      line  23, Send start    -> queue 2 (out)
proc  4 (station)      line  23, Send start    -> queue 1 (out)
proc  3 (station)      line  13, Recv start    <- queue 2 (in)
proc  2 (station)      line  13, Recv start    <- queue 1 (in)
proc  1 (station)      line  13, Recv start    <- queue 3 (in)

#processes: 7
proc  6 (station)      line 24 (state 19)
proc  5 (station)      line 24 (state 19)
proc  4 (station)      line 24 (state 19)
proc  3 (station)      line 14 (state 4)
proc  2 (station)      line 14 (state 4)
proc  1 (station)      line 14 (state 4)
proc  0 (_init) line 44 (state 8)
7 processes created
```

The simulation gets stuck after all three stations simultaneously send out the start message. The three messages are received, but then the deadlock trap closes. Three operators are waiting for a confirmation of their start messages, the other three are waiting for the telegraph to be released by their colleagues before they can sent the required attention signal. In the deadlock state, three processes are at line 14 and the other three at line 24 in the source of proctype station.

The deadlock problem is a curious variant of Dijkstra's well-known *dining philosophers'* problem.

14.3 DEKKER's ALGORITHM

To build a useful validation model, we extend Dekker's algorithm with two boolean variables, abin and bin, as follows:

```
 1 #define true       1
 2 #define false      0
 3 #define Aturn       false
 4 #define Bturn       true
 5
 6 bool x, y, t;
 7 bool ain, bin;
 8
 9 proctype A()
10 {   x = true;
11     t = Bturn;
12     (y == false || t == Aturn);
13     ain = true;
14     assert(bin == false);    /* critical section */
```

```
15      ain = false;
16      x = false
17 }
18
19 proctype B()
20 {    y = true;
21      t = Aturn;
22      (x == false || t == Bturn);
23      bin = true;
24      assert(ain == false);    /* critical section */
25      bin = false;
26      y = false
27 }
28
29 init
30 {    run A(); run B()
31 }
```

The variables `ain` and `bin` are set to `true` only when process `A()` or `B()`, respectively, enters its critical section. A simple `assert()` statement can be used to verify that both processes cannot be in their critical sections at the same time.

First, let us do a random simulation. The above validation model is stored in a file named "dekker." We try

```
$ spin dekker
3 processes created
```

No assertion violations are reported, but the run is not very informative. We try again, this time printing out all statements.

```
$ spin -p dekker
proc  0 (_init) line 31 (state 2)
proc  1 (A)     line 11 (state 2)
proc  0 (_init) line 31 (state 3)
proc  2 (B)     line 21 (state 2)
proc  1 (A)     line 12 (state 3)
proc  2 (B)     line 22 (state 3)
proc  1 (A)     line 13 (state 4)
proc  1 (A)     line 14 (state 5)
proc  1 (A)     line 15 (state 6)
proc  1 (A)     line 16 (state 7)
proc  1 (A)     line 17 (state 8)
proc  2 (B)     line 23 (state 4)
proc  2 (B)     line 24 (state 5)
proc  2 (B)     line 25 (state 6)
proc  2 (B)     line 26 (state 7)
proc  2 (B)     line 27 (state 8)
proc  2 (B)     terminates
proc  1 (A)     terminates
proc  0 (_init) terminates
3 processes created
```

We can repeat this a few times to gain confidence that indeed the algorithm seems to perform as advertised. But that is no proof. We can easily do an exhaustive search to establish once and for all that the algorithm is correct. First we generate and compile the analyzer.

```
$ spin -a dekker
$ cc -o pan pan.c
```

That is all there is to it; except for the exhaustive validation run itself of course.

```
$ pan
full state space search for:
        assertion violations and invalid endstates
vector 16 byte, depth reached 19, errors: 0
      81 states, stored
       0 states, linked
      36 states, matched              total:       117
hash conflicts: 0 (resolved)
(max size 2^18 states, stackframes: 3/0)
unreached in proctype _init:
        reached all 3 states
unreached in proctype B:
        reached all 8 states
unreached in proctype A:
        reached all 8 states
```

The first two lines tell us what type of validation is being performed. Since no temporal claims or progress states were defined, a basic search for assertion violations and invalid end-states is performed. The next line says that the state vector for this validation model took up 16 bytes of memory, the longest unique execution sequence was 19 steps long, and, alas, there were no errors found. A total of 81 reachable system states was logged. 36 times the symbolic executions performed by the validator returned the system to a reachable state that was analyzed before. There were no hash conflicts. If there had been any, since this is a full state space search, they would have been resolved with a linked list in the hash table. All states in all processes, finally, were found to be reachable and, implicitly, we proved that no execution sequence can violate the correctness assertions: the validator tried them all. No doubt about it, the algorithm enforces mutual exclusion.

14.4 A LARGER VALIDATION

A validation of the design of the file transfer protocol from Chapter 7 is a larger job. The complete design required us to address a large number of small problems, all of which could be solved with some degree of confidence. But having solved these sub-problems our job is not done. The logical consistency of the complete design is hard to assess. All the small solutions together define the behavior of a larger composite machine that can interact with its environment in an astounding number of ways. After we complete the design, the composite machine will respond in one way or another to all the possible sequences of events that the environment can offer: the ones we had in mind when we made the initial design, and all the ones we never thought of. A protocol designer quickly learns that the second class of sequences is usually larger than the first. Our job here is to find out if, despite this, the design criteria for the protocol are met.

A full listing of the protocol model, as validated here, is given in Appendix F. If all goes well, we can either prove or disprove, for instance, that this protocol is free from deadlocks, can recover gracefully from user aborts, and reliably transmits data in the presence of transmission errors.

The full protocol contains 12 asynchronous processes and 20 message channels. The model is of a realistic complexity and provides a good test case for the applicability of our tools. It is tempting to begin by trying to perform an exhaustive validation of the complete model. A straight exhaustive validation of the model, however, runs unavoidably into the traps discussed in Chapter 11; there cannot ever be enough memory or enough time to complete it. An arbitrarily placed memory limit of 16 Mbytes, for instance, is exhausted quickly and produces the following result. The maximum search depth was guessed.

```
$ spin -a pftp                  # the full model, as listed in App. F
$ cc -DMEMCNT=24 -o  pan pan.c  # set memory bound at 2^24 bytes
$ pan -m15000                   # max search depth 15,000 steps
pan: out of memory
full statespace search for:
        assertion violations and invalid endstates
search was not completed
vector 256 byte, depth reached 7047, errors: 0
   57316 states, stored
   44880 states, linked
   76300 states, matched        total:    178496
hash conflicts: 10319 (resolved)
(max size 2^18 states, stackframes: 0/1009)

memory used: 16777241
```

The exhaustive search deteriorated into an uncontrolled partial search when it exhausted the 16 Mbytes of available memory. As argued in Chapter 11, a bit state space technique can achieve better coverage in these cases, even within stricter memory bounds. For instance, with a memory arena 8 times smaller than before, a bit state space analysis reaches approximately 40 times more states:

```
$ cc -DMEMCNT=21 -DBITSTATE -o pan pan.c  # 8 times less memory
$ pan -w22 -m15000       # 2^22 = 4 Mbit = 0.5 Mbyte state space
bit state space search for:
        assertion violations and invalid endstates
vector 256 byte, depth reached 14,999, errors: 0
 2136023 states, stored
 1987936 states, linked
 3499761 states, matched        total:   7623720
hash factor: 1.963603 (best coverage if >100)
(max size 2^22 states, stackframes: 0/2365)
```

```
memory used: 1507425    # state space + 15,000 slot stack
unreached in proctype _init:
        reached all 13 states
unreached in proctype data_link:
        line 20 (state 14)
        reached: 13 of 14 states
unreached in proctype fc:
        ...
        reached: 61 of 73 states
unreached in proctype fserver:
        line 29 (state 30)
        reached: 29 of 30 states
unreached in proctype session:
        ...
        reached: 96 of 99 states
unreached in proctype present:
        ...
        reached: 32 of 34 states
unreached in proctype userprc:
        reached all 17 states
```

The analyzer inspected 7.6 million composite system states, of which more than 2 million were distinct. The state descriptions were 256 bytes long. There are, however, a number of indications that the analysis was incomplete.

☐ The hash factor is too low. The hash factor must be over a hundred, before we can be confident of sufficient coverage (Chapter 13).

☐ The depth limit of 15,000 steps was too small (note the depth-reached of 14,999 steps). The search would have to be repeated with a larger depth limit to avoid truncation.

☐ The list of unreached code, abbreviated above, shows that not all parts of the model were exercised.

We can boost the coverage a little bit by picking a larger memory arena, but the results are not encouraging:

```
$ cc -DMEMCNT=23 -DBITSTATE -o pan pan.c        # use more memory
$ pan -w25 -m45000              # allow up to 32 million states
bit state space search for:
        assertion violations and invalid endstates
vector 256 byte, depth reached 36569, errors: 0
18302437 states, stored
19482180 states, linked
33989843 states, matched           total: 71774460
hash factor: 1.833331 (best coverage if >100)
(max size 2^25 states, stackframes: 0/6167)

memory used: 6857209
...
```

This time, in less than half the memory arena of the first, "full search" we analyzed over 300 times more states using the supertrace algorithm. Still, however, the indications are that the coverage is poor. If we want to do better, we have to take a different approach. Rather than performing a single monolithic test of all layers at the same time, we can break up the validation problem into smaller, more manageable pieces. (See also the discussion of complexity management techniques such as reduction and generalization in Chapters 8 and 11.) In the design phase we already made an effort to separate orthogonal issues, such as error control, flow control, and session control. This effort can pay off now. The correctness of the flow control layer, for instance, is completely independent of the correctness of the session control layer. We can therefore reduce the complexity of the validation substantially by validating protocol modules separately.

Design by stepwise refinement and validation by stepwise abstraction are complementary techniques.

Each separate validation can achieve a much better coverage than a monolithic validation of all layers put together.

Let's look at the layers one by one. The correctness of the error control depends on the accuracy of the checksumming method, which was discussed in Chapter 3. Validation of a checksum algorithm by exhaustive reachability analysis would be inappropriate; it is a mere computation. We look at the validation of the core protocol layers: flow control, session control, and presentation. We base the validation on the assumptions that were made earlier about the behavior of the three environment processes: the user, the file server, and the data link.

14.5 FLOW CONTROL VALIDATION

The main correctness requirement for the flow control layer is that it cannot lose or reorder messages, despite the fact that the lower protocol module does lose messages. In Chapter 7 we expressed a correctness of the flow control layer, using a labeling of messages with three colors, red, white, and blue. To perform the validation we use the test sender and receiver process described in Chapter 7, extended with some extra code. Before any data are transferred, the test sender must synchronize the two flow control layer processes. The code is borrowed from the original session layer (see Chapter 7 and Appendix F).

```
proctype test_sender(bit n)
{       byte par, toggle;
        ses_to_flow[n]!sync,toggle;
        do
        :: flow_to_ses[n]?sync_ack,par ->
                if
                :: (par != toggle)
                :: (par == toggle) -> break
                fi
        :: timeout ->
                ses_to_flow[n]!sync,toggle
        od;
```

```
        toggle = 1 - toggle;
        do
        :: ses_to_flow[n]!white
        :: ses_to_flow[n]!red -> break
        od;
        do
        :: ses_to_flow[n]!white
        :: ses_to_flow[n]!blue -> break
        od;
        do
        :: ses_to_flow[n]!white
        :: break
        od
}
proctype test_receiver(bit n)
{
        do
        :: flow_to_ses[n]?white
        :: flow_to_ses[n]?red -> break
        :: flow_to_ses[n]?blue -> assert(0)
        od;
        do
        :: flow_to_ses[n]?white
        :: flow_to_ses[n]?red -> assert(0)
        :: flow_to_ses[n]?blue -> break
        od;
end:    do
        :: flow_to_ses[n]?white
        :: flow_to_ses[n]?red -> assert(0)
        :: flow_to_ses[n]?blue -> assert(0)
        od
}
```

The last cycle in the receiver was labeled as an end-state. It is where we would expect the receiver process to be in all valid end-states of the system. It is not wise to rely on the system reaching a deadlock state when an incorrect message is received. The receiver process blocks on unspecified receptions, but the other processes may continue, e.g., with retransmissions. For this reason, an explicit assertion violation is forced in the above validation model.

This test sender and receiver model the upper protocol layer for the flow control layer process. The lower protocol layer is the data link. It was modeled as follows:

```
proctype data_link()
{   byte type, seq;
end:    do
        :: flow_to_dll[0]?type,seq ->
                if
                :: dll_to_flow[1]!type,seq
                :: skip /* lose */
                fi
        :: flow_to_dll[1]?type,seq ->
```

```
                    if
                    :: dll_to_flow[0]!type,seq
                    :: skip /* lose */
                    fi
          od
}
```

The only function of the data link model is to simulate the loss of messages. There is, however, an equivalent and simpler way to model the same behavior. We can connect the two flow control processes directly and modify them to randomly discard any messages that arrive. This reduction allows us to remove two processes and two message channels from the model by the addition of just one clause to the receiver part of the flow control layer process (see Appendix F).

```
#if LOSS
        :: err_to_flow[N]?type,m /* lose any message */
#endif
```

We have used a preprocessor directive LOSS to enable or disable the possibility of message loss in validations. (The message is received, but not responded to.) In the flow control layer validation model listed in Appendix F there is one other preprocessor directive, named DUPS. It can be used to model the possibility of duplicate messages by triggering premature retransmissions, i.e., the retransmission of messages that are not really lost. Another step in our effort to reduce the complexity of the validation can be to group code into atomic statements wherever we can safely do so, and to combine the test sender and receiver into a single upper level tester. (See incremental composition, discussed in Chapters 8 and 11.) The complete code for the upper tester then looks as follows:

```
1 proctype upper()
2 {   byte s_state, r_state;
3     byte type, toggle;
4
5     ses_to_flow[0]!sync,toggle;
6     do
7     :: flow_to_ses[0]?sync_ack,type ->
8             if
9             :: (type != toggle)
10            :: (type == toggle) -> break
11            fi
12    :: timeout ->
13            ses_to_flow[0]!sync,toggle
14    od;
15    toggle = 1 - toggle;
16
17    do
18    /* sender */
19    :: ses_to_flow[0]!white,0
```

```
20       :: atomic {
21               (s_state == 0 && len (ses_to_flow[0]) < QSZ) ->
22               ses_to_flow[0]!red,0 ->
23               s_state = 1
24       }
25       :: atomic {
26               (s_state == 1 && len (ses_to_flow[0]) < QSZ) ->
27               ses_to_flow[0]!blue,0 ->
28               s_state = 2
29       }
30       /* receiver */
31       :: flow_to_ses[1]?white,0
32       :: atomic {
33               (r_state == 0 && flow_to_ses[1]?[red]) ->
34               flow_to_ses[1]?red,0 ->
35               r_state = 1
36       }
37       :: atomic {
38               (r_state == 0 && flow_to_ses[1]?[blue]) ->
39               assert(0)
40       }
41       :: atomic {
42               (r_state == 1 && flow_to_ses[1]?[blue]) ->
43               flow_to_ses[1]?blue,0;
44               break
45       }
46       :: atomic {
47               (r_state == 1 && flow_to_ses[1]?[red]) ->
48               assert(0)
49       }
50       od;
51 end:
52       do
53       :: flow_to_ses[1]?white,0
54       :: flow_to_ses[1]?red,0 -> assert(0)
55       :: flow_to_ses[1]?blue,0 -> assert(0)
56       od
57 }
```

The structure of the test system we have described is shown in Figure 14.1.

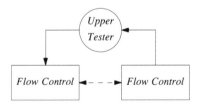

Figure 14.1 — Validation of the Flow Control Layer

The circle represents the upper level model that was added specifically for this validation. The two boxes are the flow control layer processes being validated. By the
construction of the upper tester we know that if there is any error in the flow control layer, the upper tester module will trip on a false assertion.

IDEAL CHANNELS

In a first validation run we check that in the absence of errors, data are transferred
correctly and the temporal claim cannot be violated. The startup script looks as
follows:

```
 1 /*
 2  * PROMELA Validation Model
 3  * FLOW CONTROL LAYER VALIDATION
 4  */
 5
 6 #define LOSS              0       /* message loss   */
 7 #define DUPS              0       /* duplicate msgs */
 8 #define QSZ         2      /* queue size     */
 9
10 mtype = {
11     red, white, blue,
12     abort, accept, ack, sync_ack, close, connect,
13     create, data, eof, open, reject, sync, transfer,
14     FATAL, NON_FATAL, COMPLETE
15     }
16
17 chan ses_to_flow[2] = [QSZ] of { byte, byte };
18 chan flow_to_ses[2] = [QSZ] of { byte, byte };
19 chan dll_to_flow[2] = [QSZ] of { byte, byte };
20 chan flow_to_dll[2];
21
22 #include "flow_cl"
23 #include "upper_tester"
24
25 init
26 {
27     atomic {
28       flow_to_dll[0] = dll_to_flow[1];
29       flow_to_dll[1] = dll_to_flow[0];
30       run fc(0); run fc(1);
31       run upper()
32     }
33 }
```

The include files contain the model definitions we have just discussed. The flow
control layer processes are directly linked with the first two assignments in the initial process, and they are started in the two subsequent run statements. The following numbered listing of the flow control layer, as tested, is useful for cross
referencing the unreachable code.

```
1  /*
2   * Flow Control Layer Validation Model
3   */
4
5  #define true        1
6  #define false       0
7
8  #define M    4        /* range sequence numbers    */
9  #define W    2        /* window size: M/2          */
10
11  proctype fc(bit n)
12  {   bool    busy[M];          /* outstanding messages    */
13      byte    q;                /* seq# oldest unacked msg */
14      byte    m;                /* seq# last msg received  */
15      byte    s;                /* seq# next msg to send   */
16      byte    window;           /* nr of outstanding msgs  */
17      byte    type;             /* msg type                */
18      bit     received[M];      /* receiver housekeeping   */
19      bit     x;                /* scratch variable        */
20      byte    p;                /* seq# of last msg acked  */
21      byte    I_buf[M], O_buf[M];       /* message buffers */
22
23      /* sender part */
24  end:        do
25      :: atomic {
26          (window < W  && len(ses_to_flow[n]) >  0
27                      && len(flow_to_dll[n]) < QSZ) ->
28                      ses_to_flow[n]?type,x;
29                      window = window + 1;
30                      busy[s] = true;
31                      O_buf[s] = type;
32                      flow_to_dll[n]!type,s;
33                      if
34                      :: (type != sync) ->
35                              s = (s+1)%M
36                      :: (type == sync) ->
37                              window = 0;
38                              s = M;
39                              do
40                              :: (s > 0) ->
41                                      s = s-1;
42                                      busy[s] = false
43                              :: (s == 0) ->
44                                      break
45                              od
46                      fi
47          }
48      :: atomic {
49              (window > 0 && busy[q] == false) ->
50              window = window - 1;
51              q = (q+1)%M
52          }
53  #if DUPS
```

```
54      :: atomic {
55              (len(flow_to_dll[n]) < QSZ
56              && window > 0 && busy[q] == true) ->
57              flow_to_dll[n]! O_buf[q],q
58          }
59 #endif
60      :: atomic {
61              (timeout && len(flow_to_dll[n]) < QSZ
62              && window > 0 && busy[q] == true) ->
63              flow_to_dll[n]! O_buf[q],q
64          }
65
66      /* receiver part */
67 #if LOSS
68      :: dll_to_flow[n]?type,m /* lose any message */
69 #endif
70      :: dll_to_flow[n]?type,m ->
71              if
72              :: atomic {
73                      (type == ack) ->
74                      busy[m] = false
75                  }
76              :: atomic {
77                      (type == sync) ->
78                      m = 0;
79                      do
80                      :: (m < M) ->
81                              received[m] = 0;
82                              m = m+1
83                      :: (m == M) ->
84                              break
85                      od
86                  };   flow_to_dll[n]!sync_ack,0
87              :: (type == sync_ack) ->
88                      flow_to_ses[n]!sync_ack,0
89              :: (type != ack && type != sync && type != sync_ack)->
90                      if
91                      :: atomic {
92                              (received[m] == true) ->
93                                      x = ((0<p-m    && p-m<=W)
94                                      ||   (0<p-m-M && p-m-M<=W)) };
95                              if
96                              :: (x) -> flow_to_dll[n]!ack,m
97                              :: (!x) /* else skip */
98                              fi
99                      :: atomic {
100                             (received[m] == false) ->
101                                     I_buf[m] = type;
102                                     received[m] = true;
103                                     received[(m-W+M)%M] = false
104                         }
105                     fi
106             fi
```

```
107      :: (received[p] == true && len(flow_to_ses[n])<QSZ
108                              && len(flow_to_dll[n])<QSZ) ->
109             flow_to_ses[n]!I_buf[p],0;
110             flow_to_dll[n]!ack,p;
111             p = (p+1)%M
112      od
113 }
```

Not knowing anything about the complexity of the model that we have constructed for the validation, the best approach is to run a quick supertrace (bit state space) analysis and check the hash factor and the number of reachable states. By multiplying the number of states stored with the number of bytes required per state we can then get an estimate of the amount of memory that would be required for an exhaustive search. For instance, a supertrace analysis of the flow control layer validation model from Figure 14.1 is performed as follows, using a memory arena of roughly 4.5 Mbytes:

```
$ spin -a pftp.flow
$ cc -DMEMCNT=23 -DBITSTATE -o pan pan.c
$ pan -w25
bit statespace search for:
        assertion violations and invalid endstates
vector 128 byte, depth reached 3781, errors: 0
   90843 states, stored
  317124 states, linked
  182422 states, matched        total:    590389
hash factor: 369.363216 (best coverage if >100)
(max size 2^25 states, stackframes: 0/418)

memory used: 4463832
...
```

The search was of good quality (the hash factor is high) so the number of states reached should be a good approximation of the true number of reachable states in the full state space. A quick calculation shows that we would need 90843×128, or roughly 12 Mbytes to store the complete state space. Having a machine with 64 Mbytes available, we can decide to repeat the analysis with an exhaustive check.

```
$ cc -DMEMCNT=24 -o pan pan.c   # memory bound 2^24
$ pan -w16                      # hash table of 2^16 slots
full state space search for:
        assertion violations and invalid endstates
vector 128 byte, depth reached 5580, errors: 0
   90845 states, stored
  317134 states, linked
  182425 states, matched        total:    590404
hash conflicts: 154271 (resolved)
(max size 2^16 states, stackframes: 0/418)

memory used: 12886356
unreached in proctype _init:
        reached all 7 states
```

```
unreached in proctype upper:
        line 13 (state 9)
        line 39 (state 29)
        line 48 (state 36)
        line 54 (state 43)
        line 55 (state 45)
        line 57 (state 49)
        reached: 43 of 49 states
unreached in proctype fc:
        line 63 (state 28)
        line 93 (state 50)
        line 96 (state 53)
        line 95 (state 55)
        line 113 (state 73)
        reached: 68 of 73 states
```

The state space built held 90,845 reachable system states, with 317,134 linked states (intermediate states in atomic sequences), and a longest unique execution sequence of 3781 steps. A total of 182,425 times a state was reached that was previously analyzed in the depth first search. The earlier bit state space analysis had 99.997% coverage.

Next, let us consider the states that are reported to be unreachable. Four of the six unreachable states in the upper tester correspond to the assertion violations that we *want* to be unreachable: lines 39, 48, 54, and 55. Line 13 specifies the action to be taken if a timeout occurs while the upper tester is waiting for a response to its initial sync message. It is readily checked that indeed this code should also be unreachable: if there is no message loss, the timeout should never occur. Line 57, finally, is the normal stop state of the upper tester, at the end of its code. Since the code for the upper tester is written as an infinite loop, we would also not expect that state to be reachable.

Five states are reported to be unreachable in the flow control layer protocol. The unreached code tells us that no timeout's can occur (line 63). This is correct, in the absence of message loss timeouts are redundant. It also confirms that, in the absence of all errors, acknowledgments always arrive in the exact order in which the data messages are sent (lines 93-97). Line 113, finally, is the normal end-state of the flow control layer process. Since the process never terminates, it is also correctly labeled as unreachable.

In examining the listings, remember that the line numbers are approximate, off-by-one errors are sometimes hard to avoid. In case of doubt, the state numbers given in parentheses can be used to look up the precise statement of the process in the file pan.m.

In the absence of message loss in the underlying data link, then, the flow control layer meets its correctness requirements. Since the assertions in the temporal claim cannot be violated, no messages can ever be lost or reordered.

MESSAGE LOSS AND DUPLICATION ERRORS

In the next validation runs we check the working of the flow control layer in the presence of two different types of errors: message loss and duplicate messages. First we check for message loss by giving the preprocessor directive LOSS a non-zero value. It is just within the reach of a full state space analysis.

```
$ spin -a pftp.flow1
$ cc -o pan pan.c
$ pan -w20
full state space search for:
        assertion violations and invalid endstates
vector 128 byte, depth reached 4421, errors: 0
  396123 states, stored
 1046768 states, linked
  748273 states, matched          total:  2191164
hash conflicts: 186761 (resolved)
(max size 2^20 states, stackframes: 0/543)
unreached in proctype _init:
        reached all 7 states
unreached in proctype upper:
        line 39 (state 29)
        line 48 (state 36)
        line 54 (state 43)
        line 55 (state 45)
        line 57 (state 49)
        reached: 44 of 49 states
unreached in proctype fc:
        line 113 (state 74)
        reached: 73 of 74 states
```

The timeout option in the upper tester has now been exercised, and all states of the flow control layer process were reached. All remaining unreachable states in the upper tester correspond to the error states that should be unreachable.

A next test is for duplicate messages. We enable this test with the preprocessor directive DUPS. This type of error dramatically increases the complexity of the model. A validation is now solidly outside the range of exhaustive searches. Only a bit state space search can still be performed with reasonable coverage.

```
$ spin -a pftp.flow2
$ cc -DMEMCNT=27 -DBITSTATE -o pan pan.c
$ pan -w29 -m100000
vector 128 byte, depth reached 56089, errors: 0
 8241456 states, stored
22946550 states, linked
21143649 states, matched          total: 52331655
hash factor: 65.142718 (best coverage if >100)
(max size 2^29 states, stackframes: 0/7621)

memory used: 70073429
unreached in proctype _init:
        reached all 7 states
```

```
unreached in proctype upper:
        line 13 (state 9)
        line 39 (state 29)
        line 48 (state 36)
        line 54 (state 43)
        line 55 (state 45)
        line 57 (state 49)
        reached: 43 of 49 states
unreached in proctype fc:
        line 63 (state 31)
        line 113 (state 76)
        reached: 74 of 76 states
```

Storing a full state space of 8,241,456 states of 128 bytes each would take a Giga-byte of memory. The bit state space search above used 70 Mbytes and completed with a hash factor of 65, thus with a reasonable guarantee of complete coverage (see Chapter 13). The longest unique execution sequence has now grown to 56,089 steps. All protocol states except those corresponding to errors and retransmission timeouts have been exercised. The flow control layer passes also this test, that is, in the absence of the other types of errors, the flow control layer seems able to cope successfully with arbitrary amounts of duplication errors.

This validation test is, of course, a rather drastic one. Premature retransmission timeouts can occur perhaps several times during a file transfer session, but very unlikely hundreds of times or more. Many other variations of validation runs are possible. We could, for instance, reduce the complexity of the search by counting and restricting the number of duplication errors per session. We can also test for combinations of loss and duplication errors, and we could intersperse the sending of white, red, and blue messages with flow control resynchronizations. We consider just one variant of a validation run below.

VIOLATIONS OF THE WINDOW INVARIANT

To make sure that errors are properly caught in the validation runs, we can try to tamper with the window size and replace the correct parameters:

```
#define M      4            /* range sequence numbers */
#define W      2            /* window size: M/2       */
```

in the flow control layer protocol, with, for instance

```
#define M      4            /* range sequence numbers */
#define W      3            /* window size:  > M/2    */
```

In the presence of message loss this should reveal errors, because it violates the window protocol invariant we proved earlier. We first try a search without the pos-sibility of message loss:

```
$ spin -a pftp.flow3
$ cc -o pan pan.c
$ pan -m20000
full statespace search for:
        assertion violations and invalid endstates
vector 128 byte, depth reached 10194, errors: 0
  287445 states, stored
 1181892 states, linked
  664505 states, matched           total:  2133842
hash conflicts: 487165 (resolved)
(max size 2^18 states, stackframes: 0/1130)
```

There are more states than before, because there can be more messages outstanding at the same time, but, as expected, no errors just yet. Next, we turn on message loss by setting the compiler directive LOSS to 1.

```
$ spin -a pftp.flow4
$ cc -o pan pan.c
$ pan
assertion violated 0
pan: aborted (at depth 656)
pan: wrote pan.trail
full statespace search for:
        assertion violations and invalid endstates
search was not completed
vector 128 byte, depth reached 1290, errors: 1
   22469 states, stored
   45816 states, linked
   28041 states, matched           total:    96326
hash conflicts: 3267 (resolved)
(max size 2^18 states, stackframes: 0/199)
...
```

As expected, the tampering with the window protocol invariant introduces an error that is discovered in the reachability analysis after only a few thousand states are checked. It can be tracked down with a guided simulation, using the error trail produced by the analyzer.

14.6 SESSION LAYER VALIDATION

Having convinced ourselves that, with the right window size parameters, the flow control layer correctly mimics the behavior of an ideal transmission channel to the upper protocol layers, we can now use that result to simplify the validation of the session layer. We can build a validation model for this test as follows, omitting everything that was tested before:

```
/*
 * PROMELA Validation Model
 * Session Layer
 */
```

```
#include "defines2"
#include "user"
#include "present"
#include "session"
#include "fserver"
init
{       atomic {
            run userprc(0); run userprc(1);
            run present(0); run present(1);
            run session(0); run session(1);
            run fserver(0); run fserver(1);
            flow_to_ses[0] = ses_to_flow[1];
            flow_to_ses[1] = ses_to_flow[0]
        }
}
```

The session layers are connected directly, as if connected by an ideal channel that never loses, distorts or reorders messages. Since no flow control layer is present, we can comment out the code in the session layer that is specifically meant for the initialization of the flow control layer sequence numbers. The resulting code looks as follows:

```
 1 /*
 2  * Session Layer Validation Model
 3  */
 4
 5 proctype session(bit n)
 6 {    bit toggle;
 7      byte type, status;
 8
 9 endIDLE:
10     do
11     :: pres_to_ses[n]?type ->
12             if
13             :: (type == transfer) ->
14                     goto DATA_OUT
15             :: (type != transfer)    /* ignore */
16             fi
17     :: flow_to_ses[n]?type,0 ->
18             if
19             :: (type == connect) ->
20                     goto DATA_IN
21             :: (type != connect)     /* ignore */
22             fi
23     od;
24
25 DATA_IN:               /* 1. prepare local file fsrver */
26     ses_to_fsrv[n]!create;
27     do
28     :: fsrv_to_ses[n]?reject ->
29             ses_to_flow[n]!reject,0;
30             goto endIDLE
31     :: fsrv_to_ses[n]?accept ->
```

```
32                   ses_to_flow[n]!accept,0;
33                   break
34      od;
35                           /* 2. Receive the data, upto eof */
36      do
37      :: flow_to_ses[n]?data,0 ->
38                   ses_to_fsrv[n]!data
39      :: flow_to_ses[n]?eof,0 ->
40                   ses_to_fsrv[n]!eof;
41                   break
42      :: pres_to_ses[n]?transfer ->
43                   ses_to_pres[n]!reject(NON_FATAL)
44      :: flow_to_ses[n]?close,0 ->    /* remote user aborted */
45                   ses_to_fsrv[n]!close;
46                   break
47      :: timeout ->           /* got disconnected */
48                   ses_to_fsrv[n]!close;
49                   goto endIDLE
50      od;
51                           /* 3. Close the connection */
52      ses_to_flow[n]!close,0;
53      goto endIDLE;
54
55 DATA_OUT:               /* 1. prepare local file fsrver */
56      ses_to_fsrv[n]!open;
57      if
58      :: fsrv_to_ses[n]?reject ->
59                   ses_to_pres[n]!reject(FATAL);
60                   goto endIDLE
61      :: fsrv_to_ses[n]?accept ->
62                   skip
63      fi;
64                           /* 2. initialize flow control *** disabled
65      ses_to_flow[n]!sync,toggle;
66      do
67      :: atomic {
68              flow_to_ses[n]?sync_ack,type ->
69              if
70              :: (type != toggle)
71              :: (type == toggle) -> break
72              fi
73        }
74      :: timeout ->
75              ses_to_fsrv[n]!close;
76              ses_to_pres[n]!reject(FATAL);
77              goto endIDLE
78      od;
79      toggle = 1 - toggle;
80                       /* 3. prepare remote file fsrver */
81      ses_to_flow[n]!connect,0;
82      if
83      :: flow_to_ses[n]?reject,0 ->
84              ses_to_fsrv[n]!close;
85              ses_to_pres[n]!reject(FATAL);
```

```
 86                 goto endIDLE
 87     :: flow_to_ses[n]?connect,0 ->
 88                 ses_to_fsrv[n]!close;
 89                 ses_to_pres[n]!reject(NON_FATAL);
 90                 goto endIDLE
 91     :: flow_to_ses[n]?accept,0 ->
 92                 skip
 93     :: timeout ->
 94                 ses_to_fsrv[n]!close;
 95                 ses_to_pres[n]!reject(FATAL);
 96                 goto endIDLE
 97     fi;
 98                         /* 4. Transmit the data, upto eof */
 99     do
100     :: fsrv_to_ses[n]?data ->
101                 ses_to_flow[n]!data,0
102     :: fsrv_to_ses[n]?eof ->
103                 ses_to_flow[n]!eof,0;
104                 status = COMPLETE;
105                 break
106     :: pres_to_ses[n]?abort ->      /* local user aborted */
107                 ses_to_fsrv[n]!close;
108                 ses_to_flow[n]!close,0;
109                 status = FATAL;
110                 break
111     od;
112                         /* 5. Close the connection */
113     do
114     :: pres_to_ses[n]?abort         /* ignore */
115     :: flow_to_ses[n]?close,0 ->
116                 if
117                 :: (status == COMPLETE) ->
118                         ses_to_pres[n]!accept,0
119                 :: (status != COMPLETE) ->
120                         ses_to_pres[n]!reject(status)
121                 fi;
122                 break
123     :: timeout ->
124                 ses_to_pres[n]!reject(FATAL);
125                 break
126     od;
127     goto endIDLE
128 }
```

The user code is:

```
1 /*
2  * User Layer Validation Model
3  */
4
5 proctype userprc(bit n)
6 {
7     use_to_pres[n]!transfer;
8     if
9     :: pres_to_use[n]?accept -> goto Done
```

```
10        :: pres_to_use[n]?reject -> goto Done
11        :: use_to_pres[n]!abort  -> goto Aborted
12     fi;
13 Aborted:
14     if
15     :: pres_to_use[n]?accept -> goto Done
16     :: pres_to_use[n]?reject -> goto Done
17     fi;
18 Done:
19     skip
20 }
```

And, finally, the presentation layer code is:

```
 1 /*
 2  * Presentation Layer Validation Model
 3  */
 4
 5 proctype present(bit n)
 6 {   byte status, uabort;
 7
 8 endIDLE:
 9     do
10     :: use_to_pres[n]?transfer ->
11             uabort = 0;
12             break
13     :: use_to_pres[n]?abort ->
14             skip
15     od;
16
17 TRANSFER:
18     pres_to_ses[n]!transfer;
19     do
20     :: use_to_pres[n]?abort ->
21             if
22             :: (!uabort) ->
23                     uabort = 1;
24                     pres_to_ses[n]!abort
25             :: (uabort) ->
26                     assert(1+1!=2)
27             fi
28     :: ses_to_pres[n]?accept,0 ->
29             goto DONE
30     :: ses_to_pres[n]?reject(status) ->
31             if
32             :: (status == FATAL || uabort) ->
33                     goto FAIL
34             :: (status == NON_FATAL && !uabort) ->
35                     goto TRANSFER
36             fi
37     od;
```

```
38 DONE:
39      pres_to_use[n]!accept;
40      goto endIDLE;
41 FAIL:
42      pres_to_use[n]!reject;
43      goto endIDLE
44 }
```

We will do a validation in two separate steps. The file server, session, and presentation layer processes are all cyclic: they should never terminate. The initial process and the user processes, however, are terminating, and once they have completed their execution, the other processes must have reached a well-defined end-
state. In the first validation, therefore, we can try to make sure that the system has
no reachable invalid end-states. We can do this with an exhaustive validation, as
follows:

```
$ spin -a pftp.ses
$ cc -o pan pan.c
$ pan -w19
full state space search for:
        assertion violations and invalid endstates
vector 144 byte, depth reached 451, errors: 0
  509179 states, stored
       9 states, linked
  576192 states, matched            total:   1085380
hash conflicts: 369417 (resolved)
(max size 2^19 states, stackframes: 0/23)
unreached in proctype _init:
        reached all 12 states
unreached in proctype fserver:
        line 29 (state 30)
        reached: 29 of 30 states
unreached in proctype session:
        line 48 (state 37)
        line 94 (state 64)
        line 95 (state 65)
        line 124 (state 93)
        line 128 (state 99)
        reached: 94 of 99 states
unreached in proctype present:
        line 26 (state 15)
        line 44 (state 34)
        reached: 32 of 34 states
unreached in proctype userprc:
        reached all 17 states
```

The unreached code in the presentation layer (line 26) indicates that no case was
found in which two subsequent abort messages are received from the user process.
Checking the user process, we can quickly see why that is: the user process does
not allow it. The unreached code in the session layer protocol, however, flags an
incompleteness in this first validation test. The unreached lines 48, 94, 95, 124,
and line 128 are responses to timeout conditions that were included to allow the

session layer to recover from a sudden loss of communication with its peer process. This possibility, however, is not modeled as part of the channel behavior and cannot be exercised.

To verify also that these `timeout` conditions cannot cause havoc, we must revise the validation model. We can do so by adding a few lines to the initialization code in the `init` process given above:

```
          atomic
          {         byte any;
                    chan foo = [1] of { byte, byte };
                    ses_to_flow[0] = foo;
                    ses_to_flow[1] = foo
          };
end:      do
          :: foo?any,any
          od
    }
```

At any time after the initial start-up of the protocol, these extra lines can now be executed. The effect is that the two peer session layer processes are disconnected. The loop at the end removes all the messages that the two session layers produce. The extension increases the complexity of the test somewhat more, but a bit state space analysis is still feasible. The result is now

```
$ spin -a pftp.ses1
$ cc -DBITSTATE -o pan pan.c
$ pan -w29
bit state space search for:
        assertion violations and invalid endstates
vector 148 byte, depth reached 456, errors: 0
 1686543 states, stored
  246135 states, linked
 1960294 states, matched          total:   3892972
hash factor: 318.326063 (best coverage if >100)
(max size 2^29 states, stackframes: 0/25)
unreached in proctype _init:
        line 31 (state 19)
        reached: 18 of 19 states
unreached in proctype fserver:
        line 29 (state 30)
        reached: 29 of 30 states
unreached in proctype session:
        line 128 (state 99)
        reached: 98 of 99 states
unreached in proctype present:
        line 26 (state 15)
        line 44 (state 34)
        reached: 32 of 34 states
unreached in proctype userprc:
        reached all 17 states
```

Compared to the first test, we have now explored over three times as many states and effectively reached all relevant protocol states. The hash factor is large enough to be confident that close to 100% of the reachable system states have been tested within the memory arena that is available. An exhaustive search would have required at least 1,686,543×148 or 249 Mbytes of memory, four times more than we have used.

THE TEMPORAL CLAIM

In the second validation of the session layer protocol that we undertake here, we consider the temporal claim that was formulated in Chapter 7.

```
never {
        do
        :: !pres_to_ses[n]?[transfer]
        && !flow_to_ses[n]?[connect]
        :: pres_to_ses[n]?[transfer] ->
                goto accept0
        :: flow_to_ses[n]?[connect] ->
                goto accept1
        od;
accept0:
        do
        :: !ses_to_pres[n]?[accept]
        && !ses_to_pres[n]?[reject]
        od;
accept1:
        do
        :: !ses_to_pres[1-n]?[accept]
        && !ses_to_pres[1-n]?[reject]
        od
}
```

Since the protocol is symmetric, it suffices to validate this claim for just one value of n, e.g., zero. The result is as follows:

```
$ spin -a pftp.ses2
$ cc -o pan pan.c
$ pan
cycle of length 6 (99) 104
pan: accept state in cycle (at depth 99)
pan: wrote pan.trail
full statespace search on behavior restricted to claim for:
        assertion violations
        and absence of acceptance labels in all cycles
search was not completed
vector 148 byte, depth reached 100, errors: 1
     151 states, stored
       9 states, linked
      16 states, matched            total:        176
hash conflicts: 0 (resolved)
(max size 2^18 states, stackframes: 0/4)
```

An acceptance cycle was detected, which means that the claim can be violated. A closer look with the simulator can reveal the cause.

```
$ spin -t -r -s pftp.ses2        # -t: follow trail produced by pan
proc  3 (userprc) line   8, Send transfer -> queue 6 (use_to_pres[1])
proc  5 (present) line  11, Recv transfer <- queue 6 (use_to_pres[1])
proc  5 (present) line  19, Send transfer -> queue 4 (pres_to_ses[1])
proc  7 (session) line  11, Recv 13      <- queue 4 (pres_to_ses[1])
proc  7 (session) line  56, Sent open    -> queue 8 (ses_to_fsrv[1])
...
<<<<<START OF CYCLE>>>>>
proc  9 (fserver) line  13, Recv data    <- queue 8 (ses_to_fsrv[1])
proc  6 (session) line 101, Send data,0 -> queue 1 (ses_to_flow[0])
proc  8 (fserver) line  23, Sent data    -> queue 9 (fsrv_to_ses[0])
proc  6 (session) line 100, Recv data    <- queue 9 (fsrv_to_ses[0])
proc  7 (session) line  37, Recv data,0 <- queue 1 (flow_to_ses[1])
spin: trail ends after 179 steps
step 179, #processes: 10
...
```

The validator discovered here that the number of data messages that is exchanged during a file transfer session is not bounded. This means that the sending of a final accept or reject message to the presentation layer can be postponed indefinitely, which is a direct violation of our correctness requirement.

To fix this problem we can try telling the temporal claim to ignore data messages, that is, to consider only zero-length file transfers.

```
never {
        do
        :: !pres_to_ses[0]?[transfer]
        && !flow_to_ses[0]?[connect]
        :: pres_to_ses[0]?[transfer] ->
                goto accept0
        :: flow_to_ses[0]?[connect] ->
                goto accept1
        od;
accept0:
        do
        :: !ses_to_pres[0]?[accept]
        && !ses_to_pres[0]?[reject]
        && !ses_to_flow[0]?[data]
        od;
accept1:
        do
        :: !ses_to_pres[1]?[accept]
        && !ses_to_pres[1]?[reject]
        && !ses_to_flow[1]?[data]
        od
}
```

The validation with this new claim proceeds as follows:

```
$ spin -a pftp.ses3
$ cc -o pan pan.c
$ pan
cycle of length 5 (99) 103
pan: accept state in cycle (at depth 99)
pan: wrote pan.trail
full state space search on behavior restricted to claim for:
        assertion violations
        and absence of accept states in all cycles
search was not completed
vector 148 byte, depth reached 132, errors: 1
   21645 states, stored
       9 states, linked
   20316 states, matched         total:     41970
hash conflicts: 2293 (resolved)
(size 2^18 states, stackframes: 0/5)
```

Again, the validator discovered that the correctness requirement can be violated. The relevant part of the trail is as follows:

```
$ spin -t -r -s pftp.ses3
...
proc  4 (present) line 19, Send transfer -> queue 3 (pres_to_ses[0])
proc  6 (session) line 42, Recv transfer <- queue 3 (pres_to_ses[0])
<<<<<START OF CYCLE>>>>>
proc  6 (session) line 43, Send reject,NON_FATAL -> \
                                        queue 11 (ses_to_pres[0])
proc  4 (present) line 31, Recv reject,15 <- queue 11 (ses_to_pres[0])
proc  4 (present) line 19, Send transfer -> queue 3 (pres_to_ses[0])
spin: trail ends after 176 steps
...
```

After a file transfer has started, there can be an unbounded number of conflicting transfer requests from the remote peer process. Again, processing these requests as non-fatal rejects can postpone for arbitrarily long the sending of the final accept or reject message for the active file transfer.

This time it is much harder to modify the temporal claim to remove this pattern from consideration. An acceptance-state label identifies events as potentially bad. In this case, however, we can work more effectively with a method for labeling a small set of events as good and focus on others. The right tool for that is the progress-state label. If we can rephrase the temporal claim as a correctness requirement on the absence of non-progress cycles it becomes easier to exclude certain patterns from consideration.

Note that, if we disregard the two patterns discovered earlier, all executions of the session layer protocol must terminate. Any cycle that can be identified, therefore, will become a non-progress cycle and thus a detectable a violation of the correctness requirements. We label the states DATA_IN and DATA_OUT in the session layer protocol as progress states. To exclude the two patterns discovered above, we also label the data exchanges with the file server as progress states, plus one state in the presentation layer protocol. A new listing of the presentation layer is given below:

```
proctype present(bit n)
{       byte status, uabort;
endIDLE:
        do
        :: use_to_pres[n]?transfer ->
                uabort = 0;
                break
        :: use_to_pres[n]?abort ->
                skip
        od;
TRANSFER:
        pres_to_ses[n]!transfer;
        do
        :: use_to_pres[n]?abort ->
                if
                :: (!uabort) ->
                        uabort = 1;
                        pres_to_ses[n]!abort
                :: (uabort) ->
                        assert(1+1!=2)
                fi
        :: ses_to_pres[n]?accept ->
                goto DONE
        :: ses_to_pres[n]?reject(status) ->
progress:       if
                :: (status == FATAL || uabort) ->
                        goto FAIL
                :: (status == NON_FATAL && !uabort) ->
                        goto TRANSFER
                fi
        od;
DONE:
        pres_to_use[n]!accept;
        goto endIDLE;
FAIL:
        pres_to_use[n]!reject;
        goto endIDLE
}
```

The validation is straightforward from this point on.

```
$ spin -a pftp.ses4
$ cc -DBITSTATE -o pan pan.c
$ pan -l -w28
bit state space search for:
        assertion violations and non-progress loops
vector 148 byte, depth reached 458, non-progress loops: 0
  847134 states, stored
      18 states, linked
 1104341 states, matched          total:  1951493
```

```
hash factor: 316.874472 (best coverage if >100)
(size 2^28 states, stackframes: 0/489)
```

A bit state space analysis completed with good coverage. No non-progress cycles were discovered, which means that with good probability the correctness requirements are met.

FURTHER REDUCTIONS

To confirm the earlier results with an exhaustive validation, we could pursue several options. Incremental composition and generalization can be used to combine the user and presentation layer processes into a single environment process to the session layer. This model may look as follows, appropriately labeled with progress tags:

```
/*
 * PROMELA Validation Model
 * Presentation & User Layer - combined and reduced
 */
proctype present(bit n)
{       byte status;
progress0:
        pres_to_ses[n]!transfer ->
        do
        :: pres_to_ses[n]!abort;
progress1:      skip
        :: ses_to_pres[n]?accept,status ->
                        break
        :: ses_to_pres[n]?reject,status ->
                if
                :: (status == NON_FATAL) ->
                        goto progress0
                :: (status != NON_FATAL) ->
                        break
                fi
        od
}
```

The external behavior of this process is indistinguishable from the external behavior of the two separate processes, with one important exception: the new model is less well-behaved. The reduced model can spark an arbitrary number of abort messages while a transfer request is outstanding. If the session layer protocol is correct for this environment, it must also be correct with respect to the original one, simply because the original behavior is a subset of the new one. The validation can now be done exhaustively and produces the following result:

```
$ spin -a pftp.ses5
$ cc -DMEMCNT=27 -o pan pan.c
$ pan -l -m2000
full state space search for:
        assertion violations and non-progress loops
```

```
vector 132 byte, depth reached 1783, non-progress loops: 0
   553987 states, stored
        8 states, linked
   798367 states, matched              total:   1352362
hash conflicts: 990275 (resolved)
(size 2^18 states, stackframes: 0/325)

memory used: 70872461
```

The validation run confirms that the correctness requirement of the session layer protocol is properly met. Had this first reduction been insufficient, further reduction steps could still be taken to force an exhaustive validation. All interactions of the session layer with the file server, for instance, could be removed and replaced with equivalent nondeterministic choices within the session layer. Similarly, the combined user and presentation layer could be merged into the session layer protocol to produce a single process that represents the behavior of one protocol session layer entity. The combinations can be made manually, carefully preserving the equivalence with the original model, or automatically with an incremental composition method as discussed in Chapters 8 and 11.

14.7 SUMMARY

Our admiration for programmers who can design and debug a protocol using only tools developed for sequential systems can only grow after the first experience with an automated protocol validation system. It is, of course, not really surprising that the validation runs reported in this chapter have failed to reveal serious errors in the design from Chapter 7. The errors were certainly present in the initial versions of the protocol, but were found with SPIN and removed before these final tests were performed. Most of the errors found in the earlier stages of the design were cases of incompleteness that are very hard to find by manual inspection of the code.

Given a machine of reasonable size, the basic protocols for session control and flow control can fairly easily be validated with purely exhaustive searches of all reachable system states. This much is well within the power of the automated tools. The tools are severely tested by the exception conditions that must be validated: message loss, duplication errors, and hangups. The increase in complexity makes it impossible to perform the traditional completely exhaustive validations. Bit state space hashing proves to be a powerful alternative here. As an example, one test performed for an earlier version of the session layer protocol generated 15,462,939 system states of 472 bytes each. A full state space that stores all these states would be over 7 Gigabytes (7,298,507,208 bytes), well beyond what can effectively be stored or processed. On a machine with 64 Mbytes of memory available for the search, no more than 142,179 of these states can be stored in a full state space search: a coverage of less than 1%. The bit state space technique, using the same amount of memory, can accommodate over 250,000,000 states, more than 15 times what is required. With this method we could effectively increase the coverage of that search from less than 1% to one that, with high probability, is close to 100%. No other method known to date can do better.

EXERCISES

14-1 Validate your favorite protocol with the tools described here.

14-2 Develop and implement more specific tools for automating the generalization or incremental composition of PROMELA models (research project).

BIBLIOGRAPHIC NOTES

A detailed validation study as performed in this chapter is rarely documented. The first automated validations were reported in West and Zafiropulo [1978], though the analytical power of our tools has grown substantially since then. The validation method applied in this chapter was originally described in Holzmann [1987b, 1988]. Its capabilities are compared with more conventional approaches to the protocol validation problem in Holzmann [1990]. It has been applied to systems that are ordinarily well outside the range of exhaustive validation, as reported in Holzmann and Patti [1989].

CONCLUSION

While the performance of computers and the speed of data networks continues to improve steadily, our ability to utilize these resources effectively does not. Data communications software has become a bottleneck in many high performance systems; it is often much slower than the hardware permits and it can be hard to establish its logical consistency.

It is notoriously difficult to write software for a distributed system. It is even harder to prove rigorously the correctness of such software. In its simplest form, the problem is to design methods that allow asynchronously executing communicating machines to exchange information quickly and reliably and to prove that these methods, or protocols, have certain desirable properties.

Today, most protocols are designed in an *ad hoc* matter. There is a known set of protocol standards, whose description is faithfully copied in most textbooks. There is, however, little understanding of why some protocols work and what is wrong with others. A designer needs to know how a correct protocol can be constructed from scratch and how that design can be matched to specific design and correctness criteria. The techniques that can be used to prove that a new protocol design is correct have long been considered too esoteric for real day-to-day use. This book is meant to show that the tools have come of age.

The design methods and tools that we have discussed allow the designer to attack fundamental process coordination problems in a rigorous and a practical manner. To design reliable protocols, no matter what your application is, you need tools to test your ideas. This book should convince you that the right tools are available. The capabilities of the new validation tools is sometimes justifiably regarded with scepticism. A generous number of pages is therefore devoted in this text to a detailed discussion of tools. For the first time, the complete source to these tools is now made available, both in this text and in electronic form. Your critical evaluation, experiments, applications, and comparisons are eagerly invited.

REFERENCES

Adi, W. [1984], "Fast burst error-correction scheme with Fire code," *IEEE Trans. on Computers*, Vol. C-33, No. 7, July 1984, pp. 613-618.

Agerwala, T.K.M. [1975], *Towards a Theory for the Analysis and Synthesis of Systems Exhibiting Concurrency*, Ph.D. Thesis, Johns Hopkins University, Baltimore, Md., 241 pgs.

Aggarwal, S., Courcoubetis, C., and Wolper, P. [1990], "Adding liveness properties to coupled finite state machines," *ACM Trans. on Programming Languages and Systems*, Vol 12, No. 2, pp. 303-339.

Aggarwal, S., Kurshan, R.P., and Sharma, D. [1983], "A language for protocol specification and verification," *Proc. 3rd IFIP WG 6.1 Int. Workshop on Protocol Specification,, Testing, and Verification*, North-Holland Publ., Amsterdam, pp. 35-50.

Aho, A.V., Dahbura, A.T., Lee, D., and Uyar, M.U. [1988], "An optimization technique for protocol conformance test generation based on UIO sequences and rural Chinese Postman Tours," *Proc. 8th IFIP WG 6.1 Int. Workshop on Protocol Specification, Testing, and Verification*, North-Holland Publ., Amsterdam.

Aho, A.V., Hopcroft, J.E., Ullman, J.D. [1974], *The Design and Analysis of Computer Algorithms*, Addison-Wesley, Reading, Mass., 470 pgs. ISBN 0-201-00029-6.

Aho, A.V., Hopcroft, J.E., Ullman, J.D. [1983], *Data Structures and Algorithms*, Addison-Wesley, Reading, Mass., 427 pgs. ISBN 0-201-00023-7.

Aho, A.V., Sethi, R., Ullman, J.D. [1986], *Compilers — Principles, Techniques and Tools*, Addison-Wesley, Reading, Mass., 796 pgs. ISBN 0-201-10088-6.

Aho, A.V., and Ullman, J.D. [1977], *Principles of Compiler Design*, Addison-Wesley, Reading, Mass., 604 pgs. ISBN 0-201-00022-9.

Apt, K.R., and Kozen, D.Z. [1986], "Limits for automatic verification of finite state concurrent systems," *Inf. Processing Letters*, Vol. 22, No. 6, May 1986, pp. 307-309.

Arthurs, E., Chesson, G.L., and Stuck, B.W. [1983], "Theoretical performance analysis of sliding window flow control," *IEEE Journal on Selected Areas in Comm.*, Vol. SAC-1, No. 5, pp. 947-959.

Balkovic, M.D., Klancer, H.W., Klare, S.W., and McGruther, W.G. [1971], "1969-1970 Connection survey: high speed voiceband data transmission Performance on the Switched Telecommunications Network," *Bell System Technical Journal*, Vol. 50, No. 4, 1349-1384.

Bartlett, K.A., Scantlebury, R.A., and Wilkinson, P.T. [1969], "A note on reliable full-duplex transmission over half-duplex lines," *Comm. of the ACM*, Vol. 12, No. 5, 260-265.

Beeforth, T.H., Grimsdale, R.L., Halsall, F., and Woolons, D.J. [1972], "Proposed organization for packet switched data communication network." *Proc. IEEE*, Vol. 119, No. 12, Dec. 1972, pp. 1677-1682.

Bennet, W.R., and Davey, J.R. [1965], *Data Transmission*, McGraw-Hill, New York.

Berlekamp, E.R. [1968], *Algebraic Coding Theory*, McGraw-Hill, New York.

Bertsekas, D., and Gallager, R. [1987], *Data Networks*, Prentice Hall, Englewood Cliffs, N.J., 486 pgs. ISBN 0-13-196825-4.

Bochmann, G. von [1983], *Concepts for Distributed Systems Design*, Springer-Verlag, New York.

Bochmann, G. von [1986], *Methods and tools for the design and validation of protocol specifications and implementations*, Report 596, October 1986, University of Montreal, Canada, 56 pgs.

Bochmann, G. von, and Sunshine, C.A. [1980], "Formal methods in communication protocol design," *IEEE Trans. on Communications*, Vol. COM-28, No. 4, pp. 624-631.

Bolognesi, T., and Brinksma, E. [1987], "Introduction to the ISO specification language Lotos," *Computer Networks and ISDN Systems*, Vol. 14, pp. 25-59.

Bond, D.J. [1987], "A theoretical study of burst noise," *British Telecom Technology Journal*, Vol. 5, No. 4, October 1987.

Bose, R.C., and Ray-Chaudhuri, D.K. [1960], "On a class of error correcting binary group codes," *Inform. Control*, Vol. 3, pp. 68-79, 279-290.

Bourguet, A. [1986], "A Petri Net tool for service verification in protocols," *Proc. 6th Workshop on Protocol Specification, Testing, and Verification*, Montreal, North-Holland Publ., Amsterdam, pp. 281-292.

Brand, D., and Joyner, W.H., Jr. [1978], "Verification of protocols using symbolic execution," *Computer Networks*, Vol. 2, pp. 351-360.

Brand, D., and Zafiropulo, P. [1980], "Synthesis of protocols for an unlimited number of processes," *Proc. Computer Network Protocols Conf.*, IEEE, pp. 29-40.

Brand, D., and Zafiropulo, P. [1983], "On communicating finite state machines," *Journal of the ACM*, Vol. 30, No. 2, pp. 323-342.

Bredt, T.H. [1970], *The Mutual Exclusion Problem*, Report SU-STAN-CS-70-173, Stanford University, Calif., Aug. 1970, 71 pgs.

Brilliant, M.B. [1978], "Observations of errors and error rates on T1 digital repeatered lines," *Bell System Technical Journal*, Vol. 57, No. 3, March 1978, pp. 711-747.

Brinksma, E. [1987], "An introduction to Lotos," *Proc. 7th IFIP WG 6.1 Int. Workshop on Protocol Specification, Testing, and Verification*, North-Holland Publ., Amsterdam.

Brinksma, E. [1988], *On the Design of Extended Lotos*, Ph.D. Thesis, University of Twente, The Netherlands, 240 pgs.

Brinksma, E., Alderden, R., Langerak, R., Tretmans, J., and Lagemaat, J. van de, [1989], *A Formal Approach to Conformance Testing*, Report 89-45, Dept. of Computer Science, University of Twente, The Netherlands, 18 pgs.

Brown, G.M., Gouda, M.G., and Miller, R.E. [1989], "Block acknowledgments: redesigning the window protocol," *Proc. ACM SIGCOMM '89*, Austin, Texas.

Brown, G.M., Gouda, M.G., and Wu, C. [1989], "Token systems that self-stabilize," *IEEE Trans. on Computers*, Vol. 36, No. 6, pp. 845-852.

Browne, M.C., Clarke, E.M., Dill, D.L., and Mishra, B. "Automatic verification of sequential circuits using temporal logic," *IEEE Trans. on Computers*, Vol. C-35, No. 12, pp. 1035-1043.

deBruyn, N.G. [1967], "Additional comments on a problem in concurrent programming control," *Comm. of the ACM*, Vol. 10, No. 3, pp. 137-138.

Budkowski, S., and Dembinski, P. [1987], "An introduction to Estelle: a specification language for distributed systems," *Computer Networks and ISDN Systems*, Vol. 14, pp. 3-23.

Byte [1989], Vol. 14, No. 1, January 1989, pp. 363-376.

CCITT [1977], *Orange Book VIII.2*, Recommendation X.25, "Interface between DTE and DCE for terminals operating in the packet mode on public data networks," International Telecommunications Union (ITU), Geneva.

CCITT [1988], *Blue Book*, Recommendation Z.100, International Telecommunications Union (ITU), Geneva.

Campbell-Kelly, M. [1988], "Data communications at NPL," in *Annals of the History of Computing*, Vol. 9, No. 3.

Cerf, V.G., and Kahn, R.E. [1974], "A protocol for packet network intercommunication," *IEEE Trans. on Communications*, Vol. COM-22, No. 5, pp. 637-648.

Chappe, C. [1798], *Lettres sur le nouveau télégraph*, (in French), Paris, France.

Chappe, I.U.J. [1824], *Histoire de la télégraphy*, by Claude Chappe's brother Ignace, (in French), Paris, France.

Chesson, G. [1987], "The protocol engine project," *Unix Review*, Vol. 5, No. 9, Sept. 1987, pp. 70-77.

Choi, T.Y., and Miller, R.E. [1986], "Protocol analysis and synthesis by structured partitioning," *Computer Networks and ISDN Systems*, Vol. 11, No. 5, pp. 367-383.

Chow, T. [1978], "Testing software design modeled by finite state machines," *IEEE Trans. on Software Engineering*, Vol. SE-4, No. 3, pp. 178-187.

Chu, P.M., and Liu, M.T. [1988], "Protocol synthesis in a state transition model," *Proc IEEE Compsac Conf.*, October 1988, pp. 505-512.

Chu, P.M. [1989], *Towards Automating Protocol Synthesis and Analysis*, Ph.D. Thesis, Ohio State University, Dept. of Computer and Information Science, 1989, 168 pgs.

Clark, D. [1985], *NETBLT: A bulk data transfer protocol*, Report RFC-275, MIT, Lab. for Computer Science, February 1985.

Clark, D., Lambert, M., and Zhang, L. [1988], "NETBLT: A high throughput transport protocol," *ACM Computer Communication Review*, Vol 17., No. 5, pp. 353-359.

Clarke, E.M., Emerson, E.A., Sistla, A.P. [1983], "Automatic verification of finite state concurrent systems using temporal logic specifications: a practical approach," *Proc. 10th ACM Symposium on Principles of Programming Languages*, Austin, Tx.

Cole, R. [1987], *Computer Communications*, Springer Verlag, New York, ISBN 0-387-91306-8, 173 pgs.

Cooke, W.F. [1842], *Telegraphic Railways or the single way recommended by safety, economy, and efficiency, under the safeguard and control of the electric telegraph — with particular reference to railway communication with Scotland, and to Irish Railways*, W. Lewis and Son, Finch-Lane, London, England.

Courcoubetis, C., Vardi, M., Wolper, P., and Yannakakis, M. [1990], "Memory efficient algorithms for the verification of temporal properties," *2nd Workshop on Computer-Aided Verification*, Rutgers University, New Brunswick, N.J., June 18-20, 1990.

Cunha, P.R.F., and Maibaum, T.S.E. [1981], "A synchronization calculus for message oriented programming," *Proc. Int. Conf. on Distributed Systems*, IEEE, pp. 433-445.

Dahbura, A., and Sabnani, K. [1988], "Experience in estimating the coverage of a protocol test," *Proc. IEEE INFOCOM '88*, March 1988, pp.71-85.

Dahl, O.J., Dijkstra, E.W., and Hoare, C.A.R. [1972], *Structured Programming*, Academic Press, New York.

Decina, M., and Julio, U. de [1982], "Performance of integrated digital networks: international standards," *IEEE 1982 Int. Communications Conference*, ICC, Vol. 1, pp. 2D1.1-6

Dijkstra, E.W. [1959], "A note on two problems in connection with graphs," *Numerische Mathematik*, Vol. 1, pp. 269-271.

Dijkstra, E.W. [1965], "Solution of a problem in concurrent programming control," *Comm. of the ACM*, Vol. 8, No. 9, p. 569.

Dijkstra, E.W. [1968], "Cooperating sequential processes," in: *Programming Languages*, F. Genuys (Ed.), Academic Press, New York.

Dijkstra, E.W. [1968a], "Go To considered harmful," *Comm. of the ACM*, Vol. 11, No. 3, pp. 147-148, 538, 541.

Dijkstra, E.W. [1968b], "The structure of the 'THE' multiprogramming system," *Comm. of the ACM*, Vol. 11, No. 5, pp. 341-346.

Dijkstra, E.W. [1969a], "Complexity controlled by hierarchical ordering of function and variability," in *Software Engineering*, P. Naur and B. Randell (eds.), Sc. Aff. Div., NATO, Brussels, pp. 114-116.

Dijkstra, E.W. [1969b], *Notes on Structured Programming*, THE Report EWD-249 (70-Wsk-03), University of Technology Eindhoven, The Netherlands. Also published in: Dahl et al. [1972].

Dijkstra, E.W. [1972], "Hierarchical ordering of sequential processes," in: *Operating Systems Techniques*, Academic Press, New York.

Dijkstra, E.W. [1974], "Self-stabilizing systems in spite of distributed control," *Comm. of the ACM*, Vol. 17, No. 11, pp. 643-644.

Dijkstra, E.W. [1975], "Guarded commands, nondeterminacy and formal derivation of programs," *Comm. of the ACM*, Vol. 18, No. 8, pp. 453-457.

Dijkstra, E.W. [1976], *A Discipline of Programming*, Prentice Hall, Englewood Cliffs, N.J.

Dijkstra, E.W. [1986], "A belated proof to self-stabilization," *Distributed Computing*, Vol. 1, January 1986, pp. 5-6.

Duke, R., Hayes, I., King, P., and Rose, G. [1988], "Protocol verification and specification using Z," *Proc. 8th IFIP WG 6.1 Int. Workshop on Protocol Specification, Testing, and Verification*, North-Holland Publ., Amsterdam, pp. 33-46.

Duke, R., Hayes, I., and Rose, G. [1988], *Verification of a cyclic retransmission protocol*, Technical Report No. 92, July 1988, Computer Science Department, University of Queensland, Australia, 23 pgs.

Edelcrantz, A.N. [1796], *Avhandling om Telegrapher, och Försök Til en ny Inrättning däraf*, Johan Pehr Lind, Stockholm, (in Swedish).

Edmonds, J., and Johnson, E.L. [1973], "Matching, Euler tours and the Chinese postman," *Mathematical Programming*, Vol. 5, pp. 88-124.

Eijk, P. van, Vissers, C.A., and Diaz, M. [1989], *The Formal Description Technique Lotos*, North-Holland Publ., Amsterdam, 1989. 451 pgs.

Eisenberg, M.A., and McGuire, M.R. [1972], "Further comments on Dijkstra's concurrent programming control problem," *Comm. of the ACM*, Vol. 15, No. 11, p. 999.

Field, J.A. [1976], "Efficient computer-computer communication," *Proc. IEEE*, Vol. 123, August 1976, pp. 756-760.

Finkel, A., and Rosier, L. [1987], *A Survey of FIFO Nets*, Publ. 632, October 1987, University of Montreal, Dept. d'Informatique et de Recherche Operationelle, 37 pgs.

Fleming, H.C., and Hutchinson, R.M., Jr. [1971], "1969-1970 Connection survey: low speed data transmission performance on the switched telecommunications network," *Bell System Technical Journal*, Vol. 50, No. 4, 1385-1405.

Fletcher, J.G. [1982], "An arithmetic checksum for serial transmission," *IEEE Trans. on Communications*, Vol. COM-30, No. 1, January 1982.

Floyd, R.W. [1967], "Assigning meanings to programs," *Proc. Symposia in Applied Mathematics*, American Mathematical Society, Vol. 19, pp. 19-32.

Fraser, A.G. and Marshall, W.T. [1989], "Data Transport in a Byte Stream Network," *IEEE Journal on Selected Areas in Comm.*, Vol. 7, No. 7, pp. 1020-1033.

Friedman, A.D., and Menon, P.R. [1971], *Fault Detection in Digital Circuits*, Prentice Hall, Englewood Cliffs, N.J., 220 pgs.

Garey, M.G., and Johnson, D.S. [1979], *Computers and Intractability: a Guide to the Theory of NP-completeness*, Freeman, San Fransisco.

Gerla, M., and Kleinrock, L. [1980], "Flow control: a comparative survey," *IEEE Trans. on Communications*, Vol. COM-28, No. 4, April 1980, pp. 553-574.

Gibbons, A. [1985], *Algorithmic Graph Theory*, Cambridge University Press, 260 pgs.

Gill, A. [1962], *Introduction to the Theory of Finite State Machines*, McGraw-Hill, New York.

Gobershtein, S.M. [1974], "Check words for the states of a finite automaton," *Kibernetika*, No. 1, pp. 46-49, (original in Russian).

Godefroid, P. [1990], "Using partial orders to improve automatic verification methods," *Proc. 2nd Workshop on Computer-Aided Verification*, R.P. Kurshan, and E.M. Clarke (Eds.), Rutgers University, Springer Verlag, New York.

Gotzheim, R., and Bochmann, G. von [1986], *Deriving Protocol Specifications from Service Specifications*, University of Montreal, Report #562.

Gouda, M.G. [1983], "An example for constructing communicating machines by stepwise refinement," *Proc. 3rd IFIP WG 6.1 Int. Workshop on Protocol Specification, Testing, and Verification*, North-Holland Publ., Amsterdam, pp. 63-74.

Gouda, M.G. [1987], *The Stabilizing Philosopher: Asymmetry by Memory and by Action*, Report TR-87-12, April 1987, Dept. of Computer Sciences, University of Texas at Austin.

Gouda, M.G. and Han, J.Y. [1985], "Protocol validation by fair progress state exploration," *Computer Networks and ISDN Systems*, Vol. 9, pp. 353-361.

Gouda, M.G. and Yu, Y.T. [1984], "Protocol validation by maximal progress state exploration," *IEEE Trans. on Communications*, Vol. COM-32, No. 1, pp. 94-97.

Griffiths, G., and Stones, G.C. [1987], "The tea-leaf reader algorithm: an efficient implementation of CRC-16 and CRC-32," *Comm. of the ACM*, Vol. 30, No. 7, pp. 617-620.

Hajek, J. [1978], "Automatically verified data transfer protocols," *Proc. 4th ICCC*, Kyoto, pp. 749-756.

Hamming, R.W. [1950], "Error detecting and error correcting codes," *Bell System Technical Journal*, Vol. 29, pp. 147-160.

Har'El, Zri, and Kurshan, R.P. [1990], "Software for analytical development of communications protocols," *AT&T Technical Journal*, Special issue on Protocol Testing and Verification. Vol 69, No 1, pp. 45-59.

Harbison, S.P., and Steele, G.L., Jr. [1987], *C — a Reference Manual*, Prentice Hall, Englewood Cliffs, N.J., 2nd ed., ISBN 0-13-109802-0.

Harrison, M.A. [1965], *Introduction to Switching and Automata Theory*, McGraw-Hill, New York, Series in Systems Science.

Hartley, R.V.L. [1928], "Transmission of information," *Bell System Technical Journal*, Vol 7, pp. 535-563.

Hartmanis, J., and Stearns, R.E. [1966], *Algebraic Structure Theory of Sequential Machines*, Prentice Hall, Englewood Cliffs, N.J. Int. Series in Appl. Mathematics.

Harvard University, Computation Laboratory Staff, [1951], *Synthesis of Electronic Computing and Control Circuits*, Harvard University Press, Massachusetts.

Hayes, I., Mowbray, M., and Rose, G.A. [1989], "Signalling system No. 7, the network layer," *Proc. 9th IFIP WG 6.1 Int. Workshop on Protocol Specification, Testing, and Verification*, North-Holland Publ., Amsterdam.

Hennie, F.C. [1964], "Fault detecting experiments for sequential circuits," *Proc. 5th Annual Symp. Switching Circuit Theory and Logical Design*, Princeton University, Princeton, N.J., Nov. 11-13 1964, pp. 95-110.

Herbarth, D. [1978], *Die Entwicklung der Optischen Telegrafie in Preussen*, Arbeitsheft 15, Landeskonservator Rheinland, Rheinland-Verlag, Koln 1978, in German, ISBN 3-7927-0247-9, 200 pgs.

Hoare, C.A.R. [1978], "Communicating sequential processes," *Comm. of the ACM*, Vol. 21, No. 8, pp. 666-677.

Hocquenghem, A. [1959], "Codes correcteurs d'erreurs," *Chiffres (Paris)*, Vol. 2, pp. 147-156.

Hodge, F.W. [1910], *Handbook of American Indians North of Mexico*, Part 2, Smithsonian Institution, Bureau of Ethnology, Bulletin 30.

Holzmann, G.J. [1979], *Coordination Problems in Multiprocessing Systems*, Ph.D. Thesis, Delft University of Technology, The Netherlands, 315 pgs.

Holzmann, G.J. [1982a], "A Theory for protocol validation," *IEEE Trans. on Computers*, Vol. C-31, No.8, pp. 730-738.

Holzmann, G.J. [1982b], "Algebraic validation methods," *Proc. 2nd IFIP WG 6.1 Int. Workshop on Protocol Specification, Testing, and Verification*, North-Holland Publ., Amsterdam, pp. 383-390.

Holzmann, G.J. [1984a], "The Pandora system — an interactive system for the design of data communication protocols," *Computer Networks*, Vol. 8, No. 2, pp. 71-81.

Holzmann, G.J. [1984b], "Backward symbolic execution of protocols," *Proc. 4th IFIP WG 6.1 Int. Workshop on Protocol Specification, Testing, and Verification*, North-Holland Publ., Amsterdam, pp. 19-30.

Holzmann, G.J. [1985], "Tracing protocols", *AT&T Technical Journal*, Vol 64, December 1985, pp. 2413-2434.

Holzmann, G.J. [1987a], "Automated protocol validation in 'Argos,' assertion proving and scatter searching," *IEEE Trans. on Software Engineering*, Vol. 13, No. 6, June 1987, pp. 683-697.

Holzmann, G.J. [1987b], "On limits and possibilities of automated protocol analysis," *Proc. 7th IFIP WG 6.1 Int. Workshop on Protocol Specification,, Testing, and Verification*, North-Holland Publ., Amsterdam, pp. 137-161.

Holzmann, G.J. [1988], "An improved protocol reachability analysis technique," *Software, Practice and Experience*, Vol 18, No. 2, February 1988, pp. 137-161.

Holzmann, G.J. [1990], "Algorithms for automated protocol validation," *AT&T Technical Journal*, Special issue on Protocol Testing and Verification. Vol 69, No 1, pp. 32-44.

Holzmann, G.J., and Patti, J. [1989], "Validating SDL specifications: an experiment," *Proc. 9th IFIP WG 6.1 Int. Workshop on Protocol Specification, Testing, and Verification*, North-Holland Publ., Amsterdam.

Hsieh, E.P. [1971], "Checking experiments for sequential machines," *IEEE Trans. on Computers*, Vol C-20, No. 10, pp. 1152-1166.

Hubbard, G. [1965], *Cooke and Wheatstone and the Invention of the Electric Telegraph*, Routledge & Kegan Paul, London.

Huffman, D.A. [1954], "The synthesis of sequential circuits," *Jour. Franklin Inst.*, Vol. 257, March-April 1954, No. 3-4, pp. 161-190, 275-303.

Huffman, D.A. [1964], "Canonical forms for information-lossless finite state logical machines," in *Sequential Machines: Selected Papers*, E.F. Moore (Ed.), Addison-Wesley, Reading, Mass.

Hutchinson, N.C., Peterson, L.L., and Rao, H. [1989], "The X-kernel: an open operating system design," *Proc. 2nd Workshop on Workstation Operating Systems*, IEEE Computer Society, WWOS-II, Sept. 27-29, 1989, pp. 55-59.

Hyman, H. [1966], "Comments on a problem in concurrent programming control," *Comm. of the ACM*, Vol 9, No. 1, p. 45.

IBM [1964], *Error Control through Coding*, Technical Documentary Report No. RADC-TDR-64-149, Vol. 1 - 9, July 1964, Griffis AFB, N.Y.

IFIP [1982-present], *Proc. IFIP WG 6.1 Int. Workshops on Protocol Specification, Testing, and Verification*, The proceedings of this annual conference are published by: North-Holland Publ., Amsterdam.

ISO [1979], *Reference Model of Open Systems Interconnection*, Doc. ISO/TC97/SC16 N227.

ISO [1983], *Connection Oriented Transport Protocol*, Doc. DP 8073.

ISO [1987], *OSI Conformance Testing Methodology and Framework*, ISO/TC97/SC21, Part 2: Abstract test suite specification," Annex E: "The tree and tabular combined notation."

Jacobson, V. [1988], "Congestion avoidance and control," *ACM Computer Communication Review*, Vol. 18, No. 4, pp. 314-329.

Jain, R. [1986], "A timeout based congestion control scheme for window flow-controlled networks," *IEEE Journal on Selected Areas in Comm.*, Vol. SAC-4, No. 7, October 1986, pp. 1162-1167.

Jain, R., Ramakrishan, K.K., and Chiu, D.M. [1987], *Congestion Avoidance in Computer Networks with a Connectionless Network Layer*, Report DEC-TR-506, Digital Equipment Corp., 17 pgs.

Kain, R.Y. [1972], *Automata Theory: Machines and Languages*, McGraw-Hill, New York, Computer Science Series.

Kanellakis, P.C., and Smolka, S.A. [1990], "CCS expressions, finite state processes, and three problems of equivalence," *Information and Computation*, Vol 86, No. 1, pp. 43-68.

Karn, P., and Partridge, C. [1987], "Improving round-trip time estimates in reliable transport protocols," *Proc. ACM SIGCOMM '87*, pp. 2-7.

Kendall, D.G. [1951], "Some problems in the theory of queues," *J. Royal. Statist. Society.*, Ser. B, Vol 13, p. 151.

Kernighan, B.W, and Pike, R. [1984], *The UNIX Programming Environment*, Prentice Hall, Englewood Cliffs, N.J., ISBN 0-13-937699-2.

Kernighan, B.W., and Ritchie, D.M. [1978], *The C Programming Language*, Prentice Hall, Englewood Cliffs, N.J. 2nd ed. 1988, ISBN 0-13-110362-8.

Klee, V. [1980], "Combinatorial optimization: what is the state of the art?," *Math. Oper. Res.*, Vol 5, pp. 1-26.

Knudsen, H.K. [1983], *Linked-state Machines*, Report LA-9770-MS, Los Alamos National Laboratory, Los Alamos, N.M., July 1983, 84 pgs.

Knuth, D.E. [1966], "Additional comments on a problem in concurrent programming control," *Comm. of the ACM*, Vol. 9, No. 5, pp. 321-322.

Knuth, D.E. [1981], "Verification of link level protocols," *BIT*, Vol. 21, pp. 31-36.

Kohavi, Z. [1978] *Switching and Finite Automata Theory*, 2nd ed., McGraw-Hill, New York, Computer Science Series, 658 pgs.

Krogdahl, S. [1978], "Verification of a class of link level protocols," *BIT*, Vol. 18, pp. 436-448.

Kruijer, H.S.M. [1979], "Self-stabilization (in spite of distributed control) in tree-structured systems," *Information Processing Letters*, Vol. 8, No. 2, pp. 91-95.

Kuan, M-K. [1962], "Graphic programming using odd or even points," *Chinese Math.*, Vol. 1, pp. 273-277.

Kuo, F.F. [1981], *Protocols and Techniques for Data Communications Networks*, F.F. Kuo (Ed.), Prentice Hall, Englewood Cliffs, N.J.

Lam, S.S., and Shankar, A.U. [1984], "Protocol verification via projections," *IEEE Trans. on Software Engineering*, Vol. 10, No. 4, pp. 325-342.

Lamport, L. [1974], "A new solution to Dijkstra's concurrent programming problem," *Comm. of the ACM*, Vol. 17, No. 8, pp. 453-455.

Lamport, L. [1976], "The synchronization of independent processes," *Acta Informatica*, Vol. 7, pp. 15-34.

Lamport, L. [1977], "Proving the correctness of multiprocess programs" *IEEE Trans. on Software Engineering*, Vol SE-3, No. 2, pp 125-143.

Lamport, L. [1984], "Unsolved problems, and non-problems in concurrency," Invited address, *Proc. 3rd ACM Symposium on Principles of Distributed Computing*, Vancouver, Canada, August 1984, pp. 1-11.

Lamport, L. [1986], "The mutual exclusion problem — parts I and II", *Journal of the ACM*, Vol. 33, No. 2, April 1986, pp. 313-347.

Lin, F.J., Chu, P.M., and Liu, M.T. [1987], "Protocol verification using reachability analysis," *Computer Communication Review*, Vol. 17, No. 5, pp. 126-135.

Lin, S., and Rado, T. [1965], "Computer studies of Turing machine problems," *Journal of the ACM*, Vol. 12, No. 2, pp. 196-212.

Lindgren, B. [1987], *The X.25 Handbook*, Kalmar Publ., Sweden.

Linn, R.J., and McCoy, W.H. [1983], "Producing tests for implementations of OSI protocols," *Proc. 3rd IFIP WG 6.1 Int. Workshop on Protocol Specification, Testing, and Verification*, North-Holland Publ., Amsterdam, pp. 505-520.

Lint, J.H. van [1971], *Coding Theory*, Lecture Notes in Mathematics, Springer Verlag, New York, 136 pgs.

Lynch, W.C. [1968], "Reliable full duplex file transmission over half-duplex telephone lines," *Comm. of the ACM*, Vol. 11, No. 6, pp. 407-410.

MacWilliams, F.J., and Sloane, N.J.A. [1977], *Theory of Error-correcting Codes*, North-Holland Publ., Amsterdam.

Mallery, J. [1881], "Sign Language among North American Indians," *Bureau of Ethnology Annual Report*, Vol. 1, 1879-1880, Washington, GPO.

Malmgren, E. [1964], "Den optiska telegrafen i Furusund," in *Daedalus*, Annual Publ. of the Swedish National Museum of Science and Technology, Stockholm, (in Swedish).

Mandelbrot, B. [1965], "Self similar error clusters in communications systems and the concept of conditional stationarity," *IEEE Trans. on Communications Technology*, Vol COM-13, No. 1, pp. 71-90.

Manna, Z., and Pnueli, A. [1987], "Specification and verification of concurrent programs by $\forall$ automata," *Proc. ACM Conf. on Principles of Programming Languages*, POPL'87, 21-23 January 1987, Munich, W.Germany, pp. 1-12.

Manna, Z., and Wolper, P. [1984], "Synthesis of communication processes from temporal logic specifications," *ACM Trans. on Programming Languages and Systems*, Vol. 6, No. 1, January 1984, pp. 68-93.

Marland, E.A. [1964], *Early Electrical Communication*, Abelard-Schuman, New York, 220 pgs.

Maxemchuck, N., and Sabnani, K. [1987], "Probabilistic verification of communications protocols," *Proc. 7th IFIP WG 6.1 Int. Workshop on Protocol Specification, Testing, and Verification*, North-Holland Publ., Amsterdam, pp. 307-320.

McCulloch, W.S., and Pitts, W. [1943], "A logical calculus of the ideas immanent in nervous activity," *Bulletin of Mathematical Biophysics*, Vol. 5, pp. 115-133.

McIlroy, M.D. [1982], "Development of a Spelling List," *IEEE Trans. on Communications*, Vol. 30, pp. 91-99.

McNamara, J.E. [1982], *Technical Aspects of Data Communication*, 2nd ed., Digital Press, DEC, Bedford, Mass.

McQuillan, J.M., and Walden, D.C. [1977], "The ARPA network design decisions," *Computer Networks*, Vol. 1, pp. 243-289.

Mealy, G.H. [1955], "A method for synthesizing sequential circuits," *Bell System Technical Journal*, Vol. 34, Sept. 1955, pp. 1045-1079.

Merlin, P.M. [1979], "Specification and validation of protocols," *IEEE Trans. on Communications*, Vol. COM-27, 1761-1780.

Merlin, P.M., and Bochmann, G. von [1983], "On the construction of submodule specifications and communication protocols," *ACM Trans. on Programming Languages and Systems*, Jan 1983, pp. 1-25.

Michaelis, A.R. [1965], *From Semaphore to Satellite*, International Telecommunication Union, Geneva.

Milner, R. [1980], "A calculus for communicating systems," *Lecture Notes in Computer Science*, Vol. 92.

Moitra, A. [1985], "Automatic construction of CSP programs from sequential non-deterministic programs," *Science of Computer Programming* , Vol. 5 (1985), pp. 277-307.

Moore, E.F. [1956], "Gedanken-experiments on sequential machines," *Automata Studies, Annals of Mathematics Studies*, No. 34, Princeton University Press, Princeton, N.J., pp. 129-153.

Moore, E.F. [1964], *Sequential Machines: Selected Papers*, Addison-Wesley, Reading, Mass.

Morris, R. [1968], "Scatter Storage Techniques," *Comm. of the ACM*, Vol. 11, No. 1, pp. 38-44.

Multari, N. [1989], *Towards a Theory of Self-stabilizing Protocols*, Ph.D. Thesis, Dept. of Computer Science, University of Texas at Austin.

Naito, S., and Tsunoyama, M. [1981], "Fault detection for sequential machines by transition tours," *Proc. IEEE Fault Tolerant Computing Conf.*.

Nakassis, A. [1988], "Fletcher's error detection algorithm: how to implement it efficiently and how to avoid the most common pitfalls," *Computer Communication Review*, Vol. 18, No. 5, October 1988, pp. 63-88.

Needham, R.M., and Herbert, A.J. [1982], *The Cambridge Distributed Computing System*, International Computer Science Series, Addison-Wesley, ISBN 0-201-14092-6, 170 pgs.

Nightingale, J.S. [1982], "Protocol testing using a reference implementation," in: *Proc. 2nd IFIP WG 6.1 Int. Workshop on Protocol Specification, Testing, and Verification*, North-Holland Publ., Amsterdam, pp. 513-522.

Nock, O.S. [1967], *Historic Railway Disasters*, Ian Allan, London.

Nyquist, H. [1924], "Certain factors affecting telegraph speed," *Bell System Technical Journal*, Vol. 3, pp. 324-346.

Owicki, S., and Lamport, L. [1982] "Proving liveness properties of concurrent programs," *ACM Trans. on Programming Languages and Systems*, Vol. 4, No. 3, July 1982, pp. 455-495.

Pageot, J.M., and Jard, C. [1988], "Experience in guiding simulation," *Proc. VIII-th Workshop on Protocol Specification, Testing, and Verification*, Atlantic City, 1988, North-Holland Publ., Amsterdam.

Perez, A. [1983], "Byte-wise CRC calculations," *IEEE Micro*, June 1983, pp. 40-50.

Peterson, W.W., and Weldon, E.J., Jr. [1972], *Error-correcting Codes*, 2nd ed., MIT Press, Cambridge, Mass.

Petri, C.A. [1962], *Kommunikation mit Automaten*, In German, University of Bonn, Germany. Reprinted in English as *Communication with Automata*, Suppl. 1 to Techn. Report RADC-TR-65-377, Vol. 1, Griffis AFB, New York, 1966.

Pike, R., and Kernighan, B.W. [1984]. "Program design in the Unix environment," *AT&T Technical Journal*, Vol. 63, No. 8, October 1984, pp. 1595-1605.

Pnueli, A. [1977], "The temporal logic of programs," *Proc. 18th IEEE Symposium on Foundations of Computer Science*, Providence, R.I., pp. 46-57.

Pouzin, L. [1976], "Flow control in data networks — methods and tools," *Proc. Int. Conf. Comp. Comm.*, Toronto, Ont., Canada, August 1976.

Pouzin, L., and Zimmerman, H. [1978], "A Tutorial on protocols," *Proc. IEEE*, Vol. 66, No. 11, 1346-1370.

Prescott, G.B. [1877], *Electricity and the Electric Telegraph*, New York, 1877.

Price, W.L. [1971], *Graphs and Networks*, Auerbach Publ., ISBN 0-8876-128-2, 108 pgs.

Prinoth, R. [1982], "An algorithm to construct distributed systems from state machines," *Proc. 2nd IFIP WG 6.1 Int. Workshop on Protocol Specification, Testing, and Verification*, North-Holland Publ., Amsterdam, pp. 261-282.

Probert, R.L., and Ural, H. [1983], "Requirements for a test specification language for protocol implementation testing," in: *Proc. 3rd IFIP WG 6.1 Int. Workshop on Protocol Specification, Testing, and Verification*, North-Holland Publ., Amsterdam. pp. 437-436.

Probst, D.K. [1990], "Using partial-order semantics to avoid the state explosion problem in asynchronous systems," *Proc. 2nd Workshop on Computer-Aided Verification*, R.P. Kurshan, and E.M. Clarke (Eds.), Rutgers University, Springer Verlag, New York.

Puzman, J., and Porizek, R. [1980], *Communication Control in Computer Networks*, Wiley & Sons, New York.

Queille, J.P. [1982], *Le systeme Cesar: description, specification et analyse des applications reparties*, Ph.D. Thesis, Computer Science Dept., University of Grenoble, France,

Rado, T. [1962], "On non-computable functions," *Bell System Technical Journal*, Vol. 41, May 1962, pp. 977-884.

Rafiq, O., and Ansart, J.P. [1983], "A protocol validator and its applications," *Proc. 3rd Workshop on Protocol Specification, Testing, and Verification*, Zurich, North-Holland Publ., Amsterdam, pp. 189-198.

Rayner, D. [1982], "A system for testing protocol implementations," in: *Proc. 2nd IFIP WG 6.1 Int. Workshop on Protocol Specification, Testing, and Verification*, North-Holland Publ., Amsterdam, pp. 539-554.

Rayner, D. [1987], "OSI conformance testing," *Computer Networks and ISDN Systems*, Special issue on Conformance Testing, Vol. 14, No. 1, pp. 79-98.

Razouk, B.B., and Estrin, G. [1980], "Modeling and verification of communication protocols in SARA: the X.21 interface," *IEEE Trans. on Computers*, Vol. C-29, No. 12, pp. 1038-1052.

Reid, J.D. [1886], *Telegraph in America*, John Polhemus Publ., New York, 881 pgs.

Reif, J.H., and Smolka, S.A. [1988], "The complexity of reachability in distributed communicating processes," *Acta Informatica*, Vol. 25, pp. 333-354.

Richier, J.L., Rodriguez, C., Sifakis, J., and Voiron, J., [1987], "Verification in Xesar of the sliding window protocol," *Proc. 7th Workshop on Protocol Specification, Testing, and Verification*, Zurich, North-Holland Publ., Amsterdam, pp. 235-250.

Ritchie, G.R., and Scheffler, P.E. [1982], "Projecting the error performance of the Bell system digital network," *IEEE 1982 Int. Communications Conference*, ICC, Vol. 1, pp. 2D2.1-6

Rockstrom, A., and Saracco, R. [1982], "SDL — CCITT Specification and Description Language," *IEEE Trans. on Communications*, Vol. COM-30, No. 6, pp. 1310-1318.

Rolt, L.T.C. [1976], *Red for Danger, a History of Railway Accidents and Railway Safety*, David & Charles, London.

Rubin, J., and West, C.H. [1982], "An improved protocol validation technique," *Computer Networks*, Vol. 6, Nr. 2, pp. 65-74.

Rudie, K., and Wonham, W.M. [1990], *Proc. 10th IFIP WG 6.1 Int. Workshop on Protocol Specification*, North-Holland Publ., Amsterdam.

SDL [1987], "Special issue on the CCITT language SDL," *Computer Networks and ISDN Systems*, Vol. 13, No. 2, pp. 65-134.

Sabnani, K., and Dahbura, A. [1985], "A new technique for generating protocol tests," *ACM Computer Communication Review*, Vol. 15, No. 4, September 1985.

Sabnani, K. and Dahbura, A. [1988], "A protocol test generation procedure," *Computer Networks and ISDN Systems*, Vol. 15, pp. 285-297.

Saracco, R., Smith, J.R.W., and Reed, R. [1989], *Telecommunications Systems Engineering using SDL*, North-Holland Publ., Amsterdam, 633 pgs, ISBN 0 444 88084 4.

Saracco, R., and Tilanus, P.A.J. [1987], "CCITT SDL: overview of the language and its applications," *Computer Networks and ISDN Systems*, Vol. 13, No. 2, pp. 65-74.

Sarikaya, B. [1984], *Test Design for Computer Network Protocols*, Ph.D. Thesis, McGill University, Montreal, Canada, March 1984.

Scantlebury, R.A., Bartlett, K.A. [1967], "A protocol for use in the NPL data communications network," Technical Memorandum, National Physical Laboratory.

Schneider, A., and Mase, A. [1968], *Railway Accidents of Great Brittain and Europe, their Causes and Consequences*, David & Charles, London.

Schreiner, A.T., and Friedman, H.G., Jr. [1985], *Introduction to Compiler Construction with UNIX*, Prentice Hall, Englewood Cliffs, N.J., 194 pgs. ISBN 0-13-474396-2.

Schwabe, D. [1981], "Formal specification and verification of a connection establishment protocol," *Proc. Seventh Data Comm. Symp.*, Mexico City, (IEEE), pp. 11-26.

Shannon, C.E. [1948], "A mathematical theory of communication," *Bell System Technical Journal*, Vol. 27, pp. 379-423, 623-656.

Shannon, C.E. and McCarthy, J. (eds.) [1956], *Automata Studies*, Princeton University Press, Princeton, N.J.

Shaw, R.B. [1978], *A History of Railroad Accidents, Safety Precautions and Operating Practices*, Northern Press, Postdam, New York.

Shen, Y-N, and Lombardi, F. [1989], "Protocol conformance testing using multiple UIO sequences," *Proc. 9th Workshop on Protocol Specification, Testing, and Verification*, Twente, The Netherlands, North-Holland Publ., Amsterdam.

Shih, T., and Sidhu, D. [1986], *A technique for generating test sequences for protocols*, Report TR 86-23, Iowa State University.

Sidhu, D., and Leung, T. [1989], "Formal methods for protocol testing: a detailed study," *IEEE Trans. on Software Engineering*, Vol. 15, No. 4, pp. 413-426.

Sidhu, D. [1990], "Protocol testing, the first ten years, the next ten years," *Proc. 10th IFIP WG 6.1 Int. Workshop on Protocol Specification*, North-Holland Publ., Amsterdam.

Slepian, D. (ed.) [1973], *Key papers in the development of information theory*, IEEE Press, New York.

Snepscheut, J.L.A. van den [1985], *Trace Theory and VLSI Design*, Ph.D. Thesis, Eindhoven University of Technology, The Netherlands, also in: Lecture Notes in Computer Science, Vol 200, Springer Verlag, New York.

Stallings, W. [1985], *Data and Computer Communications*, Macmillan, New York, London, 594 pgs. 2nd ed., 1988, 653 pgs.

Stallings, W., Mockapetris, P., McLeod S., and Michel, T. [1988], *Handbook of Computer Communications Standards*, Macmillan, New York, London, ISBN 0-02-948072-8, 206 pgs.

Stenning, N.V. [1976], "Data transfer protocol," *Computer Networks*, Vol 1, pp. 99-110.

Still, A. [1946], *Communication through the Ages; from Sign Language to Television*, Murray Hill Books, New York, 201 pgs.

Sunshine, C.A., and Smallberg, D.A. [1982], *Automated Protocol Verification*, USC/ISI report RR-83-110, October 1982.

Tanenbaum, A.S. [1981], *Computer Networks*, Prentice Hall, Englewood Cliffs, N.J., 2nd ed., 1988.

Tarjan, R.E. [1983], *Data Structures and Network Algorithms*, Philadelphia, Pa., 1983, Soc. of Industrial and Applied Mathematics, 131 pgs.

Tugal, D. and Tugal, O. [1982], *Data Transmission, Analysis, Design and Applications*, McGraw-Hill, New York.

Turing, A.M. [1936], "On computable numbers, with an application to the Entscheidungsproblem," *Proc. London Math. Soc.*, Ser. 2, Vol. 42, pp. 230-265; correction Vol. 43, pp. 544-546.

Ural, H., and Probert, R.L. [1986], "Step-wise validation of communication protocols and services," *Computer Networks and ISDN Systems*, Vol. 11, No. 3, pp. 367-383.

Uyar, M.U., and Dahbura, A.T. [1986], "Optimal test sequence generation for protocols: the Chinese Postman Algorithm applied to Q.931," *Proc. IEEE Global Telecommunications Conference, 1986*, Houston, Texas, Vol. 1, pp. 3.1.1-5.

Valmari, A. [1990], "A stubborn attack on state explosion," *Proc. 2nd Workshop on Computer-Aided Verification*, R.P. Kurshan, and E.M. Clarke (Eds.), Rutgers University, Springer Verlag, New York.

Vasilevskii, M.P. [1973], "Failure diagnosis of automata," *Kibernetika*, No. 4, pp. 98-108, (original in Russian).

Vissers, C. and Logrippo, L. [1985] "The importance of the service concept in the design of data communications protocols," *Proc. 5th IFIP WG 6.1 Int. Workshop on Protocol Specification, Testing, and Verification*, North-Holland Publ., Amsterdam, pp. 3-17.

Vissers, C. [1990] "FDT's for open distributed systems, a retrospective and a prospective view," *Proc. 10th IFIP WG 6.1 Int. Workshop on Protocol Specification, Testing, and Verification*, North-Holland Publ., Amsterdam.

Wang, B., and Hutchinson, D. [1987], "Protocol testing techniques," *Computer Communications*, Vol 10, No. 2, April 1987, pp. 79-87.

West, C.H., and Zafiropulo, P. [1978], "Automated validation of a communications protocol: the CCITT X.21 recommendation," *IBM J. Res. Develop.*, Vol. 22, No. 1, pp. 60-71.

West, C.H [1978], "General technique for communications protocol validation," *IBM J. Res. Develop.*, Vol. 22, No. 3, pp. 393-404.

West, C.H. [1982], "Applications and limitations of automated protocol validation," *Proc. 2nd IFIP WG 6.1 Int. Workshop on Protocol Specification, Testing, and Verification*, North-Holland Publ., Amsterdam, pp. 361-372.

West, C.H. [1986a], "A validation of the OSI session layer protocol," *Computer Networks and ISDN Systems*, Vol 11, No. 3, pp. 173-183.

West, C.H. [1986b], "Protocol validation by random state exploration," *Proc. 6th IFIP WG 6.1 Int. Workshop on Protocol Specification, Testing, and Verification*, North-Holland Publ., Amsterdam, pp. 233-242.

West, C.H. [1989], "Protocol validation in complex systems," *Proc. 8th ACM Symposium on Principles of Distributed Computing*, Austin, Texas, August 1989.

Wirth, N. [1971], "Program development by stepwise refinement," *Comm. of the ACM*, Vol. 14, No. 4, pp. 221-227.

Wirth, N. [1974], "On the composition of well structured programs," *Computing Surveys*, Vol. 6, No. 4, pp. 247-259.

Wolper, P. [1981], "Temporal logic can now be more expressive," *Proc. 22nd IEEE Symposium on Foundations of Computer Science*, pp. 340-348.

Wolper, P. [1986], "Specifying interesting properties of programs in propositional temporal logic," *Proc. 13th ACM Symposium on Principles of Programming Languages*, St. Petersburg Beach, Fla., January 1986, pp. 148-193.

Yannakakis, M., and Lee, D. [1990], "Testing finite state machines," to appear.

Zafiropulo, P. [1978], "Protocol validation by duologue-matrix analysis," *IEEE Trans. on Communications*, Vol. COM-26, No. 8, pp. 1187-1194.

Zafiropulo, P., West, C.H., Rudin, H., Cowan, D.D., and Brand, D. [1980], "Toward analyzing and synthesizing protocols," *IEEE Trans. on Communications*, Vol. COM-28, No. 4, pp. 651-661.

Zhang, L. [1986], "Why TCP timers don't work well," *Proc. ACM SIGCOMM '86*, pp. 397-405.

DATA TRANSMISSION   A

For the purposes of protocol design, it can suffice to model a physical channel as a black box with just one interesting feature: it can distort the data that passes through it. We will understand a *channel* to be any medium capable of transferring signals from sender to receiver. The physical realization of the channel can be anything from a twisted pair of copper wires to a satellite link. The only thing we are interested in is the behavior of the channel in so far as it can modify the signals it transfers.

Trusted Data → Distortion Box → Untrusted Data

Figure A.1 — Channel Behavior

The distortion that is introduced by the channel is typically defined by an error distribution function with known characteristics. For a given medium, the average probability of bit errors can be looked up in a table (see Table A.1 at the end of this Appendix). With this information we can devise an error detection scheme that encodes the trusted data in such a way that its integrity can be checked after it has passed through the distortion box (Chapter 3). Such an error detection scheme intercepts most of the distortions, but is transparent to undistorted data. This transforms the *distortion box* into a *deletion box*.

Deletion errors can be dealt with straightforwardly in a flow control protocol that numbers messages (Chapter 4). Because the error control schemes are based on an estimate of the *average* bit error rate, there is always some probability that distorted data are not intercepted. The purpose of error control is to make the probability of these events acceptably small (Chapter 3).

To gain a better insight into the nature of transmission errors, however, we do take a peek into the distortion box in this appendix. We will see how the behavior of the physical channel is influenced by factors such as

- ○ The data encoding method
- ○ The channel quality (bandwidth, noise level)

○ The physical dimensions of the channel
○ The signaling speed

With this background, it will be easier to make the right assessment about the protocol requirements for different types of channels. For instance, it would be utter folly to devise an elaborate protocol with forward error control (Chapter 3) on a 10 foot fiber-optic link. Similarly, it would be unwise to attempt to send data at 100 Mbps on a twisted pair cable, no matter what error control scheme is used.

TYPES OF CHANNELS

In practice, three different types of data transmission channels are used. A *simplex* channel can only be used for data transfer in one direction. The sender typically has a "modulator" to translate binary data into analog signals, and the receiver has a "demodulator" for the reverse translation. A *duplex*, or *full-duplex*, channel can transfer information in both directions simultaneously. Each station has both a "modulator" and a "demodulator" combined into a single instrument called a "modem." A *half-duplex* channel, finally, can transfer data in both directions, but not simultaneously. The stations have to be switched from sending to receiving or back. The switch usually takes about 200 msec.

SERIAL AND PARALLEL

Depending on the available hardware, the raw data bits may be transmitted on a physical channel with several bits at a time in parallel, or one bit at a time in series. Parallel transmission is normally only used on short distances, e.g., from a machine to a peripheral. In parallel transmissions one extra line is used to carry a special clock or "strobe" signal that will indicate when precisely the signals on the other lines constitute a valid data word. Due to variations in propagation delays, and the range of possible distortions, it becomes increasingly difficult on longer lines to synchronize the strobe signal and the various bit-streams. For long distances serial transmission is therefore more common.

ASYNCHRONOUS AND SYNCHRONOUS

On a serial line both the sender and the receiver have a separate clock that sets the transmission rate. The sender uses its clock to *drive* the line (i.e., to transmit the bits), and the receiver uses its clock to *scan* it. In asynchronous transmissions the two clocks need not be in perfect synchrony when no data are transmitted. Data is transmitted in chunks of, for instance, 7 or 8 bits, preceded by a special *start* symbol and followed by a *stop* symbol. The receiver uses the start symbol to synchronize its clock with the sender.

It is sufficient if the two clocks can stay in synchrony for only the 7 or 8 bits that make up a data word. The length of the data word is sometimes called the "synchronization gap," the period of time that the two clocks must stay in synchrony. The stop symbol is usually either 1.5 or 2 bits long, to allow the receiver to process the data and catch up with the sender and to restore synchrony at the next start symbol. The period of time that passes between the stop symbol and the next start symbol, however, need not be an integral number of bit times.

Figure A.2 — Asynchronous Transmission

Figure A.2 shows the asynchronous transmission of an 8 bit ASCII character: 7 bits of data followed by a parity bit, labeled *P* (see Chapter 3). The idle state of the line is indicated by a high voltage, a logical one. The one symbol is sometimes called a *mark* and the zero symbol a *space*.

The asynchronous transmission method is self-stabilizing, even when the receiver erroneously starts its clock at a data bit instead of the start symbol. The number of data bits scanned will come out wrong, producing a "framing error." But since the assumed start of a data word can only move forward in time sooner or later the receiver will re-synchronize.

In synchronous transmission the sender and receiver's clock must stay in synchrony at all times. When no data are transmitted, the two clocks can be kept synchronous with special "SYNC" characters.

Data can also be encoded in such a way that the signal always has a sufficient number of transitions to keep the receiver's clock synchronized with the sender's. With this method the bits are encoded in the *transitions* of a binary signal, rather than in absolute signal levels. The best known method of this type is the Manchester encoding. A one symbol is encoded in the Manchester code by a downward transition (one to zero) and a zero is encoded by an upward (zero to one) transition. This method uses two Baud (signal elements) to encode one bit of information. Figure A.3 illustrates this process.

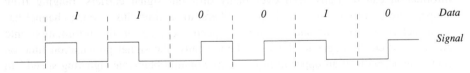

Figure A.3 — Manchester Encoding

The Manchester code is called a "self-clocking code." The receiver's clock can synchronize on the transition that is guaranteed to occur in the middle of each symbol. The Manchester code has another important property: it creates a "balanced" signal. The average value of the signal over time approaches zero, even if a continuous sequence of equal bits is transmitted. The distortion of a balanced signal on the physical data link is generally smaller than that of an unbalanced signal. The electrical properties of media such as a twisted pair or a coaxial cable are relatively unfavorable for DC (direct current) signals, but more favorable for AC (alternating current), or balanced signals.

Experiment has shown that the maximum signaling speed on a twisted pair cable can be increased by a factor of *ten* if an unbalanced code is replaced with a balanced one.

SIGNALING SPEED

Signals are normally transmitted on channels as sequences of signal elements of some fixed duration[1]. Each signal element can have a finite value chosen from V distinct signal levels. When $V = 2$, the signal is called a *binary* signal. The duration of each signal determines the signaling speed. This speed is expressed in the unit *Baud*[2] which is defined as the number of signal elements that can be transmitted per second. The signaling speed of a channel, however, is more appropriately measured by the rate at which "information" can be transferred. A *bit*[3] is the smallest unit of information. It has one of two possible values. If one signal level is used to encode one symbol, V discrete signal levels trivially allow the encoding of $\log_2 V$ bits of information per signal element, so

$$1 \quad \text{Baud} \quad = \quad \log_2 V \quad \text{bits per second (bps)}$$

For binary signals the signaling speed in Baud therefore always equals the signaling speed in bps. Note, however, that in the Manchester code a sequence of two signal levels is used to encode a single symbol. For the Manchester codes, therefore, 2 Baud = 1 bps.

It is understandable that these units are easily confused. Note carefully what the difference is between a signaling speed of, for instance, 1200 Baud, 1200 bps, and 1200 char/sec.

SIGNAL PROPAGATION

Information can be transferred over many different signal carriers, ranging from copper wires, coaxial cables, and optical fibers, to satellite links. Each channel has a characteristic behavior and requires a specific coding of the information into electrical or electromagnetic signals. Theoretically, the signal propagation time on each channel will set an upper limit to the maximum obtainable signaling speed. In practice, we will see that other factors, such as "noise" and bandwidth limitations, have a larger limiting effect. For electromagnetic waves, e.g., satellite links and

---

1. A notable exception is the Morse code. The familiar dot and dash signals are of unequal length.

2. The word "Baud" honors the French telegraph operator Emil Baudot who invented a five bit code for telegraph transmissions in 1874.

3. The term "bit" was coined by J.W. Tukey of AT&T Bell Laboratories as a shorthand for 'binary digit' Shannon [1948].

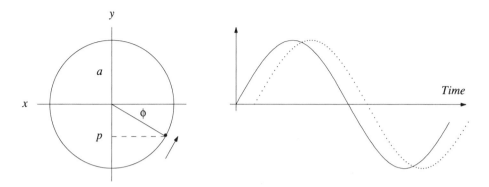

Figure A.4 — Sine Curve

optical fibers, the signal propagation time is roughly $3 \cdot 10^8$ meter/sec. For electrical signals in cables it is about a factor of ten less.

Consider, in Figure A.4, the projection p of an imaginary dot that moves around the circle. On the right it is shown how the projection on the y-axis changes with time when the dot moves with constant velocity: a perfect *sine* curve. One complete traversal of circle produces one "period" or "cycle" of the sine. The maximum "amplitude" of the curve equals the radius of the circle a. If the curve is interpreted as an electrical signal, the velocity of the dot determines the signal "frequency." The unit for measuring frequency is Hertz (Hz). One Hertz equals one cycle per second.

Figure A.4 also shows a dotted curve that would correspond to the projection of a second dot that would follow the first one at a fixed distance, given by the angle ϕ. The angle is called the "phase-shift" between the first and the second signal. Obviously, the maximum phase-shift will be one complete circle traversal, or 2π radians. Formally, a sine curve is described by

$$a \; sin(2\pi ft - \phi)$$

where a is the amplitude, f the frequency, t the time, and ϕ the phase shift.

The sine curve has two properties that make it attractive to theoreticians: it is continuous and it is periodic. The signal in Figure A.5, for instance, is neither, but it does seem to be a more likely representation of a binary bit stream.

FOURIER SERIES

Fortunately, when we study the characteristics of transmission channels we do not have to consider all possible waveforms, like the complicated one in Figure A.5. We can achieve a very good approximation by considering only sine waves. Let us consider an arbitrary periodic signal like the one in Figure A.5. There are two problems with this signal: it is not periodic, and it is not continuous. The first

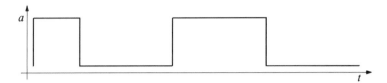

Figure A.5 — Discrete, Non-periodic Signal

problem is easy to fix, at least for modeling purposes. If we want to describe this fragment of the signal elegantly, we can model it as part of a longer, periodic, signal that is obtained by repeating the signal fragment infinitely often. The second problem is a non-problem: the ideal discontinuous square wave is just an abstraction. In practice, any change in signal levels takes a non-zero amount of time, and no discontinuity exists.

Fourier discovered that every continuous periodic signal can be described by a sum of simple sine waves, each with a frequency that is an integer multiple of a "base frequency" f.

$$\sum_{n=1}^{\infty} a_n \sin(2\pi nft - \phi_n)$$

In this formula, a_n is a coefficient that determines the amplitude of the n-th frequency component and ϕ_n is the corresponding phase shift. For aperiodic signals the discrete series of frequency components changes into a continuum of frequencies, but in principle the same type of analysis can be performed.

Figure A.6 gives an example of the approximation of a discrete square wave by the sum of two sine components.

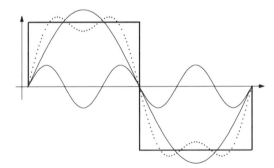

Figure A.6 — Fourier Series

The more sine components we add, the better the approximation. The composite signal is again constructed from one base frequency and a range of "harmonics," of which we have used only the first one. The complete composite is defined by

$$\sum_{n=0}^{\infty} \frac{1}{2n+1} \sin((2n+1)2\pi ft)$$

BANDWIDTH

If we set out signal frequency along the x-axis and amplitude along the y-axis, we can describe this signal in the "frequency domain" as shown in Figure A.7.

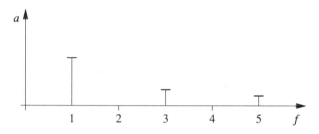

Figure A.7 — Frequency Domain

If we increase the signaling speed, the base frequency and all its harmonics will also increase. Unfortunately, a real transmission channel can only transfer a limited range of signal frequencies. A voice-grade telephone line, for instance, can only transfer signals between 300 Hz and 3400 Hz. If we increase the signaling speed, the higher frequency components may fall outside the signaling band and disappear from the signal transmitted. If we decrease the signaling speed the same may happen with the lower frequency components, having an even more detrimental effect on the signal quality.

The "bandwidth" of the channel determines its quality. Bandwidth is defined as the difference between the highest and the lowest frequency that the channel can reliably transfer. The larger the bandwidth, the more information the channel can carry.

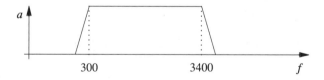

Figure A.8 — Cutoff Frequencies

In general, if we transmit a composite signal over a bandwidth-limited channel some frequency components will be attenuated more than others, and some will be lost completely. The result will be a distorted signal. If we try to transmit the binary signal from Figure A.5 directly as an electrical signal, the distorted signal that will arrive at the receiver may well look like the dotted line in Figure A.6.

Figure A.8 shows the bandwidth of a standard switched telephone line. No signal with a frequency less than 300 Hz will get through it, and no signal with a frequency higher than 3400 Hz. The bandwidth is 3.1 kHz. To transfer an arbitrary binary signal across a telephone channel, it must be translated into frequencies that do pass the channel effortlessly. This process, called *modulation*, is discussed below. For now, it should be noticed that every physical transmission medium has a finite bandwidth, and consequently distorts the signals transmitted on it. An ordinary wire pair has a bandwidth of roughly 250 kHz (see Table A.1). The cutoff frequency is roughly at 200 kHz, with the attenuation of signals of a higher frequency rising exponentially. For coaxial cables the high cutoff frequency is about an order of magnitude higher. The distortion will increase with the signaling speed, simply because the higher data rates cause higher signal frequencies.

A sequence of binary signals will deteriorate from a nice clean square wave to a smooth waveform in which the individual bits may be hard to recognize. The dotted line in Figure A.9 shows the ''decision level'' below which a signal is classified as a zero. The accuracy of the receiver is severely tested by the signal distortion. A small amount of noise can immediately cause classification errors in the receiver. Note also that the presence of the two one signals surrounding the isolated zero signal in Figure A.9, contribute to the distortion of the zero. This ''inter-symbol interference'' becomes worse as the signaling speed goes up, and the ''symbols'' are more closely spaced.

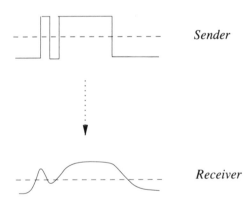

Figure A.9 — Distorted Signal

MODULATION

Modulation is used to adapt the signals to the characteristics of a channel. On a phone line, for instance, we can transmit a binary one as a frequency (a sine) of 1270 Hz, and a zero as 1070 Hz. To make a full-duplex channel, we can choose 2225 Hz and 2025 Hz for the transmission of respectively a one and a zero on the return channel[4]. All these frequencies are within the range that is transmitted with little or no signal attenuation on a phone line (Figure A.8), in order to avoid some of the effects of harmonic distortions on signal quality.

This modulation method is known as *frequency shift keying*, or also simply as *frequency modulation*. As we noted earlier, not too many channels can transmit DC signals conveniently. A balanced, or AC, signal can survive the damage done by the channel much better. If we take a standard sine wave as a basic carrier signal to transmit the data, there are three different ways in which we can change (modulate) that carrier to encode the information. We can use the data signal to vary the carrier's

○ Amplitude
○ Frequency
○ Phase angle

Amplitude modulation for a binary signal would be achieved if we chose two representative amplitudes, e.g., 5 Volts and 10 Volts, to encode binary data. The frequency transmitted is constant, and can be chosen in the middle of the band of frequencies that is accepted by the channel. Any noise on the channel, however, is added to the signal as transmitted and can cause bit errors. Signal attenuation, especially time dependent variations in attenuations can cause extra errors.

Frequency modulation is more robust against noise and direct attenuation of the signal. But now, frequency dependent propagation delays and subtle frequency interference patterns caused by echo and cross talk can cause problems (see below). By using multiple frequencies, however, it is easy to increase the signaling speed in bits per second, for a given baud rate.

The third method, using phase shift keying, or phase modulation, is the most complicated one of the three. Every signal element is now encoded by a phase shift from the previous signal element. In these *quadrature amplitude modulation* techniques (Figure A.10) a combination of amplitude and phase modulation is used. A simple version of this uses four different phase shifts: at 90° increments: 45°, 135°,

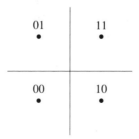

Figure A.10 — Quadrature Amplitude Modulation

---

4. These are in fact the frequencies used on a 300 Baud Bell 108 modem.

225°, and 315°. Since this is a one out of four choice, every new symbol now encodes two bits of information, and the data rate in bits per second will be twice the data rate measured in Baud.

DISTORTION

A signal transmitted on a bandwidth-limited channel incurs a frequency-dependent attenuation. This type of signal distortion is a linear distortion. It can be measured and can, to an extent, be compensated for with special filters that flatten the response curve in the frequency domain.

The signal propagation time can be different for each frequency component in a composite signal. This causes an unintended phase shift between harmonics: the higher frequencies usually travel faster than the others. For a given channel, this phase distortion can also be corrected with special filters.

Transmission channels can also add new waveforms of varying frequencies to a signal. These non-linear distortions can be completely unrelated to the original signal and are much harder to counter.

Signal echoes are an example of non-linear distortions. Wherever there is a sudden change of impedance in the channel, e.g., at the terminals, the signal may bounce back onto the line and travel in the opposite direction, distorting the original signal. A similar type of non-linear distortion is caused by cross-talk. The distortion comes from other channels that are physically close enough to cause shadow signals by electromagnetic induction. In modulated signals the same type of problem can occur as inter-modulation noise.

Still more drastic causes of error are electric spikes and sparks: short, powerful, and unpredictable electric discharges. They can be caused by switches, engines, or simply by spontaneous discharges in the atmosphere. They are hard to avoid, other than by thorough insulation.

NYQUIST's SAMPLING THEOREM

The relation between signaling speed and bandwidth was first studied by H. Nyquist in 1924. He showed that if samples are taken from an arbitrary signal that is transmitted across a channel with a bandwidth B, the original signal can be completely reconstructed if at least $2B$ samples per second are taken. This *sampling theorem* can be used to determine the maximum signaling speed. $2B$ samples can maximally define $2B$ different signal elements. The maximum signaling speed on a channel with a bandwidth of B Hz is then

$$2B \, \log_2 V \quad \text{bps}$$

According to this estimate, the signaling speed can be increased arbitrarily by increasing the number of signal values V. Below we will see that there is yet another factor that limits the signaling speed: noise.

NOISE

Noise is a fundamental and unavoidable cause of signal distortion. Thermal noise is caused by thermal fluctuations of electrons in conductors. It has no preference for any particular frequency: it is equally present in all. It is therefore sometimes referred to as *white noise*. An important measure for the quality of a signal is the signal-to-noise ratio.

The strength, or power, of a signal is expressed in watts (energy per second). Signal ratios are most conveniently defined in *decibel*. If P_1 and P_2 give the power of two signals in watts, then

$$10 \log_{10} \frac{P_1}{P_2} \quad \text{dB}$$

is their ratio in decibels. Decibels are used, for instance, to express the signal attenuation on a channel. If R_1 is the signal attenuation on one channel in dB, and R_2 is the attenuation on another channel, the combined loss if both channels are used in series will simply be $R_1 + R_2$.

SHANNON-HARTLEY LIMIT

In 1948, Claude E. Shannon studied the precise effect of the signal-to-noise ratio on data transmission. He showed, for instance, that the maximum signaling speed in on a channel with bandwidth B and signal-to-noise ratio S/N, with S and N in watts, is

$$C = B \log_2 (1 + \frac{S}{N}) \quad \text{bps}$$

This result is known as the Shannon-Hartley limit. C is called the channel capacity. For a telephone line we have $B = 3100$ Hz and a signal-to-noise ratio of 30 dB (1000:1), giving a maximum signaling speed of 30 Kbit/sec. Above this limit is in general not possible to distinguish the signal transmitted from the background noise: the information content of the signal is too low.

Figure A.11 shows the values that can be calculated from the Shannon-Hartley limit for a telephone line, for signal-to-noise ratios from 1 to 30 dB. The dotted line shows the asymptote $B \log_2 (S/N)$. Signaling speeds above the drawn line cannot be realized, not even with the most clever encoding of data one can imagine.

For *binary* signals the Nyquist rate of *2B* bps (about 6 Kbit/sec) can be achieved, theoretically, for a signal-to-noise ratio of only 2.5 dB.

To even approach the Shannon-Hartley limit we must make optimal use of statistical information about the data to be transmitted. The transfer of English text, for instance, can be optimized by taking the frequency of occurrence of certain letters and letter combinations into account, assigning the shortest code to the most frequent ones.

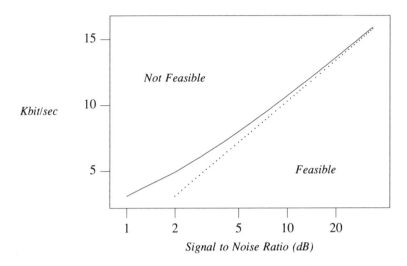

Figure A.11 — Shannon-Hartley Limit

The Nyquist rate for a bandwidth-limited channel was $2B$, or, for $B = 3100$ Hz, 6200 Baud. This means that to realize a signaling speed of 30 Kbit/sec we must also use 32 different signal levels: it cannot be realized with a binary signal.

In practice, the signaling speeds that are used are much lower than both the Nyquist and the Shannon-Hartley limit. One reason is that all other causes of distortion (echo, cross-talk, non-linear distortions, and so on) are not taken into account in these results. Furthermore, it is not always worthwhile or possible to include very elaborate coding schemes that can truly optimize the transmission rates. In practice the maximum signaling speed on voice-grade phone lines is not higher than 1200 to 2400 Baud.

The simplest way to obtain a higher signaling speed on a bandwidth-limited channel is, of course, to increase the bandwidth. This is precisely what the phone company does with the new *voice over data* (Co-Lan) services on specially equipped telephone lines, offering both normal phone service and simultaneous duplex data transfers at signaling speeds up to 19.2 Kbit/sec.

OVERVIEW

A signal that is transmitted on a physical channel can be affected by two main types of distortion:

○ The transformation of the original signal
○ The addition of information unrelated to the original signal

Examples of the first type of distortion are frequency dependent attenuation, and the loss of high and low frequency signal components due to bandwidth limitations.

Examples of the second type of distortion are noise, echoes, crosstalk, and interference patterns caused by non-linear signal distortions.

The effect of the first type of distortion can be reduced by using proper data encoding, modulation, and signal filtering techniques.

Typical data and error rates for three common types of physical media are given in Table A.1.

Table A.1

	Twisted Pair	Coaxial Cable	Optical Fiber
Data Rate in Mbps	10	100	1000
Bit Error Rate	10^{-5}	10^{-6}	10^{-9}
Bandwidth	250 kHz	350 MHz	1 GHz

Note, however, that many other factors besides bandwidth affect the data and error rates: the particular method of data encoding used, the length of the data line and hence its susceptibility to noise, echoes, cross-talk, non-linear distortions, etc. For a twisted pair cable, for instance, the quoted rate of 10 Mbps holds for a line length up to about 30 ft, for "balanced transmissions" (for example, with a Manchester encoding). At 300 ft, the data rate drops to 1 Mbps; at 3000 ft it drops to 100 Kbit/sec. Transmission at 1 Mbps on a 3000 ft twisted pair cable, therefore, requires signal regenerators (repeaters).

BIBLIOGRAPHIC NOTES

A detailed study of line characteristics and data transmission theory is given in Bennet and Davey [1965]. An excellent tutorial on modems, data lines and protocol standards is McNamara [1982]; a well recommended practical reference book. An application oriented treatment of data transmission techniques is presented in Tugal and Tugal [1982]. Other solid treatments of data transmission theory and techniques can be found in Bertsekas and Gallager [1987], [Stallings '85], and, of course, Tanenbaum [1981, 1988]. A pleasant introduction to some of the details of data transmission can also be found in Byte [1989].

FLOW CHART LANGUAGE **B**

The flow chart language used in Part I is based on a small subset of the CCITT Specification and Description Language SDL, CCITT [1988], Rockstrom and Saracco [1982], SDL [1987], Saracco, Smith and Reed [1989]. There are a few deviations that bring its semantics closer to that of the PROMELA language discussed in Chapters 5, 6 and Appendix C.

Each self-contained flow chart defines a process that, at least conceptually, is executed concurrently with all other similarly defined processes. Each flow chart has one entry point that is labeled either with a process name or with the symbol *start*.

As in a traditional flow chart, the actions of a process are specified with symbols of various shapes linked by directed arcs. Six different types of symbols are used, as illustrated in Figure B.1.

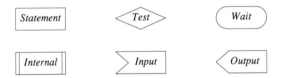

Figure B.1 — Flow Chart Symbols

These symbols represent:

- ○ Statements, e.g, assignments
- ○ Boolean tests, e.g., expressions
- ○ Wait conditions, e.g., receives
- ○ Internal events, e.g., timeouts
- ○ Message inputs and outputs

The boolean tests are evaluated without delay. Wait conditions, however, are used to model process synchronizations. They specify that the executing process does not proceed beyond that point in the program unless a specific condition holds. The two remaining flow chart elements, used for connecting the symbols from Figure B.1, are:

○ Directed arcs

○ Connectors

This gives us a total of eight basic building blocks to construct charts.

The directed arcs indicating the control flow can only converge in connectors, as illustrated in Figure B.2. They can diverge, without connectors, at wait conditions and at boolean tests.

Figure B.2 — Connector and Arcs

Each flow chart process has associated with it an implicit message queue, theoretically of infinite capacity, that is used to store the incoming messages. Messages are appended to the queues in output statements and they are retrieved from the queues in input statements. Message names must uniquely identify the receiving process. Note that a message name can always be extended with the name of a process to guarantee this.

Outputs, statements, wait conditions, internal events, and boolean tests may appear anywhere in a flow chart. Inputs may only follow a wait symbol labeled *receive*. More than one input may appear.

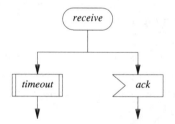

Figure B.3 — Inputs and Timeouts

A wait condition labeled *receive* will delay the executing process until the implicit message queue of that process contains, in its first slot, a message of a type specified in one of the inputs that follow the wait symbol in the flow chart. It is a protocol error if the message in the first slot of the queue is of another type.

A timeout is an internal synchronizing condition that is represented as an internal event. The corresponding condition will always eventually become true. If a timeout event is specified following a wait symbol labeled *receive*, the executing process can abort the wait for an incoming message and continue with the execution of the statements following the timeout.

The wait symbol can also be labeled with an expression. In this case the executing process will be delayed until the expression, when evaluated, yields the boolean value *true* (or any non-zero integer value).

A boolean test must be labeled with an expression, but in this case the expression is evaluated once and the resulting value is used to select an outgoing link with the corresponding label. The process is not delayed. It is an error if the evaluation of the expression yields a value for which there is no matching label on any of the outgoing arcs. The effect of such an error is undefined.

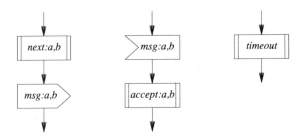

Figure B.4 — Internal Events

Two special internal actions modeling file access are predefined: *next* and *accept*. The notation *next:a,b* indicates the internal retrieval of data items *a* and *b* from an internal data base. Similarly, *accept:a,b* indicates the storage of the data items in an internal data base. The two actions *next* and *accept* include all background processing that is associated with the retrieval and storage of data items, respectively. Their usage is illustrated in Figure B.4.

The use of variables and abstract data types is not restricted by the flow chart language. Similarly, the contents of a statement box can be anything that does not involve wait conditions, receiving or sending messages, timeouts and boolean tests.

For examples, refer to the flow charts in Chapters 2 and 4.

PROMELA LANGUAGE REPORT   C

This appendix is a reference manual for PROMELA, the language for describing protocol validation models introduced in this book. It gives a terse overview of the main syntax requirements of the language. Semantics and usage is more fully explained in Chapters 5 and 6. This manual describes the language proper. It does not cover possible restrictions or extensions of specific implementations. In case of doubt, for instance when you have to find out what the precise effect is of an expression such as $(-10)\%(-9)$ or $(-10)<<(-2)$ on your machine, the quickest way to learn is to execute a little PROMELA test program, like

```
init { printf("%d\t%d\n", (-10)%(-9), (-10)<<(-2)) }
```

using the PROMELA simulator (Chapter 12). The meaning of all binary, arithmetic, and relational operators matches that of ANSI standard C.

LEXICAL CONVENTIONS

There are five classes of tokens: identifiers, keywords, constants, operators and statement separators. Blanks, tabs, newlines, and comments serve only to separate tokens. If more than one interpretation is possible, a token is taken to be the longest string of characters that can constitute a token.

COMMENTS

Any string started with /* and terminated with */ is a comment. Comments cannot be nested.

IDENTIFIERS

An identifier is a single letter or underscore, followed by zero or more letters, digits, or underscores.

KEYWORDS

The following identifiers are reserved for use as keywords:

```
assert        atomic        bit           bool
break         byte          chan          do
```

385

```
fi              goto            if              init
int             len             mtype           never
od              of              printf          proctype
run             short           skip            timeout
```

CONSTANTS

There are three types of constants.

- ○ String constants
- ○ Enumeration constants
- ○ Integer constants

String constants can only be used in `printf` statements.

Enumeration constants can be used to define symbolic names for message types. They can be defined in `mtype` declarations of the type

```
mtype = { namelist }
```

where `namelist` is a comma separated list of symbolic names. Only one `mtype` declaration per program can be used.

An integer constant is a sequence of digits representing a decimal integer. There are no floating point numbers in PROMELA.

EXPRESSIONS

The evaluation of expressions is defined in integer arithmetic. Unsigned data, that is all variables declared with type `bit`, `byte`, or `bool`, are cast to signed integers before being used in expressions. For example, the value of expression $(p-1)$, with p a variable of type byte (unsigned char) and value zero, is the signed value -1 in PROMELA, and not the unsigned equivalent 255. On assignments, however, the type of the destination always prevails. The value -1 is cast to 255 when it is stored in a unsigned variable, but it remains -1 when stored in a signed variable.

The following operators can be used to build expressions.

`+, -, *, /, %,`	arithmetic operators
`>, >=, <, <=, ==, !=,`	relational operators
`&&, ||, !`	logical AND, OR, NOT
`&, |, ~, >>, <<`	C-style bit operators
`!, ?`	send and receive operators
`(), []`	grouping, indexing
`len, run`	special operators

The syntax, semantics, side effects, and machine dependencies of all operators match ANSI standard C. Table C.1 defines the precedence levels. The operators on the first line in the table have the highest precedence. Most operators, including assignment =, take two operands. The boolean negation ! and the unary minus − operator can be both unary and binary, depending on context. The assignment operator takes an expression on the right, and a variable reference on the left:

Table C.1 — Precedence and Associativity

Operators	Associativity
`()` `[]`	left to right
`~` `-` *(unary minus)* `!` *(boolean negation)*	left to right
`*` `/` `%`	left to right
`+` `-`	left to right
`>>` `<<`	left to right
`>` `<` `>=` `<=`	left to right
`==` `!=`	left to right
`&`	left to right
`|`	left to right
`&&`	left to right
`||`	left to right
`!` *(send)* `?` *(receive)*	left to right
`len` `run`	left to right
`=`	right to left

```
varref = expression
```

Unlike C, the assignment operator cannot be used in expressions in PROMELA. The unary operator, `len`, applies to message channels only, and the unary operator `run` applies to process types. Informally, we talk about `len`- or `run`- statements, and similarly about send- and receive-statements, for statements that contain these operators.

REMOTE REFERENCING

Global variables and local variables declared within the same process type can be referred to by name. For instance

```
byte glob;

proctype same()
{       bool loc;

here:   (loc+glob)
}
```

Local variables of other processes can be referred to as follows:

```
proctype other()
{
        assert(same[2].loc > 3)
}
```

Here a process of type `other` refer to the local variable `loc` of the process with `pid` two, i.e., the second process that was instantiated. It is a run-time error if the type of that process is different from the specified type `same`.

The process state of a remote process can be tested with boolean colon expressions. For instance, the condition

```
same[2]:here
```

is true if and only if the process referred to is currently in the state that was labeled here. Remote referencing of variables and control flow states is intended to be used only in assertions and in temporal claims. The language definition, however, does not prevent other applications.

DECLARATIONS

Processes and variables must be declared before they can be used. Variables can be declared either locally, within a process type, or globally. A process can only be declared globally in a proctype declaration. Proctype declarations cannot be nested. Local declarations may appear anywhere in a process body. The scope of a local variable is the complete process body, irrespective where its declaration is placed. It is not accessible, though, until execution has passed the point of declaration at least once. There are six data types:

```
bit, bool, byte, chan, short, int
```

VARIABLES

A variable declaration begins with a keyword indicating the data type of the variable followed by a list of identifier names, each one optionally followed by an initializer.

```
byte name1, name2 = 4, name3;
chan qname; chan a = [3] of { byte };
```

The initializer must be an expression for a variable of a basic data type, and a channel specification for variables of type chan. By default, variables of all types except chan are initialized to zero. Variables of type chan must be initialized explicitly before they can be used for message passing. It is undefined what the result is of using an uninitialized channel variable. Most likely, it causes a fatal runtime error.

Table C.2 summarizes the width and attributes of the five basic data types.

Table C.2 — Basic Data Types

Name	Size (bits)	Usage
bit	1	unsigned
bool	1	unsigned
byte	8	unsigned
short	16	signed
int	32	signed

The names `bit` and `bool` are synonyms for a single bit of information. A `byte` is an unsigned quantity that can store a value between 0 and 255. `Shorts` and `ints` are signed quantities that differ only in the range of values they can hold.

An array of variables is declared as follows:

```
int name1[N];
chan q[M];
```

where `N` and `M` are constants. An array declaration may have an initializer, which initializes all elements of the array. If the array is a channel, one message channel of the given type per array element is created. In the channel initializer

```
chan q[M] = [x] of { types }
```

`M` is a constant, `x` is an expression that specifies the size of the channel, and `types` is a comma separated list of one or more data types that defines the format of each message that can be passed through the channel. All channels are initialized to be empty. Initialized channel identifiers can be passed from one process to another in messages or in `run` statements.

PROCESSES AND TEMPORAL CLAIMS

A process declaration starts with the keyword `proctype` followed by a name, a list of formal parameters enclosed in round braces, and a sequence of statements and local variable declarations. The body of a process declaration is enclosed in parentheses.

```
proctype name( /* parameter declarations */ )
{
        /* declarations and statements */
}
```

The parameter declarations cannot have initializers. One process declaration is required in every PROMELA model: the initial process. It is declared without the keyword `proctype` and without a parameter list.

```
init {
        /* declarations and statements */
}
```

It is the first process running and it has `pid` zero.

A temporal claim starts with the keyword `never` and can contain any PROMELA text

```
never {
        /* declarations and statements */
}
```

There can be at most one temporal claim per PROMELA model. It is used to specify a correctness requirement about the executions of the system specified. The temporal claim specifies a behavior that is claimed to be impossible. The claim will normally only contain conditions, though it is valid to allow the temporal claim to contain variable declarations, atomic sequences, and send and receive statements. To violate a correctness claim, it must be possible to execute one statement, or one atomic sequence of statements, for every statement that is executed by any of the other processes in the model. By using the temporal claim in combination with acceptance-state labels, any linear-time propositional temporal logic formula on the system behavior can be expressed (see Chapter 6).

STATEMENTS

There are twelve types of statements:

assertion	assignment	atomic	break
expression	goto	printf	receive
selection	repetition	send	timeout

Any statement can be preceded by one or more declarations. A statement can only be passed if it is executable. To determine its executability the statement can be evaluated: if evaluation returns a zero value the statement is blocked. In all other cases the statement is executable and can be passed. The evaluation of a compound expression is always indivisible. This means that the statement

```
(a == b && a != b)
```

will always be unexecutable, but the sequence

```
(a == b); (a != b)
```

may be executable in that order.

The act of passing the statement after a successful evaluation is called the "execution" of the statement. There is one *pseudo* statement, skip, which is syntactically equivalent to the condition (1). Skip, is a null statement; it is always executable and has no effect when executed. It may be needed to satisfy syntax requirements.

Goto statements can be used to transfer control to any labeled statement within the same process or procedure. They are always executable. Assignments and declarations are also always executable. Expressions are only executable if they return a non-zero value. That is, the expression 0 (zero) is never executable, and similarly 1 is always executable.

Each statement may be preceded by a label: a name followed by a colon. Each label may be used as the destination of a goto. Three types of labels have predefined meanings in validations: end-state labels, progress-state labels, and acceptance-state labels. The semantics are explained in Chapter 6.

The remaining statements, selection, repetition, send, receive, break, timeout, and atomic sequences, are discussed below.

SELECTION

A selection statement begins with the keyword if, is followed by a list of one or more options and ends with the keyword fi. Every option begins with the flag : : followed by any sequence of statements. One and only one option from a selection statement will be selected for execution. The first statement of an option determines whether the option can be selected or not. If more than one option is executable, one will be selected at random. Thus the language defines nondeterministic machines as defined on page 165.

REPETITION AND BREAK

A repetition or do statement is similar to a selection statement, but is executed repeatedly until either a break statement is executed or a goto jump transfers control outside the cycle. The keywords of the repetition statement are do and od instead of if and fi. The break statement will terminate the innermost repetition statement in which it is executed. The use of a break statement outside a repetition statement is illegal.

ATOMIC SEQUENCE

The keyword atomic introduces an atomic sequence of statements that is to be executed as one indivisible step. The syntax is as follows:

```
atomic { sequence };
```

Logically the sequence of statements is now equivalent to one single statement. It is a run-time error if any statement in an atomic sequence other than the first one is found to be unexecutable. The first statement is called the *guard* of the sequence. If it is executable, so should be the rest of the sequence. In general, therefore, the guard of an atomic sequence is followed only with local assignments and local conditions, but not with any send or receive statements.

SEND

The syntax of a send statement is

```
q!expr
```

where q is the name of a channel, and the evaluation of expression expr returns a value to be appended to the channel. The send statement is not executable (blocks) if the channel is full or does not exist. If more than one value is to be passed from sender to receiver, the expressions are written in a comma-separated list:

```
q!expr1,expr2,expr3
```

Equivalently, this may be written

```
q!expr1(expr2,expr3)
```

RECEIVE

The syntax of the receive statement is

```
q?name
```

where `q` is the name of a channel and `name` is a variable or a constant. If a constant is specified the receive statement is only executable if the channel exists and the oldest message stored in the channel contains the same value. If a variable is specified, the receive statement is executable if the channel exists and contains any message at all. The variable in that case will receive the value of the message that is retrieved. If more than one value is sent per message, the receive statement also take a comma-separated list of variables and constants,

```
q?name1,name2,...
```

which again is syntactically equivalent to

```
q?name1(name2,...)
```

Each constant in this list puts an extra condition on the executability of the receive: it must be matched by the value of the corresponding message field of the message to be retrieved. The variable fields retrieve the values of the corresponding message fields on a receive. It is an error to attempt to receive a value when none was transferred, and vice versa.

Any receive statement can be used as a side-effect free condition by enclosing its parameter list in square braces:

```
q?[name1,name2,...]
q?[name1(name2,...)]
```

The statement is executable (returns a non-zero result) only if the corresponding receive operation is executable, but it has no effect on the variables or the channel.

The only other type of operation allowed on channels is

```
len(varref)
```

where `varref` identifies an instantiated channel. The operation returns the number of messages in the channel specified, or zero if the channel does not exist.

TIMEOUT

The keyword `timeout` represents a condition that becomes true if and only if no other statement in the system is executable. A timeout statement has no effect when executed. Timeouts can be included in expressions.

MACROS AND INCLUDE FILES

The source text of a specification is processed by the C preprocessor for macro-expansion and file inclusions, Kernighan and Ritchie [1978].

PROMELA GRAMMAR

The grammar is listed in BNF-style. Parenthesis are used for grouping. A plus indicates a repetition of one or more times of the last syntactical unit; a star indicates a repetition of zero or more times. Square brackets are used to indicate optional elements. A vertical bar separates options. Literals are quoted. Terminals are written in upper-case, non-terminals in lower-case.

```
program     ::= { unit } +
unit        ::=  PROCTYPE NAME '(' [ decl_lst ] ')' body
            | CLAIM body
            | INIT body
            | one_decl
            | MTYPE ASGN '{' NAME { ',' NAME } * '}'
            | ';'
body        ::=  '{' sequence '}'
sequence    ::=  step { ';' step } *
step        ::=  [ decl_lst ] stmnt
one_decl    ::=  [ TYPE ivar { ',' ivar } * ]
decl_lst    ::=  one_decl { ';' one_decl } *
ivar        ::=  var_dcl | var_dcl ASGN expr | var_dcl ASGN ch_init
ch_init     ::=  '[' CONST ']' OF '{' TYPE { ',' TYPE } * '}'
var_dcl     ::=  NAME [ '[' CONST ']' ]
var_ref     ::=  NAME [ '[' expr ']' ]
stmnt       ::=  var_ref ASGN expr
            | var_ref RCV margs
            | var_ref SND margs
            | PRINT '(' STRING { ',' expr } * ')'
            | ASSERT expr
            | GOTO NAME
            | expr
            | NAME ':' stmnt
            | IF options FI
            | DO options OD
            | BREAK
            | ATOMIC '{' sequence '}'
options     ::= { SEP sequence } +
binop       ::=  '+' | '-' | '*' | '/' | '%' | '&' | '|' | '>' | '<'
            | GE  | LE  | EQ  | NE  | AND | OR | LSHIFT | RSHIFT
unop        ::= '~' | '-' | SND
expr        ::=  '(' expr ')'
            | expr binop expr
            | unop expr
            | RUN NAME '(' [ arg_lst ] ')'
            | LEN '(' var_ref ')'
            | var_ref RCV '[' margs ']'
            | var_ref
            | CONST
            | TIMEOUT
            | var_ref '.' var_ref
            | var_ref ':' NAME
arg_lst     ::=  expr { ',' expr } *
margs       ::=  arg_lst | expr '(' arg_lst ')'
```

SPIN SIMULATOR SOURCE D

The *makefile* for the final version of SPIN, discussed in Chapter 12, is defined as follows.

```
CC=cc            # ANSI C compiler
CFLAGS=-O        # optimizer
YFLAGS=-v -d -D # verbose, debugging
OFILES= spin.o lex.o sym.o vars.o main.o debug.o \
        mesg.o flow.o sched.o run.o dummy.o

spin:   $(OFILES)
        $(CC) $(CFLAGS) -o spin $(OFILES) -lm

%.o:    %.c spin.h
        $(CC) $(CFLAGS) -c $%.c
```

The remainder of this Appendix lists the contents of the 11 source files (see Table D.1) that are required to compile the program, plus one dummy file as temporary place holder for the analysis routines that are added in Chapter 13 and listed in Appendix E. The program should run on any UNIX system with an ANSI-standard compatible C compiler.

Table D.1 – Source File Index

File	Line Number
dummy.c	1901
flow.c	1137
lex.l	194
main.c	487
mesg.c	867
run.c	1378
sched.c	1553
spin.h	1
spin.y	283
sym.c	626
vars.c	717

Table D.2 – Procedures Listed – Appendix D

Procedure	Line	Procedure	Line
a_rcv(q, n, full)	1001	a_snd(q, n)	969
add_el(e, s)	1232	add_seq(n)	1256
addsymbol(r, s)	1717	break_dest()	1348
cast_val(t, v)	791	check_name(s)	268
checkvar(s, n)	745	close_seq()	1158
cnt_mpars(n)	882	complete_rendez()	1686
doq(s, n)	1111	dumpglobals()	815
dumplocal(s)	847	emalloc(n)	582
enable(s, n)	1601	eval(now)	1455
eval_sub(e)	1385	eval_sync(now)	1435
fatal(s1, s2)	573	find_lab(s, c)	1322
findloc(s, n)	1799	gensrc()	1903
get_lab(s)	1287	getglobal(s, n)	769
getlocal(s, n)	1819	getval(s, n)	725
has_lab(e)	1298	hash(s)	634
if_seq(s, tok, lnno)	1209	interprint(n)	1511
ismtype(str)	703	lookup(s)	649
main(argc, argv)	502	make_atomic(s)	1355
match_trail()	1908	mov_lab(z, e, y)	1309
naddsymbol(r, s, k)	1739	new_el(n)	1195
nn(s, v, t, l, r)	592	open_seq(top)	1148
p_talk(e)	1858	pushbreak()	1335
q_is_sync(n)	935	qlen(n)	925
qmake(s)	893	qrecv(n, full)	959
qsend(n)	945	ready(n, p, s)	1588
rem_lab(a, b, c)	607	rem_var(a, b, c)	617
remotelab(n)	1866	remotevar(n)	1878
runnable(s, n)	1574	s_snd(q, n)	1039
sched()	1629	seqlist(s, r)	1184
set_lab(s, e)	1272	setglobal(v, m)	804
setlocal(p, m)	1829	setmtype(m)	686
setparams(r, p, q)	1776	settype(n, t)	670
setval(v, n)	735	sr_mesg(v, j)	1098
sr_talk(n, v, s, a, j, mx, named)	1073	start_claim(n)	1616
talk(e, s)	1846	typck(n, t, s)	1759
typex(n, t)	783	walk_atomic(a, b)	1364
whoruns()	1840	wrapup()	1672
yyerror(s1, s2)	561		

Table D.3 – Procedures Explained – Chapter 12

Procedure	Page	Procedure	Page
a_rcv()	275	a_snd()	274
add_el()	280	add_seq()	280
addsymbol()	289	break_dest()	283
cast_val()	268	check_name()	260
check_name()	269	check_name()	286
checkvar()	267	close_seq()	279
complete_rendez()	276	emalloc()	262
enable()	288	eval()	254
eval()	267	eval()	272
eval()	289	eval()	291
eval_sub()	281	eval_sub()	290
eval_sync()	277	findloc()	291
get_lab()	281	getglobal()	268
getlocal()	291	hash()	263
if_seq()	284	interprint()	271
ismtype()	286	lookup()	262
lookup()	263	main()	293
new_el()	279	nn()	253
nn()	265	open_seq()	279
pushbreak()	282	qlen()	273
qmake()	268	qmake()	273
qrecv()	274	qsend()	274
ready()	287	rem_lab()	292
rem_var()	292	runnable()	287
s_snd()	275	sched()	289
seqlist()	279	set_lab()	281
setglobal()	267	setlocal()	291
setmtype()	286	setparams()	288
setparams()	288		

```
 1 /***** spin: spin.h *****/
 2
 3 /* Copyright (c) 1991 by AT&T Bell Telephone Laboratories, Inc.
 4  * written by Gerard J. Holzmann, as part of the book
 5  * ''Design and Validation of Computer Protocols,''
 6  * Prentice Hall, Englewood Cliffs, NJ, 07632
 7  * Send bug-reports to: gerard@research.att.com
 8  */
 9
10 typedef struct Symbol {
11     char    *name;
12     short   type;           /* variable or chan type     */
13     int     nel;            /* 1 if scalar, >1 if array   */
14     int     *val;           /* runtime value(s), initl 0  */
15     struct Node     *ini;   /* initial value, or chan-def */
16     struct Symbol   *context; /* 0 if global, or procname */
17     struct Symbol   *next;  /* linked list */
18 } Symbol;
19
20 typedef struct Node {
21     int     nval;           /* value attribute            */
22     short   ntyp;           /* node type                  */
23     Symbol *nsym;           /* new attribute              */
24     Symbol *fname;          /* filename of src            */
25     struct SeqList  *seql;  /* list of sequences          */
26     struct Node     *lft, *rgt; /* children in parse tree */
27 } Node;
28
29 typedef struct Queue {
30     short   qid;            /* runtime q index     */
31     short   qlen;           /* nr messages stored  */
32     short   nslots, nflds;  /* capacity, flds/slot */
33     short   *fld_width;     /* type of each field  */
34     int     *contents;      /* the actual buffer   */
35     struct Queue    *nxt;   /* linked list */
36 } Queue;
37
38 typedef struct Element {
39     Node    *n;             /* defines the type & contents */
40     int     seqno;          /* uniquely identifies this el */
41     unsigned char   status; /* used by analyzer generator  */
42     struct SeqList  *sub;   /* subsequences, for compounds */
43     struct Element  *nxt;   /* linked list */
44 } Element;
45
46 typedef struct Sequence {
47     Element *frst;
48     Element *last;
49 } Sequence;
50
51 typedef struct SeqList {
52     Sequence        *this;  /* one sequence */
53     struct SeqList  *nxt;   /* linked list  */
```

```
 54 } SeqList;
 55
 56 typedef struct Label {
 57     Symbol  *s;
 58     Symbol  *c;
 59     Element *e;
 60     struct Label    *nxt;
 61 } Label;
 62
 63 typedef struct Lbreak {
 64     Symbol  *l;
 65     struct Lbreak   *nxt;
 66 } Lbreak;
 67
 68 typedef struct RunList {
 69     Symbol  *n;             /* name           */
 70     int     pid;            /* process id     */
 71     int     maxseq;         /* used by analyzer generator */
 72     Element *pc;            /* current stmnt  */
 73     Symbol  *symtab;        /* local variables */
 74     struct RunList  *nxt;   /* linked list */
 75 } RunList;
 76
 77 typedef struct ProcList {
 78     Symbol  *n;             /* name           */
 79     Node    *p;             /* parameters */
 80     Sequence *s;            /* body           */
 81     struct ProcList *nxt;   /* linked list */
 82 } ProcList;
 83
 84 #define DONE        1               /* status bits of elements */
 85 #define ATOM        2               /* part of an atomic chain */
 86 #define L_ATOM      4               /* last element in a chain */
 87 #define Nhash       255             /* size of hash table */
 88
 89 #define PREDEF      5               /* predefined identifier */
 90 #define BIT   1                 /* data types     */
 91 #define BYTE        8               /* width in bits */
 92 #define SHORT       16
 93 #define INT   32
 94 #define     CHAN    64
 95
 96 #define max(a,b)  (((a)<(b)) ? (b) : (a))
 97
 98 /***** Old-Style C - prototype definitions *****/
 99 extern char *malloc();
100 extern char *memcpy();
101 extern char *memset();
102 extern char *mktemp();
103 extern char *strcat();
104 extern char *strcpy();
105 extern long time();
106 extern void exit();
107 extern int  srand();
```

```
108
109 extern Element      *d_eval_sub();
110 extern Element      *eval_sub();
111 extern Element      *get_lab();
112 extern Element      *huntele();
113 extern Element      *if_seq();
114 extern Element      *new_el();
115 extern Element      *walk_sub();
116 extern Node *nn();
117 extern Node *rem_var();
118 extern Node *rem_lab();
119 extern SeqList      *seqlist();
120 extern Sequence     *close_seq();
121 extern Symbol       *break_dest();
122 extern Symbol       *findloc();
123 extern Symbol       *has_lab();
124 extern Symbol       *lookup();
125 extern char *emalloc();
126 extern void add_el();
127 extern void add_seq();
128 extern void addsymbol();
129 #ifdef DEBUGa
130 extern void auto2();
131 extern void auto_atomic();
132 extern void blurb();
133 extern void check_proc();
134 extern void cnt_mpars();
135 extern void do_var();
136 extern void doglobal();
137 extern void do_init();
138 extern void dolocal();
139 extern void doq();
140 extern void dumpglobals();
141 extern void dumplocal();
142 extern void dumpskip();
143 extern void dumpsrc();
144 extern void end_labs();
145 extern void explain();
146 extern void fatal();
147 extern void genaddproc();
148 extern void genaddqueue();
149 extern void genaddclaim();
150 extern void genheader();
151 extern void genother();
152 extern void gensrc();
153 extern void genunio();
154 extern void lost_trail();
155 extern void main();
156 extern void make_atomic();
157 extern void match_trail();
158 extern void mov_lab();
159 extern void naddsymbol();
160 extern void ncases();
161 extern void ntimes();
```

```
162 extern void open_seq();
163 extern void p_talk();
164 extern void patch_atomic();
165 extern void pushbreak();
166 extern void put_pinit();
167 extern void put_ptype();
168 extern void putname();
169 extern void putnr();
170 extern void putremote();
171 extern void putproc();
172 extern void putprogress();
173 extern void putseq();
174 extern void putskip();
175 extern void putsrc();
176 extern void putstmnt();
177 extern void ready();
178 extern void runnable();
179 extern void sched();
180 extern void set_lab();
181 extern void setmtype();
182 extern void setparams();
183 extern void settype();
184 extern void sr_mesg();
185 extern void sr_talk();
186 extern void start_claim();
187 extern void talk();
188 extern void typ2c();
189 extern void typex();
190 extern void undostmnt();
191 extern void walk_atomic();
192 extern void whoruns();
193
194 /***** spin: lex.l *****/
195
196 %{
197 #include "spin.h"
198 #include "y.tab.h"
199
200 int            lineno=1;
201 unsigned char        in_comment=0;
202 extern Symbol        *Fname;
203
204 #define Token        if (!in_comment) return
205 %}
206
207 %%
208 "/*"        { in_comment=1; }
209 "*/"        { in_comment=0; }
210 \n          { lineno++; }
211 [ \t]       { /* ignore white space */ }
212 [0-9]+      { yylval.val = atoi(yytext); Token CONST; }
213 \#\ [0-9]+\ \"[^\"]*\" {    /* preprocessor directive */
214             int i=1;
215             while (yytext[i] == ' ') i++;
```

```
216                lineno = atoi(&yytext[i])-1;
217                while (yytext[i] != ' ') i++;
218                Fname = lookup(&yytext[i+1]);
219     }
220 \".*\"       { yylval.sym = lookup(yytext); Token STRING; }
221 "never" { yylval.sym = lookup(":never:"); Token CLAIM; }
222 "init"       { yylval.sym = lookup("_init"); Token INIT; }
223 "int"        { yylval.val =    INT; Token TYPE; }
224 "short"      { yylval.val = SHORT; Token TYPE; }
225 "byte"       { yylval.val =   BYTE; Token TYPE; }
226 "bool"       { yylval.val =    BIT; Token TYPE; }
227 "bit"        { yylval.val =    BIT; Token TYPE; }
228 "chan"       { yylval.val =   CHAN; Token TYPE; }
229 "skip"       { yylval.val = 1; Token CONST; }
230 [a-zA-Z_][a-zA-Z_0-9]* { Token check_name(yytext); }
231 "::"         { yylval.val = lineno; Token SEP; }
232 "="          { yylval.val = lineno; Token ASGN; }
233 "!"          { yylval.val = lineno; Token SND; }
234 "?"          { yylval.val = lineno; Token RCV; }
235 "->"         { Token ';'; /* statement separator */ }
236 "<<"         { Token LSHIFT; /* shift bits left   */ }
237 ">>"         { Token RSHIFT; /* shift bits right */ }
238 "<="         { Token     LE; /* less than or equal to */ }
239 ">="         { Token     GE; /* greater than or equal to */ }
240 "=="         { Token     EQ; /* equal to */ }
241 "!="         { Token     NE; /* not equal to */ }
242 "&&"         { Token    AND; /* logical and */ }
243 "||"         { Token     OR; /* logical or */ }
244 .            { Token yytext[0]; }
245 %%
246
247 static struct {
248     char *s;          int tok;
249 } Names[] = {
250     "assert",         ASSERT,
251     "atomic",         ATOMIC,
252     "break",          BREAK,
253     "do",             DO,
254     "fi",             FI,
255     "goto",           GOTO,
256     "if",             IF,
257     "len",            LEN,
258     "mtype",          MTYPE,
259     "od",             OD,
260     "of",             OF,
261     "printf",         PRINT,
262     "proctype",       PROCTYPE,
263     "run",            RUN,
264     "timeout",        TIMEOUT,
265     0,                0,
266 };
267
268 check_name(s)
269     char *s;
```

```
270 {
271     register int i;
272     for (i = 0; Names[i].s; i++)
273             if (strcmp(s, Names[i].s) == 0)
274             {       yylval.val = lineno;
275                     return Names[i].tok;
276             }
277     if (yylval.val = ismtype(s))
278             return CONST;
279     yylval.sym = lookup(s); /* symbol table */
280     return NAME;
281 }
282
283 /***** spin: spin.y *****/
284
285 %{
286 #include "spin.h"
287 #define YYDEBUG     0
288 #define Stop        nn(0,lineno,'@',0,0)
289 extern Symbol      *context;
290 extern int  lineno, u_sync, u_async;
291 char               *claimproc = (char *) 0;
292 %}
293
294 %union{
295         int     val;
296         Node    *node;
297         Symbol  *sym;
298         Sequence *seq;
299         SeqList *seql;
300 }
301
302 %token     <val>    RUN LEN OF
303 %token     <val>    CONST TYPE ASGN
304 %token     <sym>    NAME CLAIM
305 %token     <sym>    STRING INIT
306 %token     <val>    ASSERT
307 %token     <val>    GOTO BREAK MTYPE SEP
308 %token     <val>    IF FI DO OD ATOMIC
309 %token     <val>    SND RCV PRINT TIMEOUT
310 %token     <val>    PROCTYPE
311
312 %type      <sym>    var ivar
313 %type      <node>   expr var_list stmnt
314 %type      <node>   args arg typ_list decl
315 %type      <node>   decl_lst one_decl any_decl
316 %type      <node>   prargs margs varref step ch_init
317 %type      <seql>   options
318 %type      <seq>    option body
319
320 %right              ASGN
321 %left               SND RCV
322 %left               OR
323 %left               AND
```

```
324 %left                  '|'
325 %left                  '&'
326 %left                  EQ NE
327 %left                  '>' '<' GE LE
328 %left                  LSHIFT RSHIFT
329 %left                  '+' '-'
330 %left                  '*' '/' '%'
331 %right                 '~' UMIN NEG
332 %%
333
334 /** PROMELA Grammar Rules **/
335
336 program : units             { sched(); }
337         ;
338 units   : unit | units unit
339         ;
340 unit    : proc
341         | claim
342         | init
343         | one_decl
344         | mtype
345         ;
346 proc    : PROCTYPE NAME     { context = $2; }
347             '(' decl ')'
348         body               { ready($2, $5, $7);
349                              context = (Symbol *) 0;
350                            }
351         ;
352 claim   : CLAIM            { context = $1;
353                              if (claimproc)
354                                yyerror("claim %s redefined",
355                                           claimproc);
356                              claimproc = $1->name;
357                            }
358         body               { ready($1, (Node *) 0, $3);
359                              context = (Symbol *) 0;
360                            }
361         ;
362 init    : INIT             { context = $1; }
363         body               { runnable($3, $1);
364                              context = (Symbol *) 0;
365                            }
366         ;
367 mtype   : MTYPE ASGN '{' args '}' { setmtype($4); }
368         | ';'        /* optional ; as separator of units */
369         ;
370 body    : '{'               { open_seq(1); }
371             sequence       { add_seq(Stop); }
372         '}'                { $$ = close_seq();
373                            }
374         ;
375 sequence: step             { add_seq($1); }
376         | sequence ';' step { add_seq($3); }
377         ;
```

```
378 step    : any_decl stmnt     { $$ = $2; }
379         ;
380 any_decl: /* empty */        { $$ = (Node *) 0; }
381         | one_decl ';' any_decl { $$ = nn(0, 0, ',', $1, $3); }
382         ;
383 one_decl: TYPE var_list       { settype($2, $1); $$ = $2; }
384         ;
385 decl_lst: one_decl            { $$ = nn(0, 0, ',', $1,  0); }
386         | one_decl ';' decl_lst { $$ = nn(0, 0, ',', $1, $3); }
387         ;
388 decl    : /* empty */         { $$ = (Node *) 0; }
389         | decl_lst            { $$ = $1; }
390         ;
391 var_list: ivar                { $$ = nn($1, 0, TYPE,  0,  0); }
392         | ivar ',' var_list   { $$ = nn($1, 0, TYPE,  0, $3); }
393         ;
394 ivar    : var                 { $$ = $1; }
395         | var ASGN expr        { $1->ini = $3; $$ = $1; }
396         | var ASGN ch_init     { $1->ini = $3; $$ = $1; }
397         ;
398 ch_init : '[' CONST ']' OF '{' typ_list '}'
399                               { if ($2) u_async++; else u_sync++;
400                                 cnt_mpars($6);
401                                 $$ = nn(0, $2, CHAN, 0, $6);
402                               }
403         ;
404 var     : NAME                { $1->nel =  1; $$ = $1; }
405         | NAME '[' CONST ']'  { $1->nel = $3; $$ = $1; }
406         ;
407 varref  : NAME                { $$ = nn($1, 0,  NAME,  0,  0); }
408         | NAME '[' expr ']'   { $$ = nn($1, 0,  NAME, $3,  0); }
409         ;
410 stmnt   : varref ASGN expr  { $$ = nn($1->nsym, $2, ASGN, $1, $3); }
411         | varref RCV margs  { $$ = nn($1->nsym, $2, 'r', $1, $3); }
412         | varref SND margs  { $$ = nn($1->nsym, $2, 's', $1, $3); }
413         | PRINT '(' STRING prargs ')' { $$ = nn($3, $1,PRINT, $4, 0); }
414         | ASSERT expr       { $$ = nn(0, $1, ASSERT, $2, 0); }
415         | GOTO NAME         { $$ = nn($2, $1, GOTO, 0, 0); }
416         | expr              { $$ = nn(0, lineno, 'c', $1, 0); }
417         | NAME ':' stmnt    { $$ = nn($1, $3->nval,':',$3, 0); }
418         | IF options FI     { $$ = nn(0, $1, IF, 0, 0);
419                               $$->seql = $2;
420                             }
421         | DO               { pushbreak(); }
422           options OD       { $$ = nn(0, $1, DO, 0, 0);
423                               $$->seql = $3;
424                             }
425         | BREAK             { $$ = nn(break_dest(),$1,GOTO,0,0); }
426         | ATOMIC
427           '{'              { open_seq(0); }
428             sequence
429           '}'              { $$ = nn(0, $1, ATOMIC, 0, 0);
430                              $$->seql = seqlist(close_seq(), 0);
431                              make_atomic($$->seql->this);
```

```
432                                   }
433           ;
434 options : option            { $$ = seqlist($1, 0); }
435         | option options    { $$ = seqlist($1, $2); }
436         ;
437 option  : SEP               { open_seq(0); }
438           sequence          { $$ = close_seq(); }
439         ;
440 expr    : '(' expr ')'              { $$ = $2; }
441         | expr '+' expr            { $$ = nn(0, 0,   '+', $1, $3); }
442         | expr '-' expr            { $$ = nn(0, 0,   '-', $1, $3); }
443         | expr '*' expr            { $$ = nn(0, 0,   '*', $1, $3); }
444         | expr '/' expr            { $$ = nn(0, 0,   '/', $1, $3); }
445         | expr '%' expr            { $$ = nn(0, 0,   '%', $1, $3); }
446         | expr '&' expr            { $$ = nn(0, 0,   '&', $1, $3); }
447         | expr '|' expr            { $$ = nn(0, 0,   '|', $1, $3); }
448         | expr '>' expr            { $$ = nn(0, 0,   '>', $1, $3); }
449         | expr '<' expr            { $$ = nn(0, 0,   '<', $1, $3); }
450         | expr GE expr             { $$ = nn(0, 0,    GE, $1, $3); }
451         | expr LE expr             { $$ = nn(0, 0,    LE, $1, $3); }
452         | expr EQ expr             { $$ = nn(0, 0,    EQ, $1, $3); }
453         | expr NE expr             { $$ = nn(0, 0,    NE, $1, $3); }
454         | expr AND expr            { $$ = nn(0, 0,   AND, $1, $3); }
455         | expr OR  expr            { $$ = nn(0, 0,    OR, $1, $3); }
456         | expr LSHIFT expr         { $$ = nn(0, 0,LSHIFT,$1, $3); }
457         | expr RSHIFT expr         { $$ = nn(0, 0,RSHIFT,$1, $3); }
458         | '~' expr                 { $$ = nn(0, 0,   '~', $2,  0); }
459         | '-' expr %prec UMIN      { $$ = nn(0, 0,  UMIN, $2,  0); }
460         | SND expr %prec NEG       { $$ = nn(0, 0,   '!', $2,  0); }
461         | RUN NAME '(' args ')'    { $$ = nn($2,$1, RUN, $4,  0); }
462         | LEN '(' varref ')'       { $$ = nn($3->nsym, $1, LEN, $3,  0); }
463         | varref RCV '[' margs ']' { $$ = nn($1->nsym,$2,'R',$1,$4); }
464         | varref                   { $$ = $1; }
465         | CONST                    { $$ = nn(0,$1,  CONST,  0,  0); }
466         | TIMEOUT                  { $$ = nn(0,$1,TIMEOUT,  0,  0); }
467         | NAME '[' expr ']' '.' varref { $$ = rem_var($1, $3, $6); }
468         | NAME '[' expr ']' ':' NAME   { $$ = rem_lab($1, $3, $6); }
469         ;
470 typ_list: TYPE                     { $$ = nn(0, 0, $1, 0,  0); }
471         | TYPE ',' typ_list        { $$ = nn(0, 0, $1, 0, $3); }
472         ;
473 args    : /* empty */              { $$ = (Node *) 0; }
474         | arg                      { $$ = $1; }
475         ;
476 arg     : expr                     { $$ = nn(0, 0, ',', $1,  0); }
477         | expr ',' arg             { $$ = nn(0, 0, ',', $1, $3); }
478         ;
479 prargs  : /* empty */              { $$ = (Node *) 0; }
480         | ',' arg                  { $$ = $2; }
481         ;
482 margs   : arg                      { $$ = $1; }
483         | expr '(' arg ')'         { $$ = nn(0, 0, ',', $1, $3); }
484         ;
485 %%
```

```
486
487 /***** spin: main.c *****/
488
489 #include <stdio.h>
490 #include "spin.h"
491 #include "y.tab.h"
492
493 extern int lineno;
494 FILE        *yyin;
495 Symbol      *Fname;
496 int verbose = 0;
497 int analyze = 0;
498 int s_trail = 0;
499 int m_loss  = 0;
500
501 void
502 main(argc, argv)
503     char *argv[];
504 {
505     Symbol *s;
506     int T = (int) time((long *)0);
507
508     while (argc > 1 && argv[1][0] == '-')
509     {       switch (argv[1][1]) {
510             case 'a': analyze  = 1; break;
511             case 'g': verbose +=  1; break;
512             case 'l': verbose +=  2; break;
513             case 'm': m_loss   = 1; break;
514             case 'n': T = atoi(&argv[1][2]); break;
515             case 'p': verbose +=  4; break;
516             case 'r': verbose +=  8; break;
517             case 's': verbose += 16; break;
518             case 'v': verbose += 32; break;
519             case 't': s_trail  = 1; break;
520             default : printf("use: spin -[agmlpqrst] [-nN] file\n");
521                       printf("\t-a produce an analyzer\n");
522                       printf("\t-g print all global variables\n");
523                       printf("\t-l print all local variables\n");
524                       printf("\t-m lose msgs sent to full queues\n");
525                       printf("\t-nN seed for random nr generator\n");
526                       printf("\t-p print all statements\n");
527                       printf("\t-r print receive events\n");
528                       printf("\t-s print send events\n");
529                       printf("\t-v verbose, more warnings\n");
530                       printf("\t-t follow a simulation trail\n");
531                       exit(1);
532             }
533             argc--, argv++;
534     }
535     if (argc > 1)
536     {       char outfile[17], cmd[64];
537             Fname = lookup(argv[1]);
538             mktemp(strcpy(outfile, "/tmp/spin.XXXXXX"));
539             sprintf(cmd, "/lib/cpp %s > %s", argv[1], outfile);
```

```
540              if (system(cmd))
541              {       unlink(outfile);
542                      exit(1);
543              } else if (!(yyin = fopen(outfile, "r")))
544              {       printf("cannot open %s\n", outfile);
545                      exit(1);
546              }
547              unlink(outfile);
548      } else
549              Fname = lookup("<stdin>");
550      srand(T);
551      s = lookup("_p"); s->type = PREDEF;
552      yyparse();
553      exit(0);
554 }
555
556 yywrap()     /* dummy routine */
557 {
558      return 1;
559 }
560
561 yyerror(s1, s2)
562      char *s1, *s2;
563 {
564      printf("spin: %s line %d: ", Fname->name, lineno);
565      if (s2)
566              printf(s1, s2);
567      else
568              printf(s1);
569      printf("\n"); fflush(stdout);
570 }
571
572 void
573 fatal(s1, s2)
574      char *s1, *s2;
575 {
576      yyerror(s1, s2);
577      fflush(stdout);
578      exit(1);
579 }
580
581 char *
582 emalloc(n)
583 {    char *tmp = malloc(n);
584
585      if (!tmp)
586              fatal("not enough memory", (char *)0);
587      memset(tmp, 0, n);
588      return tmp;
589 }
590
591 Node *
592 nn(s, v, t, l, r)
593      Symbol *s;
```

```
594        Node *l, *r;
595   {
596        Node *n = (Node *) emalloc(sizeof(Node));
597        n->nval = v;
598        n->ntyp = t;
599        n->nsym = s;
600        n->fname = Fname;
601        n->lft  = l;
602        n->rgt  = r;
603        return n;
604   }
605
606   Node *
607   rem_lab(a, b, c)
608        Symbol *a, *c;
609        Node *b;
610   {
611        return  nn(0, 0, EQ,
612                nn(lookup("_p"), 0, 'p', nn(a, 0, '?', b, 0), 0),
613                nn(c, 0, 'q', nn(a, 0, NAME, 0, 0), 0));
614   }
615
616   Node *
617   rem_var(a, b, c)
618        Symbol *a;
619        Node *b, *c;
620   {
621        Node *tmp;
622        tmp = nn(a, 0, '?', b, 0);
623        return nn(c->nsym, 0, 'p', tmp, c->lft);
624   }
625
626   /***** spin: sym.c *****/
627
628   #include "spin.h"
629   #include "y.tab.h"
630
631   Symbol      *symtab[Nhash+1];
632   Symbol      *context = (Symbol *) 0;
633
634   hash(s)
635        char *s;
636   {
637        int h=0;
638
639        while (*s)
640        {       h += *s++;
641                h <<= 1;
642                if (h&(Nhash+1))
643                        h |= 1;
644        }
645        return h&Nhash;
646   }
647
```

```
648 Symbol *
649 lookup(s)
650     char *s;
651 {
652     Symbol *sp;
653     int h=hash(s);
654
655     for (sp = symtab[h]; sp; sp = sp->next)
656             if (strcmp(sp->name, s) == 0 && sp->context == context)
657                     return sp;                      /* found */
658     sp = (Symbol *) emalloc(sizeof(Symbol));        /* add */
659     sp->name = (char *) emalloc(strlen(s) + 1);
660     strcpy(sp->name, s);
661     sp->nel = 1;
662     sp->context = context;
663     sp->next = symtab[h];
664     symtab[h] = sp;
665
666     return sp;
667 }
668
669 void
670 settype(n, t)
671     Node *n;
672 {
673     while (n)
674     {       if (n->nsym->type)
675                 yyerror("redeclaration of '%s'", n->nsym->name);
676             n->nsym->type = t;
677             if (n->nsym->nel <= 0)
678                 yyerror("bad array size for '%s'", n->nsym->name);
679             n = n->rgt;
680     }
681 }
682
683 Node *Mtype = (Node *) 0;
684
685 void
686 setmtype(m)
687     Node *m;
688 {
689     Node *n = m;
690     if (Mtype)
691             yyerror("mtype redeclared", (char *)0);
692
693     Mtype = n;
694     while (n)        /* syntax check */
695     {       if (!n->lft || !n->lft->nsym
696             ||  (n->lft->ntyp != NAME)
697             ||   n->lft->lft)         /* indexed variable */
698                     fatal("bad mtype definition", (char *)0);
699             n = n->rgt;
700     }
701 }
```

```
702
703 ismtype(str)
704     char *str;
705 {
706     Node *n;
707     int cnt = 1;
708
709     for (n = Mtype; n; n = n->rgt)
710     {       if (strcmp(str, n->lft->nsym->name) == 0)
711                     return cnt;
712             cnt++;
713     }
714     return 0;
715 }
716
717 /***** spin: vars.c *****/
718
719 #include <stdio.h>
720 #include "spin.h"
721 #include "y.tab.h"
722
723 extern RunList      *X;
724
725 getval(s, n)
726     Symbol *s;
727 {
728     if (s->context && s->type)
729             return getlocal(s, n);
730     if (!s->type)   /* not declared locally */
731             s = lookup(s->name); /* try global */
732     return getglobal(s, n);
733 }
734
735 setval(v, n)
736     Node *v;
737 {
738     if (v->nsym->context && v->nsym->type)
739             return setlocal(v, n);
740     if (!v->nsym->type)
741             v->nsym = lookup(v->nsym->name);
742     return setglobal(v, n);
743 }
744
745 checkvar(s, n)
746     Symbol *s;
747 {
748     int i;
749
750     if (n >= s->nel || n < 0)
751     {       yyerror("array indexing error, '%s'", s->name);
752             return 0;
753     }
754     if (s->type == 0)
755     {       yyerror("undecl var '%s' (assuming int)", s->name);
```

```
756                 s->type = INT;
757     }
758     if (s->val == (int *) 0)          /* uninitialized */
759     {       s->val = (int *) emalloc(s->nel*sizeof(int));
760             for (i = 0; i < s->nel; i++)
761             {       if (s->type != CHAN)
762                             s->val[i] = eval(s->ini);
763                     else
764                             s->val[i] = qmake(s);
765     }       }
766     return 1;
767 }
768
769 getglobal(s, n)
770     Symbol *s;
771 {
772     int i;
773     if (strcmp(s->name, "_p") == 0)
774             return (X && X->pc)?X->pc->seqno:0;
775     if (s->type == 0 && X && (i = find_lab(s, X->n)))
776             return i;
777     if (checkvar(s, n))
778             return cast_val(s->type, s->val[n]);
779     return 0;
780 }
781
782 void
783 typex(n, t)
784     Node *n;
785 {
786     if (n->ntyp == NAME && n->nsym->type != t
787     && (t == CHAN || n->nsym->type == CHAN))
788             yyerror("type clash (chan) in mesg pars");
789 }
790
791 cast_val(t, v)
792 {   int i=0; short s=0; unsigned char u=0;
793
794     if (t == INT || t == CHAN) i = v;
795     else if (t == SHORT) s = (short) v;
796     else if (t == BYTE)  u = (unsigned char)v;
797     else if (t == BIT)   u = (unsigned char)(v&1);
798
799     if (v != i+s+u)
800             yyerror("value %d truncated in assignment", v);
801     return (int)(i+s+u);
802 }
803
804 setglobal(v, m)
805     Node *v;
806 {
807     int n = eval(v->lft);
808
809     if (checkvar(v->nsym, n))
```

```
810                 v->nsym->val[n] = m;
811     return 1;
812 }
813
814 void
815 dumpglobals()
816 {   extern Symbol *symtab[Nhash+1];
817     register Symbol *sp;
818     register int i, j, k, n, m;
819
820     for (i = 0; i <= Nhash; i++)
821     for (sp = symtab[i]; sp; sp = sp->next)
822     {       if (!sp->type || sp->context)
823                 continue;
824             for (j = 0, m = -1; j < sp->nel; j++)
825             {       if (sp->type == CHAN)
826                     {       doq(sp, j);
827                             k = 0;
828                             continue;
829                     }
830                     n = getglobal(sp, j);
831                     if (j == 0 || n != k)
832                     {       if (m != j-1)
833                                     printf("\t\t...\n");
834                             if (sp->nel > 1)
835                               printf("\t\t%s[%d] = %d\n",
836                                     sp->name, j, n);
837                             else
838                               printf("\t\t%s = %d\n",
839                                     sp->name, n);
840                             m = j;
841                     }
842                     k = n;
843     }       }
844 }
845
846 void
847 dumplocal(s)
848     Symbol *s;
849 {
850     Symbol *z;
851     int i;
852
853     for (z = s; z; z = z->next)
854     for (i = 0; i < z->nel; i++)
855     {       if (z->type == CHAN)
856                 doq(z, i);
857             else
858             {       if (z->nel > 1)
859                     printf("\t\t%s[%d] = %d\n",
860                     z->name, i, getval(z,i));
861                 else
862                     printf("\t\t%s = %d\n",
863                     z->name, getval(z,0));
```

```
864      }          }
865 }
866
867 /***** spin: mesg.c *****/
868
869 #include <stdio.h>
870 #include "spin.h"
871 #include "y.tab.h"
872
873 #define MAXQ         2500              /* default max # queues  */
874
875 extern       int lineno, verbose;
876 Queue        *qtab = (Queue *) 0;      /* linked list of queues */
877 Queue        *ltab[MAXQ];              /* linear list of queues */
878 int nqs=0;
879 int Mpars=0;         /* max nr of message parameters  */
880
881 void
882 cnt_mpars(n)
883     Node *n;
884 {
885     Node *m;
886     int i=0;
887
888     for (m=n; m; m = m->rgt)
889             i++;
890     Mpars = max(Mpars, i);
891 }
892
893 qmake(s)
894     Symbol *s;
895 {
896     Node *m;
897     Queue *q;
898     int i; extern int analyze;
899
900     if (!s->ini)
901             return 0;
902     if (s->ini->ntyp != CHAN)
903             fatal("bad channel initializer for %s\n", s->name);
904     if (nqs >= MAXQ)
905             fatal("too many queues (%s)", s->name);
906
907     q = (Queue *) emalloc(sizeof(Queue));
908     q->qid = ++nqs;
909     q->nslots = s->ini->nval;
910     for (m = s->ini->rgt; m; m = m->rgt)
911             q->nflds++;
912     i = max(1, q->nslots);  /* 0-slot qs get 1 slot minimum */
913
914     q->contents  = (int *) emalloc(q->nflds*i*sizeof(int));
915     q->fld_width = (short *) emalloc(q->nflds*sizeof(short));
916     for (m = s->ini->rgt, i = 0; m; m = m->rgt)
917             q->fld_width[i++] = m->ntyp;
```

```
918        q->nxt = qtab;
919        qtab = q;
920        ltab[q->qid-1] = q;
921
922        return q->qid;
923 }
924
925 qlen(n)
926        Node *n;
927 {
928        int whichq = eval(n->lft)-1;
929
930        if (whichq < MAXQ && whichq >= 0 && ltab[whichq])
931                return ltab[whichq]->qlen;
932        return 0;
933 }
934
935 q_is_sync(n)
936        Node *n;
937 {
938        int whichq = eval(n->lft)-1;
939
940        if (whichq < MAXQ && whichq >= 0 && ltab[whichq])
941                return (ltab[whichq]->nslots == 0);
942        return 0;
943 }
944
945 qsend(n)
946        Node *n;
947 {
948        int whichq = eval(n->lft)-1;
949
950        if (whichq < MAXQ && whichq >= 0 && ltab[whichq])
951        {       if (ltab[whichq]->nslots > 0)
952                        return a_snd(ltab[whichq], n);
953                else
954                        return s_snd(ltab[whichq], n);
955        }
956        return 0;
957 }
958
959 qrecv(n, full)
960        Node *n;
961 {
962        int whichq = eval(n->lft)-1;
963
964        if (whichq < MAXQ && whichq >= 0 && ltab[whichq])
965                return a_rcv(ltab[whichq], n, full);
966        return 0;
967 }
968
969 a_snd(q, n)
970        Queue *q;
971        Node *n;
```

```
972  {
973      Node *m; extern int m_loss;
974      int i = q->qlen*q->nflds;        /* q offset */
975      int j = 0;                       /* q field# */
976
977      if (q->nslots > 0 && q->qlen >= q->nslots)
978              return m_loss;  /* q is full */
979
980      for (m = n->rgt; m && j < q->nflds; m = m->rgt, j++)
981      {       typex(m->lft, q->fld_width[j]);
982              q->contents[i+j] =
983                      cast_val(q->fld_width[j], eval(m->lft));
984              if (verbose&16)
985                      sr_talk(n, eval(m->lft), "Send", "->", j,
986                          q->nflds, m->lft && m->lft->ntyp == CONST);
987      }
988      if (verbose&16)
989      {       for (i = j; i < q->nflds; i++)
990                      sr_talk(n, 0, "Send", "->", i, q->nflds, 0);
991              if (verbose&32)
992              { if (j < q->nflds)
993                      printf("\twarning: missing params in send\n");
994                if (m)
995                      printf("\twarning: too many params in send\n");
996      }       }
997      q->qlen++;
998      return 1;
999  }
1000
1001 a_rcv(q, n, full)
1002    Queue *q;
1003    Node *n;
1004 {
1005    Node *m;
1006    int j, k;
1007    if (q->qlen == 0)
1008            return 0;        /* q is empty */
1009
1010    for (m = n->rgt, j=0; m && j < q->nflds; m = m->rgt, j++)
1011    {       if (m->lft->ntyp == CONST)
1012            {       if (q->contents[j] != m->lft->nval)
1013                            return 0;        /* no match */
1014            } else if (m->lft->ntyp != NAME)
1015                    fatal("bad arg in receive", (char *)0);
1016    }
1017    if (verbose&8 && verbose&32)
1018    {       if (j < q->nflds)
1019                printf("\twarning: missing params in next recv\n");
1020            else if (m)
1021                printf("\twarning: too many params in next recv\n");
1022    }
1023    for (m = n->rgt, j=0; j<q->nflds; m = (m)?m->rgt:m, j++)
1024    {       if (verbose&8)
1025                    sr_talk(n, q->contents[j], "Recv", "<-", j,
```

```
1026                            q->nflds, m && m->lft->ntyp == CONST);
1027               if (m && m->lft->ntyp == NAME)
1028               {       typex(m->lft, q->fld_width[j]);
1029                       setval(m->lft, q->contents[j]);
1030               }
1031               for (k = 0; full && k < q->qlen-1; k++)
1032                       q->contents[k*q->nflds+j] =
1033                           q->contents[(k+1)*q->nflds+j];
1034       }
1035       if (full) q->qlen--;
1036       return 1;
1037 }
1038
1039 s_snd(q, n)
1040     Queue *q;
1041     Node *n;
1042 {
1043     Node *m;
1044     int i, j = 0;    /* q field# */
1045
1046     for (m = n->rgt; m && j < q->nflds; m = m->rgt, j++)
1047             q->contents[j] = cast_val(q->fld_width[j], eval(m->lft));
1048
1049     q->qlen = 1;
1050     if (!complete_rendez())
1051     {       q->qlen = 0;
1052             return 0;
1053     }
1054     if (verbose&16)
1055     {       m = n->rgt;
1056             for (j = 0; m && j < q->nflds; m = m->rgt, j++)
1057             {       typex(m->lft, q->fld_width[j]);
1058                     sr_talk(n, eval(m->lft), "Sent", "->", j,
1059                       q->nflds, m->lft && m->lft->ntyp == CONST);
1060             }
1061             for (i = j; i < q->nflds; i++)
1062                     sr_talk(n, 0, "Sent", "->", i, q->nflds, 0);
1063             if (verbose&32)
1064             {       if (j < q->nflds)
1065                     printf("\twarning: missing params in send\n");
1066                     if (m)
1067                     printf("\twarning: too many params in send\n");
1068     }       }
1069     return 1;
1070 }
1071
1072 void
1073 sr_talk(n, v, s, a, j, mx, named)
1074     Node *n;
1075     char *s, *a;
1076 {
1077     if (j == 0)
1078     {       whoruns();
1079             printf("line %3d, %s ", n->nval, s);
```

```
1080    } else
1081            printf(",");
1082    sr_mesg(v, named);
1083
1084    if (j == mx-1)
1085    {       printf("\t%s queue %d", a, eval(n->lft));
1086            if (n->nsym->type == CHAN)
1087                    printf(" (%s", n->nsym->name);
1088            else
1089                    printf(" (%s", lookup(n->nsym->name)->name);
1090            if (n->lft->lft)
1091                    printf("[%d]", eval(n->lft->lft));
1092            printf(")\n");
1093    }
1094    fflush(stdout);
1095 }
1096
1097 void
1098 sr_mesg(v, j)
1099 {  extern Node *Mtype;
1100    int cnt = 1;
1101    Node *n;
1102    for (n = Mtype; n && j; n = n->rgt, cnt++)
1103            if (cnt == v)
1104            {       printf("%s", n->lft->nsym->name);
1105                    return;
1106            }
1107    printf("%d", v);
1108 }
1109
1110 void
1111 doq(s, n)
1112    Symbol *s;
1113 {
1114    Queue *q;
1115    int j, k;
1116    if (!s->val)    /* uninitialized queue */
1117            return;
1118    for (q = qtab; q; q = q->nxt)
1119    if (q->qid == s->val[n])
1120    {       if (s->nel != 1)
1121              printf("\t\tqueue %d (%s[%d]): ", q->qid, s->name, n);
1122            else
1123              printf("\t\tqueue %d (%s): ", q->qid, s->name);
1124            for (k = 0; k < q->qlen; k++)
1125            {       printf("[");
1126                    for (j = 0; j < q->nflds; j++)
1127                    {       if (j > 0) printf(",");
1128                            sr_mesg(q->contents[k*q->nflds+j], j==0);
1129                    }
1130                    printf("]");
1131            }
1132            printf("\n");
1133            break;
```

```
1134    }
1135 }
1136
1137 /***** spin: flow.c *****/
1138
1139 #include "spin.h"
1140 #include "y.tab.h"
1141
1142 Label       *labtab = (Label *) 0;
1143 Lbreak      *breakstack = (Lbreak *) 0;
1144 SeqList     *cur_s = (SeqList *) 0;
1145 int         Elcnt, break_id=0;
1146
1147 void
1148 open_seq(top)
1149 {   SeqList *t;
1150     Sequence *s = (Sequence *) emalloc(sizeof(Sequence));
1151
1152     t = seqlist(s, cur_s);
1153     cur_s = t;
1154     if (top) Elcnt = 1;
1155 }
1156
1157 Sequence *
1158 close_seq()
1159 {   Sequence *s = cur_s->this;
1160     Symbol *z;
1161
1162     if (s->frst == s->last)
1163     {       if ((z = has_lab(s->frst))
1164             && (strncmp(z->name, "progress", 8) == 0
1165             ||  strncmp(z->name, "accept", 6) == 0
1166             ||  strncmp(z->name, "end", 3) == 0))
1167             {       Element *y =    /* insert a skip */
1168                     new_el(nn(0, s->frst->n->nval, 'c',
1169                             nn(0, 1, CONST, 0, 0), 0));
1170                 if (s->frst->n->ntyp == GOTO
1171                 ||  s->frst->n->ntyp == BREAK)
1172                 {       s->frst = y;
1173                         y->nxt = s->last;
1174                 } else
1175                 {       mov_lab(z, s->frst, y);
1176                         s->frst->nxt = y;
1177                         s->last = y;
1178     }       }           }
1179     cur_s = cur_s->nxt;
1180     return s;
1181 }
1182
1183 SeqList *
1184 seqlist(s, r)
1185     Sequence *s;
1186     SeqList *r;
1187 {
```

```
1188    SeqList *t = (SeqList *) emalloc(sizeof(SeqList));
1189    t->this = s;
1190    t->nxt = r;
1191    return t;
1192 }
1193
1194 Element *
1195 new_el(n)
1196    Node *n;
1197 {
1198    Element *m;
1199
1200    if (n && (n->ntyp == IF || n->ntyp == DO))
1201            return if_seq(n->seql, n->ntyp, n->nval);
1202    m = (Element *) emalloc(sizeof(Element));
1203    m->n = n;
1204    m->seqno = Elcnt++;
1205    return m;
1206 }
1207
1208 Element *
1209 if_seq(s, tok, lnno)
1210    SeqList *s;
1211 {
1212    Element *e = new_el((Node *) 0);
1213    Element *t = new_el(nn(0, lnno, '.', 0, 0)); /* target */
1214    SeqList *z;
1215
1216    e->n = nn(0, lnno, tok, 0, 0);
1217    e->sub = s;
1218    for (z = s; z; z = z->nxt)
1219            add_el(t, z->this);
1220    if (tok == DO)
1221    {       add_el(t, cur_s->this);
1222            t = new_el(nn(0, lnno, BREAK, 0, 0));
1223            set_lab(break_dest(), t);
1224            breakstack = breakstack->nxt;   /* pop stack */
1225    }
1226    add_el(e, cur_s->this);
1227    add_el(t, cur_s->this);
1228    return e;        /* destination node for label */
1229 }
1230
1231 void
1232 add_el(e, s)
1233    Element *e;
1234    Sequence *s;
1235 {
1236    if (e->n->ntyp == GOTO)
1237    {       Symbol *z;
1238            if ((z = has_lab(e))
1239            && (strncmp(z->name, "progress", 8) == 0
1240            || strncmp(z->name, "accept", 6) == 0
1241            || strncmp(z->name, "end", 3) == 0))
```

```
1242              {          Element *y =     /* insert a skip */
1243                         new_el(nn(0, e->n->nval, 'c',
1244                              nn(0, 1, CONST, 0, 0), 0));
1245                         mov_lab(z, e, y); /* gets its label */
1246                         add_el(y, s);
1247         }          }
1248     if (!s->frst)
1249              s->frst = e;
1250     else
1251              s->last->nxt = e;
1252     s->last = e;
1253 }
1254
1255 void
1256 add_seq(n)
1257     Node *n;
1258 {
1259     Element *e;
1260     if (!n) return;
1261     if (n->ntyp == ':')
1262     {        e = new_el(n->lft);
1263              set_lab(n->nsym, e);
1264              n = n->lft;
1265     } else
1266              e = new_el(n);
1267     if (n->ntyp != IF && n->ntyp != DO)
1268              add_el(e, cur_s->this);
1269 }
1270
1271 void
1272 set_lab(s, e)
1273     Symbol *s;
1274     Element *e;
1275 {
1276     Label *l; extern Symbol *context;
1277     if (!s) return;
1278     l = (Label *) emalloc(sizeof(Label));
1279     l->s = s;
1280     l->c = context;
1281     l->e = e;
1282     l->nxt = labtab;
1283     labtab = l;
1284 }
1285
1286 Element *
1287 get_lab(s)
1288     Symbol *s;
1289 {
1290     Label *l;
1291     for (l = labtab; l; l = l->nxt)
1292              if (s == l->s)
1293                      return (l->e);
1294     fatal("undefined label %s", s->name);
1295 }
```

```
1296
1297 Symbol *
1298 has_lab(e)
1299     Element *e;
1300 {
1301     Label *l;
1302     for (l = labtab; l; l = l->nxt)
1303             if (e == l->e)
1304                     return (l->s);
1305     return (Symbol *) 0;
1306 }
1307
1308 void
1309 mov_lab(z, e, y)
1310     Symbol *z;
1311     Element *e, *y;
1312 {
1313     Label *l;
1314     for (l = labtab; l; l = l->nxt)
1315             if (e == l->e)
1316             {       l->e = y;
1317                     return;
1318             }
1319     fatal("cannot happen - mov_lab %s", z->name);
1320 }
1321
1322 find_lab(s, c)
1323     Symbol *s, *c;
1324 {
1325     Label *l;
1326     for (l = labtab; l; l = l->nxt)
1327     {       if (strcmp(s->name, l->s->name) == 0
1328             &&  strcmp(c->name, l->c->name) == 0)
1329                     return (l->e->seqno);
1330     }
1331     return 0;
1332 }
1333
1334 void
1335 pushbreak()
1336 {   Lbreak *r = (Lbreak *) emalloc(sizeof(Lbreak));
1337     Symbol *l;
1338     char buf[32];
1339
1340     sprintf(buf, ":b%d", break_id++);
1341     l = lookup(buf);
1342     r->l = l;
1343     r->nxt = breakstack;
1344     breakstack = r;
1345 }
1346
1347 Symbol *
1348 break_dest()
1349 {   if (!breakstack)
```

```
1350              fatal("misplaced break statement", (char *)0);
1351     return breakstack->l;
1352 }
1353
1354 void
1355 make_atomic(s)
1356     Sequence *s;
1357 {
1358     walk_atomic(s->frst, s->last);
1359     s->last->status &= ~ATOM;
1360     s->last->status |= L_ATOM;
1361 }
1362
1363 void
1364 walk_atomic(a, b)
1365     Element *a, *b;
1366 {
1367     Element *f;
1368     SeqList *h;
1369     for (f = a; ; f = f->nxt)
1370     {       f->status |= ATOM;
1371             for (h = f->sub; h; h = h->nxt)
1372                     walk_atomic(h->this->frst, h->this->last);
1373             if (f == b)
1374                     break;
1375     }
1376 }
1377
1378 /***** spin: run.c *****/
1379
1380 #include <stdio.h>
1381 #include "spin.h"
1382 #include "y.tab.h"
1383
1384 Element *
1385 eval_sub(e)
1386     Element *e;
1387 {
1388     Element *f, *g;
1389     SeqList *z;
1390     int i, j, k;
1391     extern int Rvous, lineno;
1392     extern Symbol *Fname;
1393
1394     if (!e->n)
1395             return (Element *)0;
1396     if (e->n->ntyp == GOTO)
1397             return (!Rvous)?get_lab(e->n->nsym):(Element *)0;
1398     if (e->sub)
1399     {       for (z = e->sub, j=0; z; z = z->nxt)
1400                     j++;
1401             k = rand()%j;   /* nondeterminism */
1402             for (i = 0, z = e->sub; i < j+k; i++)
1403             {       if (i >= k && (f = eval_sub(z->this->frst)))
```

```
1404                              return f;
1405                      z = (z->nxt)?z->nxt:e->sub;
1406              }
1407      } else
1408      {        if (e->n->ntyp == ATOMIC)
1409              {        f = e->n->seql->this->frst;
1410                       g = e->n->seql->this->last;
1411                       g->nxt = e->nxt;
1412                       if (!(g = eval_sub(f))) /* atomic guard */
1413                               return (Element *)0;
1414                       Rvous=0;
1415                       while (g && (g->status & (ATOM|L_ATOM))
1416                       && !(f->status & L_ATOM))
1417                       {        f = g;
1418                                g = eval_sub(f);
1419                       }
1420                       if (!g)
1421                       {        wrapup();
1422                                lineno = f->n->nval;
1423                                fatal("atomic seq blocks", (char *)0);
1424                       }
1425                       return g;
1426              } else if (Rvous)
1427              {        if (eval_sync(e->n))
1428                               return e->nxt;
1429              } else
1430                       return (eval(e->n))?e->nxt:(Element *)0;
1431      }
1432      return (Element *)0;
1433 }
1434
1435 eval_sync(now)
1436      Node *now;
1437 {  /* allow only synchronous receives
1438     /* and related node types    */
1439
1440      if (now)
1441      switch (now->ntyp) {
1442      case TIMEOUT:   case PRINT:     case ASSERT:
1443      case RUN:       case LEN:       case 's':
1444      case 'c':       case ASGN:      case BREAK:
1445      case IF:        case DO:        case '.':
1446              return 0;
1447      case 'R':
1448      case 'r':
1449              if (!q_is_sync(now))
1450                      return 0;
1451      }
1452      return eval(now);
1453 }
1454
1455 eval(now)
1456      Node *now;
1457 {
```

```
1458    extern int Tval, lineno;
1459    extern Symbol *Fname;
1460    if (now)
1461    switch (now->ntyp) {
1462    case CONST: return now->nval;
1463    case   '!': return !eval(now->lft);
1464    case  UMIN: return -eval(now->lft);
1465    case   '~': return ~eval(now->lft);
1466
1467    case   '/': return (eval(now->lft) / eval(now->rgt));
1468    case   '*': return (eval(now->lft) * eval(now->rgt));
1469    case   '-': return (eval(now->lft) - eval(now->rgt));
1470    case   '+': return (eval(now->lft) + eval(now->rgt));
1471    case   '%': return (eval(now->lft) % eval(now->rgt));
1472    case   '<': return (eval(now->lft) <  eval(now->rgt));
1473    case   '>': return (eval(now->lft) >  eval(now->rgt));
1474    case   '&': return (eval(now->lft) &  eval(now->rgt));
1475    case   '|': return (eval(now->lft) |  eval(now->rgt));
1476    case    LE: return (eval(now->lft) <= eval(now->rgt));
1477    case    GE: return (eval(now->lft) >= eval(now->rgt));
1478    case    NE: return (eval(now->lft) != eval(now->rgt));
1479    case    EQ: return (eval(now->lft) == eval(now->rgt));
1480    case    OR: return (eval(now->lft) || eval(now->rgt));
1481    case   AND: return (eval(now->lft) && eval(now->rgt));
1482    case LSHIFT: return (eval(now->lft) << eval(now->rgt));
1483    case RSHIFT: return (eval(now->lft) >> eval(now->rgt));
1484
1485    case TIMEOUT: return Tval;
1486
1487    case   RUN: return enable(now->nsym, now->lft);
1488    case   LEN: return qlen(now);
1489    case   's': return qsend(now);              /* send          */
1490    case   'r': return qrecv(now, 1);           /* full-receive */
1491    case   'R': return qrecv(now, 0);           /* test only     */
1492    case   'c': return eval(now->lft);          /* condition     */
1493    case   'p': return remotevar(now);
1494    case   'q': return remotelab(now);
1495    case PRINT: return interprint(now);
1496    case  ASGN: return setval(now->lft, eval(now->rgt));
1497    case  NAME: return getval(now->nsym, eval(now->lft));
1498    case ASSERT: if (eval(now->lft)) return 1;
1499                 yyerror("assertion violated", (char *) 0);
1500                 wrapup(); exit(1);
1501    case  IF: case DO: case BREAK:  /* compound structure */
1502    case   '.': return 1;   /* return label for compound */
1503    case   '@': return 0;   /* stop state */
1504    default  : printf("spin: bad node type %d (run)\n", now->ntyp);
1505                 fflush(stdout);
1506                 exit(1);
1507    }
1508    return 0;
1509 }
1510
1511 interprint(n)
```

```
1512    Node *n;
1513 {
1514    Node *tmp = n->lft;
1515    char c, *s = n->nsym->name;
1516    int i, j;
1517
1518    for (i = 0; i < strlen(s); i++)
1519            switch (s[i]) {
1520            default:  putchar(s[i]); break;
1521            case '\"': break; /* ignore */
1522            case '\\':
1523                    switch(s[++i]) {
1524                    case 't': putchar('\t'); break;
1525                    case 'n': putchar('\n'); break;
1526                    default:  putchar(s[i]); break;
1527                    }
1528                    break;
1529            case  '%':
1530                    if ((c = s[++i]) == '%')
1531                    {       putchar('%'); /* literal */
1532                            break;
1533                    }
1534                    if (!tmp)
1535                    {       yyerror("too few print args %s", s);
1536                            break;
1537                    }
1538                    j = eval(tmp->lft);
1539                    tmp = tmp->rgt;
1540                    switch(c) {
1541                    case 'd': printf("%d", j); break;
1542                    case 'o': printf("%o", j); break;
1543                    case 'u': printf("%u", j); break;
1544                    case 'x': printf("%x", j); break;
1545                    default:  break; /* ignore */
1546                    }
1547                    break;
1548            }
1549    fflush(stdout);
1550    return 1;
1551 }
1552
1553 /***** spin: sched.c *****/
1554
1555 #include <stdio.h>
1556 #include "spin.h"
1557 #include "y.tab.h"
1558
1559 int nproc = 0;
1560 int nstop = 0;
1561 int Tval  = 0;
1562 int Rvous = 0;
1563 int depth = 0;
1564
1565 RunList              *X   = (RunList  *) 0;
```

```
1566 RunList              *run = (RunList  *) 0;
1567 ProcList    *rdy = (ProcList *) 0;
1568 Element              *eval_sub();
1569 extern int verbose, lineno, s_trail, analyze;
1570 extern Symbol       *Fname;
1571 extern char         *claimproc;
1572
1573 void
1574 runnable(s, n)
1575    Sequence *s;    /* body */
1576    Symbol *n;      /* name */
1577 {
1578    RunList *r = (RunList *) emalloc(sizeof(RunList));
1579    r->n = n;
1580    r->pid = nproc++;
1581    r->pc = s->frst;
1582    r->maxseq = s->last->seqno;
1583    r->nxt = run;
1584    run = r;
1585 }
1586
1587 void
1588 ready(n, p, s)
1589    Symbol *n;       /* process name */
1590    Node *p;         /* formal parameters */
1591    Sequence *s;     /* process body */
1592 {
1593    ProcList *r = (ProcList *) emalloc(sizeof(ProcList));
1594    r->n = n;
1595    r->p = p;
1596    r->s = s;
1597    r->nxt = rdy;
1598    rdy = r;
1599 }
1600
1601 enable(s, n)
1602    Symbol *s;       /* process name */
1603    Node *n;         /* actual parameters */
1604 {
1605    ProcList *p;
1606    for (p = rdy; p; p = p->nxt)
1607            if (strcmp(s->name, p->n->name) == 0)
1608            {       runnable(p->s, p->n);
1609                    setparams(run, p, n);
1610                    return (nproc-nstop-1); /* pid */
1611            }
1612    return 0; /* process not found */
1613 }
1614
1615 void
1616 start_claim(n)
1617 { ProcList *p;
1618    int i;
1619
```

```
1620     for (p = rdy, i=1; p; p = p->nxt, i++)
1621             if (i == n)
1622             {       runnable(p->s, p->n);
1623                     return;
1624             }
1625     fatal("couldn't find claim", (char *) 0);
1626 }
1627
1628 void
1629 sched()
1630 { Element *e;
1631     RunList *Y;      /* previous process in run queue */
1632     int i;
1633
1634     if (analyze)
1635     {       gensrc();
1636             return;
1637     } else if (s_trail)
1638     {       match_trail();
1639             return;
1640     }
1641     if (claimproc)
1642             printf("warning: claims are ignored in simulations\n");
1643
1644     for (Tval=i=0; Tval < 2; Tval++, i=0)
1645     {       while (i < nproc-nstop)
1646             for (X=run, Y=0, i=0; X; X = X->nxt)
1647             {       lineno = X->pc->n->nval;
1648                     Fname  = X->pc->n->fname;
1649                     if (e = eval_sub(X->pc))
1650                     {       X->pc = e; Tval=0;
1651                             talk(e, X->symtab);
1652                     } else
1653                     {       if (X->pc->n->ntyp == '@'
1654                             &&   X->pid == (nproc-nstop-1))
1655                             {       if (Y)
1656                                             Y->nxt = X->nxt;
1657                                     else
1658                                             run = X->nxt;
1659                                     nstop++; Tval=0;
1660                                     if (verbose&4)
1661                                     {       whoruns();
1662                                             printf("terminates\n");
1663                                     }
1664                             } else
1665                                     i++;
1666                     }
1667                     Y = X;
1668     }       }
1669     wrapup();
1670 }
1671
1672 wrapup()
1673 { if (depth)       /* for guided simulations, Chapter 12 */
```

```
1674              printf("step %d, ", depth);
1675     if (nproc != nstop)
1676     {        printf("#processes: %d\n", nproc-nstop);
1677              dumpglobals();
1678              verbose &= ~1;  /* no more globals */
1679              verbose |= 4;   /* add process states */
1680              for (X = run; X; X = X->nxt)
1681                      talk(X->pc, X->symtab);
1682     }
1683     printf("%d processes created\n", nproc);
1684 }
1685
1686 complete_rendez()
1687 {  RunList *orun = X;
1688    Element *e;
1689    int res=0;
1690
1691    if (s_trail)    /* for guided simulations, Chapter 12 */
1692             return 1;
1693    Rvous = 1;
1694    for (X = run; X; X = X->nxt)
1695             if (X != orun && (e = eval_sub(X->pc)))
1696             {       X->pc = e;
1697                     if (verbose&4)
1698                     {       printf("rendezvous: %s ",X->n->name);
1699                             printf("<-> %s\n", orun->n->name);
1700                             printf("=r==:   ");
1701                             talk(e, X->symtab);
1702                             printf("=s==:   ");
1703                             X = orun;
1704                             talk(X->pc, X->symtab);
1705                     }
1706                     res = 1;
1707                     break;
1708             }
1709    Rvous = 0;
1710    X = orun;
1711    return res;
1712 }
1713
1714 /***** Runtime - Local Variables *****/
1715
1716 void
1717 addsymbol(r, s)
1718    RunList *r;
1719    Symbol  *s;
1720 {
1721    Symbol *t = (Symbol *) emalloc(sizeof(Symbol));
1722    int i;
1723
1724    t->name = s->name;
1725    t->type = s->type;
1726    t->nel  = s->nel;
1727    t->ini  = s->ini;
```

```
1728    if (s->val)                 /* if initialized, copy it */
1729    {       t->val = (int *) emalloc(s->nel*sizeof(int));
1730            for (i = 0; i < s->nel; i++)
1731                    t->val[i] = s->val[i];
1732    } else
1733            checkvar(t, 0); /* initialize it */
1734    t->next = r->symtab;    /* add it */
1735    r->symtab = t;
1736 }
1737
1738 void
1739 naddsymbol(r, s, k)
1740    RunList *r;
1741    Symbol  *s;
1742 {
1743    Symbol *t = (Symbol *) emalloc(sizeof(Symbol));
1744    int i;
1745
1746    t->name = s->name;
1747    t->type = s->type;
1748    t->nel  = s->nel;
1749    t->ini  = s->ini;
1750    t->val = (int *) emalloc(s->nel*sizeof(int));
1751    if (s->nel != 1)
1752    fatal("array in formal parameter list, %s", s->name);
1753    for (i = 0; i < s->nel; i++)
1754            t->val[i] = k;
1755    t->next = r->symtab;
1756    r->symtab = t;
1757 }
1758
1759 typck(n, t, s)
1760    Node *n;
1761    char *s;
1762 {
1763    if (!n || !n->lft
1764    || (n->lft->ntyp == NAME && n->lft->nsym->type != t
1765        && n->lft->nsym->type != 0
1766        && (t == CHAN || n->lft->nsym->type == CHAN))
1767    || (n->lft->ntyp == NAME && n->lft->nsym->type == 0
1768        && lookup(n->lft->nsym->name)->type != t) )
1769    {       yyerror("error in parameters of run %s(...)", s);
1770            return 0;
1771    }
1772    return 1;
1773 }
1774
1775 void
1776 setparams(r, p, q)
1777    RunList *r;
1778    ProcList *p;
1779    Node *q;
1780 {
1781    Node *f, *a;    /* formal and actual pars */
```

```
1782    Node *t;          /* list of pars of 1 type */
1783
1784    for (f = p->p, a = q; f; f = f->rgt) /* one type at a time */
1785    for (t = f->lft; t; t = t->rgt, a = (a)?a->rgt:a)
1786    {       int k = eval(a->lft);          /* must be initialized*/
1787            if (typck(a, t->nsym->type, p->n->name))
1788            {       if (t->nsym->type == CHAN)
1789                            naddsymbol(r, t->nsym, k); /* copy */
1790                    else
1791                    {       t->nsym->ini = a->lft;
1792                            addsymbol(r, t->nsym);
1793                    }
1794            }
1795    }
1796 }
1797
1798 Symbol *
1799 findloc(s, n)
1800     Symbol *s;
1801 {
1802     Symbol *r;
1803
1804     if (n >= s->nel || n < 0)
1805     {       yyerror("array indexing error %s", s->name);
1806             return (Symbol *) 0;
1807     }
1808
1809     for (r = X->symtab; r; r = r->next)
1810             if (strcmp(r->name, s->name) == 0)
1811                     break;
1812     if (!r)
1813     {       addsymbol(X, s);
1814             r = X->symtab;
1815     }
1816     return r;
1817 }
1818
1819 getlocal(s, n)
1820     Symbol *s;
1821 {
1822     Symbol *r;
1823
1824     r = findloc(s, n);
1825     if (r) return cast_val(r->type, r->val[n]);
1826     return 0;
1827 }
1828
1829 setlocal(p, m)
1830     Node *p;
1831 {
1832     int n = eval(p->lft);
1833     Symbol *r = findloc(p->nsym, n);
1834
1835     if (r) r->val[n] = m;
```

```
1836     return 1;
1837 }
1838
1839 void
1840 whoruns()
1841 {
1842     if (X) printf("proc %2d (%s)      ", X->pid, X->n->name);
1843 }
1844
1845 void
1846 talk(e, s)
1847     Element *e;
1848     Symbol *s;
1849 {
1850     if (verbose&4)
1851     {       p_talk(e);
1852             if (verbose&1) dumpglobals();
1853             if (verbose&2) dumplocal(s);
1854     }
1855 }
1856
1857 void
1858 p_talk(e)
1859     Element *e;
1860 {
1861     whoruns();
1862     printf("line %d (state %d)\n",
1863             (e && e->n && e->n->nval)?e->n->nval:-1, e->seqno);
1864 }
1865
1866 remotelab(n)
1867     Node *n;
1868 {
1869     int i;
1870
1871     if (n->nsym->type)
1872             fatal("not a labelname: '%s'", n->nsym->name);
1873     if ((i = find_lab(n->nsym, n->lft->nsym)) == 0)
1874             fatal("unknown labelname: %s", n->nsym->name);
1875     return i;
1876 }
1877
1878 remotevar(n)
1879     Node *n;
1880 {
1881     int pno, i, j;
1882     RunList *Y, *oX = X;
1883
1884     if (!n->lft->lft)
1885     {       yyerror("missing pid in %s", n->nsym->name);
1886             return 0;
1887     }
1888     pno = eval(n->lft->lft); /* pid */
1889     i = nproc - nstop;
```

```
1890    for (Y = run; Y; Y = Y->nxt)
1891    if (--i == pno)
1892    {       if (strcmp(Y->n->name, n->lft->nsym->name))
1893                    yyerror("wrong proctype %s", Y->n->name);
1894            X = Y; j = getval(n->nsym, eval(n->rgt)); X = oX;
1895            return j;
1896    }
1897    yyerror("remote ref: proc %s not found", n->nsym->name);
1898    return 0;
1899 }
1900
1901 /***** spin: dummy.c *****/
1902
1903 gensrc()
1904 {
1905    printf("analyze: not defined\n");
1906 }
1907
1908 match_trail()
1909 {
1910    printf("trails: not defined\n");
1911 }
```

SPIN VALIDATOR SOURCE   **E**

The program listings that follow are the program segments that are added to the simulator code described in Chapter 12 and listed in Appendix D. The code from this appendix is used to generate a protocol-specific validator for any protocol validation model that is described in PROMELA. The extensions are discussed in Chapter 13.

The new *makefile* for this version of SPIN looks as follows.

```
CC=cc           # ANSI C compiler
CFLAGS=-O       # optimizer
YFLAGS=-v -d -D # verbose, debugging
OFILES= spin.o lex.o sym.o vars.o main.o debug.o \
        mesg.o flow.o sched.o run.o pangen1.o pangen2.o \
        pangen3.o pangen4.o pangen5.o

spin:   $(OFILES)
        $(CC) $(CFLAGS) -o spin $(OFILES) -lm

%.o:    %.c spin.h
        $(CC) $(CFLAGS) -c $%.c

pangen1.o:      pangen1.c pangen1.h pangen3.h
pangen2.o:      pangen2.c pangen2.h
```

The remainder of this Appendix lists the contents of the 8 additional source files (see Table E.1). A large part of the code is contained in header files and copied into a protocol specific validator generated with SPIN.

Two pre-processor directives are generated for optional manipulation by the user. By default, all validators generated by SPIN perform an exhaustive search. If the name BITSTATE is defined at compile-time, this search strategy is replaced with a supertrace analysis (see Chapter 14 for examples). Similarly, by default there is no predefined maximum to the amount of memory that an exhaustive analysis can use. If, however, the name MEMCNT is defined at compile-time, it numeric value will be used to set an upper-bound. If, for instance, MEMCNT=20 the upper-bound used is 2^{20} bytes (see also Chapter 14 for examples).

Table E.1 – Source File Index

File	Line Number
pangen1.c	1149
pangen1.h	1
pangen2.h	911
pangen2.c	1575
pangen3.c	2096
pangen3.h	1156
pangen4.c	2201
pangen5.c	2381

ELECTRONIC VERSION OF SPIN

The source code listed in Appendices D and E is available, for a fee, in electronic form from AT&T's UNIX® System Toolchest software distribution system.

To obtain the code, call 1-201-522-6900 and login as *guest*. In Europe, contact AT&T UNIX Europe in London at 44-81-567-7711, and in the Far East, contact AT&T UNIX Pacific in Tokyo at 81-3-431-3670.

All future revisions, additions, and fixes to the source will be also be made available via Toolchest. Send bug reports to the author via electronic mail at: gerard@research.att.com.

Table E.2 – Procedures Listed – Appendix E

Procedure	Line	Procedure	Line
any_proc(now)	2298	any_undo(now)	2281
blurb(fd, t, n)	2071	check_proc(now, m)	2308
d_eval_sub(s, pno, nst)	2501	do_init(sp)	1326
do_var(dowhat, s, sp)	1300	doglobal(dowhat)	1289
dolocal(dowhat, p, s)	1272	dumpskip(n, m)	2143
dumpsrc(n, m)	2167	end_labs(s, i)	1241
genaddproc()	1191	genaddqueue()	1476
genheader()	1172	genother(cnt)	1211
genunio()	2322	getweight(n)	2048
has_tau(n)	2060	huntele(f, o)	1404
huntstart(f)	1389	lost_trail()	2459
match_trail()	2395	ncases(fd, p, n, m, c)	1463
ntimes(fd, n, m, c)	1259	put_pinit(e, s, p, i)	1364
put_ptype(s, p, i, m0, m1)	1344	putnr(n)	2192
putstmnt(fd, now, m)	1825	typ2c(sp)	1433
undostmnt(now, m)	2214	walk_sub(e, pno, nst)	2469

Table E.3 – Procedures Explained – Chapter 13

Procedure	Page	Procedure	Page
addproc()	306	assert()	307
checkchan()	309	d_hash()	300
d_hash()	307	delproc()	306
endstate()	307	gensrc()	298
gensrc()	308	hstore()	306
huntini()	308	match_trail()	298
match_trail()	310	new_state()	306
new_state()	300	new_state()	300
new_state()	305	p_restor()	306
putproc()	308	putseq()	308
putstmnt()	308	putstmnt()	309
q_restor()	305	qrecv()	305
qsend()	305	r_ck()	307
retrans()	307	s_hash()	300
s_hash()	307	settable()	307
uerror()	300	uerror()	303
undostmnt()	308	undostmnt()	309
unrecv()	306	unsend()	306

```
1 /***** spin: pangen1.h *****/
2
3 char *Header[] = {
4     "#define qptr(x)        (((uchar *)&now)+q_offset[x])",
5     "#define pptr(x)         (((uchar *)&now)+proc_offset[x])",
6     "#define Pptr(x)         ((proc_offset[x])?pptr(x):noptr)",
7     "#define q_sz(x)         (((Q0 *)qptr(x))->Qlen)\n",
8     "#define MAXQ            255",
9     "#define MAXPROC         255",
10    "#define WS              sizeof(long)   /* word size in bytes */",
11    "#ifndef VECTORSZ",
12    "#define VECTORSZ        1024           /* sv   size in bytes */",
13    "#endif",
14    "extern char *malloc(), *memcpy(), *memset();",
15    "extern void exit();",
16    "extern int abort();\n",
17    "typedef struct Stack  {           /* for queues and processes */",
18    "        short o_delta;",
19    "        short o_offset;",
20    "        short o_delqs;",
21    "        char *body;",
22    "        struct Stack *nxt;",
23    "        struct Stack *lst;",
24    "} Stack;\n",
25    "typedef struct Svtack { /* for complete state vector */",
26    "        short o_delta;   /* current size of frame */",
27    "        short m_delta;   /* maximum size of frame */",
28    "#if SYNC",
29    "        short o_boq;",
30    "#endif",
31    "        int j1, j2;      /* loop detection */",
32    "        char *body;",
33    "        struct Svtack *nxt;",
34    "        struct Svtack *lst;",
35    "} Svtack;\n",
36    "typedef struct Trans {",
37    "        short atom;      /* is this an atomic transition */",
38    "        short st;        /* the nextstate */",
39    "        short ist;       /* intermediate state */",
40    "        int forw;        /* index for forward transition */",
41    "        int back;        /* index for return  transition */",
42    "        struct Trans *nxt;",
43    "} Trans;\n",
44    "Trans ***trans;          /* 1 ptr per state per proctype */\n",
45    "int proc_offset[MAXPROC];",
46    "int q_offset[MAXQ];",
47    "int depthfound = -1;   /* loop detection */",
48    "short vsize;             /* vector size in bytes */",
49    "short boq = -1;          /* blocked_on_queue status */",
50    "typedef struct State {",
51    "        uchar _nr_pr;",
52    "        uchar _nr_qs;",
53    "        uchar _p_t; /* loop detection */",
```

```
 54      0,
 55 };
 56
 57 char *Addp0[] = {
 58      /* addproc(....parlist... */ ")",
 59      "{",
 60      "        int j, h = now._nr_pr;",
 61      "        if (h >= MAXPROC)",
 62      "                Uerror(\"too many processes\");",
 63      "        switch (n) {",
 64      "        case 0: j = sizeof(P0); break;",
 65      0,
 66 };
 67
 68 char *Addp1[] = {
 69      "        default: Uerror(\"bad proc - addproc\");",
 70      "        }",
 71      "        if (vsize%%WS && (j > WS-(vsize%%WS)))",
 72      "                vsize += WS-(vsize%%WS);",
 73      "        proc_offset[h] = vsize;",
 74      "        now._nr_pr += 1;",
 75      "        vsize += j;",
 76      "        hmax = max(hmax, vsize);",
 77      "        if (vsize >= VECTORSZ)",
 78      "                Uerror(\"VECTORSZ is too small, edit pan.h\");",
 79      "        memset((char *)pptr(h), 0, j);",
 80      "        switch (n) {",
 81      0,
 82 };
 83
 84 char *Addq0[] = {
 85      "addqueue(n)",
 86      "{        int j=0, i = now._nr_qs;",
 87      "        if (i >= MAXQ)",
 88      "                Uerror(\"too many queues\");",
 89      "        switch (n) {",
 90      0,
 91 };
 92
 93 char *Addq1[] = {
 94      "        case -1: printf(\"queue was deleted\\n\");",
 95      "        default: Uerror(\"bad queue - addqueue\");",
 96      "        }",
 97      "        if (vsize%%WS && (j > WS-(vsize%%WS)))",
 98      "                vsize += WS-(vsize%%WS);",
 99      "        q_offset[i] = vsize;",
100      "        now._nr_qs += 1;",
101      "        vsize += j;",
102      "        hmax = max(hmax, vsize);",
103      "        if (vsize >= VECTORSZ)",
104      "                Uerror(\"VECTORSZ is too small, edit pan.h\");",
105      "        memset((char *)qptr(i), 0, j);",
106      "        ((Q0 *)qptr(i))->_t = n;",
107      "        return i;",
```

```
108    "}\n",
109    0,
110 };
111
112 char *Addq11[] = {
113    "{        int j; uchar *z;\n",
114    "         if (into >= now._nr_qs || into < 0)",
115    "                 Uerror(\"qsend bad queue#\");",
116    "         z = qptr(into);",
117    "         switch (((Q0 *)qptr(into))->_t) {",
118    0,
119 };
120
121 char *Addq2[] = {
122    "         case -1: printf(\"queue was deleted\\n\");",
123    "         default: Uerror(\"bad queue - qsend\");",
124    "         }",
125    "}\n",
126    "#if SYNC",
127    "q_zero(from)",
128    "{",
129    "         switch(((Q0 *)qptr(from))->_t) {",
130    0,
131 };
132
133 char *Addq3[] = {
134    "         case -1: printf(\"queue was deleted\\n\");",
135    "         }",
136    "         Uerror(\"bad queue q-zero\");",
137    "}",
138    "#endif",
139    "q_full(from)",
140    "{",
141    "         switch(((Q0 *)qptr(from))->_t) {",
142    0,
143 };
144
145 char *Addq4[] = {
146    "         case -1: printf(\"queue was deleted\\n\");",
147    "         }",
148    "         Uerror(\"bad queue - q_full\");",
149    "}\n",
150    "qrecv(from, slot, fld, done)",
151    "{        uchar *z;",
152    "         int j, k, r=0;",
153    "         if (from >= now._nr_qs || from < 0)",
154    "                 Uerror(\"qrecv bad queue#\");",
155    "         z = qptr(from);",
156    "         switch (((Q0 *)qptr(from))->_t) {",
157    0,
158 };
159
160 char *Addq5[] = {
161    "         case -1: printf(\"queue was deleted\\n\");",
```

```
162     "          default: Uerror(\"bad queue - qrecv\");",
163     "          }",
164     "          return r;",
165     "}\n",
166     0,
167 };
168
169 char *Code0[] = {
170     "run()",
171     "{        memset((char *)&now, 0, sizeof(State));",
172     "         vsize = sizeof(State) - VECTORSZ;",
173     "         settable();",
174     0,
175 };
176 char *Code1[] = {
177     "#define CONNECT        %d /* accept labels */",
178     0,
179 };
180 char *Code2[] = {
181     "        UnBlock;        /* disable rendez-vous */",
182     "#ifdef BITSTATE",
183     "        SS = (uchar *) emalloc(1<<(ssize-3));",
184     "        if (loops)",
185     "        LL = (uchar *) emalloc(1<<(ssize-3));",
186     "#if CONNECT>0",
187     "        printf(\"warning: acceptance labels are\");",
188     "        printf(\" ignored in bit-state mode\\n\");",
189     "#endif",
190     "#else",
191     "        hinit();",
192     "#endif",
193     "        stack   = ( Stack *) emalloc(sizeof(Stack));",
194     "        svtack  = (Svtack *) emalloc(sizeof(Svtack));",
195     "        /* a place to point for Pptr of non-running procs: */",
196     "        noptr   = (uchar *) emalloc(Maxbody * sizeof(char));",
197     "        addproc(0);     /* init */",
198     "        depth=mreached=0;",
199     "        trpt = &trail[depth];",
200     "        new_state();",
201     "}\n",
202     "new_state()",
203     "{        register Trans *t;",
204     "         char n, m, ot;",
205     "         short II, tt;\n",
206     "         short From = now._nr_pr-1;",
207     "         short To = 0;",
208     "Down:",
209     "        if (now._p_t && prognow()) /* loop detection */",
210     "                goto Up;",
211     "        if (depth >= maxdepth)",
212     "        {       truncs++;",
213     "#if SYNC",
214     "                (trpt+1)->o_n = 1; /* not a deadlock */",
215     "#endif",
```

```
216     "                    goto Up;",
217     "          }",
218     "#if CONNECT>0",
219     "#ifndef BITSTATE",
220     "          trpt->parent = 0;",
221     "#endif",
222     "#endif",
223     "#ifdef VERI",
224     "          if (!(trpt->tau&4))      /* if no claim move */",
225     "#endif",
226     "          if (To == 0)",
227     "          {",
228     "#ifdef BITSTATE",
229     "                    d_hash((uchar *) &now, vsize);",
230     "                    j3 = (1<<(J1&7)); j1 = J1>>3;",
231     "                    j4 = (1<<(J2&7)); j2 = J2>>3;",
232     "                    if ((SS[j2]&j3) && (SS[j1]&j4))",
233     "#else",
234     "                    if (hstore((char *)&now, vsize))",
235     "#endif",
236     "                    {        truncs++;",
237     "#ifdef BITSTATE",
238     "                         if (loops && now._p_t",
239     "                         && LL[j1] && LL[j2] && onstack())",
240     "                              uerror(\"non-progress cycle\");",
241     "#else",
242     "#if CONNECT>0",
243     "                         setparent((char *)&now, vsize);",
244     "#endif",
245     "#endif",
246     "#if SYNC",
247     "/* mid rendezvous */  if (boq != -1 && !(((trpt-1)->tau)&1))",
248     "                         (trpt+1)->o_m = 1; /* not stuck */",
249     "#endif",
250     "                         goto Up;",
251     "                    }",
252     "#ifdef BITSTATE",
253     "                    SS[j2] |= j3; SS[j1] |= j4;",
254     "                    if (loops)",
255     "                    {        sv_save();",
256     "                         LL[j1]++; LL[j2]++;",
257     "                         svtack->j1 = J1;",
258     "                         svtack->j2 = J2;",
259     "                    }",
260     "#else",
261     "#if CONNECT>0",
262     "                    setparent((char *)&now, vsize);",
263     "#endif",
264     "#endif",
265     "                    nstates++;",
266     "          }",
267     "          if (depth > mreached)",
268     "                    mreached = depth;",
269     "          trpt->tau &= ~1; n = 0;",
```

```
270     "#if SYNC",
271     "          (trpt+1)->o_n = 0;",
272     "#endif",
273     "#ifdef VERI",
274     "          if (now._nr_pr < 2",
275     "          || ((P0 *)pptr(1))->_p == endstate1)",
276     "                  uerror(\"claim violated!\");",
277     "          if (trpt->tau&4)        /* must make a claimmove */",
278     "          {       II = 1;",
279     "                  goto Veri0;",
280     "          }",
281     "#endif",
282     "\nAgain:",
283     "          for (II = From; II >= To; II -= 1)",
284     "          {",
285     "#ifdef VERI",
286     "                  if (II == 1) continue;",
287     "#endif",
288     "Veri0:          this = pptr(II);",
289     "                tt = (short) ((P0 *)this)->_p;",
290     "                ot = (uchar) ((P0 *)this)->_t;",
291     "                for (t = trans[ot][tt]; t; t = t->nxt)",
292     "                {",
293     "#include \"pan.m\"",
294     "P999:           /* jumps here when move succeeds */",
295     "                depth++; trpt++;",
296     "                trpt->pr = II;",
297     "                trpt->st = tt;",
298     "                if (t->st)",
299     "                {       ((P0 *)this)->_p = t->st;",
300     "                        reached[ot][t->st] = 1;",
301     "                }",
302     "                trpt->o_t  = t; trpt->o_n  = n;",
303     "                trpt->o_ot = ot; trpt->o_tt = tt;",
304     "                trpt->o_To = To; trpt->o_m  = m;",
305     "                if (t->atom&2)",
306     "                {       From = To = II; nlinks++;",
307     "#ifdef VERI",
308     "                        trpt->tau = (trpt-1)->tau&4;",
309     "                } else",
310     "                {       if ((trpt-1)->tau&4)",
311     "                                trpt->tau = 0;",
312     "                        else",
313     "                                trpt->tau = 4;",
314     "#else",
315     "                } else",
316     "                {",
317     "#endif",
318     "                        From = now._nr_pr-1; To = 0;",
319     "                }",
320     "                goto Down;      /* pseudo-recursion */",
321     "Up:",
322     "                t  = trpt->o_t;  n  = trpt->o_n;",
323     "                ot = trpt->o_ot; II = trpt->pr;",
```

```
324        "                            tt = trpt->o_tt; this = pptr(II);",
325        "                            To = trpt->o_To; m  = trpt->o_m;",
326        "#ifdef VERI",
327        "#if SYNC",
328        "/* preserve rendez-vous completion status: */",
329        "/* if the next level was a claim, copy through */",
330        "                            if (trpt->tau&4)",
331        "                                    trpt->o_n = (trpt+1)->o_n;",
332        "#endif",
333        "#endif",
334        "#include \"pan.b\"",
335        "R999:                       /* jumps here when done */",
336        "                    depth--; trpt--;",
337        "                    if (m>n||(n>3&&m!=0)) n=m;",
338        "                    ((P0 *)this)->_p = tt;",
339        "                } /* all options */",
340        "#ifdef VERI",
341        "                    if (II == 1) break;",
342        "#endif",
343        "            } /* all processes */",
344        "            if (n == 0)",
345        "            {",
346        "#ifdef VERI",
347        "                    if (trpt->tau&4)",
348        "                            goto Done;",
349        "#endif",
350        "#if SYNC",
351        "                    if (boq == -1)",
352        "#endif",
353        "                    if (!endstate() && now._nr_pr ",
354        "                    &&  depth < maxdepth-1)",
355        "                    {       if (!((trpt->tau)&1))   /* timeout */",
356        "                            {       trpt->tau |= 1;",
357        "                                    goto Again;",
358        "                            }",
359        "                            if (loops) /* loop det. only */",
360        "                                    goto Done;",
361        "                            if (To == 0)",
362        "                            {",
363        "#ifdef VERI",
364        "                                    printf(\"claim at line %%d \",",
365        "                                            claimline);",
366        "                                    printf(\"(state %%d)\\n\",",
367        "                                            ((P0 *)pptr(1))->_p);",
368        "#endif",
369        "                                    uerror(\"invalid endstate\");",
370        "                            } else",
371        "                                    Uerror(\"atomic seq blocks\");",
372        "                    }",
373        "            }",
374        "Done:",
375        "            if (depth > 0)",
376        "            {       if (loops && To == 0)",
377        "#ifdef VERI",
```

```
378     "                   if (!(trpt->tau&4))",
379     "#endif",
380     "#ifdef BITSTATE",
381     "           {           LL[(svtack->j1)>>3]--;",
382     "                       LL[(svtack->j2)>>3]--;",
383     "                       svtack = svtack->lst;",
384     "           }",
385     "#else",
386     "                       htag((char *)&now, vsize);",
387     "#endif",
388     "#if CONNECT>0",
389     "#ifndef BITSTATE",
390     "                   checkaccept();",
391     "#endif",
392     "#endif",
393     "               goto Up;",
394     "           }",
395     "}\n",
396     "assert(a, s, ii, tt, t)",
397     "       char *s;",
398     "       Trans *t;",
399     "{      if (!a)",
400     "       {           printf(\"assertion violated %%s\", s);",
401     "                   depth++; trpt++;",
402     "                   trpt->pr = ii;",
403     "                   trpt->st = tt;",
404     "                   trpt->o_t = t;",
405     "                   uerror(\"aborted\");",
406     "                   depth--; trpt--;",
407     "           }",
408     "}\n",
409     "#ifdef MEMCNT",
410     "int memcnt=0;",
411     "#endif",
412     "void",
413     "wrapup()",
414     "{",
415     "#ifdef BITSTATE",
416     "       double a, b;\n",
417     "       printf(\"bit statespace search \");",
418     "#else",
419     "       printf(\"full statespace search \");",
420     "#endif",
421     "#ifdef VERI",
422     "       printf(\"on behavior restricted to claim \");",
423     "#endif",
424     "       printf(\"for:\\n\tassertion violations\");",
425     "#ifndef VERI",
426     "       if (loops)",
427     "               printf(\" and non-progress loops\");",
428     "       else",
429     "               printf(\" and invalid endstates\");",
430     "#endif",
431     "#if CONNECT>0",
```

```
432    "        printf(\"\\n\\tand absence of acceptance labels\");",
433    "        printf(\" in all cycles\");",
434    "#endif",
435    "        if (!done) printf(\"\\nsearch was not completed\");",
436    "        printf(\"\\nvector %%d byte, depth reached %%d\", ",
437    "                                    hmax, mreached);",
438    "        if (loops)",
439    "          printf(\", non-progress loops: %%d\\n\", errors);",
440    "        else",
441    "          printf(\", errors: %%d\\n\", errors);",
442    "        printf(\"%%8d states, stored\\n\", nstates);",
443    "        printf(\"%%8d states, linked\\n\", nlinks);",
444    "        printf(\"%%8d states, matched\t   total: %%8d\\n\",",
445    "        truncs, nstates+nlinks+truncs);",
446    "#ifdef BITSTATE",
447    "        a = (double) (1<<ssize);",
448    "        b = (double) nstates+1.;",
449    "        printf(\"hash factor: %%f \", a/b);",
450    "        printf(\"(best coverage if >100)\\n\");",
451    "#else",
452    "        printf(\"hash conflicts: %%d (resolved)\\n\", hcmp);",
453    "#endif",
454    "        printf(\"(max size 2^%%d states, \", ssize);",
455    "        printf(\"stackframes: %%d/%%d)\\n\\n\", smax, svmax);",
456    "#ifdef MEMCNT",
457    "        printf(\"memory used: %%d\\n\", memcnt);",
458    "#endif",
459    "        if (done && !loops) do_reach();",
460    "        exit(0);",
461    "}\n",
462    "d_hash(cp, om)",
463    "        uchar *cp;",
464    "{",
465    "        register long z = 0x88888EEFL;",
466    "        register long *q, *r;",
467    "        register int h;",
468    "        register m, n;\n",
469    "        h = (om+3)/4;",
470    "        m = n = -1;",
471    "        q = r = (long *) cp;",
472    "        r += (long) h;",
473    "        do {",
474    "                m += m;",
475    "                if (m < 0)",
476    "                        m ^= z;",
477    "                m ^= *q++;",
478    "                n += n;",
479    "                if (n < 0)",
480    "                        n ^= z;",
481    "                n ^= *--r;",
482    "        } while (--h > 0);",
483    "        J1 = (m ^ (m>>(8*sizeof(unsigned)-ssize)))&mask;",
484    "        J2 = (n ^ (n>>(8*sizeof(unsigned)-ssize)))&mask;",
485    "}\n",
```

```
486    "s_hash(cp, om)",
487    "        uchar *cp;",
488    "{",
489    "        register long z = 0x88888EEFL;",
490    "        register long *q;",
491    "        register int h;\n",
492    "        register m = -1;",
493    "        h = (om+3)/4;",
494    "        q = (long *) cp;",
495    "        do {",
496    "                m += m;",
497    "                if (m < 0)",
498    "                        m ^= z;",
499    "                m ^= *q++;",
500    "        } while (--h > 0);",
501    "        j1 = (m ^ (m>>(8*sizeof(unsigned)-ssize)))&mask;",
502    "}\n",
503    "main(argc, argv)",
504    "        char *argv[];",
505    "{",
506    "        while (argc > 1 && argv[1][0] == '-')",
507    "        {       switch (argv[1][1]) {",
508    "                case 'c': upto  = atoi(&argv[1][2]); break;",
509    "#ifndef VERI",
510    "                case 'l': loops = 1; break;",
511    "#endif",
512    "                case 'm': maxdepth = atoi(&argv[1][2]); break;",
513    "                case 'w': ssize = atoi(&argv[1][2]); break;",
514    "                default : usage(); exit(1);",
515    "                }",
516    "                argc--; argv++;",
517    "        }",
518    "        signal(SIGINT, wrapup);",
519    "        mask = ((1<<ssize)-1);  /* hash init */",
520    "        trail = (Trail *) emalloc((maxdepth+2)*sizeof(Trail));",
521    "        run();",
522    "        done = 1;",
523    "        wrapup();",
524    "}\n",
525    "usage()",
526    "{       fprintf(stderr, \"unknown option\\n\");",
527    "        fprintf(stderr, \"-cN stop at Nth error \");",
528    "        fprintf(stderr, \"(default=1)\\n\");",
529    "#ifndef VERI",
530    "        fprintf(stderr, \"-l  find non-progress loops\\n\");",
531    "#endif",
532    "        fprintf(stderr, \"-mN max depth N (default=10k)\\n\");",
533    "        fprintf(stderr, \"-wN hashtable of 2^N entries \");",
534    "        fprintf(stderr, \"(default=%%d)\\n\", ssize);",
535    "}\n",
536    "char *",
537    "emalloc(n)",
538    "{       char *tmp = malloc(n);",
539    "#ifdef MEMCNT",
```

```
540        "        if (!tmp || memcnt > 1<<MEMCNT)",
541     "#else",
542        "        if (!tmp)",
543     "#endif",
544        "        {       printf(\"pan: out of memory\\n\");",
545        "                wrapup();",
546        "        }",
547     "#ifdef MEMCNT",
548        "        memcnt += n;",
549     "#endif",
550        "        memset(tmp, 0, n);",
551        "        return tmp;",
552     "}\n",
553     "Uerror(str)",
554        "        char *str;",
555     "{      /* always fatal */",
556        "        uerror(str);",
557        "        wrapup();",
558     "}\n",
559     "uerror(str)",
560        "        char *str;",
561     "{",
562        "        if (++errors == upto)",
563        "        {       printf(\"pan: %%s (at depth %%d)\\n\", str,",
564        "                (depthfound==-1)?depth:depthfound);",
565        "                putrail();",
566        "                wrapup();",
567        "        }",
568        "        return 1;",
569     "}\n",
570     "r_ck(which, N, M, src)",
571        "        uchar *which;",
572        "        short *src;",
573     "{      int i, m=0;\n",
574     "#ifdef VERI",
575        "        if (M == VERI) return;  /* no useful info there */",
576     "#endif",
577        "        printf(\"unreached in proctype %%s:\\n\", procname[M]);",
578        "        for (i = 1; i < N; i++)",
579        "          if (which[i] == 0)",
580        "            printf(\"\\tline %%d (state %%d)\\n\", src[i],i);",
581        "          else",
582        "            m++;",
583        "        if (m == N-1)",
584        "                printf(\"\\treached all %%d states\\n\", m);",
585        "        else",
586        "        printf(\"\treached: %%d of %%d states\\n\", m, N-1);",
587     "}\n",
588     "putrail()",
589     "{      int fd, i, j, q;",
590        "        char snap[64];\n",
591        "        if ((fd = creat(\"pan.trail\", 0666)) <= 0)",
592        "        {       printf(\"cannot create pan.trail\\n\");",
593        "                return;",
```

```
594         "         }",
595         "#ifdef VERI",
596         "         sprintf(snap, \"-2:%%d:-2:-2\\n\", VERI);",
597         "         write(fd, snap, strlen(snap));",
598         "#endif",
599         "         for (i = 1, j = 0; i <= depth; i++)",
600         "         {       q = trail[i].pr;",
601         "                 if (i == depthfound)",
602         "                     write(fd, \"-1:-1:-1:-1\\n\", 12);",
603         "                 if (loops)",
604         "#ifdef VERI",
605         "                 {       if (q == 2) continue;",
606         "                         if (q  > 2) q -= 2;",
607         "                 }",
608         "#else",
609         "                 {       if (q == 1) continue;",
610         "                         if (q  > 1) q--;",
611         "                 }",
612         "#endif",
613         "                 if (trail[i].o_t->ist)",
614         "                 { sprintf(snap, \"%%d:%%d:%%d:%%d\\n\", j++,",
615         "                                 q, trail[i].o_t->ist, i);",
616         "                   write(fd, snap, strlen(snap));",
617         "                 }",
618         "                 sprintf(snap, \"%%d:%%d:%%d:%%d\\n\", j++, ",
619         "                                 q, trail[i].o_t->st, i);",
620         "                 write(fd, snap, strlen(snap));",
621         "         }",
622         "         printf(\"pan: wrote pan.trail\\n\");",
623         "         close(fd);",
624         "}\n",
625         "sv_save()       /* push state vector onto save stack */",
626         "{       if (!svtack->nxt)",
627         "        {  svtack->nxt = (Svtack *) emalloc(sizeof(Svtack));",
628         "           svtack->nxt->body = emalloc(vsize*sizeof(char));",
629         "           svtack->nxt->lst = svtack;",
630         "           svtack->nxt->m_delta = vsize;",
631         "           svmax++;",
632         "        } else if (vsize > svtack->nxt->m_delta)",
633         "        {  svtack->nxt->body = emalloc(vsize*sizeof(char));",
634         "           svtack->nxt->lst = svtack;",
635         "           svtack->nxt->m_delta = vsize;",
636         "           svmax++;",
637         "        }",
638         "        svtack = svtack->nxt;",
639         "#if SYNC",
640         "        svtack->o_boq = boq;",
641         "#endif",
642         "        svtack->o_delta = vsize;",
643         "        memcpy((char *)(svtack->body), (char *)&now, vsize);",
644         "}\n",
645         "sv_restor()     /* pop state vector from save stack */",
646         "{       memcpy((char *)&now, svtack->body, svtack->o_delta);",
647         "#if SYNC",
```

```
648         "        boq = svtack->o_boq;",
649         "#endif",
650         "        if (vsize != svtack->o_delta)",
651         "                Uerror(\"sv_restor\");",
652         "        if (!svtack->lst)",
653         "                Uerror(\"error: v_restor\");",
654         "        svtack  = svtack->lst;",
655         "}\n",
656         "p_restor(h)",
657         "{       int i; char *z = (char *) &now;",
658         "        proc_offset[h] = stack->o_offset;",
659         "        memcpy(z+vsize, stack->body, stack->o_delta);",
660         "        vsize += stack->o_delta;",
661         "        i = stack->o_delqs;",
662         "        now._nr_pr += 1;",
663         "        if (!stack->lst)        /* debugging */",
664         "                Uerror(\"error: p_restor\");",
665         "        stack = stack->lst;",
666         "        this = pptr(h);",
667         "        while (i-- > 0)",
668         "                q_restor();",
669         "}\n",
670         "q_restor()",
671         "{       char *z = (char *) &now;",
672         "        q_offset[now._nr_qs] = stack->o_offset;",
673         "        memcpy(z+vsize, stack->body, stack->o_delta);",
674         "        vsize += stack->o_delta;",
675         "        now._nr_qs += 1;",
676         "        if (!stack->lst)        /* debugging */",
677         "                Uerror(\"error: q_restor\");",
678         "        stack = stack->lst;",
679         "}\n",
680         "delproc(sav, h)",
681         "{       int d, i=0;",
682         "",
683         "        if (h+1 != now._nr_pr) return 0;",
684         "",
685         "        while (now._nr_qs",
686         "        &&      q_offset[now._nr_qs-1] > proc_offset[h])",
687         "        {       delq(sav);",
688         "                i++;",
689         "        }",
690         "        d = vsize - proc_offset[h];",
691         "        if (sav)",
692         "        {       if (!stack->nxt)",
693         "                {       stack->nxt = (Stack *)",
694         "                                emalloc(sizeof(Stack));",
695         "                        stack->nxt->body = ",
696         "                                emalloc(Maxbody*sizeof(char));",
697         "                        stack->nxt->lst = stack;",
698         "                        smax++;",
699         "                }",
700         "                stack = stack->nxt;",
701         "                stack->o_offset = proc_offset[h];",
```

```
702    "             stack->o_delta   = d;",
703    "             stack->o_delqs   = i;",
704    "             memcpy(stack->body, (char *)pptr(h), d);",
705    "       }",
706    "       vsize = proc_offset[h];",
707    "       now._nr_pr = now._nr_pr - 1;",
708    "       memset((char *)pptr(h), 0, d);",
709    "       return 1;",
710    "}\n",
711    "delq(sav)",
712    "{      int h = now._nr_qs - 1;",
713    "       int d = vsize - q_offset[now._nr_qs - 1];",
714    "       if (sav)",
715    "       {      if (!stack->nxt)",
716    "              {      stack->nxt = (Stack *)",
717    "                          emalloc(sizeof(Stack));",
718    "                     stack->nxt->body = ",
719    "                          emalloc(Maxbody*sizeof(char));",
720    "                     stack->nxt->lst = stack;",
721    "                     smax++;",
722    "              }",
723    "              stack = stack->nxt;",
724    "              stack->o_offset = q_offset[h];",
725    "              stack->o_delta  = d;",
726    "              memcpy(stack->body, (char *)qptr(h), d);",
727    "       }",
728    "       vsize = q_offset[h];",
729    "       now._nr_qs = now._nr_qs - 1;",
730    "       memset((char *)qptr(h), 0, d);",
731    "}\n",
732    "prognow()",
733    "{",
734    "       int i; P0 *ptr;",
735    "       for (i = 0; i < now._nr_pr; i++)",
736    "       {      ptr = (P0 *) pptr(i);",
737    "              if (progstate[ptr->_t][ptr->_p])",
738    "                     return 1;",
739    "       }",
740    "       return 0;",
741    "}\n",
742    "endstate()",
743    "{      int i; P0 *ptr;",
744    "       for (i = 0; i < now._nr_pr; i++)",
745    "       {",
746    "#ifdef VERI",
747    "                     if (i == 1) continue;",
748    "#endif",
749    "                     ptr = (P0 *) pptr(i);",
750    "              if (!stopstate[ptr->_t][ptr->_p])",
751    "                     return 0;",
752    "       }",
753    "       if (loops)",
754    "              uerror(\"non progress sequence\");",
755    "       return 1;",
```

```
756    "}\n",
757    "onstack()",
758    "{        register Svtack *ptr;",
759    "         register char *won = (char *)&now;",
760    "         register int j=depth;",
761    "         for (ptr = svtack; ptr; ptr = ptr->lst, j--)",
762    "         if (ptr->o_delta == vsize)",
763    "         && ptr->j1 == J1 && ptr->j2 == J2",
764    "         && memcmp(ptr->body, won, vsize) == 0)",
765    "         {         depthfound = j;",
766    "                   return 1;",
767    "         }",
768    "         return 0;",
769    "}\n",
770    "#ifndef BITSTATE",
771    "#if CONNECT>0",
772    "struct H_succ {",
773    "         struct H_el *succ;      /* a successor state   */",
774    "         Trans *how;             /* how you get there   */",
775    "         int who;                /* who got us there    */",
776    "         struct H_succ *nsucc;   /* linked list, if >1 */",
777    "};",
778    "#endif",
779    "struct H_el {",
780    "         struct H_el *nxt;",
781    "#if CONNECT>0",
782    "         struct H_succ *slst;    /* list of successors */",
783    "#endif",
784    "         unsigned tagged;", /* bit 30 used in CONNECT mode */
785    "         unsigned state;",
786    "} **H_tab;\n",
787    "hinit()",
788    "{        H_tab = (struct H_el **)",
789    "                emalloc((1<<ssize)*sizeof(struct H_el *));",
790    "}\n",
791
792    "#if CONNECT>0",
793    "setparent(v, n)",
794    "         char *v;",
795    "{",
796    "         register struct H_el *tmp;",
797    "         struct H_succ *yy;",
798    "         struct Trail *TR;",
799    "         s_hash(v, n);",
800    "         for (tmp = H_tab[j1]; tmp; tmp = tmp->nxt)",
801    "         {        if (memcmp(((char *)&(tmp->state)), v, n) == 0)",
802    "                  {        trpt->parent = tmp;",
803    "                  /* next: enlist as a child */",
804    "                           for (TR = trpt-1; !TR->parent; TR--)",
805    "                                   if (TR < trail) return;",
806    "                           yy = (struct H_succ *)",
807    "                                   emalloc(sizeof(struct H_succ));",
808    "                           yy->succ = tmp;",
809    "                           yy->how  = (TR+1)->o_t;",
```

```
810      "                             yy->who   = (TR+1)->pr;",
811      "                             yy->nsucc = TR->parent->slst;",
812      "                             TR->parent->slst = yy;",
813      "                             return;",
814      "                    }",
815      "            }",
816      "       Uerror(\"cannot happen, setparent\");",
817      "}\n",
818
819      "struct H_el *acc_root;",
820      "checkaccept()",
821      "{      int i; P0 *ptr;",
822      "       if (trpt->parent)",
823      "       for (i = 0; i < now._nr_pr; i++)",
824      "       {      ptr = (P0 *) pptr(i);",
825      "              if (accpstate[ptr->_t][ptr->_p])",
826      "              {      acc_root = trpt->parent;",
827      "                     depthfound = depth;",
828      "                     dfs_acc(acc_root);",
829      "                     depthfound = -1;",
830      "                     break;",
831      "       }          }",
832      "}\n",
833      "int maxl=0;",
834      "dfs_acc(acc)    /* is 'acc' part of a cycle? */",
835      "       struct H_el *acc;",
836      "{              /* tag all non-tagged successors */",
837      "       struct H_succ *zz;",
838      "       maxl++;",
839      "       for (zz = acc->slst; zz; zz = zz->nsucc)",
840      "              if (!(zz->succ->tagged & (1<<30)))",
841      "              {      zz->succ->tagged |= (1<<30);",
842      "                     if (zz->succ == acc_root)",
843      "                     {  printf(\"cycle of length \");",
844      "                        printf(\"%%d (%%d) %%d\\n\",",
845      "                             maxl, depthfound, depth);",
846      "                        uerror(\"accept state in cycle\");",
847      "                     } else",
848      "                     {  trpt++; depth++;",
849      "                        trpt->pr  = zz->who;",
850      "                        trpt->o_t = zz->how;",
851      "                        dfs_acc(zz->succ);",
852      "                        trpt--; depth--;",
853      "              }          }",
854      "       maxl--;",
855      "}",
856      "#endif\n",
857      "htag(v, n)",
858      "       char *v;",
859      "       short n;",
860      "{",
861      "       register struct H_el *tmp;",
862      "       s_hash(v, n);",
863      "       for (tmp = H_tab[j1]; tmp; tmp = tmp->nxt)",
```

```
864    "          {            if (memcmp(((char *)&(tmp->state)), v, n) == 0)",
865    "                       {        tmp->tagged &= (1<<30);",
866    "                                return;",
867    "                       }",
868    "          }",
869    "          Uerror(\"cannot happen, htag\");",
870    "}\n",
871    "hstore(v, n)",
872    "          char *v;",
873    "          short n;",
874    "{",
875    "          register struct H_el *tmp;\n",
876    "          s_hash((uchar *)v, n);",
877    "          tmp = H_tab[j1];",
878    "          if (!tmp)",
879    "          { tmp = (struct H_el *)",
880    "              emalloc(sizeof(struct H_el)+n-sizeof(unsigned));",
881    "            H_tab[j1] = tmp;",
882    "          } else",
883    "          { for (;; hcmp++)",
884    "            { if (memcmp(&(tmp->state), v, n) == 0)",
885    "              { if (loops && now._p_t",
886    "                &&  (tmp->tagged & ~(1<<30)))",
887    "                { depthfound = tmp->tagged&~(1<<30);",
888    "                  uerror(\"non-progress cycle\");",
889    "                }",
890    "                return 1;",
891    "              }",
892    "              if (!tmp->nxt) break;",
893    "              tmp = tmp->nxt;",
894    "            }",
895    "            tmp->nxt = (struct H_el *)",
896    "              emalloc(sizeof(struct H_el)+n-sizeof(unsigned));",
897    "            tmp = tmp->nxt;",
898    "          }",
899    "          tmp->tagged = depth+1; /* non-zero while on stack */",
900    "          memcpy(((char *)&(tmp->state)), v, n);",
901    "          return 0;",
902    "}",
903    "#endif",
904    "#include \"pan.t\"",
905    "",
906    "do_reach()",
907    "{",
908    0,
909 };
910
911 /***** spin: pangen2.h *****/
912
913 char *Preamble[] = {
914    "#include        <stdio.h>",
915    "#include        <signal.h>",
916    "#include        \"pan.h\"\n",
917    "#define max(a,b) (((a)<(b)) ? (b) : (a))",
```

```
918    "typedef struct Trail {",
919    "        short pr;       /* process id    */",
920    "        short st;       /* current state */",
921    "        char o_n, o_ot, o_m, tau;", /* to save locals */
922    "        short o_tt, o_To;", /* used in new_state() */
923    "#if CONNECT>0",
924    "#ifndef BITSTATE",
925    "        struct H_el *parent;",
926    "#endif",
927    "#endif",
928    "        Trans *o_t;",    /* transition fct, next state  */
929    "        int oval;",      /* backup value of a variable */
930    "} Trail;",
931    "Trail *trail, *trpt;",
932    "uchar *this;\n",
933    "int maxdepth=10000;",
934    "uchar *SS, *LL;",
935    "char *emalloc(), *malloc(), *memset();",
936    "int mreached=0, done=0, nstates=0;",
937    "int nlinks=0, truncs=0, errors=0;",
938    "int mask, hcmp=0, loops=0, upto=1;",
939    "#ifdef BITSTATE",
940    "int ssize=22;",
941    "#else",
942    "int ssize=18;",
943    "#endif",
944    "int hmax=0, svmax=0, smax=0;",
945    "int Maxbody=0;",
946    "uchar *noptr;  /* used by macro Pptr(x) */",
947    "State  now;             /* the full state vector */",
948    "Stack  *stack;          /* for queues, processes */",
949    "Svtack *svtack;         /* for old state vectors */",
950    "int J1, J2, j1, j2, j3, j4;",
951    "int depth=0;\n",
952    "#if SYNC",
953    "#define IfNotBlocked    if (boq != -1) continue;",
954    "#define UnBlock         boq = -1",
955    "#else",
956    "#define IfNotBlocked    /* cannot block */",
957    "#define UnBlock         /* don't bother */",
958    "#endif\n",
959    0,
960 };
961
962 char *Tail[] = {
963    "Trans *",
964    "settr(a, b, c, d)",
965    "{       Trans *tmp = (Trans *) emalloc(sizeof(Trans));\n",
966    "        tmp->atom = a&6;",
967    "        tmp->st = b;",
968    "        tmp->forw = c;",
969    "        tmp->back = d;",
970    "        return tmp;",
971    "}\n",
```

```
972     "Trans *",
973     "cpytr(a)",
974     "       Trans *a;",
975     "{      Trans *tmp = (Trans *) emalloc(sizeof(Trans));\n",
976     "       tmp->atom = a->atom;",
977     "       tmp->st = a->st;",
978     "       tmp->ist = a->ist;",
979     "       tmp->forw = a->forw;",
980     "       tmp->back = a->back;",
981     "       return tmp;",
982     "}\n",
983     "int cnt;",
984     "retrans(n, m)   /* proc n, m states */",
985     "{      Trans *T0, *T1, *T2, *T3;",
986     "       int i, j=0;",
987     "       do {    j++;",
988     "               for (i = 1, cnt = 0; i < m; i++)",
989     "               {       T1 = trans[n][i]->nxt;",
990     "                       T2 = trans[n][i];",
991     "/* prescan: */          for (T0 = T1; T0; T0 = T0->nxt)",
992     "/* choice inside choice */     if (trans[n][T0->st]->nxt)",
993     "                               break;",
994     "                       if (T0)",
995     "                       for (T0 = T1; T0; T0 = T0->nxt)",
996     "                       {       T3 = trans[n][T0->st];",
997     "                               if (!T3->nxt)",
998     "                               {       T2->nxt = cpytr(T0);",
999     "                                       T2 = T2->nxt;",
1000    "                                       imed(T2, T0->st, n);",
1001    "                                       continue;",
1002    "                               }",
1003    "                               do {    T3 = T3->nxt;",
1004    "                                       T2->nxt = cpytr(T3);",
1005    "                                       T2 = T2->nxt;",
1006    "                                       imed(T2, T0->st, n);",
1007    "                               } while (T3->nxt);",
1008    "                               cnt++;",
1009    "                       }",
1010    "               }",
1011    "       } while (cnt);",
1012    "       for (i = 1; i < m; i++)",
1013    "       if (trans[n][i]->nxt)   /* optimize the list a bit */",
1014    "       {       T1 = trans[n][i]->nxt;",
1015    "               T0 = trans[n][i] = cpytr(trans[n][T1->st]);",
1016    "               imed(T0, T1->st, n);",
1017    "               for (T1 = T1->nxt; T1; T1 = T1->nxt)",
1018    "               {       T0->nxt = cpytr(trans[n][T1->st]);",
1019    "                       T0 = T0->nxt;",
1020    "                       imed(T0, T1->st, n);",
1021    "               }       }",
1022    "}",
1023    "imed(T, v, n)   /* set intermediate state */",
1024    "       Trans *T;",
1025    "{      static uchar warned=0;",
```

```
1026    "        if (T->ist && !warned)",
1027    "        {       warned=1;",
1028    "                printf(\"warning: %%s has \", procname[n]);",
1029    "                printf(\"ambiguous flow ctl structures, \");",
1030    "                printf(\"revise model\\n\");",
1031    "        }",
1032    "        progstate[n][T->st]  |= progstate[n][v];",
1033    "        accpstate[n][T->st]  |= accpstate[n][v];",
1034    "        stopstate[n][T->st]  |= stopstate[n][v];",
1035    "        T->ist = v;",
1036    "}",
1037    0,
1038 };
1039
1040
1041 char *R0[] = {
1042    "        Maxbody = max(Maxbody, sizeof(P%d));",
1043    "        reached[%d] = reached%d;",
1044    "        accpstate[%d] = (uchar *) emalloc(nstates%d);",
1045    "        progstate[%d] = (uchar *) emalloc(nstates%d);",
1046    "        stopstate[%d] = (uchar *) emalloc(nstates%d);",
1047    "        stopstate[%d][endstate%d] = 1;",
1048    "        retrans(%d, nstates%d);",
1049    0,
1050 };
1051 char *R1[] = {
1052    "        reached[%d] = (uchar *) emalloc(4*sizeof(uchar));",
1053    "        stopstate[%d] = (uchar *) emalloc(4*sizeof(uchar));",
1054    "        progstate[%d] = stopstate[%d];",
1055    "        accpstate[%d] = stopstate[%d];",
1056    0,
1057 };
1058 char *R2[] = {
1059    "uchar *accpstate[%d];",
1060    "uchar *progstate[%d];",
1061    "uchar *reached[%d];",
1062    "uchar *stopstate[%d];",
1063    0,
1064 };
1065 char *R3[] = {
1066    "        Maxbody = max(Maxbody, sizeof(Q%d));",
1067    0,
1068 };
1069 char *R4[] = {
1070    "        r_ck(reached%d, nstates%d, %d, src_ln%d);",
1071    0,
1072 };
1073 char *R5[] = {
1074    "        case %d: j = sizeof(P%d); break;",
1075    0,
1076 };
1077 char *R6[] = {
1078    "        case %d: /* progress checker */",
1079    "                ((P%d *)pptr(h))->_t = %d;",
```

```
1080    "                    ((P%d *)pptr(h))->_p = 1;",
1081    "                    now._p_t = 0;",
1082    "                    break;",
1083    "            }",
1084    "#ifdef VERI",
1085    "            if (h == 0 && !addproc(VERI))",
1086    "                    return 0;",
1087    "#endif",
1088    "            if (h == 0 && loops && !addproc(%d))",
1089    "                    return 0;",
1090    "#ifdef VERI",
1091    "            return (h>0)?h-loops-1:0;",
1092    "#else",
1093    "            return (h>0)?h-loops:0;",
1094    "#endif",
1095    "}\n",
1096    0,
1097 };
1098 char *R8[] = {
1099    "            case %d: j = sizeof(Q%d); break;",
1100    0,
1101 };
1102 char *R9[] = {
1103    "typedef struct Q%d {",
1104    "            uchar Qlen;        /* q_size */",
1105    "            uchar _t;          /* q_type */",
1106    "            struct {",
1107    0,
1108 };
1109 char *R10[] = {
1110    "typedef struct Q0 {\t/* generic q */",
1111    "            uchar Qlen, _t;",
1112    "} Q0;",
1113    0,
1114 };
1115 char *R12[] = {
1116    "\t\tcase %d: r = ((Q%d *)z)->contents[slot].fld%d; break;",
1117    0,
1118 };
1119 char *R13[] = {
1120    "unsend(into)",
1121    "{       int m=0, j; uchar *z;",
1122    "        z = qptr(into);",
1123    "        j = ((Q0 *)z)->Qlen;",
1124    "        ((Q0 *)z)->Qlen = --j;",
1125    "        switch (((Q0 *)qptr(into))->_t) {",
1126    0,
1127 };
1128 char *R14[] = {
1129    "        default: Uerror(\"bad queue - unsend\");",
1130    "        }",
1131    "        return m;",
1132    "}",
1133    "",
```

```
1134    "unrecv(from, slot, fld, fldvar, strt)",
1135    "{       int j;",
1136    "        uchar *z = qptr(from);",
1137    "        j = ((Q0 *)z)->Qlen;",
1138    "        if (strt) ((Q0 *)z)->Qlen = j+1;",
1139    "        switch (((Q0 *)qptr(from))->_t) {",
1140    0,
1141 };
1142 char *R15[] = {
1143    "        default: Uerror(\"bad queue - qrecv\");",
1144    "        }",
1145    "}",
1146    0,
1147 };
1148
1149 /***** spin: pangen1.c *****/
1150
1151 #include <stdio.h>
1152 #include <math.h>
1153 #include "spin.h"
1154 #include "y.tab.h"
1155 #include "pangen1.h"
1156 #include "pangen3.h"
1157
1158 extern FILE        *tc, *th;
1159 extern Node        *Mtype;
1160 extern ProcList    *rdy;
1161 extern Queue       *qtab;
1162 extern RunList     *run;
1163 extern Symbol      *symtab[Nhash+1];
1164 extern int nqs, nps, mst, Mpars;
1165 extern char        *claimproc;
1166
1167 enum { INIV, PUTV };
1168 int Npars=0, u_sync=0, u_async=0;
1169 int acceptors=0;
1170
1171 void
1172 genheader()
1173 {  ProcList *p;
1174    int i;
1175    fprintf(th, "#define SYNC       %d\n", u_sync);
1176    fprintf(th, "#define ASYNC      %d\n\n", u_async);
1177
1178    fprintf(tc, "char *procname[] = {\n");
1179    put_ptype(run->n->name, (Node *) 0, 0, mst, nps);
1180    for (p = rdy, i = 1; p; p = p->nxt, i++)
1181            put_ptype(p->n->name, p->p, i, mst, nps);
1182    put_ptype("_progress", (Node *) 0, i, mst, nps);
1183    fprintf(tc, "};\n\n");
1184    ntimes(th, 0, 1, Header);
1185    doglobal(PUTV);
1186    fprintf(th, "   uchar sv[VECTORSZ];\n");
1187    fprintf(th, "} State;\n");
```

```
1188 }
1189
1190 void
1191 genaddproc()
1192 { ProcList *p;
1193    int i;
1194
1195    fprintf(tc, "addproc(n");
1196    for (i = 0; i < Npars; i++)
1197            fprintf(tc, ", par%d", i);
1198
1199    ntimes(tc, 0, 1, Addp0);
1200    ntimes(tc, 1, nps, R5);
1201    ntimes(tc, 0, 1, Addp1);
1202
1203    put_pinit(run->pc, run->n, (Node *) 0, 0);
1204    for (p = rdy, i = 1; p; p = p->nxt, i++)
1205            put_pinit(p->s->frst, p->n, p->p, i);
1206
1207    ntimes(tc, i, i+1, R6);
1208 }
1209
1210 void
1211 genother(cnt)
1212 { ProcList *p;
1213    int i;
1214
1215    ntimes(tc,   0,   1, Code0);
1216    ntimes(tc,   0, cnt,    R0);
1217    ntimes(tc, cnt, cnt+1, R1);
1218    end_labs(run->n, 0);
1219    for (p = rdy, i = 1; p; p = p->nxt, i++)
1220            end_labs(p->n, i);
1221    ntimes(th, acceptors, acceptors+1, Code1);
1222    ntimes(th, i+1, i+2, R2);
1223
1224    doglobal(INIV);
1225    ntimes(tc, 1, nqs+1, R3);
1226    ntimes(tc, 0,     1, Code2);
1227    ntimes(tc, 0,     i, R4);
1228    fprintf(tc, "}\n\n");
1229 }
1230
1231 static struct {
1232    char *s, *t; int n, m;
1233 } ln[] = {
1234    "end",          "stopstate",    3,      0,
1235    "progress",     "progstate",    8,      0,
1236    "accept",       "accpstate",    6,      1,
1237    0,              0,              0,      0,
1238 };
1239
1240 void
1241 end_labs(s, i)
```

```
1242    Symbol *s;
1243  {
1244     extern Label *labtab;
1245     Label *l;
1246     int j;
1247
1248     for (l = labtab; l; l = l->nxt)
1249     for (j = 0; ln[j].n; j++)
1250             if (strncmp(l->s->name, ln[j].s, ln[j].n) == 0
1251             &&  strcmp(l->s->context->name, s->name) == 0)
1252             {       fprintf(tc, "\t%s[%d][%d] = 1;\n",
1253                             ln[j].t, i, l->e->seqno);
1254                     acceptors += ln[j].m;
1255             }
1256  }
1257
1258  void
1259  ntimes(fd, n, m, c)
1260     FILE *fd;
1261     char *c[];
1262  {
1263     int i, j;
1264     for (j = 0; c[j]; j++)
1265     for (i = n; i < m; i++)
1266     {       fprintf(fd, c[j], i, i, i, i);
1267             fprintf(fd, "\n");
1268     }
1269  }
1270
1271  void
1272  dolocal(dowhat, p, s)
1273     char *s;
1274  {
1275     int i;
1276     Symbol *sp;
1277     char buf[64];
1278
1279     for (i = 0; i <= Nhash; i++)
1280     for (sp = symtab[i]; sp; sp = sp->next)
1281             if (sp->context && sp->type != 0
1282             &&  strcmp(s, sp->context->name) == 0)
1283             {       sprintf(buf, "((P%d *)pptr(h))->", p);
1284                     do_var(dowhat, buf, sp);
1285             }
1286  }
1287
1288  void
1289  doglobal(dowhat)
1290  { Symbol *sp;
1291     int i;
1292
1293     for (i = 0; i <= Nhash; i++)
1294     for (sp = symtab[i]; sp; sp = sp->next)
1295             if (!sp->context && sp->type)
```

```
1296                        do_var(dowhat, "now.", sp);
1297 }
1298
1299 void
1300 do_var(dowhat, s, sp)
1301    char *s;
1302    Symbol *sp;
1303 {
1304    int i;
1305
1306    switch(dowhat) {
1307    case PUTV:
1308            typ2c(sp);
1309            break;
1310    case INIV:
1311            if (!sp->ini)
1312                    break;
1313            if (sp->nel == 1)
1314            {       fprintf(tc, "\t\t%s%s = ", s, sp->name);
1315                    do_init(sp);
1316            } else
1317            for (i = 0; i < sp->nel; i++)
1318            {       fprintf(tc, "\t\t%s%s[%d] = ", s, sp->name, i);
1319                    do_init(sp);
1320            }
1321            break;
1322    }
1323 }
1324
1325 void
1326 do_init(sp)
1327    Symbol *sp;
1328 {
1329    int i;
1330
1331    if (sp->type == CHAN && ((i = qmake(sp)) > 0))
1332            fprintf(tc, "addqueue(%d);\n", i);
1333    else
1334            fprintf(tc, "%d;\n", eval(sp->ini));
1335 }
1336
1337 blog(n)     /* for small log2 without rounding problems */
1338 {   int m=1, r=2;
1339    while (r < n) { m++; r *= 2; }
1340    return 1+m;
1341 }
1342
1343 void
1344 put_ptype(s, p, i, m0, m1)
1345    char *s;
1346    Node *p;
1347 {
1348    Node *fp, *fpt;
1349    int j;
```

```
1350    fprintf(tc, "    \"%s\",\n", s);
1351    fprintf(th, "typedef struct P%d { /* %s */\n", i, s);
1352    fprintf(th, "    unsigned _t : %d; /* proctype */\n", blog(m1));
1353    fprintf(th, "    unsigned _p : %d; /* state    */\n", blog(m0));
1354    dolocal(PUTV, i, s);      /* includes pars */
1355    fprintf(th, "} P%d;\n", i);
1356
1357    for (fp  = p, j = 0;  fp;  fp = fp->rgt)
1358    for (fpt = fp->lft; fpt; fpt = fpt->rgt)
1359            j++;      /* count # of parameters */
1360    Npars = max(Npars, j);
1361 }
1362
1363 void
1364 put_pinit(e, s, p, i)
1365    Element *e;
1366    Symbol *s;
1367    Node *p;
1368 {
1369    Node *fp, *fpt;
1370    int ini, j;
1371
1372    ini = huntele(e, e->status)->seqno;
1373
1374    fprintf(tc, "\tcase %d: /* %s */\n", i, s->name);
1375    fprintf(tc, "\t\t((P%d *)pptr(h))->_t = %d;\n", i, i);
1376    fprintf(tc, "\t\t((P%d *)pptr(h))->_p = %d;", i, ini);
1377    fprintf(tc, " reached%d[%d]=1;\n", i, ini);
1378    dolocal(INIV, i, s->name);
1379    for (fp  = p, j=0; fp; fp = fp->rgt)
1380    for (fpt = fp->lft; fpt; fpt = fpt->rgt, j++)
1381    {       if (fpt->nsym->nel != 1)
1382            fatal("array in parameter list, %s", fpt->nsym->name);
1383            fprintf(tc, "\t\t((P%d *)pptr(h))->%s = par%d;\n",
1384                            i, fpt->nsym->name, j);
1385    }
1386    fprintf(tc, "\t break;\n");
1387 }
1388
1389 huntstart(f)
1390    Element *f;
1391 {
1392    Element *e = f;
1393
1394    if (e->n)
1395    {       if (e->n->ntyp=='.' && e->nxt)
1396                    e = e->nxt;
1397            else if (e->n->ntyp == ATOMIC)
1398                    e->n->seql->this->last->nxt = e->nxt;
1399    }
1400    return e->seqno;
1401 }
1402
1403 Element *
```

```
1404 huntele(f, o)
1405     Element *f;
1406 {
1407     Element *g, *e = f;
1408     int cnt; /* a precaution against loops */
1409     for (cnt=0; cnt < 10 && e->n; cnt++)
1410     {       switch (e->n->ntyp) {
1411             case GOTO:
1412                     g = get_lab(e->n->nsym);
1413                     break;
1414             case '.':
1415             case BREAK:
1416                     if (!e->nxt)
1417                             return e;
1418                     g = e->nxt;
1419                     break;
1420             case ATOMIC:
1421                     e->n->seql->this->last->nxt = e->nxt;
1422             default:        /* fall through */
1423                     return e;
1424             }
1425             if ((o & ATOM) && !(g->status & ATOM))
1426                     return e;
1427             e = g;
1428     }
1429     return e;
1430 }
1431
1432 void
1433 typ2c(sp)
1434     Symbol *sp;
1435 {
1436     switch (sp->type) {
1437     case BIT:
1438             if (sp->nel == 1)
1439             {       fprintf(th, "\tunsigned %s : 1", sp->name);
1440                     break;
1441             } /* else fall through */
1442     case CHAN:      /* good for up to 255 channels */
1443     case BYTE:
1444             fprintf(th, "\tuchar %s", sp->name);
1445             break;
1446     case SHORT:
1447             fprintf(th, "\tshort %s", sp->name);
1448             break;
1449     case INT:
1450             fprintf(th, "\tint %s", sp->name);
1451             break;
1452     case PREDEF:
1453             return;
1454     default:
1455             fatal("variable %s undeclared", sp->name);
1456     }
1457     if (sp->nel != 1)
```

```
1458                fprintf(th, "[%d]", sp->nel);
1459      fprintf(th, ";\n");
1460  }
1461
1462  void
1463  ncases(fd, p, n, m, c)
1464      FILE *fd;
1465      char *c[];
1466  {
1467      int i, j;
1468      for (j = 0; c[j]; j++)
1469      for (i = n; i < m; i++)
1470      {       fprintf(fd, c[j], i, p, i);
1471              fprintf(fd, "\n");
1472      }
1473  }
1474
1475  void
1476  genaddqueue()
1477  {   char *buf0;
1478      int j;
1479      Queue *q;
1480
1481      buf0 = (char *) emalloc(32);
1482      ntimes(tc, 0, 1, Addq0);
1483      for (q = qtab; q; q = q->nxt)
1484      {       ntimes(tc, q->qid, q->qid+1, R8);
1485              ntimes(th, q->qid, q->qid+1, R9);
1486              for (j = 0; j < q->nflds; j++)
1487              {       switch (q->fld_width[j]) {
1488                      case BIT:
1489                              fprintf(th, "\t\tunsigned");
1490                              fprintf(th, " fld%d : 1;\n", j);
1491                              break;
1492                      case CHAN:
1493                      case BYTE:
1494                              fprintf(th, "\t\tuchar fld%d;\n", j);
1495                              break;
1496                      case SHORT:
1497                              fprintf(th, "\t\tshort fld%d;\n", j);
1498                              break;
1499                      case INT:
1500                              fprintf(th, "\t\tint fld%d;\n", j);
1501                              break;
1502                      default:
1503                              fatal("bad channel spec", "");
1504                      }
1505              }
1506              fprintf(th, "  } contents[%d];\n", max(1, q->nslots));
1507              fprintf(th, "} Q%d;\n", q->qid);
1508      }
1509      ntimes(th, 0, 1, R10);
1510      ntimes(tc, 0, 1, Addq1);
1511
```

```
1512    fprintf(tc, "qsend(into");
1513    for (j = 0; j < Mpars; j++)
1514            fprintf(tc, ", fld%d", j);
1515    fprintf(tc, ")\n");
1516    ntimes(tc, 0, 1, Addq11);

1518    for (q = qtab; q; q = q->nxt)
1519    {       sprintf(buf0, "((Q%d *)z)->", q->qid);
1520            fprintf(tc, "\tcase %d: j = %sQlen;\n", q->qid, buf0);
1521            fprintf(tc, "\t\t%sQlen = j+1;\n", buf0);
1522            if (q->nslots == 0)     /* reset handshake point */
1523                    fprintf(tc, "\t\t(trpt+2)->o_m = 0;\n");
1524            sprintf(buf0, "((Q%d *)z)->contents[j].fld", q->qid);
1525            for (j = 0; j < q->nflds; j++)
1526                    fprintf(tc, "\t\t%s%d = fld%d;\n", buf0, j, j);
1527            fprintf(tc, "\t\tbreak;\n");
1528    }
1529    ntimes(tc, 0, 1, Addq2);

1531    for (q = qtab; q; q = q->nxt)
1532    fprintf(tc, "\tcase %d: return %d;\n", q->qid, (!q->nslots));

1534    ntimes(tc, 0, 1, Addq3);

1536    for (q = qtab; q; q = q->nxt)
1537    fprintf(tc, "\tcase %d: return (q_sz(from) == %d);\n",
1538                    q->qid, max(1, q->nslots));

1540    ntimes(tc, 0, 1, Addq4);
1541    for (q = qtab; q; q = q->nxt)
1542    {       sprintf(buf0, "((Q%d *)z)->", q->qid);
1543            fprintf(tc, "   case %d:", q->qid);
1544            if (q->nflds == 1)
1545            {       fprintf(tc, "\tif (fld == 0) r = %s", buf0);
1546                    fprintf(tc, "contents[slot].fld0;\n");
1547            } else
1548            {       fprintf(tc, "\tswitch (fld) {\n");
1549                    ncases(tc, q->qid, 0, q->nflds, R12);
1550                    fprintf(tc, "\t\t}\n");
1551            }
1552            fprintf(tc, "\t\tif (done)\n");
1553            fprintf(tc, "\t\t{       j = %sQlen;\n", buf0);
1554            fprintf(tc, "\t\t        %sQlen = --j;\n", buf0);
1555            fprintf(tc, "\t\t        for (k=0; k<j; k++)\n", q->qid);
1556            fprintf(tc, "\t\t        {\n");

1558            sprintf(buf0, "\t\t\t((Q%d *)z)->contents", q->qid);
1559            for (j = 0; j < q->nflds; j++)
1560            {       fprintf(tc, "\t%s[k].fld%d = \n", buf0, j);
1561                    fprintf(tc, "\t\t%s[k+1].fld%d;\n", buf0, j);
1562            }
1563            fprintf(tc, "\t\t        }\n");
1564            for (j = 0; j < q->nflds; j++)
1565                    fprintf(tc, "%s[j].fld%d = 0;\n", buf0, j);
```

```
1566                    fprintf(tc, "\t\t\tif (fld+1 != %d)\n\t\t\t", q->nflds);
1567                    fprintf(tc, "\tuerror(\"missing pars in receive\");\n");
1568                    /* incompletely received msgs cannot be unrecv'ed */
1569                    fprintf(tc, "\t\t}\n");
1570                    fprintf(tc, "\t\tbreak;\n");
1571      }
1572      ntimes(tc, 0, 1, Addq5);
1573 }
1574
1575 /***** spin: pangen2.c *****/
1576
1577 #include <stdio.h>
1578 #include "spin.h"
1579 #include "y.tab.h"
1580 #include "pangen2.h"
1581
1582 extern ProcList    *rdy;
1583 extern RunList     *run;
1584 extern Symbol      *Fname;
1585 extern char        *claimproc;
1586 extern int lineno;
1587 extern int Mpars;
1588
1589 FILE       *tc, *th, *tt, *tm, *tb;
1590 int        uniq=1;
1591 int        nocast=0;        /* to turn off casts in lvalues */
1592 int        terse=0;         /* terse printing of varnames */
1593 int        nps=0;           /* number of processes */
1594 int        mst=0;           /* max nr of state/process */
1595 int        claimnr = -1;    /* claim process, if any */
1596 int        Pid;             /* proc currently processed */
1597
1598 fproc(s)
1599     char *s;
1600 {
1601     ProcList *p;
1602     int i;
1603
1604     if (strcmp("_init", s) == 0)
1605             return 0;
1606     for (p = rdy, i = 1; p; p = p->nxt, i++)
1607             if (strcmp(p->n->name, s) == 0)
1608                     return i;
1609     fatal("proctype %s not found", s);
1610 }
1611
1612 void
1613 gensrc()
1614 { ProcList *p;
1615     int i;
1616
1617     if (!(tc = fopen("pan.c", "w"))          /* main routines */
1618     || !(th = fopen("pan.h", "w"))          /* header file   */
1619     || !(tt = fopen("pan.t", "w"))          /* transition matrix */
```

```
1620       ||  !(tm = fopen("pan.m", "w"))              /* forward  moves */
1621       ||  !(tb = fopen("pan.b", "w")))             /* backward moves */
1622       {         printf("spin: cannot create pan.[chtmb]\n");
1623                 exit(1);
1624       }
1625       fprintf(th, "/*** %s ***/\n", Fname->name);
1626       fprintf(th, "#define uchar       unsigned char\n");
1627       if (claimproc)
1628       {         claimnr = fproc(claimproc);
1629                 fprintf(th, "#define VERI       %d\n",  claimnr);
1630                 fprintf(th, "#define claimline");
1631                 fprintf(th, "  src_ln%d[((P0 *)pptr(1))->_p]\n",
1632                                                       claimnr);
1633       }
1634       ntimes(tc, 0, 1, Preamble);
1635
1636       mst = run->maxseq;
1637       for (p = rdy, i = 1; p; p = p->nxt, i++)
1638                 mst = max(p->s->last->seqno, mst);
1639       nps = i+1;        /* add progress checker */
1640
1641       fprintf(tt, "settable()\n{\tTrans *T, *settr();\n\n");
1642       fprintf(tt, "\ttrans = (Trans ***) ");
1643       fprintf(tt, "emalloc(%d*sizeof(Trans **));\n", nps);
1644
1645       fprintf(tm, "  switch (t->forw) {\n");
1646       fprintf(tm, "  default: Uerror(\"bad forward move\");\n");
1647
1648       fprintf(tb, "  switch (t->back) {\n");
1649       fprintf(tb, "  default: Uerror(\"bad return move\");\n");
1650       fprintf(tb, "  case 0: goto R999; /* nothing to undo */\n");
1651
1652       if (!run) fatal("no runable process", (char *)0);
1653
1654       putproc(run->n, run->pc, 0, run->maxseq);
1655       for (p = rdy, i = 1; p; p = p->nxt, i++)
1656                 putproc(p->n, p->s->frst, i, p->s->last->seqno);
1657       putprogress(i, 2);
1658       ntimes(tt, 0, 1, Tail);
1659       genheader();
1660       genaddproc();
1661       genother(i);
1662       genaddqueue();
1663       genunio();
1664 }
1665
1666 void
1667 putproc(n, e, i, j)
1668    Symbol *n;
1669    Element *e;
1670 {
1671    Pid = i;
1672    fprintf(th, "\nshort nstates%d=%d;\t/* %s */\n", i, j+1, n->name);
1673    fprintf(tm, "\n            /* PROC %s */\n", n->name);
```

```
1674     fprintf(tb, "\n                    /* PROC %s */\n", n->name);
1675     fprintf(tt, "\n /* proctype %d: %s */\n", i, n->name);
1676     fprintf(tt, "\n trans[%d] = (Trans **)", i);
1677     fprintf(tt, " emalloc(%d*sizeof(Trans *));\n\n", j+1);
1678     putseq(e);
1679     dumpsrc(j, i);
1680 }
1681
1682 void
1683 putprogress(i, j)   /* loop detector */
1684 {
1685     fprintf(th, "\nshort nstates%d=%d;\t/* _progress */\n", i, j+1);
1686
1687     fprintf(tt, "\n /* proctype %d: _progress */\n", i);
1688     fprintf(tt, "\n trans[%d] = (Trans **)", i);
1689     fprintf(tt, " emalloc(%d*sizeof(Trans *));\n\n", j+1);
1690     fprintf(tt, "    trans[%d][1]    = settr(1,2,%d,%d);\n",
1691                                    i, uniq+1, uniq+1);
1692     fprintf(tt, "    trans[%d][2]    = settr(1,0,%d,%d);\n",
1693                                    i, uniq+2, uniq+2);
1694     fprintf(tt, "}\n");
1695
1696     fprintf(tm, "\n                /* _progress */\n");
1697     fprintf(tm, "    case %d:          /* progress */\n", uniq+1);
1698     fprintf(tm, "             IfNotBlocked\n");
1699     fprintf(tm, "             now._p_t = 1;\n");
1700     fprintf(tm, "             m = 3; goto P999;\n");
1701     fprintf(tm, "    case %d:\n", uniq+2);
1702     fprintf(tm, "             continue;\n");
1703     fprintf(tm, "    }\n\n");
1704
1705     fprintf(tb, "\n                /* _progress */\n");
1706     fprintf(tb, "    case %d:          /* progress */\n", uniq+1);
1707     fprintf(tb, "             now._p_t = 0;\n");
1708     fprintf(tb, "             goto R999;\n");
1709     fprintf(tb, "    case %d:\n", uniq+2);
1710     fprintf(tb, "             goto R999;\n");
1711     fprintf(tb, "    }\n\n");
1712 }
1713
1714 void
1715 putseq(f)
1716     Element *f;
1717 {
1718     Element *e;
1719     SeqList *h;
1720     int n, a;
1721
1722     for (e = f; e; e = e->nxt)
1723     {       if (e->status & DONE) continue;
1724             e->status |= DONE;
1725             if (e->n->nval) putsrc(e->n->nval, e->seqno);
1726             if (e->sub)
1727             {       fprintf(tt, "\tT = trans[%d][%d] = ",
```

```
1728                                                 Pid, e->seqno);
1729                 fprintf(tt, "settr(%d,0,0,0);", e->status);
1730                 blurb(tt, e->n->ntyp, e->n->nval);
1731                 for (h = e->sub; h; h = h->nxt)
1732                 {       putskip(h->this->frst->seqno);
1733                         a = huntstart(h->this->frst);
1734                         if (h->nxt)
1735                                 fprintf(tt, "\tT = T->nxt\t= ");
1736                         else
1737                                 fprintf(tt, "\t    T->nxt\t= ");
1738                         fprintf(tt, "settr(%d,%d,0,0);",
1739                                         e->status, a);
1740                         blurb(tt, e->n->ntyp, e->n->nval);
1741                 }
1742                 for (h = e->sub; h; h = h->nxt)
1743                         putseq(h->this->frst);
1744         } else
1745         {       if (e->n && e->n->ntyp == ATOMIC)
1746                 {       patch_atomic(e->n->seql->this);
1747                         putskip(e->n->seql->this->frst->seqno);
1748                         a = huntstart(e->n->seql->this->frst);
1749                         fprintf(tt, "\tT = trans[%d][%d] = ",
1750                                         Pid, e->seqno);
1751                         fprintf(tt, "settr(%d,0,0,0);", ATOM);
1752                         blurb(tt, e->n->ntyp, e->n->nval);
1753                         fprintf(tt, "\t    T->nxt\t= ");
1754                         fprintf(tt, "settr(%d,%d,0,0);", ATOM,a);
1755                         blurb(tt, e->n->ntyp, e->n->nval);
1756                         e->n->seql->this->last->nxt = e->nxt;

1758                         putseq(e->n->seql->this->frst);
1759                         break;
1760                 }
1761                 if (e->n->ntyp == GOTO)
1762                         a = huntele(get_lab(e->n->nsym),
1763                                         e->status)->seqno;
1764                 else if (e->nxt)
1765                         a = huntele(e->nxt, e->status)->seqno;
1766                 else
1767                         a = 0;
1768                 fprintf(tt, "\ttrans[%d][%d]\t= ",
1769                                         Pid, e->seqno);
1770                 if (any_undo(e->n))
1771                         fprintf(tt, "settr(%d,%d,%d,%d);",
1772                                 e->status, a, uniq, uniq);
1773                 else
1774                         fprintf(tt, "settr(%d,%d,%d,0);",
1775                                 e->status, a, uniq);
1776                 blurb(tt, e->n->ntyp, e->n->nval);
1777                 fprintf(tm, "\tcase  %d: /* STATE ", uniq++);
1778                 fprintf(tm, "%d - type %d - line %d */\n\t\t",
1779                                 e->seqno, e->n->ntyp, e->n->nval);
1780                 if (e->n && e->n->ntyp != 'r' && Pid != claimnr)
1781                         fprintf(tm, "IfNotBlocked\n\t\t");
```

```
1782                          putstmnt(tm, e->n, e->seqno);
1783                          n = getweight(e->n);
1784                          fprintf(tm, ";\n\t\tm = %d; goto P999;\n", n);
1785                          if (any_undo(e->n))
1786                          {       fprintf(tb, "\tcase  %d: ", uniq-1);
1787                                  fprintf(tb, "/* STATE %d */\n\t\t",
1788                                                          e->seqno);
1789                                  undostmnt(e->n, e->seqno);
1790                                  fprintf(tb, ";\n\t\tgoto R999;\n", n);
1791                          }
1792                  }
1793          }
1794 }
1795
1796 void
1797 patch_atomic(s)
1798      Sequence *s;
1799 {  /* catch goto's that break the chain */
1800      Element *f, *g;
1801      SeqList *h;
1802      for (f = s->frst; ; f = f->nxt)
1803      {       if (f->n && f->n->ntyp == GOTO)
1804              {       g = get_lab(f->n->nsym);
1805                      if ((f->status & ATOM)
1806                      && !(g->status & ATOM))
1807                      {       f->status &= ~ATOM;
1808                              f->status |= L_ATOM;
1809                      }
1810              } else
1811              for (h = f->sub; h; h = h->nxt)
1812                      patch_atomic(h->this);
1813              if (f == s->last)
1814                      break;
1815      }
1816 }
1817
1818 #define cat0(x)    putstmnt(fd,now->lft,m); fprintf(fd, x); \
1819                    putstmnt(fd,now->rgt,m)
1820 #define cat1(x)            fprintf(fd,"("); cat0(x); fprintf(fd,")")
1821 #define cat2(x,y)          fprintf(fd,x); putstmnt(fd,y,m)
1822 #define cat3(x,y,z)        fprintf(fd,x); putstmnt(fd,y,m); fprintf(fd,z)
1823
1824 void
1825 putstmnt(fd, now, m)
1826      FILE *fd;
1827      Node *now;
1828 {
1829      Node *v;
1830      int i, j; extern int m_loss;
1831
1832      if (!now) { fprintf(fd, "0"); return; }
1833      if (now->ntyp != CONST) lineno = now->nval;
1834      switch (now->ntyp) {
1835      case CONST:    fprintf(fd, "%d", now->nval); break;
```

```
1836    case '!':       cat3("!(", now->lft, ")"); break;
1837    case UMIN:      cat3("-(", now->lft, ")"); break;
1838    case '~':       cat3("~(", now->lft, ")"); break;
1839
1840    case '/':       cat1("/");  break;
1841    case '*':       cat1("*");  break;
1842    case '-':       cat1("-");  break;
1843    case '+':       cat1("+");  break;
1844    case '%':       cat1("%%"); break;
1845    case '<':       cat1("<");  break;
1846    case '>':       cat1(">");  break;
1847    case '&':       cat1("&");  break;
1848    case '|':       cat1("|");  break;
1849    case LE:        cat1("<="); break;
1850    case GE:        cat1(">="); break;
1851    case NE:        cat1("!="); break;
1852    case EQ:        cat1("=="); break;
1853    case OR:        cat1("||"); break;
1854    case AND:       cat1("&&"); break;
1855    case LSHIFT:    cat1("<<"); break;
1856    case RSHIFT:    cat1(">>"); break;
1857
1858    case TIMEOUT:   fprintf(fd, "((trpt->tau)&1)"); break;
1859
1860    case RUN:       if (claimproc
1861                    &&  strcmp(now->nsym->name, claimproc) == 0)
1862                            fatal("%s is claim, not runnable",
1863                                                    claimproc);
1864                    fprintf(fd,"addproc(%d", fproc(now->nsym->name));
1865                    for (v = now->lft; v; v = v->rgt)
1866                    {       cat2(", ", v->lft);
1867                    }
1868                    fprintf(fd, ")");
1869                    break;
1870    case LEN:       putname(fd, "q_sz(", now->lft, m, ")");
1871                    break;
1872
1873    case 's':       fprintf(fd, "\n#if (SYNC>0 && ASYNC==0)\n\t\t");
1874                    putname(fd, "if (q_sz(", now->lft, m, "))\n");
1875                    fprintf(fd, "#else\n\t\t");
1876                    putname(fd, "if (q_full(", now->lft, m, "))\n");
1877                    fprintf(fd, "#endif\n");
1878                    if (m_loss)
1879                            fprintf(fd, "\t\t{ m=3; goto P999; }\n");
1880                    else
1881                            fprintf(fd, "\t\t\tcontinue;\n");
1882                    putname(fd, "\t\tqsend(", now->lft, m, "");
1883                    for (v = now->rgt, i = 0; v; v = v->rgt, i++)
1884                    {       cat2(", ", v->lft);
1885                    }
1886                    if (i > Mpars)
1887                            fatal("too many pars in send", "");
1888                    for ( ; i < Mpars; i++)
1889                            fprintf(fd, ", 0");
```

```
1890                          fprintf(fd, ");\n");
1891                          fprintf(fd, "#if SYNC\n#if ASYNC==0\n");
1892                          putname(fd, "\t\tboq = ", now->lft, m, ";\n");
1893                          fprintf(fd, "#else\n\t\t");
1894                          putname(fd, "if (q_zero(", now->lft, m, ")) ");
1895                          putname(fd, "boq = ",now->lft,m,";\n");
1896                          fprintf(fd, "#endif\n#endif\n\t\t");
1897                          break;
1898      case 'r':           fprintf(fd, "\n#if SYNC\n#if ASYNC==0\n");
1899                          putname(fd, "\t\tif (boq != ", now->lft,m,")");
1900                          fprintf(fd, " continue;\n#else\n");
1901                          putname(fd, "\t\tif (q_zero(", now->lft,m,"))");
1902                          fprintf(fd, "\n\t\t");
1903                          putname(fd, "{  if (boq != ",  now->lft,m,")");
1904                          fprintf(fd, " continue;\n\t\t} else\n\t\t");
1905                          fprintf(fd, "{  if (boq != -1) continue;\n\t\t");
1906                          fprintf(fd, "}\n#endif\n#endif\n\t\t");
1907                          putname(fd, "if (q_sz(", now->lft, m, ") == 0)");
1908                          fprintf(fd, " continue");
1909      /* test */          for (v = now->rgt, i=j=0; v; v = v->rgt, i++)
1910                          {       if (v->lft->ntyp != CONST)
1911                                  {       j++; continue;
1912                                  }
1913                                  fprintf(fd, ";\n\t\t");
1914                                  cat3("if (",  v->lft, " != ");
1915                                  putname(fd, "qrecv(", now->lft, m, ", ");
1916                                  fprintf(fd, "0, %d, 0)) continue", i);
1917                          }
1918                          if (j > 0)
1919                                  fprintf(fd, ";\n\t\tsv_save()");
1920      /* set */           for (v = now->rgt, i = 0; v; v = v->rgt, i++)
1921                          {       if (v->lft->ntyp == CONST && v->rgt)
1922                                          continue;
1923                                  fprintf(fd, ";\n\t\t");
1924                                  if (v->lft->ntyp != CONST)
1925                                  {       nocast=1;
1926                                          putstmnt(fd, v->lft, m);
1927                                          nocast=0; fprintf(fd, " = ");
1928                                  }
1929                                  putname(fd, "qrecv(", now->lft, m, "");
1930                                  fprintf(fd, ", 0, %d, ", i);
1931                                  fprintf(fd, "%d)", (v->rgt)?0:1);
1932                          }
1933                          fprintf(fd, ";\n#if SYNC\n");
1934                          putname(fd, "\t\tif (q_zero(", now->lft, m, "");
1935                          fprintf(fd, ")) boq = -1;\n#endif\n\t\t");
1936                          break;
1937      case 'R':           putname(fd, "(q_sz(", now->lft, m, ") > 0)");
1938      /* test */          for (v = now->rgt, i=j=0; v; v = v->rgt, i++)
1939                          {       if (v->lft->ntyp != CONST)
1940                                  {       j++; continue;
1941                                  }
1942                                  fprintf(fd, "\n\t\t&& qrecv(");
1943                                  putname(fd, "", now->lft, m, "");
```

```
1944                              fprintf(fd, ", 0, %d, 0) == ", i);
1945                              putstmnt(fd, v->lft, m);
1946                      }
1947                 fprintf(fd, ")");
1948                 break;
1949
1950     case 'c':   cat3("if (!(", now->lft, "))\n");
1951                 fprintf(fd, "\t\t\tcontinue");
1952                 break;
1953     case ASGN:  cat3("(trpt+1)->oval = ", now->lft, ";\n\t\t");
1954                 nocast = 1; putstmnt(fd,now->lft,m); nocast = 0;
1955                 fprintf(fd," = ");
1956                 putstmnt(fd,now->rgt,m);
1957                 break;
1958     case PRINT: fprintf(fd, "printf(%s", now->nsym->name);
1959                 for (v = now->lft; v; v = v->rgt)
1960                 {       cat2(", ", v->lft);
1961                 }
1962                 fprintf(fd, ")");
1963                 break;
1964     case NAME:  if (!nocast && now->nsym
1965                 &&  now->nsym->type < SHORT)
1966                         putname(fd, "((int)", now, m, ")");
1967                 else
1968                         putname(fd, "", now, m, "");
1969                 break;
1970     case  'p':  putremote(fd, now, m);
1971                 break;
1972     case  'q':  if (terse)
1973                         fprintf(fd, "%s", now->nsym->name);
1974                 else
1975                         fprintf(fd, "%d", remotelab(now));
1976                 break;
1977     case ASSERT: cat3("assert(", now->lft, ", ");
1978                 terse = nocast = 1;
1979                 cat3("\"", now->lft, "\\n\", II, tt, t)");
1980                 terse = nocast = 0;
1981                 break;
1982     case  '.':
1983     case BREAK:
1984     case  GOTO:  putskip(m);
1985                 break;
1986     case  '@':  fprintf(fd, "if (!delproc(1, II)) continue");
1987                 fprintf(th, "#define endstate%d %d\n", Pid, m);
1988                 break;
1989     default  :  printf("spin: bad node type %d (.m)\n",
1990                                               now->ntyp);
1991                 exit(1);
1992     }
1993 }
1994
1995 void
1996 putname(fd, pre, n, m, suff)              /* varref */
1997     FILE *fd;
```

```
1998    Node *n;
1999    char *pre, *suff;
2000 {
2001    Symbol *s = n->nsym;
2002    if (!s)
2003            fatal("no name - putname", "");
2004    if (s->context && !s->type)      /* not a local name */
2005            s = lookup(s->name);      /* must be a global */
2006    if (!s->type)
2007            yyerror("undeclared name '%s'", s->name);
2008    fprintf(fd, pre);
2009    if (s->context || !strcmp(s->name, "_p"))
2010    {       if (!terse) fprintf(fd, "((P%d *)this)->", Pid);
2011            fprintf(fd, "%s", s->name);
2012    } else
2013    {       if (!terse) fprintf(fd, "now.");
2014            fprintf(fd, "%s", s->name);
2015    }
2016    if (s->nel != 1)
2017    {       cat3("[", n->lft, "]");
2018    }
2019    fprintf(fd, suff);
2020 }
2021
2022 void
2023 putremote(fd, n, m)                     /* remote reference */
2024    FILE *fd;
2025    Node *n;
2026 {
2027    if (terse)
2028    {       fprintf(fd, "%s[", n->lft->nsym->name);
2029            putstmnt(fd, n->lft->lft, m);
2030            if (strcmp(n->nsym->name, "_p") == 0)
2031                    fprintf(fd, "]:");
2032            else
2033                    fprintf(fd, "].%s", n->nsym->name);
2034    } else
2035    {       fprintf(fd, "((P%d *)Pptr(loops+",
2036                    fproc(n->lft->nsym->name));
2037            if (claimproc) fprintf(fd, "1+");
2038            putstmnt(fd, n->lft->lft, m);
2039            fprintf(fd, "))->%s", n->nsym->name);
2040    }
2041    if (n->rgt)
2042    {       fprintf(fd, "[");
2043            putstmnt(fd, n->rgt, m);
2044            fprintf(fd, "]");
2045    }
2046 }
2047
2048 getweight(n)
2049    Node *n;
2050 {
2051    switch (n->ntyp) {
```

```
2052    case 'r':     return 4;
2053    case 's':     return 2;
2054    case TIMEOUT: return 1; /* lowest priority */
2055    case 'c':     if (has_tau(n->lft)) return 1;
2056    }
2057    return 3;
2058 }
2059
2060 has_tau(n)
2061    Node *n;
2062 {
2063    if (!n) return 0;
2064    if (n->ntyp == TIMEOUT) return 1;
2065    return (has_tau(n->lft) || has_tau(n->rgt));
2066 }
2067
2068 #include <ctype.h>
2069
2070 void
2071 blurb(fd, t, n)
2072    FILE *fd;
2073 {
2074    fprintf(fd, "   /* ");
2075    switch (t) {
2076    case ATOMIC:    fprintf(fd, "ATOMIC"); break;
2077    case IF:        fprintf(fd, "IF"); break;
2078    case DO:        fprintf(fd, "DO"); break;
2079    case BREAK:     fprintf(fd, "BREAK"); break;
2080    case GOTO:      fprintf(fd, "GOTO"); break;
2081    case ASSERT:    fprintf(fd, "ASSERT"); break;
2082    case TIMEOUT:   fprintf(fd, "TIMEOUT"); break;
2083    case LEN:       fprintf(fd, "LEN"); break;
2084    case RUN:       fprintf(fd, "RUN"); break;
2085    case PRINT:     fprintf(fd, "PRINT"); break;
2086    case NAME:      fprintf(fd, "NAME"); break;
2087    default:        if (isprint(t))
2088                            fprintf(fd, "'%c'", t);
2089                    else
2090                            fprintf(fd, "%d", t);
2091                    break;
2092    }
2093    fprintf(fd, " line %d */\n", n);
2094 }
2095
2096 /***** spin: pangen3.c *****/
2097
2098 #include <stdio.h>
2099 #include "spin.h"
2100
2101 extern FILE       *th;
2102
2103 typedef struct SRC {
2104    short ln, st;
2105    struct SRC *nxt;
```

```
2106 } SRC;
2107
2108 SRC          *frst = (SRC *) 0;
2109 SRC          *skip = (SRC *) 0;
2110 int          col;
2111
2112 void
2113 putskip(m) /* states that need not be reached */
2114 {   SRC *tmp;
2115
2116     for (tmp = skip; tmp; tmp = tmp->nxt)
2117             if (tmp->st == m)
2118                     return;
2119     tmp = (SRC *) emalloc(sizeof(SRC));
2120     tmp->st = (short) m;
2121     tmp->nxt = skip;
2122     skip = tmp;
2123 }
2124
2125 void
2126 putsrc(n, m)          /* match states to source lines */
2127 {   SRC *tmp;
2128
2129     for (tmp = frst; tmp; tmp = tmp->nxt)
2130             if (tmp->st == m)
2131             {       if (tmp->ln != n)
2132                             printf("putsrc mismatch %d - %d\n");
2133                     return;
2134             }
2135     tmp = (SRC *) emalloc(sizeof(SRC));
2136     tmp->ln = (short) n;
2137     tmp->st = (short) m;
2138     tmp->nxt = frst;
2139     frst = tmp;
2140 }
2141
2142 void
2143 dumpskip(n, m)
2144 {   SRC *tmp, *lst;
2145     int j;
2146
2147     fprintf(th, "uchar reached%d [] = {\n\t", m);
2148     for (j = 0, col = 0; j <= n; j++)
2149     {       lst = (SRC *) 0;
2150             for (tmp = skip; tmp; lst = tmp, tmp = tmp->nxt)
2151                     if (tmp->st == j)
2152                     {       putnr(1);
2153                             if (lst)
2154                                     lst->nxt = tmp->nxt;
2155                             else
2156                                     skip = tmp->nxt;
2157                             break;
2158                     }
2159             if (!tmp)
```

```
2160                        putnr(0);
2161     }
2162     fprintf(th, "};\n");
2163     skip = (SRC *) 0;
2164 }
2165
2166 void
2167 dumpsrc(n, m)
2168 {  SRC *tmp, *lst;
2169    int j;
2170
2171    fprintf(th, "short src_ln%d [] = {\n\t", m);
2172    for (j = 0, col = 0; j <= n; j++)
2173    {       lst = (SRC *) 0;
2174            for (tmp = frst; tmp; lst = tmp, tmp = tmp->nxt)
2175                    if (tmp->st == j)
2176                    {       putnr(tmp->ln);
2177                            if (lst)
2178                                    lst->nxt = tmp->nxt;
2179                            else
2180                                    frst = tmp->nxt;
2181                            break;
2182                    }
2183            if (!tmp)
2184                    putnr(0);
2185    }
2186    fprintf(th, "};\n");
2187    frst = (SRC *) 0;
2188    dumpskip(n, m);
2189 }
2190
2191 void
2192 putnr(n)
2193 {
2194    if (col++ == 8)
2195    {       fprintf(th, "\n\t");
2196            col = 1;
2197    }
2198    fprintf(th, "%3d, ", n);
2199 }
2200
2201 /***** spin: pangen4.c *****/
2202
2203 #include <stdio.h>
2204 #include "spin.h"
2205 #include "y.tab.h"
2206
2207 extern FILE      *tc, *tb;
2208 extern Queue     *qtab;
2209 extern int nocast;
2210 extern int lineno;
2211 extern char      *R13[], *R14[], *R15[];
2212
2213 void
```

```
2214  undostmnt(now, m)
2215     Node *now;
2216  {
2217     Node *v;
2218     int i, j; extern int m_loss;
2219
2220     if (!now)
2221     {       fprintf(tb, "0");
2222             return;
2223     }
2224     lineno = now->nval;
2225     switch (now->ntyp) {
2226     case CONST:     case '!':        case UMIN:
2227     case '~':       case '/':        case '*':
2228     case '-':       case '+':        case '%':
2229     case '<':       case '>':        case '&':
2230     case '|':       case LE:         case GE:
2231     case NE:        case EQ:         case OR:
2232     case AND:       case LSHIFT:     case RSHIFT:
2233     case TIMEOUT:   case LEN:        case NAME:
2234     case 'R':       putstmnt(tb, now, m);
2235                     break;
2236     case RUN:       fprintf(tb, "delproc(0, now._nr_pr-1)");
2237                     break;
2238     case 's':       if (m_loss)
2239                     {       fprintf(tb, "if (m == 2) m = unsend");
2240                             putname(tb, "(", now->lft, m, ")");
2241                     } else
2242                     {       fprintf(tb, "m = unsend");
2243                             putname(tb, "(", now->lft, m, ")");
2244                     }
2245                     break;
2246     case 'r':       for (v = now->rgt, j = 0; v; v = v->rgt)
2247                             if (v->lft->ntyp != CONST)
2248                                     j++;
2249                     if (j > 0)      /* variables were set */
2250                     {       fprintf(tb, "sv_restor()");
2251                             break;
2252                     }
2253                     for (v = now->rgt, i = 0; v; v = v->rgt, i++)
2254                     {       fprintf(tb, "unrecv");
2255                             putname(tb, "(", now->lft, m, ", 0, ");
2256                             fprintf(tb, "%d, ", i);
2257                             undostmnt(v->lft, m);
2258                             fprintf(tb, ", %d);\n\t\t", (i==0)?1:0);
2259                     }
2260                     break;
2261     case '@':       fprintf(tb, "p_restor(II)");
2262                     break;
2263     case ASGN:      nocast=1; putstmnt(tb,now->lft,m);
2264                     nocast=0; fprintf(tb, " = trpt->oval");
2265                     check_proc(now->rgt, m);
2266                     break;
2267     case 'c':       check_proc(now->lft, m);
```

```
2268                        break;
2269    case '.':
2270    case GOTO:
2271    case BREAK:        break;
2272    case ASSERT:
2273    case PRINT:        check_proc(now, m);
2274                        break;
2275    default:           printf("spin: bad node type %d (.b)\n",
2276                                                    now->ntyp);
2277                        exit(1);
2278    }
2279 }
2280
2281 any_undo(now)
2282    Node *now;
2283 {  /* is there anything to undo on a return move? */
2284
2285    if (!now) return 1;
2286    switch (now->ntyp) {
2287    case 'c':          return any_proc(now->lft);
2288    case ASSERT:
2289    case PRINT:        return any_proc(now);
2290
2291    case '.':
2292    case GOTO:
2293    case BREAK:        return 0;
2294    default:           return 1;
2295    }
2296 }
2297
2298 any_proc(now)
2299    Node *now;
2300 {  /* check if an expression refers to a process */
2301    if (!now) return 0;
2302    if (now->ntyp == '@' || now->ntyp == RUN)
2303            return 1;
2304    return (any_proc(now->lft) || any_proc(now->rgt));
2305 }
2306
2307 void
2308 check_proc(now, m)
2309    Node *now;
2310 {
2311    if (!now)
2312            return;
2313    if (now->ntyp == '@' || now->ntyp == RUN)
2314    {       fprintf(tb, ";\n\t\t");
2315            undostmnt(now, m);
2316    }
2317    check_proc(now->lft, m);
2318    check_proc(now->rgt, m);
2319 }
2320
2321 void
```

```
2322 genunio()
2323 {   char *buf1;
2324     Queue *q; int i;
2325
2326     buf1 = (char *) emalloc(128);
2327     ntimes(tc, 0, 1, R13);
2328     for (q = qtab; q; q = q->nxt)
2329     {       sprintf(buf1, "((Q%d *)z)->contents[j].fld", q->qid);
2330             fprintf(tc, "  case %d:\n", q->qid);
2331             for (i = 0; i < q->nflds; i++)
2332                     fprintf(tc, "\t\t%s%d = 0;\n", buf1, i);
2333             if (q->nslots==0)
2334             {       /* check if rendezvous succeeded, 1 level down */
2335                     fprintf(tc, "\t\tm = (trpt+1)->o_m;\n");
2336                     fprintf(tc, "\t\tUnBlock;\n");
2337             } else
2338                     fprintf(tc, "\t\tm = trpt->o_m;\n");
2339             fprintf(tc, "\t\tbreak;\n");
2340     }
2341     ntimes(tc, 0, 1, R14);
2342     for (q = qtab; q; q = q->nxt)
2343     {       sprintf(buf1, "((Q%d *)z)->contents", q->qid);
2344             fprintf(tc, "  case %d:\n", q->qid);
2345             if (q->nslots == 0)
2346                     fprintf(tc, "\t\tif (strt) boq = from;\n");
2347             else if (q->nslots > 1) /* shift */
2348             {       fprintf(tc, "\t\tif (strt && slot<%d)\n",
2349                                                 q->nslots-1);
2350                     fprintf(tc, "\t\t{\tfor (j--; j>=slot; j--)\n");
2351                     fprintf(tc, "\t\t\t{");
2352                     for (i = 0; i < q->nflds; i++)
2353                     {       fprintf(tc, "\t%s[j+1].fld%d =\n\t\t\t",
2354                                                 buf1, i);
2355                             fprintf(tc, "\t%s[j].fld%d;\n\t\t\t",
2356                                                 buf1, i);
2357                     }
2358                     fprintf(tc, "}\n\t\t}\n");
2359             }
2360             strcat(buf1, "[slot].fld");
2361             fprintf(tc, "\t\tif (strt) {\n");
2362             for (i = 0; i < q->nflds; i++)
2363                     fprintf(tc, "\t\t\t%s%d = 0;\n", buf1, i);
2364             fprintf(tc, "\t\t}\n");
2365             if (q->nflds == 1)      /* set */
2366                     fprintf(tc, "\t\tif (fld == 0) %s0 = fldvar;\n",
2367                                                 buf1);
2368             else
2369             {       fprintf(tc, "\t\tswitch (fld) {\n");
2370                     for (i = 0; i < q->nflds; i++)
2371                     {       fprintf(tc, "\t\tcase %d:\t%s", i, buf1);
2372                             fprintf(tc, "%d = fldvar; break;\n", i);
2373                     }
2374                     fprintf(tc, "\t\t}\n");
2375             }
```

```
2376                fprintf(tc, "\t\tbreak;\n");
2377     }
2378     ntimes(tc, 0, 1, R15);
2379 }
2380
2381 /***** spin: pangen5.c *****/
2382
2383 #include <stdio.h>
2384 #include "spin.h"
2385 #include "y.tab.h"
2386
2387 extern int nproc, nstop, Tval, Rvous;
2388 extern RunList     *run, *X;
2389 extern int verbose, lineno;
2390 extern int depth;
2391
2392 FILE *fd;
2393
2394 void
2395 match_trail()
2396 {  int i, pno, nst, lv0=0, lv1=0;
2397
2398     if (!(fd = fopen("pan.trail", "r")))
2399     {       printf("spin -t: cannot find 'pan.trail'\n");
2400             exit(1);
2401     }
2402     Tval = 1; /* timeouts may be part of the trail */
2403     while (fscanf(fd, "%d:%d:%d:%d\n", &depth, &pno, &nst, &lv0)
2404                                                         == 4)
2405     {       if (lv1 >= 0 && depth > 0 && (verbose&32 || lv1 != lv0))
2406                     talk(X->pc, X->symtab);
2407             lv1=lv0;         /* non-verbose in intermediate steps */
2408             if (depth == -1)
2409             {       if (verbose)
2410                     printf("<<<<<START OF CYCLE>>>>>\n");
2411                     continue;
2412             }
2413             if (depth == -2)
2414             {
2415                     start_claim(pno);
2416                     continue;
2417             }
2418             i = nproc - nstop;
2419             if (nst == 0)
2420             {       if (pno == i-1 && run->pc->n->ntyp == '@')
2421                     {       run = run->nxt;
2422                             nstop++;
2423                             continue;
2424                     } else
2425                     {       printf("step %d: stop error, %d %d %c\n",
2426                                     depth, pno, i, run->pc->n->ntyp);
2427                             exit(1);
2428                     }       }
2429             for (X = run; X; X = X->nxt)
```

```
2430                {
2431                        if (--i == pno)
2432                                break;
2433                }
2434            if (!X)
2435            {       printf("step %d: lost trail ", depth);
2436                    printf("(proc .%d state %d)\n", pno, nst);
2437                    lost_trail();
2438                    wrapup();
2439                    exit(1);
2440            }
2441            lineno = X->pc->n->nval;
2442            do
2443            {       X->pc = d_eval_sub(X->pc, pno, nst);
2444            } while (X && X->pc && X->pc->seqno != nst);
2445            if (!X || !X->pc)
2446            {       printf("step %d: lost trail ", depth);
2447                    printf("(proc %d state %d.)\n", pno, nst);
2448                    lost_trail();
2449                    wrapup();
2450                    exit(1);
2451            }
2452    }
2453    talk(X->pc, X->symtab);
2454    printf("spin: trail ends after %d steps\n", depth);
2455    wrapup();
2456 }
2457
2458 void
2459 lost_trail()
2460 {  int d, p, n, l;
2461
2462    while (fscanf(fd, "%d:%d:%d:%d\n", &d, &p, &n, &l) == 4)
2463    {       printf("step %d: proc  %d ", d, p);
2464            printf("(state %d) - d %d\n", n, l);
2465    }
2466 }
2467
2468 Element *
2469 walk_sub(e, pno, nst)
2470    Element *e;
2471 {
2472    SeqList *z;
2473    Element *f;
2474    for (z = e->sub; z; z = z->nxt)
2475    {
2476            if (z->this->frst->seqno == nst)
2477                    return z->this->frst;
2478            if (!z->this->frst->nxt)
2479                    fatal("cannot happen", "walk_sub");
2480            if (z->this->frst->sub)
2481            {       f = walk_sub(z->this->frst, pno, nst);
2482                    if (f) return f;
2483            }
```

```
2484                f = huntele(z->this->frst, z->this->frst->status);
2485                if (f->seqno == nst)
2486                        return f;
2487                if (f->seqno == X->pc->seqno)            /* looping */
2488                        continue;                        /* fails */
2489                if (f->sub && (f = walk_sub(f, pno, nst)))
2490                        return f;
2491                if (f && f->n->ntyp == ATOMIC)
2492                {       f = f->n->seql->this->frst;
2493                        if (f->seqno == nst)
2494                                return f;
2495                }
2496        }
2497        return (Element *) 0;
2498 }
2499
2500 Element *
2501 d_eval_sub(s, pno, nst)
2502        Element *s;
2503 {
2504        Element *e=s;
2505
2506        if (e->n->ntyp == GOTO)
2507        {
2508                return get_lab(e->n->nsym);
2509        }
2510        if (e->sub)
2511        {       if (e = walk_sub(e, pno, nst))
2512                {
2513                        return e;
2514                }
2515        } else if (e->n && e->n->ntyp == ATOMIC)
2516        {       e->n->seql->this->last->nxt = e->nxt;
2517                if (e->n->seql->this->frst->seqno == nst)
2518                        return e->n->seql->this->frst;
2519                return d_eval_sub(e->n->seql->this->frst, pno, nst);
2520        } else if (eval(e->n))
2521        {
2522                return e->nxt;
2523        }
2524        if (e && (nst == e->seqno))
2525                return e;
2526        if (s && (nst == s->seqno))
2527                return s;
2528        printf("step %d: lost trail (proc %d ", depth, pno);
2529        printf("state .%d) [stuck in %d]\n", nst, (e)?e->seqno:-1);
2530        lost_trail();
2531        wrapup();
2532        exit(1);
2533 }
```

PROMELA FILE TRANSFER PROTOCOL F

Here is a complete listing of the set of file transfer protocol validation models that were developed in Chapter 7, with the modifications discussed in Chapter 14. It is an error to retrieve fewer parameters in a message input from a channel than defined in the corresponding channel declaration. Unused parameter fields are therefore set to zero in sends and receives.

```
 1 /*
 2  * PROMELA Validation Model - startup script
 3  */
 4
 5 #include "defines"
 6 #include "user"
 7 #include "present"
 8 #include "session"
 9 #include "fserver"
10 #include "flow_cl"
11 #include "datalink"
12
13 init
14 {   atomic {
15         run userprc(0); run userprc(1);
16         run present(0); run present(1);
17         run session(0); run session(1);
18         run fserver(0); run fserver(1);
19         run fc(0);      run fc(1);
20         run data_link()
21     }
22 }
23
24 /*
25  * Global Definitions
26  */
27
28 #define LOSS            0       /* message loss  */
29 #define DUPS            0       /* duplicate msgs */
30 #define QSZ      2      /* queue size    */
31
```

```
32 mtype = {
33     red, white, blue,
34     abort, accept, ack, sync_ack, close, connect,
35     create, data, eof, open, reject, sync, transfer,
36     FATAL, NON_FATAL, COMPLETE
37     }
38
39 chan use_to_pres[2] = [QSZ] of { byte };
40 chan pres_to_use[2] = [QSZ] of { byte };
41 chan pres_to_ses[2] = [QSZ] of { byte };
42 chan ses_to_pres[2] = [QSZ] of { byte, byte };
43 chan ses_to_flow[2] = [QSZ] of { byte, byte };
44 chan flow_to_ses[2] = [QSZ] of { byte, byte };
45 chan dll_to_flow[2] = [QSZ] of { byte, byte };
46 chan flow_to_dll[2] = [QSZ] of { byte, byte };
47 chan ses_to_fsrv[2] = [0] of { byte };
48 chan fsrv_to_ses[2] = [0] of { byte };
49
50 /*
51  * User Layer Validation Model
52  */
53
54 proctype userprc(bit n)
55 {
56     use_to_pres[n]!transfer;
57     if
58     :: pres_to_use[n]?accept -> goto Done
59     :: pres_to_use[n]?reject -> goto Done
60     :: use_to_pres[n]!abort  -> goto Aborted
61     fi;
62 Aborted:
63     if
64     :: pres_to_use[n]?accept -> goto Done
65     :: pres_to_use[n]?reject -> goto Done
66     fi;
67 Done:
68     skip
69 }
70
71 /*
72  * Presentation Layer Validation Model
73  */
74
75 proctype present(bit n)
76 {   byte status, uabort;
77
78 endIDLE:
79     do
80     :: use_to_pres[n]?transfer ->
81             uabort = 0;
82             break
83     :: use_to_pres[n]?abort ->
84             skip
85     od;
```

```
86
87 TRANSFER:
88     pres_to_ses[n]!transfer;
89     do
90     :: use_to_pres[n]?abort ->
91             if
92             :: (!uabort) ->
93                     uabort = 1;
94                     pres_to_ses[n]!abort
95             :: (uabort) ->
96                     assert(1+1!=2)
97             fi
98     :: ses_to_pres[n]?accept,0 ->
99             goto DONE
100    :: ses_to_pres[n]?reject(status) ->
101            if
102            :: (status == FATAL || uabort) ->
103                    goto FAIL
104            :: (status == NON_FATAL && !uabort) ->
105                    goto TRANSFER
106            fi
107    od;
108 DONE:
109    pres_to_use[n]!accept;
110    goto endIDLE;
111 FAIL:
112    pres_to_use[n]!reject;
113    goto endIDLE
114 }
115
116 /*
117  * Session Layer Validation Model
118  */
119
120 proctype session(bit n)
121 {   bit toggle;
122     byte type, status;
123
124 endIDLE:
125    do
126    :: pres_to_ses[n]?type ->
127            if
128            :: (type == transfer) ->
129                    goto DATA_OUT
130            :: (type != transfer)   /* ignore */
131            fi
132    :: flow_to_ses[n]?type,0 ->
133            if
134            :: (type == connect) ->
135                    goto DATA_IN
136            :: (type != connect)    /* ignore */
137            fi
138    od;
139
```

```
140 DATA_IN:                /* 1. prepare local file fsrver */
141     ses_to_fsrv[n]!create;
142     do
143     :: fsrv_to_ses[n]?reject ->
144             ses_to_flow[n]!reject,0;
145             goto endIDLE
146     :: fsrv_to_ses[n]?accept ->
147             ses_to_flow[n]!accept,0;
148             break
149     od;
150                         /* 2. Receive the data, upto eof */
151     do
152     :: flow_to_ses[n]?data,0 ->
153             ses_to_fsrv[n]!data
154     :: flow_to_ses[n]?eof,0 ->
155             ses_to_fsrv[n]!eof;
156             break
157     :: pres_to_ses[n]?transfer ->
158             ses_to_pres[n]!reject(NON_FATAL)
159     :: flow_to_ses[n]?close,0 ->    /* remote user aborted */
160             ses_to_fsrv[n]!close;
161             break
162     :: timeout ->           /* got disconnected */
163             ses_to_fsrv[n]!close;
164             goto endIDLE
165     od;
166                         /* 3. Close the connection */
167     ses_to_flow[n]!close,0;
168     goto endIDLE;
169
170 DATA_OUT:               /* 1. prepare local file fsrver */
171     ses_to_fsrv[n]!open;
172     if
173     :: fsrv_to_ses[n]?reject ->
174             ses_to_pres[n]!reject(FATAL);
175             goto endIDLE
176     :: fsrv_to_ses[n]?accept ->
177             skip
178     fi;
179                         /* 2. initialize flow control */
180     ses_to_flow[n]!sync,toggle;
181     do
182     :: atomic {
183             flow_to_ses[n]?sync_ack,type ->
184             if
185             :: (type != toggle)
186             :: (type == toggle) -> break
187             fi
188         }
189     :: timeout ->
190             ses_to_fsrv[n]!close;
191             ses_to_pres[n]!reject(FATAL);
192             goto endIDLE
193     od;
```

```
194     toggle = 1 - toggle;
195                     /* 3. prepare remote file fsrver */
196     ses_to_flow[n]!connect,0;
197     if
198     :: flow_to_ses[n]?reject,0 ->
199             ses_to_fsrv[n]!close;
200             ses_to_pres[n]!reject(FATAL);
201             goto endIDLE
202     :: flow_to_ses[n]?connect,0 ->
203             ses_to_fsrv[n]!close;
204             ses_to_pres[n]!reject(NON_FATAL);
205             goto endIDLE
206     :: flow_to_ses[n]?accept,0 ->
207             skip
208     :: timeout ->
209             ses_to_fsrv[n]!close;
210             ses_to_pres[n]!reject(FATAL);
211             goto endIDLE
212     fi;
213                     /* 4. Transmit the data, upto eof */
214     do
215     :: fsrv_to_ses[n]?data ->
216             ses_to_flow[n]!data,0
217     :: fsrv_to_ses[n]?eof ->
218             ses_to_flow[n]!eof,0;
219             status = COMPLETE;
220             break
221     :: pres_to_ses[n]?abort ->      /* local user aborted */
222             ses_to_fsrv[n]!close;
223             ses_to_flow[n]!close,0;
224             status = FATAL;
225             break
226     od;
227                     /* 5. Close the connection */
228     do
229     :: pres_to_ses[n]?abort         /* ignore */
230     :: flow_to_ses[n]?close,0 ->
231             if
232             :: (status == COMPLETE) ->
233                     ses_to_pres[n]!accept,0
234             :: (status != COMPLETE) ->
235                     ses_to_pres[n]!reject(status)
236             fi;
237             break
238     :: timeout ->
239             ses_to_pres[n]!reject(FATAL);
240             break
241     od;
242     goto endIDLE
243 }
244
245 /*
246  * File Server Validation Model
247  */
```

```
248
249 proctype fserver(bit n)
250 {
251 end:        do
252     :: ses_to_fsrv[n]?create ->      /* incoming */
253             if
254             :: fsrv_to_ses[n]!reject
255             :: fsrv_to_ses[n]!accept ->
256                     do
257                     :: ses_to_fsrv[n]?data
258                     :: ses_to_fsrv[n]?eof -> break
259                     :: ses_to_fsrv[n]?close -> break
260                     od
261             fi
262     :: ses_to_fsrv[n]?open ->                   /* outgoing */
263             if
264             :: fsrv_to_ses[n]!reject
265             :: fsrv_to_ses[n]!accept ->
266                     do
267                     :: fsrv_to_ses[n]!data
268                     :: ses_to_fsrv[n]?close -> break
269                     :: fsrv_to_ses[n]!eof -> break
270                     od
271             fi
272     od
273 }
274
275 /*
276  * Flow Control Layer Validation Model
277  */
278
279 #define true      1
280 #define false     0
281
282 #define M    4       /* range sequence numbers    */
283 #define W    2       /* window size: M/2          */
284
285 proctype fc(bit n)
286 {   bool    busy[M];        /* outstanding messages     */
287     byte    q;             /* seq# oldest unacked msg */
288     byte    m;             /* seq# last msg received   */
289     byte    s;             /* seq# next msg to send    */
290     byte    window;        /* nr of outstanding msgs   */
291     byte    type;          /* msg type                 */
292     bit     received[M];   /* receiver housekeeping    */
293     bit     x;             /* scratch variable         */
294     byte    p;             /* seq# of last msg acked   */
295     byte    I_buf[M], O_buf[M];   /* message buffers */
296
297     /* sender part */
298 end:        do
299     :: atomic {
300         (window < W  && len(ses_to_flow[n]) >  0
301                     && len(flow_to_dll[n]) < QSZ) ->
```

```
302                    ses_to_flow[n]?type,x;
303                    window = window + 1;
304                    busy[s] = true;
305                    O_buf[s] = type;
306                    flow_to_dll[n]!type,s;
307                    if
308                    :: (type != sync) ->
309                            s = (s+1)%M
310                    :: (type == sync) ->
311                            window = 0;
312                            s = M;
313                            do
314                            :: (s > 0) ->
315                                    s = s-1;
316                                    busy[s] = false
317                            :: (s == 0) ->
318                                    break
319                            od
320                    fi
321              }
322    :: atomic {
323            (window > 0 && busy[q] == false) ->
324            window = window - 1;
325            q = (q+1)%M
326       }
327 #if DUPS
328    :: atomic {
329            (len(flow_to_dll[n]) < QSZ
330             && window > 0 && busy[q] == true) ->
331            flow_to_dll[n]! O_buf[q],q
332       }
333 #endif
334    :: atomic {
335            (timeout && len(flow_to_dll[n]) < QSZ
336             && window > 0 && busy[q] == true) ->
337            flow_to_dll[n]! O_buf[q],q
338       }
339
340     /* receiver part */
341 #if LOSS
342    :: dll_to_flow[n]?type,m /* lose any message */
343 #endif
344    :: dll_to_flow[n]?type,m ->
345            if
346            :: atomic {
347                    (type == ack) ->
348                    busy[m] = false
349              }
350            :: atomic {
351                    (type == sync) ->
352                    m = 0;
353                    do
354                    :: (m < M) ->
355                            received[m] = 0;
```

```
356                           m = m+1
357                   :: (m == M) ->
358                           break
359               od
360           };   flow_to_dll[n]!sync_ack,0
361       :: (type == sync_ack) ->
362               flow_to_ses[n]!sync_ack,0
363       :: (type != ack && type != sync && type != sync_ack)->
364           if
365           :: atomic {
366                   (received[m] == true) ->
367                           x = ((0<p-m   && p-m<=W)
368                           ||   (0<p-m-M && p-m-M<=W)) };
369                   if
370                   :: (x) -> flow_to_dll[n]!ack,m
371                   :: (!x) /* else skip */
372                   fi
373           :: atomic {
374                   (received[m] == false) ->
375                           I_buf[m] = type;
376                           received[m] = true;
377                           received[(m-W+M)%M] = false
378               }
379           fi
380       fi
381   :: (received[p] == true && len(flow_to_ses[n])<QSZ
382                       && len(flow_to_dll[n])<QSZ) ->
383           flow_to_ses[n]!I_buf[p],0;
384           flow_to_dll[n]!ack,p;
385           p = (p+1)%M
386   od
387 }
388
389 /*
390  * Datalink Layer Validation Model
391  */
392
393 proctype data_link()
394 {   byte type, seq;
395
396 end:    do
397     :: flow_to_dll[0]?type,seq ->
398             if
399             :: dll_to_flow[1]!type,seq
400             :: skip /* lose message */
401             fi
402     :: flow_to_dll[1]?type,seq ->
403             if
404             :: dll_to_flow[0]!type,seq
405             :: skip /* lose message */
406             fi
407     od
408 }
```

NAME INDEX

491

SUBJECT INDEX